POLITICS IN THE POST-WELFARE STATE

RESPONSES TO THE NEW INDIVIDUALISM

Edited by

M. DONALD HANCOCK

and GIDEON SJOBERG

COLUMBIA UNIVERSITY PRESS

NEW YORK and LONDON   1972

M. Donald Hancock
is Associate Professor of Government at the University of Texas.

Gideon Sjoberg
is Professor of Sociology at the University of Texas.

Copyright © 1972 Columbia University Press
Cloth-bound edition ISBN: 0-231-03127-0
Paper-bound edition ISBN: 0-231-08667-9
Library of Congress Catalog Card Number: 79-165181
Printed in the United States of America

To Erik

Preface

THIS VOLUME OF ORIGINAL ESSAYS reflects a continuing interest on the part of the editors with the future political and social organization of industrial-urban societies. Some years ago we, along with Orion White, Jr., wrote a short monograph, *Politics in the Post-Welfare State: A Comparison of the United States and Sweden* (Bloomington, Ind.: Carnegie Seminar for Political and Administrative Development and the Department of Government, 1967). We believe our concerns are even more relevant for the 1970s than they were for the 1960s.

The United States, as well as various European nations, passed through an era of protest during the 1960s. The resultant crisis of authority seems to be paving the way for fundamental changes in the political systems of these nations. It is no longer possible to write uncritically about basic tenets of the welfare state as did political sociologists such as S. M. Lipset and William Kornhauser, among others, in the 1960s and many political scientists—including Harry Eckstein, Gabriel A. Almond, and Sidney Verba—during the same decade.

Political scientists and sociologists are increasingly aware that we require more satisfactory answers to old questions and that we must raise new questions about the emergent political order. Moreover, we are convinced that new methodologies must be developed for studies of the future. A mere extrapolation of the past into the future is no guide for understanding the future and building a better tomorrow.

We organized this volume with the firm conviction that men and women can wield an element of control over their destiny and that they therefore must delineate and critically analyze the possible options that may be open to them. Our contributors were invited to write chapters because of their differing views and because of their critical spirit. We believe they define the range of issues that the United States, England, and Sweden will face in the post-welfare period, and they highlight some of the possible consequences of various courses that political action may take.

We thank the contributors for their patience and understanding and for their willingness to challenge us on points of disagreement. Most of all we want to thank each of them for their commitment to reasoned disputation in an era when rhetoric can so readily be substituted for critical analysis.

We acknowledge the University Research Institute at the University of Texas in Austin for research support and financial assistance in typing the manuscript. And to Bernard Gronert of Columbia University Press we express our appreciation for his helpfulness in making this effort a reality.

M. D. H.

G. S.

July, 1971

Contents

Contributors

JON ALEXANDER, Department of Political Science, Carleton University, Ottawa, Canada.

ERIK ANNERS, Faculty of Law, University of Stockholm, Stockholm, Sweden.

KAJ BJÖRK, Member of Parliament, Stockholm, Sweden.

DOUGLAS L. CAPPS, Office of the Ombudsman, Eugene, Oregon.

JOHN MILTON COOPER, JR., Department of History, University of Wisconsin, Madison, Wisconsin.

NILS ELVANDER, Department of Political Science, University of Uppsala, Sweden.

LARS GYLLENSTEN, Novelist, Stockholm, Sweden.

M. DONALD HANCOCK, Department of Government, University of Texas, Austin, Texas.

DAVID HOWELL, Member of Parliament, London, England.

TERRY LACEY, former Vice-Chairman, National Union of Liberal Students, London, England.

CHRISTOPHER LASCH, Department of History, University of Rochester, Rochester, New York.

D. MCQUAIL, Department of Sociology and Social Administration, University of Southampton, Southampton, England.

GIDEON SJOBERG, Department of Sociology, University of Texas, Austin, Texas.

DUSKY LEE SMITH, Department of Sociology, McMaster University, Hamilton, Canada.

J. H. SMITH, Department of Sociology and Social Administration, University of Southampton, Southampton, England.

ORION WHITE, JR., Department of Political Science, Syracuse University, Syracuse, New York.

Politics in the Post-Welfare State: Responses to the New Individualism

M. Donald Hancock and
Gideon Sjoberg, Editors

Modern industrial systems, and more narrowly the welfare states of North America and Western Europe, are undergoing a serious socio-political crisis. A salient feature of the current upheaval is the struggle to provide the individual with a more meaningful place in the society of the future. Although technological change in the advanced nations has closed certain socio-economic options, it has simultaneously created new possibilities for restructuring society. On the one hand modern technology provides more efficient means for political repression; on the other, it enhances the capacity of the individual for seeking personal fulfillment. One of the basic premises of this volume is that persons in advanced industrial nations confront a choice between these two alternatives.

Distinctive in a number of respects, this is the first work that presents a variety of views on the politics of the future. To provide a cross-national perspective on the prospects of socio-political change in advanced nations, the volume encompasses essays on the United States, England, and Sweden.

Each of the authors addresses himself to the relation of the individual to broader society. The result is a set of essays with both theoretical and practical significance. Throughout the volume the contributors' assumptions concerning group-individual relations clearly emerge as a principal factor

tate:

lualism

e future
re state.
sed will
in both
s in the

Associate
Director
tudies at
stin. He
 Politics
co-editor
in Inter-
Compara-
Reader in

y Profes-
ersity of
fessor of
ersity of
dition to
icles and
author of
co-author
Social

Introduction: Images of the Future

THE MODERN INDUSTRIAL SYSTEMS, and more narrowly the welfare states of North America and Western Europe, are undergoing a serious social crisis. The maturation of the industrial-welfare states has led to the exposure of significant contradictions in their value systems and authority structures. Consequently, these nations are being subjected to a variety of challenges that call for a fundamental reappraisal of contemporary social and political conditions.

A salient feature of this current upheaval is the struggle to provide the individual with a more meaningful place in the society of the future. While technological change in the advanced nations has closed certain socio-economic options, such as dismantling the industrial system or retreating to autarchy, it has simultaneously created new possibilities for restructuring society. And whereas, on the one hand, modern technology provides more efficient means for political repression, it also enhances the capacity of the individual for seeking personal fulfillment. One of our basic premises in this book is that modern man confronts a choice between these alternatives. Standing at a major crossroad in the continuing development of society, man can either lapse into a totalitarian condition or he can fashion new socio-political alternatives previously denied him.

The issue of the role of the individual in relation to society has been a long-standing one in Western political and sociological debate. In the emerging era of post-industrial affluence and automation, the inherent tension between individual interests and the claims of society for collective action has assumed new forms. Attesting to this transformation are the appearance of diverse protest groups, including various student and militant minority movements, and the revival of ideological debate in the 1960s. This volume addresses itself to the implications of the "new individualism" that these forces for change herald in the post-welfare state.

The prospects of a new individualism are not confined to any single nation-state. The crisis of modern society is international in scope, and the responses to the challenge of post-industrial change are likely to vary from one advanced nation to another. Hence we deliberately approached the problem of the new individualism from a cross-national perspective, selecting the United States, Great Britain, and Sweden as the focus for our study.

These particular countries were chosen for both theoretical and practical reasons. Despite national differences in size, regionalism, governmental structures, and ideological tradition, all three are highly industrialized, affluent, and bureaucratized. Each has in its own way experimented with different variations of the welfare system model. Then, too, each is an important case study of a modern system in transition from the modern industrial stage to a post-industrial or post-welfare order. Few other advanced societies would be as useful for our purposes. For instance, we might have selected West Germany, but the situation there is confounded by the particular problem of national division.

A second criterion of selection was more practical and personal. The United States, Great Britain, and Sweden were the countries with which we had become most familiar through our earlier research and writing. Even so, the theoretical considerations loom larger than the practical one.

With respect to each of the nations, we have chosen contributors who would accept the challenge of analyzing the future of the post-welfare state. Just as significant, we have included authors who represent diverse viewpoints. Equally diverse are their backgrounds—social scientists, political philosophers, political activists. Some of them, as anticipated, perceive the new individualism as a nonviable pattern for the future while others write in support of it. Their varying responses are clearly reflected in the essays in this volume.

Specifically we posed the following questions to our contributors:

1. What are the differences (if any) between the new individualism and the individualism of the nineteenth century?

2. Do you believe that this emphasis on the individual will play a part in the future ideological struggles within the nation you are discussing?

3. Do you believe that this emphasis on the individual will play a part in bringing about structural changes (e.g., decentralization of certain kinds of government activities) in the nation you are discussing? And why?

4. What are the specific political implications of the new individualism? Will it become the focus for new political parties and opposition? Or will traditional political parties take over the issues involved? Or will individualism simply become an apolitical movement concerned only with "self?"

THE CONCEPT OF THE WELFARE STATE

Political analysts have for decades debated the concept of the welfare state without reaching a generally accepted agreement on its precise definition. Some argue, for example, that in comparison with the wide range of social services provided by most West European governments, those offered in the United States scarcely qualify it to be ranked as a welfare state at all.[1] Yet, to consider the future of politics in the post-welfare state, one presumably must have a fairly clear notion of what is meant by both the welfare and the post-welfare states.

In our prospectus to the authors, we deliberately did not define the term "welfare state." As the essays reveal, this has had definite advantages. It is clear that the contributors (as might be expected) define the welfare state in somewhat different ways. Their conception of what is meant by the welfare state is often in turn associated with their image of politics in the post-welfare state.

Christopher Lasch sees contemporary American society as a post-industrial state, while Dusky Lee Smith tends to equate the post-welfare state with the new industrial state. In contrast, John Cooper and Terry Lacey perceive the welfare state as yet imperfectly achieved. A majority of our contributors—including Jon Alexander, D. McQuail, J. H.

Smith, Douglas L. Capps, David Howell, Kaj Björk, Erik Anners, Lars Gyllensten, and Nils Elvander—maintain that the welfare state has already been largely attained but that the course of post-welfare change remains open. In each case these diverse views of the welfare state have led to differing perceptions of the potential of politics in the future.

IMAGES OF MAN AND REALITY

Not all our contributors have addressed themselves consistently to the specific questions we raised about the effect of the new individualism on the politics of the future. Yet the very statement of this problem has prompted all of them to consider, either explicitly or implicity, the central issue of group-individual relations. At least three major views on this question emerge, and each of them reflects a different image of human nature and social reality.

Lasch and Dusky Smith tend to separate the individual from the collectivity. They see the system as ubiquitous, totally dominating the individual. In their view the individual consequently has no real place in modern societies that are dominated by large-scale organizations. Because they do not believe that the individual has any real influence on developments in modern society, both Lasch and Smith are social pessimists. This position is much in keeping with the writings of such diverse theorists as Max Weber and Herbert Marcuse. In one form or another all these writers have perceived the individual as buffeted by the forces of organizational circumstances and compelled to accept a totally subordinate position within modern society.

A second theme which characterizes some of the chapters is that the individual gains his self-esteem and personal meaning through participation in the collectivity. Hancock, Björk, and Elvander are aligned with this school of thought. This perspective, too, is deeply rooted in modern social thought. One has only to look at the writings of Emile Durkheim, among others, to find expression of a similar theoretical perspective.

A third theme is that of inherent strain between the individual and the group. This viewpoint, which has several dimensions, is reflected in the essays by Orion White, Jr., and Sjoberg, Alexander, Lacey, Anners, and Gyllensten. Employing various interpretations, they stress the ongoing tension between the individual and the group and the constant struggle to work out an accommodation between the two.

More broadly, the views that the authors hold regarding the relation of the individual to the collectivity structures to a considerable degree the manner in which they analyze the future course of politics. In turn, this pattern suggests a link between a scholar's world view and his social analysis, as well as his prescription for what ought to be. This relation, so frequently ignored by contemporary social scientists, is of considerable import in understanding political theorizing. Few studies have revealed the relation as dramatically as the essays in this volume.

Out of these differing conceptions of the welfare state and the nature of individual-group relations emerges a continuum of views toward the politics of the future. Some of our contributing authors consider the new individualism only a passing phenomenon, while others envision it as the possible basis for revolutionizing society.

The most pessimistic perception of future change is that expressed by Lasch and Dusky Smith. They emphasize the disintegrative forces of post-industrial society and its subjugation of the individual, and they conclude that modern systems may either collapse or revert to extreme forms of repression in an attempt to sustain themselves. On the other hand, those contributors who posit a continuing tension between society and the individual and those who see the individual achieving fulfillment within the group generally assume a more optimistic view of the future.

White and Sjoberg, Cooper, McQuail and J. H. Smith, Howell, Lacey, Björk, and Gyllensten foresee a future politics of modifying change. Through dialectical processes of group-individual accommodation and partial reforms of the existing system, the post-welfare state can in their view successively overcome the contemporary crisis of modern industrial society.

An alternative vision of the future—that of transforming change —is suggested in the essays by Alexander, Hancock, and Elvander. According to their interpretations of the evolving nature of contemporary industrial-welfare society, the post-welfare state will conceivably involve the radical restructuring of group-individual relations on behalf of greater individual participation and choice.

A CHALLENGE TO DEBATE

In raising issues of the new individualism and the post-welfare state, this volume supplements a growing body of literature on the future of politics. The publication of Daniel Bell's *Toward the Year 2000,* Herman Kahn and Anthony Wiener's *The Year 2000,* and Alain Touraine's *La Société Post-Industrielle,* as well as scattered articles in periodicals and the popular press, testifies to the increasing interest among social scientists in the society of tomorrow.[2]

While this volume forms part of this emergent body of scientific literature, it is distinctive in its own right. In contrast to the primary emphasis in existing studies on the national dimensions of contemporary socio-economic and technological change, our approach is cross-national. Only by appraising the prospects of future change from a cross-cultural perspective is it possible, we believe, to generalize about the post-industrial order. We shall return to this theme in the epilogue.

Moreover, this compilation of essays focuses on politics in the post-welfare state and more specifically on the role of the individual therein. Thus the volume goes beyond current assessments of technological and social change to various appraisals of future forms of socio-political organization. By making the potential range of options for reshaping group-individual relations more explicit, this study provides a link between the struggle by individuals to secure greater dignity and freedom for themselves and broader efforts to restructure society as a whole.

The views expressed in the following essays are neither definitive nor exhaustive. An analysis of much greater length would be required to explore fully the implications of post-industrial change even in the three countries we have included, not to mention in other advanced systems of Europe and North America. Assuming that modern men and women indeed confront a variety of possible futures, we nevertheless hope that this volume can serve to stimulate a constructive debate on the alternatives open to them.

So, too, we hope that the analysis of post-welfare politics will contribute to a broader understanding of social science itself. Alvin Gouldner, in *The Coming Crisis of Western Sociology,*[3] suggests that many of the present-day debates in social science reflect the struggles within the broader social order. Assuming this, an analysis of the emerging political system is a necessary condition for the reordering of social inquiry. Just as social science knowledge may inform our knowledge of politics, so our knowledge of politics may inform our knowledge of social science.

Notes

1. Particularly useful treatments of the welfare state concept, including ambiguities in its meaning, include Richard M. Titmuss, *Essays on 'The Welfare State'* (London, 1958), David Marsh, *The Future of the Welfare State* (London, 1964), Maurice Bruce, *The Coming of the Welfare State,* rev. ed. (New York, 1966), Piet Thoenes, *The Elite in the Welfare State,* trans. by J. E. Bingham (New York, 1966), Asa Briggs, "The Welfare State in Historical Perspective," *European Journal of Sociology,* II, No. 2 (1961), 221–58, and T. H. Marshall, "The Welfare State: A Sociological Interpretation," *European Journal of Sociology,* 284–300. Critical Swedish views of contemporary welfare society are expressed in Torsten Eliasson, *Är välfärd nog?* (Arboga, Sweden, 1963) and Gunnar and Maj-Britt Inghe, *Den ofärdiga välfärden* (Stockholm, 1967).

2. In addition to the compilation of essays edited by Bell (Boston, 1969) and the studies written by Kahn and Wiener (New York, 1967) and by Touraine (Paris, 1969), see Andrew Schonfield, "Thinking About the Future," *Encounter,* XXXII, No. 2 (February, 1969), 15–26, and Herbert J. Gans, "We Won't End the Urban Crisis Until We End 'Majority Rule,'" *New York Times Magazine* (August 3, 1969), 12–15, 20, 24, 26–28. An earlier version of our own view on the future is presented in Gideon Sjoberg, M. Donald Hancock, and Orion White, Jr., *Politics in the Post-Welfare State: A Comparison of the United States and Sweden* (Bloomington, Ind., 1967).

3. New York, 1970.

United States

ORION WHITE, JR., AND
GIDEON SJOBERG

The Emerging "New Politics" in America

CONSIDERABLE EVIDENCE can be adduced in support of the proposition that a fundamental readjustment of American political patterns is now taking place. Herein we are concerned with analyzing the social preconditions leading to this change, and, then, most important of all, with attempting to delineate the possible shape of the political system over the next several decades.

THE SOCIAL BASES FOR POLITICAL CHANGE

The present-day concern with a "new politics" has not emerged within a vacuum. Quite the contrary. Certain shifts in the value system, as well as structural realignments during the past several decades, have not only laid the basis for the rise of new political patterns but have done much to foster them.[1] The new structures and values have resulted in turn from the rise of an affluent society—an affluent order that rests upon the continuing development of science and technology.

Still, the social consequences of scientific and technological change have been contradictory in the extreme. Many of them can be viewed as socially and morally undesirable. As a result most of the leading social theorists in the Western world during the nineteenth and twentieth centuries have deplored the impact of science and technology, especially as these have destroyed the moral fabric of man's relationship to man.[2] And the criticism continues. Science and technology, after all, have been employed for the most nonhumanitarian ends: by the Germans against the Jews and by Americans at Hiroshima and Nagasaki, and now in Vietnam.

But we cannot ignore the fact that because of the scientific revolution, which preceded the industrial one, man is no longer completely at the mercy of a not always beneficent nature, as he was in the preliterate and the preindustrial eras. Without the creative efforts of the scientific revolution the welfare state and its effort to provide the citizenry with minimal economic and social amenities would never have come into existence. Nor without the unending scientific and technological changes of the past several decades could men have gained relative freedom from the immediate concerns of the productive process, to the extent that they can now afford the luxury of discussing the "new individualism" and the "new politics"—of searching for a better life in post-welfare society. In the preliterate world the idea of individualism hardly exists, and in preindustrial civilizations only a handful of the elite (and then only in certain cultures and eras) have been able to devote themselves to this question.

The relation between the scientific and technological systems and the political order is a complex one. It still awaits clarification by social scientists. However, some broad patterns can be delineated. With respect to the American scene we must begin by examining the changes in social organization that have taken place over the past few decades— notably in the spheres of bureaucracy and social stratification—as well as modifications in the societal value system.

To restate our argument, the scientific-industrial revolution has made possible a more affluent welfare state; this affluence has been associated with bureaucratic and stratificational rearrangements as well as with modifications in the society's value orientations.[3] Because of these upheavals we can and must reflect upon the emergence of a "new individualism" and its relation to the future of American politics.

Structural Realignments. One of the most obvious and widely discussed changes in the American social structure since the Depression of

the 1930s, and more especially after World War II, has been an increase in the size and complexity of large-scale organizations or
bureaucratic systems. The business sector has come to be dominated by
corporate giants.[4] Concomitantly the power of labor unions has been
enhanced. So too, large-scale government has come into its own. Governmental bureaucracies have expanded in size and complexity on almost every level and, perhaps most significant of all, an enormous increase in political power has accrued to those bureaucracies that
dominate the national scene.

Although most students of organizational change in American society have focused on the emergence of big business, big labor, and big
government—and rightly so—modifications of considerable magnitude
have occurred in other spheres as well. The latter, however, can only be
understood within the context of the restructuring of the economic
sphere. Social scientists and policy makers, by and large, still retain an
image of the American economy as dominated by the manufacturing
sector with the blue-collar worker constituting the major element in the
labor force. But the data force us to visualize the economy in quite different terms.

Beginning in about the mid-1950s we saw for the first time in
American history more white-collar than blue-collar workers.[5] This
trend toward a white-collar labor force is associated with the growing
dominance of the service over the manufacturing sector. Although the
actual number of personnel in the "goods-producing industries" has remained relatively stable over the past several decades, an impressive increase in employment in the "service-producing industries" of the
"urban economy" has taken place.[6]

As is true with most concepts relating to social life, what is meant
by "services" or "the service sector" is ambiguous and subject to debate. Nonetheless, it is apparent that in relative terms manufacturing
has experienced a marked decline. And the service sector—much of
which is closely associated with the rise of the educational complex—
seems destined to become an ever more dominant force on the American economic scene in the years and decades ahead.[7]

We must also recognize that the shift in the nature and function of
the labor force is related to the changing class structure and the organizational revolution. What is clear is that increasingly more large-scale

bureaucracies—governmental, educational, and the like—are oriented toward providing services for the citizenry. In turn, these bureaucracies have become the key vehicle for sustaining the present-day class system in American society.

In elaborating upon this argument we should recognize that social scientists, including many sociologists whose field of specialization is in social class, are so caught up in the concern with individual mobility that they have lost sight of the structural rearrangements on the societal level—revisions that are essential for understanding what is happening to the class system, and indirectly to the future of politics. The stress upon individual rather than structural change is symbolized by the widely praised work of Peter M. Blau and Otis Dudley Duncan, *The American Occupational Structure*.[8] The authors, utilizing data collected in a survey in the early 1960s, studied the mobility patterns of individuals. But one can read this book and remain almost totally oblivious to the facts that the United States has experienced fundamental realignments in its social structure and that these changes have affected mobility patterns on the macro level. One of these structural changes has been the shift in the nature of the labor force.

Of more immediate relevance for us is the relation of the organizational system to the labor force and to the existing class and power alignments. With the shift in emphasis from production-centered to service-centered bureaucracies, the latter became the scene of much of the social and political controversy that dominated the domestic scene in the 1960s, and it is here that the key political battles of the 1970s are likely to be fought. However, the rise of client-centered bureaucracies has exposed many of the contradictions inherent in Weber's bureaucratic model. The system Weber analyzed was oriented toward an economy of scarcity rather than an economy of plenty. Although he cannot be faulted for failing to anticipate the future in all of its complexities, many of his admirers still fail to recognize that the bureaucratic system Weber portrayed—one geared to hierarchy and dominance—does not and cannot provide clients, especially in the realm of health, education, and welfare, with the kinds of services called for by the ideals of modern society. In the area of social services, more clearly than in the mass production of goods, some elements of the citizenry have come to recognize that bureaucratic organizations serve the interests not of clients but rather of persons who command the positions of power within those organizations. They also perceive that these bureaucratic organizations, instead of facilitating their clients' claim to a fair share of the goods and services of the affluent society, have acted to keep these clients in their place.[9]

Lower-class or disadvantaged clients constantly encounter highly complex rules they do not understand, for they are the ones with the least knowledge of the system. Yet frequently they are the persons standing in the greatest need of these services. Typically these clients are shunted from one agency to another, or from one sector to another within a particular agency, since the bureaucrats route the client and his problems on a more or less assembly-line basis. Each member of the bureaucracy encountered performs a specialized service and thus is unable to view the client as a total person. On the other hand, the privileged members of society have access to the upper echelons of the bureaucratic order and so come to be viewed as whole persons. The higher officials stand in the bureaucracy, the less constrained they are by the formal rules of the system and the more readily they can bypass the tangle of red tape.

We could go on to document the fact that bureaucratic organizations are perhaps the major vehicle for producing and sustaining the class system in the modern welfare state. Nowhere is this more transparent than in the income tax structure. Persons who have the means are able to take advantage of the organizational apparatus and, in a proper and legal manner, employ specialists with the expertise necessary to help them take advantage of the rules. It seems that the more disadvantaged the person, the less able he is to make use of provisions in the regulations that might permit him to retain more of his income. Similar patterns are apparent in the field of education, so that education and income are closely associated with the ability to understand and make profitable use of the normative order. Although the rules call for universalism and ideally encourage mobility, in practice they tend to maintain the existing status and power arrangements which have emerged in the welfare state. The rational and universalistic standards of bureaucracies also tend to maintain existing patterns of social stratification in the realm of minority relations. This is especially obvious in educational bureaucracies. Thus in universities, given the "logic" of "objective" standards, it seems irrational, impractical, and therefore "impossible" to recruit representative members of Blacks and other minority group members who live in worlds that do not fully socialize them into the performance standards of educational bureaucracies.

The Value System. With the growing affluence of American society fundamental changes have taken place not only in the social organization but in the value orientation as well. Among the most pervasive of the changes has been an increased emphasis upon individualism. Although the Western world has had a tradition emphasizing the importance of the individual, the meaning of "individualism" has varied somewhat in different historical contexts. The individualism of John Stuart Mill and England of the nineteenth century is not the individualism that many members of American society are espousing today (although even in the latter instance members of the New Left and the New Right differ somewhat in their views). Still, in different historical eras, a theme concerning respect for the individual, as apart from the collectivity, has been an integral feature of the Western value system.

Most significant for our understanding of the contemporary scene is the fact that in a highly affluent society a large number of individuals can take advantage of the call for individual dignity and can strive to implement this ideal. More American citizens than ever before have been freed from the traditional economic constraints that were once so binding. Consequently the concern with individual self-determination or self-expression is a major force leading to the questioning of bureaucratic structures and the status arrangements supported by them. The challenge results from the fact that the ideals of the system are in many cases not attained—i.e., the constraints of modern bureaucracies often inhibit the search for self-determination.

This fact is increasingly being illustrated by trends in the organizational world of government, business, and education. The recent reshaping of the "human relations" orientation in management into a humanistic framework has made many persons or groups aware that they can legitimately achieve individual fulfillment through work. Various subgroups have launched internal attacks upon bureaucracies (including professional associations), inasmuch as members of these groups seek increased monetary rewards and power and greater freedom for program innovations that will enhance their fulfillment as individuals through work and the usefulness of organizations to their clients.[10]

In part the opening up of work as a means of self-actualization has led to the development of heterogeneous life styles outside of organizations. As meaning in work is sought through more direct focus upon human objectives rather than through institutional aggrandizement, so too individual fulfillment is sought beyond traditional motivations. It is this quest for self-actualization that is a distinctive aspect of the new individualism and that is leading many persons to seek self-expression within the context of broad religious or nationalistic values. But these values are no longer as meaningful as formerly, and the search for identity often leads to a kind of tribalism that erects protective walls around the individual's experiential world. Thus the search for self-expression typically lacks any sense of relative transcendence over immediate experience, a fact that takes on considerable significance in any attempt to assess the course of politics in the future.

POLITICS IN TRANSITION

We have discussed in broad outline the social forces that we believe are laying the foundation for, and demanding, a new kind of political system in the United States. At the present time the American system is in a state of flux; the new politics has yet to emerge in full-blown form. As a result, before we analyze what we believe will be the political order of the post-welfare state, we must carefully examine the present political patterns as they appear in the state of transition.

Two social patterns that are in some respects contradictory, in other respects mutually supportive, have dominated the scene during the past decade or so. One is the emergence of new organizational forms, notably in the educational service sector and to some degree among the clients who are served by this sector. The other is the delegitimation of formal (including governmental) organizations, a process that has led some social scientists to speak of a "crisis of institutions" (or, more narrowly, a crisis of authority) in American society.

We should recognize that new organizational forms can emerge only when the traditional authority system has been delegitimized to a degree. The rising militancy of high school teachers in many parts of America is a major case in point. The strikes of the late 1960s in New York City, various communities in New Jersey, Los Angeles, and elsewhere dramatize the once-passive teacher's revolt against previously honored authority relations such as those between the school principal and the teacher, or the teacher and the community.

So marked is this trend toward the organization of professions that some form of "unionization" of college-level teachers seems on the horizon. Already the staid American Association of University Professors has offered itself as a collective bargaining agent dedicated to the protection of faculty prerogatives, be these salaries or other occupational benefits.

In the educational service sector it is not only professionals who are challenging the once-sacred authority structure. In some urban centers paraprofessionals in schools and hospitals are on the verge of becoming a potent organizational force. Add to this the emergence of organizations among clients themselves—be these students or welfare recipients. The result is a burgeoning of organizational structures in the service sector on a variety of levels at the very time when traditional organizations (and even formal organizations in general) are being called into question.

We can expect many more of these organizations to emerge in the decade to come. The rise of unions or unionlike organizations in government—on both the federal and the local levels—is another striking dimension of this movement.[11] Only a few years ago government was considered off-limits to organizations whose purpose was to further the special interests of employees through some form of collective bargaining.

Yet it is not just that new organizations in the service sector will strive to achieve greater economic gains for their members. They also seem destined to enter the political arena, directly or indirectly, as a means of attaining their economic and other objectives. The potential political impact of these organizations cannot be ignored in any analysis of politics in the post-welfare state.

At the same time we must not overlook the fact that such organizations are emerging in an era characterized by widespread delegitimation of traditional forms of authority and a questioning of authority in general. This suggests that the new organizations may not follow in the footsteps of the traditional bureaucratic forms. The former may instead be more transitory and flexible.

Although the industrial-urban order, or the welfare state in particular, has never before experienced such widespread skepticism concerning its authority system, sociologists and political scientists who analyze formal organizations continue to emphasize the role of legitimation. We know of no systematic effort to examine the delegitimation process, although a recent work by Hazel S. Fisher on the Women's Liberation Movement deals with this issue at some length.[12] Then, too, many writers who comment on the crisis of authority seem to have overemphasized the role of youth in this process, both in America and throughout the Western world. Although the youth protest has had widespread impact, we cannot overlook such a movement as that led by Pope John, a man of considerable age, to revise the authority patterns of the Catholic Church. A deep-seated social process seems to be at work, in part related to the breakup of traditional religious and nationalistic values, in part related to the rise of the "new individualism" and the search for a more meaningful value system that is in keeping with the emergent social order.

In attempting to understand the delegitimation process, we must distinguish between delegitimation promoted by advantaged members of the society and that instigated by the more disadvantaged sectors.

Many advantaged citizens have challenged the system through such diverse tactics as overconformity to the rules, picketing, protest rallies, the guerrilla theater, and even "dropping out." In effect they are saying that the system as presently constituted is not worth preserving, or at the very least that the existing authority structure must be revised. A crisis of authority has been experienced by universities, the structure of news media, governmental agencies, and so on. It has diffused outward to hitherto unlikely spheres such as athletic organizations and even the military.

The direct confrontation with persons occupying positions of authority has often exposed the fact that not all norms are designed to help the organization achieve its ideal goals. That many serve simply to entrench individuals in the seats of power has been revealed, for example, when university students have challenged the educational authority structure. It is here that the charge of hypocrisy, so freely bandied about, becomes relevant. Persons in authority positions come to be viewed as hypocritical, not necessarily because of their adherence to actual, in contrast to ideal, norms, but because the actual norms, by supporting special privileges, are perceived as undermining such ideal goals as equality and justice.

This confrontation also has exposed to public view norms that have not been articulated either by members of the system or by outsiders, especially the norm that system maintenance overrides all other considerations. Thus the delegitimation process is often heightened when persons in positions of power and authority in bureaucratic organizations are overly rigid in their defense of the status quo, even when faced with reasonable grievances that demand some modification in the normative order. The leadership's overresponse to the challenge dramatizes their orientation to system maintenance as an end in itself.

The delegitimation process is accentuated when citizens who confront organizations (or the system as a whole) find that they can do so without destroying their own existence. Bureaucratic leaders have argued time and again that critics of the existing arrangements will lose the benefits that would otherwise accrue to them. While some dissidents have been penalized, and a few severely so, others have been left unscathed. Many persons from privileged groups have been able to escape reprisals because they live in an affluent society wherein the traditional controls, such as withholding employment or cutting off goods and services, are simply not as effective as in a society based upon an economy of scarcity.

To an appreciable degree the social structure has been delegitimized not only for the privileged but for the less privileged as well. However, the process by which the latter, particularly lower-middle-class persons, come to question the ongoing order is quite different from that experienced by the more advantaged sectors of the society.

One challenge to the system's authority resides in the fact that the disadvantaged have internalized the norm of equality and are demanding a greater share of the society's economic rewards as well as increased social power.[13] The 1970 strike of postal workers was an historic occasion since these workers, members of the so-called silent majority, launched a significant protest against the government of the United States. Although social and political protest has had a long history in American society, this particular affront against governmental authority by workers within the system appears to have been unprecedented in nature, as postal workers called for greater economic equality and political power in an emerging affluent society.

Still another factor has led lower-middle-class persons to question the existing authority arrangements. They observe the contradictory manner in which bureaucratic leaders deal with privileged groups who challenge the system. Students, for instance, are seen as "biting the hand that feeds them," of taking undue advantage of their special position. Inasmuch as college students reap the rewards of the system even when they engage in acts that the less advantaged regard as illegitimate, the latter come to lose faith in the authority structure, viewing it as too tolerant of deviants.

THE NEW POLITICS

Given the shifting structural arrangements in American society and the upsurge of the "new individualism," with its questioning of the authority structure of formal organizations, what will be the future of American politics, especially in the decades just ahead? Two extreme counter-system models present themselves as possibilities.[14] On the one hand we may see a major effort to fit the emerging social patterns into pre-existing molds, leading to repression as the dominant form of politics. Or we may witness the rise of a new kind of political action: what we term "mobilization politics."

We cannot ignore the possibility of a movement dominated by "repression politics" whereby traditional categories and traditional power arrangements, including the political organization and the process of pluralist politics, will be sustained in coming decades. Already we hear of the stifling of dissent through increasingly sophisticated police methods—including the use of computers, wire tapping, and infiltration techniques—as a means of ensuring the maintenance of traditional structures.[15] Such repression will in general be accentuated by the actions of persons who resort to violence when seeking to change the system.

Although police power will form an integral part of repression politics, should the latter prove to be the course of the future, we believe that most forms of coercion employed will be far more subtle in nature. Modern bureaucracy, upon which the power elite depends, is not without resilience in the face of shifting social circumstances. By allowing some new forms of participation by dissidents and then establishing more and more levels of bureaucracy between themselves and their clients, as is happening in many universities, organizational leaders may frequently be able to isolate themselves from their increasingly rebellious clients. Thus bureaucracy fights back by creating more bureaucracy.

Moreover, the counterculture that attracts so many young people today may only serve to reinforce certain traditional structures. If, as is being proposed by certain social reformers, the system provides everyone with a minimum annual income, members of the "drop out" subculture will survive more easily in isolation from the established order. Being cut off in many respects from the mainstream of society, they are the most likely to heed the prescription laid down by the political scientist Banfield [16] that citizens should realistically limit their aspirations and be satisfied with less than complete justice and equality for all. Under these circumstances the pluralist model of politics, wherein the leaders of special interest groups compete in making key decisions, will prevail.

Obviously a major world crisis which conceivably could lead to a new constitutional convention would crystallize many of the social forces that reinforce the status quo. Such a convention would shore up, in a legalistic manner, the structure that is weakening under rapidly changing social conditions.

While we do not rule out the possibility of repression and containment of the new individualism within the existing organizational and political format, we believe that the pressures for major structural revisions are too powerful to be stifled or ignored. Our argument rests upon the thesis that the structural changes sketched above are taking place within a relatively flexible legal framework. The English common law tradition which underlies American political institutions is conducive to, and supportive of, adjustment—far more so than the legal tradition of continental Europe, which has instead fostered political closure. And whereas democracy in continental Europe is based upon a tradition of equality in contrast to the British notion of liberty under the law, the American constitutional heritage is a mixture of both of these traditions.[17] Although the ideals of both liberty and equality have fallen far short of actualization in the United States, the fact remains that the American value system forces members of the society to confront both of these standards.

Just as significant in the long run for sustaining an open society is the very complexity of the American social order. Although this has led to confusion and disarray and many confounding tensions, it has also militated against widespread political repression. Every power group in America is faced with extensive ethnic and regional diversity and a complex division of labor. Moreover, the division of labor itself is typified by a wide variety of mediator roles. Such mediators serve as buffers against possible repression. While some mediators, such as lawyers, psychiatrists, and social workers, have typically served as agents of social control for modern bureaucratic organizations, they are also in a position in times of crisis to interpret the arguments of dissenters to persons in authority, as well as members of the broader public who may often be adverse to accepting fundamental structural revisions. Although the effectiveness of various Presidential commissions, for instance, has rightly been questioned, these have filled the function of sensitizing the power groups and the broader citizenry to the struggles of the disadvantaged and even, to some degree, to the meaning of the "new individualism." Granted that it is difficult to define in any operationally acceptable manner the impact of these commissions, it seems plausible to assume that without such mediator groups the existing tensions would be far more destructive.

In the end, then, we believe that large-scale repression is not the most likely outcome of the current social and political crisis (though, admittedly, selected groups and individuals seem destined to experience social harm). Our argument leads to the conclusion that a new kind of political system, in contrast to the pluralistic one, is in the offing. This countermodel we have termed "mobilization politics."

In order to clarify our position we must briefly relate the fundamental structural and value changes in American society more explicitly to this emerging political form. Our argument relies heavily upon the premise that with growing affluence—and an expanding privileged class whose members strive to attain individual self-expression—there will be a mounting separation between old-line political and economic controls. This separation will foster as well as demand a mobilization type of politics which is more responsive to the ever-changing concerns of individuals in the modern world.

As suggested earlier, in the bureaucracy-dominated society as described by Weber the political sector has used economic coercion, such as the loss of one's job or job security, as the major means of controlling a large section of the populace. But with increasing affluence this threat is no longer as compelling and will become even less so if a guaranteed annual income is implemented.

Stated differently, scholars and citizens who think and act in terms of traditional political arrangements view dissidents, be they youths or other persons, with both scorn and envy. Attackers of the system can ignore or reject the old-line status and authority hierarchies with considerable impunity. Because a significant sector of the populace has already gained access to the economic resources by which they can at least sustain a minimal level of subsistence, those in positions of authority cannot as readily disburse or withhold economic rewards as a means of sustaining the social order. This pattern in turn reinforces the decline of one's occupation, and achievement therein, as an important source of personal values.

It is the separation of economic from political controls that has facilitated the emergence of new and varied life styles among the privileged. In other eras the development of new life styles was hardly feasible on any large-scale basis. In the past, deviant life-style patterns have been associated with a few avant-garde artist groups, the poor, or the members of ethnic enclaves. But, significantly, these life styles were rarely the result of "free choice."

Nowadays many urban subcultures are emerging more or less spontaneously among members of the advantaged sectors as they seek to establish a sense of community in what has come to be regarded as a largely inhuman technological environment.[18] And it seems evident that a significant number of those persons who have rejected the dominant middle-class life styles and status arrangements will find it increasingly difficult to return to the "straight world" in their later years.

The new life-style subcultures seem destined to become permanent features of American society. With the relative decline of the blue-collar worker and the rise of the educational service sector, these life styles are more likely to cut across status (including ethnic) boundaries and across the organizational structures that are coming into existence. We are not suggesting that all status differences will dissolve but rather that the structural shift toward an educational service economy will result in a variety of overlapping life styles among members of the society.

The emergence of these life styles takes on broader political and social import in that they accentuate still further the rupture between the political and the economic spheres. Not only do they make it more difficult for persons who command political power to manipulate others through traditional bureaucratic rules, and not only do they reinforce disrespect for traditional authority, but the champions of these life styles must, if they are to sustain the new patterns, enter the political arena in order to revise the political and economic rules that affect their way of life. Such a situation already obtains among some elements within the Women's Liberation Movement. And it is emerging as well among members of the Gay Liberation Movement.

The decline of occupation as a central feature of a person's values and the flowering of a wide range of life styles may prove "functional" for the survival of the post-welfare social order. In a society characterized by drastic scientific and technological innovations, as well as the emergence of new organizations, even highly educated persons must prepare for the possibility of shifting their occupational goals and cultural styles at some time in their life cycle. The economic difficulties confronting some highly trained physicists, engineers, and corporate executives in the late 1960s and early 1970s point to the dilemmas that many advantaged members of society may face in the years ahead.

To reiterate: The basic changes in the class system and the emergence of a new individualism made possible by affluence are leading to a basic reorientation of politics, in large part because the traditional controls, largely dependent upon economic coercion, are no longer feasible. Major readjustments are both possible and necessary if industrial man is to survive and sustain his humanity.

This is the context for the new politics—the evolution of mobilization politics. Inasmuch as the condition of social pluralism, with new but fragile life styles, is increasing greatly, a politics wherein flexibility is the dominant orientation is deemed the reasonable outcome. The current political structure, oriented toward assumptions of social stability, is based upon rather narrow, fixed lines of representation—via the party electoral and interest-group systems. Inasmuch as this structure presupposes order and stability, the leaders bargain and compromise for their respective constituencies. The political outcomes (laws) are refined through compromise decisions which are reached in the process of administrative politics. Such a political style fits a stable social-economic order, wherein issues are defined by relatively permanent economic and political interest groups. But under conditions of social pluralism and flux, the issues must constantly be redefined as different organizations and life styles come and go.

A major characteristic of mobilization politics will be a highly flexible electoral structure that goes beyond such traditional mechanisms for flexibility as referendum and recall. Particularly, provisions will have to be made for greater participation by citizens in the selection of candidates and the framing of issues. A step in this direction seems to have been initiated in Wisconsin, where a citizen, under very special circumstances, can not only mark for a given candidate but can also vote "None of the Names Shown." Even such a simple move as this can have a major impact upon political outcomes, for in this situation voters would be able to record their dissatisfaction with the existing candidates or the issues as framed by the political leadership.

Mobilization politics also calls for a marked reformulation of the party system. There are indications that such is occurring on various levels. More and more Americans identify themselves by some special group designation or as independents rather than as Democrats or Republicans. Illustrative of this development is what was called the "six-party system" that emerged in the 1969 mayoralty contest in New York City.[19] So too, the crisis of party allegiance and organization is reflected in the struggles by the Democrats to incorporate a wider variety of subgroups into the decision-making process that selects candidates for office.

Overall we can look forward to a fluid system wherein the successful political leadership is one that can put together shifting coalitions of individuals and groups as issues and interests among voters are constantly evolving.

Along with increased flexibility in electoral participation will come a tendency to define issues in macro-political terms rather than within

the present lower-level framework of administrative politics. The new
politics will deem unacceptable the "sublimation" of issues to solution
by the administrative process.[20] Already some citizens are demanding
that even many of the technical issues of economic regulation that are
now handled at the agency level be thrown back into the political arena.
Commitments to policy will therefore become more general. Instead of
fighting, for instance, over the specifics of a program such as Medicare,
the issue will tend to be defined and settled politically in terms of a general debate on the needs for public health. Only after that will the specifics be considered (although even the latter will be open periodically
to political debate).

As a corollary of mobilization politics, bureaucratic discretion and
the implementation of policy through the development of elaborate administrative procedures will not be as heavily relied upon as they are
today. Instead, there will be self-administering policies such as the family allowance measure recently proposed in the United States Congress,
which would eliminate the casework load of welfare programs by making a certain "per child" stipend to mothers of *all* children in the nation, and then taxing families differentially, according to their ability to
pay, for the financing of the program.

Related to an increased reliance upon self-administering programs
would be a more general dependence upon "the rule of law" as a means
for attaining social justice. In keeping with the decline of bureaucratic
discretion in the management of welfare programs, psychiatric and
other professional psychological forms of discretion will take on less
and less importance in the definition of what is regarded as deviant social action. In a society marked by divergent and overlapping life styles,
as practiced by a wide spectrum of the population, only specific legal
standards defining the minimum rules of social organization can probably be maintained.[21]

It further seems likely that as a means of mobilizing political
groups to accomodate their own temporariness and heterogeneity, some
novel organizational and influential strategies will evolve. The "nonhier-
archical," "nonbureaucratic" structures espoused by some social scientists for carrying out special tasks in society are likely to assume a definite place in the political sphere.[22] And such new forms of influence
and pressure tactics as overcompliance with administrative rules, para-

compliance, and the guerrilla theater will become legitimized. The citizenry will likely build upon some of the strategies that have delegitimized traditional authority systems as a means of sustaining a greater responsiveness to the electorate on the part of those who command positions of power.

The founding fathers established a constitutional structure for controlling factions, or special interest groups, through such devices as the separation of powers and checks and balances, and they set in motion the subsequent development of party and electoral politics, patterns that are increasingly difficult to sustain in a society wherein social pluralism and flux are the order of the day. In the 1960s pluralistic politics came under increasing attack. Pluralist elitism (resulting from the likemindedness of policy makers and a bias against social sectors that cannot afford to organize and play the pluralist game), mass powerlessness (resulting from too-narrow paths for representation), and apathy (resulting from the sublimation of politics into administration) are all potentially resolved by mobilization politics.

However, mobilization politics, as it has been sketched, is a *countersystem model*. What will actually result in the post-industrial, or post-welfare, era is a combination of this kind of political pattern with that of the present day. The new formal organizations arising in the service sector, though more flexible than those in the past, will nonetheless serve as a significant brake upon the rise of mobilization politics in its pure form. So, too, the demand for technical expertise will sustain certain bureaucratic operations. And politics as a mass encounter group is not without its own sense of boredom and frustration.

The specific form that the political structure of the future will take will most likely vary according to the particular kinds of policy encountered. Lowi's analysis of American politics links various policies—those related to distributive, regulatory, and redistributive functions—to separate political styles. We shall build upon his informative discussion.[23]

Distributive policy is that which is made "without regard to limited resources"—river and harbor legislation, public land and resource policy, tariffs, etc. It involves "stakes" which can be broken down into smaller and smaller parts. This process facilitates the use of such policy standards as equality, consistency, impartiality, and uniformity. These standards, one could argue, are what might be expected in a political system of the popular democratic-representational sort, and indeed Lowi views the structure and process of this political form as associated with distributive policy-making. Coalitions of specific individuals with diverse interests (those having little or nothing in common) are formed under "mutual noninterference" pacts for purposes of policy-making, where each part seeks indulgences for himself yet tolerates the seeking of indulgences by others. Such a process has multiple facets, as in congressional committees and stable logrolling relations. The very nature of these relations leads to a kind of decentralization in decision-making.

Regulatory policy, a second type, involves decisions over scarce resources that directly determine who will be indulged and who will be deprived. Unlike distributive policy, regulatory politics involves a pie that can be sliced and divided into relatively few parts rather than into many small ones—hence some groups win and others lose. Allocations of air routes, television channels, and the imposition of rules such as those governing labor-management relations are examples of regulatory policies. In contract to the specific issues that develop around the pay-offs of distributive politics, regulatory politics creates interest aggregations around sectors of society. These sectors are defined by general rules that are the outcome of the regulatory process, in that individual parties group with others that are similarly affected. Coalitions are formed through conflict and compromise among tangential interests in a sector, and an unstable balance of power is created wherein realignments occur constantly as the issues are modified. The pattern here is most like the pluralist ideal with its "policy clusters."

A third kind of policy, the redistributive one, involves broad categories of social classes. The purposes of this policy are "not use of property itself, not equal treatment but equal possession, not behavior but being." Examples of this type are welfare programs and income taxes. In their structure and process such policies most closely approach the power elite model, wherein there is much cohesion along social class lines and among peak associations. The shared interests are stable and consistent enough to provide an ideological base for the institutionalization of the system that sets these policies. In this sphere of political action there are only two sides, and negotiation is limited to strengthening or softening the impact of redistribution.

In the post-industrial order, characterized by affluence and the emerging social structure we have described above, the relative emphases given the various types of politics within American society must shift considerably. Of the various political forms described by Lowi,[24] regulatory politics seems most likely to persist in somewhat its present form. For some degree of scarcity in certain policy areas appears destined to remain. Yet even here, as is suggested by the present-day efforts of various subgroups to challenge the regulation of mass media, the basic value orientation and social priorities of the regulators will periodically be forced into open debate. It is through these challenges that the technical decisions can be placed in their broader social context. At the same time the technical expertise associated with regulatory decisions, notably with respect to an automated economy, will continue to conceal many of these actions from broader public scrutiny.

Distributive and redistributive politics seem certain to undergo more fundamental changes in nature and extent than regulatory politics. Given a high degree of affluence, distributive politics will cover a much broader range of human issues than it did in times of relative scarcity. The emergent social conditions will cause a shift in the basic value orientation toward the distributive process. Today all political issues tend to be considered in terms of a scarcity model, even in the realm of distributive politics where there are no direct gains or losses for political participants. Public works programs—the epitome of the distributive model—are viewed as solutions to the problem of public or social saving and development. In contrast, the distributive politics of the future will be oriented not toward problem solving but toward the formulation and attainment of broader societal goals—such as the achievement of a better quality of life for all.

The space program is another example of the current distributive policy. The difficulties encountered in space policy-making so far augur a shift to the mobilization politics model as a means for reaching distributive policy decisions in the future. To relate such an exotic program as space exploration to the issues of the everyday world poses a challenge to the modern politician.

Distributive politics in the post-industrial era will demand that the political leadership define broader societal goals—not just in a negative way but also in a positive way—so that programs can be placed into some more meaningful context for the members of subcommunities within the society and so that the populace can be mobilized in terms of a broader social cause.

Redistributive politics will undergo changes of similar depth. The issues will begin to shift away from the reallocation of economic resources among social classes to adjustments among members of differing life-style subgroupings. Even today the "law and order issue" overrides many social class and socio-economic considerations.

Mobilization politics will have its most visible impact in the redistributive realm. It has been widely noted that the locus of the most intense political activity has moved significantly from the executive-legislative level to the administrative one. The people of Resurrection City approached Capitol Hill only at the end of their summer of demonstration—after months of first seeking to confront the administrative departments. Administrative agencies are a natural target for mobilized political groups, for they impinge most directly upon a person's daily life and his group's life style. Furthermore, these agencies are often highly vulnerable to the strategies and tactics that are associated with certain forms of mobilization politics.

The administrative system will serve as the locus for the transitional phase of development into mobilization politics. These organizations will be forced to become more sensitive to clients and to the demands for revision that will be created by the conditions of the new social and cultural pluralism. In the longer run, however, the entire political system will have to undergo change. The pressures of a highly pluralist society can be dealt with only partially by administration since the basic requisite for the viability of social and cultural pluralism is full citizenship and participation for the society's members. The mobilization politics model that we have discussed seems to be the most likely vehicle for revitalizing the role of the citizen in the society of the future.

SOME CRITICAL REFLECTIONS

We have elaborated herein our thesis that fundamental structural changes and basic shifts in values have been occurring in American society and that these are both laying the basis for and demanding a new kind of political apparatus. Although a major world crisis could enable the contemporary power structure to force its critics back into the traditional mold, we believe that the social pressures lie mainly in the opposite direction: They call for a new politics that not only will provide for greater humanism but also will serve to sustain the highly developed scientific and technological order.

Thus a mobilization politics seems likely to emerge—not in its ideal form but in some modified version. It can be attained in a society dominated by the educational service sector wherein social class lines are vague, organizational commitments are minimal, and overlapping life styles are the rule.

But we would be remiss if we did not consider the inherent dangers of this new political form. Mobilization politics opens up the possibility of manipulation of the electorate. It poses a problem that has haunted political thinkers such as Hannah Arendt who, after analyzing the totalitarian movements of Europe in this century, found no viable organizations standing between the individual and the state.[25] Without organizational buffers individuals are vulnerable to charismatic leaders who are adept at manipulation through effective use of the mass media. This danger has perhaps been heightened with the prevalence of television.

The use of mobilization politics for potentially authoritarian ends cannot be lightly dismissed. Even a highly educated electorate which doubts and questions authority structures is not a sufficient deterrent. If man is to overcome the dangers posed by mobilization politics and yet be able to take advantage of this political activity to enhance his participation in the decision-making process, he must devise a new authority system. If man is to attain freedom through increased control over his life's chances, he must also construct and maintain an order which provides him with significant structural alternatives.

We stand in desperate need of a new kind of authority structure, one not built upon Weber's categories of charismatic, traditional, or legal-rational authority. The authority system we envisage would foster and sustain tensions between individuals and the authority structure. But it would do more than this. It would lead to built-in tensions for persons who occupy positions of authority: fundamental dilemmas between the action they must take in the here-and-now, through participation in mobilization or ad hoc politics, and a utopian vision that would place these actions in a more meaningful context.

Mobilization politics without proper structural constraints could lead citizens to focus upon issues that are of only momentary or narrow personal concern. A growing emphasis upon the experiential world, dramatized among counterculture groups, could lead men to lose sight of the struggles of persons who live in quite different social and cultural spheres.

It is through tensions between individuals and the groups in which they participate, and between actions oriented toward the here-and-now and some utopian dream, that the leadership and the citizenry can attain relative transcendence over their own and their society's immediate concerns. Just how the new political structure can encourage political leaders and the broader citizenry to continue the "moral struggle" we have described is the major challenge confronting those who seek to create political systems that will be not only viable in the post-welfare state but also of lasting value to humankind everywhere.

Notes

1. Two current works which have been widely read describe aspects of this shift in the value system: Theodore Roszak, *The Making of a Counter Culture: Reflections on the Technocratic Society and Its Youthful Opposition* (Garden City, N.Y., 1969), and Charles Reich, *The Greening of America* (New York, 1970). Our analysis goes beyond that of Roszak and Reich and at points diverges markedly from their conclusions about the direction and outcome of shifts in the normative order.

2. One of the most challenging accounts can be found in Jacques Ellul, *The Technological Society* (New York, 1964).

3. On the class stratification basis of the bureaucratized professional management movement, see Judith A. Merkle, "The Taylor Strategy: Organizational Innovation and Class Structure," *Berkeley Journal of Sociology*, XIII (1968), 59–81.

4. Michael Reagan, *The Managed Economy* (New York, 1963), and John Kenneth Galbraith, *The New Industrial State* (Boston, 1967).

5. See *Occupational Outlook Handbook, 1970–1971 Edition,* U.S. Department of Labor, Bureau of Labor Statistics, Bulletin No. 1650 (Washington, D.C., 1970), p. 15.

6. *Ibid.,* p. 12.

7. Victor R. Fuchs, *The Service Economy* (New York, 1968). The author contends that during the period following World War II the United States became the world's first service economy, p. 1.

8. New York, 1968.

9. Gideon Sjoberg, Richard Brymer, and Buford Farris, "Bureaucracy and the Lower Class," *Sociology and Social Research,* L (April 1966), 325–37.

10. This humanistic development in management philosophy is well stated in Warren G. Bennis, *Changing Organizations* (New York, 1966). An example of an internal attack on the national bureaucracy which reflects this point of view can be seen in the activities of the Federal Employees for a Democratic Society, which is apparently a growing organization. See, for a statement of the "FEDS Manifesto," "The Condition of the Federal Employee and How to Change It," *Public Administration Review,* XXIX (July–August 1969), 435–40. The dissent which is occurring within virtually all the traditional academic, practicing, and newer professions (such as journalism) is also quite pertinent evidence to this point. See, for example, a symposium on "The Coming Newsroom Revolution," *Columbia Journalism Review,* IX (Summer 1970). Note especially the articles by Jean Schwoebel and Edwin Diamond.

11. "Symposium on Collective Negotiations in the Public Service," *Public Administration Review,* XXVIII (March–April 1968), 111–47.

12. Hazel S. Fisher, *The Women's Liberation Movement in the Process of Emergence* (unpublished dissertation, City University of New York, 1971).

13. Cf. Herbert J. Gans, "The 'Equality' Revolution," *New York Times Magazine* (November 3, 1968), 36 f.

14. For a discussion of countersystem analysis see Sjoberg and Leonard D. Cain, "Negative Values, Countersystem Models, and the Analysis of Social Systems," in Herman Turk and Richard Simpson, eds., *Institutions and Social Exchange: The Sociologies of Talcott Parsons and George C. Homans* (Indianapolis, 1971), Chapter 14.

15. Alan F. Westin, *Privacy and Freedom* (New York, 1967).

16. Edward C. Banfield, *The Unheavenly City* (Boston, 1968).

17. George H. Sabine, "The Two Democratic Traditions," *Philosophical Review,* LXI (October 1952), 451–74.

18. Emerging life styles were already being discussed in a wide range of newspapers and magazines during the latter part of the 1960s. See such New York newspapers and magazines as *The Village Voice, The Rat,* and *New York Magazine.* And these phenomena are now being discussed in more traditional circles. See, for example, Ken Harnett (Associated Press), "The Alternative Society," *Houston Chronicle* (April 26, 1971), 1–2. This is the first of a five-part series of articles.

19. Richard Reeves, "The Six-Party System," *New York Times* (September 29, 1969), 41.

20. Sheldon S. Wolin, *Politics and Vision* (Boston, 1960), 352–434, and Jack L. Walker, "A Critique of the Elitist Theory of Democracy," *American Political Science Review,* LX (June 1966), 285–95.

21. Thomas Szasz, *Law, Liberty, and Psychiatry* (New York, 1968), and Szasz, *Myth of Mental Illness* (New York, 1961).

22. For one example, see Orion F. White, Jr., "The Dialectical Organization—An Alternative to Bureaucracy," *Public Administration Review,* XXIX (January–February 1969), 32–42.

23. Theodore J. Lowi, "American Business, Public Policy, Case Studies, and Political Theory," *World Politics,* XVI (July 1964), 673–715, and Lowi, *The End of Liberalism: Ideology, Policy, and the Crisis of Public Authority* (New York, 1969).

24. Lowi, *The End of Liberalism.*

25. Hannah Arendt, *The Origins of Totalitarianism* (New York, 1951).

CHRISTOPHER LASCH

Toward a Theory of Post-Industrial Society

POST-INDUSTRIAL SOCIETY may be said to come into being when capital accumulation has reached the point where scarcity is no longer a major social problem—that is, when the industrial system has developed the capacity to satisfy all the basic human needs. Only capitalism has achieved this level of productivity—notably in the United States and in the more advanced states of Western Europe, like Sweden. The term "post-industrial," therefore, designates a particular stage in the historical development of capitalism which is distinguishable from earlier stages in important respects but is still capitalist in its essential features. Post-industrial society is still capitalist in the sense that the industrial system produces commodities rather than objects for use and that the important decisions concerning production remain in "private" hands rather than being socially determined.

In the United States, the advent of post-industrial society can be dated roughly from the end of World War II, while the period approximately from 1865 to 1945 may be designated as the industrial stage of American history—the period of necessary capital accumulation.

The post-industrial phase of capitalist development—if American history offers any clues to a theory that might be more generally applicable—differs from the industrial phase in a number of ways, of which the following seem to be the most important.

The Changing Character of Poverty. Poverty is no longer a general and pervasive condition. In industrial society masses of people lived in poverty, and poverty was aggravated by periodic business depressions with widespread unemployment. The consciousness of poverty was therefore as generalized as poverty itself. In post-industrial society, poverty is found isolated in "pockets" or "islands" and tends to become "invisible."

This point, which has been given wide circulation by Galbraith's *The Affluent Society* and Harrington's *The Other America,* can be put more precisely. In industrial society poverty was the condition of the most numerous class, the industrial working class, and the struggles of this class to organize itself in the face of oppression and misery formed one of the central threads in the history of industrial societies. In post-industrial society the working class has achieved relative affluence and economic security in the form of pensions, social security, medical care, and a guaranteed annual wage. Wherever it has penetrated, the industrial system tends to eliminate poverty. In post-industrial society, therefore, poverty is the lot of those whom the industrial system has failed to absorb: migrant and seasonal workers, the chronically unemployed, and workers in the shops of petty capitalism. The fact that poverty is increasingly identified with certain racial and ethnic differences contributes to its marginality and isolation.

The Class Structure of Post-Industrial Society. The changing character of poverty is closely related to the changing class structure of post-industrial society. The industrial working class is no longer the largest class. As industry rationalizes itself, the demand for white-collar workers outruns the demand for unskilled and semiskilled workers. People without skills consequently find themselves not only excluded from industry altogether but also excluded, for a variety of reasons, from the educational opportunities that would enable them to acquire skills necessary to enter the industrial working force (even though their children are forced to spend many years in school). Post-industrial society gives rise to a sizable class of new poor who live, as noted, on the margins of the industrial system, with access only to the most menial jobs. The new poor are not a proletariat in the strict sense because they are not engaged in industrial production; instead they constitute a new kind of *lumpenproletariat,* alienated and resentful.

The growing demand for skilled and highly trained personnel gives rise, on the other hand, to the so-called new middle class of clerks, salesmen, and technicians—a class that also includes teachers and other employees of the state. Because this class has very limited access to property, and very limited control over the social decisions that shape the lives of its members, it resembles a new kind of proletariat more nearly than it resembles a middle class. At the same time its members reject identification with the working class. Although the members of this class think of themselves as "middle class," they do not share the ideology of the old bourgeoisie.[1] As Louis Boudin pointed out many years ago, " 'governmental interference' has no terrors for . . ." the new middle class. "It feels the need of a stronger hand than that of the individual in arranging the field of battle for the struggle for existence. If such a makeshift may be dignified into an ideology, its ideology is State Socialism . . ." or, what is the same thing, the ideology of the welfare state.[2]

Whereas the class structure of industrial society tended to be polarized between bourgeois and proletarians, post-industrial society consists of five distinct classes, of which the first is steadily diminishing in size and importance:

(i) the traditional middle class, declining in status and increasingly attracted, in its insecurity and despair, to racist versions of its old *laissez faire* ideology;

(ii) the traditional working class, now somewhat diminished in size, unionized, relatively affluent, and integrated into the industrial system;

(iii) the new *lumpenproletariat*, swollen by recent migrants from rural areas where mechanization has eliminated the need for unskilled labor, who collect in the ghettos of decaying cities;

(iv) the "new middle class" or white-collar proletariat; and finally,

(v) the ruling class, an amalgam of the *haute bourgeoisie* and the new managerial elite, that controls the great corporations, most of the land, and the higher reaches of government (especially the military). In both its functions and ideology the ruling class is predominantly managerial. The term "ruling class" is misleading, however, if it suggests too sharp a distinction between those who control the giant corporations and those who own them. The theory of the managerial revolution notwithstanding, ownership even today—as C. Wright Mills pointed out in *The Power Elite*—is by no means wholly divorced from control. Nor has the managerial class developed an antibourgeois ideology, as so many writers over the years have predicted it would.[3] On the contrary, it has developed a variant of bourgeois ideology, a variant of liberalism best described as corporate liberalism and exemplified in progressivism, the New Deal, the Fair Deal, the New Frontier, and the Great Society. Corporate liberalism, sometimes confused with socialism by those who do not know any better and even by those who should (like William F. Buckley), differs from traditional liberalism in its acceptance of a managed economy, its recognition of Labor unions as legitimate bargaining agents, its commitment to the welfare state, and its devotion to a Liberalized imperialism abroad. It shares with traditional liberalism a fundamental commitment to the "free enterprise economy"—that is, to the system of commodity production for "private" profit known as capitalism.

The ruling class has disseminated the ideology of corporate liberalism with such success that "Liberal" values pervade all classes, even the marginal poor. The only challenge to it comes, as noted, from remnants of the old middle class who are declining in status or, on the other hand, from independent capitalists who have not yet achieved full membership in the ruling elite. But the laissez faire ideology articulated by Goldwater and Wallace is itself informed by many assumptions of corporate liberalism. Thus it condemns "government interference" but advocates a militaristic foreign policy that would lead to more centralization of power, not less. The ideological congruence, at certain points, of Goldwaterism and the dominant liberalism suggests that the old middle class, on which a laissez faire ideology necessarily rests, is tending to disappear as an independent entity. At its upper level, it tends to merge with the managerial class and to become managerial in outlook, while on its lower levels it melts imperceptibly into the "new middle class" or white-collar proletariat. That is why a reactionary movement in post-industrial society cannot base itself purely on the ideology of laissez faire.

Insofar as reactionary movements speak to a pervasive dissatisfaction with centralization, with bureaucratic control, and with the rootlessness and emptiness of modern life, they find potential recruits among all classes and in all sections of the country—even among members of the working class, as George Wallace has demonstrated. But in identifying themselves with a laissez faire and antiwelfare ideology, reactionary movements alienate their potential supporters in the old working class as well as the new. While many members of those classes readily respond to appeals to their sense of powerlessness, their overt or latent racism, their jingoism, and their need for "law and order," they are nevertheless too well integrated into the industrial system and too heavily dependent on the welfare state to welcome an ideology that glorifies the entrepreneur and denounces government intervention in the economy. To be successful a rightist or Fascist movement in the United States would have to come to terms with the welfare state—something which is difficult to imagine. Rather than welling up out of a popular upheaval, it is more likely that Fascist or quasi-Fascist measures would be imposed, in a period of extreme crisis, by the managerial elite itself in the guise of corporate liberalism.

The Decay of the City. Whereas industrial society was built around the industrial city, a central feature of post-industrial society is the decay of the city and the vast growth of suburbs. In the United States this process is far advanced, while in Europe it is just beginning. In both cases the most important agent of this fundamental social change is the automobile, around whose peculiar needs the modern city increasingly organizes itself. The automobile devours space in the form of superhighways and parking lots, pollutes the air, destroys public transportation, and above all makes possible the flight of masses of people and later of industry and capital from the cities to the suburbs. Even recreational and cultural facilities eventually leave the city. These facts, like those concerning the changing character of poverty, are familiar enough. What is not generally recognized is that they are by no means accidental or secondary phenomena correctable at will, but reflect the central needs of the industrial system in a post-industrial age.

In such a system the automobile industry has a position of unusual importance because of the automobile's insatiable appetite for roads, parking garages, gasoline, roadside establishments of all kinds, and innumerable other goods and services ancillary to itself (to say nothing of its appetite for steel, rubber, glass, and all the other materials that are required to produce cars in the first place). No other industry has such seemingly unlimited capacity to stimulate a wide range of other industries. In an economy oriented around the production of consumer goods, the automobile plays the same role as the railroad played in an economy oriented around heavy industry. It is the most appropriate and glamorous symbol of the consumer culture and the values it embodies: personal mobility and the private satisfaction of culturally stimulated needs and wants. In a society in which the consumption of goods has been raised to the level of an ethical imperative, and in which consumption has been closely tied to the privatization of life, the automobile, which is an indispensable means of access to the consumption of everything from symphonies to hot dogs (as well as to work) and which epitomizes privatization, comes to be regarded as a *deus ex machina* on which the successful resolution of all life's cares depends—even the attainment of sexual satisfaction.

Superfluous Production. The needs of the automobile, which are destroying not only the city but also much of the countryside as well, exemplify the needs of the industrial or corporate system as a whole in a period when it has achieved the capacity to satisfy all the basic material needs. The continuing growth of the system now depends on the creation and satisfaction of false needs, and even then the system finds itself unable to run at full capacity.

Because of its own efficiency, the system of "private" industry has outrun the need for its own existence and can survive only through the production of waste, whether in the form of goods that people do not need or in the form of goods designed to become prematurely obsolescent. The need for waste has given rise to entire new industries such as advertising, market research, and public relations. It has also led to governmental subsidization of waste in the form of highways, urban "renewal" programs accommodated to the needs of the automobile industry, and other concealed subsidies to that industry, the space program, and most spectacularly, unprecedented expenditures for defense. The need for subsidized waste, together with federally imposed restrictions against the "unfair trade practices" of smaller competitors, has greatly increased the dependence of the great corporations on the state. The ideology of corporate liberalism is a reflection of this dependence.[4]

The state has grown to enormous size and its activities have proliferated in all directions. Yet the same developments that have led to this growth have had the curious effect of impoverishing the state which depends for revenue on a base of taxable wealth that is steadily shrinking. The corporations produce an ever-growing surplus, but it takes the form not of taxable wealth but of waste built into consumer goods. Hence the well-known disparity between the affluence of the private sector and the impoverishment of the public.[5] In the partnership between government and the great corporations, the former performs all the functions indispensable to the survival of the corporations, while the corporations retain the profits. While surplus wealth accumulates at an unheard-of rate, schools, public transportation, and cultural facilities decay; the landscape is devastated, rivers and lakes are polluted, and the whole quality of civic life deteriorates.

Neo-colonialism. The same conditions that force the corporations to seek new markets in the form of waste also force them to seek new markets abroad. Since 1945 the United States has steadily expanded into the former colonial areas vacated by the declining empires of Europe. Because this expansion has brought the United States into conflict with the forces of communism and nationalism in the third world, as well as the military power of the Soviet Union, it has served to justify the creation of a vast arsenal of destruction. Armament development and production serve in turn to justify the foreign policies that called them into being, even when those policies have become obsolescent in their own terms. The diplomatic needs of the United States—that is, of the great corporations—would best be served by a *detente* with the Soviet Union, a withdrawal not only from South Vietnam but also from all of southeast Asia, and a division of the world into spheres of influence in which the entire Western hemisphere would be assigned to the United States on condition that she not meddle with the rest of the world. Since this policy would lead to a reduction in arms expenditures, the dismantling of the machinery of nuclear deterrence, and a global arms accord, however, it threatens the growth of the military establishment which plays a major role in sustaining a corporate economy geared to the production of waste. Even if it is no longer necessary, from a strictly economic point of view, that the United States maintain a worldwide colonial empire, it is necessary for military spending not only to be sustained at its present levels but also to grow. Hence for reasons having little to do with the immediate requirements of diplomacy, the United States finds itself locked into the archaic policy of "containment."

Post-industrial society, in short, demands a continual state of military emergency and a global crusade against an enemy, the "international communist conspiracy," with which there can be no compromise. The old imperialism of the industrial epoch could coexist, for a time at least, with balance-of-power diplomacy among the great powers. In contrast, the peculiar requirements of the new colonialism preclude a worldwide accord that would guarantee periods of peace and stability. Neo-Conservative critics of American diplomacy, who advocate such an accord under the name of disengagement, are demanding, in effect, a return to nineteenth-century power politics. Yet they raise such demands at a time when the social order requires precisely the "messianic" diplomacy they deplore, and which they erroneously attribute not to the need for greater and greater military spending but to the eccentricities of the American "national character." [6]

The Central Importance of Education. Perhaps the most striking feature of post-industrial society is the degree to which formal education has become a universal phenomenon. Even a college education has come to be defined as a right to which all people are entitled (though the system still falls short of that goal), while increasing numbers of college graduates go on to some sort of postgraduate training. The most obvious reason for this is the demand of the industrial system for trained personnel. A less obvious reason is that mass education is a precondition for mass propaganda on the part of both the state, which seeks to maintain a constant air of crisis, and the corporations, which need to create sophisticated consumers.[7] In other words, mass education is a political even more than it is a strictly economic necessity. Otherwise it would be difficult to explain the mass education of women, particularly at the higher levels, at a time when women are actively discouraged from entering the professions or managerial careers. It is apparent that higher education is extended to women not because their skills are needed in production but because they are consumers par excellence—and the more educated the consumer, the more voracious his appetites. (In addition, women are needed as teachers. An increasing number of college graduates and postgraduates go back into the educational system; thus to a certain degree the system is needed simply to feed itself.)

Mass education also reflects the degree to which post-industrial society has rendered young people superfluous. In a highly developed technological society, young people suffer the fate of all workers without skills: They are displaced by machines. In the nineteenth century the demand for universal education originated, in part, in a protest of humanitarian reformers against the horrors of child labor. It is unlikely that the reformers would have succeeded, however, if the industrial system had not simultaneously outgrown the need for child labor. From one point of view, mass education can be regarded as a custodial system designated to administer a class of persons displaced by technology. This helps to explain why schools, particularly secondary schools, so often take on the character of detention camps. Their custodial function becomes doubly apparent at a time when the schools, as purveyors of managerial values and attitudes, find themselves in conflict not only with the newly self-conscious black movement but also with the new youth culture (as when school authorities attempt to impose their own standards regarding dress and hair). Young people then perceive the schools as, in effect, prisons; hence the growing revolt among high school students.

The revolt of college students derives from the same general conditions, but it is colored by the peculiarities of the university, which alone among the institutions of post-industrial society still stands for values that run counter to the dominant values. In order to create an atmosphere attractive to serious scholars, the university must do more than pay lip service to its traditional ideals. It must not only permit the free exchange of ideas but to some degree it must govern itself in accord with the humane and civilized values it claims to embody. The conflict between the social role of the university and the values it continues to represent, however imperfectly, makes the university a battleground on which the political tensions latent in post-industrial capitalism come into open conflict. The very freedom of the university, which makes this conflict possible, comes under attack. "Paradoxically, the university offered its students the freedom to say much of what they wanted. . . . But they [members of the Free Speech Movement at Berkeley] felt patronized by this approach, for to them it appeared that the university tolerated all of this talk as long as it did not interfere with the production of the educational corporation." [8]

THE INHERENT INSTABILITY OF
POST-INDUSTRIAL SOCIETY

The foregoing analysis, while little more than a skeleton, has the advantage of suggesting explanations for things that are otherwise inexplicable. In particular it provides a way of understanding the turbulent politics of the post-industrial era—the student revolt, the black revolt, the "new politics," the right-wing revival—and of assessing the character and probable consequences of these movements. Other theories of post-industrial society are unable to explain why such a society should be susceptible to change. The weakness of theories that were proposed a few years ago, when the subject of post-industrial society was just beginning to excite speculation about its distinctive character, is nowhere more glaringly exposed than in the failure of those theories to anticipate or account for the political and cultural chaos that has since come to characterize the American scene.

On the contrary, the early theories of post-industrial society postulated a static social order marvelously resistant to change. Resistance to change, indeed, was supposed to be precisely the defining characteristic of post-industrial society. So pervasive was this view that it was shared by structuralists and behaviorists alike, by those who emphasized "mass society" and those who spoke of "pluralism," by those who criticized American society from the left and by those who celebrated it from the center. In one way or another critics of all schools labored under the spell of "the end of ideology." Together they shared the belief that the age of deep political conflict was dead and that the Western world had entered a post-revolutionary era in which the only threat to its continuing stability would come from outside—from the revolutionary forces in the premodern world. For Liberals, accordingly, the chief task of post-industrial or post-modern politics would be to contain those revolutionary pressures while outflanking them by exporting to poor countries the tranquilizing benefits of industrial progress. For radicals, on the other hand, political pressures from the third world represented the only hope in an otherwise hopeless prospect.

At bottom, both Liberal and leftist critics postulated a social order in which all political—that is, ideological—questions had been translated into administrative questions soluble through manipulation, propaganda ("education"), and social engineering—although Liberals were quick to repudiate any utopian overtones that might still cling to this last concept. The belief that administration had replaced politics informed the celebration of American "pragmatism" that was explicit in the works of Liberal or Social Democratic ideologues like Daniel Bell, Sidney Hook, and Daniel Boorstin and was implicit in most academic

sociology, economics, and political science. The belief in the primacy of
administration also informed the works of left-wing critics like Mills,
Herbert Marcuse, and Jacques Ellul. "Contemporary society seems to
be capable of containing social change . . . ," wrote Marcuse in *One
Dimensional Man*. "This containment of social change is perhaps the
most singular achievement of advanced industrial society."

Behind all such statements one senses the formidable weight of a
long tradition of twentieth-century social thought, or, rather, of several
traditions converging to produce the modern critique of "mass society."
This critique encompasses the theory of the managerial revolution, the
existentialist vision of the absurdity of modern life and the impossibility
of rational choice, the antiutopian fantasies of Huxley, Koestler, and
Orwell, and the critique of totalitarianism (by Hannah Arendt and others) as the prototype of the mass society of the future. All these influences, together with the deceptive calm of early post-industrial society
itself, contributed in the 1950s and early 1960s to the formation of an
intellectual climate in which major social change—which ever since the
French Revolution had been one of the constant expectations of Western life—had ceased to appear as an historical possibility. The unreal-
ity of the prospect of change might be regarded as itself one of the
characteristic traits of post-industrial society which distinguishes it further from industrial society. For the assumption of stability, however
unjustified, has penetrated deep into the consciousness not just of intellectuals but of the masses, where it works, not to prevent change as
such, but to prevent the kind of change that could lead to a new social
order based on human needs and humane values. For most people,
post-industrial capitalism appears to represent the furthest limits of social development.

Post-industrial society contains many mechanisms that inhibit the
political expression of underlying social conflict—that is, prevent those
conflicts from assuming a political form. The tendency of political
grievances to present themselves as personal grievances, the tendency
for repressive authority to assume the guise of benevolence, the substitution of psychology for politics, and the pervasiveness of the managerial mode of thought help prevent conflicts from coming to the surface
and contribute to the illusion that ideology has exhausted itself. But, in
spite of all these factors, post-industrial society—in the United States as

well as in Western Europe—is torn by political conflict. It is the nature of that society, as we have seen, that it creates new classes of marginal and technologically superfluous people, notably the ethnic minorities who make up the "new poor" and the students, who are removed from the working force and placed in educational custody where they are exposed to a combination of bureaucratic repression and dangerous ideas. These groups whom post-industrial society has been unable to absorb make up an increasingly alienated and subversive force within it.

Nor is discontent confined to the marginal classes. It has begun to enter the lives of the working classes as well, both the traditional working class and the new white-collar proletariat. Post-industrial society has given those classes a high degree of economic security, but it has exacted from them a heavy price for their security. The same corporate institutions that sustain the celebrated American standard of living require for their continuing growth policies that are making the cities uninhabitable, polluting the air and water, impoverishing cultural life, creating an apparently endless series of international emergencies, and breeding riot and rebellion at home. In order to make these anxieties tolerable, the post-industrial order offers to the working classes the pleasures of consumption on an unprecedented scale, but it is not always successful in concealing the emptiness of those pleasures or their social cost.

Faced with mounting tensions and threats on every side, the working classes will increasingly demand the solution of problems that the existing order cannot solve. In trying to satisfy their demand for the restoration of "law and order," the authorities will face a growing rebellion among students and blacks. The working classes themselves represent a potentially revolutionary threat to the system, insofar as the demands they make cannot be met under the existing institutions. Given the absence in the United States of a Socialist movement that can articulate the democratic values implicit in those demands (even the demand for "law and order"), the working classes will become increasingly a force for reaction. In either case the emergence of political consciousness among them will contribute to the polarization of post-industrial politics.

The post-industrial order, far from transcending the contradictions inherent in capitalism, embodies them in an acute form. Having out-

lasted its principal historical function—that of capital accumulation—
the system of privately owned production for profit can only survive by
devoting itself more and more to the production of waste. Yet the social
effect of waste is to generate mounting political tensions. How these
tensions will be resolved—whether in the long run they will furnish the
basis of a socialism of abundance or whether efforts to resolve them
will usher in a new age of barbarism—no one can say with any confidence. What can be said is that the post-industrial order is an inherently
unstable form of society. There are good reasons to think that it may
not even survive the twentieth century.

Notes

1. A social class is defined by its social and economic function (its relationship to the means of production) but above all by its ideology, that is, its
collective consciousness of itself and of the experiences and interests that
distinguish it from other classes. Class is thus a *historical* concept, because it
is only in the course of historical struggle that classes, as self-conscious entities, emerge from the welter of hierarchical distinctions that characterize all
societies except the most rudimentary. "In its characteristic modern sense
the notion of class—as distinct from that of rank or estate—may be said to
have arisen in the course of the French Revolution, from an empirical
awareness that the removal of legal privileges did not by itself result in social equality, but rather laid bare an enduring conflict of interest dividing
the propertied minority from the bulk of the labouring poor." (George
Lichtheim, *Marxism* [New York, 1961], p. 381).

Recent academic sociology, under the guise of a conceptual advance, has
retreated to the obscurantist idea of class as rank or status. This can be seen
in the very terminology that sociologists since Lloyd Warner have employed: upper, lower-upper, upper-middle, etc. In modern sociological research these hierarchical rankings—which purport to describe the "class
structure" of a community—are arrived at by asking people to rank themselves and others on a scale sometimes furnished by the investigators, sometimes by the subjects themselves. Richard Centers ("Social Class, Occupation, and Imputed Belief," *American Journal of Sociology*, May 1953) asked
people to classify various occupations as "upper," "middle," or "working"
class. Other investigators, objecting to this procedure not because it is ahistorical but because it prejudices the results of the poll, use an open-ended
questionnaire, asking people whether they believe social classes exist, and if

so, how they would define them, etc. In a study by Joseph A. Kahl and James A. Davis ("A Comparison of Indexes of Socio-Economic Status," *American Sociological Review*, June 1955), 77 per cent of those interviewed believed that classes could be said to exist; 8 per cent believed that the main determinant of class was occupation, 61 per cent believed it was money, and 16 per cent thought there was no single criterion.

These polls measure attitudes expressed by individuals in the hope that a collective picture will emerge from the sum of those attitudes. Quite apart from the difficulty that the attitudes themselves are highly colored by official attitudes, conclusions about class consciousness cannot be based on any such arithmetical procedure. (Modern sociologists would do well to remember Durkheim's dictum that in social life, the whole is more than the sum of its parts.) Class-consciousness manifests itself not in quantifiable "attitudes" or "beliefs" but in the way classes collectively *act*. No poll that can be devised by sociologists will so much as detect the existence of the new middle class or white-collar proletariat, much less tell us anything about the way it conceives of itself. In the Kohl-Davis study, the members of this class drop completely out of sight, losing themselves in an impenetrable thicket of occupational and hierarchical categories. If asked by centers to classify themselves, they would classify themselves as "middle class" on the strength of their jobs. But the new "middle class" does not *act* like a middle class or bourgeoisie, even though individually its members identify themselves as middle class and unhesitatingly reject identification with the proletariat. As a class, they correctly perceive that their job security and general well-being depend on the welfare state. As a class, they are "Liberal" (in the modern American sense) rather than "Conservative" (which in the United States describes the laissez faire liberalism that *is* the ideology of the traditional middle class).

2. Louis B. Boudin, *The Theoretical System of Karl Marx in the Light of Recent Criticism* (Chicago, 1907), p. 210.

3. See, among others, Walter Lippmann, *A Preface to Politics* (New York, 1914); Thorstein Veblen, *The Engineers and the Price System* (New York, 1919); James Burnham, *The Managerial Revolution* (New York, 1941); David T. Bazelon, *Power in America: The Politics of the New Class* (New York, 1967); Galbraith, *The New Industrial State* (Boston, 1967).

4. For the growing dependence of the corporations on the state and the origins of corporate liberalism, see Gabriel Kolko, *The Triumph of Conservatism* (New York, 1963), and James Weinstein, *The Corporate Ideal in the Liberal State* (Boston, 1968).

5. See Galbraith, *The Affluent Society* (Boston, 1958).

6. For the critique of American diplomacy from the point of view of the "new realism," see, e.g., George F. Kennan, *American Diplomacy* (Chicago,

=42

1951) and *Russia, The Atom and the West* (New York, 1958); Lippmann, *The Public Philosophy* (New York, 1955) and more recently, *Conversations with Walter Lippmann* (Boston, 1965); also Louis J. Halle, *Dream and Reality, Aspects of American Foreign Policy* (New York, 1959).

7. On the connection between mass education and propaganda, see Ellul, *Propaganda* (New York, 1965), which deals, however, only with the propaganda of the state.

8. Paul Jacobs and Saul Landau, eds., *The New Radicals: A Report with Documents* (New York, 1966), p. 60.

JOHN MILTON COOPER, JR.

Neo-progressivism and "Slack-Water Politics"

COMPARED WITH OTHER WESTERN COUNTRIES, the United States has presented a Janus face toward welfare politics. It has been at once the most conservative and most progressive of highly developed industrial nations. In establishing the institutions of the welfare state, America still lags conspicuously behind Sweden and Great Britain and even France and West Germany. Yet most of the goals of modern welfare politics—such as creation of social equality through erasure of inherited rank and privilege, provision of a decent living standard for all citizens, and assurance of positive social mobility through good mass education—have come closer to realization in the United States. These twin conditions describe the characteristic ambivalence of American politics.

This ambivalence shows every sign of enduring, and it shapes the three basic conditions of the emergence of post-welfare politics in America. The first condition is that post-welfare politics is emerging while the controversies of welfare politics continue in full force. Despite the growth of an area of tacit agreement between moderate and liberal Democrats and Republicans on some welfare issues, established conflicts remain lively. That the right wing especially contests these issues is illustrated by the spectacular rises of Ronald Reagan and George Wallace. The second condition is that post-welfare concerns have emerged through the reassertion of a traditional American political style. Focused on what are regarded as spiritual shortcomings, cultural emptiness, and the enervating scale of a highly bureaucratized society, these concerns elicit a spirit of moralistic exhortation common to earlier reform movements. The final condition is a measure of mutual harm to both welfare and post-welfare politics caused by their overlap. The intrusion of post-welfare concerns may delay the completion of the welfare state in America. Yet since those concerns presuppose at least partial fulfillment of the welfare state, their premature emergence can also inhibit the full development of post-welfare politics.

Post-welfare concerns are arising in two areas—one within and the other outside the lines of controversy over welfare issues. As a part of welfare politics, these concerns have emerged principally from the dire warnings of the Conservative opposition about the decay of personal and national morality, the sapping of individual initiative and creativity, and the dehumanization of men caught in the grip of a vast social machine. Although the American right wing has almost willfully made itself difficult to take seriously, it does deserve some credit for uttering more than the cant of the privileged and the curses of the ignorant. As Theodore H. White observed, Barry Goldwater touched on important problems in 1964 but strayed into outdated fantasies in trying "to deal with the faceless newer enemies of the Digital Society." [1] Goldwater's failure epitomized the role of the right wing in American welfare politics. After drawing prescient observations about moral and spiritual dangers inherent in mass society, it has then invalidated those observations with a narrowly economic definition of individualism and an obdurate refusal to admit that the evils it decries might spring from deeper causes than misguided or sinister actions on the part of government.

The conflicts of welfare politics have taken place on two fairly distinct levels in the United States. The familiar struggle of social classes and economic interest groups for the enhancement of opportunities and the defense of entrenched positions has formed the staple of politics since the 1930s in America just as in other countries. In contrast with Europe, however, this struggle has not aligned two clear-cut ideological camps against each other. Only the right in the United States has been truly ideological. Conservative opponents of welfare measures have consistently linked the defense of their interests with ideals, moral principles, and hallowed creeds. Liberal proponents have, on the other hand, tended to stress little more than realism, necessity, and action.[2] These circumstances are now contributing to the peculiar features of the emergence of post-welfare issues.

Each side has gained and suffered from its position. Becoming ideological has harmed the right, which has too often preferred to invoke well-worn pieties, rather than mount a more effective opposition by examining the needs served by the welfare state and devising alternative programs. Conversely, the avoidance of ideology has given such flexibility to proponents of welfare measures that they have absorbed nearly all the remaining positions on the political spectrum. By the same token, however, ideology has enabled the right to carry on the most vital tradition of American politics, dating back to the progressive era earlier in this century and even to the antislavery movement in the 1800s. The tradition is that of democratic evangelism and moral reformation. Because Americans' deepest values consist almost entirely of a libertarian individualism heavily suffused with Protestant morality, the Conservatives' ideology has made them unwitting forerunners of post-welfare politics. Despite the efforts of spokesmen like Arthur Schlesinger, Jr., to invest welfare liberalism with an aura of moral purposefulness, its credo has never amounted to much more than the vaguely humanitarian feelings of an interest-group coalition imbued with success and practicality. Vexation over this lack of transcendent values has contributed importantly to the response of the American left to the concerns of post-welfare politics.

An emerging left-wing response forms the thrust of post-welfare politics originating outside the established lines of controversy. It sprang first from the civil rights movement. As late as 1960, H. Stuart Hughes worried that for the American left Karl Mannheim's prediction of "a world without utopia—without any notion of transcendence in social and cultural pursuits" had come true, leaving "a cold, bleak world, a world drained of meaning." [3] The civil rights movement changed that situation overnight. It brought everything that morally famished Liberals could desire. Especially in its first phases in the South, the movement furnished an inspiring struggle of acute moral clarity for the highest of human goals. Even more important, perhaps, it afforded significant activity on a satisfying human scale. In a highly organized, specialized society, the freedom rides, sit-ins, and protest marches opened opportunities for positive action by individuals and small groups of people with little or no prior training. This moral shot-in-the-arm for the left has, in turn, shaped its attitudes toward emerging post-welfare issues.

The critical effect of the civil rights experience can be seen most strikingly in the formation of the "New Left." This loose collection of groups of young radicals came into being in the early 1960s, drawing its membership chiefly from those who had participated in freedom rides and sit-ins. Most of these organizations have remained concerned in one way or another with racial problems. The distinction between the two movements is that the New Left seeks to extend the perspective of the civil rights effort to other problems such as peace, poverty, and cultural alienation. The New Left views all of American society as an extension of the treatment of the Negro in the 1950s: A "power structure" abets active oppression by hiding the evils of discrimination and exploitation from a smugly contented middle class; direct action offers the only solution, both because the situation is crystal clear and because plans and programs are the ruses used by the discredited "Liberal establishment" to avoid real confrontations with evils. That, in a skeletal form, is the vision of the New Left.[4]

Its importance lies in representing the beginning of a left-wing approach to post-welfare concerns heretofore touched upon in Conservative rhetoric. Attunement to these new issues can be seen in the centrality of direct action and individual commitment in New Left canons and in the insistence upon grass-roots solutions to social problems, as exemplified in the slogan of the Students for a Democratic Society (SDS) of "participatory democracy." The New Left does not merely display an impatient juvenile radicalism within the context of earlier leftist doctrines, as many critics have charged. The New Left also addresses itself to the same problems of moral lassitude in and the dehumanizing scale of modern society that the right earlier decried. These newer concerns, together with a certain inescapable chiliasm at the outset of radical movements, help to explain the apparent anti-intellectualism of the stress upon direct action.

Yet in its novelty the New Left ironically recaptures the same traditional evangelical spirit and moral reformatory style that have distinguished conservatism in the last three decades. This represents a partial return to an accustomed hortatory stance among American reformers. The nineteenth-century abolitionists, for example, denounced slavery as a sinful institution and allied themselves with temperance, peace, and woman-suffrage movements. The Progressives of the early part of this century railed against the evils of big business and political machines, while linking their crusades with later phases of the temperance and woman-suffrage movements. This reform evangelism has seldom been truly ideological, since its transcendent moral principles have not been based upon economic class interests or social positions of different groups.[5] Abolitionist and civil rights' organizations led by Negroes have been clear exceptions, but most American reform efforts have sprung from cultural sources among such middle-class elements as Protestant ministers and laymen and "alienated" intellectuals. Self-interested class politics in America has either coexisted on a different plane or clashed with this form of evangelical politics.

The New Left, for all its various claims to advance the cause of a kind of proletariat, does not depart from this pattern of evangelical reform in either the social origins or the basically cultural orientation of its members. Moreover, it follows the traditional pattern closely in pursuing grass-roots activities to ameliorate the lot of the underprivileged. Direct action against social ills, often outside normal political channels, has been a hallmark of moral reform in America. The abolitionists not only denounced slavery; they also set up the underground railroad to help slaves escape. After emancipation, they mounted a massive effort to educate and organize Negroes politically in the Southern states. Similarly, the Progressives worked through such agencies as settlement houses to help immigrants in the cities establish themselves as fully participating citizens, while the suffragettes pioneered the technique of protest marching. Both the moral stance and the techniques of the New Left have venerable precedents in the history of American reform.

This consonance of the New Left with those traditional positions makes it the cutting edge of a Liberal response to post-welfare issues. The almost pathetic respect shown to it by veterans of the left, usually in spite of sharp disagreements with its approaches, attests a widespread gratitude for the revival of the evangelical posture. Some approaches of the New Left have also found broader acceptance. Several younger American historians have recently begun to assail previous generations of Liberals for compromising their principles and relying too much upon the power of the state.[6] Significant spokesmen for established welfare liberalism have espoused post-welfare concerns like those of the New Left. Schlesinger has urged the discarding of older "quantitative liberalism" in favor of attention to issues "no longer social and economic as much as they are cultural and moral." Richard N. Goodwin has called for the redirection of liberalism to mount an attack on "the most troubling fact of our age: that the growth in central power has been accompanied by a continual diminution in the significance of the individual citizen. . . ."[7]

Yet, at the same time, the established controversies of welfare politics display no likelihood of early disappearance. Welfare issues remain ideologically divisive for the right wing, and they also retain a high potential for self-interested conflict. Almost any predictable extension of the welfare state would arouse both kinds of controversy. Lines have already begun to form over suggestions for federal assumption of relief and unemployment insurance. Establishment of a national, medical insurance scheme or tax relief for low-income families would precipitate conflicts between the desires of the less advantaged for larger benefits and the clamor of business and better-off elements against the taxes needed to pay for such measures. In addition, as the Vietnam War has shown, other areas of government activity can rival and curtail welfare expenditures.

The intrusion of post-welfare concerns has already brought some major alterations in established lines of controversy over the welfare state. Race has always tended to distort simple class divisions in American politics. The Wallace candidacy illustrated particularly well how poorer Southern white men can defy their economic interests to form a bastion of opposition to the welfare state.[8] On the other side, comfortable, educated whites have often lent greater support to civil rights drives than workers or lower middle-class groups. Certainly, the bases for Liberal positions can differ markedly on welfare and post-welfare issues. Whereas welfare liberalism has usually reflected class interests, post-welfare liberalism (or radicalism) seems to spring from a higher level of education or, often as a consequence, from a heightened moral conscience. These differences have led Schlesinger, for one, to predict that a newer, "qualitative liberalism" will gather its following principally from colleges, universities, churches, and social service organizations.[9] The support given to Eugene McCarthy's bid for the 1968 Democratic nomination would appear to bear out such an analysis. But whether a durable following has formed remains open to question.

The safest prediction that one can make about American politics in coming years is that it will be confused. The overlap of welfare and post-welfare issues will lead to debates and divisions along complicated, unclear lines. These conflicts will elicit kinds of political participation that will be, by turns, exciting and creative, frustrating and futile. But this form of politics will not be new to America. Instead, it will be a return to what has been a familiar form of politics in the nation's history since at least the 1830s and 1840s. American politics is reverting to an accustomed condition of being at once enlivened and disoriented by agitation over profound moral and cultural concerns.

This development can best be understood by recalling the situation existing in the United States at the beginning of this century. In certain broad outlines, that situation presented a mirror image of the one prevailing today. In the last election of the preceding century—1896—the country witnessed the decisive defeat of a party dominated by an ideological faction. William Jennings Bryan had run on a Democratic platform written by representatives of staple-producing and silver-mining interests of the South and West. They borrowed heavily from the Populists, the third party, which espoused a small-capitalist, sometimes agrarian, ideology uniting economic interests with claims about the moral undermining of America by growing urban, immigrant population and the machinations of the big business.[10] Three factors—the stake of the more substantial middle classes in a stable currency, the Democrats' severely limited appeal outside the staple-agricultural and mining areas of the South and West, and widespread revulsion toward Bryan as a harebrained candidate with reactionary ideas—combined to bring about the most decisive defeat of a Presidential candidate in forty years.[11]

What happened after 1896 suggests further similarities with current developments. The issues of that election and the interests behind them did not disappear, but they were partially subsumed and redirected under a different form of politics. The Populist and Democratic concern for the moral and cultural state of the nation, coupled with some of their programs, began to attract support from leaders of the staunchest opposition elements. Middle-class and patrician spokesmen, led by men like Theodore Roosevelt, now attacked big business and political corruption. They gradually formed the Progressive movement, at first mainly within the Republican party, but drawing also upon the urban and state-reform drives of such men as Robert M. La Follette in Wisconsin. By 1912 the spirit of progressivism had grown so pervasive that it dominated both parties and split the Republicans, with Roosevelt as a third-party Progressive outpolling the regular ticket.

Despite common programs and rhetoric, however, progressivism was hardly a metamorphosed version of populism or Bryanite democracy. Progressivism did not become ideological, because it embodied only the moral superstructure of the earlier movements without their self-interested underpinnings. Offering cultural and ethical objections to a burgeoning urban, industrial society, progressivism gained support and leadership from middle-class citizens who wished merely to exorcise ill-defined feelings of discontent without effecting deep social or economic changes. Significantly, it displayed a marked propensity for crusading against sins and punishing evildoers in preference to reforming systems or changing structures. Not surprisingly, the Progressive era appears from the perspective of subsequent welfare politics to have left few substantial accomplishments.[12]

These experiences offer clues to what we can expect from the interaction between welfare and post-welfare politics. The differences between the Progressive era and today are readily apparent. Political directions have reversed. Ideology and initial concern then lay on the left with the Populists; now they lie on the right. Styles have also altered drastically. Buoyancy and underlying complacency characterized progressivism, whereas suspicion and self-proclaimed "alienation" are now the stigmata of the New Left and the intellectual milieu generally. Yet significant similarities remain. Today opposite sides of the political spectrum also focus on the same concerns from conflicting perspectives. One side again adopts the other's moral concern while scorning the self-interested bias of its ideology.

On a deeper level, the Liberal response to post-welfare issues ap-

pears to revive the most significant aspect of progressivism. As Richard
Hofstadter has pointed out, the fundamental Progressive thrust was a
"struggle against organization," which expressed a desire to reassert
man's control over his life in an increasingly collectivized and impersonal society.[13] The individual, in the Progressives' view, was pitted
against all kinds of organizations—political machines, corporations,
Labor unions. Morality was always a matter of the exercise of individual conscience in unremitting hostility to the demands of those organizations. Progressives usually depicted individualism in economic terms
and revealed a stubborn insensitivity to infringements of civil liberties
and social inequalities. But their underlying concern was the same as
the striving today for a reassertion of individual competence and moral
responsibility. At bottom, post-welfare liberalism appears to be a kind
of neo-progressivism.

The Progressive experience illuminates both strengths and weaknesses in this kind of politics. On the positive side, progressivism made
politics exciting and meaningful for informed citizens. Their attitude toward previous issues was best described by the term "slack-water politics," created in the 1880s by a former abolitionist who lamented the
displacement of momentous Civil War movements by interest-group coalitions dominated by professionals.[14] Progressivism was what finally
agitated those "slack-water politics" for the majority of Americans.
Similarly, such arousal over moral and cultural problems can encourage
the kind of grass-roots, sometimes extrapolitical efforts that can be most
effective in dealing with them. The settlement houses of the Progressive
era served to teach urban immigrants how to become effective citizens,
thereby raising the tone of politics and helping to eliminate the need for
political machines. Some of today's activities of a local and regional nature may also work toward restoring both the feeling and the reality of
men's control over their society.

Neo-progressivism may also instill a healthier attitude toward
power on the part of intellectuals. Since the end of World War II a
number of American intellectuals have sought to maintain that the basically self-interested Liberal position in welfare politics has contained
transcendent moral purpose. This is not to say that an ideology could be
constructed from that position. Indeed, American liberalism suffers
from the lack of such an ideology. But these intellectuals have touted

"pragmatism" and "tough-mindedness" as if those were goals in themselves, and they have too often mistaken style for performance. This attempt to render self-interested welfare liberalism morally transcendent
reached its apex under John F. Kennedy's "New Frontier," which combined baldly practical interest-group politics with sophisticated rhetoric.[15] Since then, in part because of post-welfare concerns, intellectuals
appear to have recovered a sense of separation from power. Unfortunately, the Kennedy legend, reinforced by Robert Kennedy's martyrdom, now serves as the myth of the lost golden age for many intellectuals in their new mood of alienation from power.

As the attitude of the intellectuals indicates, the weaknesses of this
increasingly prevalent form of politics can outweigh its strengths. The
most serious disadvantage of post-welfare neo-progressivism is precisely
that it overlaps with continuing welfare controversies. It has arisen at a
critical moment in America's drive to extend the welfare state, when the
most difficult and serious problems of hard-core poverty and racial discrimination are just beginning to be touched. These are problems for
which, except for some organizational activities and local efforts, post-
welfare concerns can be a distinct hindrance. Although post-welfare
Liberal criticism contains valid points in questioning moral purposes,
condemning the lack of a sense of participation, or scoring inefficiencies
of overcentralization, none of these objections obviates the overriding
need for completion of the welfare state. The shift of concern to post-
welfare issues may forestall the benefits of the welfare state from reaching those who need them most.

Moreover, this shift threatens to leave important questions only
half-explored. One could concede every specific point that critics raise
about shortcomings not only of the welfare state but also of modern
mass society in general and still question whether the over-all drift of
their arguments is correct. It seems highly debatable, for example,
whether society in recent years has failed to rise, much less declined, either in cultural level or moral purposes. Culture is exceedingly difficult
to measure, and much of the condemnation of modern popular culture
rests upon false comparisons with previous "high" cultures.[16] So, too,
the recognition of the immoralities of poverty and racial discrimination
springs from greater awareness of those conditions, rather than from
their worsening. With regard to the dehumanizing scale of modern so-

ciety, it is possible to argue that in some cases greater size enhances the possibilities for direct individual action. The civil rights movement has made many of its gains through the vivid means afforded by mass communications, especially television, for bringing the struggles of its members to the attention of millions. Nor does governmental centralization necessarily diminish opportunities for individual action. Local protests against school segregation have received great boosts from threats of cutting off federal funds.

The basic consideration, of course, continues to be the relation between size and effective freedom. Despite the almost unshakeable Platonic assumption that democracies can exist only in small units, it can be argued with equal plausibility that smallness enhances tyranny. Impersonality even appears in some instances, as in the modern corporation and factory, to be a necessary precondition for greater individual latitude. These observations, though by no means denying the points raised by post-welfare critics, show that their analysis of the problems of modern society is far from incontrovertible. America suffers here from the failure to construct welfare ideologies. Because only right-wing opposition has linked its stand to moral absolutes, its formulations of transcendent values seem to have prevailed by default. This is particularly unfortunate now when Americans need compelling welfare ideologies in order to justify the commitments essential to an attack upon the most serious social and economic inequities in the nation. It is not difficult to see how the intrusion of post-welfare concerns will impede these efforts.

The arousal of such moral questions introduces a form of politics with weaknesses that are the defects of its strengths. A high level of citizen participation, for instance, can be a decidedly mixed blessing. "Slack-water politics" has the advantage of assuring relative stability and promoting disciplined, effective organizations. Likewise, although one might translate to politics Napoleon's dictum about war being too important to be left to the generals, professionalism has virtues that should never be underrated, especially in a complex society. The most negative aspect of widespread citizen arousal over these concerns is the fostering of the notion that politics is a matter of simple moral conflict. If morality cannot be banished from politics, neither can other equally valid considerations, and moral questions, which do crop up, are usually intertwined with conflicting self-interests. Post-welfare concerns seem, however, to be resurrecting many of the old illusions of the Progressives about the primacy of simple, individual morality in politics.

For intellectuals this form of politics encourages the exchange of one uncritical bias toward power for another. Hans Morgenthau has spoken of the necessity for intellectuals to maintain a "prophetic" posture toward power.[17] Such an admonition contains the obvious pitfall of glorifying powerlessness, a tendency already amply disclosed in the prevalent celebration of "alienation." In that celebration, moreover, some intellectuals have mixed welfare and post-welfare issues in bizarre ways. The New Left and sympathetic intellectuals have tried to cast the poor and blacks in the role of a radical moral and cultural alternative to dominant middle-class ways. This effort has met with rebuke from many quarters; even Stokely Carmichael has complained, "Too many young middle-class Americans, like some sort of Pepsi generation, have wanted to come alive through the black community. . . ."[18]

Emphasis on direct, individual action also brings problems. Such action and local initiative, though valuable, are hardly basic. The existence of powerful welfare-state insitutions is what permits these recourses to be effective. Without the revenues, expertise, and standard setting of a strong central government, it would be pointless to talk about disbursing funds or management of programs to cities and states. Properly viewed, these post-welfare concerns are refinements of the welfare state, but the already present danger is that they will be regarded as sources of conflict against it.

Post-welfare concerns have entered American politics in a manner entirely in keeping with its characteristic ambivalence. The prospects for the future are muddled. The overlap of post-welfare concerns with continuing welfare controversies will bring some strengths but, I believe, more weaknesses to American politics. It is particularly unfortunate that an evangelistic, neo-Progressive attitude seems to be on the rise among the intellectual left. Its energies would be better expended in efforts to construct Liberal welfare ideologies.[19] These are sorely needed in the United States. Equally necessary are comparable conservative ideologies favorable to the welfare state, like that of the Conservative party in Britain.[20] Thus far, Republican thinking has produced only a desire to imitate earlier Democratic "pragmatism" in order to win elections. If such ideologies were present, the welfare state would be well on its way to completion. Then one could greet the emergence of post-welfare concerns with relish.

As matters now stand, however, the most important consideration is the danger that post-welfare concerns will hamper the extension of the welfare state just when greater advances to attack the roots of poverty and discrimination have become the nation's most pressing task. Conflict between welfare and post-welfare concerns will be doubly unfortunate because the two areas really ought to be viewed as complementary. Yet such conflict appears all too probable. For once, Americans seem to be badly served by the characteristic ambivalence of their politics. They would do much better to attend to first things first.

Notes

1. Theodore H. White, *The Making of the President 1964* (New York, 1965), pp. 313–14.

2. This ideological one-sidedness is discussed in Richard Hofstadter, *The Age of Reform: From Bryan to F.D.R.* (New York, 1960), pp. 316–18, and Christopher Lasch, *The New Radicalism in America, 1889–1963: The Intellectual as a Social Type* (New York, 1965), pp. 288–90.

3. H. Stuart Hughes, "Mass Culture and Social Criticism," *Daedalus,* LXXXIX (Spring 1960), 393.

4. For authentic expressions of the New Left, see Jacobs and Landau, eds., *The New Radicals: A Report with Documents* (New York, 1966), and Jack Newfield, ed., *The Prophetic Minority* (New York, 1966).

5. Some historians have tried to connect abolitionism and progressivism with status anxieties of middle-class groups. Such interpretations remain controversial, but even if they were accepted, they would not prove that these movements were ideological. Nor would they detract from the strong cultural motivation behind these reform movements.

6. See, especially, Barton J. Bernstein, ed., *Towards a New Past: Dissenting Essays in American History* (New York, 1968).

7. Arthur M. Schlesinger, Jr., "The New Liberal Coalition," *The Progressive,* XXXI (April 1967), pp. 15–19; Richard N. Goodwin, "The Shape of American Politics," *Commentary,* XLIII (June 1967), 25–40.

8. Wallace's campaign positions reflected the contradictory wishes of poor whites not only in the South but also throughout the country. The major thrust of his appeal lay in standard right-wing attacks on the welfare state, yet Wallace also took the most radical position on taxation of any Presidential candidate since the 1930s, demanding that the rich be made to pay their "fair share."

9. Schlesinger, "The New Liberal Coalition," pp. 16–17.

10. On the Populists' thought see Hofstadter, *The Age of Reform*, especially pp. 60–93, and Walter T. K. Nugent, *The Tolerant Populists: Kansas Populism and Nativism* (Chicago, 1963).

11. On the 1896 election, see Paul W. Glad, *McKinley, Bryan and the People* (Philadelphia, 1963); Carl N. Degler, "American Political Parties and the Rise of the City: An Interpretation," *Journal of American History*, XLVI (June 1964), 41–59; William Diamond, "Urban and Rural Voting in 1896," *American Historical Review*, LI (January 1941), 281–305.

12. There is a heated debate among American historians over the degree to which progressivism did or did not lay the basis for the welfare liberalism of the New Deal. An excellent treatment of the problem, which on balance stresses differences between progressivism and the New Deal, is Otis G. Graham, Jr., *An Encore to Reform: The Old Progressives and the New Deal* (New York, 1967).

13. Hofstadter, *The Age of Reform*, pp. 215–21.

14. George W. Julian, *Political Recollections, 1840 to 1872* (Chicago, 1883), p. 372.

15. The New Frontier cult is dissected in Lasch, *The New Radicalism in America*, pp. 310–22.

16. Cf. Daniel Bell, *The End of Ideology* (Glencoe, 1960), especially pp. 26–27, 36, 44, 67, and Edward Shils, "Daydreams and Nightmares: Reflections on the Criticism of Mass Culture," *Sewanee Review*, LXII (October–December 1957), 587–608.

17. Hans J. Morgenthau, "Truth and Power," *New Republic*, CLV (November 14, 1966), 42.

18. Stokely Carmichael, "What We Want," *New York Review of Books*, VII (September 22, 1966), 8.

19. Some have called for such efforts. See, e.g., Doris Kearns and Sanford Levison, "How to Remove LBJ in 1968," *New Republic*, CLVI (May 13, 1967), 13–14; Irving Howe, "Is This Country Cracking Up?," *Dissent*, XIV (May–June 1967), 259–63. Another distinct possibility, already manifested in the McCarthy candidacy, is that the neo-Progressive spirit may be di-

rected more toward foreign affairs. Since post-welfare concerns over morals, culture, and individual responsibility do not lend themselves easily to political action, this tendency could become paramount.

20. The lack of a Conservative pro-welfare ideology is a great missed opportunity of modern American politics. The basis for such an ideology was laid in the "New Nationalism" of Theodore Roosevelt, which resembled the British "Tory Democracy" of such spokesmen as Lord Randolph Churchill. Roosevelt advocated reforms that anticipated the welfare state from the point of view of a responsible Conservative who wished to mollify discontent and prevent upheavals. For him, such reforms were also necessary in order to maintain a strong, efficient government that would defend the nation's interests abroad.

DUSKY LEE SMITH

Scientific Liberalism: Ward, Galbraith, and the Welfare State

FOR ONE REASON or another many capitalists do not like to refer to themselves as capitalists. Instead, they often prefer some euphemism such as "Liberal" which seems to reduce their burden. Beleaguered throughout history they have invented and/or discovered deity, human instincts, natural laws, rationality, and mysticism to vindicate much of their activity. With God, biology, history, reason, and the invisible hand of the market place on their side, the Liberals could look toward the golden future with much confidence. However, it was not until liberalism had become an established reality with political and military power to defend its structure that the Liberal became sanguine.*

Regardless of their buoyant and enthusiastic perspective many liberals still seem quite perplexed. They have family problems within capitalism that lead to violent and aggressive activities such as the case of Germany and Japan in World War II. They have problems with those who disagree about the nature of the Good Society—that is, the Eternal Enemy (from within and from without). Liberals also seem plagued by the humanistic tradition of their culture, with its emphasis upon the worth and dignity of the individual. Their endeavor to reconcile the hu-

* I want to thank Donna Longtin, Rainer Knopff, and Neill Kroeger (McMaster University) for their criticisms of this chapter.

manistic tradition with their cherished economic goals and practices consumes much of their time and energy.

The Liberal struggle with the humanistic tradition involves a number of potential contradictions. For example, Liberals seek to reconcile the expectation of private gain with the anticipation of a day-to-day life in which the individual personality is of priceless value; the search for profits with the search for a public sensitivity in which the self-development of the personality is supreme; and the pursuit of personal financial wealth with the quest for a form of public policy in which each individual has an equal voice. Additional facets of this struggle encompass tension between the power of private property and the power of individuals to determine, insofar as it is possible, their own life fates; the mysterious (irrational) market place which regulates the production, price, and purchases of goods and services and the belief that each individual should be dealt with according to rational and understandable laws; the maintenance of high profits and judgments concerning events and governmental policies in view of their bad or good results for men; and the rationality of the capitalistic enterprise and the rationality of the individual.

Liberals have been concerned with maximizing high profits, as well as convincing people that the rationality of the business enterprise should take precedence over all other forms of reason. For decades Liberal capitalism has been the dominant form of economic enterprise in the United States, and its values and form of rationality have played a powerful role in determining the directions in which the rest of society has evolved. Liberal capitalism has, for example, restricted and contained the impulses and trends toward the establishment of a society based upon the ethics and values of a humanistic society. Goods and services exist primarily for profit rather than the enhancement of the individual and his personality. Many protagonists of Liberal capitalism dominate, among other things, the social thought taught and dispensed in the universities. Academic Liberals have helped to explain and justify human behavior, providing a very effective ideology in the guise of social science. Social thought often reflects the major socio-historical forces and trends in which it is developed. Symbolic of some of the major socio-historical forces which have been active during two key periods in the development of liberalism in the United States are the so-

cial theories of Lester Frank Ward (1831–1913) and John Kenneth
Galbraith (1908–   ). As such they provide important insights into
the past and future economic and political conditions of the United
States.

Lester Frank Ward, the father of sociology in the United States
and a leading Liberal at the turn of the century, discovered certain social principles, that is, invented a sociology that justified the institutions
and behavior consistent with what was eventually described as the New
Deal. Thirty-seven years after his death, Ward was eulogized in 1950 as
"the Prophet of the New Deal" in appreciation for his theoretical-ideo-
logical contributions.[1] Ward's sociology probably represents one set of
historical trends of its time better than any other sociology. His views
provided the intellectual weapons which were used by many neo-Liberals during the latter part of the nineteenth century to defeat the old liberalism that found defense and justification in the sociology of William
Graham Sumner. Likewise, the neo-liberalism of John Kenneth Galbraith's social theory represents certain historical forces that can possibly offer insight into the nature of politics in the post-welfare state.

Ward: Moses and the New Deal

Ward's neo-Liberal sociology can be partially understood as a reaction against the old liberalism represented by Sumner's sociology.
These two sociologies symbolized many of the issues of their era, as
well as many of the social forces dominating social thought at the turn
of the century. Divested of their scholarly elaborations and terminology,
the issues they discussed were simplified into political slogans—such as
free silver, sound money, rugged individualism, state intervention,
planned economy, and regimentation—and were discussed and debated
for half a century from Grange Halls to the cotton fields and from legislative chambers to the prairies.[2]

Sumner's social theories defended a social order in which business
virtues were to dominate—a social order of old liberalism, however,
that did take into account large industrial organizations. Ward's social

theories offered an alternative to the Social Darwinism of Sumner, making room for governmental intrusion and melioristic intervention. Sumner and Ward's sociologies both justified the wealth of the elite and the increased well-being of the middle class, but Ward did offer some relief to the poor who were caught in the "theater of woe." The ideologies and social theories of these two men endeavored to salvage capitalism from its threatened demise.

Because they did not justify, among other things, the growing ties between military, government, and business, Sumner's sociological doctrines proved unfavorable to capitalism in transition. His sociology thus had to be declared socially and historically bankrupt.[3]

New liberalism was not to be directed by natural development, as Sumner would have it, but rather by men—intelligent and powerful men who were part of large-scale organizations that furnished them most of their power. This new liberalism needed a new image of man, society, and history. Ward's sociology provided these images.

THE PROGRESSIVE PLOD

History, evolution, and progress were deeply intertwined in Ward's sociology. In his view the history of man was an evolution from a genetic state to a telic (artificial) state in which a progressive civilization could exist. The evolutionary crawl or the progressive plod is exceedingly slow in the natural or genetic state—which coincides with the basic notions of laissez faire including natural selection, survival of the fittest, and the economics of nature. If progress was to occur, if new liberalism was to dominate, then the old notions had to be dispelled.

Not only was genetic socio-historical change slow; because it occured by ebbs and flows it was also very costly. After the ebb tide was over a great amount of waste remained. The law of natural selection, in which the individual utilized nature's unlimited resources to act in his own self-interest, produced a redundant supply and trusted to the environment to select the most fit. Thus, the new liberalism as sociology argued that the survival of the fittest involved a sacrifice of whatever was eventually produced by its method of trial and error—which aimed at success through the indefinite multiplication of chances. Moreover, economics of nature were costly in that the same amount of energy was required, for example, to keep a person alive until he reached (say) twenty-one, whether or not he survives beyond that age.[4] Old liberalism was based upon doctrines which supported nature's exaggerated cost of whatever is produced. In contrast, the new liberalism maintained that only through conscious effort, through telic effort, through intelligent foresight, and through planning—that is, through new liberalism itself —civilization is produced.

The telic process which new liberalism promoted sought to improve society by employing intelligent foresight, seizing upon the laws of nature and directing the natural forces to society's ends. The logical extension of laissez faire, of genetic laws, suggests that one should not interfere with the natural flow of the wind or water. Man in the telic stage interferes with the wind by building a windmill and with the water by building a dam. He interferes with the natural economy and social laws and uses them according to his intellectual dictates. The new individual is rational but he is also a bundle of desires which need to be gratified, desires which should be freed.

FREEDOM AND THE CENTRAL NERVOUS SYSTEM

Rooted deeply in the individual's central nervous system are his desires which form the true social forces that make society possible. These desires are, however, directed, influenced, and given form by their sociohistorical context. The individual has a propensity to seek gratification of his natural faculties but this propensity was blocked by the essentially plutocratic structure of old liberalism. "To be free is the great object which all men seek, and this means physical freedom—to have the power to do as they please, to act according to their desires, is the end aimed at." [5] A new individual is possible, but this depends upon the artificial (telic) production of economic surplus. Surplus was necessary, Ward argued, because it generated more and more desires that serve to increase the demand for more and more freedom. An increase in both production and consumption is very important in Ward's scheme.

Fortunately for capitalism and especially the new liberalism, Ward's social science discovered that each individual desires permanent ownership or possession—that each individual desires to own private property, to be a capitalist.[6] It is this desire for acquisition, the pursuit of wealth, that makes civilization possible.

CIVILIZATION AND ITS DISCONTENTED

The basic structure of capitalism, with certain adjustments, was the social order that the new liberalism sought to maintain. The social order of old capitalism created the social forces which were threatening to destroy it, and if these forces were not brought more in line with man's intellect, then the whole of capitalism might well be destroyed. These threatening social forces—including extremists, the abuse of wealth, ignorance, and deception—introduced chaos in the midst of capitalist society and hence created an impending crisis entailing the risk of open revolt.[7]

The ripening spirit of revolt existed primarily because of underpaid labor, wasted strength, misery and squalor, groveling and prolonged drudgery, disease, and premature deaths. These abuses grew out of the inequitable economic system of old liberalism which had been produced by astute management of shrewd businessmen who for centuries had secured for themselves an undue share of the world's products.[8] Through application of the telic means of melioristic intervention, new liberalism offered a revised capitalism whereby the abuse of wealth could be eliminated and capitalism could be salvaged.

SOCIOLOGY AS A SAVIOR

"The problem of today," Ward contended, "is how to help on a certain evolution by averting an otherwise equally certain revolution." [9] As the essential prerequisite for successful evolution he posited a "widespread acquaintance with the principles of sociology." [10] Sociology became the scientific means of maintaining capitalism against its enemies and internal weaknesses, but to accomplish this goal sociology needed the help of the wealthy just as the wealthy required the assistance of sociology.

In 1886, when Ward warned of the impending crisis, the United States had spent nine of the past thirteen years in depression, and the Haymarket bomb was just about to blow open many of the issues about which Ward had been writing. It was at this time that he scientifically discovered the role of the wealthy. In his "Use and Abuse of Wealth" [11] he asked that the wealthy join in directly with the governing of society and to use their wisdom so as to not force the people "into open revolt." [12] Suggesting that if they take the leadership in instituting systematic reforms, "no one will dispute their title to the means employed." [13]

Intelligent minds realized that wealth made possible the necessary leisure by which creative and capable individuals carried on the tasks of creating civilization. Ward argued that "no right-minded artisan begrudges the millionaire his millions." [14] The merchant, the railroad king, and the manufacturer are industrious men who organize "production, exchange, and distribution of wealth, and are essential to society." [15] But the wealthy capitalists cannot handle the task by themselves. Hence they need the neo-Liberal as scientist who possesses a widespread acquaintance with the principles of sociology.

Scientific sociology discovered that desires can exceed their proper bounds and threaten the capitalist social order. Therefore, they need effective guidance into channels through which they can flow in harmony with the safety of the social order. [16] The control of the individual's desires is but a logical extension of the scientific motif, "predict in order to control." Control is contained in the "logical history of all science; and as sociology is a science, such must be its destiny and its legitimate function." [17] Finding that science's conquest of the material world is to be duplicated in the social world, the founding father of sociology and prophet of the New Deal argued that "the statement of the problem is its theoretical solution, which can be nothing less than the conquest by science of the domain of the social as it has conquered that of the physical forces." [18]

The new liberalism based upon sociological principles does not presuppose a change in human nature as do "all socialistic schemes" and does not require any radical structural change in the capitalist order. New liberalism and its governmental process will be different, but "that difference will not be so radical as to require a revolution." [19]

"If government could be in the hands of the social scientists . . . it might be elevated to the rank of an applied science, or the simple application of the scientific principles of social phenomena." [20] The legislator as a scientific investigator or a person with scientific advisers "would then set for himself the task of devising means to render harmless those forces now running to waste." [21] If the laws given by sociology "were always carefully studied it would soon be discovered that man is as easily managed by intelligence as . . . nature was shown to be." [22] Education was the telic means by which the values of new liberalism were to be instilled.

Ward's subsequent celebration as the Prophet of the New Deal is not entirely divorced from some of Ward's own thoughts. He entitled one of his articles "The Gospel of Action," and said that "the laboring classes of both England and America, and to a large extent the poor and oppressed of all lands . . . regard the teachings of [my book] Dynamic Sociology as tending to liberate them from their chains." After some thought he was more or less compelled to admit that he "had become a sort of Moses to them to lead them out of the wilderness of human thraldom." [23] By advocating a planned economy, a planned society, and the increased functions of the state, Ward, as a scientific Moses, did endeavor to lead the people to the promised land of what has come to be called the New Deal.

Galbraith: Patron Saint of the Revised Deal

Liberalism has now come under attack from various sources, and the intensity of these attacks seems to have increased. Students who in the past supplied liberalism with much vitality and energy have become disillusioned in the face of the manifest contradictions of liberalism and have joined groups that are highly critical of liberalism. Even a few college professors, who for many decades found much reward in defending liberalism, have turned into its bitter opponents. The myth of a monolithic communist conspiracy which the Liberals used for several decades to justify their position has begun to lose its popular charm and appeal. Countries that once could be counted on to support Liberal forays into the frontiers of near and not so near countries are not offering their formerly enthusiastic support. Liberalism appears to be in another crisis.

Galbraith's social theory can be viewed as an endeavor to rejuvenate liberalism—an effort to masquerade liberalism's contradictions, an attempt to make liberalism more attractive to the defecting youth, an adventure to gap the obvious disparity between Liberal theory and Liberal practice, and an experiment to retain liberalism's irrationality as the seat of reason for a new individualism.

THEORY AND PRACTICE

Galbraith suggests that Liberal theory and Liberal practice are not always consistent; what economic textbooks describe and what actually exists are different. Textbook theories describe the world of the small entrepreneur, repair man, independent craftsman, barber, market gardener, bookmaker, independent retailer, the farmer, the shoe repairman, narcotics peddler, pizza merchant, the car and dog laundry—in short the world outside of the industrial system. These theories are based upon a world in which prices are not controlled and where pecuniary motivation is unimpaired. However, this is not the world of the most significant forces—the world of the new industrial state such as of General Motors, General Electric, Standard Oil, Du Pont, and the other less than four hundred corporations that account for over 85 per cent of all industrial research and development. Over 250,000 corporations accounted for only 7 per cent. The five largest industrial corporations, in 1962 for example, possessed over 12 per cent of all manufacturing assets.

MANAGED DEMANDS, TUTORED RESPONSES, AND CONTROLLED BEHAVIOR

Size, according to Galbraith, is the general servant of technology and not the special servant of profits. Accordingly, planning itself is produced by the demands of technology. To reject planning and large-scale organizations is to reject technology. Technology under "all circumstances, leads to planning." [24] Planning, which played an integral part in Ward's scheme for new individualism, remains central to the new individualism of Galbraith. High technology and heavy capital use ". . . require planning," and for this reason even "prices cannot be left to the vagaries of the unmanaged market." [25] The new industrial state cannot rely on the "untutored responses" of the consumer who must be carefully conditioned to want the blessings of new liberalism; "it is the essence of planning that public behavior be made predictable—that it be subject to control." [26] Men's desire for technology leads to their own management, their own control. The increased activity of the state that Ward promoted is still relevant to the new liberalism as it is instrumental in planning and directing men's lives.

THE NEW LIBERAL STATE

The state now functions to force the consuming citizen to save money to invest in the growth of technology. If people are allowed to save freely rather than purchase goods, the result can be a serious and cumulative reduction in aggregate demand. If this happens the industrial state of new liberalism becomes quite vulnerable. Effective regulation of the aggregate demand is thus an "imperative" of new liberalism while the domination of individual needs, of individual demands, "is an organic requirement of the industrial system." [27]

To guarantee consumers for the large corporations the state plans and gathers the forced savings—the taxes—and becomes an important consumer through public expenditures, using its power over taxation and expenditures to provide the balance between savings and their use that the industrialized system of liberalism cannot maintain for itself.[28] The Liberal state supplies the missing element in the planning of savings. Ward's insistence that the wealthy industrialists join the government is quite relevant to decisions concerning where the forced savings are to be spent. Industrial personnel and representatives in key governmental positions are very important to neo-liberalism.

The state must be quite large if its expenditures are to be effective. An adequate scale of government expenditures is the "fulcrum" for the regulation of aggregate demand, and military expenditures are the pivot on which the fulcrum rests and serves as the main crutch for Liberal industrialization.[29] The state becomes "an instrument of the industrial system" and underwrites the corporations' commitments in the areas of advanced technology.[30] At the same time, however, the industrial system becomes an extension of the federal bureaucracy. The line between public and private, which is celebrated in the textbooks, fades in practice.[31]

TECHNOSTRUCTURED DEMOCRACY

The power of industrial apparatus, Galbraith maintains, does not lie with the directors of the "mature" corporations. Instead it is "lodged deeply" within the technical planning and other specialized staff—that is, among the technicians, engineers, sales executives, scientists, designers, market analysts, computer programmers, industrial stylists, and other specialists. In combination all employees make up what he calls the technostructure.

Because of the development of advanced technology and the concomitant rise of the technostructure, the distinctions between employer and employee are obscured. Power passes down into the organization, effectively making it a democratic organization even though formal chains of command might be established.[32] But this is not the technostructure's only positive aspect; it also becomes "the guiding intelligence —the brain—of the enterprise." [33]

The technostructure brings additional Liberal blessings. Since the unstable market has been eliminated by the management of taste, the tutoring of responses, careful conditioning, and forced savings and forced investments, there is a reliable flow of earnings which makes the maximization of profits "no longer necessary." [34] Moreover, the dispersion of power and intelligence into the technostructure prohibits the personal profit-making, prescribes the privacy that malfeasance and misfeasance requires, and makes it difficult to deploy financial resources for political purposes.[35] The development of the technostructure also guarantees that it will select its theater of influence "with discrimination and intelligence." [36] With the development of the technostructure the technological apparatus becomes more democratic and intelligent.

Presumably the only reason the technostructure endeavors to make any profit at all is for its own survival. If it fails to make a profit, stockholders and other "outsiders" will come in and cause all kinds of problems.[37] An additional blessing of new liberalism is that its technostructure only tries to secure a "minimum of profits." [38] New liberalism, consequently, is a much better world to live in than old liberalism. *But* it is still not the best of all possible worlds.

LIBERAL DISASTER

The technostructure is brought about by the demands of increased technology; that is, increased technology needs more and more specialized personnel. The development of this personnel—the technostructure—ultimately makes the industrial apparatus more democratic and more intelligent. Yet the technostructure seeks to guarantee its survival through the expansion of output, the parallel increase in consumption, technological advancement, and the public images that sustain it. This can lead to some very disastrous consequences. There is a danger, Galbraith discovers, that the goals of the industrial apparatus, the industrial system, will become the goals of society.[39] This he feels, should not occur.

If it does, individuals will only be allowed what is consistent with these goals. Wants will be managed in accordance with the industrial system's needs; the state's policies will be subject to similar influence; education will be molded to the needs of the technostructure; the morality required by the industrial system will be the conventional morality of the community; liberty will be endangered by the subordination of belief to the needs of the industrial system; and goals not related to the growth and development of the technostructure and industrial system will become unimportant or deviant.[40]

INTELLECTUAL AS SAVIOR

For neo-liberalism, the intellectuals comprising the scientific and educational elite *must* take the lead in avoiding these dangers. For, as Gal-

braith maintains, "there are no other saviors." [41] The means whereby
the individual can be liberated from the disaster of old liberalism is the
same that Ward chose: Emancipation of the individual from the management of his demands to which he is subjected "lies with
education." [42]

Galbraith realizes that modern education is "extensively accommodated to the needs of the industrial system . . . and possesses a strong
tendency to surrender to the goals of the industrial system before the
battle is joined." [43] However, since the educational and scientific estate
acquires prestige and status which the industrial apparatus supplies,
Galbraith believes that the educational community gains potential
power that hopefully can be exerted "not on behalf of the industrial system but on behalf of the entire human personality." [44]

The intellectual, it turns out, is already a commonplace figure in
American politics. In several states—including Michigan, Wisconsin,
Minnesota, and California—the "educational and scientific estate has a
strong hold on the state and local organization of the Democratic
Party." [45] These saviors of the entire human personality will find added
support in the "great philanthropic organizations" which have given
"grants to groups duly constituted to re-examine the purposes of the
society." [46] (Galbraith admits he is aware that "such re-examination has
invariably led to a strong affirmation of the goals that serve the needs
of the industrial system.")

The educational and scientific estate can assist emancipation by reducing the industrial system's domination of social purposes. Many people, including the industrialists, will recognize that this step is designed
to reduce the role of the industrial system in life "but it is not inconsistent with the continued existence of that system." [47]

ROUND TRIP TO INFINITY

Neo-liberalism will be safer than old liberalism because the method of
underwriting technology will shift from destructive weapons to the
space race. Neo-liberalism accepts as given the need of the existing
technological apparatus for the production of waste, but desires a shift
toward a nondestructive alternative. Galbraith's social theory recognizes

that public expenditures for parks, schools, and the poor do not require the needed technological sophistication that will maintain the techno-structure. Consequently, the space-race waste is a necessity for a peace-oriented liberalism since it also requires high spending and intensified planning. Pouring large public outlays down the industrial drain perpet-uates the technological apparatus which the Liberals control. Not only is the space race relatively harmless but also journeys to Jupiter, salvos to Saturn, and round-trip excursions to infinity serve "an organic need of the industrial system as *now constituted.*" [48]

TO WORK OR NOT TO WORK

Neo-liberalism will permit the employee a wider set of options between working to receive goods and taking more leisure time. If a person only wants to work (say) ten to twenty hours a week and forego the goods and services he could otherwise receive, this choice should be possible. Other alternatives should exist in the form of extended paid vacations or extended leaves of absence. To fail to give employees these options "is to make the needs of the industrial system, not the opportunity of the individual to fashion his own existence, the ruling concern." [49]

CULTIVATED CAPITALISM

The technological apparatus and the Liberals who control it cannot identify themselves with aesthetic goals and simultaneously regard them as relatively unimportant, otherwise they would sanction hideous power lines and power plants, strip mining operations' ruins, shopping centers, billboards, and radio and television commercials. To mitigate these unaesthetic consequences of modern technology neo-liberalism actively supports landscapes, open spaces, virgin mountain sides, antique squares, and tranquility on earth and in the skies as part of the Liberal way of life.

To assert the aesthetic goals of neo-liberalism, however, is "to in-terfere seriously with the management of the consumer." [50] In applying the aesthetic principle to the advertising billboard, for example, neo-liberalism would require that such advertisements blend gracefully with the landscape rather than contrast with its surroundings. Similarly the jarring effect of radio and television commercials, as well as the design and packaging of products, would have to be reduced. (Presumably, pickled pig's feet could be purchased wrapped in a Picasso print.)

Aesthetic goals will, of course, be asserted by the educational and scientific estate and by the state itself since the latter is the only organization available with the political strength to protect and enforce the aesthetic goals. Under new liberalism the use of the aesthetic principle will affect the location of industrial plants, the odors they dispense and the wastes they deposit. The new Liberal state would also support painting, sculpture, music, and good architecture.[51]

LIBERAL FUTURITY: THE TWO-EDGED SWORD

Little suggests that politics in the immediate future of the United States is going to be anything other than what it has been for decades—namely, an extension of Liberal capitalism. Just as the New Deal contained some of the major aspects of Ward's sociology, there is a good chance that the next few decades will contain many of the key features of Galbraith's social thought. Those emphasizing the humanistic tradition—where, for example, men are the measure of all things, where the social order as well as social change are judged according to what it means to and for the individual person, where men should control their life fates and authority exists by their consent, where men's loyalties are conditional upon their individual principles, and where the economy is not seen as an end but as a means of advancing individual and social welfare—will be remembered by that small minority attending free universities, but it will be Galbraith's theories which will be examined for credit toward the degrees. The winners still write the official history.

THE POWER STRUCTURE

The power structure of Liberal capitalism and the bureaucratic organization which supports it is vast and has the ability to restrict or contain the humanistic impulses and tradition within the boundaries of its own nation-state (as well as a few others). Liberalism is now anchored to a military and industrial organization that imposes its definitions of reality through ideology, diplomacy, brute force, and threats both at home and abroad. However, it also incorporates certain elements from the humanistic tradition and uses them as ideological devices.

Given the complexities of the disastrous world situation which liberalism has helped to create, its humanistic rhetoric is both a constant irritation and a source of satisfaction. It is, in short, a double-edged sword. The worth and dignity of the individual, for example, helps defend liberalism, yet also provides a source for criticism as liberalism continually fails to achieve its humanistic goals. The contradictions between the humanistic theory and nonhumanistic practice of liberalism is quite perplexing to the practicing Liberal. Internal and external pressures from those who question liberalism, changes in the technological and economic realms, and changes in the world situation force Liberal spokesmen to suggest accommodations that must be made to reduce the obvious contradictions of theory and practice.

SAINT JOHN'S LIBERALISM

In the approaching decades organized liberalism will make certain accommodations to the humanistic tradition to keep itself in line with the economic imperatives of the present and the future. These accommodations will also serve to quiet the critics who base their arguments on the humanistic tradition. For a long time, for example, Liberals have forced scarcity upon men. Today, however, Liberals can argue that extended leisure should be a goal of modern society and that advancing technology can eliminate scarcity. As the technological advancements increase material abundance, scarcity as an ideology is beginning to lose its force as a means of social control. A new means of social control is needed and is found in leisure and increased abundance.

By using the existing technology to dominate men's leisure time— through the diffusion of motorboats and fishing tackle, television and TV dinners, workshops in the basements and playgrounds in the parks —the technological apparatus and the Liberals who control it are re-enforcing the reality that they have helped construct. At a time when men are no longer needed in the productive process, neo-Liberals are advocating the guaranteed annual income and other such programs to blunt any incipient or potential threats to the Liberal system. Liberal technology itself becomes ideological, prompting men to define many of their own needs. Men desire what is to be produced by the technological apparatus and are satisfied by consuming its wares. Television with its vulgarity and unaesthetic advertisements has helped promote these desires, and television aesthetic advertisements are going to re-enforce the existing Liberal technology as well. Galbraith's plea for leisure and aesthetic advertisements to help fill that leisure serves to maintain liberalism.

Galbraith eliminated the search for maximum profits and the irrational notion of the market place from his new social theory and made liberalism an almost noncapitalist experiment in which the capitalists were all but replaced in the power structure by the technostructure—a nonprofit or very low profit-oriented group that is primarily concerned with consumption, growth, and increased technology. Saint John also attempted to show how the industrial apparatus was the source of rationality. At the same time he has attempted to demonstrate how the individual, especially the intellectual, was the source of reason pitted against the irrationality of organized liberalism. His attempt to reconcile this contradiction was more commendable than his achievement.

DO-IT-TO-YOURSELF KITS

Galbraith admitted that the scholars and their academic community had a strong tendency to surrender to liberalism before any battle was even started, pointing out that the community was extensively accommodated to the needs of the industrial system. The only hope he could find in these intellectuals was that they might utilize their power, which is based upon their affiliation with organized liberalism, and use it to promote man as the measure for needed socio-historical change.

The brutality which has historically accompanied liberalism in the United States will be greatly reduced as economists, sociologists, and psychologists contribute to the social control devices, reflected in their social control concepts, that are required by a sophisticated liberalism.

Complex technology is expensive and not easily replaced if it is destroyed by the aggressiveness of internal or external deviants. This Liberal technology will be used to make life more pleasurable and liberalism more palatable, even for deviants.

The do-it-to-yourself kits that Liberal technology produces in the form of desires and needs serve to make liberalism and its technology a vital part of the individual's self-image. To attack the law and order of organized liberalism is to attack oneself. The fate of the individual under new liberalism will be to remain an extension of the technological apparatus.

DEMOCRATIC DOMINATION

Streamlined domination of Liberal technocracy is still domination but one which is more aesthetically pleasing. Since the power of the capitalists has been removed—since the United States is no longer a capitalist society but rather a society with a wide dispersion of power—to protest against one's domination is to protest against democracy, Liberal democracy. Democratic domination will obviously be a better form of liberalism than any which has existed in the past. After the present phase when protesting minorities are beaten and consumed into submission, subsequent attempts to castigate liberalism will become more and more quaint, and more and more meaningless. The bureaucratized structure of liberalism will contain and pervert the humanistic tradition with greater and more streamlined ease.

The structure of Liberal capitalism has dominated the issues raised in the three branches of government to such an extent that the democratic checks and balances effectively check the development of any consciousness that could serve to move the issues outside the Liberal reality. Existing checks and balances also work to state the issues in favor of maintaining liberalism as the *Weltanschauung.* To place hope for meaningful change in the government is like placing that hope in the technostructure that is an extension of the government. Together they form a unity against which the humanistic tradition will not be able to advance in any meaningful sense in the near future.

UNTUTORED RATIONALITY

Tutored needs are the *sine qua non* of the technostructure that represents the democratic and intelligent nature of the technological apparatus. This is the very apparatus that makes contemporary and future liberalism possible, yet it is for the existence of untutored needs that Galbraith pleads. It is the intellectual who will emancipate the individual's need by making him conscious of his domination by the technological apparatus, but this emancipation seems to have certain limits consistent to the existence of the Liberal system. This contradiction of liberalism—the necessity for tutored needs and the desire for untutored needs—is not resolved by Galbraithian logic. The possibility exists that the free and untutored individual might not desire to live under the Liberal system. Consequently, the emancipation from untutored needs will be extended to the individual to the degree that liberalism is not threatened. Untutored needs will still be tutored, anchored in the intelligence upon which the technostructure is based—the rationality of the Liberal system.

LIBERAL RATIONALITY

The technostructure, based upon a complex technology and heavy capital investment in the production of waste, is a manifestation of Liberal rationality. Liberal rationality is dependent on and consistent with the production of goods which continually wear out. The largest expenditure of wasteful production would be the space program. Liberal reason is a wasteful irrationality.

The identity of the citizen with the (his) space program is an essential part of the technostructure's public image. Moreover, it is necessary as a means to obtain his forced savings. The financial contributions to this wasteful enterprise will be great and much time and effort will be directed at the individual to convince him that he *needs* the space program. (Galbraith did not suggest what might happen to liberalism if the individual was freed from this tutored need.)

THE LIBERAL HOURS

Liberalism assumed, at one time, that freedom existed in the world of the small entrepreneur living in rural or small communities, that the different institutions—economic, political, military, educational, kinship, and religious—were autonomous, that the individual was the seat of rationality, and that authority should be explicit. It became obvious to even the most dedicated Liberal that these characteristics no longer existed. The economy no longer consisted of small units of production but instead was dominated by a few—two or three hundred—large corporations. Government was no longer just a guardian, but had become a manager in the form of a large bureaucracy. No longer another aspect under the control of the public, the military had grown into a centralized force of powerful lobbyists. Education also became bureaucratized, serving as a training ground for these other institutions. Liberalism, with its giant corporations based on a military capitalism, became a power structure of international relevance, and required a new theory to rationalize its new role in history.

The social theories of Galbraith were but one response to the socio-historical imperatives that helped to bring about the change in liberalism which had to be explained, justified, and analyzed by a conceptual framework with scientific validity. Since social sciences had come of age, sociology, economics, and psychology supplied the needed concepts and theories in the name of objectivity and neutrality.

The old notion of the self-balancing society was a good ideology and served the vested interests well. When the theory was obviously no longer adequate, Galbraith and many others merely switched the emphasis from the small entrepreneurs and small farmers to the large corporations, calling them countervailing powers. The world of corporate capitalism was also self-balancing.

When it became obvious that the existing powers were no longer countering each other—that they were part of a unified whole—a new theory was needed and once again Galbraith became the man of the liberal hours. The world situation was changing drastically. Communism had moved only ninety miles from Miami and, in general, the world was becoming smaller. Some critics of liberalism revealed it for what it was, corporate and military capitalism. *The New Industrial State* serves the needs of liberalism and to some extent suggests the path that the welfare-warfare state of liberalism must take if it is to survive.

To maintain itself, liberalism must contend with the forces that threaten and confront it. One of these forces is represented in the image of man put forth by the humanistic tradition which liberalism has historically been able to contain. Man as the measure of socio-historical phenomena serves as the criterion by which institutions can be judged according to their effectiveness in bettering the welfare of the individuals comprising them. Liberalism has always been plagued by humanistic values and has had to contend with them throughout its history.

In attempting to prove the worthiness of the existing capitalistic enterprise Galbraith's neo-liberalism argues that existing structures are indeed the best set of arrangements for rational democracy and the best means whereby men's needs can be fulfilled. *The New Industrial State* attempts to demonstrate that the warfare nature of the Liberal welfare state is not a permanent military capitalism.

Galbraith not only fails to suggest the possibility of a relationship between imperialism and the Liberal *Weltanschauung* but he also will not even acknowledge the existence of the Liberal exploitation of other countries as a historically specific event. The sanguineness of Galbraith's theories does not permit him to approach many of those key issues confronting liberalism that are manifested in the behavior of those protesting against his system.

Of course, this inadequacy does reveal a weakness of Liberal theory, but it attests to the power and strength of Liberal practice. The discontent of a minority of workers, students, blacks, women in their own liberation groups, and, for example, the Vietnamese exists in a world far removed from Liberal theory (except for those daring academicians who proclaim them as "problems"). To ignore the social forces of which these groups are manifestations reflects the inadequacy of Liberal theory, but where Liberal theory fails to "handle" these "problems," Liberal practice does not. The liberalism of Galbraith's sanguine theory is not the liberalism which is imposing its comfortable but oppressive reality upon a large segment of the earth. Liberalism in practice cannot rely (as yet) on the conceptual schemes of the social scientists and must depend ever so often on its local, state, national, and international police force to handle those disquieting "elements" of the world population.

Because of its brute force, liberalism is able to contain qualitative socio-historical change to a degree, but its major thrust at containment has come through its technological advancement. Modernized technology with all its comfort has served to reconcile and accommodate the alternative forces opposing liberalism. Yesterday's malcontents become today's defenders. Liberalism consumes the very forces that militate against it, leaving the representatives of these forces as subjects of folk-songs and posters and as examples of its powers of containment.

Through technology and the bureaucratic structure which surrounds it, the oppositional forces are eventually unified into a whole. Yet liberalism's containment of these different forms of dissent leaves them impotent and celebrating their own existence, sometimes on prime-time television and quite frequently through the Liberal press. Technology, which has the potential to set men free by bursting through the Liberal techniques of domination, is transformed into the Liberal forces that perpetuate servitude. Liberalism has transformed its domination into administrative objectivity where "society," the "social system," or "social order," for example, become the embodiment of rationality. To protest liberalism becomes utopian, unpractical, and, of course, irrational.

The unrealistic and impractical of the alternatives presented to liberalism do not reveal any inherent weakness of the alternatives, but they attest on the contrary to the strength of liberalism which actually prevents and perverts the actualization of the alternatives. Liberal insanity —the Liberal lunacy exemplified by the servitude it perpetuates, the ill-health and premature deaths it creates, the waste it demands, the poverty it generates, and the crimes against humanity it commits—is absolved and transformed into rationality by the liberties it bestows, the comforts it delivers, the leisure it dispenses, the aestheticism it contributes, and the style of life it presents.

Liberalism has become more and more capable of providing the products to be consumed and, consequently, more able to unite the population within its bureaucratic structure. It has also modernized its powers of containment and is able to make the necessary accommodations of its military capitalism to the welfare state—increased public expenditures, increased governmental planning, enlarged public works, larger foreign aid, the growth of multinational corporations and investment, and extended security programs. These accommodations have increased the power and ability of liberalism to widen its scope of streamlined domination.

Liberalism contains the seeds of its own destruction, but it also contains the seeds of its own construction—namely, the ability to accommodate and contain. The collapse of liberalism might well lie in the future, but it is not the impending doom or the imminent inevitability of the near future. Liberalism's containment capacity will divert many oppositional forces into a more comfortable life and its accommodation ability will help men celebrate their own unfreedom for many years to come.

Notes

1. Henry Steele Commager, *The American Mind* (New Haven, 1962), p. 214.

2. *Ibid.*, p. 216.

3. For the most part, Sumner's central concepts evolved around economic and industrial criteria. Private property, and even liberty, were incorporated into several of his basic concepts. The recognition of good mores was related to the advancement of economic power and material well-being; progress was correlated to the achievements of a business world freed of political contamination; and the social elite which nature used to guide the masses emerged from a process of natural selection operating primarily within the business realm.

Sumner feared that his generation had created social problems that it was incompetent to solve, and that both the social problems and this incompetency threatened the basic structure of the good and true socio-economic system. Plutocracy with its military-business-political elite was destroying this socio-economic system, introducing a bevy of parasites—lawyers, militarists, bureaucrats, lobbyists, and part politicians—and evoking not only a century-long social war but also a century-armed war with "a frightful effusion of blood." Sumner too had prophetic powers.

4. Lester Frank Ward, *Pure Sociology* (New York, 1903), p. 469, and Ward, *Dynamic Sociology* (New York, 1911), I, 30 and 75.

5. Ward, *Glimpses of the Cosmos* (New York, 1935), I, 237.

6. Dusky Lee Smith, *Some Socio-economic Influences of the Founding Fathers of Sociology, 1865–1917* (unpublished dissertation), pp. 326–28.

7. Ward, *Glimpses,* IV, 55 and 312.

8. Ward, *The Psychic Factors of Civilization* (New York, 1906).

9. *Ibid.* 10. *Ibid.* 11. Ward, *Glimpses,* I, 55. 12. *Ibid.*

13. *Ibid.* 14. *Ibid.,* p. 53. 15. *Ibid.* 16. *Ibid.,* IV, 263.

17. Ward, *Dynamic Sociology,* I, 81. 18. Ward, *Glimpses,* IV, 14.

19. Ward, *The Psychic Factors of Civilization,* p. 325.

20. Ward, *Dynamic Sociology,* I, 249. 21. *Ibid.*

22. Ward, *Pure Sociology,* p. 570. 23. Ward, *Glimpses,* IV, 231.

24. Galbraith, *The New Industrial State* (Boston, 1967), p. 20 and 319.

25. *Ibid.,* pp. 12, 20, 23, 189, and 319. 26. *Ibid.,* p. 319.

27. *Ibid.,* pp. 222–23. 28. *Ibid.,* p. 261. 29. *Ibid.,* p. 228.

30. *Ibid.,* pp. 251, 296, and 309. 31. *Ibid.,* p. 379.

32. *Ibid.,* pp. 71, 116, 153, and 268. 33. *Ibid.,* p. 71.

34. *Ibid.,* p. 110. 35. *Ibid.,* p. 149.

36. *Ibid.,* pp. 117, 302, and 316. 37. *Ibid.,* p. 168. 38. *Ibid.*

39. *Ibid.,* pp. 153 and 323. 40. *Ibid.,* p. 398. 41. *Ibid.,* p. 385.

42. *Ibid.,* p. 366. 43. *Ibid.,* p. 383. 44. *Ibid.,* pp. 283–372.

45. *Ibid.,* p. 381.

46. *Ibid.,* p. 344. The fact that the "dissenter" from the industrial system "had had little problem in expressing his dissent. . . ." (besides that "those who claim they have been censored in the United States usually turn out, on examination to have had nothing much to say. . . ."), in combination with the fact that most instruments of literary communication are manned by intellectuals who have a natural libertarian bias, "insures that the goals of the intellectuals will be respected." *Ibid.,* p. 377.

47. *Ibid.,* p. 380. 48. *Ibid.,* p. 342. 49. *Ibid.,* p. 367.

50. *Ibid.,* p. 348. 51. *Ibid.,* p. 352.

JON ALEXANDER

The Soft Cell

THE FINAL TRIUMPH of the bureaucratic welfare state in
America—its almost universal acceptance—was consolidated in what
Eric Goldman has called the Crucial Decade following World War II.[1]
By the mid-1950s, Liberals were uneasily proclaiming their "victory" as
the end of ideology. Not only did ideology subside but also politics itself began to disappear from the public forum. Outwardly politics was
replaced by a manipulative "pseudopolitics" suppressing the individual's capacity and opportunity for rational choice. The political system
was increasingly absorbed into a more general system of social control,
of which the welfare state apparatus formed a major part. A century-
old prophecy was fulfilled.*

In the nineteenth century Alexis de Tocqueville looked forward
with grave apprehension to the eventual consolidation of the democratic
welfare state. His nightmare vision was that of a soft cell. Majoritarian
government by public opinion, he saw, would come "to the same thing
as if the majority itself held its deliberation in the market-place."[2] The
despotism which democratic nations had to fear would be that of an administered, manipulated, political market.

This despotism would not be the tyranny of old: "It would be
more extensive and more mild. It would degrade men without torment-

* The writer acknowledges a general intellectual debt to Dr. Harvey Wheeler of
the Center for the Study of Democratic Institutions, many of whose ideas have
been used or misused in this essay.

ing them." The citizenry would become massified status seekers "incessantly endeavoring to procure the petty and paltry pleasures with which they glut their lives." They would be alienated in a lonely crowd: "Each of them, living apart, is a stranger to the fate of all the rest,—his children and his private friends constitute to him the whole of mankind; as for the rest of his fellow citizens, he is close to them, but he sees them not; he touches them, but he feels them not; he exists for himself alone. . . ." Lives would be bureaucratically controlled by a state power which is "absolute, minute, regular, provident, and mild, . . ." bestowing security while robbing individual independence and autonomy. "The will of man is not shattered, but softened, bent, and guided; men are seldom forced to act, but they are constantly restrained from acting: such a power does not destroy, but it prevents existence; it does not tryannize, but it compresses, enervates, extinguishes, and stupifies a people, till each nation is reduced to be nothing better than a flock of timid and industrious animals, of which the government is the shepherd." [3]

De Tocqueville was an aristocrat, yet his prophecy is strikingly similar to descriptions of the present condition advanced by contemporary radical, Liberal, and Conservative social critics alike: the brave new world of organization men in a nation of sheep where growing up is absurd, a managerial revolution establishing a power elite that "administers" a consumer society. When de Tocqueville wrote that "I have always thought that servitude of the regular, quiet, and gentle kind . . . might be combined more easily than is commonly believed with some of the outward forms of freedom, and that it might even establish itself under the wing of the sovereignty of the people, . . ." [4] he was expressing views which are today reflected in Barbara Garson's brutal satire *MacBird,* a parody on Lyndon Johnson's Great Society, and Herbert Marcuse's critical philosophy. As Marcuse argues, "A comfortable, smooth, reasonable, democratic unfreedom prevails in advanced industrial civilization, a token of technical progress." [5]

But contemporary political scientists have typically failed to come to grips with the warnings of de Tocqueville or the frontal attacks against the system by today's social critics. This is because of a bias of political science, namely, a concern with distributive notions: Politics is defined as who gets what, when, and how. Political scientists see large numbers of competing interest groups and assume that all is well with our pluralistic society.

Herein I shall attempt to assess the prospects for a new individualism. But to do so, I must first examine the structure and dynamics of modern society, the integrative and absorptive powers of which are tremendous. I shall argue that with the merger of the political-corporate power system we have come to the end of politics—to the end of debate. But in turn, I believe, this structure is giving rise to new social patterns which in the end will revise the political-corporate system. Modern man will function outside the existing political framework and thereby change it.

THE SMOOTH SOCIETY

We are returning to an age where—as with primitive tribes—it is the society that controls the individual, not law, not politics. But the new forms of social control are artificial and bureaucratic rather than natural and customary. Modern man in a technological society feels unfree to the extent that he perceives the manipulativeness and social coercion of the whole system.

Natural community is born historically of the necessities from which man now has freed himself. Organization, impersonality, and efficiency are hallmarks of technological society; these are characteristics not of community but of its negation. Freed from necessity, man is freed as well from community. Instead of an organic community of which he is a part, he is now faced with the system, an entity from which he is alienated but which demands conformity. This is why members of the New Left, as well as the man in the street, refer not to government but vaguely to the "system" as the oppressor. Its control is pervasive and is not confined to those who work for large bureaucratic organizations. Bernard Asbell interviewed a farmer who understood something of the "system":

I have the feeling I'm being pushed around by somebody bigger than me, but I don't know who he is. Sometimes I feel like I live in one of those Western towns you see in the movies where a man with a big gun struts around and says, 'I run this place. My name is Tex spelled with a capital T, and you all do what I say.' Trouble is, if you ask me who's Tex, I don't know. . . . I don't know who's to blame. I just know if you put them all together—the milk companies, the Department of Agriculture, the marketing orders, the credit companies, even the retired farmers who run the big farm organizations that never seem to get us anywhere—they're all Tex. They tell me what to do, how much I collect, who to pay, how fast to pay it. They all have more to say about running my farm than I do.[6]

Like this unhappy farmer, most social critics—Conservative, Liberal, and radical—have focused attention and concern primarily upon the "system's" aggregative tendencies. They describe the manipulative power of large private corporate enterprise: They see that collectivization and rationalization of production require an irrational collectivization of public taste, based upon massive conditioning by advertising which leads to involuntary behavior.

Modern technological society is indeed capable of "delivering the goods" in great quantity, but this has been achieved only through increased organization of both economic-government processes and people. Because the distributive concern of brokerage politics has fostered centripetal and organizational forces, pluralism has actually legitimized central control. As Herbert Marcuse says, "Our society distinguishes itself by conquering the centrifugal social forces with Technology rather than Terror, on the dual basis of an overwhelming efficiency and an increasing standard of living." [7]

However, the preoccupation with distributive processes has led many contemporary political scientists to postulate a free market in politics much like the free market of classical economics. Since pluralism is the invisible hand for most political scientists today, political theory has lagged far behind economic theory. The most significant advances in modern macroeconomic theory derive from a shift in focus from distributive notions to aggregative concerns. Economists have come to be concerned with the dynamics of organization, planning, and control of the economic world by large corporate structures. This shift corresponds to the powerful organizational and aggregative forces now at work in American society.

Any new individualism will necessarily be concerned with these aggregative tendencies, and it will necessarily be radical. For the new individualism must question not only the faulty distribution but also, more importantly, the faulty organization of society.

THE DEATH OF POLITICS

A fundamental characteristic of contemporary American society is the mutual interest among private corporations and government in preserving security at the expense of individual liberty. As the welfare state has developed, its aims have been subtly perverted. Rather than seeking equality or the enlargement of freedom, the contemporary welfare state strives for social and national security.

Big business requires large stable markets. Accordingly it has accepted the welfare state and the new economics. The middle-class welfare state provides stable markets, but it does not involve any major redistribution of wealth from those at the top. The awesome fact of truly massive privilege remains. In fact, during the last decade the total distributional effect of taxes and benefits by American government at all levels was to increase inequality.[8] As it was during these years that the "end of ideology" was proclaimed! Michael Harrington did not exaggerate when he said that the American welfare state is a system of socialism for the rich and capitalism for the poor.

John Kenneth Galbraith shows in his *New Industrial State* that big business also requires and secures administered (controlled) markets and administered prices. This means that organizational control is necessary not only of products but also of consumers. Integration propaganda is necessary to the degree to which our society is economically rationalized and organized. Given a pecuniary society, a high degree of organization of productive forces would be useless unless organization of the consumptive forces occurs simultaneously. Mass consumption requires that Everyman has an identical definition of the necessities of life. Conformity of action in a soft cell requires conformity of thought.

Similarly, government needs "administered markets" for rational decision-making. By the mid-1960s more than four-fifths of the nation's work force were employed by corporations.[9] With this percentage edging upward annually, the government has sought to control the activities of corporate enterprises through more extensive planning. The result has been a merger of business and government. At least two-thirds of American industry and much of American finance are now controlled by federal industrial plans. Virtually all industry, finance, and foreign business investment is subject to informal government "guidelines." [10] Through the growth of the military, the scientific establishment (which now works largely for the government or is financed by it), and government itself, the government has absorbed huge areas of private enterprise. Former Presidential Adviser Richard N. Goodwin cites some illuminating data that indicate the scope of government-economic activities:

The federal government spends about one-seventh of our national wealth and creates more of it. Between 1950 and 1960, nine out of ten new jobs were created by the public and the private not-for-profit sectors, and only one out of ten by private enterprise. Today [1967], one-third of the entire labor force works for someone other than a profit-making institution. [11]

This merger of business and government has resulted in the death of politics. Advertising techniques employed by both partners in their pursuit of security have conditioned consensus on two basic levels of mass consciousness. The first is general opinion. The second is what we may call the inarticulate major premises of a society. Government and business attempt to manipulate both kinds of consensus. In the first instance they may seek to sell a particular product or policy. In the second case, they may attempt—whether consciously or not—to affect the very standards by which citizens judge or identify themselves with a system of business or government.

Advertising campaigns may not be successful in selling a particular product, but their cumulative effect is to make compulsive consumers of most of us. Whatever brand we choose, we do in fact consume the goods that the industrial system offers. Likewise government propaganda prepares us to accept the imperatives and propensities under which our government operates. Whatever we may have thought about Korea or Vietnam, many Americans accept uncritically the garrison state we have become.

As political manipulation increases, a pseudopolitical freedom increases as well. One is more free to engage in political action that is either meaningless, designed to reinforce consensus, or concerned purely with distribution. Because political organization (just as mass production) does deliver the goods, one is more free to obey what he considers to be good, legitimate, and beneficial control. But in a manipulative political system the obligations of citizenship create merely a pseudo-involvement. Citizens are engaged in politics in the same sense that a transmission's gears are engaged in a moving automobile.

With the death of politics in contemporary America, political citizenship has thus become transformed into corporate citizenship. The corporate citizenship requires closer analysis, for it involves a fundamental change in the nature of politics.

BUREAUCRACY AND THE
CORPORATE CITIZENSHIP

As societal collectivization proceeds, citizens find themselves excluded from political participation as they become absorbed into the bureaucratic system of the welfare state. Bureaucratic organizations possess two major means to "neutralize" their environment so that their work may proceed unimpaired. The first is information control, which involves secrecy, the development of esoteric languages and procedures, and manipulative publicity or news management. This set of procedures is favored more by the public or political bureaucracies. The second method, which is favored more by the corporate structures, is the socialization process. Through inducements ranging from patent coercion to the most subtle appeals to conformity, people are "taught" or conditioned to behave in ways that serve organizational goals of size, power, and survival of bureaucratic structures. Hence, corporate citizens thwart their own self-realization and, in varying degrees, become willing accomplices of their controllers.[12]

Organization theory, as expressed by such leading exponents as Phillip Selznick and Herbert Simon, postulates a wide separation between elite and follower, i.e., between the manager and the managed. The organizational values are determined by elites without "political" participation by others. The value system is controlled, first through establishing a strong institutional core, then through indoctrination and positive reinforcement to foster personal acceptance of and commitment to the institutional values, and finally through expulsion of nonconformists.[13] Elite manipulation, a subordinate mass, and powerful sanctions against dissenters thus preclude meaningful citizen sovereignty. "Citizens" simply are not involved in questions of purpose.

As societal collectivization proceeds, we may now begin to apply organization theory to gain an understanding not only of large bureaucracies but also of the present organizational society as a whole. With the merger of public and private governments, their mutually reinforcing methods of control have hardened the walls of the soft cell of corporate citizenship. De Tocqueville foresaw the development of organizational citizenship and described the fate—one far softer than that imposed by the old-style tyranny—of those who opt out of the organizational society:

The master no longer says, 'You shall think as I do, or you shall die; but he says, 'You are free to think differently from me, and to retain your life, your property, and all you possess; but you are henceforth a stranger among your people. You may retain your civil rights, but they will be useless to you. . . . You will remain among men, but you will be deprived of the rights of mankind. Your fellow-creatures who believe in your innocence will abandon you, lest they should be shunned in their turn. Go in peace! I have given you life, but it is an existence worse than death.[14]

Herbert Marcuse despairs of the possibility of escaping the soft cell, and freedom is escape:

Thus economic freedom would mean freedom *from* the economy—from being controlled by economic forces and relationships, freedom from the daily struggle for existence, from earning a living. Political freedom would mean liberation of the individuals *from* politics over which they have no effective control. Similarly, intellectual freedom would mean the restoration of individual thought now absorbed by mass communication and indoctrination, abolition of 'public opinion' together with its makers. The unrealistic sound of these propositions is indicative, not of their utopian character, but of the strength of the forces which prevent their realization.

The soft cell is, in the final analysis, created in men's minds. But its psychological nature merely adds to the difficulty. Marcuse asks, "How can the administered individuals—who have made their mutilation into their own liberties and satisfactions, and thus reproduce it on an enlarged scale—liberate themselves from themselves as well as from their masters? How is it even thinkable that the vicious circle be broken?" [15]

The great danger of the soft cell is that in an effect-oriented society we will be so seduced by the products of technology that we will willingly acquiesce to both the necessity for consuming its byproducts and the loss of meaningful choice, spontaneity, and creativity. In that case we will feel no great constraint and little sense of loss, for our prisons will be supremely comfortable, and we will have many technological diversions. Our senses will be massaged electronically, our physical needs met synthetically, and our sexual and spiritual needs satisfied vicariously. But we will not be individual human persons. We will be treated as merely Kantian phenomena—mind-constructs, not each a thing-in-itself—and hence reduced to parts of men in roles. This is happening today to the men in large bureaucratic organizations, both governmental and private. In government this is especially degrading, for bureaucratic people-parts tend to treat citizens—the "clients" of bureaucracy—as people-parts as well. The bureaucratic process thus destroys the integral wholeness of citizen and bureaucrat alike.

Because bureaucratic control is in effect the "rule of nobody," there are no rascals to throw out; bureaucracy is characterized by people in interchangeable roles. Fire x; put in y, and y must do what x had been doing. To the extent that bureaucratic organization and technical procedure determine what government does—and these influences are profound—morality simply disappears from the governmental process. Technicians at work are rigidly amoral. If they were to become moralists, they would cease to be good technicians. Technical procedure lies in the realm of integral causality, evolving in a purely causal way and pursuing no end, professed or unprofessed. Thus bureaucratic government has abdicated responsibility for the pursuit of the good society. This abdication gives free play to manipulative social forces.

Who is in charge here? Who governs? The frenetic search for a "national purpose" in the late 1950s and early 1960s was an expression of the apprehension created by our new condition. As politics dissolves into administration, and as the political and economic spheres merge, we have a new situation which is difficult to comprehend. Yet we have some historical evidence that may be instructive as we attempt to grapple with this phenomenon. The entire government seems now to be following a pattern long-established in the independent regulatory commissions.

The concept of the independent regulatory commission, or at least the original rationale for this new form of government, was to remove regulation from politics. Political scientist Marver Bernstein wrote the now classic description of this pattern in terms of a typical "life cycle": gestation, youth, maturity, and old age. The agencies of government in which politics is disappearing more or less naturally, i.e., without conscious intention and design, are mostly still in their "youth" period. The furthest advanced is the Department of Defense, where adoption of technical decision-making has proceeded fastest. Bernstein describes the mature period for the commissions:

> Gradually the spirit of controversy fades out of the regulatory setting, and the commission adjusts to conflict among the parties in interest. It relies more and more on settled procedures and adapts itself to the need to fight its own political battles unassisted by informed public opinion and effective national political leadership. . . . In the period of maturity, regulation usually becomes more positive in its approach. Its functions are less those of a policeman and more like that of a manager of an industry. The approach and point of view of the regulatory process begin to partake of those of business management. The commission becomes accepted as an essential part of the industrial system. . . . Cut off from the mainstream of political life the commission's standards of regulation are determined in the light of the desires of the industry affected. . . . [in the case of the Defense Department, by the military-industrial complex.] The close of the period of maturity is marked by the commission's surrender to the regulated . . . ; the commission finally becomes a captive of the regulated groups.

Bernstein concludes that this pattern is not uniquely applicable to regulatory commissions: "Acceptance by government officials of an alliance with regulated groups is an abdication of responsibility and must be considered a blow to democratic government and responsible political institutions." [16]

AMERICA'S NEW CONSERVATISM

Thus government and business merge, and to what purpose? Apparently the only public purpose is growthmanship. The private purpose is simply the maintenance of this symbiotic relationship against substantial change. Coupled with the Conservative bias of this symbiosis is the general timidity of bureaucracy. The security state officials develop institutions that mainly seek security for themselves. Government becomes incapable of attending the public good and mobilizing resources to further qualitative ends.

This new conservatism is not reactionary; it does not want to keep things the way they are. It wants to preserve the rate of "progress," i.e., the sort of growth that can be measured quantitatively as Gross National Product and consumption figures. Nevertheless the new conservatism is a force opposed to real progress toward human happiness and human development and growth.

Who is in charge here? The symbiosis of government and big-business creates an urge for defense of the status quo in an institutional sense. But who is concerned with what technology is doing to us? We must now face the very real possibility that no one in a position of power is so concerned.

Critics pointed out that C. Wright Mills, who demonstrated the existence of a "power elite," was unable to demonstrate what this elite did with its power. This criticism must be based on the assumption that an elite will want to do something beyond simply maintaining its position of privilege. The unchecked rush of technology should lead us to question this assumption. Bachrach and Baratz argue convincingly that there are in fact two faces of power:

Of course power is exercised when A participates in the making of decisions that affect B. But power is also exercised when A devotes his energies to creating or reinforcing social and political values and institutional practices that limit the scope of the political process to public consideration of only those issues which are comparatively innocuous to A.[17]

This second face of power has come to prevail in an age of impotent government and pseudopolitics.

The end of ideology does not mean that the problems of politics have been solved. Traditional problems of freedom, justice, peace, and order are more acute than ever, but we can no longer look to bureaucracy to treat them. Bureaucratic government has abandoned the public interest, and so has lost its legitimacy.

In a bureaucracy each man has become a functionary performing his assigned role with impersonal detachment. He is concerned with form not substance, with legality not justice, with procedure not product. In the course of his duties the individual bureaucrat may be required to engage in behavior that he considers personally reprehensible. Yet he performs his duty with little sense of personal responsibility or guilt. For he knows that the logic of bureaucratic functioning is not the logic of individual morality. Thus bureaucracy is the very embodiment of collective irresponsibility. By way of contrast let us recall, as John Dewey formulates them, the classic ideals of democratic liberalism: "the conception of a common good as the measure of political organization and policy, of liberty as the most precious trait and very seal of individuality, of the claim of every individual to the full development of his capacities." [18]

The Liberal democratic ideal represents a government founded in reason and in philosophy. According to this ideal, doctrine is both the criterion of action and the judge of the quality of governmental activities. In contrast bureaucracy is a vast assortment of highly specialized compartments that engage in a collective decision-making process. On major decisions "ambassadors" from several of the segments come together to produce a committee report that often appears to be integrated but in reality is a "satisficing" compromise interweaving majority and minority views. In cases of strong dissention, the "policy" may be purposely ambiguous or even contradictory. This tendency toward collective irrationality and collective contradiction produces policies that are difficult or even impossible to administer. No doctrine is the criterion of action, for doctrine becomes merely explicative and justifying. It is paradoxical that as technical operations become more efficient, the governmental process becomes less able to give direction to this massive societal intervention. As man succeeds in overcoming many of the laws of nature, he is less able to provide reasoned humanistic purposes to the use of his power.

Faced with this dilemma, the standard response of the "Liberal establishment" is that our salvation will be found in rational planning. Planning is indeed necessary, but given the present structure of our business-government symbiosis, planning is more likely to regiment rather than liberate man. The prospect that planning will serve manipulated wants instead of human needs of society is an outgrowth of the transformation of liberalism in contemporary America. Conditioned by its technological-bureaucratic environment, liberalism has abandoned its once-radical passion for justice in favor of a pervasive concern with efficiency. This decline has been described by John Roche as a descent into a "technocratic liberalism" which would favor urban renewal as a means to beautify America's cities by replacing Negroes with trees. Let us see how this technocratic liberalism would "solve" our highway beautification problem. William Wheaton, urban planner at Berkeley, explains:

[Beside future expressways] a corridor 600 to 1,000 feet could be landscaped to create the impression of countryside, forests, and woods even while it traversed a densely developed urban area. It is ridiculous to propose the preservation of greenbelts or mile-wide scenic corridors if the purpose is to provide visual recreation. That purpose can be efficiently achieved with comparatively narrow rights of way properly landscaped. If there are those who desire to see rural land uses, cows can be stationed in the highway corridor to simulate the traditional image of the countryside without wasting useful urban land. We might even install plastic cows and sheep to create a simulation of the desired rusticity. . . . It should be reasonable . . . to insist that all future expressways conform to such standards.[19]

This is a counsel of despair. It assumes that we cannot recreate a humanistic environment and must instead be satisfied with a pseudo-environment. No greater perversion of human values can be imagined.

Bureaucratic "rationalization" of society is rapidly reaching a point where the governmental process will have passed out of the possibility of human experience altogether. If we fail to establish a firm basis for the new individualism, we should reconcile ourselves to a synthetic world from which human meaning has disappeared—to be replaced by plastic cows. There would be no need then to place plastic sheep *beside* the highways; we will be driving the cars.

DISSENT AND PROSPECTS OF CHANGE

By the late 1960s, while complacency and inertia still were rampant in America, some people were beginning to opt out of the system. Among them were members of the New Left, the hippies, the black-power Negroes, and disillusioned intellectuals. Clearly a new individualism had stirred violent passions and deep anxieties across the land. Born in the Negro ghettos and nurtured on university campuses by society's youth, the reaction against regimentation and manipulation spread even to the staid suburbs of America. In face of the increasing pressures toward conformity, the nation seemed to be making a last attempt to retain its sanity and resist its transformation into plastic sheep.

The soft cell was still "delivering the goods," but the costs were becoming increasingly apparent. Reality was beginning to intrude upon the contrived images of the smooth society. The seemingly endless bloodshed in Vietnam, the continued oppression of society's rejects, and the impotence of government stood in glaring contrast to the traditional American idea of inevitable unilinear progress. A few cracks were beginning to appear in the walls of the soft cell. Perhaps the ability of a free people to adapt to regimentation was beginning to reach its breaking point. The selling pitch, both governmental and corporate, had reached the intensity of hard sell. And buyer resistance was increasing.

William Safire, speechwriter and adviser to President Nixon, has modestly proclaimed *Safire's Law* to read as follows: "Acquiescence to manipulation decreases in direct ratio to the developing technique of sophisticated persuasion." [20] The best example of this reaction is the government's Vietnam-War-policy hard sell which has not united but divided the American people. But the credibility gap is larger than Vietnam. In 1967, Secretary of Labor Wirtz wrote in the *New York Times:* "A considerable part of what the public reads and sees and hears about the conduct of its public affairs is such a diluted and artificially colored version of fact and truth that if it were a mouthwash, the Federal Trade Commission would divide three-to-two on whether to let it on the market." More and more the people know this. Government lying and manipulation, business propaganda and regimentation, are increasingly perceived as fundamental aspects of a soulless machinelike system which is losing its appeal for some Americans. Not all were opting out of the system, only a few; many were simply turning to crime or escaping into psychosis. America was a study in contradictions:

In terms of sheer productive quantity, the United States is the miracle of civilization. In this calendar year [1968] we will have 14 million families earning more than $10,000—*yet* 60 million of us will live in poverty. We will have 100,000 millionaires—*still* 360,000 personal bankruptcies will be declared. We will have 57 million homes—*but* 70% of our population will crowd itself onto 1% of our land. We will have 95 million motor vehicles—*however,* almost 2 million of us will be injured, and 52,000 killed, by them. We will have 10 million college graduates—*and*

5 million mentally ill. This nation will have a real, total wealth of 4 trillion dollars—*nevertheless*, we will have 4 million crimes, 21 thousand suicides, 5 million alcoholics, 23 births out of a thousand will be illegitimate, 1 marriage out of four will fail.[21]

To those who look backward, much has been accomplished. To those who look critically at the present society—with affluence assumed —it seems clear we have traded quality for quantity. The welfare state, so confidently, so hopefully if haphazardly erected, had begun to display its limitations and inadequacies. The technological society which sustained it began to reveal its tremendous social costs. Today the welfare state in America is mature. On its own terms it has largely succeeded; wealth, education, leisure, all are increasing. We have come a long way. The middle class is huge. By and large the Liberal reformers have had their way. But the welfare state has seemingly reached some sort of upper limit; it has failed to satisfy the expectations it aroused. It has balked far short of the just society it promised.

In 1954 the Supreme Court, in declaring school segregation unconstitutional, initiated a war on racial discrimination and inequality, and the civil rights movement was called into being to respond. It was a reformist movement, much in the American tradition. The stirring rhetoric of John Kennedy roused the nation from complacency, calling for a New Frontier, calling for national adventure of inner reform. Lyndon Johnson declared a war on poverty to bring society's rejects into the mainstream of American life. Affirming solidarity with the poor, the blacks, the President of the United States insisted: "We *shall* overcome!"—and the nation was moved. Two Presidents and such reformers as Martin Luther King touched the deep strain of idealism in America that has never been expunged. Hundreds of thousands of Americans listened as King spoke in the nation's capitol, "I have a dream," he said. And later, "I have been to the mountaintop, and I have seen the promised land," and his vision was shared by many. It was a vision of justice for all, to which the security state could not respond.

As accurately as he predicted its shape, de Tocqueville foresaw the limitations of the welfare state. He said:

The sufferings that are endured patiently, as being inevitable, become intolerable the moment it appears there might be an escape. Reform then only serves to reveal more clearly what still remains oppressive and now all the more unbearable. The suffering, it is true, has been reduced, but one's sensitivity has become more acute.[22]

Most Americans, of course, accept the welfare state so completely that for them ideology has no place. Yet a significant number have now "seen the promised land," and there is emerging among them a new ideology. It is not the average middle-class citizen who is dissatisfied. Although many members of the middle class share an uneasy sense of malaise, it is primarily the young who are alienated. This is surprising, for we have turned the American child, as David Riesman says, into a "consumer trainee." [23]

Perhaps the advertising machine has done its job too well. Mass-consumption psychology is the psychology of hedonism, but hedonism may well be incompatible with regimentation. Conditioned by hedonistic manipulation, middle-class youth in America is beginning to turn on its manipulators. As one young New Leftist explains, they are now taking hedonism seriously:

The American economic system says: work hard so you can retire for a good life in the future! The American school system says: study hard so you can get a degree and become a big something in the future!
In America a revolutionary movement could be built around the idea: I want to live life now! Ecstacy now!
Now! has become our rallying cry.[24]

Perhaps adult middle-class America will follow the lead of youth here, as in so many other respects. Even now many tens of thousands, possibly hundreds of thousands, of respectable middle-class American adults have joined this hedonism to the extent of illegally smoking marijuana. It was a small step from the nicotine, caffeine, pep pills, diet pills, tranquilizers, and alcohol with which they make their empty lives a bit more bearable.

This inclination toward hedonism is a reflection of the success of the soft cell in replacing traditional sources of transmitting values in American society—the family and the church. The present ferment on college campuses, even high schools, too is a reflection of youth's questioning the legitimacy of institutions which in large part are designed to inculcate a set of values determined by the organizational society. We have said that mass-media advertising sells not only goods but also a complete set of values. It is ironic that the great success of the mass media has been to free today's youth from the indoctrination of all traditional institutions. That this consequence of the mass media, of advertising, was not intended is obvious! Its implications have scarcely been explored. What it means basically is that during at least the past decade all American institutions have been drained inexorably of their very legitimacy in the eyes of large numbers of the young in America. Business and government, by their own doing—their advertising and propaganda—have become objects to be despised rather than venerated by significant segments of today's youth.

Because of the default of political scientists, who refuse to recognize and study present aggregative forces, we do not have any sophisticated analysis of the political dynamics of such forces, and our understanding of the soft cell is both hazy and fragmentary. But, because they have been so grossly "oversold," the most perceptive of America's youth acutely *feel* the shortcomings of the system. They feel the impossibility of direct reform of the system through political participation, not because of its evil, but because of its vastness, remoteness, and subtlety. As an exceptional political scientist, Emmette Redford says:

> The first characteristic of the great body of men subject to the administrative state is that they are dormant regarding most of the decisions being made with respect to them. Their participation cannot in any manner equal their subjection. Subjection comes from too many directions for man's span of attention, much less his active participation, to extend to all that affects him. Any effort of the subject to participate in all that affects him would engulf him in confusion, dissipate his activity, and destroy the unity of his personality. Democracy in the sense of man's participation in all that affects him is impossible in the administered society.[25]

The new individualism must, however, necessarily be concerned with the aggregative tendencies of modern society. It is profoundly anti-institutional, antiorganizational, even antipolitical. It mainly seeks escape from the perceived oppressiveness of all institutions; it seeks nothing less than the survival of the person.

There are two separate aspects to this new individualism, the public and the communal. Although they are emerging spontaneously, they are as subtle and effective as the forces they oppose. They attack the aggregative forces and underlying premises of the soft cell directly, and they focus upon the individual. The new individualists recognize the strength of the organizational society, and they confront it in its totality with their own sensitive morality. Beginning with the universities, they reproach our outmoded institutions for their hypocrisy. As one New Left theoretician explains:

The technological society, with its war and exploitation and control, cannot survive unless it is able to keep its component parts from asserting themselves in their totality. If the religions choose to be religious; if the politicians choose to be political; if education chooses to be educational—all in their true human meaning—then the structure is doomed.[26]

But this is more than just a tactic. It is a moral stance taken by those whom our society has driven to a point of existential nausea.

The public action is based upon an apparently intuitive understanding of the power of the mass media and of their weakness for sensationalism. The new individualists understand and use television especially well, for, after all, it was their babysitter. The form of this public action is educational rather than political in the traditional sense. Through provocation and confrontation such actions attempt to expose the repressiveness and unresponsiveness of the "Establishment," the "Technostructure," and the "System." Public action was surprisingly successful at the 1968 Democratic Convention in Chicago in that it resulted in a televised "police riot." As the establishment moves to counter this tactic, the new individualists broaden their efforts to make the general public aware of the social costs of the operation of a politics of scarcity in an age of affluence. Their political activity will be to attack bureaucratic institutions, enticing their members to join the new individualists in an "inner immigration" from the blandishments of the soft cell.

The new individualists are striving to restrict the control of large-scale organizations over the individual so that the actions of corporate and governmental systems will become less and less important for a person's daily life—to create "life space," as they say. This has been one consequence of the radical resistance to authority, which has taken the form of deglorification of the state and passive resistance measures such as ridicule or "consumer" boycotts. And there has been open defiance of the authority structure of modern bureaucracies. The challenging of various types of recruiters on college campuses has been carried

out by some of the most intelligent and sensitive youth in American society. The Vietnam War patriotic hard sell has exaggerated this resistance. Thus American jails hold numerous young men who have refused
induction into the army. These direct confrontations with traditional authority systems are likely to continue for some time (even after the end
of the Vietnam War). However, the new individualists recognize America as not a prerevolutionary, but a post-revolutionary society. Therefore they will engage not in guerrilla warfare, but in "guerrilla theater."
They are revolutionaries, to be sure, but what they seek is a cultural
rather than a political revolution. They recognize that America has
come to the end of politics but not to the end of ideology. They also
perceive that the revitalization of politics will occur outside the present-day political arena, notably the existing manipulated party apparatus and electoral structure.

The communal aspect of the new movement has been made possible by the increasingly affluent society. A small, though socially
significant number of individualists has sought to escape communes in
the sparsely populated countryside in an attempt to recreate life on a
more human scale. More important is the movement in cities and
around universities toward cooperative or communal "developments."
This aspect of the new individualism in the United States generally involves an attempt to redefine the political and the social so that freedom
will come to mean, as Marcuse says, the liberation of individuals *from*
politics over which they presently have no effective control. Today
there are many ways people can live, can modify their environment and
change their life conditions. For these persons what is socially meaningful is taking place outside the established social order that is so dominated by the bureaucratic imperative. It is in these nonbureaucratic set-
tings that the participants attain a greater control over their life
chances. At the same time they hold up to the public a highly visible
example of alternative life styles, which in its seductiveness rivals the
soft cell. Their dress, their art, their music, and their sexual behavior all
stand in taunting opposition to the sublimated repressiveness of the
smooth society. It is as if they were saying, as Whitman once said, "I
and mine do not convince by arguments, we convince by our
presence." [27]

Those who are choosing to live outside of, or marginal to, the system are far less vulnerable to the traditional forms of social control. These persons are not acting in accordance with the occupational expectations of the bureaucratic game, and therefore traditional punitive measures, such as threats of the loss of job, no longer carry with them once-powerful sanctions. Persons committed to a hedonistic or existentialist life style are not subject to controls which assume that men will always strive to conform to narrow system expectations.

Philosopher Raghavan Iyer applauds this development, observing that bureaucratic employment is, and—in the interests of a new individualism—should be, disagreeable:

> Let the people who really can't do anything else, those conventional people who always need to rely on the big machine, let them become the bureaucrats, let them run the machine. The people who enjoy doing this sort of thing are the people who really can't do very much else. This is tolerable provided that outside the civic sector the really important things go on. . . .[28]

CONCLUSIONS

We are now in a position to isolate the three main issues with respect to the emergence of the new individualism: the quest for quality in human life, the quest for community, and the general opposition to the bureaucratic system as it now functions. The contemporary political system has failed dismally to cope with the first two issues. And this failure stems from the fact that politics has become subservient to the workings of bureaucratic organizations in both the public and the private sectors.

The key to the future of American society lies in what happens to the aggregative tendencies inherent in modern bureaucratic structures. If it is to be meaningful and successful, the new individualism must force the large-scale bureaucracies to contract. Parkinson's Law, which has much to recommend it, indicates that bureaucracies tend to expand even when infected with injelitis (a high concentration of incompetence and jealousy) or palsied paralysis. To treat these diseases, Parkinson prescribes measured injections of Intolerance, Ridicule, and Castigation.[29] It is unlikely that Parkinson foresaw a new generation would actually inject such social medicine into the mainstream of bureaucratic life.

While persons are challenging bureaucracies on various fronts, the system itself has unleashed another potent force that will aid in the transformation of society—technology. The computer makes miniaturized and more easily manageable bureacracies possible. The technological complexity of modern society makes traditional forms obsolescent and impotent as problem solvers. In 1965, Warren Bennis, a student of industrial management, said:

It is my premise that the bureaucratic form of organization is becoming less and less effective; that it is hopelessly out of joint with contemporary realities; that new shapes, patterns, and models are emerging which promise drastic changes in the conduct of the corporation and of managerial practices in general. In the next 25 to 50 years we should witness, and participate in, the end of bureaucracy and the rise of new social systems better suited to twentieth century demands of industrialization.[30]

Bureaucracy will (and should) contract not only because it is inhuman but also because it is too rigid and inflexible to fulfill its function in an age of rapid social and technical change. The new structures, to succeed and to be effective, must be flexibly arranged on organic rather than mechanical models. Rigid vertical hierarchies of rank and status having little to do with competence must be dissolved and replaced by small units of highly trained persons, often functioning as ad hoc task forces, loosely coordinated along the lines of "think tanks" and scientific laboratories. Is this a real possibility? By 1969, Warren Bennis was able to say:

Ironically, the bold future I had predicted is now routine and can be observed wherever the most interesting and advanced practices exist. Most of these trends are visible and have been surfacing for years in the aerospace, construction, drug, and consulting industries as well as professional and research and development organizations, which only shows that the distant future has a way of arriving before the forecast is fully comprehended.[31]

But the question arises: When bureaucracies are thus replaced, and when cybernated systems come to operate the industrial machine, what will most of us do? A guaranteed annual wage means that people will not be forced to work in order to sustain themselves. And leisure for learning, service to others, and self-fulfillment will become possible. Thus larger numbers of people will be able to build their own communities and thereby attain a quality of life removed from the pressures exerted by traditional bureaucratic controls. These new communal life styles then will facilitate the decline of the bureaucratic structure and will be alternative forms of existence for those persons who are no longer needed by the system.

The lesson is clear: Liberalism, if it is to pursue its historic ideals, must become radical. Liberals, if they are to support the ideals inherent in the new individualism must, through various means, encourage the withering away of the bureaucratic state. They must not only oppose the faulty distribution of the system but must also attack the faulty organization of the smooth society. They must rip away the walls of the soft cell and restore the Liberal polity. Although the task will not be an easy one, the forces of technology are on the side of drastic change, and so we must create a new political science which strives to understand these forces. We must seize this opportunity to remake the "future." It is just possible that we can thereby restore politics to its proper place—so that its central concern will again be with freedom, justice, peace, and order.

Notes

1. Eric F. Goldman, *The Crucial Decade—and After, 1945–60* (New York, 1960).

2. Alexis de Tocqueville, *Democracy in America,* ed. and abr. by Andrew Hacker (New York, 1964), p. 91. Reprinted by permission of Simon and Schuster, Inc.

3. *Ibid.,* pp. 314, 315, 316.   4. *Ibid.,* p. 316.

5. Herbert Marcuse, *One-Dimensional Man* (Boston, 1964), p. 1. Reprinted by permission of Beacon Press.

6. Bernard Asbell, *The New Improved American* (New York, 1965), pp. 110–11. Reprinted by permission of McGraw-Hill Book Company.

7. Marcuse, *One-Dimensional Man,* p. x.

8. William J. Newman, *Liberalism and the Retreat from Politics* (New York, 1964), pp. 164–65.

9. W. H. Ferry, "Disarmament, Anyone?," in Andrew Hacker, ed., *The Corporation Take-Over* (Garden City, New York, 1965) p. 111.

10. A. A. Berle, "Economic Power and the Free Society," *The Corporation Take-Over*, p. 100. Also see George P. Schultz and Robert Z. Alber, eds., *Guidelines, Informal Controls and the Market Place* (Chicago, 1966).

11. Goodwin, "The Shape of American Politics," *Commentary*, XLIII (June 1967), 26.

12. See Robert Presthus, *The Organizational Society* (New York, 1962).

13. See Robert B. Denkart, "Organizational Citizenship and Personal Freedom," *Public Administration Review*, XXVIII (January–February 1968).

14. de Tocqueville, *Democracy in America*, pp. 97–98.

15. Marcuse, *One-Dimensional Man*, pp. 4, 250–51.

16. Marver H. Bernstein, *Regulating Business by Independent Commission* (Princeton, 1955), pp. 86–90. Reprinted by permission of Princeton University Press.

17. Peter Bachrach and Morton S. Baratz, "Two Faces of Power," *American Political Science Review*, LVI (December 1962), 948.

18. John Dewey, *Liberalism and Social Action* (New York, 1935), p. 24.

19. William L. C. Wheaton, "Form and Structure of the Metropolitan Area," in William R. Ewald, Jr., ed., *Environment and Policy: The Next Fifty Years* (Bloomington, 1968), pp. 176–77. Reprinted by permission of Indiana University Press.

20. William L. Safire, *The Relations Explosion* (New York, 1963), p. 161. David Ogilvy, dean of Madison Avenue advertisers, has expressed similar "concerns" in typically colorful language: "The average person is seeing about 40,000 commercials a year. And they have developed an ability to screen out commercials. You've got to bring on a couple copulating elephants or something to stop people from tuning out." "The View from the Chateau," *Newsweek* (August 18, 1969), p. 66.

21. "The Quality of Our Lives," *Newsweek* (Copyright Newsweek, Inc., February 19, 1968), p. 97.

22. Quoted by John V. Lindsay, in "The Decent Society: Race Relations," *Playboy* (January 1969), p. 272.

23. In large part this is a result of television. By 1968, the average child in America was watching TV an average of fifty-four hours a week, thus learning far more about the joys of consumership than about all academic subjects combined. See "Brightening the Boob Tube," *Newsweek* (April 1, 1968), p. 67.

24. Jerry Rubin, "Elvis Kills Ike," *Berkeley Barb* (March 8–14, 1968), p. 12.

25. Emmette S. Redford, *Democracy in the Administrative State* (New York, 1969), p. 66. Reprinted by permission of Oxford University Press.

26. Henry Milner, "To Whom the Future?" (Washington, D.C., August, 1969, mimeographed manuscript), p. 125.

27. Whitman is quoted in another context by Lewis Mumford in *The Transformations of Man* (New York, 1956), p. 74.

28. Walter A. Weisskopf, Raghavan Iyer, et. al., *Looking Forward: The Abundant Society* (Santa Barbara, 1966), p. 32.

29. See C. Northcote Parkinson, "Injelitis or Palsied Paralysis," *Parkinson's Law and Other Studies in Administration* (New York, 1957), pp. 100–14.

30. Bennis, "Beyond Bureaucracy," *Trans-action* (July–August 1965), p. 31.

31. Bennis, "Post-Bureaucratic Leadership," *Trans-action* (July–August 1969), p. 45. For a fascinating argument concerning both the possibilities, and necessity for transcending bureaucratic structures, see S. H. Maslow, *Eupsychian Management: A Journal* (Homewood, Ill., 1965).

Great Britain

D. MCQUAIL AND J. H. SMITH

Britain – A Post-Welfare Society?

ANY ASSESSMENT of Britain as a society moving into a "post-welfare" phase of political thought and alignment encounters an immediate obstacle in the attitude of the British themselves. For it is abundantly clear that they regard the welfare state as one of their better inventions, so that pride of ownership, or of paternity, nurtures an ingrained reluctance to reappraise objectives and performance in the welfare field.[1] Furthermore, for many Britons the welfare state was an event, rather than a development. As something that happened during their own lifetime, the welfare state has the emotional appeal of a victory recalled with pride and satisfaction. It is not without significance that the Beveridge report, the outline strategy for postwar social legislation, appeared in the year of El Alamein.[2] This identification of the welfare state as "one of the things we fought for" inhibits the British in contemplating new structures or in considering alternatives to existing welfare policy. Reinforced by the recognition among political parties of its strong emotional appeal to the voter, the durability of the welfare state as a political reference point seems assured for many years to come.

THE WELFARE STATE AS A
POLITICAL EQUILIBRIUM

Social policies and their effectiveness have, of course, been major factors in British politics since the beginning of the century. The first important steps in health, housing, and social security had all been taken by the Liberals before World War I. Thereafter the pressures for state intervention were as irreversible as the decline of the Liberal party itself, since the working class movement gave its loyalty to Labor and Conservatives found universal social services consistent with the duties of responsible government. This is not the place to chart the eclipse of the Liberal party; we may simply note that its ideas and assumptions about social policy commanded more support than did its candidates.[3] Some of the most influential writers on social policy—notably Beveridge and Seebohm Rowntree—were professed Liberal supporters; but as we shall see, the rapid adoption of common assumptions and purposes in social policy made the Liberal origins or sponsorship of the welfare state irrelevant as political facts.

Both world wars greatly strengthened arguments for state intervention in the identification and satisfaction of social needs.[4] The 1939–1945 war drastically altered both the facts of politics and the problems facing the political parties. The wartime coalition government gave Labor politicians experience in office and a chance to become nationally known, and also helped dispel some of the wilder fears of what socialism might involve. The war itself, in which the home front ranked equally with other theaters of operations, exposed gross inequalities in health and living standards while creating its own priorities for the more effective care and control of the civilian population. Inevitably this led to the formulation of goals for social reform to be pursued after the war, which would fulfill the promise of the democratic institutions then being defended. In addition, the consequences of war-destroyed and neglected homes, the deterioration of many less essential services, the dislocation of industry, and a much-weakened economy confronted politicians with a range of immense and urgent problems.

The general election of August 1945 was held under unprecedented circumstances. No general election had taken place for ten years, and substantial economic and social changes had occurred. Agreement had been reached on major reforms in education, health, and social security, and both parties were committed to their completion. The Conservative party's main asset, and a considerable one, was to have Churchill as a leader. The Labor party—which stood to gain from the contemporary desire for change—intended in particular to claim the fruits of victory in the form of a more just society. Labor was a party with a newly acquired image of success in handling social and industrial questions, a party of moderate reform, closely allied to established trade union interests, but with important middle-class reformist elements. The election was unusual in the uniqueness of historical circumstances, the unpredictability of the outcome, and the resounding nature of the Labor party victory.

On taking office in 1945, Attlee's government could be said to have a mandate to reconstruct British society on lines of greater equality—in particular, to tip the balance toward the ordinary wage earner and his family in the allocation of the essentials of homes, food, employment opportunities, and the provision of health and education services. The Labor government was committed as well to the extension of public ownership to basic industries. These were its distinctive policies. Labor shared with the Conservative party a commitment to carry out necessary postwar reconstruction. The party was challenged by Conservatives and Liberals mainly because of its attachment to an ideology of state control. Indeed it was reaction against the extension of public ownership that provided the most effective weapon of opposition to Labor rather than concrete alternative proposals.[5]

The most striking feature of British political history in the decades following 1945 is its continuity—a product in turn of the stability of party positions. This equilibrium between two major parties requires emphasis since it does much to explain the continuing importance of social welfare in British politics. While no party can claim any monopoly of achievement in establishing the welfare state, and while the factors that have contributed to growth in welfare often lie outside of party politics, the future of welfare remains among the most enduring and potent of issues in British politics.

On what evidence is the assertion of continuity in British politics based? First of all, the balance between the major parties, in terms of popular support, has been very even during the period, much more so than changes in parliamentary representation of the parties would suggest. Thus even in the so-called landslide victory of 1945, Labor obtained less than half of the twenty-five million votes cast, and the largest "swing" between the main parties at any of the six general elections since 1945 was no more than 3.1 per cent (e.g., in the 1964 election, which yielded a Labor victory). In all postwar elections the Labor and Conservative parties have never been separated by more than approximately one and one-half million votes—some 5 per cent of the electorate.[6] Second, electoral survey data reveal a high degree of loyalty over time to a chosen party and tend to indicate that the rate of change from one party to another is both small and constant over time—at least up to 1964.[7] Quantitatively, the most significant change of party allegiance has involved the minority Liberal party.[8] Third, some features of the "swing" between parties from one election to another provide evidence of stability: It is remarkably uniform in its range and extent throughout the United Kingdom, and appears subject to very gradual, progressive movements over long periods of time. Any reverses have never been large enough to alter the over-all balance between parties.[9] Finally, the perennial nature of the major issues which have preoccupied election campaigns from 1945 to 1966 also attests to continuity in British politics. While a close inspection can, as we shall see later, detect significant changes in the content of the political debate, the major themes have continued to be those of the cost of living, the country's economic prospects, employment, housing, pensions, and social services, and education, in approximately that order.[10]

It is true that the fact of balance does not tell us much in itself about the strength of opposing forces or the gap which separates the two parties. An even division can indicate a persistent and implacable hostility across fixed lines, with clear differences of ideology and aims inhibiting maneuver. We know, however, that this is not the case in Britain. The principles dividing the parties are expressed in a somewhat open-ended form, often with overlapping aims. Disagreements may exist as to the appropriate method of achieving rather similar purposes, but these may arise within parties as well as between them. As a result, on specific policy issues, "progressive" Conservatives and Labor "loyalists" will often have more in common with each other than with the extremists of their respective parties.

A lack of partisanship may also be detected among the electors themselves. On many issues (especially those concerned with foreign affairs and noneconomic matters) attitudes and opinions appear not to be shaped by party loyalty at all. Even in social and economic issues, in which the parties seek to emphasize different approaches, the divergences among supporters are often as great as the differences between the parties. The priorities attached by voters to problems facing governments are very much the same, whatever their party allegiance.[11] Indeed, most voters do not seem to regard the political color of the party in office as vitally important for themselves or the country.[12]

This absence of fluidity and partisanship in the electorate at large requires some explanation. The postwar period has not been lacking in events or in changes important to British society. It has included a recovery from war, the anxieties of the Cold War, a shedding of empire and world power status, a series of endemic economic crises, a novel experiment in socialism, however moderate, and a need to respond to far-reaching technological change. Equally important, the latent disagreements over the nature of the good life and good society in Britain are more powerful than the content of formal politics might lead one to suppose: there are persistent class antagonisms, and there has been ample scope for the expression of radical viewpoints ranging from far left to far right.

At the risk of oversimplification, one major explanation for this persisting equilibrium is the British political situation. The key may be found, paradoxically, in the fact that Britain remains a class-divided society—divided in the sense that real and important variations exist in standards of living, life style, and status, between major social strata. The notable feature is that this division does not correspond to the division of political loyalty, despite the fact that the political parties derive whatever distinctive identity they have from their positions as class parties. The history, name, and composition of the Labor party leave no doubt that it is a working-class party; the principles, composition, and policies of the Conservative party make it primarily a middle-class party. The views of electors themselves as reported in numerous surveys also make it clear that the parties are most clearly differentiated according to social class associations, and this is especially true in the case of working-class attitudes.[13]

However, the discrepancy between the class images of the parties and actual voting behavior has been very marked. Throughout the postwar period, the evidence of opinion polls and academic surveys has shown that a steady third of the manual working class has voted Conservative, along with about 80 per cent of the middle and upper classes.[14] Because of the larger size of the working class (65 to 70 per cent of the population) this means that roughly half of the Conservative party support comes from the working class, while the Labor party gets relatively few middle-class votes.[15] The curious fact then presents itself that the Conservative party is both more representative of the nation in class terms than Labor *and* more closely identified with specific social interests and attitudes.

Explanations of working-class support of the Conservative party have been assiduously sought since the war.[16] The composite answer which emerges suggests that significant numbers of working-class people perceive the Conservative party either as possessing the elite qualities necessary to govern (these constitute the so-called deferential voters) or as having greater executive ability to handle problems relevant to working-class economic interests. According to McKenzie and Silver, the latter attitude is more prevalent among younger and higher income working-class Conservatives and thus is likely to predominate over "deferential" attitudes. If this is so, the Conservative party must increasingly be judged by its working-class supporters in terms of its performance on matters that affect their own lives.

The nature of the equilibrium in British politics can now be better appreciated. The party system fits obliquely on a class structure that is changing only slowly and lacks elements of open conflict. The nature of the fit is itself a source of stability, but as a consequence both major parties face a dilemma. Each is nothing if not a class party, yet the stability of the class structure rules out explicit class ideologies as impractical politics. The Labor party cannot publicize itself as the party of organized labor or emphasize its working-class image—partly because of its own record, traditions, and leadership, and partly because it cannot afford to alienate its small but highly important body of middle-class support. In any case the facts of political behavior seem to suggest that a loss of working-class support to the *right* is much more likely than a loss to the *left*. The position of the Conservative party is, at least in theory, even more vulnerable, with half its support coming from working-class voters (often those most sensitive to their own personal well-being) and with no real prospect of gaining more middle-class support than it has already. The position of the Liberal party in the party system serves only to emphasize the determining role of class in British politics. Lacking a class identification, the Liberal party is mainly distinctive in the public mind as a halfway house between Labor and Conservative.[17] Thus all three main parties must seek to present a "classless image," although their respective reasons for doing so are very different.

This balance of forces has considerable relevance for the future of social welfare policies. The Labor party must perform particularly well in any matters affecting the living standards of the working class. Important components of that living standard have increasingly been provided in the form of welfare state benefits—including health, education, and housing subsidies, family allowances, and income security in sickness, old age, and unemployment. The Conservative party must also respect existing welfare arrangements and make good any well-demonstrated inadequacies, if they are to be assured of working-class support. The record of both parties since 1945 demonstrates that major modifications of welfare institutions are not undertaken with enthusiasm. Moreover, when reforms are attempted, they are implemented within a framework of shared assumptions.

Given such a definite equilibrium in British politics, what factors might disturb it? And what prospects exist that politics in Britain will move into a distinct "post-welfare" phase? These questions provide the major focus for the remainder of this chapter. In attempting to answer them, we have to consider the nature of recent economic, social, and political trends in Britain, as well as current arguments for change in the organization and purposes of welfare institutions. We take the view that possibilities for major political changes exist only insofar as they arise from major shifts in social structure and values. In particular, we believe that speculation about changes in the objectives and administrative systems typical of the welfare state must be related to specific changes in patterns of social need and expectations. We turn next, therefore, to a brief consideration of recent socio-economic trends in Britain, followed by an assessment of political developments. In each case our concern is with the consequences for the present political equilibrium that we call the welfare state. So far, we have avoided defining the latter term. Although we share Titmuss' dislike of that "indefinable abstraction," we would suggest that the essential characteristics of the welfare state in Britain include:

(1) A highly developed framework of central administration capable of imposing universalist solutions.

(2) A comprehensive system of services designed to guarantee "appropriate" standards of provision in "basic" areas. These would be generally agreed to include health, social security, housing, and special welfare needs for, e.g., the handicapped, the elderly, and the delinquent. Many would add education and associated services.

(3) An assumption that state provision is essential to meet the needs of all individuals and their families. This does not exclude, however, voluntary initiative by individuals or groups; indeed such initiative may be state-subsidized.[18]

RECENT SOCIAL TRENDS

The period since the creation of the British welfare state has been one of considerable change, though change so lacking in drama that it is easily underestimated. There has been no economic miracle nor any sharp discontinuity in economic and social life. Instead, there has been a steady rise in industrial output, accompanied by rising earnings which slowly outdistance price rises. The evidence of solid, if modest, prosperity is contained in Table 1, and would immediately be apparent even to the casual observer familiar with life in Britain in the late 1940s.[19] The relative prosperity of Britain today reveals itself in similar ways as in all advanced urban-industrial societies. The number of private cars has risen, for example, from two and one-half million to over eleven million, which means that 65 per cent of all families own a car. At the same time, expenditure on new road construction or major road improvements increased by a factor of 9 between 1957 and 1967. Approximately 50 per cent of all households now own or are buying their own home, compared to an estimated 29 per cent in 1948. The housing problem no longer takes the form of an acute general shortage, but is rather one of replacing the heritage of past inadequacy and neglect. The average number of persons living in each housing unit is slightly lower than in the United States. Since 1951 over six million new houses have been constructed, so that 34 per cent of all households now occupy what is considered a modern home. A noticeable feature of development in Britain has been the establishment of new towns. While new towns presently house little more than 2 per cent of the population, the

TABLE 1. INCOME, PRICES, AND UNEMPLOYMENT IN UNITED KINGDOM, 1950–1969 *

	1950	1952	1954	1956	1958	1960	1962	1964	1966	1968	1969
Average Weekly Earnings 1955 = 100	68.1	80.9	91.5	108.0	116.9	130.1	142.9	161.8	185.0	208.1	220.5†
Average Salary Earnings 1955 = 100				107.3	118.5	133.4	147.7	164.5	186.1	206.9	
Monthly Average of Total Registered Unemployed (thousands)		498.6	284.8	257.0	457.4	360.4	463.2	380.6	359.7	564.1	506.6†
Conservative or Labor Party in Office	Lab.	Con.	Con.	Con.	Con.	Con.	Con.	Con./Lab.	Lab.	Lab.	Lab.

* *Employment and Productivity Gazette*, LXXVII, No. 11 (November, 1969), Tables 129 and 132.
† Estimated.

pattern of living that they represent and encourage is becoming increasingly typical of modern Britain.

The aspects of social structure most relevant to the present discussion are those concerning changes in class and occupational pattern and in population size and composition. The total population of the United Kingdom rose from 50.3 million in 1951 to 55.3 million in 1968, confounding early projections, and is now expected to reach at least 68 million within thirty years. The immediate prospect is for a constant proportion of the economically active to be supporting a rising proportion of retired persons, but this pattern will alter within a generation. Despite the publicity given to immigration, the net inflow into the United Kingdom has been very small in recent years and is unlikely to rise again in the foreseeable future. Certain movements of population have taken place within the country, notably a move from the large cities and conurbations to peripheral areas, and the so-called drift, now largely halted, from the north to the south and southeast. Differential rates of population growth persist between the regions, with the reasons for this appearing to be mainly economic.

The general rise in prosperity has not basically affected the pattern of income distribution between social class and occupational groups, a fact that is apparent both from the very high correlation between rises in earnings by wage earners and salaried employees and from such evidence as we have about property ownership. Such evidence does, however, leave out of account some important changes which have occurred, and are occurring at present at a rapid rate—notably, changes that concern investment in welfare. An increasingly important component of the average citizen's standard of living is provided, or guaranteed, by state welfare services. This results in greater real equality than income differentials imply, and also provides a possible increased impetus toward future equality.

All the main forms of welfare expenditure have shown a rise in real terms since the mid-1950s, and a very substantial rise as a proportion of Gross National Product since Labor took office in 1964. The changes shown in Table 2 represent a marked shift from the private to the public sector. In practice they have meant real improvements in pensions and other social security benefits, and an appreciable extension of educational provision. The educational revolution has been late in

TABLE 2. EXPENDITURE ON SOCIAL SERVICES AND WELFARE, U.K., 1950–1968: PROPORTIONS OF GNP EXPENDED BY ALL PUBLIC AUTHORITIES *

	1950	1952	1954	1956	1958	1960	1962	1964	1966	1968
Housing	2.9	3.1	2.9	2.3	2.0	2.1	2.1	2.8	2.9	3.0
Education	3.1	3.3	3.3	3.7	3.9	4.0	4.6	4.8	5.4	5.9
National Health Service	4.1	3.6	3.4	3.5	3.6	3.8	3.8	3.9	4.2	4.6
Social Security	5.7	5.9	5.7	5.9	6.6	6.5	6.8	7.1	7.8	9.1
All Social Services†					14.6	14.9	15.9	16.5	18.2	20.5
GNP (£1000 million)	11,752	13,982	15,923	18,359	20,408	22,794	25,563	29,373	33,006	36,686
Conservative or Labor Party in Office	Lab.	Con.	Con.	Con.	Con.	Con.	Con.	Con./Lab.	Lab.	Lab.

* *Reports on National Income and Expenditure*, 1960, 1969.
† The total for all social services excludes housing and includes certain heads of expenditure not shown separately in the table.

coming and has many causes, but there is little doubt about its extent and its implications for the future. Between 1958 and 1968 the proportion of the 15–19 age group attending grant-aided schools rose from 11.5 to 21.3 per cent, and shows every sign of continuing to rise as educational policies actively encourage the trend. Higher education shows comparable growth rates. In the university sector alone, the number of full-time students rose from 95,442 to 220,000 between 1958 and 1969. By 1980 it is now expected that the present total in full-time education will be almost doubled. The origins of this trend lie in the extension and encouragement of education by public policy, the demands of employment, and rising aspirations and expectations of parents and children. The force of these tendencies makes any reversal of public policy neither politically feasible nor even very thinkable. In the next twenty to thirty years, the British way of life and standards of social provision must be decisively influenced by the results of this educational leap forward. At present, however, it would be difficult to conclude that the social structure of Britain in the late 1960s showed any striking divergences from the pattern characteristic of Britain since 1945; or, for that matter, from the Britain of the interwar years.

CHANGES IN THE PATTERN OF POLITICS

Since the early 1950s a number of subtle shifts have occurred in the pattern of politics which could have important consequences for the present balance between the Labor and Conservative parties. Given the social and economic changes already described, traditional party loyalties— and old animosities—might become less important as prosperity increases, new expectations arise concerning the role of government, and relations alter between politicians and people. Present trends apparently pointing in such a direction include a growing belief that Parliament is losing its power to influence events; an increasing emphasis on the need for citizen participation in decisions; some evidence of decreasing partisanship; a growth in an "instrumental" approach to politics; and, finally, an increase in the importance of public relations and mass media in forging party images.[20]

The supposed decline in the power of Parliament may be traced to a number of sources. Whether this belief is mistaken or not is less important than the fact that it is widely held. Parliament today operates under evident disadvantages. It is clearly constrained by external economic factors, both national and international. The administrative processes which it generates have become increasingly complex and difficult to reform in a simple manner. At a time when technological change and the flow of information are speeding up, the processes of democratic government are visibly slowing down. As a result, less is seen to be done, promised changes are slow to materialize, and confident forecasts are overtaken by events. More effective action and speedier decisions are attributed to business concerns, local authorities, experts of various kinds, and pressure groups. At the same time, pressures for local autonomy and effective participation by individual citizens present a "democratic" challenge to the authority of central government and its agencies.

Some decrease in partisanship can be inferred from the behavior of politicians and voters alike. A shift toward the center of the political spectrum has occurred in the two major parties. Voters now seem to attach less importance to party differences or to the political color of the government in office. The supporters of both parties express fewer fears concerning the other side than they did in the late 1940s. Related to this is the growth in "instrumentalism" on the part of voters. In other words, more interest is attached to effective performance than to ideological correctness. A reflection of this change—which the parties appear to have encouraged—may be seen in survey evidence obtained under comparable circumstances in 1959 and 1964. In 1959 the main dimension of political attitudes could be described as a "traditional versus radical" axis, emphasising the Labor party's role as a working-class reforming party and the Conservative party as a guardian of national tradition. By 1964 this dimension appeared to have been displaced by one conceived in terms of competent and efficient government. The Labor party was claiming the right to govern on the grounds of conservative economic mismanagement, presenting itself on the eve of the 1970 General Election as "the party of government." [21] Rising prosperity may have something to do with this change, which has considerable implications for the way voters are likely to respond to government successes and failures in the future.

It is generally accepted that from the late 1950s political parties in Britain have become greatly dependent on market-research experts and publicity advisers. Advertising campaigns, the organized release of information, and television and radio broadcasting have been used on a larger scale and with far more care than in the past. The intention of such efforts has been to gain control over the public or political image that is presented by parties and leaders.[22] These developments are results of both the availability of new kinds of expertise and the relative impotence in making or shaping needs that afflict government and parties in a society whose communications' media enjoy freedom and independence. The effects of this professional "image-making" are difficult to ascertain, and they may be considered less important than the hard realities of political life. They do, however, reinforce the decline in partisanship that has already been noted. Moreover, they have consequences for the relations between people and party and heighten the voters' awareness of manipulation.

CONTINUITY AND CHANGE IN BRITISH WELFARE

We have noted the extent and effects of rising prosperity in Britain, particularly during the 1960s, and evidence of disenchantment with established forms of political orientation and action. Both trends are commonly assumed to have implications for the future of the welfare state. It is important to decide, therefore, whether the present political scene shows signs of substantial modifications in the fabric of welfare—especially to allow for rising affluence—or progress toward a "post-welfare" society in which welfare policies are of diminished importance.

The first, and in fact most lasting, impression is of a close preoccupation with the deficiencies of the present administrative framework of welfare policy and administration. We have already noted the belief that Parliament has less control over the machinery of government. Certainly the complexities of social service ministries and their coordination have received considerable attention from all postwar governments. At the time of writing, new social security legislation is before Parliament. Few members claim to understand its technical provisions, and there has been little sign so far that voters are pressing their representatives for enlightenment.[23] Following the Maud and Seebohm reports and a second Green Paper on health services' reorganization, Parliament is also grappling with vital decisions concerning local government reforms and a more effective basis for the administration of social services.[24] In a real sense, the necessity for these decisions and the torturous procedures required before they can be implemented illustrates not only the complexity of the welfare state but also the fundamental implausibility of dismantling it—at least by the normal procedures of parliamentary government. In this connection, it is chastening to recall that the reform of the Poor Law was accomplished—from the appointment of the Royal Commission in 1832 to the passage of the Poor Law Amendment Act—in just over two years.[25]

Today, the sheer scale of the welfare system and its administrative entourage induce an inertia for which local participation and contact are now recommended as remedies. Other panaceas include modern management techniques, the introduction of market mechanisms to channel supply and demand in welfare, more drastic curbs and penalties for persistent abusers or manipulators of services, purges by captains of industry or financial wizards skilled in takeovers, and business surgery.[26] What is lacking in these discussions are any realistic proposals to replace the present welfare framework. The truth is that the apparatus of British welfare is now so firmly built into social structure and social values that alternative forms of a radical kind have become unthinkable.

What prospects exist that one of the parties might veer to the unthinkable and thus break the present deadlock? We have already observed how welfare policies have been fostered in the present century by all parties. T. H. Marshall has written of the political philosophy of the welfare state: "It belonged, in fact, to that area of politics in which the proximate wings of all the parties meet and overlap. It appealed to enlightened Tories, progressive Liberals, most Radicals and moderate Socialists." [27]

Not surprisingly, this universal appeal has led to a major synthesis of thought and actions among the parties—even, for a period, to a point where the welfare state could be regarded as "above politics." [28]

As a result, there exists among politicians a shared set of assumptions concerning the welfare state, which inevitably set political and administrative limits to the discussion of reform.

These assumptions deserve detailed consideration since they bear directly on the question of attitudes to the nature of welfare and its political significance. Here we may distinguish between assumptions that are historical and those that may be called predictive. The first kind of assumptions are those made about the nature of social problems arising from industrialization; knowledge of these problems is derived from a study of their history and from the institution of procedures, such as surveys and statistical reviews, designed to keep that history up-to-date. This historical orientation rests on the belief that welfare policies are essentially responses to the effect of industrialization on a stable, communal-based society.

The second set of assumptions may be called predictive in the sense that predictions of the future are introduced in terms of the opportunities and constraints inherent in existing services. It is difficult at present to detect assumptions bearing on major changes or reversals of policy—with the possible exception of those envisaging wider scope for private provision to meet individual needs, especially in the field of health care, which presently enjoy limited support in the Conservative party.[29] Even here, acceptance of the analytical framework of human needs and social objectives permeates the British conception of the welfare state.

British politicians of all parties have invested so heavily in the welfare state that few would jeopardize possible electoral dividends by suggesting radical departures. All politicians are anxious to remind the voter of their supposed achievements, and a great deal of effort has been expended by all three parties to advertise their claims to be the true founder and protector of the welfare system. Although a full examination would reveal differences of emphasis, especially in terms of specific services, it is sufficient for our purpose to accept that all parties played a part in fashioning the present system and they are committed to the maintenance of its essentials.

In the immediate future, therefore, we must conclude that the trends in politics discussed earlier are unlikely to affect greatly the character of welfare policies. Some modification of existing administrative institutions may allow greater decentralization and local participation in decisions: Diminished partisanship could only accentuate the emphasis on administrative efficiency and the satisfaction of needs. Assuming no more than the trends mentioned above, the "end of ideology" conclusion might be seen to apply to the politics of welfare in Britain. Does this mean that no meaningful or dynamic political disagreements are likely to divide the parties?

It will be clear that consensus on the purposes and organization of the welfare state is more than an historical accident and corresponds fully with the pragmatic basis of British politics. This consensus reflects not only an ideological convergence (or more accurately an agreement to avoid an ideological approach to such questions) but also continuities in social structure which merit closer consideration. We have already asserted a connection between social structure, prevailing values, and the pattern of welfare objectives. At this point we would add that ideological agreement and disagreement directly reflect continuities and discontinuities in social structure, and reiterate that speculations about major changes in social policy must, in our view, be based on firm evidence of a shift toward a post-welfare society. In other words, changes in social structure—such as the emergence of new social groups and values of a dynamic character—must logically accompany moves for fundamental appraisals of social welfare and the transformation of existing institutions. To identify such changes in Britain today, or alternatively to suggest factors encouraging or inhibiting them, is an indispensable step in the argument about the post-welfare society.

At the same time the evidence for these changes in social structure must be viewed against prevailing assumptions about objectives and methods within the agreed framework of the welfare state. Here we would suggest that in political terms there *are* differences of some importance, and further, that they fall into three distinct sets of attitudes. These may be summarized as follows:

(1) that the "welfare state" solves all major social problems, or is capable of doing so, given the resources necessary to match rising population and rising standards.

(2) that the "welfare state" provides a minimum standard of living through social security provisions, together with minimum guarantee of "access to opportunity," in the shape of health services and educa-

tion; but that individuals should be encouraged to exercise "choice" in raising these standards if they wish to do so.

(3) that the "welfare state" is incapable of dealing with specific problems of the needy and disadvantaged—e.g., poverty among the elderly and homeless in major cities—and that solutions have to be sought outside traditional party lines.

Broadly speaking, these different attitudes can be identified with specific political and parapolitical groups. The first is still broadly the attitude adopted by the Labor party; the second accurately reflects the present Conservative approach to social policy, while the third is typified by current 'activists' movements such as Shelter and the Child Poverty Action Group.[30]

With these assumptions in mind, we can now consider some of the main pressures for change in the present structure of welfare services in Britain. These come mainly in two forms—arguments concerning overdue administrative reforms and arguments for shifting responsibility for welfare toward the individual and away from the state.

As it happens, both kinds of argument raise crucial questions concerning the scope of social welfare, its ideological justification, its implicit values, and its administrative structures and procedures. In contrast to the immediate response to the Beveridge report, the present pattern of state-guaranteed rights and services in Britain does not automatically appear either necessary or good. State provisions can be attacked from opposite ends of the political spectrum—on the one hand, because they reduce individual choice, and on the other, because they remove decisions from the sphere of influence of the ordinary citizen. At the same time the revelation that greater expectations accompany greater provisions indicates a crisis for administrative measures geared to the provision of minimum standards; it also brings widespread misgivings about the escalation of social service expenditure and the need to find alternative sources of finance. Health, housing, education, and pensions are all fields in which administrative and fiscal uncertainties are currently emphasized.

For example, during the 1960s, the cost of National Health Service went up 2.3 times, Social Security 2.6, and education 2.8.[31] During the same period, major reorganizations were undertaken in the administration of social security and most sectors of education. The case for administrative reform of the health services was generally conceded and a preliminary step was taken with the preparation of the first Green Paper.

There are signs, therefore, of concern over the present organization and objectives of the welfare state in that an increasing number of questions are raised. If we consider those with a direct bearing on changes in the present pattern, we find, first of all, questions directly concerned with standards and performance. As the standard of living rises, how should the state-guaranteed minimum in the field of income maintenance and provision of social services be adjusted? How far can variations in the quality of provision be tolerated? What should be the role of the state in setting and maintaining standards? A further set of questions is concerned with priorities. On what basis should choices be made in allocating resources to different areas of social expenditure? "Left" and "right" agree on the need to discriminate, but little common ground exists between them on the principles that should govern "choice." Next comes questions focused on cost, specifically, (a) the degree to which contributions should be related to benefits received, (b) the means by which remittances should be allowed to those who need them, and (c) the extent to which individual welfare should remain predominantly a matter of state financial responsibility rather than one of individual choice and provision through the private sector.

A fourth type of question is concerned with organization and control. This stems from evidence of dissatisfaction with existing arrangements for consumer representation and the sweeping review of many welfare arrangements contained in the Seebohm Committee Report, the Report of the Royal Commission on *Local Government in England,* and the Green Paper on health-service organization. Finally, there is a whole range of questions expressing continuing uncertainties about the values to be upheld and institutionalized in welfare services. Are the latter to be judged by such criteria as cost-efficiency, the effective deployment of resources, and consumer satisfaction? Or are they much more than that, namely, a means to achieve social equality or, as it has been put by Labor party enthusiasts, "communal services as a badge of citizenship?"

All these questions can be reduced to a set of fairly precise alternatives facing present and future governments, on the assumption that they remain committed to the underlying objectives of the "welfare state":

(1) Should there be further channeling of national incomes away from private consumption and towards social expenditure, or should positive limits (e.g., a fixed proportion of Gross National Product) be set to the cost of welfare?

(2) Should the higher cost of meeting welfare needs, in bridging the gap between objectives and performance, be met in part by asking people to pay more directly for welfare, either through applying charges for services (with more extensive means tests) or by increasing contributions levied on a progressive basis?

(3) Should private provision in the field of health, education, and superannuation be given positive encouragement and support?

(4) Should existing structures of administration and control be modified or drastically reformed?

The political context at the time of writing provides some useful leads in considering these questions. The hope once held by Labor that the expansion of welfare could be comfortably financed out of economic growth now seems a vain one, not so much because of economic performance as of immediate and future tasks. The Wilson government, despite the demands of recurrent economic crises, increased social-service expenditure in real terms, especially in education and health. Even so, the climate of political opinion now seems distinctly unfavorable to suggestions that further burdens should be added to general taxation in the interests of improved welfare services.

The alternative of allowing and even encouraging people to purchase their own welfare entitlements and standards beyond a compulsory minimum has undoubted ideological significance, as has the whole question of means testing and charging for services.[32] So far these issues have been debated mainly in academic terms, but given certain conditions this ideological significance could readily be communicated to the electorate. The spectres of the double standard of provision and the double standard of citizenship are readily conjured up. In practice, however, neither a shift toward more use of income-related contributions and benefits or toward more extensive means tests would be a radical departure *in principle*. More critical would be how far the balance might shift and what the traumatic implications would be for a Labor party still professing Socialist ideals.

THE DIRECTION OF SOCIAL CHANGE

In the longer term, the prospects of change in British social structure are more decisive. We may now consider whether changes are visible in social structure that could foster the socio-political trends with which this volume is concerned. We noted earlier the extent to which developments in population, employment, income distribution, and (though to a lesser extent) class structure were in line with trends in other advanced industrial societies. In other words, population—especially of dependents—is increasing; employment in white-collar and service occupations is generally rising, at the expense of traditional manual jobs; the transition from a low-wage, subsistence-centered economy to a high-wage, consumption-centered economy is virtually completed; and the more extreme social divisions between the classes have largely disappeared, although the language of class and the political assumptions derived from past inequalities remain important.

On the face of it, the trend toward affluence and "privatization" is indisputable. It must certainly be accepted that material prosperity, supported by greatly improved health, education, and other services, has already transformed the lot of the typical family in Britain and will continue to do so. There is already a good deal of evidence to suggest that a distinctive working-class way of life is in decline and that some convergence between the classes is taking place in terms of patterns of consumption, housing, and leisure. There seems no doubt that this process will continue and that the goals and standards set for society as a whole will increasingly be concerned and measured in middle-class terms.[33]

Much of this is in keeping with the social pattern suggested for the post-welfare society. It is also consistent with the feasibility of greater individual provision, or a "new individualism" in welfare. At a conservative estimate, average real income per head in Britain will have doubled by the end of the century. At the same time, it is doubtful whether social costs (including new ones) will be avoided. A greater homogeneity of life styles may be accompanied by the persistence of poverty among the elderly and disadvantaged, and by a sharper sense of relative deprivation. A greater emphasis on economic growth and material prosperity may widen the gap between affluence and poverty and sharpen social divisions.

Another intangible is the effect of increased women's employment on the values attached to different types of expenditure.[34] It is now a commonplace that expenditure in the home has increased as married women's employment has risen, but there is very little evidence to suggest how feminine values and objectives may channel the benefits of rising affluence—not only in terms of private consumption but also in terms of public policy. A resultant focus on the family unit, its satisfactions and security, may reinforce present welfare systems.

The political implications of this development have already given rise to speculation—some of it bordering on fantasy. White-collar unionism has for some years been regarded as a threat to the traditional character of the T. U. C., as well as the potential disruption of the power base of the Labor party. At the same time, affluence for the manual worker would, by conferring upon him a bourgeois style of life, produce an irreversible swing to the right.[35] Yet white-collar unions have shown increasing militancy and the manual worker who votes conservative is at least as established a phenomenon as the party itself. The question of the emasculation of the Labor party through the transformation of the working class is not a particularly new one. During the latter 1950s, when Labor seemed destined to permanent opposition, it flustered Labor politicians and political commentators. The thesis of working-class "embourgeoisement" has since that time been subjected to rigorous testing by events. In 1964 and 1966 Labor recovered those working-class voters who seemed to have deserted it.[36] During the same period, detailed examination by sociologists revealed the weakness of the proposition that higher living standards bring lower working-class identification or loss of loyalty to the Labor party. A study of "affluent" workers carried out in 1962–1963 demonstrated that high wages are not on their own associated with decline in Labor voting and suggested that there are no good grounds for supposing that they will in the absence of major changes in social structure.[37] Of particular relevance to the present discussion is the conclusion of the authors of that study that a shift may be occurring to what is called a more "instrumental" form of collectivism, a preoccupation with the economic goals of collective action. Trade unionism is thus likely to be strengthened rather than weakened and to be more loyal to the Labor party. "Instrumentalism" involves not only a concern with wages but also a concern with welfare benefits; and, in addition, instrumental attitudes having to do with the "payoff" to be expected from a Labor government in the way of higher living standards and better social services were clearly in evidence.[38]

What is perhaps more important than the effect on political alignments are the consequences of a changing class structure for the style of politics itself. Counterelites such as the Young Liberals and new forms of political action such as nonviolent protest are significant in themselves and cannot be overlooked as sources of institutional change.

TOWARD A POST-WELFARE SOCIETY
IN BRITAIN?

We have now reviewed some major developments in politics and society in Britain with particular reference to the complex of institutions and values which we call the welfare state. The question to be considered is whether these developments may generate sufficient momentum to redefine the central issues of the welfare state and to transform its institutions. We have noted the close interaction between welfare and politics during the present century and the limited room for maneuver at present available to the parties. However, rising affluence and trends in politics reacting against monolithic systems of government suggest possibilities of a new "individualism" in welfare as in other fields. In our view, the question of change in the political change to a post-welfare society hinges on (1) gaps between objectives and performance in present welfare systems leading to a fundamental reappraisal of the "welfare state," and (2) changes in social structure and values favoring different institutional arrangements.

If we wish to evaluate the probable course of events, we must consider first the constants. In the field of welfare it is the extent of old and familiar problems that must be most striking. There is still much poverty —in the sense of large numbers living below an acceptable minimum standard of living, with a high proportion of children affected. There is a shortage of housing for those with low incomes and a problem of bad

housing which outpaces present efforts at replacement. There are too
many old, crowded, and ill-equipped schools and hospitals. In this and
other respects the world of the affluent wage earner does not show such
a marked discontinuity with the Britain of thirty or forty years ago.
This implies that the problem remains one of allocating sufficient resources to combat inequality and squalor; also for many wage earners
the prospect of self-support in welfare is economically unrealistic. Little
scope exists at present for any initiatives that are not directly addressed
to continuing problems of bad social conditions and substandard ways
of life.

The realities of politics similarly suggest that no fundamental
changes are in prospect. While the postwar equilibrium in British politics may not last indefinitely, and some reasons for expecting a change
have been noted, it is difficult to see what unfamiliar moves could be
made by either the Labor or Conservative parties during the next few
years. The Labor party is uniquely committed to maintaining the welfare state in very much its present form—i.e., as a system of near-
universal benefits and services. It can at most edge forward, and it
cannot go back. To move in a significant direction toward alternative
forms of financing welfare provision would be a painful road. In one
direction, it might cost Labor important middle-class support, while in
another, to apply charges and enlarge the scope of means tests would
compromise its role as defender of working-class interests. The ideological temptations for the Conservatives to tamper with the welfare
state are far greater, but the electoral costs would be out of all proportion to possible gains in support or even morale.

The emphasis placed here on the balance between parties as a key
to change in social welfare institutions may seem exaggerated. It should
be remembered, however, that the situation in Britain is unusual. Unlike most European countries, virtually all welfare is a *government* responsibility, and the party in power must answer for all changes in the
level and manner of charges and the level and standard of benefits and
services. Different systems involving insurance and independent public
agencies to a large degree remove social welfare from the forefront of
politics, since the expenditure involved is not in competition with other
forms of public spending. There is little immediate likelihood of any
shift away from this situation in Britain, since foreign systems offer no

obvious advantages apart from the greater possibility of raising money for certain categories of welfare provision, and of responding to consumer demand.

The situation is akin to the meteorological conditions of a col—an area bounded by stationary pressure centers. Social policy in Britain has emerged through the identification and recognition of new needs and shifts in the balance of power between different groups in society. At the present, few of the more specific demands for change (for more selectivity, more participation, and further diversions of national resources to welfare) are backed by real political power. Even arguments based on grounds of efficiency lack force. The system is not as a whole demonstrably inadequate and the benefits to society of a change in welfare policy are not self-evident. However appropriate or eloquent their claims, the self-appointed agents of change lack teeth. And the sheer complexity of the welfare state in Britain deters the advocate of even moderate reform.

Nonetheless, there are developments favorable to change, although these lie outside the limits of conventional party politics. First, there is an increasing professionalization of welfare which is marked by a greater degree of organization and articulateness among employees, as well as the rapid development of social administration as a major academic subject and field of inquiry for the social sciences. The roles of the expert, the pressure group, and the professional have never been unimportant, but the widening of questions involved, coupled with assertions of greater autonomy, could appreciably enlarge their influence.

It seems highly probable that new channels of communication between professionals and the public may be opened, thus bypassing the politicians. Second, the current movement toward participation and involvement, toward politics by pressure group and consumer organization, will effect the control of a wide range of services, e.g., schools, housing, and hospitals. Public involvement could lead to a greater valuation of welfare services and an increased willingness to pay for higher quality.

A final consideration is that welfare problems are subject to a continual process of redefinition and extension. In advanced industrial societies three main kinds of problem have increased in intensity—those concerning the physical environment, those relating to work and leisure, including the control of technical change, and finally those of social cohesion, arising from new deviant subcultures, the fragmentation of society, the accentuation of such issues as race relations and individual freedom. The more seriously these questions are taken, the more they will create demands for increased social expenditure. Because they are problems calling for solutions on a societal rather than on an individual basis, pressures may develop for public expenditure to be diverted toward their solution, at the expense of welfare systems which can be organized on the basis of individual provision. In this way, socio-economic change and the recognition of new and pressing social priorities may map out new boundaries for political discussion and determine new social objectives.

Notes

1. On the development of the welfare state in Britain, see Titmuss, *Essays on 'The Welfare State'* (London, 1958), M. P. Hall, *The Social Services of Modern England* (London, 1968), and Morris Ginsberg, ed., *Law and Opinion in England in the 20th Century* (London, 1959).

2. Report on *Social Insurance and Allied Services* (the Beveridge Report), Cmd. 6404 (London, 1942).

3. The best single treatment of the history of party organization is R. T. McKenzie, *British Political Parties* (London, 1955). Two useful general introductions are G. C. Moodie, *The Government of Great Britain* (New York, 1961) and J. Blondel, *Voters, Parties and Leaders* (London, 1963).

4. For a concise account of the civilian experience in World War I, see Arthur Marwick, *The Deluge* (London, 1967). The standard work for 1939–1945 is Titmuss, *Problems of Social Policy* (London, 1950). See also A. Calder, *The People's War* (London, 1969).

5. Blondel, *Voters, Parties and Leaders,* Chapter 3. See also C. A. R. Crosland, *The Future of Socialism* (London, 1956) and William A. Robson, *Nationalised Industry and Public Ownership* (London, 1960).

6. Documented in R. L. Leonard, *Election in Britain* (London, 1968). See also D. E. Butler and J. Freeman, *British Political Facts, 1900–1968* (London, 1969).

7. A typical survey-finding can be consulted in J. M. Trenaman and D. McQuail, *Television and the Political Image* (London, 1961), which shows

(pp. 130–31) that 93 per cent reporting a Conservative vote at an election four years earlier held to this allegiance, with a comparable figure of 78 per cent for Labor voters. More recently, the accepted version of a stable electorate has been subjected to close scrutiny and in part demolished: It ignores the many sources of change additional to conversions between major parties, leaves out of account the cumulative effect of change, and is too often based on unreliable evidence about past political behavior and opinions. See, in particular, Butler and D. Stokes, *Political Change in Britain* (London, 1969), pp. 275–312.

8. Butler and Stokes, *ibid.,* pp. 313–38, Butler and A. King, *The British General Election of 1964* (London, 1965), and Butler and King, *The British General Election of 1966* (London, 1967).

9. According to Butler and Stokes, "No electoral phenomenon in Britain has been more widely remarked on than that of 'uniform national swing.' In election after election since World War II, the net shift of strength between the parties has amounted to a remarkably similar fraction of the electorate in the great bulk of constituencies across the country." Butler and Stokes, *Political Change,* p. 303. See also pp. 135–43.

10. See Blondel, *Voters, Parties and Leaders,* pp. 74 ff., R. Rose, *Politics in England* (London, 1965), and the series of Nuffield College election studies, many edited by D. E. Butler.

11. Blondel, *ibid.,* pp. 75–79, presents evidence to show that Labor and Conservative voters hold identical viewpoints on many individual issues, with divergence occurring on matters to do with industrial relations and social welfare. Butler and Stokes have recently demolished the notion that a simple left-right ideological dimension is useful in distinguishing electors' preferences and opinions.

12. See Rose, *Politics in England,* for discussion on this point. Of the sample interviewed by Butler and Stokes, *Political Change,* 33 per cent said in 1963 that they did not usually care which party won an election, while 50 per cent said they did not feel the government pays much attention to what people think.

13. See Rose, *Politics in England,* and Leonard, *Election in Britain.* Among a sample of electors interviewed in 1959, 55 per cent agreed that the Conservative party "stands mainly for the upper classes, . . ." and 54 per cent thought the Labor party "stands mainly for the working classes. . . ." Trenaman and McQuail, *Television,* p. 276.

14. See H. Durant, "Voting Behaviour in Britain, 1945–66," in Rose, ed., *Studies in British Politics* (London, 1969), pp. 165–71.

15. The actual share of middle-class votes obtained by Labor has ranged from 16 per cent (1959) to 24 per cent (1945 and 1966). Durant, *ibid.,* p. 166.

16. See R. McKenzie and A. Silver, *Angels in Marble* (London, 1968), E. A. Nordlinger, *The Working-Class Tories* (London, 1967), and M. Abrams, R. Rose, and R. Hinden, *Must Labour Lose?* (London, 1960).

17. J. G. Blumler and D. McQuail, *Television in Politics* (Chicago, 1970), pp. 277–80.

18. Examples include the availability of financial inducements for housing associations and house purchase; tax reliefs granted for providing care for relatives at home; and tax concessions for a wide range of welfare benefits offered by employers.

19. The evidence cited in the ensuing pages is derived principally from *Annual Abstract of Statistics,* No. 106, 1969 (London, H.M.S.O., 1969); Central Statistical Office, *National Income and Expenditure, 1960,* and *National Income and Expenditure, 1969* (London, H.M.S.O., 1960, 1969); *Employment and Productivity Gazette* (London, H.M.S.O.); and Ministry of Housing and Local Government, *Housing Statistics* (London, H.M.S.O., quarterly).

20. Evidence for these points can be cited in numerous sources, including Butler and Stokes, *Political Change,* D. Hill, *Participating in Local Affairs* (London, 1970), Rose, *Politics in England,* and Rose, *Influencing Voters* (New York, 1967).

21. Blumler and McQuail, *Television in Politics,* pp. 191 and 326.

22. See Rose, *Influencing Voters.*

23. *National Superannuation and Social Insurance,* Cmnd. 3883 (London, H.M.S.O., 1969) and *National Superannuation and Social Insurance Bill* (Bill 69 of session 1969–1970).

24. Report of the Committee on the *Management of Local Government* (London, H.M.S.O. 1967); Report of the Royal Commission on *Local Government in England,* I Report, II Memorandum of Dissent, Cmnd. 4040, Cmnd. 4040–I (London, H.M.S.O., 1969); Report of the Committee on *Local Authority and Allied Personal Social Services,* Cmnd. 3703 (London, H.M.S.O., 1968); Ministry of Health, *National Health Service. The Administrative Structure of the Medical and Related Services in England and Wales* (London, H.M.S.O., 1968); and Department of Health and Social Security, *National Health Service. The Future Structure of the National Health Service* (London, H.M.S.O., 1970).

25. S. E. Finer, *The Life and Times of Sir Edwin Chadwick* (London, 1952) and P. Ford, *Social Theory and Social Practice* (Dublin, 1969).

26. See, in particular, publications by the Institute of Economic Affairs, London, e.g., D. S. Lees, *Health Through Choice* (London, 1961) and E. G.

West, *Education and the State* (London, 1965), and the rejoinders in Titmuss, *Commitment to Welfare* (London, 1968).

27. T. H. Marshall, *Sociology at the Crossroads* (London, 1963), p. 273.

28. Titmuss, *Essays on 'The Welfare State,'* p. 34.

29. For pointers to these developments, see Institute of Economic Affairs, *Monopoly or Choice in Health Services* (London, 1964).

30. *Shelter* is concerned with improvements in the supply of housing, especially for the homeless. Its director has specialized in contesting official statistics and estimates and in large-scale charity-style collections. The *Child Poverty Action Group* has been closely concerned with establishing the extent of need among families receiving social security benefits or with low incomes.

31. Central Statistical Office, *National Income and Expenditure 1960* and *National Income and Expenditure 1969.*

32. See reports of the Institute of Economic Affairs cited above.

33. There is already a sizable literature on the "embourgeoisement" thesis. For two contrary approaches, see F. Zweig, *The Worker in an Affluent Society* (London, 1961) and J. H. Goldthorpe, *et al., The Affluent Worker,* Vols. 1–3 (Cambridge, 1968–1970).

34. V. Klein, *Britain's Married Women Workers* (London, 1965) and P. Jephcott, N. Seear, and J. H. Smith, *Married Women Working* (London, 1962).

35. For an early statement of the problem, see Abrams, Rose, and Hinden, *Must Labour Lose?* More recent evidence is presented in Goldthorpe, *et al., The Affluent Worker.*

36. Butler and Stokes, *Political Change.*

37. Goldthorpe, *et al., The Affluent Worker.*   38. *Ibid.*

DOUGLAS L. CAPPS

The Citizen, Administration, and Politics in Post-Welfare Britain

> *"Would you please tell me which way I ought to walk from here?" said Alice.*
> *"That depends a good deal on where you want to get to," said the Cat.*
> —LEWIS CARROLL, *Alice's Adventures in Wonderland*

IT HAS BEEN SAID that bureaucratic systems will become a major focal point of tension and political debate in the post-welfare state. Organizations have been identified as the qualitatively, socially, and morally decisive realm. "It is in organizations that our values will be achieved, that individual freedom will be attained." [1] These observations have generated a new interest in bureaucracy. Analysis of bureaucracy has become crucial not only because the complexity of decision-making in technologically advanced societies places bureaucracy (with a momentum of its own) at the helm; it has also become crucial because "man in conflict with bureaucracy is in large part a description of the modern human condition." [2]

These assertions differ greatly from those used to defend individual freedom in the Britain of the past. A reconciliation between language and fact has pushed Britain on to the threshold of major reform. Motivated by a growing awareness of the role modern bureaucracy plays, combined with an awareness of the inadequacies of traditional responses, Britain is witnessing increased demands that suggest, directly or indirectly, the need for changing the nature of the growing administrative state.

This chapter involves a time perspective. Time is used here in an Augustinian three-fold sense: the present as we experience it, the past as present memory, and the future as present expectation. Specifically, the following discussion will review the growth of administrative power in Britain and efforts to do something about it. I shall then examine the concept of individualism in relation to administrative growth and the intellectual language used to voice reactions to perceived patterns. Finally, I shall assess the nature of contemporary relations between governors and governed, and the demands, which arise from the implications of these relations, that comprise the "futuribles" of the post-welfare era. The first half of the twentieth century provides the "realm of present memory."

THE BUREAUCRATIC REVOLUTION

Whether or not the contention is valid, Britain is thought to have emerged from the first half of the twentieth century with the full status of a welfare state. As such, it has experienced a proliferation of complex bureaucratic systems. The so-called organizational revolution was well under way in Britain by the turn of the century.

The revolutionary character of organizational growth is verified by contrasting the administrative system with the "civil administration" of earlier times. Toward the end of the eighteenth century the English administrative arrangement could be described as "decentralized, non-professional—save for Whitehall officials—non-bureaucratic, liberal, with a dispersed and incoherent arbitrariness." [3] The nineteenth century marked the beginning of a "system," generated by the insistence that the Civil Service be manned by men "innocent of professional qualifications" but well schooled in the classical and other then-conventional subjects of secondary and university education.[4]

The system which created the Admirality and War Office for defense and the Foreign and Colonial Office for external political relations was soon augmented by a Home Office for general internal affairs and the Board of Trade for commercial and industrial affairs. The Treasury became the core unit, although formal recognition of its primacy was not given until 1920. Before the turn of the century a Ministry of Agriculture, a Board of Education, and a Local Government Board had joined the "civil services." Expansion during World War I was not permanent, although great numbers were needed for the immediate pressure of the problems of war and reconstruction. The Air Ministry and the Ministry of Pensions survived into peacetime. Of course, ancient common-service departments, the Post Office and the Office of Works, along with Customs and Excise, had large staffs.

During World War II a great leap forward occurred in so-called welfare legislation, particularly in the fields of National Insurance (establishing the National Health Service) and in the Town and Country Planning Act. By the middle of the twentieth century social services and the management of the economy were more or less comprehensive, providing insurance, health, pensions, family allowances, and other services on a national scale. Every individual, at least theoretically, has been brought within the scope of the welfare state, an aim motivated by the assumption that social services are necessary to achieve a reasonably high standard of living for all.

This, then, is roughly what the organizational revolution in public administration means. It is difficult to define it with any statistical precision, but we know that nonindustrial civil servants numbered 16,000 in 1800, 39,000 in 1850, 116,000 in 1900, 281,000 in 1914, 317,000 in 1922, and 637,000 in 1960. The composition of British administration has gradually but steadily changed from a "picked band of permanent officials operating under the aegis of a succession of individual Ministers to that of a succession of Ministers being grafted more or less temporarily on to the permanent and firmly structured organism of a Department of State." [5]

COUNTERMOVES AGAINST THE ADMINISTRATIVE STATE

The bureaucratic revolution wrought a gradual assumption of power which occurred as the role of the state was successively expanded in accord with pragmatic policy decisions endorsed by all the major parties. Hence, it generated no widespread backlash. Nevertheless there were some very significant shouts and murmers, particularly in protest against the expanding area of discretionary decisions and the inadequate mechanisms for airing grievances. (Of course, discretionary decisions are not the only visible activity of government and grievances are not the only relation citizens have with the state.) By focusing on the implications of both discretion and grievances, one can discern the general conflict between the rights of the citizen and the power of the welfare state, as well as the lines upon which the battle has been fought.

THE NEW DESPOTISM

Twentieth-century administrative theory generally maintains the need for the exercise of legitimate administrative discretion—but discretion controlled ultimately by law. This is the application of the familiar "rule of law" principle of the British constitution. For a number of significant reasons, however, the "judicial method" administered by the courts has not been the only means to administrative justice. While court review provides one channel to obtain justice,[6] judicial resistance to the claims of the executive has so greatly decayed in the twentieth century that any dramatic revival is a blatantly unrealistic hope.

For that reason we must look instead to those protests directed to Parliament—for it is Parliament that determines, in the last analysis, both the extent of discretionary power and the means for appealing against its day-to-day use.

The publication of the *New Despotism* by Lord Hewart in 1929 is a potent example of the dispute over sovereign administrative power. It stands as one of Britain's most significant and hard-hitting reactions to both the growth of administrative pragmatism and the extent of discretionary power in government. Lord Hewart's reaction has often been dismissed as a subtle attack on the whole collectivist trend. But we cannot overlook it, for its appearance signaled widespread concern.

Hewart's reaction was angry, sharp, and representative enough to prompt an official inquiry into the accountability of administration. The resulting Donoughmore Report is said to be a minor classic in administrative law.[7] But neither Donoughmore nor the *New Despotism* was very perceptive in assessing reality. One of the more unique features of the growing administration was the simultaneous creation of administrative tribunals to hear complaints. They were never mentioned by Hewart in his attack on administrative law as lawlessness.[8] The Donoughmore Committee regarded tribunals as somewhat exceptional, resorted to only in special circumstances. What was much more important, according to the Committee, was strengthening the rule of law and the sovereignty of Parliament.

This language is more illuminating than the practical proposals of the Donoughmore Report. (Its recommendations never found their way into legislation.) First of all, the emphasis on rights in both Hewart's book and the Donoughmore Report revealed that nineteenth-century liberalism was still breathing. The blatant appearance of communism, fascism, and nazism may have reinforced Liberal arguments about upholding individualism. But the real impetus for such arguments was the "much less dramatic but steady advance of the planned administrative state" [9] which was steadily eating away into the private rights and arrangements of the nineteenth century.

An attack on the dangerously developing relation between authority and individualism required a philosophical language with political application. This was provided by the legal constitutionalists flourishing in the late nineteenth and early twentieth centuries. Led by A. V. Dicey, the legal constitutionalists maintained a firm grip on public and legal thinking about the boundaries of power. Their principal conceptual slogans were sovereignty of Parliament and rule of law. In the view of Dicey and others, individualism—secured by the rule of law—was being destroyed by the power of Parliament to delegate authority, for this rendered the will or caprice of the executive unfettered and supreme. Similarly, the Frenchman's unhappy lot and lack of individual freedom was due to *droit administratif*—administrative law that made executive power no less than despotic.

This was good enough stuff for Lord Hewart and the Donoughmore Committee. Both translated the power of bureaucracy into a legal argument that defined individualism in terms of access to courts of law. At the same time, however, the "administrative method" continued to gain its quiet but growing pre-eminence. In contrast to Lord Hewart and the Donoughmore Committee, proponents of the administrative method assumed that "economic and social questions raise issues of policy which ought not to be frustrated by litigation in the courts, and that administrative discretion subject to parliamentary control is a flexible and necessary mode of action over a wide range of administrative policy." [10]

THE REVOLT OF THE 1950S

Why an open conflict between these two perspectives did not rise to the surface again for twenty-five years is difficult to explain. Perhaps the war conditions of the 1940s made it difficult to receive much public support for those who had grievances over discretionary, administrative decisions. Certainly serious attempts were made in the courts, but the emergency situation also made judges less ready to uphold complaints by citizens. The judiciary took shelter behind the terminology of statures which precluded review. Perhaps the relaxation of those conditions in the mid-1950s contributed to an atmosphere of protest and general concern over individual rights and administrative justice.

Whatever the reasons, one incident opened the floodgates and initiated a conflict of crisis proportions: the Crichel Down Affair. Based on administrative mishandling of Crichel Down, a piece of land obtained by compulsory order in Dorset County, this controversy publicized the predicament of the ordinary citizen when confronted with immense discretionary powers of the administration. Again the question, "What is the proper use and extent of discretionary powers of government?" (or more generally, "Who governs the government?") was loudly raised.

The rumblings of Crichel Down encouraged an official inquiry, the results of which led to new areas of awareness about administrative power. The principle of ministerial responsibility had been upheld in the past as one of the chief means by which Parliament performs its scrutinizing function. Ministers may very well be the chief executives of the bureaucracy. But at 2:30 in the afternoon on days that Parliament is sitting, those chief executives leave their cozy Whitehall offices and take their places on the front bench of the House of Commons. It is there that they and their departments are open to investigation by backbench and opposition M.P.s.

But the Crichel Down inquiry showed that vast numbers of cases were decided by civil servants without the least reference to the Minister. The bastion of administrative accountability, political control by means of ministerial responsibility, was full of holes. The Minister obviously could not be expected to review every decision. Therefore, how was he to be responsible for cases of incompetence which had never been near his desk? Yet, if the Minister could not realistically be held responsible for day-to-day decisions, who could?

This was the thrust of Crichel Down. An administrative decision had been made and the series of processes which followed were kept hidden. It became clear that there was "no process, no machinery of any kind by which a normal citizen can as a right bring before any court or any other impartial person an act done by a Ministry within its departmental powers." [11] It is not surprising that a revived awareness of administrative power generated reactions. They began to flow from all corners of the political spectrum. R. H. S. Crossman, in a pamphlet published by the Fabian Society entitled *Socialism and the New Despotism,* pointed out the threat of a vast centralized bureaucracy to social democracy. Socialist principles did not preclude attack on its excesses nor the defense of the individual against its incipient despotism. A 1958 Labor party pamphlet, *Personal Freedom,* had the originality and creativity to adopt the main recommendations of the *Donoughmore Report* of 1932! A 1956 Inns of Court and Unionist Society publication, *Rule of Law,* represented a "mild revolt from the Right at the helplessness of the citizen who seeks redress from arbitrary or unfair action by a department." [12]

Such reactions were made official in the Report of the Franks Committee, created in response to the noise made by Crichel Down. The committee did nothing to hide the fact of the extended area of governmental activity. Government had assumed increasing responsibility for the well-being of the community. But such activity increased the occasions in which the individual may be at issue with the state. The committee concentrated on the administrative tribunals and inquiries which had been created to resolve disputes between the governors and the governed.[13]

There were other differences between the Franks Committee outlook and the Donoughmore effort. The Franks Committee was not a lawyers' affair. Instead of principles, supremacy, constitutional doctrines, and balances of power, the committee spoke of citizen satisfaction, fair play, and reasonable regard for public interest. Reporting in terms of harmony, relationships, and concern, it exemplified an official concern with citizen feelings about the administrative state. It shifted the whole point of view from constitutional principles to the citizen. By 1958 we see Dicey standing on his head.

THE PAST IN A NUTSHELL:
THE QUESTION OF RIGHTS

These are significant developments. The protest in the early twentieth century focused upon *individual rights*.[14] The view was through law-colored glasses, for law in an earlier era had already proved its ability to settle disputes and protect property. The law was considered the means by which rights would continue to be determined. Saying that, it took little effort to assume that the expanding state should also be controlled by the same procedures. This was the way to restrict the growing power of the state, permitting it to interfere with the individual as little as possible. The 1920s marked a particularly strong effort to provide a constitutional defense against emerging political necessities.

The 1950s went a long way toward voicing the concern over relations between the state and the individual more realistically. The old legal, individual, negative rights were giving way to positive social rights. Rights are to be determined by subjective necessity. The very basis of administration is the attainment of social rights. "All members of the community have equal claim to them. . . . They have to be satisfied from communal resources, and to be administered by communal agencies." [15] It was no longer relevant to make the assertion of rights (property) dependent upon *reducing* the range of public power. Government had become active rather than reactive.

The nature of property has also changed. Individual goods have become increasingly available and are open to choice. But they have been joined by communal goods that are not divisible in the market sense.[16] An increasing number of goods require communal purchasing. The persistence of anachronistic beliefs, practices, and laws is little help to a society that needs to establish a system for deciding. The delivery or allocation of communal goods is a part of the process and also causes concern. What if someone dislikes the way the system has delivered the goods?

Parliament (which embodies the bias toward political and away from legal control) tried to answer that question over the years. Protection for the citizen was infused into the administrative machinery itself. But Crichel Down showed the difficulties of that, and the brave set out to find alternatives. The Franks Committee came up with *procedural safeguards*. This was fine as far as it went, but it became apparent that tribunals, while extensive, did not cover a great deal of administrative decisions. It was suggested that citizens with grievances might confront the administration personally, or alternatively refer the problem to an M.P., a representative organization, or the press.[17]

Two problems became increasingly apparent. How could citizens of a democratic state be certain that government decisions were representative? How could individuals be protected from the arbitrary exercise of administrative power? A search to provide answers to these questions spread into the courts, the administration, and Parliament itself. Many sacred positions and sacredly held notions could not stand up to the test. Analysis by such scholars as Brian Chapman and Bernard Crick made the audacious suggestion that Britain might learn from foreign experience.[18] The spirit of reform had been unleashed.

The role of the judiciary was one of the first casualties. Even if its lack of initiative could be remedied, illegal administrative decisions were not the problem. It was primarily those decisions made in the ordinary course of public business that resulted in injustice to its recipients. This, together with an Anglican preference to avoid legalism in matters of administration, shifted the focus upon political control. The constituency work of individual M.P.s seemed particularly relevant to democratic participation and individual protection. Supported by the traditional role of providing a repository for frustration and anger over administrative action, the M.P. often brings up parliamentary questions or confronts bureaucracy directly. But the Question Hour—often hailed as Britain's answer to the close legislative committee scrutiny found in other countries (particularly the United States)—is more an opportunity for scoring political points than a time for requesting information, sorting out an administrative case, or arguing a decision. Direct questioning through letters to a department or personal contact with a Minister may lead to speedier replies than the citizen would obtain on his own. But the question of impartiality is not adequately answered, and M.P.s do not have access to departmental files.

Each search party which sought ways to democratic controls from within came back empty-handed. If alternatives were available, they were not supported by the proper components for system change. The magic number was possessed, however, by *Justice,* the British Section of the International Commission of Jurists, made up of members of the legal, academic, and public fields who organized to investigate anomalies in the political and legal systems. *Justice* published a report recommending the creation of a Parliamentary commissioner.[19] It was to be a British version of the Scandinavian ombudsman, adapted to the British system. The arguments stressed the ways in which the ombudsman would plug the most glaring gaps in procedural safeguards. A grievance man seemed a particularly adaptable alternative to encompass the requirements of both participation and protection.

The ombudsman proposal, adopted by the Labor party in its 1964 Election Manifesto, was not alone in the arena of reform. The 1960s saw the cult of the generalists in the Civil Service denounced by the Report of the Fulton Committee and replaced by a more professional managerial body. The Seebohm Committee drew up a new blueprint for the country's welfare services. The Donovan Commission called for trade-union reform. The crisis of the 1950s emerged into an atmosphere of almost orthodox radical reform.

Yet as optimistically as this narrative may seem to end, close analysis suggests that any optimism would be misplaced—granted a new mode or realization had been attained, granted the immense importance of recognizing the "historical residue of grey-faced charitable paternalism; a traditional concept of them versus us which seems to permeate so many bureaucratic departments." [20] While the real conditions of the citizen were approached, the alternative structures to meet those conditions seemed out of range. For example, the Franks Committee could do little more than raise the level of bad tribunals to the level of good ones. Those who thought the ombudsman would fill the gaps were further disappointed. The relatively unstructured New Zealand plan, adopted prior to the British campaign, showed the adaptability of a mechanism—activated by citizens' complaints—to inquire into the wrongness of administrative decisions. Since New Zealand was a common-law country with a political system based upon the British example, the New Zealand precedent should have encouraged Britain to adopt an ombudsman with powers much more closely related to citizens' needs. Instead Britain chose a cautious approach. A bill strongly supported by the Civil Service and reflecting an executive mentality that precludes extensive prying into the merits of discretionary decisions was accepted by Parliament. The ombudsman was given jurisdiction over administrative procedures. If procedures were consistent with established rules, the ombudsman was powerless to return a guilty verdict regarding maladministration, regardless of the impact of the decision upon the complainant. Clearly the search for bureaucratic alternatives was heading in the wrong direction.

TURNING THE RIGHT DIRECTION

Mid-century activities have been aimed at mending the welfare state; they are attempts at catching up. To step over the threshhold into the arena of imaginative innovation requires a much more total mode of realization than has thus far been attained, corresponding to the new capabilities of society. Could it be that politics in Britain is too much dominated by nineteenth-century private minds?

Britain needs to become more aware of the *nature* of bureaucracy. Recognizing its physical or constitutional features is not enough, for it does not reveal the changing nature of the bureaucracy or the role of the individual in relation to it. Policy makers need to see the connection between bureaucractic organization and a new articulation of individualism. The protest today is predominantly centered on newly felt rights and responsibilities and on the feeling of deprivation and dissatisfaction with systems organized on a fading industrial basis.

This means, fundamentally, seeing that technological "rationality" has produced an integrated society that functions "not as the sum total of mere instruments which can be isolated from their social and political effects, but rather as a system which determines *a priori* the product of the apparatus; as well as the operations of servicing and extending it." [21] Anticipating the post-welfare state requires an examination of the internal contradictions of prevailing forms of bureaucracy and their implications within the broader social context. Both fronts are supplied by a growing source of social science research. Such research is exceeded in relevance only by readily discernible protests against the rational apparatus of bureaucracy. A growing number of citizens are realizing that politicians represent the science of "politics" more than they represent the people. The new individualism rejects the mystique of power and authority and demands a more human approach.

Britain has, in fact, contributed very little to the growing realization of either the contradictions inherent in modern bureaucracy or their implications for the future. It is in the position of having a highly influential administrative structure, but an uninfluential body of research concerning it. Britain shares this position with another pervasive administrative state, Sweden, which is also said to lack in a coherent theory of public administration. Britain, like Sweden, favors descriptive study. This can "distract attention from sources of possible social change" as much as the overattention to theory and ideology found, for example, in the United States.[22]

What is implied here is that Britain can build its future by analyzing the consistency of its formal organizations with the democratic values upon which the entire system is based. Britain must also turn its attention toward the problems of understanding and improving the relations between organizations and their clients. If serious analysis were attempted, what would we expect to find?

THE NATURE OF BRITISH BUREAUCRATIC LIFE

British administration, like other bureaucracies, is derived from the assumption that policies are carried out best by a centralized organ whose usefulness depends on its efficiency and rationality. These characteristics are to be obtained by specialization, a hierarchy of authority, a system of rules, and impersonality. All of this is strongly supported by Weber's familiar functional analysis of bureaucracy. He saw the bureaucratic form marked by technical training, merit appointments, fixed salaries, assured careers, fixed divisions of work, and most important, a clear hierarchy of subordination and superordination tied together with a set of rules and regulations. Efficiency demands coordination, and for the operations of hundreds of employees to be coordinated, "each individual must conform to the prescribed standards even in situations where a different course of action appears to him to be most rational." [23]

Authority within the organization is therefore a one-way relation. Reduction of the power of the individual is necessary to make him more responsible to formal authority. This calls for routinized jobs and eliminating individual discretion. Jobs must be defined in such a way as to provide for every contingency. Decision-making is removed to a remote level.

But the so-called Weberian model overlooks dysfunctions—those consequences in the British structure that interfere with adjustment and create problems in the structure. Internal contradictions affecting efficiency, relations with clients affecting purpose, and the nature of the organization in relation to broader societal goals are the usual dysfunctional categories.

INTERNAL CONTRADICTIONS

A preoccupation with upholding the "monistic ideal" [24] has led to rigidity and conformity, not innovation. Securing efficient operation means spending great effort to secure the appearance of consensus and agreement. The maintenance of this image is particularly difficult today. The technological society demands specialist decisions. Generalist supervisors have lost their ability, but not their right, to command. An internal imbalance is created. Tension grows, fed by the personal insecurity of personnel and fertilized by the importance of success on the hierarchical ladder. To ensure smooth operation under these conditions, regulations and quantitative standards are exaggerated. Symptoms of the tension are seen in pompous officials or autocratic superiors. "Impression management" [25] is explained by the need for accreditation. A good deal of pretense and play acting, or "dramaturgy," can be generated by the discrepancy between image and reality.[26]

Bureaucratic behavior of this kind (about which we are made aware by numerous analyses concentrating on processes and interactions instead of the official structure of bureaucracy) is directed more toward mitigating personal frustration. What could be more irrational in the organizational sense? Such activity has little to do with advancing the organization's goals. This line of reasoning is further strengthened by the contributions in the field of psychotherapy. Applied to bureaucracy, this approach emphasizes organizations as organisms, marked by a "primary mentality." [27] Organization members seek to satisfy individual needs by means of instrumental relations.

Because most people are socialized by the threat of deprivation and because resources (material or psychological) are therefore thought to be scarce, competition with others to get what one needs becomes a bargaining, trading, way of life. "Life is a game of mutual exploitation" is a familiar remark. Put another way, personal relations in situations in which the attainment of need-satisfaction seems limited are usually, in effect, antagonistic. Of course individuals *do* form cohesive groups, for they realize they cannot obtain satisfactions on their own. An individual will allow part of his behavior to be subject to hierarchical control, and that part is directed in the service of organizational directives. But this is still an instrumental relation. Any further control will be resisted. There exists a constant internal struggle to safeguard and expand the area of discretion by members at lower levels of the hierarchy. This is liable to generate intensified control arrangements from above to enforce the contract.[28]

One commentator, in less psychological terms, calls this the functioning of the incentive system in modern bureaucracies. The arrangement not only inhibits initiative but it also represses a common conscience. The act of the superior (in terms of punishment, withholding rewards, etc.) becomes an act of sheer power. The administrative system is not marked by cohesion but by an "adult-child relationship which reflects the immaturity of mankind." [29]

CLIENT RELATIONS

We have taken this excursion into bureaucratic behavior because these characteristics form the basis of client relations. After all, "it is the way in which *people* are being treated by the administrative systems . . ." [30] that has created the fuss.

Does anyone doubt, for example, that specialization within the organization also means treating the client in a segmented rather than total way? The client becomes an object of bureaucratic policy in the strict sense. As such, "the client is viewed as subordinate to the bureaucrat," [31] which suggests that the hierarchy does not stop at the bottom of the formal structure. Because bureaucracy is organized around rules and regulations, embodied in forms and "officialese," it is apparent to the client that he must adjust to policy, not the reverse. Likewise, if he requires more treatment than policy prescribes, he is not likely to be treated at all.

One of the few studies of client relations shows that bureaucratic structures are the key medium through which the middle class maintains its advantaged position vis-à-vis the lower class. The bureaucrat tends to impose his own expectations and interpretation of reality upon the client. "Lower class clients are likely to handicap the organization in the attainment of its goals . . . ," and the bureaucracy tends therefore to relate more toward compatible middle-class clients.[32] This orientation is also reflected in the hierarchy. "Better" administrative posts are given to those who are more adept at manipulating the power structure (a typically middle-class trait). Policy becomes enforced deferentially "in response to pressures by clients and in accord with the client's social class position." [33] The paradox emerges: Lower-class personnel are furthest away from the decision-making source of their instructions. At the same time, they are closer to the problems that generate issues for policies, and to the people who are bothered by these problems.[34]

BROADER SOCIETAL GOALS

Is there any doubt that the implications of internal behavior and external relations affect the aims for which the administrative state exists?

Can it be denied that the goal of the welfare state which Britain proudly articulates, equality for all citizens, is obliterated by administrative practice? Even the traditional standards by which bureaucracy judges its behavior are becoming increasingly irrelevant under the weight of normal administrative habits. Unequal status has precluded full dialogue between members, making "rationality" logically impossible. Efficiency is effected by the dominant element of status superimposed on the functional layers of the structure. Internal and external goals are not aligned.

But the most relevant and crucial question to emerge is this: Is bureaucracy master or servant? On the one hand we see bureaucratic faults so inconsistent with broader societal aims that "defects" is too small a word to describe them. (One commentator prefers "bureaucratic degeneration." [35]) On the other hand, we see a system that no longer depends on its role as servant of the primary group. The complexities of decision-making have allowed the established bureaucracy to take control at the helm. The bureaucratic organization itself exerts an independent influence on the political balance of power. At the same time, once a policy emerges from the apparatus, it becomes very difficult to affect or change it.

It is no longer realistic, therefore, to assume that faults are technical difficulties, inevitable, or subject to minor technical adjustment. We are talking about a major shift in the traditional balance of power. The organizational revolution has created a bureaucracy with independent powers, with invisibility, and beyond the reach of the traditional arms of democratic control.[36]

If this is the problem, are we not traveling down the very same road that Lord Hewart built in 1929? There are significant differences. In the first place, we recognize the need for wide discretionary power to ensure that government remains active. Destroying all bureaucracies would create more perils than were eliminated. Second, we recognize the inadequacy of formal controls which emerged from a mentality preoccupied with individual rights of a different nature. Third, we identify the crisis by looking at the nature of the administrative state itself. Fourth, the emerging awareness indicates new directions of change much more aligned with actual human conditions.

It is not altogether correct to assume that British awareness has traveled this far. A predominant proportion of the empirical evidence and analytical effort along these lines has come from the other side of the Atlantic.[37] Yet there is nothing to suggest that these assumptions are significantly out of tune with the bureaucratic state that is flourishing in Britain. One British reviewer of a study describing the more depressing features of French bureaucracy has said that "it probably applies to Britain." [38] He recognizes, for example, the defensive group action that throws up organizational rules. He mentions a "war of position" that minimizes effective communication between hierarchical positions, preserves a separate status and system of rights, and inhibits anyone from taking initiative.

ALTERNATIVES TO BUREAUCRACY

If the basic assumptions of studies of bureaucracy are applicable to the British system, then so too are the alternative forms proposed to counter them. Alternatives cover as great a range as the difficulties which have been perceived. But keeping in mind the threat of "bureaucratic degeneration," our attention will focus on those guidelines that suggest something more than merely attending to the technical weaknesses of administration on a large scale.[39]

When we reach this stage, we have two available alternatives. We can either take the high road or the low road.[40] The high road leads to macroscopic patterns for organizing massive units. High-road ideals such as capitalism, communism, and socialism have much to say for the nature of nation states, but they provide few guidelines for lower levels of organization. This accentuates the greater expediency of the second alternative, the low road. Values are not forgotten as part of the luggage on this trip, but instead are oriented to structural properties and organizational techniques.

The low road is not alien to Britain. The value traditionally placed on pragmatism would seem to encourage it. Furthermore, various recommendations have already been propounded that would accentuate its adoption. One analyst of the British welfare state notes that in Britain's "haphazard methods of development, we have neglected to consider the possibility of new methods of administration to meet the needs of a changing society, and so have become straddled with traditional administrative systems designed to serve the limited range of governmental functions in the nineteenth century." [41]

As a first step on the low road, some analysts look toward the elimination of hierarchy and the creation in its place of task coordination and mutual interdependence.[42] With no need to protect the old status positions, public officials would recognize the need for cooperation and the uselessness of competition. The hierarchical arrangement represses a common conscience. Mutual interdependence encourages one. Without status positions to clamor for, without "presentations" to worry about, esteem becomes a more important goal. "For esteem one competes with himself. For status one competes with others." [43] Cohesion allows a much greater range of innovation, as well as a much smaller range of rules and codes that inhibit initiation.

Alternative bureaucratic structures, according to some commentators, should be based on the assumption that the primary mentality and the resulting coercion-compromise pattern of behavior do not encompass the whole of human experience. If the institutions of the primary mentality frustrate the individual's attempt to grow in a self-actualizing, humanistic direction, then institutional alternatives must create a special interpersonal climate to nourish growth and diminish threat and alienation. This is possible by modeling structures on a "collaboration-consensus" basis. "In coercion-compromise systems, superordinate power is used to control behavior. In collaboration-consensus systems, control is achieved through agreement on goals, coupled with a communicative system which provides continuous feedback of results, *so that members can steer themselves*." [44]

This is not a repudiation of leadership. Rather than the leader being an agent of higher authority, he becomes a catalyst in the maintenance of communication and consensus among independent organizational units. This structure encourages the building of interpersonal and intergroup relations that support innovation and experimentation. Consistent with the broader assumptions of self-actualization, the organization member recognizes that he cannot attain his goals without the active collaboration of others and that they in turn cannot serve him as resources unless he is open and genuine in expressing his feelings and concerns. This builds mutual trust and commitment into the structure. The true freedom of the individual (defined more in terms of personal fulfillment than instrumental freedom, which the primary mentality promises) is actually encouraged by the nature of the structure.[45] It is not necessary for man to depend only on some sort of inner self-mastery or "reflective thought" to counteract the bureaucratic environment.

This sort of counterbureaucratic system suggests an obvious alignment between structure and broader social relations. If we are to assume the validity of such a redefined relation among healthy human beings, the elements of congruence, empathy, and genuineness are undoubtedly recognized as components. Congruence suggests that the inner world and outer world are in tune with each other. This relates to the individual and his organizational environment, as well as an organization of interdependent individuals and broader society. Empathy suggests the effort to understand deeply the other person. Genuineness makes incongruous any bluffing techniques, bargaining, and attempts to dominate.

To implement the spirit of these ideals into relations with clients necessitates a re-evaluation of the role of the client. The contemporary interaction, marked by subordination, segmentation of problem, rigidity, impersonality, and "efficiency," is consistent only with an increasingly irrelevant primary mentality. The proponents of the "dialectical organization" aim toward meeting the needs of the clientele—needs that are never finally established. Such an organization creates the necessity for "existential responsibility" by organization members. It also demands a constant synthesizing of goals (and conflict over them) which gives rise to behavior based on much more client participation to provide the necessary feedback.[46]

Meanwhile, as we have said, these necessities have not permeated the mentality of British analysts, much less broader public opinion. Without much absorption, the prospects of bureaucratic innovation might seem dim indeed. But its empirically tested validity suggests that a promising alternative to the perennial search for remedies exists for Britain.

RE-ENTER THE OMBUDSMAN

One might have thought that something like the ombudsman would provide the means to attain many of the organizational ideals described above. Of course the ombudsman in Britain emerged from an awareness of the inadequacy of structures to protect the individual from faulty administrative decision. It was also directed to strengthen the weaknesses of parliamentary control. We have already suggested that there is little innovation here. But regardless of what people thought the ombudsman would do, its functions seem to have far-reaching implications upon the administration of the post-welfare state. It personifies a humanistic orientation which emerged in Britain in the crisis of the mid-1950s. The search then was for a means to provide citizen satisfaction over administration.

To some the ombudsman is a negative check on bureaucratic vice. But its operation might as easily be defined as an attempt to secure a positive effort of imagination and kindness from public officials. One commentator has identified the ombudsman's proponents as the "cult of bureaucratic humanity." [47] Further consistent with twentieth-century trends, the existence of a parliamentary commissioner could theoretically encourage the initiative and sensibility of public officials, minimizing formal administrative codes of justice administered by formal bodies. Initially, then, the ombudsman in Britain would seem to satisfy a form of "existential responsibility."

This characteristic is emphasized by his method of investigation. The inquiry is not meant to expose the public official involved. Civil servants are therefore less likely to feel their positions threatened by public scrutiny. By investigating a decision wherever it goes wrong, the ombudsman could disregard the hierarchical structure. By working with officials rather than calling for public testimonial, an atmosphere of cooperation could be generated. As the ombudsman detects broader administrative deficiencies over time, his process of correction could be one of mutual collaboration with officials concerned. Gradually a system of mutual interdependence could develop by which feedback about administrative decisions from the citizens would be assured. This sort of participation cannot be overlooked. To be able to determine where administrative policies go awry in a day-to-day application and to alter practices based upon grievances is a large step toward the ideal of internal innovation, "continuous adjustive development." [48]

Much of this optimism about the ombudsman's theoretical role as a component of the counterbureaucratic model depends on its statutory design and intention. Perhaps the narrow perspective of the British office and its creators would be enough to create skepticism. If not, three years of ombudsman operations in Britain will dampen most enthusiastic proponents. Remember that the ombudsman emerged from a new concern over the rights of the individual. But remember, too, that the concern was voiced in terms of procedural safeguards. This orientation was wholly consistent, of course, with the spirit of the modified legal method. The ombudsman was to be administrative justice personified.

Not surprisingly, as a procedural watchdog Britain's ombudsman is not oriented toward bureaucratic innovation. Again, if the parliamentary commissioner can find no defect in the procedures used by officials, he will not rule on a case. Heavy criticism has been levied against the narrow interpretation of "maladministration," which the first ombudsman has assumed.[49]

Second, the parliamentary commissioner is limited by nature to the review of decisions after they have been made and after their impact is felt. Based on grievances, his influence is *a posteriori*. This is not unimportant over a wide range of governmental decisions. But active government requires something more than the attainment of *a posteriori* justice. The ombudsman might indirectly provide *a priori* participation by presenting patterns of defects from which general lessons might be learned. Yet the British office is not empowered to recommend administrative changes, even in individual cases. Furthermore, the cases are treated by the departments as somewhat exceptional.[50]

A priori participation is becoming a crucial necessity. Government action in the post-welfare state is definable in the same terms as any major technological achievement today: intricately planned, thoroughly predictable, and already done except for the mere doing of it. *A priori* participation (or governmental input) in the post-welfare state is precisely the means by which individuals determine their future. This, not mending, is the demand for the future.

Third, the ombudsman investigation is conducted within the department on the same basis as the parliamentary question. Great importance is placed on the hierarchical arrangements of the bureaucracy. While investigation is carried on behind the minister's back, it seldom reaches very deeply into the organizational structure. Both hierarchy and traditional responsibility are strengthened.[51]

Analysis of the ombudsman's client relations reveals more serious difficulties. The dialectical organization is based on client participation, but the ombudsman in Britain is not likely to help those most in need of his services. This has occurred despite a growing awareness in Britain that the working class is poor at articulating grievances. One British commentator has suggested that three conditions are necessary for the successful voicing of grievances: the will to complain and to persist in one's complaint, some knowledge of the law and where to complain, and the appropriate machinery for dealing with complaints.[52] The working class in Britain is unlikely to meet the first two conditions. Unable for generations to right grievances, they have adopted a stoic attitude of acceptance. Defeatism combined with ignorance ensure that most of the time their grievances are not even voiced, let alone righted.

While the ombudsman theoretically acts as a middle man, his operations require that the citizen come to him (complicated by the fact that complaints are sent first to M.P.s). This initiative may be beyond an individual's psychological or technical abilities. The citizen must feel motivated to write a letter and must have the ability to do so. The ombudsman is inherently passive in an emerging era that requires an active mediator willing to search out discontent and to build meaningful relations between governors and governed. As it stands today, only the advantaged classes are likely to use any improved machinery of democratic pressure.

The parliamentary commissioner in Britain is further hampered by his centralized position. It was thought that a prominent figure located at the center of power would be attractive to the citizenry. This is just another example of an attitude from a fading era. It is more reasonable to assume that this centralized position is viewed just as remotely as other organs of government are. The mystique of power has increasingly little relevance to those seeking a genuine human connection.

It is obviously impossible to look upon the ombudsman as a means to cure administrative defects. In terms of future administrative behavior, the ombudsman's operations provide little impetus for change. They can only be a partial solution to limited bureaucratic technical faults in procedure.

PROSPECTS FOR CHANGE

Bureaucratic innovation promises new facilities for growth, change, and
adaptation to future environmental challenges. But Britain's latest and
potentially most radical innovation has been watered down to such an
extent that it provides little indication of a willingness to step over the
threshold. Does this, combined with a relatively low level of awareness
of bureaucratic alternatives, indicate a bleak future for the formulation
of administrative doctrine and normative theory that squares more
closely with administrative facts?

The ombudsman is a difficult guide to the real answer. The office
has been created in Britain at a time when the responsibility of individual civil servants to the hierarchy, to Parliament, to the courts, and to
citizens generally is confused. According to one prominent sociologist,
"institutions that have not been deliberately established are more difficult in offering unequivocal standards . . ." [53] so that any change is difficult to evaluate. The ombudsman poses a further problem. It is a
transferred innovation from outside the system. Any stated objectives
were general, and the ombudsman was accepted by the political elite for
his value as a useful symbol of political advertising during a general
election.

THE PATTERN

Given the absence of recent indicators, we can only speculate about the
direction in which Britain is headed. "Some think in terms of a Cause,
a New Inspiration, an Ideal, which will burst upon the nation with overwhelming impact and generate vast new energies to overcome all events
and make good the errors and omissions of the past." [54] Yet the pattern
of future change in a traditional society will most likely have some relation to past orientations. Dramatics is not part of the British scene.

Britain is known to have a political culture marked by interpersonal trust and system support. This orientation may be affected by
contemporary mobility, demands of urban living, and diminishing com-

munity environment. Yet Britain may still be better equipped to embark upon change than its neighbor across the Atlantic. (There, the pervasive obsession with status and success, achieved through competition with others as objects, may have eroded man's ability to recognize community.) Demands for change in Britain do not seem to generate a devastating backlash, and extreme polarization over significant issues (excluding ethnic hostilities) does not yet mark patterns of change. This may allow the system to synthesize demands and to embark upon significant adjustments in relative peace. "The British are not particularly averse to even profound changes if they occur gradually over an extended period." [55]

This suggests that we cannot consider the future of public administration in a vacuum despite its growing autonomy. Not only is its *changing nature* affected by established patterns but it also receives its very legitimacy and authority from a *context:* It is a creation of the political system to administer political and social policies. A consideration of future relations between the citizen and the state should assume its broader context—the context of political and social structures.

THE POLITICS OF POST-WELFARE BRITAIN

It is no secret that governments have been slower than big business to get into speculation activity.[56] This is true in Britain. The most energetic organ, the Committee of the Next Thirty Years, is only a few years old and has produced one publication which discusses the relation between forecasting and the social sciences.[57] It is therefore impossible to rely on British initiatives at this point. Part of the difficulty is, of course, that no one can establish anything that does not exist. Futurists have no mystical means for ascertaining the shape of tomorrow. No less real, on the practical level, is the problem that while some kinds of data (i.e., econometrics) may provide a basis for quantitative speculation, it is difficult to foresee the detailed results of change in terms of changing political and social structures.

"It would be splendid if someone could, like de Tocqueville a hundred years ago, find a living model in the present which would make it possible to discern the essential elements of the society of the future." [58] Without a living model, one approach to the future is to begin with the supposition that the future will differ from the present in the same way as the present differs from the past. Extrapolation of trends would generate a set of "futuribles" about the political system from top to bottom.

CRUDE EXTRAPOLATION

Starting at the highest (i.e., the most centralized) level of the political system, we might expect the complexity of the technological system to engender greater expertise on the part of the representatives.[59] In this way representatives might understand developments in order to translate them to the citizenry and to deal with them in their deliberations. They might be better equipped to influence administrators. M.P.s are presently experts in one field—expenditure of the money Parliament votes for public purposes. In the future they can be expected to build on that expertise in broader areas. The four specialized Select Committees presently in existence (public accounts, estimates, statutory instruments, and nationalized industries) can provide a possible basis for such an extension of expertise.

Those who would seek to expand the scope of legislative competence have not issued a call for a return to "classical Parliamentarianism"—an attempt to restore the legislative role that the twentieth century has so strikingly diminished. Instead, reforms would involve new mechanisms that can only be utilized if the amateur mentality is thrown off.

Broadened government expertise is also envisioned in terms of equipping the Minister with his own experts (Cabinet du Ministre) so that he may engage in real business in his department from the outset.

Building on present expectations of future needs could lead to implications beyond better personal equipment. Proponents of parliamentary reform see in the development of small specialist committees the eventual growth of expert "hybrid committees." These committees would not only contain members of Parliament along with representatives of interest groups but civil servants as well. All interests which

CITIZEN, ADMINISTRATION, AND POLITICS 171

now participate in a disjointed process would be represented at a coherent policy-making level.

This outlook has been encouraged by the imperatives created by possible British entry into the Common Market. The prospects of broad economic cooperation between Britain and the Continent suggest the exchange of broad technical knowledge. It is not unrealistic for some to expect that such relations will encourage a more articulate band of civil servants with a new opportunity to comment on public issues (civil servants are today the largest group in Britain whose freedom of expression is so curtailed), as well as a new specimen of professional M.P. As the economic world becomes smaller, and as the need to solve environmental problems becomes a more widespread international imperative, administrators and M.P.s would be hived off for international duties in international parliaments and administrations.[60]

This may seem to many a reversal of the separation of powers doctrine. Cooperation among decision-makers increasingly develops a type of professional administrator cum political operator cum lobbyist. The separation of powers becomes a mixture of powers.

Government seen in these terms carries implications for traditional parliamentary behavior. One might expect Parliament to become irrelevant relative to the executive-administrative apparatus of superindustrial society. If Parliament provides only a battlefield for political power games, then indeed its role will be increasingly inconsistent with, for example, the work of hybrid committees. It is not an accident that the front benches of Parliament were designed to be separated by the distance of two sword lengths. But one Labor M.P. in a widely publicized book on parliamentary warfare articulated a growing awareness when he said "the official front bench struggle is 90% make believe." [61]

While Parliament might remain an important assembly place for a public debate on policy, we would expect that debate to be supplemented increasingly at other places. As for parliamentary games, the strong whip system will be seen as a method of curtailing M.P. independence and will be the object of increasing disfavor by M.P.s who desire to exercise their own judgment.

This outlook reaches the very heart of party politics. It is unrealistic to assume that a democratic nation will not maintain major competing political parties from which the people choose their government. Yet political parties will find that the mere competition for power will be inadequate for the citizens of post-welfare Britain. Already some believe that the "simplification of issues and dividing lines—allegedly required in order to help the simple minded voter to take sides—has been carried too far." [62] It is becoming increasingly apparent that the political parties are beginning to face the problem the churches have had to recognize. They cannot take faith for granted. They must demonstrate their relevance. An overwhelming orientation toward either obtaining or maintaining positions of power has forced the parties into the same behavior that divides bureaucracies and makes them inherently contradictory. Status orientation, which includes a clamor for accreditation, is increasingly exemplified by the techniques of image-advertising and the reduction of issues to symbols. [63]

Determining the genuine *needs* of society in the context of continual change will mark the role of the party in the future. While significant ideological gaps between party programs will be unlikely, preference will undoubtedly remain that tends to shade the parties differently. Yet it is unlikely that political parties will be able singlehandedly to assess the demands and needs of the post-welfare society. For this reason we must recognize their role in encouraging a more popular pluralism—citizens' groups organized to counterbalance the influence of existing power groups in the emerging "techno-structure."

A necessary goal of post-welfare society, then, is to expose the existing oligarchies in order to broaden public pressure and let the decision-makers know what the people think. The usefulness of pressure groups has already been established; they not only present ideas to decision-makers but also are used in implementing policy decisions. The increasing prevalence of popular pressure groups will act as a countervailing power to business interests and professional bodies on the one hand and bureaucracy on the other. "The scale of organization in our society has grown so large that only through large-scale organization does it seem possible to have a significant impact." [64] The creation of the National Economic Development Council (NEDC) and the Economic Development Committees (little Neddies) for individual industries have provided the pattern for semiautonomous bodies "appointed to listen for and respond to public feeling about specific problems." [65] The information provided by Abel-Smith and Townsend's *The Poor and the Poorest* generated the creation of a Child Poverty Action Group (CPAG). In turn, the group "forced the government to think about the kind of measures which were needed and . . . encouraged social workers and voluntary groups throughout the country to collect information in a form which would drive the Government to reach decisions." [66] The members of the Campaign Against Racial Discrimination (CARD) were made members of an official body, the National Committee for Commonwealth Immigrants. The Confederation of the Advancement of State Education (CASE) is regularly consulted by the Ministry of Science and Education.

Popular pressure groups (or citizen groups) have become institutionalized means on a small scale to publicize meetings between people and government. Popular groups bring government closer to the people for a more meaningful relationship. But the crucial component has been the capacity of such groups to wield countervailing force. This is a negative sort of access to democratic power and involves people only in terms of their complaints. More promising for the future are the positive features that result when groups actually engage in solving problems and running the affairs that concern the "public" of which they are a part. In the attempt to reverse resentment against the remote-controlled society, government will find it useful to encourage, even help finance, citizens' efforts to become involved. [67]

One innovation has been suggested to facilitate the contact outside party politics: a network of "consumer shops." [68] A neighborhood center, manned by a social service expert or lawyer and a consumer expert, would advise and refer, write letters, mediate between an aggrieved citizen and the local councilors or manufacturers, and provide legal aid. The shop would also maintain continuing surveys of both consumer goods and social services. Its presence would supply the government with an indication of the effectiveness of administrative efforts. Its independence would allow problems or growing needs to rise to the surface and be acted upon—providing the source for more pressure groups. The potential importance of consumer shops is heightened by growing awareness of the inadequacy of the existing Consumer Association and the cooperative movement, and the success of the Citizen's Advice Bureau and realistic efforts of the British Consumer Council.

It is difficult to envision the future of democratic participation outside the context of power. Britain can learn from the American poverty program that power without service is unstable. Giving more power to the people is only a means to an end—a means to direct any existing revulsion and anger at the present to future actions. But given a *service* mentality, administrators and politicians would realize that centralism works against service in a country of Britain's size. In order to have a self-regulating adaptive system, providing a meaningful and continuing contact between governors and governed, a greater or lesser degree of decentralization is required.

Decentralization is becoming a natural tendency, as the environment to be dealt with becomes more complex. Less centralized and more self-adaptive mechanisms are an ideal alternative to both the government that finds it increasingly difficult to administer policies from the top, and to the citizen who finds it increasingly difficult to understand and respect a complex, centralized decision-making center. In this sense devolution is a defense mechanism to downgrade complexity.

Britain has already embarked on this trip through, for example, the Town and Country Planning Act, which touches on the principle of "officer responsibility" to determine planning applications on the spot. Two crucial landmark publications with much more grandiose implications appeared in 1969: the *Report of the Royal Commission on Local Government in England* (Maude Report) and the *Report of the Royal Commission on Local Government in Scotland* (Wheatley Report). The Wheatley Report and the Maude Report both recommend a design to take government into the twenty-first century by restoring credibility to local government. Wheatley is particularly emphatic about granting power to an upper tier of local authority—the region. Wheatley also suggests that all local authorities should have a "general competence" to undertake any project that would be for the good of the community. (Presently they can only do what specific laws of Parliament empower them to do.) Both Wheatley and Maude base their recommendations on the principle that the citizen must have his say and that the system must be responsive to his demands. Devolution is seen as the key.

We have skipped our way from the very largest of representative bodies (a European Parliament or a European Civil Service) through the role of the national parties and the national representation chamber to the regions and to small areas where a sort of direct democracy seems likely to mark the post-welfare state. It must be abundantly clear by now that while important kernels of truth about the future may exist in the preceding catalogue of expectations, the approach has been based on simple extrapolation on this kind of model: "If a life span of man has become longer, it will become longer still; the number of work hours has decreased, it will decrease yet further; the standard of living has risen, it will rise even more." A good percentage of the futuribles of this method are the result of present trends. This is not altogether useless, but there are limitations. First, simple projections can be logically liable to absurd conclusions. For example, one British commentator noted that, given the orientation toward science (including graduates, societies, and publications) and the demand for electronics and aviation, "within about 100 years everyone of us would be a scientist, the entire national output would be absorbed in research, and we should be spending most of our lives airborne at 40,000 feet." [69] Second, such an approach may come up with manifestly wrong predictions. The variables chosen to determine a pattern to carry us into the future may be the wrong ones. Again, such an approach may be useful for predicting cycles of consumption, life spans, and even social stratification, but its usefulness for political-system definition seems limited. We would be better off with a more sophisticated outlook.

THE DYNAMICS OF POST-WELFARE POLITICS

Some of what we have been saying is based on the assumption that the future would be created more democratically than now seems likely. These futuribles on principle cannot be overlooked. But the larger bulk of this kind of prediction is based on the fact that institutions resist going out of business more than they resist anything else. To maintain a tolerable level of acquiescence, reforms are administered. The future in these terms is one in which the catching-up, or reactive, patterns of the welfare state are perpetuated. Such a mentality may indeed be more attuned to the people. But it is likely to be attuned to pure revulsion. Not only is this a system based upon reaction (which is a poor way to build the future) but also it will become an increasingly irrelevant mode of operation in a technological age in which change is irreversible. More important, it conditions the people to revolt against what *is* rather than effectively participating in what they want it to be. This kind of reform does not train people to worry about the future.

We have already indicated as an alternative to bureaucracy a more dynamic, less straight-line future by means of the adaptive, dialectical organization. There seems to be some seeds in this from which more open-ended yet more significant futuribles about the over-all political system might grow.

It is not impossible to see post-welfare politics in terms of a collaboration-consensus model. This model assumes a constant tension to redefine means to general goals. The political system might find it increasingly necessary to assume a more adaptive approach in which it could meet the most extreme shift in the environment. It must recognize that policy decisions may create its own opposite to which they must be able to react. But it must be prepared to do more. It must, in fact, foster diversity and dissent in order to determine the way people feel about those features of society that are likely to be in existence a generation away. Rather than having both feet firmly planted in the technostructure, political systems might find it more important to make themselves the repository of existential responsibility.

What we are dealing with, then, is a political future in which the system is not a more effective, efficient component of an increasingly complex technostructure, but a system that embodies the means to reconstruct a democratic system under the conditions of high technology. Some futurists have pointed to a specific future-oriented technique within this framework by members of the citizenry. A desirable goal is determined, and that future is simply created. Restaurant sit-ins in the United States were based on a future in which the desirability of integrated eating places was established. The technique was not to petition legislatures, not to petition the owners of segregated restaurants, but simply to integrate. The future had been created in the present, and it would rest upon those who have the power of law and the power of ownership in their hands to decide how to respond to that creation.[70]

The political system might therefore be designed to act when confronted with those who are willing to build the future now. Its relevance would increasingly be based on the ability to determine whether building any particular future in the present is either too challenging, or too irrelevant, to permit its continuation. I say "increasingly" because not only are more people going to be involved in this method of building *now* what they want to exist in the future but also the method will be more attuned to recognizable ideals which cannot be overlooked. (The 1969 squatters' movement in London is a salient, British example of creating a future to which society and the political system must react. While the massive occupation of a Piccadilly mansion was thin on ethic, the method was there.)

This final point in a rough outline of creative disorder suggests that politics in the post-welfare state will be more than a pragmatic planning affair. It must be abundantly clear that the demise of ideology is inherently impossible in post-welfare politics on this order. Instead, we will witness the death of neutrality. Some futuribles are a systematic appraisal based on the laws that govern the physical world. But what will mark the politics of the post-welfare era is decision-making that goes beyond useful sums to the vision of society and the consequent decisions over means by which societal values are realized. As contemporary consciousness accepts that the "golden age" is in front of us, it will adjust its orientation to desirable futures.

For government, orienting to the future means anticipating what people think will be desirable. This means scanning the social roots of ideologies to determine basic values and to anticipate how those values will relate to specific future issues. This is not a politics of *ad hoc* values, for values cannot periodically emerge to meet new situations. At the same time it is not a politics of timeless truths in the traditional sense. It is rather a politics in which means and end are not only consistent, but converging.

The most difficult question of all, of course, is: "Which values?" Individualism is an excellent example, for we have already seen how it has been variously extended in the changing conditions of twentieth-century Britain. Individualism has been translated into new deprivatized, active, and responsible directions in an attempt to obtain not only individual salvation but also the salvation of society. It has given meaning to a new freedom based on hope, anticipation, and openness. It has been adopted by a "new class"—those whose valued property is what they carry in their heads. The face of the new class *is* politics, and the ideology is based on education, culture, and a definition of conscience. Their property is increased not in the old way of accumulating things, but in a new way which seeks meaningful experiences.[71]

In terms of relations beyond the shores of Britain, the dynamics of the future in these terms has suggested to some that *transnational* rather than *international* arrangements would develop. McLuhan's global village concept describes the possibilities only generally. Within that global awareness would develop world associations which would be based largely on the interest-group model—meeting to associate and share experiences but sometimes resolving to influence or put pressure on this or that government. This development seems much more consistent with the firm individualistic pattern of nation states, which prohibits international conglomeration with commensurate loss of individual sovereignty.

But what are the indications that Britain is headed toward such a future at all?

THE FRONT OF DISCONTENT

First, there is an obvious growth of the "new class" mentioned above. The parliamentary system, Maine said in the mineteenth century, "was listening nervously at one end of a speaking tube which receives at its other end the suggestions of a lower intelligence." But the system will be listening all the more nervously "now that the suggestions are not couched as suggestions, the speaking tube has become an amplifier, and the democracy does not have a lower intelligence. The state has educated its masters." [72]

Second, even without a visible attack on the order of action politics in other Western countries, we can be fairly certain that the seeds of change are being nourished by discontent and alternative methods. The attack is supported most vocally by British students. Despite a certain "issue lag," the rhetoric indicates the same discontent over the "overdeveloped" society with its large bureaucracies in government, corporations, trade unions, and universities. Despite lower output, British students see not only the openly authoritarian or totalitarian society as an enemy, but the administered, bureaucratic, dehumanized one as well. The protest is a protest "against a society whose standards of behavior are determined by the exigencies of industrial planning, the domination of things." [73]

Students do not form the only front of discontent in Britain. What seems unique is that the Establishment in Britain is willing to recognize what lies beyond an often flimsy facade as "[a]n important and valid criticism of the political and social structures. . . . We are simply not adjusting our institutions fast enough to maintain the proper amount of communication and the proper balance of power between the citizen and his government." [74]

Protests have arisen from representatives of the "elite," such as the former leader of the Liberal party who recently spoke out against "technical determinism."

The characteristic of democracy is that it is open, mobile, elective, and participatory. Its motive force is, to put it crudely, protest. It is personal. It appreciates argument and dissent. The characteristics of bureaucracy are that it is secretive, rigid, non-elective, hierarchical. It does not appreciate mobility or dissent. . . . I reject the view that the bureaucratic expert knows best.[75]

Britain's former Minister of Technology, Mr. Anthony Benn, has also voiced concern. Basing the discontent of students and people in industry on modern technology, Mr. Benn said, "We are moving rapidly toward a situation where the pressure for the redistribution of political power will have to be faced as a major political issue. Beyond parliamentary democracy as we know it we will have to find a new popular democracy to replace it." [76] Mr. Benn told Rolls Royce workers that the government had underestimated the desire of the ordinary people to participate fully in the life of the community and the decisions that were made.[77]

The *Times* responded editorially that Mr. Benn's statements dealt with the greatest challenge facing democracy today. It commented further on the paradox of modern technological society: specialist knowledge and centralized decision-making versus a more highly educated population and broader desires to make decisions. This paradox has produced a dangerous gap between public opinion and government.[78]

Another respected newspaper has joined the cause. An *Observer* political writer notes that public opinion polls record considerable cynicism about the integrity of politicians. The widespread support for a coalition government—preferably of a managerial kind—indicates dissatisfaction with the party system. Sociologists are suggesting that political attitudes based on traditional class loyalty may be loosening. This is partly based on the feeling that the "politicians have worked out the mine of their own ideas." We have not reached the end of ideology—only the end of the present ideologies. "In short, the present discontents may reflect an unformulated, perhaps even unconscious awareness that the politicians are the prisoners of their own increasingly irrelevant assumptions." [79]

The writer notes that the most convincing arguments for a new pack of cards and revised rules of the game come from the people who defy neat pigeonholing. Perhaps the "collectivist" tradition and style are losing their attraction.[80] He suggests that something big is stirring. "What we are witnessing, I think, is the birth of a new kind of individualism . . . recognizably different from the collectivism of the first part of the twentieth century. This is the real challenge to the political system." [81]

The tyranny of governmental power has been noted by others within the British Establishment. Yet what is particularly significant is that these attacks against the paternalism which influenced social reform in the past are being joined by demands from the deprived themselves. Organizations *of* the poor are growing. Action politics is being mobilized by unmarried mothers, the handicapped, immigrants, and those in poverty. "Although in Britain client organizations are in their infancy, the fact of their birth means that a new social power is at hand." [82]

New groups of people are recognizing the advantages of indigenous organizations. Their threat can be more effective pressure on government than the academic findings of middle-class pressure groups. Second, they are much better equipped to communicate knowledge of existing rights and benefits. These developments follow what has become established as an active force in the United States—the so-called Welfare Rights Movement. The spirit, if not the name, of Saul Alinsky has been transferred to Britain, and client power groups are encouraged by the fact that an administrative fortress suddenly becomes responsive to its clients after an Alinsky-type campaign. Social workers are beginning to realize that they must take a stand regarding client power. If they identify with the groups from the start, the credibility gap between social work and social reform need not be perpetuated. All of this suggests an emerging transnationalism.

SUMMARY

It would seem as if the ingredients for change are at hand. People are agreed that they have had enough. Future alternatives are unique in providing a means, from the highest to the lowest unit of government, by which efficiency and participation might converge. A technology of social rebellion is emerging, which not only allows grievances to be voiced but also allows a future to be built.

"What matters most about the year 2000 are not the gadgets . . . but the kinds of social arrangements that can deal adequately with the problems we shall confront." [83] Lord Campbell of Eskan recently said, "It is intelligible and justifiable to encourage efficiency in order to achieve humanity, but never to permit inhumanity for the sake of disembodied efficiency." On the basis of the ingredients present in Britain, one might easily view Britain's future with hope, a hope sustained by the presence of a basic humanistic orientation within the political system and a faith in the dignity of the individual. Yet that hope must be nurtured so that the continuously adaptive society can be instated before society is overcome by events. If it is not, the means by which the freedom of the individual is attained—a freedom that means nonmanipulative self-fulfillment through genuine relations with others—will fade beyond revival, and with it man's ability to be Man.

Notes

1. Robert T. Golembiewski, *Men, Management, and Morality: Toward a New Organizational Ethic* (New York, 1965), p. 4.

2. William Krasner, "How to Live with Bureaucracy, and Win," *New Society* (July 25, 1968), p. 115.

3. H. Finer, *The Theory and Practice of Modern Government* (London, 1954), p. 29.

4. Mac Nicholson, *The System: The Misgovernment of Modern Britain* (London, 1967), p. 181.

5. *Ibid.,* p. 184.

6. Landmarks in attempts to use the courts to provide administrative justice are found, for example, in the House of Lords decision in *Local Government Board v. Arlidge* (1915), A. C. 120 (which involved a closing order); *Errington v. Minister of Health* (1935), I. K. B. 249 (which also involved a closing order); and *Liversidge v. Anderson* (1942), A.C. 206 (which concerned wide ministerial power granted by arbitrary statutory language that excluded review by the courts).

7. *Report on the Committee on Ministers' Powers,* Cmd. 4060 (London, H.M.S.O., 1932).

8. Hewart held a conspiratorial theory which "gave the impression that when honest men were abed civil servants were stalking the streets in the dead of night disguised in masks and cloaks and with dagger in hand waiting to pounce on any undefended powers which they might be able to snatch for their fell purposes." See William A. Robson, "Administrative Law," in Morris Ginsberg, ed., *Law and Opinion in England in the 20th Century* (London, 1959), p. 198.

9. From private correspondence with Professor David Mitrany during 1968.

10. Geoffrey Marshall, "Administration, Administrative Law and Administrative Discretion: The United Kingdom," *International Political Science Association Proceedings* (Brussels, 1967), p. 10.

11. C. H. Hamson, "The Real Lesson of Crichel Down," *Public Administration,* 32 (1954), 385. For the details, see *Public Inquiry into the Disposal of Land at Crichel Down,* Cmd. 9176 (London, H.M.S.O., 1954).

12. Robson, "Administrative Law," p. 199.

13. *Report of the Committee on Administrative Tribunals and Inquiries,* Cmnd. 4060 (London, H.M.S.O., 1957). Recognizing that "Tribunals are not ordinary courts, but neither are they appendages of Government departments, . . ." (para. 40), the committee recommended the application of natural justice to all tribunal proceedings. To assure that publicity of proceedings, clear procedures, and independence from departments were achieved, the committee recommended a Council on Tribunals system to keep the constitution and working of tribunals under continuous review. This and other recommendations were carried into effect by the *Tribunals and Inquires Act, 1958.*

14. Individual rights can be understood in the context of the so-called individualistic ethic, which stresses the laws of God and nature and the survival of the fittest. This ethic was a great boost for anything that was trying to get started, like business. But it turned out to be inadequate for keeping the enterprise going. See Golembiewski, *Men, Management, and Morality,* especially Chapter 1.

15. David Mitrany, "Comment on Contributed Papers," *International Political Science Association Proceedings* (Geneva, 1964).

16. It is not difficult to identify communal goods, particularly with a growing emphasis today on the environment. Clean air is an example. See Bell, "Toward the Year 2000—Work in Progress," *Daedalus,* 96 (1967), 964.

17. For an analysis of unofficial bodies to speak for the citizen, see Luch Syson and Rosiland Brooke, "The Voice of the Consumer," in Brian Lapping and Giles Radice, eds., *More Power to the People* (London, 1968), pp. 57–75.

18. Brian Chapman, *British Government Observed* (London, 1959) and Bernard Crick, *The Reform of Parliament* (London, 1964).

19. *Justice, the Citizen and the Administration: The Redress of Grievances* (The Whyatt Report) (London, 1961).

20. Ben Whitaker, *Participation and Poverty* (London, 1963).

21. Herbert Marcuse, *One-Dimensional Man* (Boston, 1964), p. xv.

22. Sjoberg, Hancock, and White, *Politics in the Post-Welfare State: A Comparison of the United States and Sweden* (Bloomington, Ind., 1967), p. 9.

23. Peter Blau, *Bureaucracy in a Modern Society* (New York, 1956), p. 18.

24. Victor A. Thompson, *Modern Organization* (New York, 1961), p. 19.

25. For the analyses supporting this terminology, see Erving Goffman, *The Presentation of Self in Everyday Life* (New York, 1959).

26. Thompson, *Modern Organization,* especially Chapter 7.

27. A summary article presents the dominant arguments. See Herbert A. Shepard, "Changing Interpersonal and Intergroup Relationships in Organizations," in James C. Marsh, ed., *Handbook of Organizations* (Chicago, 1965), pp. 1115–43.

28. The effort to minimize tension has generated less blatant, more persuasive techniques. Note the application of "human relations," "employee participation," and employee communication schemes in modern bureaucracies. "These programs are functional because they supply management with a human technology entirely consistent with the values of *La Technique.*"

William G. Scott, "Organization Government: The Prospects for a Truly Participative System," *Public Administration Review,* 29 (1969), 48. As long as the coercion-compromise structure remains, these innovations only "add one more manipulative complication to an already somewhat paranoid world." Shepard, *Changing Relationships,* p. 1124.

29. Thompson, *Modern Organization,* p. 193.

30. White, "The Dialectical Organization: An Alternative to Bureaucracy," *Public Administration Review,* 29 (1969), 33. This contribution marks a firm guidepost in an area little touched by analysts of the bureaucratic process and personality.

31. *Ibid.,* p. 36. White bases his value judgments on an empirical study of a client-centered agency. See Sjoberg, Richard Brymer, and Buford Farris, "Bureaucracy and the Lower Class," *Sociology and Social Research,* 50 (April 1966), 325–37.

32. *Ibid.,* p. 327.

33. White, "The Dialectical Organization," p. 34.

34. Herbert J. Spiro, *Government by Constitution* (New York, 1959), p. 259.

35. E. Strauss, *The Ruling Servants* (London, 1961), p. 85.

36. For one of the latest analyses of the central role of bureaucratic power, see Henry A. Kissinger, *American Foreign Policy* (New York, 1969).

37. This is not to say that the American stuff stays put. The experiments of I.B.M. and the California-based Security Pacific Bank have generated widespread interest; both turned their organization charts on the side and added a rating for competence. The publication of the book on which such "radical" moves are based was anticipated by Britain in late 1969. See Laurence J. Peter, *The Peter Principle: Why Things Always Go Wrong* (New York, 1969), in which the author analyzes the formula, "In a Hierarchy Every Employee Tends to Rise to his Level of Incompetence," and presents "Creative Incompetence" as an alternative to existing patterns of "hierarchiology" and bureaucratic escalation without a purpose.

38. Peter Self, reviewing Michael Crozier's *The Bureaucratic Phenomenon* in *Public Administration,* 43 (1965), 103–104.

39. There is nothing wrong with finding defects and Britain is not immune to the practice. See *Report of the Training of Civil Servants,* Cmnd. 6525, and *Committee on Civil Service Reform,* Cmnd. 7686. Such searching is important, but, as suggested here, it must be placed in broader perspective.

40. Golembiewski, *Men, Management, and Morality,* especially Chapter 1, uses the terminology in this context.

41. Marsh, *The Future of the Welfare State* (London, 1964) analyzes the "administrative juggernaut" in Britain.

42. Thompson, *Modern Organization,* especially Chapter 9.

43. *Ibid.,* p. 196.

44. Shepard, *Changing Relationships,* p. 1128. The emphasis is mine. This would seem a suitable basis for "teaching people to become self-monitoring . . ." implications in Peter, *The Peter Principle.*

45. This goal is consistent with Golembiewski's "Judeo-Christian" approach. "The primary and over-arching aim of life is Christian love—by which is meant the love of God and of neighbor. Implicit in this ideal of life is that the fulfillment of one's life is achieved through others." Golembiewski, *Men Management, and Morality,* especially Chapter 3.

46. See especially Sjoberg, Hancock, and White, *Politics in the Post-Welfare State,* pp. 28–30.

47. Schonfield, *Modern Capitalism: The Changing Balance of Public and Private Power* (London, 1965), p. 425.

48. Blau, *Bureaucracy,* p. 61.

49. Sir Edmund Compton, the first parliamentary commissioner, defined his role so narrowly as to make the first verdicts of maladministration almost trivial. The parliamentary select committee appointed to oversee his work found it necessary to recommend a broader definition. The ombudsman was encouraged to review a case in which the decision's effect was "thoroughly bad" or cases where there existed deficiencies in departmental processes for reviewing rules. (The committee emphasized that it was not for the commissioner to rewrite the government's administrative rules.) See *Second Report of the Select Committee on the P.C.A., Session 1967/68* (London, H.M.S.O., 1968).

50. Exceptional indeed! For example, a spokesman within the Ministry of Housing and Local Government told me that they had nearly 10,000 planning appeals in 1968—the main source of ombudsman complaints. Only 114 complaints were brought to the ombudsman, out of which 62 were investigated and 3 found to be cases of maladministration: a rate of .0003 per cent.

51. This would explain a certain amount of fear with which civil servants greet the ombudsman "file."

52. H. Glennerster, "Democracy and Class," in Lapping and Radice, eds., *More Power to the People,* p. 77.

53. Blau, *The Dynamics of Bureaucracy* (Chicago, 1955), p. 8.

54. Nicholson, *The System,* p. 395.

186   GREAT BRITAIN

55. Schonfield, "Thinking About the Future," *Encounter*, XXXII, No. 2 (February 1969), 19.

56. The exact label for future study has not yet been established, but several alternatives are available: "futurology" (Flechtheim), "conjecture" (de Jouvenal), and "futuristics" (World Future Society).

57. The Committee on the Next Thirty Years has been established as a wing of Britain's Social Science Research Council with Mark Abrams and Michael Young as chairmen. See Michael Young, ed., *Forecasting and the Social Sciences* (London, 1968).

58. Schonfield, "Thinking About the Future," *Encounter*, p. 15.

59. To equip the M.P. personally, some foresee such mundane but necessary steps as provisions for better facilities—including office space, secretarial staff, professional researchers, and a larger staff in the Commons library. At present there are eight graduate researchers. An M.P. may have an office and secretarial facilities only if he has a private income or is sponsored by a firm or trade union.

60. The best existing example of this is the European Commission of the E.E.C. Schonfield describes the "most radical and complicated set of reforms of our time . . ." in *Modern Capitalism*, pp. 404–10.

61. Christopher Mayhew, *Party Games* (London, 1969), p. 23.

62. Schonfield, *Modern Capitalism*, p. 403.

63. Outward manifestations of an unfortunate character are the parties' promises of greater economic growth. Such promises have raised expectations to an unrealistically high level, thereby creating a sense of national frustration.

64. Herbert Kaufman, "Administrative Decentralization and Political Power," *Public Administration Review*, 29 (January 1969), 5.

65. Lapping, "Can More Democracy Work?" in Lapping and Radice, *More Power to the People*, p. 183.

66. *Ibid.*, p. 178.

67. For its usefulness to be realized, a popular component must have open access to membership and ready access to existing political structures. If the road to post-welfare distribution is marked by discrimination in favor of the least fortunate, the road to post-welfare participation must be marked by discrimination in favor of the least articulate. But before "consumer syndicalism" (as Britain's "Open Group" terms this kind of popular participation) is achieved, governments will find it increasingly necessary to be mindful of the needs of those who are not represented in any way.

68. Consumer shops have been envisioned by Syson and Brooke in "The Voice of the Consumer," in Lapping and Radice, *More Power to the People,* pp. 73–75.

69. R. Cockburn, "Science, Defence and Society," Trueman Wood Memorial Lecture, Royal Society of Arts, London, February 1967.

70. Arthur Waskow, "Looking Forward: 1999," in Robert Jungk and Johan Galtung, eds., *Mankind 2000* (London, 1969), pp. 78–98. Waskow uses the Institute for Policy Studies as another example. The desirable future was the creation of many institutions in which social theory is learned from social action, and social action is derived from social theory. Rather than going to universities to argue for it or to foundations to set up study committees to look into it, the proponents *did* it. "And by doing it, created the strain, the tension which requires the rest of academia to attend to what we were doing, to decide whether it believed it was a good idea, and to move in that direction or against it." Waskow, p. 80.

71. For a discussion of the "new class," see Waskow, *ibid.,* p. 88.

72. The Open Group, "Social Reform in Centrifugal Society," *New Society* (September 11, 1969).

73. Stephen Spender, *The Year of the Young Rebels* (London, 1969), p. 78.

74. The *Times* (June 1, 1968).

75. Joe Grimmond, "Government vs. Governed," The *Times* (November 14, 1967).

76. The *Times* (May 27, 1968).   77. The *Times* (April 19, 1968).

78. *Ibid.*

79. Rudolf Klein, "Birth of the New Politics?" The *Observer* (March 30, 1969).

80. Golembiewski, *Men, Management, and Morality,* would, I believe, agree; his analysis of the Social Ethic depends on a positivistic scientism to achieve and guide the necessary "belongingness." See especially Chapter 2.

81. Klein, *Birth of the New Politics?*

82. Robert Holman, "Client Power," *New Society* (October 3, 1968), p. 645.

83. "The Year 2000: The Trajectory of an Idea," *Daedalus,* 97 (1967), 644.

DAVID HOWELL, M. P.

A Conservative View
of Political Change

"Only connect." The two devastatingly perceptive words
of E. M. Forster's in *Howard's End* serve as well as any to sum up the
problems and needs of British society today. Somehow the connection is
not being made. At the center, harassed and well-meaning politicians,
as well as intelligent and overworked civil servants, struggle to cope
with an absurdly overcentralized system of administration. At the regional and local levels, officials struggle to carry out their duties under
a system that encourages the maximum secrecy and the minimum popular participation.

The individual in this complex and disorganized new society of
ours can only pause and wonder. Faced with a world in which decisions
are made first and then discussed, in which the people who make public
policy seem to be denied the means to carry that policy out, in which
everyone seems responsible to his superior for preventing things from
happening but no one responsible to the public for achieving things on
their behalf, he may well wonder whose government, whose state, it is
that he reads about in the newspapers. Whose state is it that spends
such vast sums of his welfare, that appears so doggedly unresponsive to
the efforts and energies of the politicians he has elected in the belief
that they would set things right?

Everyone has his or her pet theory about the root causes of the

British crisis. There are those who see it entirely in terms of a transformation from empire. There are those who say we should never have made the mistake of winning the war, that we should have had the opportunity for a fresh start like France, West Germany, and Japan. There are those who blame it all on the reserve role of the pound. Commentators invariably go on to assert that, despite all the difficulties, the basic will and skill to put things right are there. Britain is full of serious, able, and energetic people whose talents could carry her back to greatness if only they were harnessed. All is not lost. Britain is ready to respond.

But respond through what and to what? Through which channels? A few years ago Jacques Ellul wrote a brilliant essay called *Western Man in 1970*. He described how the family man of 1970 would be bombarded with information. Through his television set he would instantaneously see pictures of everything happening throughout the world—wars, conferences, speeches, riots, treaties, development schemes, disasters, elections in other countries. He would see it all, but he would be a spectator. What would be hidden from him would be all the judgments, assessments, arguments, and decisions that lay behind these happenings, or often, the decisions that did *not* lie behind these happenings. He would see only those things so dearly beloved of popular television interviewers and popular journalists—the facts. He would look on all these facts and he would be afraid.

In Britain I am not sure that we had to wait until 1970 for this to occur. Of all advanced countries in the last twenty years, Britain has perhaps had to adapt the most, not just internally but in its view of itself toward the world, in its relations to the rest of the inhabitants of this planet. And of all countries, Britain has a system of government that is least sensitive to changing needs and least able to make the processes of adaptation widely understood and widely shared.

The best practical illustration of this is to be found in the growth, in both complexity and sheer size, of the power, responsibilities, and duties of the state. Over the last hundred years, we have swung from the all-pervading belief that the state can and should do nothing to the all-pervading belief that the state should do everything. So extensive has state activity become that in places the very concept of a public sector and a private sector have become blurred and lost.

Yet while successive governments of all persuasions have willingly and cheerfully shouldered these burdens in the name of "modern needs," the system of government—the actual mechanism required to bear all these new responsibilities—has not changed at all. The same management system that ran the corner shop is now required to cope with a gigantic department store. The same chains of command and structures that coped with Mr. Gladstone's £80 million a year budget now have to cope with Mr. Jenkins' £10,000 million budget.

The strains imposed by these changes are, of course, intolerable. Authorities have proliferated haphazardly in a desperate struggle to cope with the new burdens. Cashbook methods of controlling public spending have ceased to keep pace with the actual spending decisions being made or with the management of public affairs generally. More and more decisions from the vastly important to the utterly trivial have been piled on central Ministries, leading to chaotic overcentralization, hurried and arbitrary decisions taken on bad information, and the steady erosion of good regional and local government. If I may be forgiven for quoting from what I have written elsewhere, "modern government has acquired inherent tendencies to spread, which, like some primitive brainless organism, it lacks the managerial capacity to direct or check" (The *Times*, March 13, 1967).

I believe that these processes constitute the central threat to the free society today. If our political system has any life in it, then it is the duty of politicians to recognize the nature of this threat, to understand it, and to grapple with it. Governments that regard it as an inevitable trend, that shrug their shoulders and say that nothing can be done, or, worse still, that compound the difficulties by playing along with them, should be fought tooth and nail.

From the prejudiced position of an opposition politician, one naturally sees very great opportunities for the Conservative party in this situation. The essence of the British Conservative party is that it is not doctrinaire. It is a party of moderation and it has always been led by moderates. A classic exposition of the role of a typical Conservative has it that he should always be swimming gently against the mainstream. He should, in short, always be suspicious of "inevitable" trends and fashions. In an age of excessive centralization the mantle of devolution therefore falls naturally on Conservative shoulders. Pragmatists can combine with free-market ideologies in the party to press for delegation, devolution, and decentralization in the name of freedom and individualism.

What does this imply in practice for British politics and for British politicians? Faced with the inadequacies of both individualism and collectivism as guiding principles for good government, the politicians of the near future are going to have to recognize that they are confronted with four major tasks.

First, it must be recognized that a politician's work does not begin and end with policy. In the traditional view of functions in the British system of government, politicians looked after policy and officials looked after administration. A politician laid down the policies on the basis of certain principles; the civil servants then carried out these policies. In fact, of course, policy and the administration are intertwined. Policy is made as and while it is implemented. If credible relations between the public utterances and promises of politicians and the actual executive operations of government are to be restored, those with political power will have to accept their administrative responsibilities, i.e., not merely accept them but acquire the skills and techniques to enable them to penetrate to the heart of the administration and to reorganize it.

Second, those with political power must acquire the understanding and the skills to effect a major reform in the structure of Britain's Civil Service administration. The traditional centralized system of Treasury control of all financial decisions throughout all areas of government is the enemy of devolution, flexibility, and responsiveness to local needs and problems. It flies in the face of good management practice and ensures the minimum creative contribution to the work of government.

Third, the politicians of the near future must be prepared to re-examine and to question the whole range of responsibilities and activities currently undertaken by central government. This is, of course, an area heavy with the traditional ideologies. Through the fog of these ideologies, politicians with sufficient perception and ability must somehow focus coolly on which activities of central government should continue to be undertaken by central government; which can be redefined as programs or projects and farmed out to separate boards, commissions, or agencies; which can be handed back to private enterprise; which to regional or local authorities; and which to individuals themselves.

Fourth, politicians must ask how public accountability is to be restored. They will observe, quite rightly, that if decision-making in government is to be decentralized and delegated, traditional forms of parliamentary scrutiny of executive spending will become pointless. But they will also have to recognize that those traditional systems, as they function at present, are hopelessly ineffective. Far from ensuring that all decisions are faithfully referred to Ministers who in turn faithfully bring them before Parliament for comment, they merely ensure that everything is placed under an impenetrable shroud of secrecy. Public policy therefore exists as the private preserve of higher officials within the executive. Decisions are either never revealed at all or only revealed long after they have been taken and long after the reasoning and arguments underpinning them have been forgotten, if they were ever known in the first place.

This fourth issue really embraces the other three. The central question is how genuine democratic procedures can be geared to a technically efficient bureaucracy; or, stated in reverse, how the vast mass of decisions that a system of government is called upon to reach can be exposed most effectively to the influence of those who will be affected by those decisions. The Westminster parliamentary system is falling into disrepute because it fails to recognize these problems. The further reform of Parliament is the central task in the post-welfare state.

Let me develop some thoughts and establish a few conclusions on each of the four main areas outlined above.

First, politicians as administrators: The idea that politicians should, in principle, be interested in administration and be aware of the new tools available to improve the efficiency of government is, in Britain, a novel one. Given charge, by process of a General Election, of an organization, or set of organizations, of a size and complexity unparalleled in world history, politicians, one might expect, would utilize the most sophisticated management techniques and apply the most intense brainpower to the problems of administration. On the contrary, few politicians in Britain would admit until recently that their task was to manage anything. A far commoner point of view would be that they were elected to battle out great issues of policy on the basis of high principle according to party and to ensure that his battle took place in the House of Commons. They then left officials to get on with the job.

Given the manner in which party-political ideologies have developed, such a view is hardly surprising. For more than fifty years the political battle in Britain has been governed by two dominant, all-pervading, opposing, and stultifying beliefs. There have been those who argued that the state would provide and those who doubted whether it could and felt that things should be left to "free enterprise" of "the individual." The idea that politicians should be concerned with how the government should undertake the functions assigned to it, or how individuals should undertake the functions left to them, or, even more adventurous, how public and private resources and initiative might combine to achieve recognized policy goals simply never entered the political discussion.

The fault lies not entirely with politicians. For far too long the preoccupation of intellectuals and scholars concerned with questions of government has been with the size and role of the state rather than with questions of how to make the state more efficient in carrying out its assigned role. For instance, books have been written in great numbers on the macroeconomic question of the over-all level of public expenditure, or on the over-all level of taxation. Yet it is only in surprisingly recent times that minds have been really sharply focused on questions of choice between different types of public spending and on the mechanisms by which the decisions between one type of expenditure and another should be undertaken. It has been left to a few crusading and clear-thinking managerial types who have come into government to call attention to ideas of program evaluation and efficient application of cost-benefit analysis to public spending decisions.

It is not surprising, therefore, that without any adequate intellectual backing, politicians have been slow indeed to recognize their duties in ensuring administrative reform and efficiency of government. Is the situation now changing? I believe that it is. In a very real sense, the frustrations and protests of modern society in relation to those who govern them are beginning to have an impact on politicians and on the way in which they approach their work. In part, this was reflected in the decision by the incoming Labor Administration in 1964 to bring with it a large number of outside advisers. The hope was that these would bring to the executive machine some breath of the outside world and a greater sensitivity to outside needs and feelings. In part, too, it has been reflected in the growing debate swirling round Parliament itself. More and more, the argument has been heard that Parliament and its ministers must reassert their control of, and power to scrutinize effectively, the workings of the executive. Despite a certain reluctance from the Civil Service, elected members of Parliament have pressed with growing enthusiasm for the development of all-party committees to scrutinize government policy and cross-question policy makers, both politicians and officials.

The implications of this development are immense. Increased scrutiny by the public through Parliament, on the one hand, and increased exposure of both policy makers and policies, on the other, offer the best opportunity in Britain today for individual members of the public to be able to participate in the arguments preceding the decisions that ultimately affect their lives. The fact that these changes have only just begun and have encountered steady resistance from the administrative machine only serves to emphasize that the two prongs of reform—decentralized administration and increased public accountability—must go hand in hand if they are to make sense.

A further and more immediate influence has been on the outlook of politicians. Faced by a widening gap between promise and performance by successive administrations, the electorate has rightly begun to feel that all is not well with the political process. Politicians have thus found themselves the object of increasing criticism and confronted by a public that is less and less prepared to trust what they say. In short, the fundamental weaknesses in modern British democracy have begun to appear in definite and immediate political symptoms. This is at once alarming and encouraging. It is alarming because it brings into doubt the whole system of parliamentary democracy as it is known in Britain. It is encouraging because it at last forces politicians to face urgently the real political issues.

Second, the new techniques of government: The British system of government is centralized but not integrated. A vast range of activities, which strictly speaking are local or regional concerns, have to be dealt with in Whitehall. Within Whitehall itself, however, overloaded departments struggle with each other to carry out their separate, and often contradictory, functions. Underpinning centralized government is a centralized system of financial control. And this in turn is reinforced by the methods of parliamentary interference with the statistics of public expenditure, which the legislature still chooses to employ. Parliament looks at the figures rather than the policies. It demands that all details of expenditure be centrally checked by its watchdog, the Treasury. This automatically gives the Treasury supreme power in questions of financial control. It automatically deters civil servants from taking on their own initiative any action or making any management decision that might involve the spending of public money.

Yet management decisions and financial decisions are inseparable. Unless financial responsibility (except for the very largest spending decisions) can be delegated, no creative and efficient management is possible. And unless decisions can be devolved and decentralized, no effective public participation is possible. What chance, for instance, have the residents in a small town who want a pedestrian crossing in High Street, if the decision to spend money on it has to be referred to the Ministry of Transport in Whitehall? How can they be sure their voices will be heard? How can they be sure that the decision, if it is unfavorable, has been taken fairly and after due consideration of all their arguments?

These questions should be sufficient to show that fundamental reorganization of the management structure of government departments, coupled with important changes in the position of Parliament vis-à-vis the "management" or executive, is essential. If Parliament has no control, if, indeed, the attempt by Parliament to check the figures actively stifles governmental efficiency, then other methods for checking policy must be devised. Hence the growth of all-party specialist committees is so important.

If policy is to be scrutinized, it becomes necessary to identify those who are in fact responsible for policy and to cross-question them. Greater delegation of decisions from Whitehall would have two important effects in this area. First, it would relieve the Minister, the politician in charge, of a great burden of detail and give him time to run his department. Second, it would give him the management structure through which his own policies and wishes could be implemented. Questioning the Minister and those directly under him and appointed by him would thus become a far more fruitful exercise. It would be the Minister in charge and those under him who would have particular responsibilities for particular areas of activity. This would contrast with the present situation in which the Minister, while in theory responsible for all the actions of his department, must in fact rely on his senior civil servants to formulate policy because he has no time to do so.

The question for the would-be reformer is this: Can the understandable tendency for the Whitehall Civil Service to assume increasing responsibilities be reversed? Can regional questions be placed more in the hands of the regions, local questions more in the hands of local authorities? Can specific projects being undertaken by government be delegated to new agencies or project directors who are left to their own devices? Can civil servants contract more tasks out to private enterprise instead of setting up new and self-perpetuating departments to deal with each new problem as it arises? Even to raise these questions has hitherto been regarded as heresy by the traditionalists. For the implication is that the detailed control of spending will have to pass out of the hands of the Treasury. And if that happens, the sheltered, centralized, secret world of senior officialdom in Britain will begin to dissolve.

Third, redistributing responsibility: The starting point for decentralization of British government is to get civil servants to define exactly what they are trying to do, to identify goals. We must ask, for instance, what government officials at the regional levels are actually doing? Are they carrying out the policies desired by the region for improving its welfare and general standards, or are they busy giving advice to central government officials who in turn get together, take decisions, and hand those decisions back to the regional officials to carry out? If the latter, is this the best way of conducting business? Would it not be better if officials at the regional levels got together to coordinate and carry out policy regionally on the basis of the wishes of the elected County Council or regional body?

Or, to take another example, what are senior officials in the Ministry of Health doing? Are they building hospitals, or running a health service, or merely protecting their Minister from awkward questions? If the latter, is that their proper function or should not that be left to the Minister's personal *cabinet?* They are probably doing all three, just as in the Ministry of Transport the officials who are in charge of supervising the building of motorways are also in charge of other bits of policy and have to be constantly on tap to help the Minister with awkward questions and broader problems raised in Parliament.

The essential step is to redefine as many government activities as possible in terms of projects. Once there are identifiable goals with identifiable people responsible for achieving them, then it becomes possible for Parliament at the center or for regional elected bodies to question the officials concerned and to judge how successfully the policies are being carried out and how swiftly the goals are being attained. Once this reorientation has been achieved, it becomes possible to measure the usefulness of government activities, such as the running of research institutes or the provision of vaguely defined services, to certain industries against the specified goals in question. It would also become possible for laymen, that is M.P.s and ordinary members of the public, to find out what is happening, why it is happening, and what the reasons behind it are.

The famous story of Stansted Airport—the third London airport —serves as an ideal illustration. The identified task was to build a third London airport for the 1970s. Someone, somewhere, in the Board of Trade made the decision that it should be in Stansted. No one knew which official was in fact in charge of organizing air travel in Britain over the next twenty or thirty years, and no one knew by what reasoning the decision had been reached. Thus there could be no properly focused public debate and argument on the issue, regardless of whether it was right or wrong. Where debate and argument failed, or never had a chance, public agitation and the flexible mind of a new president of the Board of Trade succeeded. It was decided to hold another inquiry. Even then, the opportunities for discovering why and by whom the decision for Stansted had been made and what broad view of required landing facilities in the British Isles had initially governed the decision were by no means guaranteed. If no one is responsible, there can be no public accountability.

Fourth, how to make governments accountable: Those who object most strongly to any further evolution of the parliamentary system at Westminster to parallel the growth of the executive often point to the role of individual members of Parliament as champions of particular constituents and as promoters of individual causes. They cite examples in which M.P.s have taken up cases of injustice, wrong official decisions, unfair ministerial judgments and have succeeded in getting them reversed. If, the argument continues, members of Parliament were fully occupied on specialist committees, holding hearings and questioning high officials and Ministers about policy formulation, who would look after Citizen John Bull when he encounters the monolithic power of the state?

The question is entirely justified but the answer is not to leave things as they are. It is true that M.P.s do a good job in taking up the causes of individuals and in championing individual liberty. In doing so, they are, of course, carrying out a semijudicial function. In the absence of any system of law in Britain governing relations between the individual and the executive, it is left to the member of Parliament to present cases on his constituents' behalf. The M.P.s' efforts have recently been reinforced by the creation of the office of Parliamentary Commissioner for Administration. He is intended to have powers to investigate complaints against central government in a fashion not possible for busy M.P.s. Already he has run into strong opposition and obstruction from the executive department of government.

Hence the fundamental problem remains. If in theory all responsibility is with the Minister, if in theory officials are only carrying out the policies laid down by their political masters, how can any responsibility be pinned on the official? It is this basic constitutional fallacy in the British system of government today that makes the state so powerful and the position of the individual so weak. In theory, tens of thousands of officials are dutifully carrying out the policies of their political masters, and it is their masters—not they—who are answerable to Parliament during Question Hour, in debates, and in general elections.

In fact, these officials themselves formulate and carry out policy at all but the most strategic levels. Their actions, attitudes, and decisions can for better or for worse have a major impact on the lives of ordinary citizens. Without a system to expose the reasons and arguments used by officials to reach decisions, the scales are always tilted against the individual. His quarry can always disappear into a fog of undefined ministerial responsibility. The man who takes the decision that may ruin a citizen's life (viz. by allowing a gas works to be built next to his home) can always take refuge.

The essential requirement for maintaining public accountability is for a program of parliamentary reform to match the changed character of the administration. As greater numbers of high officials have acquired public responsibility for public programs, there has been increasing pressure for these people to report directly to Parliament and to be cross-examined on their thinking and intentions.

The ideal forum for this kind of exposure is an all-party select committee. In recent years the pressure on the government to set up more committees of this kind has grown strikingly. The difficulties raised by this development are of the chicken and egg variety. As long as the administration operates on traditional bureaucratic lines, officials are bound to view the prospect of being questioned by parliamentary committees with apprehension. And as long as they fear these committees, they are bound to do everything possible to frustrate them. Hence the two new committees recently established on science and technology and agriculture have had to fight a continual battle, not only to find out what they want to know about government policy but even to obtain a large enough budget to finance adequate research and secretarial staffs.

The Parliamentary Committee on Agriculture has been so successful in penetrating the administrative labyrinth that angry officials have now pressed the government to dispose of the committee altogether. But these reactions, although there will be more of them, are running against the tide. The demand by Parliamentarians for greater opportunity to scrutinize government policy on the public's behalf is now firmly established. This raises profound questions for the future role of British members of Parliament, many of whom in the past have viewed the House of Commons as a training ground rather than as a platform for the criticism of government. It also raises profound questions about relations between the government Front Bench and the chairmen of the new parliamentary committees. Are they to be given separate constitutional power and thus become impossible to dislodge, as in the American Congress? Or are they to be government placemen, obedient to every government wish when a delicate policy issue is raised? Somewhere between these two extremes lies the proper balance between a modern administration and a modern Parliament. Over the next ten or twenty years the British Parliament will expend large energies in groping toward this balance.

We come now to a fifth major issue in the post-welfare state and in the whole question of relations between the citizen and the vastly swollen executive. Hand in hand with greater expertise in the techniques of administration, with decentralized government, with delegated decision-making, and with a new system of parliamentary accountability should go a major modernization of the British system of law, indeed a creation of a new body of administrative law, akin to the *droit administratif,* which will govern the relations between the individual and officialdom.

What, then, is to be done to effect these enormous changes? For some years politicians of all parties in Britain have talked of the need for a more "open" society. What they are attacking is the system by which public decisions get taken privately and as a result of private discussions within the executive machine. Politicians out of office, or fairly far removed from office, tend to press this case more vigorously than politicians in sight of executive responsibility. For governments, or for those about to become the government, the temptations of keeping a system that prevents public debate—of opting for a quiet life—can prove irresistible.

Adaptation and change will begin when this choice is no longer open, when government-in-private leads not to a quiet life but to disturbing and demanding political pressures. In this paper I have tried to show that these pressures are at last beginning to develop significantly in Britain. They are developing first through the growing realization that overcentralized government, like overcentralized management, is simply inefficient. It fails to ensure that political commitments to the electorate are kept. Second, they are developing through the growth of individual demands from an increasingly informed electorate for more active participation in government. Third, they are developing because it is becoming increasingly clear that the link or gear is missing between the publicly elected Parliament and the main branches of an increasingly complex executive. Fourth, they are developing because people see, and have daily contact with, a vast world of officialdom with enormous power but upon which they can fasten no legal responsibility.

These developments are reflected in a number of very positive and immediate phenomena in Britain. Politicians of all parties are held in low esteem. Few of them appear to be in a position to carry out their promises. The electorate waits to be convinced by the party or group that really appears to know *how* to run the administration. This disillusion extends to the institution of Parliament itself. The fact that the nature and workings of the British parliamentary system have never been widely understood in Britain makes the dangers of irresponsible attack all the greater, and the need for response all the more urgent.

Outside the British capital, localism, regionalism, and nationalism —in Wales, Scotland, and Cornwall—are on the march. Denied the right to a full say in government decisions affecting them, people are increasingly ready to listen to appeals to local patriotism and to suggestions for open expressions of will—viz. marches, protest movements, and demonstrations.

This is the raw material out of which the post-welfare society will be built or not built. But the choice is not between "doing something" and doing nothing. The most significant feature of British life today is not its apathy but its vitality. That vitality—the new individualism as the editors of this book may wish to call it—will find its way out whether new channels are constructed for it or not. The choice is therefore between far-sighted adaptation of our systems of government and law and surrender to fractious and uncertain public impulses born of frustration and expressed in many forms. It is fairly clear in which direction wise minds should be turning, but they must hurry.

TERRY LACEY

Radical Liberalism

I WRITE THIS CHAPTER from the standpoint of a political activist. Since I have left the Liberal party I believe I can contribute a more objective analysis of the ideological approach that I helped promote when I was a leading member of it.

My experience in the Liberal party relates to the period 1962–1968, particularly to the twelve months from the summer of 1966 to the summer of 1967. During this time the Young Liberals made their maximum impact on the mass media and their greatest efforts to redefine radical liberalism. Much of the impetus for the rise of radical liberalism was provided by the increasing identity among younger party dissidents with the mobilization of student and youth organizations of the New Left both in Britain and elsewhere in the West. This sense of community included common critical attitudes toward the Vietnam War and the international and domestic aspects of racial oppression but excluded fundamental New Left attitudes such as the total rejection of capitalism and the acceptance of the necessity under certain circumstances of revolutionary violence. The Young Liberals attempted to place these New Left principles in the context of the historical tradition of radical liberalism.

Nevertheless the Young Liberals have failed in their attempt to chart a new course for the Liberal movement in Britain. This failure derives from their refusal to formulate a coherent theory of society based on economic relations rather than antiquated notions of individualism.

As a result radical liberalism is incapable of helping promote the necessary transformation of Western capitalist-welfare society.

RADICAL LIBERALISM IN
HISTORICAL PERSPECTIVE

Radical liberalism of the 1960s drew on the historical legacy of the positive liberalism of the 1890s, which in turn had its roots in classical economic liberalism. Economic liberalism was the central theme of individualistic conservatism and laissez faire and was the weapon of the rising bourgeoisie against the landed classes. The social connotation associated with contemporary liberalism in Britain first arose in the latter part of the nineteenth century. Rejecting utilitarianism on the grounds of its social irresponsibility, proponents of positive liberalism articulated a socially conscious view of liberty that attempted to relate the desires of the individual to the needs of the whole community. Since freedom was not possible in the context of poverty or ignorance (which afflicted the majority of the population whilst the utilitarians pontificated on the greatest happiness principle), the positive Liberals promoted the role of the state as the creator or guarantor of those conditions that would permit the maximum number of people to lead happy and fruitful lives. Specifically the positive Liberals advocated state intervention through legislation designed to improve working conditions and education and extend local government services.

Positive liberalism was akin to moral and Christian socialism also propagated during the late nineteenth century in Britain. Like advocates of these early variants of socialism, positive Liberals pointed to the contradictions between individual and collective interests but relied on metaphysical rather than materialist logic in their analysis. Whilst the Marxist critique of capitalism distinguished conflicting class interests, the logic of the positive Liberals rested on their view of individual man as a reasonable and moral being. John Stuart Mill, who near the end of his life called himself a "qualified Socialist" in the tradition of Robert Owen, never abandoned the view that "the individual and society somewhat stood apart from each other without organic connection." [1]

Thomas Green reinforced the individualistic and metaphysical roots of liberalism in typifying man as a disinterested and moral being: "The condition of a moral life is the possession of will and reason. All moral ideas have their origin in reason. Practical reason is the capacity in a man of conceiving of the perfection of his nature as an object to be attained by action." [2] Thus Green emphasized will and reason where Marx stressed class categories; Green's concept of progress derived from utopian optimism for which Marx provided the scientific equivalent of historical materialism. Green borrowed from Rousseau an idealist concept of the common good and from Hegel the notion of the state as the arbitrator of social conflicts. Marx incorporated the latter with a Hegelian dialectical analysis of society and history to produce dialectical and historical materialism.

The short-term effects of radical liberalism were limited. In response to the impetus of radical liberalism the Liberal party adopted a program for more state intervention in the economy and society, which resulted in such measures as the introduction of a national insurance system and Labor Exchanges. These measures ensured the more efficient operation of the capitalist system by providing for higher mobility of labor. Given greater emphasis on socially conscious policies with respect to education, local government services, and industrial legislation, the Fabian Socialists came to view the Liberals (for a time) as a potentially collectivist and state Socialist party.

In broader perspective the Liberal reforms of 1906 were not earthshaking. The movement against classical laissez faire in commerce and industry had already made considerable headway during the first half of the nineteenth century with the passage of the first education and factory acts. By the time the positive Liberals came on the scene such extension of state power was taken for granted. All that the Liberals accomplished in this period was to sanction a broader trend against classical laissez faire that was subsequently complemented by the return to protectionism in international trade. In this sense the positive Liberals admirably reflected the social and economic trends of their time which heralded the development of a much closer relation between capitalism and the state.

The positive Liberals lost their struggle to transform the Liberal party into the vehicle of reform and organized labor. Capitalists and manufacturers retained firm control of the party and the disillusioned working-class voters and organizations abandoned their temporary allegiance to the Liberals, turning instead to the newly founded Labor party. By its refusal to represent working-class interests the Liberal establishment assured the disintegration of the once powerful Liberal party and its reduction to the historical remnant that it now constitutes.

Positive liberalism served in practice to reinforce capitalism whilst the Marxists fought against the principle of capitalist organization of production and society. The Labor movement split between the anticapitalist minority and the majority who followed the Fabian line of reforming capitalism. As the Liberal party incorporated positive Liberal principles into official doctrine it thus drew closer to the consensual center of the political spectrum that was already occupied by Fabianism —leading in the 1960s to problems of differentiating the ideas and policies of the Liberal and Labor parties. The Liberal party now seeks to liberalize and humanize capitalism, providing it with a social conscience, and the right-wing policies of the Labor government have added credibility to the otherwise shaky Liberal claim to the mantle of "radical principles."

The variants of economic and social forms of liberalism demonstrate that "liberalism" as a term cannot be used in an unqualified manner. Similarly, "radical" implies getting to the roots of things but could mean either the reform of existing systems or their replacement by entirely new ones. Thus "radical" is frequently used ambiguously to avoid utilization of the Left-Right spectrum; indeed there is radicalism on both extremes of that spectrum. Therefore "radical liberalism" constitutes a range of possibilities qualified by an ambiguity. In the context of modern British politics and of this chapter, radical liberalism refers to the historical tradition of a reforming liberalism with an emphasis on social goals.

THE BRITISH WELFARE STATE
AND ITS SHORTCOMINGS

Radical liberalism gained much of its impetus from the positive Liberal objective to create a welfare state and subsequently through a criticism of the machinery of the welfare state as it developed. In talking about the welfare state I refer not only to such institutions as the National Health Service but also to the kind of society that Britain has evolved since World War II. To my mind it would be inadequate to attempt to assess the welfare state merely in terms of those institutions that are designed to contribute to a generally higher standard of living through state action. Therefore it is necessary to consider the kind of society we have in the epoch of the British-mixed economy-welfare state— including the distribution of wealth and power, as well as opportunities for the individual to rise above the difficulties of social circumstances into which he is born so as to exercise and develop his faculties to his own satisfaction and the improvement of society.

Critics of the contemporary level of welfare spending in Britain generally make four assumptions concerning the welfare state. They assume that the declared aims of social policy of the 1942 Beveridge Report have been largely achieved through legislation; that the social services have had an aggregate redistributive effect, transferring resources from rich to poor; that it is practical, desirable, or meaningful to abstract social services from the greater society; and that there is no conceptual problem in defining a "social service." [3] In reality, however, the declared aims of the Beveridge Report have not been accomplished. Resources have not been redistributed from rich to poor; the experience of the last two decades demonstrates that social services cannot be considered in isolation from general social values and problems; and there remains the problem of finding an acceptable definition of a social service. The shortcomings of the welfare state encompass two principal issues: first, the general question of the relative distribution of wealth in society in terms of taxation and wage levels; and, second, the actual operation of the machinery of the welfare state in terms of bias in favor of particular social groups and discrimination against others.

The past two decades in Britain have witnessed an increase in regressive taxation and an increasing percentage of long-term unemployment. Moreover, a substantial number of the working population still receive low wages. With respect to regressive taxation, subsidies on consumer expenditure fell from 3.5 per cent to 1.6 per cent of the G.N.P. between 1951 and 1964, whilst Local Authority rates rose from 2.8 per cent to 3.7 per cent and National Health Insurance contributions increased from 3.5 per cent to 4.9 per cent of the G.N.P. during the same period. Over-all regressive taxation—as a percentage of the G.N.P.—

rose 4 per cent, with a heavier net burden of taxation falling on working-class households.

The problem of low wages is exacerbated by the increase in the number of long-term unemployed. This arises from the fact that the unemployed worker receives the equivalent of a low wage. Between 1966 and 1967 long-term unemployment increased from 107,000 to 255,000. Over 5.8 million wage earners, meanwhile, earned less than £15 a week. This meant that in combination over six million households had to subsist on low incomes. In 1967 1.8 million men earned less than £15 per week of whom 1.5 million were laborers. In addition 14 per cent of all male clerks, 28 per cent of all male workers in extractive industries, and 24 per cent of all male workers in distributive trades earned less than £15 per week gross. Similarly, 40 per cent of women in full time employment—about two million—earned less than £10 per week, and another two million earned over £10 but under £15. Half a million children whose fathers are employed full time live below the official poverty line because their fathers' wages are less than their social security entitlement.

Parallel with the inability of the welfare state to solve problems of poverty, unemployment, and low wages, a negative redistribution of wealth has occurred. In 1954 5 per cent of the population owned 71 per cent of the dutiable wealth; by 1960 this 5 per cent owned 75 per cent of the dutiable wealth, with 1 per cent of the population owning 42 per cent of total dutiable wealth. The more money one has the faster it grows. Fifty-six per cent of the wealth of those with over £250,000 capital is in equities; thus the capital appreciation of the wealthiest group rose 114 per cent between 1950 and 1964, whilst the assets of those with between £3,000 and £10,000 grew by only 48 per cent. Meanwhile, the statistics of the Inland Revenue reveal that 60 per cent of the population hold no significant wealth at all. Regarding disparity between incomes in 1968, a Labor party discussion-document, which was produced for the Labor party's Young Socialist conference, showed that over 20 million wage earners earned less than £1,000 per year and only six million earned over £1,000 per year. Within the latter group about 10,000 earned over £15,000 per year. Under the welfare state the rich have thus become much richer, and property owners have improved their relative wealth at the cost of wage and salary earners.

Many shortcomings exist in the machinery of the welfare state that undermine its capacity to perform the tasks for which it was established. Social services in Britain are not integrated but instead are administered through different ministries and local government departments. A needy person's claim for his full entitlement may therefore involve complex bureaucratic procedures and forms in half a dozen offices situated in different localities. Nor can one assume that people are aware of their welfare rights. On the contrary, most people are not. Of men receiving supplementary benefits who have children under five, 90 per cent claim their free welfare foods—probably because an official told them about this—but of entitled men with low wages in full-time work only 4 per cent claim the same right.

Another example of the desultory use of a welfare right is that in 1968 a quarter of a million old people failed to claim their supplementary benefit enough though they were entitled to it. This failure arose partly through ignorance and partly because it has not been made clear to them that the benefit is a right and not a charity. Some administrative rules of the welfare state discriminate against most needy groups as a result of a throwback from the nineteenth-century poor laws. At least 30,000 unemployed men, mostly classified as light laborers, are victims of the "wage-stop rule" by which their dole is cut to a level below that of their assessed potential earnings level. As a consequence of this rule, another 100,000 children join the half million who are already below the official poverty line because their fathers receive low wages.

In practice the various allowances and provisions of the welfare state are utilized proportionately more by the middle income groups which are more articulate and knowledgeable as to their rights. The middle classes manipulate their incomes so as to maximize them and receive an increasing proportion of incomes in nontaxable forms through a great variety of fringe benefits. In 1955 half of all the new cars in Britain were paid for by firms and 20 per cent of all railway passengers were on expense accounts.

The family allowances account for only 25 per cent of the budget for child endowment, taking into account fiscal relief as well as allowances paid out. Whilst allowances are paid indiscriminately (although they are now becoming taxable), the tax concessions awarded in respect to children operate so that the greater the income, the greater the concession. Consequently many lower-paid workers never benefit from tax concessions because their income is too low to be taxed at all. One wage earner may receive a few shillings for the support of each child, in short, while a salary earner will receive several pounds a week. Thus the system of tax concessions for child endowment is socially regressive whilst family allowances have never been brought up to the level recommended in the Beveridge Report.

The middle class also benefits more from state education than any other group. Only 25 per cent of students from working-class backgrounds (representing 70 per cent of the population) manage to get university places, whilst the remaining 75 per cent of university places go to the children of only 30 per cent of the population. The reorganization of secondary or high school education on the basis of comprehensive schools is intended to eliminate the social bias of the old system, but the comprehensives will also discriminate against working-class children if their internal streaming systems merely repeat the errors of the old tripartite division between grammer, technical, and secondary schools initiated by the 1944 Butler Education Act.

Given these general points of criticism along with criticisms of the workings of the welfare state, it can be argued that the only distributive effect of the system after two decades has been a transfer of resources from the poorer to the poorest and the consolidation of the already privileged position of the middle classes.

THE PROGRAM OF RADICAL LIBERALISM

In response to the shortcoming of the welfare state and the problems of highly centralized industrial society the radical Liberals of the 1960s produced a series of proposals that together constitute a patchy program of reform. No single document or manifesto defined the attitudes and policies of radical liberalism. Instead the program emerged from a series of leaflets, pamphlets, and documents, not all of which were accepted into Liberal party policy. However, in describing the program that emerged from the Liberal youth movement and within the party around 1966–1967, it is possible to illustrate the mainstream of thought that produced it.

Any conscious attempt to tie this program together philosophically, or to give it intellectual coherence, was made retrospectively and was motivated by the knowledge that the inadequacy of the program as a basis for a new radicalism was rooted in the pragmatic, compartmentalized manner in which it evolved. Although the program of the radical Liberals was not worked out on the basis of a set of principles, it did have a guiding theme. That theme was "participation" expressed in the slogan, "Power to the People." The message given in speeches to summarize the new approach was as follows:

The class struggle has changed to the power struggle. It is no longer a question of a working class being forced by economic and social conditions into a struggle against the ruling capitalist class. Instead the working class and many elements of the middle and professional classes, including small entrepreneurs, are all in a similar position vis-à-vis their relation to real economic and political power. Therefore it is necessary for this natural majority of the people to realize collectively that their interest lies in mobilization to achieve genuine participation in the exercise of power, both in the field of government and in the realms of commerce and industry, through reforms in government structures and the acquisition of rights of representation in decision-making in the workplace.

The program that followed from this message comprised proposed reforms in three sectors of interest: foreign policy, the structure of government and public administration, and industrial and economic relations.

In foreign affairs the Liberal party traditionally supports a multiracial British Commonwealth; self-determination for colonial peoples and for oppressed black masses living under white supremacist rule; the establishment of a United Nations police force; British entry into the Common Market; and the maintenance of the Atlantic Alliance. The radical Liberals hardened these traditional attitudes by opposing the Rhodesian unilateral declaration of independence and calling for the bombing of rebel supply lines; by supporting the principal political objectives of the National Liberation Front of South Vietnam; and by compaigning against the renewal of the North Atlantic Treaty in 1969. The former two points were accepted into party policy; the latter was not. In general these attitudes only reflected traditional responses. Regarding opposition to NATO, which was a new departure from postwar Liberal tenets, the radicals failed to get their line adopted. It was on domestic issues that more fundamental points were raised concerning the organization of government and economic production.

Opposing the increased centralization of state power over the citizens, the radical Liberals pressed for changes in government structures that envisioned the democratization of public authorities and local government. Their program incorporated traditional Liberal demands for electoral and parliamentary reform along with proposals for the reorganization of local government to take account of increased urbanization and the need to simplify planning and administrative structures. In addition the Liberals campaigned for the regional devolution of power, advocating that a quasi-federal structure be established with the creation of Parliaments in Wales and Scotland. This proposal was fashioned more in response to Celtic nationalism than in recognition of the need for intelligent redistribution of central government authority. Nevertheless these disparate initiatives did amount to a program that was more rational than present reality.

The democratization theme was extended to many facets of national and local government and, in response to student agitation for representation in educational institutions, was also written into Liberal educational policy. The demand for democratization generated the most controversy when it was applied to the management of industry and the economy. In this sphere the radical Liberals devoted most of their attention to means of democratizing administrative structures. Virtually ignoring economic organization, they concentrated on problems of control rather than ownership of the means of production, distribution, and exchange.

The Liberals had advocated the election of worker-directors in companies as early as 1929 when the famous Yellow Book was produced as part of the last great effort by the Lloyd George Liberals to produce a program to attract the industrial working class. After World War II the Liberal party advocated various co-ownership schemes that would make workers shareholders in their companies. Throughout the 1950s another school of thought promoted a scheme of workers' participation based on the Yugoslav model, one that was once again more concerned with control than with ownership. At least three other systems of redistribution of wealth and power within the industrial framework were also promoted during the 1950s and 1960s. These included the German system of codetermination by elected worker-directors, the "pan-capitalism" of the Left Gaullists based on the ideas of Louis Vallen, and a series of plans for redistributing annual capital increases to employees. According to the latter group of proposals, an "Employees Surplus Fund" would be created that would cream-off an annual percentage of profits for redistribution to employees. Hence workers would gradually accumulate an increasing stake in their own firms.

The radical Liberals undertook two departures from previous proposals in this field: first, that workers should have representational rights in the workplace as of right and not because they were also shareholders; and, second, that elected works councils should be established throughout industry along with the election of worker-directors. Receiving widespread support within the Liberal party, these ideas led to a fundamental change in party policy. As a matter of principle, however, the party majority favored worker-participation rather than worker-control. Thus the party affirmed a program calling for (1) the redistribution of wealth and power through the election of worker-directors in the nationalized industries, thereby creating a system of worker-participation therein; (2) worker-representation in private firms, with half of the company board comprising delegates from the workers and half representing the interests of the shareholders; and (3) a system of redistribution of profits and capital increases to workers. In addition the party advocated the election of a works council in every industrial firm with over fifty employees, opposed antitrade-union legislation (then being carried out by the Labor government), and supported trade-union reform along the lines of industrial unionism (that is, one union per industry). Most of these proposals have already been quietly forgotten by the Liberal party, however, and the Young Liberal movement now displays much less enthusiasm for workers' control.

A CRITICISM OF RADICAL LIBERALISM

Proponents of radical liberalism might argue that it constituted some sort of intellectual departure from the stultifying constrictions of old-fashioned socialism and the selfishness and irresponsibility of conservatism. Taking the definition of radical liberalism as being liberalism plus social conscience and commitment to the historical tradition of the positive liberals, the radical liberalism of the 1960s was at least an attempt to form a set of ideas as to what was and what should be.

According to the pocket edition of the Oxford Dictionary, ideology constitutes a "science of ideas" or "visionary speculation." Being ideologically motivated in my conception of ideology, I prefer the former definition. Ideology must involve, in my view, an overarching theory or a theory of theories that provides a general theory of society and causation.

Radical liberalism, like Marxism, can perceive poverty, injustice, and discontent in the midst of affluence. Marxism interprets these phenomena in terms of the class structures that are concomitant with capitalism. Liberalism, on the other hand, cannot acknowledge the validity of class consciousness without undermining its own roots in individual rationality as the source of progress. Retrospectively liberalism acknowledges the primacy of class interests in the nineteenth century, but interprets the contemporary social situation approximately as follows:

The working class is basically emancipated. There are more equal educational opportunities, provisions, and safeguards to maintain minimum working conditions, and strong unions to defend Labor against exploitation and to fight for fair wages. All in all the whole benevolent machinery of the welfare state exists to aid those who through sickness, unemployment, and no fault of their own have fallen by the economic and social wayside. The principal difficulty now is that the state bureaucracy continually expands to meet the demands of the welfare state and takes over more power in economic and social planning and decision-making, thereby creating an unhealthy centralization of bureaucratic power. At the same time commercial bureaucracies have increased their power through continuing horizontal and vertical economic integration. Nearly everyone admits that whilst this centralization is inevitable and necessary it also has very serious implications for democracy. Therefore all reasonable people are prepared to accept intelligent recommendations as to how to improve the situation. Thus the principal effort of radical, Liberal, and generally intelligent thought should be to seek ways of mitigating the disadvantages of complex industrial society through the democratization and humanization of both state and commercial bureaucracies. The primary instrument of change must be the structural reform of these bureaucracies.

This "explanation" of the state of society is complacent in that poverty, unemployment, and social and economic inequalities are still with us and that the euphemistic problem of "urban renewal" remains a continuing crisis in most Western countries. During the 1960s the trade unions assumed their present role of cooperating with the government to control their members with respect to wage freezes. As a response to this policy of the union bureaucracies, the powers of shop stewards have increased and most strikes are now unofficial.

A majority of radical Liberals claimed to be "against the system," but in practice they made pessimistic assumptions in the name of practicality and reason—such as those outlined above—that prompted them to work only for the mitigation of what they saw as the inevitable development of semicorporatism. Only a few of them attacked the principles of free enterprise and private property that are the basis of the capitalist system.

Liberalism could not answer the question of what constitutes the basis of political power. Here radical liberalism confronts the same problem as contemporary social science. It must either accept the basic tenets of Marxist theory or seek an alternative overarching social and economic theory. Yet liberalism cannot admit that the basis of political power is economic power since this would undermine its roots in rationalism and individualism. To acknowledge that the capitalist system is dominated by a class that owns or controls the means of production, distribution, and exchange is to acknowledge the validity of class politics.

Since liberalism and Marxism have important characteristics in common, however, they cannot be considered in isolation from each other. They share much of the same history as well as a common secular humanism and belief in "progress." C. Wright Mills makes this clear:

Both marxism and humanism embody the ideals of Greece and Rome and Jerusalem: the humanism of the renaissance, the rationalism of the eighteenth century enlightenment. That is why to examine liberalism or marxism is to examine the politics of this humanist tradition. . . .[4]

Whereas the range of Marxist thought over time has been enriched with new experience but has nevertheless retained a rigorous analytical method that provides continuity, the theory of liberalism, in contrast, has lurched about. In attempting to respond to social and political demands as they have arisen, liberalism has abandoned its original principles of laissez faire in favor of slogans on social welfare. Economic liberalism provided at least a consistent theory of economic relations based on the manifest worth of laissez faire. Once one accepted its basic assumptions, economic liberalism provided causal explanations and a guide to action. As such it had a greater claim to be an ideology than the social liberalism that followed it.

Radical liberalism, based as it is on an idealist view of individual man, could only raise metaphysical slogans stressing tolerance, freedom, and liberalism itself—all of which evaded issues concerning the organization of production and its social consequences. From the simple straightforward position of laissez faire the radical Liberals assumed a stance by which they were not "against" the system but were for sensible reforms within it. Since capitalism with a social conscience leads some to oppose the whole system, it provokes conflict within the bourgeoisie. Thus when the radical Liberals substituted uncertainty and division for the total commitment to the system espoused by the economic Liberals, they introduced what the Marxists call a contradiction.

The radical Liberals advocated greater social commitment but not in terms of class interests. The radical Liberals of the 1960s used the concept of class interest but were careful to widen the scope of these interests to include nearly everybody. Therefore the radical Liberals are no longer distinguished from the non-Marxist (or Social Democratic) Socialists. We have witnessed this convergence in practice with the cooperation between Liberal and Labor leaders in Britain and the formation of the coalition government between the Social Democrats and the Free Democrats in West Germany. Liberalism is no longer concerned with grand principles but instead is now preoccupied with the wording of legislation and the rules of administration:

. . . [L]iberalism has become more administrative, and less political. It has become practical, flexible, realistic, pragmatic—as Liberals assert—and not at all utopian. All of which means . . . that as an ideology, as a rhetoric, liberalism has often become irrelevant to political positions having moral content.[5]

The evolution of Liberal theory reflects, then, an historical development. Classical economic liberalism was the ideology of classical capitalism. Classical liberalism has given way to radical liberalism, which recognized that attempts must be made to reconcile the form of economic organization with social goals. Within the setting of mixed economy oligopoly-capitalism the welfare state is naturally subject to controversy because it provides an arena in which contending factions can fight over the extent to which social goals must be subordinated to economic objectives (or vice versa). Radical liberalism and social democracy therefore occupy the mainstream position in Western consensus politics, which accepts contemporary trends and economic organization and promotes changes in social values to keep pace with these trends or to channel them in an effort to produce controlled social change. Consequently, a distinction can now be drawn between the Old Left, which is typified by its practical complicity with capitalism, and the New Left. Whilst it is appreciative of the trend toward technocratic oligopoly or semicorporatism, the latter looks to the earlier traditions of a cruder and uncompromising Marxism for ideological security. It is in this context that the utility of radical liberalism may be judged.

PROSPECTS FOR THE FUTURE

The welfare state is an attempt to reconcile conflicting social and economic priorities without overthrowing traditional social values or the capitalist system. It is a compromise by which those conscious of social needs continually raise the goals for greater commitment to welfare as the state responds by taking on more extensive social obligations. The welfare state can never mature in a finite sense. It is therefore preposterous to talk in terms of the post-welfare state, particularly when the Western world still has poverty, ghettos, and wretched social conditions in the midst of affluence. The welfare state has failed to resolve these problems, but social conditions would have become far worse without it. It is wrong to believe that the upsurge in demands for greater control over the human environment means the end of classical economic struggles. On the contrary, Western Europe has shown during 1969 that the Labor movement is more than ever concerned with wage levels as well as economic conditions.

It is paradoxical that the welfare state has angered so many who support the capitalist system when it has provided the means of mitigating the miseries that would follow from unbridled capitalism and in the process has greatly increased the survival capacity of the system. Similarly it is paradoxical that those who have fought for the welfare state under capitalism have often opposed the whole system but in practice have channeled their energies toward its preservation—thereby producing capitalism with a human face instead of posing alternatives to it.

The fundamental difference in approach between radical liberalism and Marxism is illustrated by the way each has sought to promote change, the former through compromise and the latter through conflict. Many Communist parties have joined the Social Democratic parties in espousing consensus politics and rejecting class conflict. Hence the British Communist party has chosen the parliamentary road to socialism, thus creating a mutual antipathy with New Left Marxism—an antipathy repeated in many countries of the world.

In assessing prospects for the political future of Britain, it is highly unlikely that the Liberal party will play any major part in political developments. The radical Liberals are an amorphous hotchpotch of Liberals, anarchosyndicalists, and utopian Socialists with little agreement amongst themselves, let alone a common perspective toward the Liberal party or the political scene. As such they are incapable of developing the kind of overarching theory that can relate the individual to the system of production and provide the basis for ideology. The Liberal party will thus be forced into a closer relation with the Labor party as the latter discards the last vestiges of "doctrinaire socialism" and assumes an increasingly pragmatic and unprincipled position.

In cross-national perspective the political center will shift slightly leftward as the Social Democratic parties lead Western Europe into the new technocratic era. Internationally the capitalist systems will become more interdependent and domestically more oligopolic. The state will play an increasingly important role in over-all economic and social planning and will ally itself with large capitalist production units to promote efficiency and economies of scale. State control of investment, research, and development decisions will increase in the private sector, particularly in the defense industries. The West will continue to develop a permanent arms economy.

No man is an island because he is part of society, and no country can be examined like a laboratory experiment in isolation from external influences. The domestic and foreign policies of states are severely limited by international considerations, more so for the allies or satellites of the two superpowers. Movements of national liberation in the third world will exert an influence that will encourage the Western powers to withdraw selectively from imperial commitments, although there remains a continued risk of Western involvement in internal security operations in Latin America and the Afro-Asian countries. Imperial retraction, the changing pattern of world trade, and the growth of an anti-Western third world bloc will provide an impetus for growing links between anticapitalist groupings in the West and third world national liberation movements. This emerging alliance will attack in turn the incipient detente between the Western powers and the Soviet Union and will attract those sections of the Labor and youth movements that reject Social Democratic leadership.

Constrained by consensual values which are in practice foisted upon society, the welfare state can never resolve the social problems it sets out to eliminate. Hence it will inevitably remain a failure. A transitional victory, the welfare state is the last major effort of social democracy before it loses its identity in the broad center of the political spectrum. Given this situation ideology is important because it provides the means of mental liberation that must precede the development of any superior social system.

Radical liberalism can never provide such an ideology, and the empty slogans for participation will carry little weight with the international corporations, Wall Street, or the gnomes of Zurich. Ideology will keep democracy alive, because democracy is meaningless if it is dominated in practice by a tiny elite that manipulates both government and "official opposition." In the context of an international system the New Left is producing an alternative to Western capitalism and Soviet bureaucracy—an international socialism that seeks to replace both by ignoring their sterile arguments and burying their sacred cows, providing instead the sort of commitment to collective humanity that is sadly dubbed nineteenth century and old-fashioned.

THE NEW LEFT AND BRITISH POLITICS

I define the New Left as a set of attitudes based on an analysis of the degeneration of the Russian Bolshevik Revolution into Stalinism. The New Left is left of the Communists in the sense that the Western Communist parties have adopted the parliamentary road to socialism and

have decided to operate within the ground rules of the capitalist system
—similar to the Social Democratic parties. The New Left does not accept these ground rules and instead encourages forms of direct action
—including the organization of militant rank and file organizations for
tenants, workers, and students; street demonstrations; and the occupation of factories and administrative buildings. The New Left seeks, in
short, to create a politically conscious mass movement based on the
working class. The New Left supports the national liberation movements of the third world but appreciates that the best way of demonstrating solidarity with such movements is to instill revolutionary
consciousness in the capitalist countries.

Paradoxically the spread of New Left and revolutionary ideology,
particularly among the young, will ultimately strengthen the Labor
party and shift it to the left. The pattern that we have seen in the universities will be repeated in society. A militant leadership will mobilize
more generally felt frustrations and through direct action provoke confrontations with authority. Although these will achieve little in themselves, they will produce, on the one hand, more activists and wider
support for the New Left and, on the other, will provide bargaining
power or political leverage to the reformers and gradualists. The latter
groups will articulate specific demands for changes in wages, working
conditions, representation, or whatever; these demands will then be partially met to head off the steam of the militants. By this process of unconscious alliance between revolutionaries and reformists, the militants
will push politics to the left. The whole effect is rather like a game of
leapfrog in which the reformist frog always remains one leap behind the
revolutionary frog.

A revolution in Britain is difficult to foresee without a revolutionary situation, and for such a situation to be created a militant leadership
must take advantage of exceptional circumstances that undermine the
capitalist state and social system. Such circumstances are not apparent
on the present political horizon. In their absence British politics will
take the course outlined above. Those New Left groups that are prone
to crisis politics will thus have to adopt similar tactics as religious organizations when the second coming continually fails to materialize: Either perpetually postpone the day (to the day after tomorrow) or proclaim new insights that reveal another long wait.

It is far more likely that revolutionary ideology will play an indirect but crucial role as a powerful lever for future political change. In this respect the New Left will prove a vital force in determining the nature and intensity of the pressures mounted against the status quo. Naturally these remarks pertain only to Britain. In the third world more directly revolutionary developments will occur. In Western European countries such as Italy and France there exists a greater possibility that traumatic political events might enable the Communists, in alliance with others, to achieve political power.

Notes

1. Quoted in Lane W. Lancaster, *Masters of Political Thought: Hegel to Dewey* (London, 1959), p. 205.

2. *Ibid.*, p. 217.

3. Titmuss, *Essays on 'The Welfare State'* (London, 1958), p. 38.

4. C. Wright Mills, *The Marxists* (New York, 1962), pp. 13–14.

5. *Ibid.*, pp. 20–21.

Sweden

M. DONALD HANCOCK

Post-Welfare Modernization in Sweden: The Quest for Cumulative Rationality and Equality

INCREASING AFFLUENCE, extensive coordination of socio-economic resources, the rise of new forms of critical consciousness, and incipient structural change among established political forces characterize Sweden's continuing process of modernization. As one of the world's most highly developed nations, Sweden provides a particularly suggestive model for the transition to the post-welfare state.

Although Sweden does not constitute an inevitable goal toward which other systems will in time evolve, the Swedish experience nevertheless appears highly relevant for the systematic analysis of alternative forms of social organization in the post-industrial order. The direction of political change in contemporary Sweden indicates the evolution of a system in which comprehensive planning of economic production and social investments will maximize (paradoxically, it may seem to some observers) the potential for individual choice and participation.

In analyzing this process of change in Sweden, I shall utilize the concept of post-welfare modernization as my theoretical framework. Applied to already highly advanced systems, modernization involves an inherent tension between contradictory quests for the cumulative rationalization of collective socio-economic resources and the cumulative equality of citizens. In the case of Sweden the potential conflict between these two aspects of modernization may conceivably be resolved in a positive synthesis of post-welfare transformation.

Specifically, I shall examine contemporary processes of economic, social, and political change as empirical manifestations of the Swedish pursuit of cumulative rationality and equality. Progress in Sweden toward attaining these goals indicates that neither is the product of chance. Both, however, are conditioned by objective socio-economic factors. "Deterministic" economic and social forces of change constitute, in short, the necessary basis for cumulative rationality and equality in the post-welfare state, but the realization of each remains subject to political choice.

MODERNIZATION IN SWEDEN

Modernization means, to paraphrase the definitions of C. E. Black and Dankwart A. Rustow, the rationalization of physical and human resources to increase man's control of his material and social environment. To promote this end, modernization necessitates (1) the creation of large-scale social organizations (including public and private bureaucracies) to mobilize masses on behalf of modernizing goals, and (2) the utilization of advanced technological and scientific methods in industry and management.[1] The modernization process is in turn a function of elite-mass receptiveness to the demands of transforming change and, as Manfred Halpern emphasizes, of the capacity of the system to absorb and sustain such change.[2]

Although modernization can thus be described in universalistic terms, it is obvious that it assumes different manifestations in specific systems. Modernization may serve as a defensive process to preserve the power and status of a traditional elite (as in contemporary Iran). Or it may provide the impetus for revolutionary change—as in many of the new nations of Africa or in Castro's Cuba—in which a new elite displaces colonial or indigenous rulers.

Moreover, modernization may or may not improve conditions of individual equality. While the modernization process does lead to higher levels of social mobility and economic productivity than those prevailing in premodern societies, the potential for individual freedom and participation in the political process remains subject to a wide array of ideological, power, and class factors. Even in advanced Western democracies that are ostensibly committed to maximizing individual equality, at least in political and legal terms, equality has been only imperfectly achieved.

An open-ended process, modernization can also yield diverse patterns of control over man's physical, social, and individual environments in the future. As Rustow justly points out, "Modernization is by definition a continuing process, so that no society can claim to be completely or definitively modern. Like the modern conception of truth, modernization itself is a series of approximations. Within this over-all process, it would seem that science, technology, and economic production have indefinite room for cumulative rationality." [3] Similarly, one must add, future modernization contains the possibility for cumulative equality—enhanced opportunities for individual fulfillment and meaningful participation in decisions affecting the individual's life.

As advanced industrial orders enter the post-industrial phase of modernization—the era of mass affluence in which a shift from the primacy of production to distribution becomes a realistic prospect—new options open up for the pursuit of both technical-scientific rationality and individual equality. But just as modernization has resulted historically in different applications of rationality on behalf of alternative forms of system change, post-welfare modernization can manifest itself in alternative models of future transformation.

How a given nation strikes a balance between the increased potential for economic and social control through the technical-scientific rationalization of its resources and the individual's capacity to influence his own environment is dependent on particular systemic characteristics. Of special importance in determining the course of modernization in specific countries is the nature of prevailing elite attitudes toward change. If national leaders are principally concerned with preserving their own social status and that of the dominant classes in society, post-welfare modernization will be limited largely to system maintenance. If, on the other hand, elites are receptive to the revolutionary potential of post-industrial change, the result of post-welfare modernization may be fundamental socio-political transformation.[4]

In Sweden modernization has embraced both the extensive rationalization of material and human resources to achieve a more ordered and productive society and the pursuit of liberty and egalitarianism. This achievement is due, in part, to a fortuitous combination of political and social factors. Thanks to 160 years of peace, early agreement on the nature of political authority, the existence of well-defined geographic boundaries, and the absence of deeply rooted social cleavages, Sweden has experienced the modernization process more rapidly and more completely than most other advanced systems. In virtually every category of modernity Sweden ranks among the most highly developed nations.[5]

But the specific course and future promise of modernization in Sweden are more than simply the chance outgrowth of history. Consistent with the remarks on modernization above, Sweden's present levels of modernity are the product of two closely related variables. The first of these is a commitment by the nation's political and organizational elites to socio-economic progress and democracy. The second is the capability of the system to translate these goals into meaningful action.

ELITE ATTITUDES IN SWEDEN:
AN HISTORICAL PERSPECTIVE

The nature of shared attitudes and values among the nation's political elites has proved crucial in determining both the particular course of modernization in Sweden and the system's characteristic patterns of pluralist democracy. Because a single party—the Social Democrats—has dominated cabinet office since 1932, much specific legislation in recent decades is the product of partisan political goals. Nevertheless, the Socialists have continually acted within the framework of a general elite consensus that embraces the majority party as well as its political opponents (members of the Communist, Center, Liberal, and Conservative parties) in Parliament.

Admittedly, important differences of ideology and sources of group support separate the Socialist, Communist, and non-Socialist parties. Theoretically the Social Democrats are committed to the nationalization of key industries and banks, although in practice they have pursued policies marked by pragmatism and moderation. Their basic pillar of electoral strength is organized labor, represented by the Swedish Federation of Trade Unions. Augmenting the Socialist share of the national vote—which has ranged from 42.2 per cent to 50.5 per cent during the postwar period—are significant numbers of white-collar workers and farmers.

More politicized than the majority Social Democrats, the minuscule Left-Party-Communists espouse social-political goals derived from classical Marxist-Leninist thought.[6] Drawing their support principally from workers in urban areas and timber-mining districts in the far north, the Communists advocate a radical restructuring of society (including the abolition of private ownership of the means of production) on behalf of extreme egalitarian norms.

In contrast, leaders of the three non-Socialist parties—the Center, the Liberals, and the Conservatives—oppose what they consider excessive state "intervention" in the nation's economy and the Socialist "concentration of power" in the political system. Their appeal is to individual initiative and the sanctity of free enterprise. Their followers include businessmen, industrialists, farmers, and middle- and upper-level white-collar workers.

Despite these cleavages, the four major parties, and, with qualifications, the Communist party as well, share common values that constitute a broad consensus on the desirability of modernization (as defined above) and pluralist processes of government. One of these is belief in progress—a product of the Enlightenment, the industrial revolution, and the diffusion of Liberal-Socialist thought in the nineteenth century. A second consensual value is political compromise. Throughout modern Swedish history, political antagonists have repeatedly demonstrated their willingness to accept reforms advanced by others or modifications in their own proposals to prevent open conflict and to preserve the continuity of political and social institutions.[7] Third, leaders of all the major parties endorse the concept of responsive government in which authority to participate in or influence decisions is widely dispersed throughout the political system.

Shared belief among Sweden's political elites in these values has greatly facilitated the nation's transformation from a relatively poor, oligarchical system at the beginning of this century to its present stage of economic prosperity and political democracy. Leaders of markedly contrasting ideological convictions and temperaments have contributed different initiatives in the process. Nineteenth-century Conservatives helped provide the foundation for subsequent economic development when they established the basis for today's state-owned national railway system in the 1850s; after the turn of the century Liberal and Socialist leaders successfully agitated for universal suffrage and a parliamentary form of government; and the Social Democrats were primarily responsible for introducing the nation's exemplary social welfare services from the mid-1930s onward.

Through their commitment to principles of socio-economic progress, Sweden's political elites thus helped contribute the first necessary condition for the rationalization of natural and human resources to achieve the material goals of modernization. Given the elite's positive endorsement of classical tenets of democratic government—including the sanctity of individual rights and the principle of open, free competition for political leadership—modernization has been accompanied by the attainment of individual legal and political equality. Finally, the elite's inclination toward political compromise has supported the evolution and maintenance of a pluralist system in which authority and influence are widely distributed among a variety of actors.

FACTORS OF SYSTEM CAPABILITY

The second basic condition of modernization—system capability to sustain change once the impetus for transformation has been introduced into the system—is a composite of material and social factors. First, ample supplies of natural resources in the form of rich iron ore deposits in the far north, extensive forest holdings, and the availability of abundant sources of inexpensive water power enabled large-scale industrialization to proceed rapidly and efficiently after its commencement in the 1890s. Second, a favorable combination of social traits—a high degree of cultural, religious, and linguistic homogeneity; mass literacy; and an emphasis on individual achievement engendered by Protestant religious values—facilitated the mobilization of human resources that were necessary to sustain Sweden's economic growth.

Social attitudes receptive to the demands of industrialization conditioned the evolution of Sweden's characteristic patterns of social organizations and political processes. A willingness to join with others in the pursuit of common objectives has nurtured the growth of multiple organizations that permeate both the economic and social systems. Nearly all industrial employees belong to the Swedish Federation of Trade Unions (abbreviated as the LO), which had a membership of 1,-607,000 in 1967, while a majority of white-collar workers (504,900) are members of the Central Organization of Salaried Employees (TCO). The Swedish Confederation of Professional Associations (SACO) claims nearly 99,000 members. Employers are organized nationally within the Swedish Employer Association (SAF), which comprises 25,800 individual firms.

In addition 1,356,000 Swedes are members of 297 retail societies that were affiliated in 1966 with the Cooperative Association, and 977,000 farmers belong to a network of agricultural cooperative associations. Over 300,000 Swedes are members of a variety of Protestant sects dissenting from the state Lutheran Church; more than one million students participate voluntarily in 134,000 study circles devoted to such subjects as philosophy, language, literature, and music; and more than two million have joined the Swedish Sports Federation.[8]

Simultaneously, a pervasive commitment by Sweden's organizational and political elites to the art of group compromise has facilitated the institutionalization of procedures and structures to resolve partisan conflict with a minimum of disruption. Within the economic sphere the two major partners in the labor market, the LO and the SAF, meet at two- or three-year intervals to negotiate nation-wide wage agreements with little direct intervention by the government. This procedure, which dates from the signing of the Saltsjöbaden Agreement in 1938,[9] is a major factor contributing to the stability of employer-employee relations in Sweden. In 1967, for example, a total of four strikes involving eighty-one workers resulted in the loss of only four hundred working days for the entire nation.[10]

Politically, structural features and decision-making processes of the parliamentary system have effectively translated the elite's consensus on compromise and pluralist democracy into stable patterns of shared influence and participation. Most policy initiatives, for example, are referred first to royal commissions composed of representatives of major interest associations and the four major parties before the national executive decides on its own proposals to Parliament. Within the Riksdag, debate is usually conducted in an informed, restrained fashion as deputies pass formal judgment on bills that have already been subjected to meticulous scrutiny in joint committees. In most cases the technical expertise of the members of these committees is a more important criterion in determining the merits of proposed legislation than is partisan affiliation.

Maintaining continual checks on the operation of the system as a whole are important extra-parliamentary and legal actors. An alert, aggressive, and generally partisan press—read by one of the world's best informed citizenries—subjects the political process to incisive, often highly critical scrutiny.[11] On a formal level of control, three ombudsmen are accorded extensive independent authority to probe the administrative, court, and military structures for instances of misconduct or unlawful acts.[12]

In combination, elite attitudes endorsing progress, compromise, and political democracy and the socio-economic and structural capacity of the system to achieve modernizing goals have yielded Sweden's present high level of modernity. Rationalization of the nation's economic and social resources has provided a positive support for the evolution of a pluralist political system in which liberty and egalitarianism serve as complementary bases for both government processes and the ends of policy.

That this achievement does not mark the end of the modernization process, however, is evident in the course of contemporary socio-economic and political change in Sweden. If there is an absence of dramatic crises and an apparent dearth of momentous social or political issues—such as the civil rights movement in the United States—Sweden has by no means attained utopia or even the "end-of-ideology." Beneath a surface of material prosperity and outward political tranquility, important forces of change at work in Sweden point toward the fundamental transformation of the existing system. From the enhanced capability of the system to achieve new goals of post-welfare society may emerge a potential alteration of present pluralist patterns in favor of radical redistributive and participative norms.

SOCIO-ECONOMIC BASIS OF CHANGE

Change in contemporary Sweden has assumed a variety of forms. Trade-union spokesmen have initiated innovative proposals for economic reform.[13] The Liberal, Center, and Conservative parties have largely abandoned their "strictly competitive" stance of past decades and moved toward closer coordination of party structures and programs.[14] In recent years "revisionists" have assumed control of the Communist party from within. Responding to these initiatives, the governing Social Democrats have proved receptive to demands for new economic, social, and political policies.

These changes, which are explored in greater detail below, are a reflection of basic processes of continuing modernization within both the socio-economic and political spheres. Corresponding increments in system capabilities have provided new opportunities for the nation's political elites to pursue rationalizing goals in both the economic and social systems.

Continued modernization in today's Sweden is, in major part, a function of increasing affluence. Between 1960 and 1965 the Swedish GNP rose an average of 5.1 per cent annually (compared with an annual growth rate of 4.2 per cent in the United States and 3.3 per cent in the United Kingdom). In absolute terms, the increase was from 62,487 million Swedish crowns (approximately $12 billion) to 101,485 million ($20 billion), for a corresponding gain in per capita GNP from 8,354 crowns ($1,670) to 13,122 crowns ($2,624). Private and public consumption rose annually 3.9 per cent and 5.0 per cent, respectively, during the same five-year period.[15]

Admittedly, the nation's economic growth has not affected all citizens equally.[16] Some strata have benefitted more than others, and structural readjustments within the economy—including automation, company mergers, the concentration of industry in urban areas, the abandonment of various industries as unproductive—have led to major problems of unemployment, reeducation, and industrial relocation.

Yet these very imbalances, combined with the increased total productivity of the economy, have proved a major stimulus to the rationalization of the nation's economy. In that aggregate affluence raises the levels of economic resources that are available for economic and social investment, Sweden's organizational and political leaders have acquired more effective means and a wider range of policy alternatives to overcome short-term disequilibrium and to plan for sustained economic growth in the future.

In contrast to the ad hoc, fragmentary efforts of American industrialists and political leaders to cope with similar problems of structural economic readjustment, the Swedish response has followed a more cogent blueprint of directed change. Sweden's Socialist political elites have not directly challenged the capitalist basis of the nation's economy. They have nevertheless drawn increasingly in recent years from their ideological heritage and from reform proposals advanced by the LO to initiate comprehensive measures to augment the role of the state in ensuring stable economic growth. The new economic program adopted by the Social Democrats in 1968 envisages the rational application of "scientific and technological advances . . ." to achieve the party's goals of full employment, individual security, a "more just distribution" of goods and services, and industrial democracy.[17] Policy innovations such as the passage of the supplementary pension legislation in 1959 (which led to the accumulation by 1967 of nearly three billion dollars in public funds that could be utilized in part for economic investment) and the creation of the state Investment Bank and Development Corporation in 1967 are examples of Socialist efforts to maximize the rationalization of guidelines and collective resources for future economic transformation.

A second major consequence of continuing economic modernization is its effect on Sweden's class structure. While Sweden remains a highly stratified society, affluence, and the prospect that in time more and more citizens will share in it, have helped blur traditional class cleavages in Sweden.[18] The emergence of a new middle class of civil servants, engineers, managers, and service personnel has eroded traditional class boundaries and engendered relatively greater social homogeneity. Equally important for the prospects of post-welfare modernization, the new middle class is well on its way toward becoming a prosperous class with a corresponding stake in the existing socio-economic system.

The growth of the new middle class or white-collar strata suggests a number of significant implications for the pursuit of cumulative rationality within both the economic and social systems. In order to preserve their status and economic security, the new middle-class strata are likely to respond favorably to changes instigated by the political elites to rationalize economic productivity. Hence, their endorsement of rationalizing policies within the economic sphere will be important for the articulation and aggregation of socio-economic interests by the political parties. At the same time spokesmen of the new middle class—especially leaders of white-collar unions such as SACO and TCO and consumer organizations—appear intent on modifying existing features of Sweden's welfare services. Specifically, they seek qualitative changes in state welfare functions such as retirement benefits, children allowances, and housing subsidies to tailor general social security provisions more to individual needs than has been the pattern in the past. That the new supplementary pension system provides benefits scaled to *individual* incomes during the fifteen most productive years of one's life and that a new office of "consumer ombudsman" was created in 1970 are indications that the cumulative rationalization of economic and social functions in Sweden will lead to greater attention to individual claims within the framework of a collective commitment to welfare and sustained economic growth.

Increasing affluence and accompanying changes in Sweden's class structure thus constitute a principal impetus for the pursuit of cumulative rationality in innovative transformation within both the economy and the social system. The steps that political, organizational, and bureaucratic leaders have taken to rationalize economic production and meet new demands for qualitative improvements in social services clearly reveal the link between economic-technological "determinism" and the freedom of political choice in advanced urban-industrial orders. Depending on the nature of prevailing elite values and attitudes, a nation's leadership can choose either to manipulate forces of systemic change to preserve established patterns of production and social status. Or they may seek to invest enhanced system capability in programs of progressive social transformation. Because of their traditional commitment to socio-economic progress and humanistic principles of classical Socialist-Liberal thought, Sweden's leaders have inclined toward the second alternative. Their receptiveness to innovative change is strength-

ened by the emergence of new forms of critical consciousness within
Swedish society that may accelerate parallel post-welfare reforms in the
political sphere.

POLITICAL ATTITUDES AND THE RISE OF
NEW FORMS OF CRITICAL CONSCIOUSNESS

Underlying changes in Sweden's socio-economic structures have not
yielded a uniformity of political attitudes toward either the existing wel-
fare-political system or the possible goals of post-welfare society. Indeed, a number of traditional ideological cleavages continue to persist
while new sets of attitudes have emerged to challenge prevailing ones.

A characteristic gradation of attitudes toward the welfare state
among supporters of the established political parties reveals a persistent
lack of popular consensus on the scope of welfare policies. In his study
of voting behavior in the 1960 election, Bo Särlvik found that 89 per
cent of the voters who strongly favored welfare measures supported the
Social Democrats or Communists while 50 per cent of those who were
most hostile to the welfare state endorsed the Conservatives. Support
for the Center and Liberal parties was concentrated among voters who
were ambivalent in their attitudes or weakly to moderately opposed to
the welfare state.[19] The decreasing endorsement of welfare measures
from left to right on the political spectrum reflects the basic cleavage
between Socialist and non-Socialist forces in Swedish politics that has
typified the political system since the early part of this century. These
differences in attitudes are primarily a function of family and group socialization patterns, and they constitute a principal source of electoral
stability among the general populace.[20]

Simultaneously the emergence in recent years of an articulate
Swedish New Left—a more ideologically coherent critique of present
socio-economic relations and political processes than its American or
German counterparts—has injected new perspectives into the continu-
ing debate on domestic welfare and political issues. Rooted in part in
international developments such as student demonstrations in the
United States and on the Continent, the importation of French and
American neo-Marxist thought, and the trend toward polycentrism in

the world Communist movement, New Left attitudes in Sweden are also a reflection of perceived contradictions between democratic-humanistic values and the actual performance of the Swedish system. As Kurt Samuelsson, an economist and member of the Social Democratic Party, has written: "There exist in this welfare society built-in contradictions and imbalances. These contradictions and imbalances reveal the fallacy of the belief that harmony and stability have been achieved. . . . Among the failures of welfare society, from a democratic socialist viewpoint, is the absence of equality." [21]

Claiming adherents among all of the traditional parties (though primarily in the Communist and Social Democratic parties), spokesmen of the Swedish New Left endorse the contemporary welfare state but at the same time urge its further development in a wide range of areas. Militant Communist and left Social Democratic ideologues advocate the abolition of private ownership of major industries and banks in favor of various models of decentralized worker-control. Although dissident members of the Liberal, Center, and Conservative parties do not share the Communist-left Socialist rejection of capitalism, they advocate with comparable intensity the diffusion of economic power (through greater incentives for private savings and investments) and the democratization of decision-making within major socio-economic organizations. In both cases the basis of ideological criticism of existing policies and political processes is the premise that socio-economic transformation has made possible new solutions to the fundamental problems of unequal distribution of status and influence among the masses.

Occupying a middle ground between the persistence of traditional political attitudes and increased politicization among New Left forces is "cultural radicalism." A product principally of a deeply rooted but accelerating process of secularization within Swedish society, cultural radicalism is an intellectual movement subjecting virtually all traditional values to critical reappraisal. Its most articulate manifestations include new experiments in movies and literature and the extensive moral debate on questions concerning sexual freedom and individual "liberation" from "repressive" social mores which has been conducted for over a decade in the columns of the daily press.[22]

With the appearance of cultural radicalism as a dominant theme of Sweden's political-moral debate, the new individualism of Swedish

post-welfare society is perhaps most clearly manifest. Its principal leaders, a number of whom identify with the New Left, are highly critical of
many aspects of the contemporary political system. But unlike the nihil-
ism of hippie subcultures, their views are generally tempered by a
strong commitment to social responsibility within the framework of existing structures and decision processes.

Modifications over time in general attitudes toward the welfare
state and the emergence of new attitudes of social protest and critical
consciousness have combined to reinforce incipient structural change
within the Swedish party system. While the outcome of this process is
by no means predetermined, one effect is likely to be progress toward
cumulative equality as a second major goal of modernization in the
Swedish post-welfare state.

STRUCTURAL CHANGE IN THE PARTY SYSTEM

The increasing capacity of the Swedish system to sustain new levels of
transformation, the growing homogenity of social classes, and the revitalization of ideological debate have prompted potentially significant
changes among the established political parties. Structural change of the
party system—apparent in the evolution of non-Socialist parties toward
relatively greater bloc cohesion and the temporary resurgence of Communist electoral strength—may serve as the principal impetus for post-
welfare political innovation.

The significance of change in the party system lies in the effect it
may have on translating the contemporary political debate in Sweden
into institutionalized reforms. What is at stake is not so much whether
the Social Democrats maintain their present parliamentary majority or
whether the non-Socialist parties can attain executive leadership as an
alternative government. The important determinant in the continued
transformation of the political system is the qualitative nature of political goals as defined and implemented by the nation's elite.

Within the non-Socialist camp the most dramatic evidence of
change is the transformation of the traditionally highly competitive
Center, Liberal, and Conservative party structures into a loose bloc alliance. Although non-Socialist leaders and most of their followers remain

less enthusiastic in their endorsement of the welfare state than Social Democrats or Communists, their attitudes have not proved rigid. First the Center, then the Liberal, and finally the Conservative leadership abandoned their ideological hostility to activist state policies initiated by the Social Democrats in the mid-1930s to provide minimal welfare services and stimulate economic growth. As non-Socialist leaders have come to endorse the principles of the welfare system, they have moved closer to a common ideological front and the basis of functional party unity.

In part their motivations were tactical. The repeated electoral successes of the Social Democrats from 1932 onward demonstrated the widespread appeal of Socialist-sponsored welfare measures which the non-Socialist leaders could ill afford to ignore. Moreover, they correctly perceived that only through tacit cooperation could the non-Socialist parties hope to secure a sufficient electoral majority to dislodge the Social Democrats from their long tenure in cabinet office.

Thus leaders of the Center, Liberal, and Conservative parties joined in a *Borgfreden* in which they pledged to refrain from intra-bloc controversy on the eve of the 1966 communal election in an attempt to demonstrate their credibility as an alternative government. Center and Liberal leaders went so far as to establish a joint executive committee that negotiated a common electoral program. Partially as a result of these efforts at non-Socialist unity, the opposition parties won a majority in the communal election as Social Democratic strength fell to its lowest point in more than three decades.[23]

An equally important factor in the transformation of non-Socialist bloc characteristics is socio-economic change. Affluence, urbanization, and the growth of new middle-class strata have significantly altered the group basis of party support. To adjust to these changes, leaders of the opposition parties have been compelled simultaneously to broaden their parties' appeal and to articulate policy innovations on behalf of the new white-collar strata (e.g., improvements in the physical-social environment of urban areas and increased state investments in housing construction).

Tactical cooperation and ideological refurbishment among the non-Socialist parties have not led to a formal merger of the bourgeois bloc (as many party activities, especially former Liberal leader Bertil

Ohlin and spokesmen of the various youth organizations, had hoped). The reluctance of Center chairman Gunner Hedlund to commit himself to a definite program of amalgamation and the insistence of the Conservative party on maintaining a distinct "profile" in taxation questions were obstacles too major for those intent on merger to overcome. Nonetheless consensus on basic ideological principles and the victory of the non-Socialist forces in the 1966 election contributed important new inputs to the process of political change in Sweden.

Parallel transformation of the Swedish Communist party provides a second major source of goal redefinition within the domestic system. Although the Communist party is far too small to pose a direct challenge as a serious contender for cabinet office, it exercises potentially important indirect influence—much in the same manner as third parties in the United States—on the majority Social Democrats. Socialist leaders fervently disavow periodic Communist offers of collaboration, but they share with the Communist party a sufficient degree of ideological affinity and commitment to the representation of working-class interests that they are not wholly insensitive to the moral content of Communist agitation.

Increasing the capacity of Communist spokesmen to influence Socialist policies was the victory of New Left forces within the Communist party at the January 1964 Congress. The transition of party authority from the discredited Stalinist leadership—widely blamed within party ranks for the persistent decline of electoral fortunes during the 1950s because of its indefatigable defense of Soviet policies—to the personable and less doctrinaire C. H. Hermansson marked a major transition in the Swedish Communist movement. Like the Socialist People's parties in neighboring Norway and Denmark, the Communist party in Sweden asserted its autonomy from Moscow and began to emphasize a distinctive national path to socialism.[24]

Capitalizing on rising New Left sentiment among political dissidents of all ideological backgrounds, Hermansson initiated a number of changes in party norms and goals in an effort to legitimize the Left Party-Communists' claim as ideological spokesmen for "renewal" in Swedish politics. In a series of moves intended to repudiate the party's Stalinist legacy, the central decision-making body (formerly the Politburo) was reconstituted as the executive committee; congress delegates reaffirmed principles of civil liberties and endorsed a multiparty system; open debate was encouraged within the party hierarchy; and concerted efforts were made to co-opt members of the Social Democratic party into local Socialist associations and electoral alliances.

Conceding that mass affluence and the integrative role of the LO and the Social Democratic party in articulating and aggregating working-class interests virtually excluded the possibility of revolutionary change, Hermansson and his lieutenants emphasized instead the need to democratize industry through evolutionary steps. Former doctrinaire insistence on the nationalization of industry under control of a party-state bureaucracy was abandoned as Communist leaders formulated alternative proposals for localized worker-ownership of factories and the extension of producer cooperatives. The goal of Communist agitation became, in short, the progressive transformation of Swedish society from a capitalistic political democracy to a decentralized form of economic democracy.

As long as the Social Democratic government remained relatively passive in the face of New Left ferment, and as long as the trend toward polycentrism in Eastern Europe continued unabated, the Communists were successful in mobilizing an increasing number of voters to their cause. Communist strength rose from 3.8 per cent to 5.4 per cent in the 1964 election (the first that was held after Hermansson's election as party chairman), and reached a peak of 6.4 per cent in the 1966 communal election. Only after the Social Democrats began to respond to the combined ideological onslaught from revitalized opponents on both the left and right, and after the Soviet Union invaded Czechoslovakia in August 1968, was the Communist advance reversed.

Together changes on both extremes of Sweden's party system contributed to the policy initiatives that the Social Democrats fashioned after their loss in the 1966 election. Cognizant that a comparable defeat in the parliamentary election in September 1968 could result in the formation of a non-Socialist coalition, as had occurred in Norway in 1965 and in Denmark in 1968, the Social Democrats responded with the adoption of their new economic program and legislation to establish the Development Corporation and state-owned Investment Bank. Both steps were intended to rationalize economic production in accordance with collective social needs and constituted a concession to New Left demands for further democratization of the economy without posing an overt threat to private enterprise. By incorporating demands for innovation from the left and avoiding direct confrontation with forces on the right, the Social Democrats succeeded in obtaining a new mandate for continued executive leadership. Their 1968 majority of 50.1 per cent was subsequently reduced to 45.3 per cent in 1970, but indirect Communist support in Parliament sustained their claim to cabinet office.

Structural change in the Swedish party system thus served to accelerate the process of goal redefinition in the political system. In the short run this will mean increased social control over economic investments and planning. The long-term prospect of political modernization in Sweden is the attainment of cumulative equality.

THE QUEST FOR CUMULATIVE EQUALITY

To the extent that Sweden's present and future leaders continue to implement New Left-inspired goals to increase collective influence over productive processes, egalitarianism in Swedish society will be further promoted. In light of elite-mass endorsement of libertarian principles —including the right of individuals to choose among a set of political alternatives in expressing preferences that are accorded equal weight in the electoral process [25]—the pursuit of egalitarianism will be coupled with the maintenance of existing guarantees of political liberty. The result would be a synthesis of egalitarian and libertarian norms in a condition of cumulative equality.

The institutionalization of cumulative equality in Sweden is likely to assume a variety of forms. Already the constitution has been amended to abolish the archaic, indirectly elected Senate and to institute a unicameral legislature. Staggered indirect elections to the Senate have for decades augmented declining parliamentary majorities in the lower house long after a party had lost its popular mandate. Rationalizing the parliamentary structure through adoption of a unicameral system based on the simultaneous election of all its members will result in the immediate translation of individual electoral preferences into effective political choice. Similarly the present consolidation of fragmented local communal governments into units of comparable size and population will lessen present disparities in the weight of individual electoral participation.

Sources of economic and class inequalities will conceivably be mitigated through advancing affluence and rationalizing measures by the state to sustain economic productivity. An important corollary of the cumulative rationalization of Sweden's socio-economic resources would include the refinement of present government policies to redistribute the nation's wealth through combined programs of progressive taxation, collective investments through the supplementary pension fund and the Investment Bank, and incentives for individual savings. A further step toward the attainment of cumulative equality in socio-economic status would be concerted joint efforts by government agencies and major groups such as the LO to re-educate workers who are displaced by structural economic readjustment and automation to assume new occupational tasks. The implementation of New Left demands for the democratization of decisions within major social organizations—including unions as well as political parties—would improve the participative opportunities of individual group members. Corresponding educational reforms and the progressive democratization of the higher educational system would fulfill in part the demands of the cultural radical movement for greater intellectual freedom.

The quest for cumulative equality will not mean the attainment of a classless society or the total elimination of unequal or political status. As Dahl cogently reminds us, specialization of functions, inherited differences among individuals, and differences in individual incentives combine to yield an uneven distribution of control over political resources in all political systems.[26] Yet when measured against the normative values of Liberal-Socialist thought, the successive reduction of socio-economic barriers to individual choice will constitute a significant advance in man's qualitative control of his social and individual environments.

Whether the achievement of cumulative equality will in fact characterize the political modernization of Sweden's post-welfare state remains for the present only a potential option among a variety of alternative courses. Theoretically the Swedish elites could actively resist the challenge of post-welfare modernization to their own status or choose merely to react to day-to-day issues without undertaking any long-range innovative steps to implement transforming change. But given the nature of shared elite receptiveness to the demands of socio-economic progress and the increasing capacity of the system to attain rationalizing goals, the quest for cumulative equality in Sweden seems a realistic prospect.

Notes

1. "Modernization," Rustow writes, "denotes widening control over nature through closer cooperation among men. . . . The modern attitude . . . assumes that man can improve his lot through systematic application of science, technology, and social organization." Dankwart A. Rustow, *A World of Nations* (Washington, D.C., 1967), pp. 3–9. Black defines modernization "as the process by which historically evolved institutions are adapted to the rapidly changing functions that reflect the unprecedented increase in man's knowledge, permitting control over his environment, that accompanied the scientific revolution." C. E. Black, *The Dynamics of Modernization* (New York, 1966), p. 7.

2. Manfred Halpern, "A Redefinition of the Revolutionary Situation," *Journal of International Affairs*, XXIII (1969), 54–75.

3. Rustow, *A World of Nations*, p. 16. An explicit definition of cumulative rationality is suggested by Tawney's concept of rational policy: "A rational policy . . . will aim at establishing, by social action, conditions of life work compatible with the standards of a civilized society, at extending the area of industrial relations subject to collective control and joint determination, and at ensuring that, on economic issues affecting the public welfare, the community can regularly and easily make its will prevail." R. H. Tawney, *Equality* (New York, 1961), p. 194.

4. I emphasize elite values and attitudes as a crucial variable in determining the course of change in particular societies because of the central role that elites play in determining national policy priorities. In that elites—by the very definition of their high socio-political status—are those "groups in the population who are better informed about policy matters and who have greater influence . . ." than the majority of citizens in a given political system, their attitudes and pursuit of particular goals have a direct bearing on how and in what direction the system develops. Quote from Karl Deutsch and Lewis Edinger, *Germany Rejoins the Powers* (Stanford, 1959), p. 60.

5. Selected indices of modernity include the following comparative data:

	Sweden	United States	Britain
Percentage of literate population aged 15 and over (1959)*	98.5	98.0	98.5
Life expectancy of females at age 0 (1968)†	75.7	74.2	74.4
Nonagricultural employment as a percentage of working-age population (1960)*	58.9	56.3	66.6
Per capita GNP (1967)†	$3,121	$3,474	$1,682
Automobiles per 1000 inhabitants (1967)†	250	398	188
Telephones per 1000 inhabitants (1967)†	473	517	217
Radio and television licenses (sets) per 1000 inhabitants (1967)†	286	387	259
Newspaper circulation per 1000 inhabitants (1967)†	514	309	488
Votes in national elections as a percentage of voting-age population (1968, 1970)	88.2‡	55.8§	72.0‡

* Bruce M. Russett, et al., *World Handbook of Political and Social Indicators* (New Haven, 1964).

† United Nations, *Statistical Yearbook* (United Nations, 1968).

‡ 1970

§ 1968

6. Reflecting the diffusion of New Left-ideological innovation from the early 1960s onward in Sweden, the Swedish Communist party adopted its present name of Left Party-Communists following the 1966 communal election.

7. Examples of Sweden's characteristic politics of compromise include the transformation of the four-estate Parliament into a bicameral legislature in the constitutional reform of 1865–1866; the adoption of manhood suffrage in the reforms of 1907–1909; and the introduction of universal suffrage in 1919–1921. In the latter two instances Swedish Conservatives acceded to Liberal-Socialist demands to abolish restrictions on the right to vote in exchange for the adoption of proportional representation and the retention of the indirectly elected upper house of Parliament. For detailed treatments of these reforms see Rustow, *The Politics of Compromise* (Princeton, 1955) and Douglas V. Verney, *Parliamentary Reform in Sweden 1866–1921* (Oxford, 1957).

8. Sweden, Statistiska centralbyrån, *Statistisk årsbok för Sverige 1968* (Stockholm, 1968).

9. The agreement is named after the resort town on Sweden's east coast, where the agreement was negotiated.

10. During the ten-year period from 1957 to 1967 an average number of fifteen strikes occurred annually. This average is inflated by a nation-wide

teachers' strike in 1966, which contributed a major portion of the loss of 352,000 working days in that year. The annual average from 1957 to 1967 was 48,000 working days lost. *Statistisk årsbok 1968, ibid.*, p. 246. In December 1969 labor peace was disrupted in an unprecedented strike by 4,700 workers in northern mine fields in and near Kiruna, which was directed less against management (in this case a state-owned enterprise) than against the centralized union bureaucracy. Although the strike was settled on compromise terms in February 1970, its very occurrence and intensity revealed the persisting tension between opposing claims of collective and individual control that characterizes contemporary processes of post-industrial modernization in Sweden. For a succinct summary of the causes and outcome of the strike, see Roland Huntford, "Why Did They Strike?" *Sweden Now*, 4 (June 1970), 36–38.

11. Sweden has the highest per capita newspaper circulation in the world (see note 5 above). Nearly all newspapers are identified with partisan political viewpoints (only 21 out of 152 formally proclaim themselves independent); most support the non-Socialist parties.

12. The office of ombudsman was created when the present constitution was adopted in 1809; a second ombudsman for military affairs was first elected by Parliament in 1915. In March 1968 the functions of the legal-administrative and military ombudsmen were combined into a single office with 3 incumbents. During the first year following this reform the ombudsmen undertook 3,128 investigations. Of this total 2,708 were based on complaints from individual citizens, 393 were made on the ombudsmen's own initiative, and 27 dealt with administrative or internal questions. The ombudsmen ordered 7 prosecutions and admonished 272 public officials; they referred the remaining cases to other government agencies or dismissed them. Sweden, *The Swedish Parliamentary Ombudsmen, Annual Report for 1969, Summary in English* (Stockholm, 1970), pp. 521–23.

13. These include efforts by the LO to promote industrial democracy and greater individual self-determination at places of work. A comprehensive analysis of the social consequences of technical change for the status of workers in contemporary Sweden is contained in Edmund Dahlström, et al., *Teknisk förändring och arbetsanpassning* (Stockholm, 1966).

14. Hancock, *Sweden: A Multiparty System in Transition?* (Denver, 1968), pp. 19–27.

15. Sweden, Ministry of Finance, *The Swedish Economy 1966–1970* (Stockholm, 1966), pp. 10 and 15; Sweden, Statistiska centralbyrån, *Statistisk årsbok för Sverige 1965* (Stockholm, 1965), p. 332; and *Statistisk årsbok 1968, ibid.*, p. 355.

16. More than one-third (37.9 per cent) of the Swedish working force, for example, earns less than $2,000 a year. In contrast the mean income for the

working force as a whole is $3,400. *Statistisk årsbok 1968, ibid.*, pp. 346 and 352.

17. Social Democratic party, *Program för aktiv näringsliv* (Stockholm, 1968).

18. Patterns of change in Swedish social structure are analyzed in Gösta Carlsson, "Social stratifiering och rörlighet," in Carlsson, et al., *Svensk samhällsstruktur i sociologisk belysning* (Stockholm, 1965), pp. 348–83, and Sten Carlsson, "Den sociala omgrupperingen i Sverige efter 1866," in Arthur Thomson, ed., *Samhälle och riksdag* (Stockholm, 1966), I, 3–371.

19. Bo Särlvik, "Party Politics and Electoral Opinion Formation: A Study of Issues in Swedish Politics 1956–1960," *Scandinavian Political Studies*, No. 2 (New York and Helsinki, 1967), 170.

20. *Ibid.*, and Bo Anderson, "Some Problems of Change in the Swedish Electorate," *Acta Sociologica*, VI, fasc. 4 (1962), 241–55.

21. Kurt Samuelsson, *Är ideologierna döda* (Stockholm, 1966), pp. 232–35.

22. An excellent discussion of the major themes of moral, social, and esthetic debate is Lars Gustafsson, *The Public Dialogue in Sweden* (Stockholm, 1964).

23. The Socialists received 42.2 per cent of the popular vote, their weakest support since 1934 when they had obtained 42.1 per cent.

24. The Socialist People's parties were founded in Denmark and Norway in 1958 and 1960, respectively. On the ideological transformation of the Left Party-Communists in Sweden, see Åke Sparring, *Från Höglund till Hermansson* (Stockholm, 1967). Hermansson elaborates his own views on revisionism in C. H. Hermansson, *Vänsterns väg* (Stockholm, 1965).

25. Robert Dahl, *A Preface to Democratic Theory* (Chicago, 1956, 1967), p. 67.

26. Dahl, *Modern Political Analysis* (Englewood Cliffs, N.J., 1963), pp. 32–35 and 55–71.

KAJ BJÖRK

Individualism and Collectivism

IN SWEDISH DEBATE the end of ideology thesis has been defended primarily by Herbert Tingsten. As editor-in-chief of Sweden's largest morning newspaper, *Dagens Nyheter,* Tingsten was able for a considerable period of time to propagate his ideas effectively. Swedish politicians within the various parties, however, never accepted Tingsten's analysis. Instead they have consistently maintained that ideologies continue to play an important role in the competition among parties.

These differences of opinion can be explained in part by the fact that the participants in the debate interpreted "ideology" in various ways. Nevertheless, those who have denied the end of ideology thesis have not maintained that the Swedish parties represent various closed ideological systems. The ordering of priorities among various political values is naturally related partially to the ideological heritage of the parties and partially to the social composition of groups to which each of the parties primarily appeals. In general most political observers in Sweden do not deny that ideological conflicts are less pronounced now than they were several decades ago, but the relative leveling of differences among the various parties does not constitute sufficient grounds to conclude that ideologies have disappeared.

Against this background the contemporary criticism against the end of ideology arguments of writers such as Daniel Bell and S. M. Lipset does not strike those Swedes who have been actively involved in our nation's politics as especially original. After Tingsten's resignation as editor of *Dagens Nyheter,* his ideas have elicited only limited interest. In fact, ideological aspects of the Swedish political debate have actually become more pronounced in recent years. This is reflected not only in the contributions of the so-called New Left, which has been accorded widespread attention in the press and other forms of mass media despite its numerical insignificance, but also in the official pronouncements of the established parties.

The recent resurgence of ideological controversy in Sweden does not strike those who stand in the midst of this process as a break with the past but only as a continuation and vitalization of movements that have long existed in Swedish political life. Undeniably one can observe a greater emphasis on equality of status and participation in the contemporary political debate. But the Social Democrats have propounded these goals for decades. All that is new in the present situation is that the other parties have seen fit to incorporate them in their own political agitation.

At the same time social developments in Sweden have hardly created new and unforeseen problems comparable to those that have arisen in the United States. Certainly politicians cannot always foresee which problems will demand their primary attention at any given time, but questions concerning participation in economic and administrative decisions and degrees of bureaucratic decentralization are of such ancient origin that it is hardly surprising when they emerge more strongly in the foreground. In general Swedes do not experience such issues as signaling a potential revolutionary break with the present—even if the ongoing debate concerning such problems might gradually lead to radical changes in Swedish society. Nor is it possible to speak in Sweden, as one might in the United States, of the failure of parties and interest groups to adapt to demands for change. On the contrary one can note active efforts within most major organizations to adapt to changing conditions. This applies not only to political parties and interest groups but to a certain degree to the state church and free church groups as well.

These factors make it especially difficult for an active Swedish politician to participate in the debate on the questions posed in the Introduction to this volume. My own contribution is therefore limited to a commentary on the proposition that a "new individualism" can radically influence the structure of modern welfare society. This commentary is a critical one. In my opinion "individualism" has too many diffuse connotations to be applied in a fruitful manner to an analysis of contemporary developments in Swedish society.

THE AMBIGUITY OF INDIVIDUALISM

It would be difficult, if not impossible, to reach any kind of agreement in Sweden on the meaning of individualism. Many, perhaps most, Swedes consider individualism as merely a slogan, and they give little thought to its content. Who doesn't wish to defend the essence of his individuality? Who would deny the right of others to develop their own individuality as well? But is this the meaning of individualism? Should individualism be considered the antithesis of solidarity? Or is it simply the opposite of a lack of independence in attitudes and practical behavior?

Naturally one can posit a tension between individualism and collectivism by maintaining that collective development implies a threat to the freedom and independence of the individual. But supporters of different forms of collectivism reply that it is only within the framework of collective efforts that the individual has the opportunity to develop fully his personality. All parties in Sweden are officially supporters of the doctrine, "man in the center." This concept has approximately the same meaning as the vague expression, "emphasis on the individual." Possibly it can be useful to discuss how strong this emphasis has been among the various political movements during the past century, and how important one can expect it to become in the future.

During the nineteenth century Sweden was a bureaucratic oligarchy in which only a small minority had any meaningful political influence. Nevertheless there was margin for limited ideological debate, even if it lacked significant breadth. The opposition to bureaucracy and conformism was individualistic in the sense that it advocated the freedom of the individual against various forms of state coercion. Within the religious realm, opposition took the form of various free associations outside the Lutheran state church. Politically, a minority of Liberals fought against the power of the king and the authority of the bureaucracy. It is doubtful, however, that the resistance of the agricultural class to various defense burdens—one of the central political problems of that day—can be viewed as an expression of any special individualism.

Even during the nineteenth century and at the beginning of the twentieth, it was difficult to demonstrate a contradiction between individualism and collectivism. Opposition movements lay behind the growth of various popular organizations such as the free-church movement, the temperance organizations, later the trade unions, cooperatives, and political parties. These organizations were, however, collectivist associations that did not always display tolerance in their outward manifestations. Nevertheless, they sought by various means to achieve the liberation of the individual. A Conservative distrust of these popular movements was usually combined with reverence for the bureaucratic, oligarchical state and its ideology. Where, then, was individualism? Among the Conservatives or their organized opponents?

During the first decades of the twentieth century it is possible that the Liberals were more individualistic, at least in a specialized sense, than other political movements. But the situation was far from unambiguous. The major strength of the Liberal movement lay within the free churches, which exercised strict discipline over their members. The type of "old individualism" that perceived a danger in the growing strength of interest associations was represented especially among the Conservatives. The Social Democrats, on the other hand, were collectivists to the extent that they strongly emphasized class and organization solidarity. Simultaneously, however, strong criticism was voiced within the Social Democratic movement against certain anti-individualistic aspects of Swedish society, such as forced membership in the state church.

CHANGED CONTEXT OF INDIVIDUALISM

The opposition of "old liberalism" to various types of interest organizations gradually weakened in the decades after World War I. Antipathy toward trade unions, which is still believed to have considerable influence in the United States, has disappeared from Swedish society. All social groups consider it natural to belong to some sort of organization. Those who choose not to belong to an organization are, in fact, considered somewhat disreputable because they are suspected of wishing to benefit from the accomplishments achieved by organizations without contributing their own support to them. Minority groups complain occasionally about the dominance of organizational leadership, but solidarity with one's own organization is generally considered a moral responsibility.

The type of "rugged individualism" that is expressed as animosity toward the government's social policies has also increasingly disappeared from the Swedish social scene. The Liberals have abandoned their earlier restrictive attitude toward costly social reforms and now strive to appear even more receptive to reform than the Social Democrats. During various periods the Conservatives played on the theme that a citizen should "stand on his own two feet" and not accept help from the state. But now even the Conservative party officially accepts all important aspects of the existing system of social security. During the supplementary pension controversy in the 1950s a number of opinions about the possibility and suitability of varying pensions, to be determined according to individual needs, were expressed. The Social Democrats, who gave priority to the principle that the system should provide sufficient pension benefits for all citizens, emerged as the victor. That obligatory supplementary pensions have been so completely achieved in Sweden does not mean, however, that one accords the individual less consideration than earlier. On the contrary, with the achievement of a comprehensive social security system it is possible to pay greater attention to the needs of the individual. When the Social Democrats, in particular, have opposed the use of the means test to determine qualifications for social support, their principal purpose has been to demonstrate their respect for the worth of the individual. From the Socialist perspective the poor should not have to submit themselves to humiliating scrutiny and control on the part of state officials simply because they need assistance. It is also typical that all parties now demonstrate a growing interest for groups such as the handicapped that do not receive sufficient support through the general insurance programs.

The debate concerning Swedish education policies also illustrates the difficulty of characterizing developments by the formula, "more or less individualism." In England, for example, it may be considered an expression of individualism when parents seek to choose a special type of education for their children. In Sweden the school system has for a long time been more unitary in nature than in numerous other countries, and it had developed in the direction of even greater uniformity. At the same time the few existing private schools with divergent educational programs have either disappeared or have been integrated into the general school system. One has sought, in short, to move away from a parallel school system in which children of better-situated parents received a better education and hence enhanced possibilities for career advancement than the children of workers and farmers. Undoubtedly there are various collectivistic aspects in the modern Swedish school system, but at the same time one of its proclaimed goals is "individualized education." Defenders of the current system can maintain, with good reason, that the unitary school in contemporary Sweden simultaneously makes it possible to view every child as an individual. There is still a certain tension between ideal and reality, but the direction of the development is clear.

INDIVIDUALISM IN THE
ECONOMY AND SOCIETY

What is the situation within the Swedish economy? Has a tendency toward collective action diminished possibilities for individual economic initiatives? That would be difficult to assert. Little nationalization of private enterprise has occurred in Sweden, and numerous examples can be cited of how a single man has built a small workshop into a large industry. On the other hand there is in Sweden, as in many other countries, a marked tendency toward the concentration of industry and retail outlets. As a result many small business firms have been forced to close their doors. To mitigate the effects of concentration in the private sector various state-sponsored measures have been implemented to promote the interests of small businessmen. Even today small businessmen continue to play an important role politically. Thus collective state actions have served not to restrict private economic initiatives but rather to encourage them.

It would be hazardous to juxtapose the two questions, "individualism-collectivism" and "decentralization-centralization." Centralization of various problems can often strengthen the position of the individual. The centrally directed Swedish labor market, for example, facilitates effective assistance to smaller groups of citizens when businesses have been abandoned. It is worth noting, however, that Swedish society has virtually always displayed strong tendencies toward both centralization and decentralization. A tradition of local self-government is more strongly developed in Sweden than in most other Western countries, and the local government units have effective means to assert themselves vis-à-vis the central government. However, the development of the welfare system has created new problems in this sphere. The traditional units of local government have proved too small to support the activities that have been delegated to them in the expansion of the educational system, for example. As a result Sweden has had to create larger communal units. This process involves a certain risk that a smaller number of people can be actively engaged in the work of local government. Questions concerning relations among the local communes, regional organs, and the national government are now under discussion. It is probable that a solution will be achieved that cannot be considered either more or less centralized than the present system.

When one discusses the possibilities of a new individualism in the industrial nations, the question in Sweden cannot be directed either toward dismantling the present system of social security or the unitary school system or toward reducing the influence of interest associations. There is no indication that any force of importance would wish to question these products of a long development. The discussion must instead focus on other questions. One can posit in Sweden, as in other countries, a persisting cleavage between an active elite in society— politicians, industrial owners, leaders of organizations, and experts— and a large mass of citizens who find it difficult to orient themselves in an increasingly complex society and who believe that they often lack sufficient influence over contemporary developments. This tension can call forth a number of inarticulate protests, for example, among young groups who do not find welfare society sufficiently stimulating. The emergence of such tensions makes it urgent that the elites continually seek to find new means to interest, activate, and engage citizens in the work of society.

Naturally one can also find examples of the opposite attitude: that those who have already achieved a degree of influence would prefer not to be challenged in their exercise of authority. But the prevailing official ethic in Sweden maintains that each citizen should interest himself in social questions and exercise influence through the channels that democracy provides him. An individualism that rejects the complicated machinery of democracy can naturally arise among certain groups, but it is difficult to see how this type of individualism can become a constructive force in the continuing development of society.

Another variant of individualism is perhaps the demand for increased sexual freedom, which has grown for decades in Sweden. It has culminated in the demand for changes in the law to make such freedom absolute. Similar tendencies have also emerged with respect to freedom of speech and publication. Public opinion and legislation are undoubtedly tending in the direction of increased freedom of expression. In practice, for example, pornography is published almost without restriction.

RELATED ISSUES OF WELFARE POLITICS

The development of Swedish welfare society has raised additional issues of a "new individualism." As a Social Democrat I have never found it difficult to interest either my own party colleagues or members of other parties in such questions as the risks connected with the right of society to determine through psychological tests the qualifications of those seeking employment with the state. At the same time I have encountered widespread agreement that society has a right to strengthen the sanctity of individual privacy through legislation banning the use of secret listening devices.

In recent years politicians have also concerned themselves with such issues as increased opportunities for adult education, greater attention to the treatment of individuals in prison, efforts to create meaningful jobs, and better opportunities for contact among the aged. All these problems reflect heightened political awareness of the changing status of the individual in contemporary welfare society, and have stimulated competition among the existing parties to fashion appropriate responses.

An increased willingness to treat women as individuals rather than simply as appendages of men is another "individual" problem that has been very much emphasized in the current Swedish political debate. Changes in the labor market leading to increased demand for female labor have emphasized the question of equal rights between the sexes. Special women's organizations, which have played an important role in Swedish society for a long time, have also contributed significantly to this development. It is above all the Social Democrats and the Liberals who compete to demonstrate their interests for employed women, and this tendency has begun to precipitate results in tax legislation, the supply of day nurseries, social insurance, and family rights. The growing political activity of women has been channeled entirely through the established parties.

Man's place in work also belongs to the problems that have aroused interest in the Swedish debate. In this context, however, I am personally doubtful whether classical concepts of industrial democracy —such as the right of codetermination by workers' councils—will play a significant role during the coming decades.

The notion of industrial democracy originated in a social era in which it could be assumed that workers would remain in a given industry for a number of years if not for their entire productive lives. Questions concerning their relations to their own company were therefore accorded special weight. But Sweden now finds itself in a period of industrial development in which employees as well as white-collar workers must anticipate changing their place of work and residence numerous times. Many will have to be retrained to assume new occupations. Under such conditions it is doubtful to what extent individuals will become particularly interested in developments within a particular company in which they might work at any given time.

As a result of these factors the general problem of trade-union influence on management decisions and production can probably only be partially resolved in the local plant level. On the other hand the position of the trade-union movement on developments within the economy as a whole remains of crucial importance. Swedish trade-union leaders have traditionally assumed a rather skeptical attitude toward proposed experiments in industrial democracy which they fear might weaken their present freedom of action in collective bargaining on the national labor market. Recently, however, increased interest in industrial democracy

on the local level has been expressed especially by younger trade union-
ists.

PROSPECTS OF A NEW INDIVIDUALISM

This brief overview suggests that Sweden hardly provides an example of
individualistic movements that can be expected to yield important
changes in existing political structures. Nevertheless, individualism will
undoubtedly affect Sweden's political vocabulary. Expressions such as
the "individual man," "common man," and "possibilities of individual
development" have already become more common in the vocabulary of
all the political parties. Simultaneously expressions such as the "working class," "agricultural class," and the "ruling elite" are gradually disappearing. The parties that traditionally appealed to particular class
interests now address themselves to a much larger public. The Social
Democrats, for example, like to speak to "wage earners" who encompass both blue-collar and white-collar workers. The earlier Agrarian
party has been rechristened the Center party and has begun to make
substantial inroads among small employers in urban areas.

Even if all parties thus place greater emphasis on the individual,
this does not mean that the possibilities for expression of individual
freedom will automatically increase. Like other modern industrial states
Sweden is engaged in a process in which a number of newspapers have
been forced to cease publication. In practice this has reduced opportunities for individual voices to make themselves heard. This problem has
aroused increased concern, and various possibilities have been discussed
to create forums for broader debate through state-supported measures.
Conflicts have also arisen over the means by which radio and television
can create conditions for a sufficiently varied and individualized debate.
Even in this context it is apparent that social efforts—that is, collective
measures—are required to protect individual interests.

One group in society has always represented a special form of
individualism—intellectuals, writers, and artists. In general Swedish society displays greater understanding today for the needs of these groups
than it did several decades ago. Intellectuals also play a more advanced
role in Sweden's social debate than they do in many comparable coun-

tries. Their political orientations have varied. There have been (and still are) intellectuals who are Conservative in orientation, but it is more usual that intellectuals identify themselves with parties or groups that, correctly or incorrectly, are designated as "leftists." Anarchism and syndicalism, which earlier played a somewhat more important role in Swedish society than they do today, have always exerted a certain attraction for a number of writers. Pacifism reached a new peak some years ago, not least among intellectuals. Since 1965, a growing number of writers have participated in the debate on the Vietnam conflict and related international questions.

It is usual that contributions by intellectuals to international questions are accorded attention—whether they are intelligent and well informed or whether they are simplistic and not well informed. To the extent that all literature in the arts and humanities is more or less concerned with individual problems, it is natural that individualistic thoughts can be discerned in the contributions of writers to the social debate. But above all their work is an expression of bad conscience and increased sensitivity to world suffering. The "individualistic" intellectuals often display a spontaneous interest for collectivist solutions to problems in other countries. This once again demonstrates the complications inherent in the "individualism-collectivism" duality.

The concept of the new individualism, in short, is unlikely to have a significant effect on the political structure in Sweden. Nevertheless the established parties will continue to reinterpret the problem of the individual's relation to the collectivity in light of major social and economic changes that will occur. As a result we will continue to witness ideological struggles over efforts to redefine the individual's role in modern society.

ERIK ANNERS

Conservatism in Sweden

A PRIMARY PURPOSE of this chapter is to survey the historical development of Conservative ideology in Sweden. In addition I shall appraise this ideology in its contemporary form and assess prospects of future political change. A reasonable adjunct of this undertaking is to attempt to explain causes for the developments that have taken place in modern Conservative thought or—given present limitations of space—at least to discuss some important causal relations.

Various methodological approaches could be utilized in such an analysis. One could, for example, base one's presentation primarily on an analysis of the literature that came to be viewed as Conservative during the course of historical events. That would be a limited and, at the same time, easily manageable task. But one would lose the opportunity to elucidate some of the relations between socio-economic change and the political superstructure that characterized the historical political debate. Therefore I shall attempt to describe Conservative ideology in Sweden as it was expressed within the political movement that called itself Conservative or interpreted its world view as Conservative. In this way it is also natural to discuss causal relations with the help of a method in which one defines political ideology as an expression of the values and conceptions of reality in a particular socio-economic milieu. Thus one can seek to explicate changes in ideological perception by examining the ways in which the socio-economic environment has undergone transformation and by inquiring how such changes have influenced politically relevant values and conceptions of reality.

CLASSICAL CONSERVATISM

Utilizing the latter method, one may observe that the history of nineteenth-century conservatism in Sweden is only of marginal interest. Similar to European conservatism in general, traditional Swedish conservatism was an expression of the reaction of the ruling classes to the radicalism of the Enlightenment and the French Revolution. As a political factor in nineteenth-century Swedish history, conservatism played the same role as did Conservative views in other countries on the European continent. Drawing their inspiration from the historical school and international Conservative authorities from Burke to Bismarck, early Conservative spokesmen in Sweden argued a point of view that is so well known that it scarcely needs to be elaborated here.

It is important to emphasize, however, two principal aspects of nineteenth-century conservatism if one is to understand the Conservative ideological developments that occurred during the twentieth century. First of all, conservatism was originally by no means an individualistic ideological movement. On the contrary, traditional conservatism was basically collectivist in the sense that the people, the nation, and the state—rather than the individual—comprised the primary focus of political action. The second premise associated with traditional conservatism was its pessimistic view of man. Since the early Conservatives did not trust man's talents or capacity for moral behavior, they regarded prospects of political reform with considerable caution and even skepticism. One should not forget that nineteenth-century conservatism rested basically on Christianity. Paradoxically, therefore, the classical Conservatives' long-term view of man was optimistic in that they perceived man as an eternal being—as a child of God. Simultaneously, however, man was biologically an animal who was governed by aggressive drives which were expressed, in the language of Christianity, as original sin. Believing that man's nature was evil—that man still had not attained a sufficiently high level in his ethical development to warrant trust in enlightened individual behavior—nineteenth-century

Conservatives thus maintained that the gains of civilization could be protected only through institutions that guaranteed cautious realism in reform policies.

CONSERVATISM AS AN ORGANIZED POLITICAL FORCE

It was only at the beginning of the twentieth century that a political movement emerged in Sweden whose views deserved to be interpreted as the expression of a Conservative ideology. During the past three decades this Conservative party was called literally the Right party; in 1969 it changed its name to Moderate Unity party. The person who played the most important role in the formation of a coherent Conservative ideology in Sweden was Harald Hjärne, a professor of history at the University of Uppsala. His influence derived from his status as both an eminent historian and an active politician. Since Hjärne was a member of Parliament for only a very short time, his political contribution lay primarily on the ideological plane. His political views cannot be described with a high degree of precision because he wrote no comprehensive summary that provides a definitive and clear expression of his beliefs. Nevertheless one can say that his political ideology—summarized in the concepts of "defense and reforms"—evolved from a compilation of the more important principles expressed earlier by Burke, Disraeli, and Bismarck. As the names Disraeli and Bismarck suggest, Hjärne's political views comprised a conservatism oriented toward social and humanitarian goals. The very basis of Hjärne's thought was an historically determined view of society and man. When he formulated the tenets of "defense and reforms," he meant that it was the nation's—i.e., the living generation's—responsibility to defend the heritage of civilization which the Swedish people, conceived as a unity through time, had attained during centuries of civilizing efforts. Simultaneously he advocated humanitarian, social, and economic reforms as means to attain social justice that the poor could experience as an achievement worthy of support and defense.

It is also important to note that there was a clear etatist tendency in Hjärne's definition of conservatism—a trait that was rooted in the

collectivist Conservative attitudes of the nineteenth century. The
fatherland—as both an idea and society itself—was conceived as the
Swedish realm which stood above parties and the individual. The responsibility of the individual was to sacrifice himself for the higher
community that the fatherland and the state embodied. Therein lay a
deeply experienced happiness, a contentment that the individual attained by fulfilling his duties rather than seeking self-assertion on the
basis of the demands and needs of his own personality. In this conservatism could be discerned something of a nationalistic heroism, an orientation that was strengthened and stimulated by historical memories of
Sweden's heroic kings. The figure of Karl XII, who had reigned during
the Great Northern War in the early eighteenth century, played an especially important role during the first decades of organized Swedish conservatism, just as he did for Swedish nationalism in general. Sweden's
historical mission—one spoke gladly of Sweden's fate—was and had always been to serve as the most extreme northern outpost of the Western
world against expansionist and tyrannical Russia, which was perceived
as the personification of Oriental suppression and injustice.

The etatist tendency also found expression in domestic policies in
that spokesmen for the Conservative party were often prepared to undertake extensive state control or the transfer of property and economic
enterprises (such as mines) to public ownership. This policy did not reflect the party's mistrust of the functional capabilities of capitalism. Instead, such measures were considered fundamental principles of a
patriarchical bureaucratic administration in which the expansion of the
state and its authority was deemed useful for society as a whole. However, the ideologically motivated etatist attitude of the early Conservatives contained the seeds of a conflict that later posed a major challenge
to the party's unity. For the classical sources of Conservative leadership
recruitment—which included large landowners and high-level salaried
employees—were complemented during the late nineteenth and early
twentieth centuries by a new, important, and powerful category of industrialists. Most of the leaders of Sweden's industries embraced emotional Conservative, nationalistic attitudes and hence naturally identified
with the Conservative party. But their political interests coincided with
the doctrines of Manchester liberalism. Therefore they viewed state intervention in the economy and direct state ownership with mixed feel-

ings. Least of all could they accept a planned economy as a central basis of the party's policies.

PARTY CONFLICT AND RECONCILIATION

It was just such a planned economy, however, that various youth organizations within the party—such as the National Youth Association—began to demand in the 1920s. During this decade political movements embracing nationalism and etatism had begun to sweep over the European continent. In their basic premises Italian fascism and German national socialism were the same product of the significantly more humanitarian and socially progressive ideology that permeated the National Youth Association in Sweden. All three ideological movements shared common demands for state measures to achieve greater social justice, enhanced security against unemployment, and more effective welfare services. The fundamental thought underlying such policies was that the state should intervene in instances in which private enterprise proved unwilling or unable to solve social questions in a judicious manner. This did not mean that the state should wholly dominate the economic system, but only that the state should assume greater responsibility in areas that had traditionally been reserved to private economic initiative. According to this view, state and economic leaders should seek means—through economic planning—to achieve cooperation between government institutions and private enterprise. Areas of government and private competence would not be rigidly determined in advance; cooperation could be extended instead from case to case as actual circumstances indicated its most practical forms. This view of the state's role stood in marked contrast to classical Socialist ideology with its demand for state ownership of the means of production and complete state control of the nation's economic system.

One can note that the 1920–1930 program of the National Youth Association—which was strongly influenced by theoretical left-wing Conservative doctrines advanced by Fahlbeck and Hjellén in the 1910s and 1920s—anticipated many of the actual policies that have been realized in contemporary Sweden through cooperation between the governing Social Democrats and private enterprise. (In the latter case cooperation has evolved under the concept of a "mixed economy" rather than the older, more provocative designation of a planned economy.) One should also add that the National Youth Association never advocated any racist doctrines. The organization was bound in a strong, almost romantic manner to the Swedish legal tradition, which consequently excluded the emergence of degenerate forms of activity—such as devotion to power and terror—that characterized national socialism and fascism.

The Swedish young Conservative movement claimed among its leaders a significant number of talented academicians, and promised in the long run to initiate a renewal of the old Conservative party—a renewal that could have led to a more rapid transformation of the party into a social reform party. Because of their positive attitude toward the state and their endorsement of state intervention to adjust and reform economic relations, the young Conservatives gradually came into conflict with the dominant attitudes prevailing among the older party members. Since the latter espoused for reasons of self-interest a Manchester Liberal orientation toward economic policies, the established leaders viewed as heresy the demands of the National Youth Association for a planned economy and state intervention to achieve social justice. As a result an open conflict emerged during the 1930s between the official party hierarchy—led by the Conservative party chairman, the industrialist Arvid Lindman, who also wanted to protect his personal political power—and the new academic-oriented movement. The result was a victory for the economically and numerically stronger groups within the party. The Conservatives severed their ties with the National Youth Association and proceeded to establish a new, more loyal youth association.

For a long time to come, this conflict severely damaged the Conservative party. The party lost a large number of talented persons and a generation of leading politicians. The conflict assumed a particularly bitter character when members of the majority faction sought to discredit the younger national and etatist-oriented academicians by charging that they had come under the influence of national socialism and fascism. Undeniably, German national socialism had exerted a certain effect on the leading ideologues of the National Youth Association. But its influence was by no means as great as established party leaders alleged. Above all the receptiveness of the National Youth Association to the doctrines of national socialism did not extend to its ideas of power and race.

In Swedish historical accounts of this period, this conflict has often been interpreted primarily as an ideological struggle, with the question of Nazi and Fascist influence standing in the foreground. In recent years, however, this historical view has been proved false. Instead, the most important factor determining its course and outcome was the refusal of the Manchester Liberal industrialists within the Conservative party to accept the "Socialist" concepts of a planned economy advocated by the young academicians. Members of the National Youth Association were ousted from the Conservative party not because they were racists or proponents of violence, but because they were simply too Conservative to accept the extreme Liberal attitudes that prevailed among the party's leading circles.

The outcome of the conflict proved tragic. Those groups that left the Conservative party founded their own political party under the name of National Association. Within this party those who were genuinely politically talented were quickly pushed to one side since they no longer possessed the means to advance their views which had existed in the Conservative party. In their place persons emerged who—because of weaknesses in their ideological training or purely personal reasons —were prepared to accept a great many aspects of German national socialism and Italian fascism which supporters of the National Youth Association had earlier rejected. When World War II broke out, this party —because of its agitation on behalf of Hitler Germany's foreign policies—became the object of general contempt. Those persons who continued to work actively within the National Association thus suffered a political death.

During World War II the domestic ideological debate in Sweden subsided in intensity. Nevertheless the period from 1939 to 1945 proved of considerable importance for the Conservative party because a new academic generation emerged that provided, through intensive organization work, strong party support among students. Toward the end of the war, party leaders undertook an ambitious attempt to create a program that could reconcile the older Manchester Liberal-oriented generation and the younger academicians who had emerged during the

war. The latter—like their ousted predecessors—advocated more classical Conservative doctrines. Above all they demanded an active role by
the state in achieving effective social policies. The latent contradiction
between the liberalism of the older generation and the social conservatism of the younger generation could have led to an open rupture during
the work on the new program. A conflict was averted, however, through
a compromise on social policies. The basis of the compromise was a
new form of party endorsement of positive attitudes toward social policies and comprehensive state measures in the area of social welfare
which even the older generation of Manchester Liberals could accept.
The justification was simply that properly formulated social policies
could further economic production.

INITIAL POSTWAR TRENDS

Buried in the 1946 Conservative party program, the latent ideological
tension within the party did not erupt in renewed controversy. A principal reason was that the cause of potential discord between generations
gradually diminished in the course of a strange and unforeseen ideological development within the party. The change was not, as one might
have expected, that the Manchester liberalism of the older generation
was modified to accord with a more socially oriented conservatism. Instead, the younger generation came to accept the individualist and anti-
state attitude of the older generation. A comprehensive analysis would
be required to explain the factors that led to this unusual development,
but none has been made. Hence it is possible in the present context only
to indicate a few personal reflections. One reason was that the Liberal
party—which had emerged as a synthesis of a free church party and an
atheistic cultural radical party under the leadership of one of the great
Swedish political leaders of the twentieth century, Professor Bertil
Ohlin—had "stolen" the social Conservative program of the younger
Conservative academicians. Describing its new postwar program as "social liberalism," the Liberal party presented the electorate with a program encompassing humanistic and socially Conservative principles.
Under Ohlin's leadership the Liberals openly advocated government intervention in the economy, the Labor market, and society to achieve in-

creased social security and justice. Thus the Liberals succeeded in accomplishing what the Conservatives had failed to do during World War II, namely, to develop in time a positive program for necessary state-sponsored measures to correct economic imbalances and promote social justice in a competitive society. It is one of the many ironies of history that because the Liberals shared a central point with the Social Democrats—namely, a positive attitude toward government responsibilities—the move of the Liberal party to the right of the Swedish Conservative party was interpreted as a step to the left. The simultaneous development of Conservative doctrines in the direction of Manchester liberalism meant, as a result, that ideologically the Conservative and Liberal parties exchanged places.

Another and perhaps more important reason for the general orientation of the Conservative party in an extreme Liberal direction was that the Conservatives, including the young academicians who had previously advocated social Conservative principles, vehemently opposed the radical Socialist program advanced by the Social Democrats. Anticipating major postwar economic dislocations, the Swedish Social Democrats had formulated in 1944 a "postwar program of the working-class movement"; it contained extensive socialization measures that would have transformed Sweden into a State Socialist society. The Conservative academicians within the Conservative party had witnessed during World War II where etatist doctrines could lead. Therefore they reacted strongly against the extensive trust in the power of government and the anti-individualistic and bureaucratic attitudes that permeated the Socialist program. Accordingly they came to view a free-market economy as a necessary safeguard against the creation of a Socialist bureaucratic state.

An additional reason for the orientation of the Conservative party in an extreme Liberal direction was that two persons came to exercise party leadership during the 1950s who were more interested in practical policies than in ideological issues. Jarl Hjalmarson, an insurance executive who was elected party chairman in the late 1940s, quickly developed close personal ties with Gunnar Svärd, the party secretary. Together they effectively agitated on behalf of individual freedom, security, and self-responsibility. Their inspiration for party proclamations came more from classical Liberal than from Conservative doctrines. Because Social Democratic policies adversely affected white-collar workers—who confronted unremitting increases in the rate of progressive taxation—and property owners—who were subjected to discernible restrictions on the right of ownership—the Liberal program of the Conservative party elicited widespread electoral support. Conservative strength increased from one election to another, and by 1958 the party had become the largest non-Socialist faction in Parliament.

In 1957 the Social Democrats assumed sole ministerial responsibility when the Center (Agrarian) party withdrew from the previous coalition cabinet, but by the end of the decade they confronted a severe political crisis because of their persisting hostility toward white-collar strata. The Socialists ultimately succeeded in maneuvering themselves out of this crisis by introducing a new system of compulsory supplementary pensions that was endorsed by Parliament in 1959. Because of the widespread popular appeal of the pension program, the Social Democrats were thus able to gain sufficient support among lower-level white-collar workers to maintain their executive status and even expand their electoral following—even though demographic developments had actually weakened their natural electoral basis. This is not the place to discuss in detail the supplementary pension issue or its political consequences in Sweden. It is sufficient to note that as a result first the Liberals and then the Conservatives suffered significant electoral declines, while the Socialists consolidated their position.

After the Conservatives suffered a major loss in the 1960 election, the party changed leadership. The new chairman was Gunnar Heckscher, a professor of political science who proved more interested in ideological issues than his predecessor. Heckscher initiated a concerted attempt to lead the party in the direction of a socially reformist and humanistically inspired conservatism. Heckscher became isolated in this endeavor, however, because the great majority of party members were not yet prepared to abandon the Liberal heritage which the Conservatives had incorporated as their own. By pursuing such policies in an isolated position, Heckscher received a large share of the blame—which was in large measure undeserved—for a Conservative defeat in the 1964 election. He felt compelled to resign as chairman in 1965, and was succeeded by Yngve Holmberg, the party secretary.

IDEOLOGICAL REAPPRAISAL

Neither under Hjalmarson nor Heckscher were serious efforts made to undertake a basic reappraisal of the party's postwar program. To be sure a so-called idea program had been formulated in 1956, but it contained little more than a number of general formulations which were compatible with the Liberal formulations of the 1950s. No attempt was made to view social developments in a larger perspective, apply scientific methods to appraise the political program, or deepen generally the political discussion. Nevertheless a number of party members perceived by the mid-1960s that programmatic efforts of such a character were necessary. Accordingly, delegates to the 1964 Conservative party convention voted to appoint a committee to compile and study material that could be utilized by a subsequent party commission to formulate a new program. The committee began deliberations only after the new chairman had published his own thoughts and issued his directives. In close cooperation with Holmberg, the committee developed a radically new method of program work by appointing a number of subcommittees— eventually twenty in all—which recruited scientific experts to serve as advisers. Similarly the program committee collaborated with scientists to undertake extensive studies of its own in a number of policy areas. Characterizing the work of the committee and the various subcommittees was an attempt to establish guidelines for long-range political goals. In this endeavor committee members paid special attention to the futurology literature that had been introduced in Sweden in the mid-1960s.

In 1967 the preliminary committee report was debated at a national party convention under the title, "Toward the Year 2000." Drawing its data in part from American and French futurology studies, the committee emphasized the decisive importance of data technology, the technological sciences, and technological innovation for future social development. Other questions which the committee considered included environmental control and foreign assistance. Through such broad programmatic considerations, the Conservatives acquired a considerable edge over other parties in Sweden—including the governing Social Democrats. Of course, this advantage could not be maintained indefinitely, and within a few years the other parties had followed the Conservatives' lead in forming their own perspectives on such questions as ecology. The importance of the committee's deliberations therefore lay on another level: Its analysis made possible the ideological reorientation of the Conservative party toward a new form of "humanistic conservatism."

HUMANISTIC CONSERVATISM

The program committee's work acquired significance as its findings were disseminated among a large number of study groups within the party. In these groups party members first became familiar with multifold interrelated social, scientific, and technological questions that had not been previously raised and whose political implications had not yet been appreciated. In particular this applied to ecological issues and policies which had been virtually ignored but soon came to acquire central political importance.

From an historical perspective, the internal ideological reaction to the committee's report proved highly complicated. Because of the transformation of Conservative tenets since the beginning of the twentieth century, most party members thought by the mid-1960s in Liberal rather than Conservative categories. Whereas Sweden's early Conservatives had based their policies on the nation, the state, and institutions —i.e., the social system as a whole—contemporary party spokesmen perceived that it was no longer possible to build on institutions or even the nation in attempting to justify a Conservative ideology. Instead they emphasized—as a fundamental principle of the historical process of civilization—that humanistic values must have precedence over more transitory social norms. Simultaneously party leaders had become accustomed to approach questions raised in the policy debates of the 1950s and 1960s from a Liberal point-of-view. Thus postwar Conservatives began their appraisal of particular policies by considering the needs and desires of individual persons; they asked first how political measures might affect the individual and only second how they might affect society.

The confrontation of classical Conservative and more recent Liberal party traditions with the futurology research contained in the program committee's report resulted in an ideological reorientation of the Conservative party. The immediate response was a revival of an historical perspective, a natural consequence for a movement with a Conservative and therefore historical tradition. Out of the combination of Conservative and Liberal thought, as well as methods of political analysis, evolved an ideological synthesis that can be described as humanistic conservatism. This conservatism is oriented toward both preserving and developing further the tradition of civilization that is historically manifest in the basic values of Western culture.

One practical political effect of this ideological reorientation was that the party changed its name in January 1969 from the Right party to the Moderate Unity party. A more accurate ideological designation would have been "Conservative Unity party," which would have indicated that the party's basic philosophy is humanistic conservatism. But the change of name occurred less for ideological reasons than for political ones. After the parliamentary elections in September 1968, which proved a catastrophe for the non-Socialist parties, the most pressing task facing Conservative leaders was to devise an opposition platform that would facilitate a subsequent electoral comeback. This necessitated in turn a better basis for cooperation with the Center and Liberal parties. Given such considerations, the name Moderate Unity party was chosen as a compromise formula.

Immediately after the 1968 defeat the Conservative leadership also began the definitive reformulation of the party's program—based on the material compiled by the 1965 program committee—to replace the programs of 1946 and 1956. A program revision committee was appointed which met until the fall of 1969 under the personal direction of the Conservative chairman. The Committee's recommendations were endorsed by the party conference and executive committee in November and December 1969.

It is not possible in this chapter to examine in detail the new principles and policy guidelines contained in the program. Accordingly, I shall restrict myself to the ideological introduction and several central points in an attempt to indicate how the new humanistic conservatism is expressed in specific political proposals.

The basic ideological tenets of the new party program are contained in the rather short statement of political ideas in the Introduction. These read as follows:

The Moderate Unity Party seeks in conformity with the Conservative tradition of ideas to promote a social development that can satisfy individual desires and needs;

The party expresses the humanistic view of human value, freedom, and social responsibility that has evolved within Western culture, and seeks in its policies to safeguard and strengthen basic democratic freedoms and human rights;

It adheres to the cultural view and ethical norms governing human relations that derive from Christianity.

With this affirmation of ideological principles, the old Conservative (Right) party has clearly disappeared from Swedish politics. From the historical perspective of political ideas it may be of interest to note that the final ideological version of the party program was preceded by an earlier draft that differed significantly from the accepted text. A subcommittee of the program committee had originally proposed the following introductory section, which the program committee initially endorsed as its own:

The Moderate Unity party is the heir to the Right party's tradition of Conservative ideas. In our time that heritage pledges us to maintain the responsibility of the present generation for the accomplishments of earlier generations. Moreover, it pledges us in practical political activities to strive to uphold a realistic view of society and man based on a clearly perceived historical perspective.

In its basic views the Moderate Unity party is a progressive party rooted in the ideals of Christianity and democratic humanism.

The party's affirmation of humanism, inspired by Christianity as the guiding principle in social relations, derives from the perception that the ethical norms of Western civilization are products of Christian tradition.

When the program committee's proposal was circulated among party spokesmen for their comments, many members reacted against what they considered the excessively academic style of its formulation. In particular such terms as "the ideals of Christianity and democratic humanism" and "humanism inspired by Christianity" evoked opposition. Many asserted that these terms demanded extensive interpretation if they were to be properly understood by party adherents. Others maintained that the strong emphasis on the importance of Christianity was inappropriate in a party whose majority believed in the separation of religion and politics and that the party could not affirm a religious ideology because this would require party members to be religiously active. Thus the less sophisticated and more easily understood version, quoted above, received overwhelming support from the party members. Most of the leading persons within the party hierarchy found it more practical to accept a popular, albeit vague, ideological program rather than a more academic and concise version. As is so often the case, tactical political considerations proved more decisive than the need for a clear expression of political ideas. Hence it is the proposal of the program committee, more than the ideological section of the new program itself, that reflects the development from conservatism to humanism within the Moderate Unity party.

Also noteworthy is that the term "conservatism" appears only in the introductory passage concerning the party's resolve to seek social developments "in conformity with the conservative tradition of ideas . . . that can satisfy individual desires and needs." With this phraseology the term "Conservative" is relegated to the background and no longer serves as a complete statement of the party's underlying attitude. Yet a party always requires ideological symbols. Such was also the case with the Conservative party. When a majority refused to accept "humanism" as an expression of the party's ideology because it seemed too academic, members chose "moderate" in its place. This decision was a compromise between those groups in the party that wanted to designate the Conservatives the "Moderate party" and those that proposed to call it the "Unity party." The political compromise accepted at the party convention, however, may assume unanticipated ideological consequences.

Now that "moderate" is used in place of "Conservative," a discernible movement has emerged within the party to elevate "moderate" as a principal ideological concept. When a political debating society made up of university graduates was formed in Stockholm shortly after the new program was adopted, various members seriously proposed that the group should be called the "Moderate Idea Club." In that "moderate" means measured or restrained, the name of the society would have suggested that it was a club for restrained ideas—which would undoubtedly have provoked considerable mirth at the party's expense. Nevertheless it is likely that party members, and in time the general public as well, will interpret the meaning of the term differently than at present. Eventually the word "moderate" will probably indicate a particular and coherent point-of-view rather than, as is now the case, merely an indication that policies should avoid political extremes.

Before I illustrate the party's ideology with specific examples concerning the program's most important principles, it is appropriate to elaborate upon the term "humanism"—which was briefly used in the party's internal program revision—even if it is presently considered too academic to describe the party's official ideology. Also of interest is to consider the ideological reasons for de-emphasizing the term "Conservative."

Classical Conservative terminology is no longer considered suitable partly because it has an antiquated sound in modern Swedish vocabulary; therefore its political attraction is weak. Equally important, the traditional Conservative terminology is considered by most Swedes to be an expression of unyielding opposition to change of all sorts. Above all the terminology is of limited value for the simple reason that it suggests an erroneous view of the principal political attitudes in the party's ideological program. This becomes apparent when one examines what humanism means within the party. As used by contemporary Conservatives in Sweden, humanism has nothing in common with the specialized academic meaning of humanism as a particular scientific school that existed prior to the Renaissance. Instead it is based on the attitudes associated with Christian humanism and can best be described as a secularized variant of the latter.

Like the premise of Christianity that the central element in history is the salvation of man's soul, humanism posits that the object of political action is the welfare of mankind and the individual citizen—not that of the state, the nation, or particular classes. For classical conservatism, the nation—encompassing persons civilized by centuries of cultural achievement—was the primary object of politics. From this was derived the conception of a community between the dead, living, and future generations which comprised the people of a nation. Thus humanism is internationalist and individualist; classical conservatism in general was nationalistic and collectivist.

Christianity maintains that man can attain salvation from his sinful nature through the grace of God—which is the symbolic description of religious language for the fact that biologically man is a predatory ape. In contrast, humanism expresses a strong belief in the ability of mankind and individuals to overcome—through insight into the power of love of mankind and the exertion of individual moral strength—the destructive forces in man's biological heritage and to solve the enormous problems that are posed by technological civilization. In this sense humanism is also optimistic. Classical conservatism, on the other hand, was skeptical—if not outright pessimistic—with respect to man's capacity for ethical development and constructive political acts.

What remains, then, of the old Conservative ideas within the Swedish political movement that now calls itself the Moderate Unity party? Actually only the Conservative method of approaching political social measures from a deeply rooted historical perspective. This is probably a considerable advantage for the party in comparison with the Liberals and the Socialists. Both of the latter ideological movements place the primary emphasis in their political thought on the nineteenth century. To the extent that the Marxists reflect further back in time, they force the complicated course of history into such a doctrinaire and simplified scheme of development that it provides no contemporary guidance—unless the historical framework is considered an absolute truth.

PARTY ATTITUDES TOWARD REFORM

The attitude of the Moderate Unity party toward reform is most clearly seen in its position on three of today's major problems: the question of broadening democracy, extending property rights to the means of production, and education policies. Concerning the first of these points, the party has advanced a number of proposals that are intended to place political responsibility as close to the individual as possible. A typical example is the demand to make more extensive use of the referendum to determine popular attitudes toward pending legislation. In the second instance, the party supports "property-owners democracy" as an alternative to the socialization of the means of production. Through new juridical-technical structures, as well as possibilities of tax-free savings and tax-free company shares available to employees, the party seeks to permit the great majority of citizens to become direct owners of their homes and co-owners of the places where they work. In this area the party has undertaken ambitious and constructive efforts to formulate detailed suggestions for reform. With respect to education policies, the party maintains, in opposition to the goals of the Social Democrats, that the school system should not be conceived as an instrument of social transformation leading toward socialism. Instead, the Moderate Unity party advocates that schools should provide a comprehensive education based on well-founded knowledge and politically neutral training to responsible citizenship. The party views contributions of individual citizens as the most important objective of education policy—not their conformity to various types of existing collective groups. Additional features of the new program which deserve attention are the party's highly positive attitudes toward foreign assistance and its determination to mold Sweden's foreign policy of neutrality into a contribution to world peace. These provisions clearly reveal the international facets of the new humanism.

The fundamental principles of the party program stand in sharp contrast to the collectivist and egalitarian policies that have been pursued for nearly four decades by the Social Democrats. This means that a change of executive power, in which the Moderate Unity party would acquire a share of cabinet office in a non-Socialist coalition, could lead to significant modifications in Sweden's economic and education policies.

PROSPECTS FOR THE FUTURE

The future of Swedish politics will depend on basic changes in the nation's socio-economic environment. At this point I shall therefore examine the framework within which ideological and political priorities for development can evolve during the coming decades. Since the seventeenth century the succession of politically dominant groups has been —with reservations concerning a certain schematization—as follows: the high nobility in the seventeenth century; the lesser nobility in the eighteenth century; the lesser nobility, bourgeoisie, and large landowners in the nineteenth century; the bourgeoisie during the first three decades of the twentieth century; and since 1933 the organized working-class movement with support of lower-level salaried employees. One can easily see how social institutions were shaped by the concepts of reality and values of the ruling social classes in each of these periods. Until the middle of the nineteenth century this occurred with relatively little group consciousness; until then both a science of politics and the formation of political opinions based on extensive ideological debate were absent in Sweden. The important political ideologies—important in the sense that they exercised influence over the great majority of citizens—first appeared with the advent of mass literacy from the 1840s onward. The interesting feature of the ideological awareness that emerged in the mid-nineteenth century was that the three leading ideologies took root in specific socio-economic environments and that their content was determined by the dominant values and conceptions of reality in each of the milieus.

Classical conservatism—with its perception of citizens as a unity of dead, living, and future generations—was a natural expression of the three-generation milieu of agrarian society. In this environment rights of inheritance and property were considered sacred and sanctioned by nature. Equally self-evident was the high esteem accorded an authoritative hierarchy. In the working milieu of landowners and farmers, who were bound to cycles of nature, the preservation of continuity as well as realism in reform efforts emerged as natural characteristics. Little could be changed in such a milieu in that those who comprised it were bound to prevailing modes of production which could only be transformed slowly and with the greatest difficulty. The contribution of classical conservatism was to project the values and conceptions of reality that had evolved within this specific socio-economic environment to society as a whole. This ideological conception was easily understood and accepted by many industrialists, as well as the higher echelons of the civil service. Both social groups were firmly rooted in the traditional agrarian society and for a long time shared its values.

Classical liberalism revealed similar tendencies. If conservatism was a philosophy of farmers, liberalism was a philosophy for merchants and industrialists. Liberalism emerged as an expression of the desire among the spokesmen for Sweden's new industrial economy to attain the classical model of a free market. The right of free competition became for them the most important right of all. In the view of nineteenth-century Liberals, this right should extend to all aspects of society.

Socialism, with its distinctive socio-economic political views, appeared as the philosophy of organized labor. Within the growing working-class movement, encompassing a proletarian mass and led by functionaries who were engaged in vehement conflict with the dominant employer interests, group solidarity became an absolute necessity and hence a primary value. In a milieu in which all were alike in status in the sense that none possessed more than their labor, equality was also an inevitable demand. Since the power of the collectivity was the individual's only protection, it was equally natural for social democracy to value the collectivity and conformity to group interests higher than the individual himself. And how could workers do anything other than oppose individual property rights when they, unlike the farmers and merchants, lacked the possibility to judge for themselves the positive social and economic functions of property? Since they could see only its disadvantages, private ownership of the means of production was for them "theft" and capitalism meant only the exploitation of the working masses. Marx was right, the workers spontaneously said. Self-righteously the Socialists also demanded that society be reorganized to accord with the values and conceptions of reality of their own milieu.

The reason that the conflict between Conservatives, Liberals, and Socialists proved so impassioned during the latter nineteenth and early twentieth century was, of course, not only because each believed it was right. Nearly all supporters of a political movement behave in such a manner. All three *were* right in the sense that each of the ideologies was an expression for what the various groups experienced in their different environments and was accordingly perceived as rational, correct, and just.

If these observations about the dependence of political ideologies on disparate socio-economic milieus are correct, one can apply the same logic to indicate the probable future of Swedish politics. Assuming it is possible to anticipate in broad outline socio-economic developments over the next twenty to thirty years, one should be able to make an intelligent prognosis about the evolution of the dominant political ideology.

A dominant ideology presupposes, according to the preceding analysis, a ruling class—which is used in this context as a socio-economic interest group. Who is likely to comprise the ruling class in the society of tomorrow? In all likelihood it will not be, as is presently the case, the political and union representatives of industrial workers and lower-level salaried employees. Through the extension of data processing and the automation of the productive-distributive apparatus, the groups forming the voting base for this political aristocracy will decline so sharply in number that they will no longer make up the largest segment of the Swedish electorate. Sooner than is commonly anticipated, the rapidly increasing number of academically trained white-collar workers—in both public and private service—will become the leading interest group in society. As they gain quantitative strength, they will become politically dominant through their considerable capacity to shape public opinion—a product of their advanced education.

Which ideology will the new university-trained white-collar strata embrace? That will depend primarily on national education policies that are pursued during the coming decades; these may become either more collectivist or more individualist in emphasis. If the Social Democrats succeed in their efforts to perpetuate one-party executive rule, future generations of academically trained personnel will be more collectivist in their orientation. This by no means guarantees, however, that they will become more egalitarian in the way envisioned by the Social Democrats. Because academic training presupposes and perpetuates classification, a university that lacks authority is equally meaningless as one without freedom of criticism. All higher education requires the classification of knowledge on the part of both teachers and students. Otherwise the results of research and education would become qualitatively deficient. Our contemporary technological civilization, with its increasingly complicated forms of social organization, will inevitably demand even greater and more exact knowledge and skills of all citizens. For this reason the necessity will remain to classify and rank persons—first in higher education and later in productive life.

Given this condition a considerable risk undoubtedly exists that a meritocracy will emerge in which advanced education and high socio-economic status will plainly become an inherited privilege among families with an academic tradition. Their children will easily acquire a significant advantage over those of others. The alternative, however, is not necessarily an egalitarian policy that seeks to level differences in talent and opportunity through gradeless schools and easily acquired academic degrees. In the long run no country can afford the loss of effectiveness that such a policy would presage. Instead the possibility to hinder the emergence of a meritocracy lies in the development of a humanistic education to citizenship, which seeks to create a deeper sense of community independent of individual training, social status, and responsibility. In an affluent society such a goal is not impossible. If it should be successfully attained, the way will be open to achieve a democracy that is governed by a new type of aristocracy for whom the meaning of life would consist of the search for scientific truth, the ethical development of their own personalities, and an humanist-inspired quest for the common good. An essential requisite for such a development is that the coming generations of university graduates succeed in acquiring and advancing the humanistic spirit contained in the Western cultural heritage. This will not be possible without the help of historical perspective.

Herein lies a significant opportunity for a party ideologically based on a humanistic and a Conservative approach to the problems of society. The merger of modern political humanism with classical conservatism might ultimately result in an ideology that is simultaneously radical and Conservative. This could come about through a more objective analysis of history as well as the contributions of modern social science. A radical Conservative ideology would thus constitute a synthesis between the most acceptable conceptions of the nineteenth-century ideologies and what is scientifically most probable in the future.

LARS GYLLENSTEN

Swedish Radicalism in the 1960s: An Experiment in Political and Cultural Debate

IN MANY AREAS of the world Sweden is viewed as an historical experiment that can provide guidelines for political programs and debate in other countries. Often Sweden has been cited in political propaganda either as a terrible example of alleged degeneration because Socialist ideas have determined socio-political developments or as an example of an exemplary social welfare state.

This view of Sweden as a political and social experiment rests on two principal factors. One is Sweden's extensive welfare services and high standard of living. The other is the long-term Social Democratic reform effort, which has led successively to greater social influence on the economy during the twentieth century, and which is viewed as radical in many countries with more capitalistic and competitive Liberal structures.

Beginning in the 1960s modern Socialist thoughts and protest movements directed against the Western industrial states and high consumption societies began to spread from Europe and the United States throughout Sweden as well. To a considerable degree these ideas have come to dominate the Swedish political and cultural debate among writers, critics, and other intellectuals.

Naturally the new trends in the contemporary cultural debate are not as significant for day-to-day politics, social relations, and opinion among the large political and social organizations as they might seem. Highly publicized activities among intellectuals and activist minority groups are not representative of the Swedish population at large. Public discussion is determined above all by those who have the capacity, will, and opportunities to express themselves in public. Much of the so-called cultural debate is thus a superficial or an elitist phenomenon among a favored few who enjoy intellectual prestige.

Paradoxically, then, the opposition minorities who have turned against society's leading political, cultural, and economic strata (the Establishment) simultaneously embody an "establishment in other positions." They are a minority who enjoy a privileged position because of their education, economic status, access to publicity media, and membership in a community of active creators of culture. This is as true of the present radical cultural debate as it was of all ideological movements that seemed to dominate earlier epochs. It would be well to keep this reservation about the unrepresentative character of intellectual minorities in mind in my analysis of the Swedish radical debate of the 1960s.

Public opinion polls show that most Swedes are relatively untouched by the ideas that are thought to dominate public discussion. A more Conservative or eclectic point of view persists beneath the more speculative engagement among intellectuals. This unformulated common sense or conformist traditionalism is largely independent of, or at best indirectly influenced by, the contemporary debate on ideas.

When I address myself in the following analysis to Swedish radicalism during the 1960s, I am primarily concerned with the more speculative movements. These are the ones with which I am best acquainted in my position as a writer and participant in the cultural debate, and I shall judge my theme in the subjective terms that apply to such a person. I am not an objective social scientist with a claim to neutrality. Instead I am myself a member of that intellectual minority I have described—talkative, but not actually very representative—and I shall discuss my subject with these reservations. My frame of reference is more that of a debater or writer than that of a scientist who wishes to document his subject.

THE NEW RADICALISM

The phenomena that I shall discuss reveal numerous contradictions. Espoused by various groups and persons who often engage in strong polemics with each other, they lack clarity and precise meaning. The word radical itself—once a term of abuse—has now become fashionable and is used to characterize that which is most conspicuous at any given time in contemporary cultural and social criticism. In this context I shall use "the new radicalism" as a common term for the internationally inspired Swedish orientation toward political discussion and social criticism (including both its Socialist and anarchistic emphases). Although the New Left has sometimes been used as a common label encompassing the group of intellectuals with Marxist orientation, this group has in reality been splintered from the very beginning. Their fragmentation has grown in recent years rather than diminished. Therefore I shall also apply the concept of the new radicalism to the entire spectrum of modern Socialist social criticism.[1]

In addition to the various radical ideologies that have sought to promote political reconstruction, an even vaguer and less definable form of avant-gardism emerged in the 1960s. Here I am referring primarily to literary and artistic tendencies with anarchistic overtones. These have grown out of experimental art such as concretism and pop art. These movements I shall include in the general term, the new radicalism, as well.

In an attempt to delineate the debate of the 1960s, I shall begin with the two characteristic features of the Swedish experiment which I mentioned above: economic welfare and radical reformism. In addition I shall seek to explicate the nature of this debate with reference to other special features, above all earlier ideas, that have contributed to the formation of Swedish cultural life.

A SWEDISH UTOPIA?

The Swedish welfare system has been described many times and in many ways. In 1966 Herbert Tingsten published his book, *Från idéer*

till idyll (*From Ideas to Utopia*), in which he depicted Sweden as a
largely homogeneous and harmonious society.[2] In his view the Swedish
political system was more or less evolving toward a purely technical political administrative state built on pragmatic and utilitarian principles.
Tingsten argued that Sweden had become, in short, a society lacking
fundamental conflicts of interest or ideology. Moreover, Tingsten denounced political ideologies, which he viewed as outmoded relics of
purely historical interest, and disputed the possibility that serious class
differences would emerge that might provide centers of strength and un-
rest for new political movements.

Ironically Tingsten's book appeared just as the New Left debate
began to generate widespread attention. The new cultural and ideological currents that ensued came to disprove his and related theses.

I will not attempt to develop or analyze all those conditions that
have contributed to Sweden's present position as an especially privileged country among the industrialized nations of the world, but I shall
touch on some of them.

Through fortunate circumstances Sweden has escaped the great
wars of the twentieth century. The country has also been spared major
ethnic and religious conflicts. To a considerable degree we are *one* people. Ethnic minorities such as the Lapps and the Finns in the northern
provinces, as well as the gypsies, refugees, and other immigrants who
have come here to escape political persecution or to work, have created
only marginal problems of social integration. From a religious point of
view virtually all Swedes are Protestant, the majority of whom are
only nominal church members. All of these circumstances have contributed to Sweden's social stability and economic progress.

Conditions also proved favorable for the advent of industrialization in democratic forms. We lacked an important class of large landowners, industrialists, and other capitalists who could monopolize industry in the nineteenth century and thereby create deep social
cleavages. Swedish industry has in large measure developed on a decentralized basis out of small handicrafts. The structure of large industrial
enterprises emerged relatively late when Liberal ideas had already been
transformed in a social Liberal direction.

These advantageous socio-economic conditions also determined the
basis for the Swedish form of Social Democracy that has dominated our

political life for the past four decades. In many areas of the world Sweden is viewed as a Socialist country. What one means by this description depends, as noted above, on one's point of view. Characterizing Sweden as a Socialist system is only possible if one judges prevailing conditions from a more private capitalistic basis such as that which existed in Sweden at the turn of the century or which exists today in West Germany, the United States, and France. Admittedly our economic system is subject to extensive public control, but the purpose of such control is to guarantee social security for all citizens regardless of their particular economic situation. Leading examples are medical care and aid for the aged. As a result we have relatively high taxes which many reactionaries—who are primarily concerned with preserving their own privileged economic status—sometimes label confiscatory with no appreciation for how these taxes are used to further common interests.

Partners in the labor market negotiate for the most part on a basis of equality. The Swedish Federation of Trade Unions encompasses virtually all workers who comprise in turn a very large portion of the Swedish electorate. As a major political force in its own right, the trade-union movement has cooperated closely with the Social Democratic party—which has maintained political power throughout the postwar period—in formulating Sweden's present system of steeply progressive taxation. These policies have served to further the common goal of organized labor and the Social Democrats to achieve social equalization. Differences in income levels have also been equalized, particularly when one takes into account the various social security measures initiated by the government.

The Swedish Social Democrats have implemented such measures in accordance with a reformist model which, from its initial point of departure, would have to be called radical. (I have referred to this model above as "radical reformism.") Initially their strategy had been ambiguous. Only after protracted controversy were the Social Democrats able during the first decade of the twentieth century to unite on a revisionist course as opposed to a revolutionary one.

A virtually continuous rise in Sweden's standard of living during the present century has facilitated the successive reduction of earlier gross disparities in social status and economic opportunity without threatening the position or progress of the nation's wealthier strata. On the contrary, Social Democratic reformism has led gradually to intensified socio-economic cooperation between the Social Democrats and private enterprise.

Practical principles have proved decisive considerations in the party's pursuit of its two major goals: to promote total economic productivity and full employment, and to provide economic and social security and a rising standard of living for workers in the name of stability, justice, and equality. Sweden's so-called mixed economy presupposes, then, a basic community of interests between the Social Democratic government and the non-Socialist opposition parties (the Center party, the Liberals, and the Conservatives). This consensus on basic values provides a major impetus for what Tingsten called the "death of ideology," i.e., the demise of major conflicts of interests, ideas, and values among the major political parties.

PERSISTING CONTRADICTIONS

This sketch of welfare society in Sweden is an optimistic and partially superficial description which requires qualification. I shall note some of the nuances in modern Swedish developments partially because the discrepancy between an optimistic and positive view of Sweden, on one hand, and a critical or pessimistic view, on the other, is important if one is to understand both the Marxist-inspired criticism that has arisen in recent years and domestic reaction to such criticism.

Critics have cited various shortcomings with respect to both economic equality and justice and the domestic distribution of power in Sweden. Above all, questions of equality have aroused considerable attention. For example, critics have asserted that major differences still exist in cultural and social behavior among various groups of citizens. And to a considerable degree it is true that those persons who have always belonged to the privileged strata have availed themselves of better education and the opportunities for social mobility which it provides to enhance their social standards, incomes, prestige, and cultural enrichment. Underlying this discrepancy in access to higher education facilities are economic conditions, traditional social roles, differences in living conditions, and other factors which influence practical possibilities to pursue advanced studies. Statistically there is also social discrimination against women with respect to educational opportunity.

Important contemporary political tasks in Sweden include broadening educational opportunities, increasing the capacity of higher education, and reforming both higher education and traditional academic programs through provisions for various types of practical professional or occupational training, adult education, and re-education. The Social Democrats have been the driving force in continuing efforts, which date back a number of years, to transform Sweden's higher educational system to achieve these goals on behalf of the ideal of equality.

The debate on higher education and what has often been called "cultural consumption" has helped focus attention on another class contradiction in modern Social Democratic Sweden. This debate began long before the New Left introduced, in Marxist terminology, class conflict as a major theme of its criticism. The New Left is a relatively new phenomenon which did not appear until the middle of the 1960s, while educational reform proposals—including demands for new educational policies arising out of the discussion concerning the distribution and values of cultural consumption—had emerged as serious topics of concern well before then. Especially after the publication in 1962 of B. Nerman's booklet, *Demokratins kultursyn* (*Democracy's Cultural View*), criticism of what has been termed "high-brow culture" aroused considerable attention. Nerman, among others, attacked cultural ambitions and values that expressed the priorities of an established hierarchical society. In his view such values served to perpetuate a form of sterile and abstract prestige in the cultural sphere, which is restricted to the existing higher classes. These early critics argued that such values constituted an ossified mandarin culture that lacked existential justification. Social Democrats of various radical hues, as well as many Liberals, participated constructively in this cultural discussion.

Perhaps even more interested in the debate on sexual roles, the Liberal critics sought to end prejudices concerning the place of women in society and to achieve greater freedom of choice for women in occupations and sexual behavior. (This debate on sexual roles has deep roots in Swedish society and flared up anew during the 1950s.) Adherents of the New Left, on the other hand, view the debate on sexual roles and the discussion of sexual freedom with a certain ambivalence. Some of them maintain that the debate is merely an apparent problem that can only be finally resolved in the broader context of Socialist assumptions about class differences. Other less dogmatic members of the New Left, however, view the debate on sexual roles as a modern radical basis for criticizing a stagnating society.

Another important question of equality that helps qualify an overly idealistic view of modern Sweden concerns economic leveling. Various government commissions have been able to demonstrate that little effective reduction has occurred since the 1940s in differences of income levels despite an indisputable increase in total consumption and wage levels. Many lower-wage groups are still disadvantaged and encounter difficulties in the labor market, for example, during periods of economic fluctuation. Various minorities such as the aged, the handicapped, and social misfits have not been accorded equality. Such groups are burdened with lower incomes, poorer service, and reduced standards of living in a society that is primarily created for those who are effective producers.

Sweden's democratic institutions have also been subjected to criticism. The attack has focused primarily on the contradiction between formal democracy and the actual exercise of political influence that is immune from democratic control. Examples include the concentration of power in various sectors of private enterprise and tendencies toward bureaucratic autonomy within political or government institutions, party-leadership echelons, large interest associations, local government units, urban planning councils, and the police force.

The Swedish radical debate which began in the middle of the 1960s must be viewed against the background of these contradictory features of contemporary welfare society. Compared with most other industrial nations, it is undeniable that Sweden is in many respects a prospering utopia. We lack racial tensions, slums, wars, a truly large capitalistic concentration of power, a proletariat, and an authoritarian regime, which in various combinations have generated the strength and mass following of Socialist protest movements in such countries as the United States, France, West Germany, Spain, and Italy. We also lack an oppressive socialism comparable to that in Poland, East Germany, or the Soviet Union, where a critical and humanistic Socialist opposition has turned against established society in much the same manner as intellectuals (especially younger intellectuals) have done in the above non-Communist countries.

A militant protest movement can thus be thought to lack justification in Sweden. Yet careful analysis reveals important shortcomings in the Swedish welfare system, some of which have been briefly mentioned above. These shortcomings might appear minor in an international perspective, and one can argue that they could be overcome in a similar fashion in which we have pursued radical reformism for the past several decades. Indeed, this is precisely the line of reasoning advanced by most Swedish Social Democrats in refuting the Marxist demands of the radical opposition for revolutionary transformation.

THE LEFT OPPOSITION

The dilemma of the left opposition in Sweden lies in the fact that Swedish society can be interpreted in two contradictory ways within the context of international events. The traditional view is suggested by the following analysis: Sweden is a fortunate country in comparison with most other nations, and the relatively unimportant shortcomings that still exist can be overcome in the same spirit of radical reformism that has determined the course of socio-economic developments for the past several decades. Probably a majority of Swedes would endorse such an interpretation which, basically, is an expression of social stability.

The second point of view interprets the Swedish "utopia" as a chimera. According to this perspective of Swedish welfare, reformism is considered a product of the same forces that dominate the political system of the United States and other great powers. Through a process of domestic and external conflicts new capitalistic and imperialistic class societies have emerged in the Western industrial states which control more or less authoritarian regimes at home and seek the military and economic exploitation of the third world. This Marxist-influenced criticism derives much of its strength from the increasing opposition in Sweden to the American war in Vietnam and American support for reactionary regimes throughout the world. (This opposition sentiment is shared by many members of all political parties.) An additional source of this form of critical reasoning is the heightened consciousness of contradictions between the poor and the affluent nations.

According to Marxist analysis all of these events are closely related; they are the contemporary expression of the mechanisms of class society. A small ruling and owning class manipulates and exploits the great majority of the citizens in its own country and extends its power through military and economic means over the third world. The Marxist interpretation of these relations is so well known that it requires no further elaboration.

When this Marxist view of events is applied to the Swedish system, Sweden's democratic and egalitarian shortcomings which I mentioned earlier assume a symptomatic content and significance that they would not otherwise possess. In an effort to explain the contradiction that Sweden constitutes a capitalist class society despite long-term Social Democratic political dominance, the New Left (in the tradition of A. Gramsci) distinguishes between political domination and political hegemony.[3] The former refers only to the exercise of formal political power, while the latter term encompasses a society's incompletely developed system of concealed ideas and values which define the leading groups in society and indirectly determine what is politically possible to implement. Although the Social Democrats thus dominate politically in Sweden, a political hegemony is nevertheless said to exist in the form of capitalistic or bourgeois thoughts, values, and behavior patterns. The Social Democratic leaders are considered merely a group of marionettes who more or less unconsciously run the errands of private, big capitalist enterprise. In the process they so mislead their supporters, the working classes, that the workers do not perceive that they are exploited and suppressed.

Sweden's high standard of living is described by dogmatic adherents of the New Left as a revisionist trick, opium for the masses, and a form of bribery which lulls the workers into false confidence that society exists for their sake and which inculcates them with bourgeois values that in reality are alien to them and prevent them from developing themselves or their true interests. The New Left sees in the mixed economy—a description which in critical Marxist parlance has become pejorative—the central point in the camouflaged and corrupted subjugation of revisionist social democracy to the bourgeois hegemony.

Other Marxists—or Leninists as they call themselves—consider theories of hegemony and dominance heretical, however, and maintain that actual political power rests in Sweden, as it does in other Western countries, in the hands of private monopoly capitalists rather than the representatives of the working class movement. Marxist critics of all ideological temperaments find support for their view that Swedish social democracy is an opportunistic revisionism which has been corrupted by capitalistic interests in the parallel compromises that the German and English working-class movements have made in the Grand Coalition and under the Wilson government, respectively. Such Marxist perspectives claim to represent a coherent and scientific "ideology."

IDEOLOGY AND CONSCIOUSNESS

Undoubtedly we are experiencing a rebirth of ideology which began about the same time that Tingsten had declared the end of ideology. The term "ideology," however, is poorly chosen. In its original conception, in the writings of Marx himself, for example, ideology designated the various forms of political propaganda and prejudices that emerged as secondary superstructures of class-determined economic aspirations and interests which served to disguise class interests in the form of pseudo-scientific formulation. For Tingsten, in contrast, ideology means a comprehensive and more or less dogmatic political doctrine—a kind of religion or metaphysics which is characterized by logical coherence but is also removed from reality and hence illusionary.

The various "ideologies" which are propounded in the contemporary Swedish political and cultural debate correspond to neither of these definitions. Instead they embrace a vague sense of political activity combined with one or another basic political attitude without simultaneously providing a comprehensive or clearly formulated political doctrine. All political parties throughout the political spectrum—from the intellectually impoverished Swedish Conservatives to the various competing factions on the extreme left—proclaim ideologies, and each maintains that its own ideology is an objective, effective, and truthful political doctrine. But their claims can be considered naïve and uncritical.

The conflicting perspectives of Sweden within the international system which I have mentioned above—Sweden as the favored welfare state of radical reformism and Sweden as a corrupted revisionistic class society—are not two articulated theoretical systems that can be objectively tested against each other. They are, instead, two different ways of elucidating the same conditions—two analytical predispositions, each of which can be elaborated in a different way and can lead to different self-fulfilling prophecies concerning the content and development of Swedish politics. This applies with even greater force to the bourgeois ideologies which provide little to correspond with the serious theoretical discussion that is being conducted within the New Left.

The conception that one's own political ideas constitute an authoritative political ideology is combined with the demand that every politically responsible person—especially writers and other intellectuals—should adopt that particular ideology as his own. Both of these claims —the intellectual claim that ideologies are objectively valid and the moral claim that fellow citizens should assert ideological convictions— contrast sharply with the pragmatic and relativistic attitude that pervades Tingsten's ideological criticism, as well as the practical, commonsense reformism that characterizes Swedish politics. These claims also contrast with the literary cultural movements that dominated in Sweden before the advent of the New Left.

A brief analysis of the changed meaning of the word "consciousness" can illustrate this difference. The concept of psychological consciousness was employed earlier, in connection with psychoanalytical thought, to mean critical awareness, self-criticism, and criticism of the biases of one's thought processes and preconceptions. In the tradition of natural science, theoretical consciousness was thus considered approximately the same as methodological insights into how systems of conception or theoretical models which one uses to describe one's experiences and to program one's actions are determined by values and premises. Consciousness embraced, in short, a form of critical knowledge.

In the terminology of the Swedish New Left, however, the word political "consciousness" is used to describe one's adherence to the

Marxist view of society as a class society composed of exploiters and exploited and to interpret social and political behavior in terms of the special form of Marxism that is now considered correct. This use applies equally to other political directions. "Consciousness" means that one rigorously applies the ideology to which one adheres in one's political thoughts and actions. This has little in common with the earlier form of critical knowledge. On the contrary, it is the latter's antithesis.

The insight that sociological, economic, political, and some of our ideological and scientific systems are ultimately based on subjective values has been utilized in an irrational manner. Many social critics have denied *a priori* the validity of competing theories, ways of thought, and institutions. Calling such systems bourgeois or capitalistic, they have rejected them out of hand in order to make room for their own conceptions and propositions. This means that many deny the possibility for critical debate, empirical tests, and argumentation in the manner in which scientific systems have evolved through social interchange among scientists. Instead they have opened the door to categorical decrees, majority decisions, and antidemocratic actions within the circle of a self-chosen elite whose status is based on power or force. Examples of this have occurred, for example, under the label of "direct democracy."

The claim that one can embrace an objectively true political doctrine corresponds to the position of Conservative communism. Such a claim is also related to Conservative or Stalinist doctrines in literary and other artistic questions which maintained that artists could provide an objective "realistic" picture of reality and were, moreover, obliged to do so. This uncritical realism also has its ardent supporters among younger critics and writers in Sweden who assert that objectively documented political propaganda should be coupled with polemics against what they call "formalism," "high-brow culture," "individualism," and "bourgeois sentimentality." Such conceptions and demands stand in contradiction to both earlier Swedish traditions and the tendency toward liberalization that intellectuals in post-Stalinist Eastern Europe are determined to defend and to strengthen. At meetings among Swedish "radical" writers and foreign writers who are directly involved in the problems of both Socialist and third-world cultures, this Swedish "radicalism"—or puritanism—has aroused both concern and scorn.

We possess in Sweden our own traditions of so-called criticism of values and semantic logical criticism of knowledge. Both have had important consequences for the social and esthetic debate for a number of decades. Through its failure to relate productively to these indigenous Swedish cultural traditions, the New Left in Sweden has missed an important opportunity to make an original contribution and to conduct an independent Swedish experiment in the political and cultural movements of the past several years. Despite some exceptions—such as members of the group of "Young Philosophers" at the University of Stockholm—a strain of provincial uncertainty has characterized much of the recent leftist debate in Sweden.

THE NEW LEFT: A CRITIQUE

The New Left has to a great extent failed to relate its ideas and programs with previous Swedish cultural traditions and with the special conditions of Swedish political and economic life—i.e., with "the Swedish experiment." There are many reasons for this failure. We lack breadth and continuity in our public cultural life. Swedish culture is sustained primarily by a small circle whose members publish in a limited number of newspapers and magazines in Stockholm and various other large cities. Small shifts of view within this group can have an important effect on the public debate. In addition we lack a healthy tradition of Marxist and radical Socialist thought. The radical socialism that existed before the advent of the New Left was represented primarily by an arid form of communism within the insignificant Communist party, which for a long time merely transmitted the various propaganda interpretations of Soviet communism. When, after the fall of Stalinism, new Liberal Socialist ideas began to make their international appearance, we were not prepared to assimilate them. We lacked the intellectual requisites. This is the weakness of a small country—to be dependent on cultural ideas originating in the larger nations.

Uncertainty concerning their own identity contributes further to the tendency in smaller countries such as Sweden to accept uncritically new cultural impulses. They seek inspiration, justification, and membership in a larger community and naïvely attempt to demonstrate—both for themselves and for others—their adherence to cultural movements that impress them. The epigone becomes, however, a caricature of that which he seeks to imitate. Because he is uncertain of his own resources to establish contact and his capacity to play the role which he assigns himself, his actions resemble the exaggerated expressionism of silent movies.

Ridiculous examples of this phenomenon in Sweden include the occupation of administration buildings at the University of Stockholm in the spring of 1968 and other similar actions and claims for "direct democracy." The former was an attempt to ape the student demonstrations in Paris and the American SDS. In the absence of authoritarian control over the educational system, cultural life, and society as in Gaullist France or explosive racial and class differences as in the United States, these and similar manifestations were unwarranted and childish.

Moreover, such so-called radical student actions combined in an absurd fashion the revolutionary Socialist ideas espoused by a radical minority of students with the traditional academic illusion that students constitute an elite who can claim freedom from society and special privileges which they themselves determine. This elitist view—resting on an ancient tradition of academic vanity and self-chosen status—is cherished by the Conservative majority of students. Undoubtedly such ill-founded applications of an uncritical and unanalyzed "radicalism" have helped generate a backlash that has harmed the serious leftist movement.

A generation gap has also contributed, of course, to the break in continuity between the Swedish New Left and earlier Swedish cultural traditions. Leaders of the New Left represent a younger generation which is seeking to establish its own identity. Related to this is the fact that our cultural life is too narrow to support, in quantitative terms, a many-faceted cultural experience. Generation shifts and alleged conflicts among various literary generations have appeared on several occasions during the past century in Sweden. Examples include the deep cleavages between the literary giants of the 1880s and 1890s, i.e., between the realists and romanticists exemplified by Strindberg and Heidenstam, respectively, and between writers of the 1940s and 1950s, i.e. the existential moralists and the public-oriented romanticists. Such watersheds in artistic and cultural life are related to a natural cycles in productive resources and possibilities. A given cultural attitude, a particular system of roles or models for artistic creation and thought, will yield with time to exhaustion or disgust. Once a cultural or artistic orientation no longer serves as a source of creative inspiration, it will be abandoned in the search for new forms.

One can discern indications that this process has occurred within the "new" Swedish cultural life even outside the New Left. During the 1940s and 1950s a mechanical and fashionable epigonism, which took the form of dogmatic antimetaphysics and logical formalism, gradually modified the prevailing traditions of semantic knowledge and criticism of values. Its spokesmen failed to recognize, however, that religious, political, and metaphysical modes of thought could not be dismissed simply as some sort of semantic foolishness. On the contrary such symbols and language systems made possible serious attempts to interpret valid experiences of reality and aspirations. These attempts have inspired, and still inspire, the creativity, insights, and behavior of innumerable persons.

Long before the appearance of the New Left we also experienced in Sweden tendencies toward a renaissance of what I might call the "logically impure languages" and of attempts to seek greater knowledge of man and his world, which these "impure" systems of ideas can provide. The general movement toward a rebirth of ideology was evidenced as well in the widespread interest that Swedish literary figures accorded existentialism during the 1940s.

The New Left has also failed to relate itself consciously to the latter aspect of Swedish cultural tradition. This failure contrasts to developments in France where the New Socialist movement has sought to renew Marxism by incorporating aspects of modern intellectual trends such as existentialism, psychoanalysis, and New Thomism. Yet if one attempts to discern continuities of Swedish tradition in the new Swedish radicalism—continuities which the most ardent spokesmen of what is considered entirely "new" do not exploit or of which they are unaware —the breaks and contrasts between cultural generations will possibly prove not to be as great as they might initially appear.

THE TRANSFORMATION OF
SWEDISH LIBERALISM

An additional reason why the New Left has emphasized its separation from earlier Swedish cultural traditions lies in the fact that such traditions were primarily represented by aggression and corruption in American foreign and defense policies. Symptomatic of this attitude was the wide reception in Sweden that was accorded F. A. von Hayek's *The Road to Serfdom.*

During the 1950s an opposition movement began to appear in Sweden, and elsewhere, against atomic armaments, a one-sided view of Soviet politics, the "myths of the Cold War," American dominance of NATO, and the global encirclement of the Eastern bloc. By the beginning of the 1950s a minority of radicals had emerged who stood in strong opposition to the old Liberals and Conservatives. This opposition continued to grow, and by the latter part of the decade had broadened its criticism to include what is called "Western indoctrination" in Sweden and other countries associated with the United States. The war in Vietnam, American dominance in the third world, and American support for reactionary regimes provided further impetus for the growth of this opposition movement.

By the mid–1960s the New Left had established a direct link with these earlier manifestations of Swedish radicalism. In contrast members of the political and cultural establishment—i.e., the leading representatives of Liberal and Conservative socio-cultural viewpoints—remained relatively passive. As a result the Liberal party and those who still claim to represent Liberal values lost much of their capacity to elicit a positive response among radical intellectuals in Sweden. The majority of Liberals, at least the political leaders among them, thus appear to have stumbled into a blind alley in this phase of the contemporary political and cultural debate. Their failure to respond to the new radical criticism has undoubtedly contributed to the break in the continuity of the Swedish cultural tradition which occurred during the 1960s and to its subsequent impoverishment as well.

The moral basis of the New Left assumes various manifestations. Among them have been a strong demand for political participation, vehement denunciation of those holding different viewpoints, rejection of literature and art that do not serve concrete political purposes (such as political analysis, propaganda, and documentation), and impatience with reforms and other programs which require more time for fruition than so-called direct democracy. Even though it is often difficult to determine whether specific actions are motivated by moral indignation or whether they are caused by other factors, moral passion constitutes an important source of strength within the New Left. Notwithstanding the usual vulgar interpretations of Sweden abroad, moral considerations determine to a considerable degree many aspects of Sweden's cultural life. (This observation applies equally to the denounced and misunderstood Swedish sexual mores, which have evolved primarily in response to demands for honesty and openness in sexual questions and not as a consequence of any greater promiscuity in Sweden than in other countries.)

Despite continuing secularization, pietistic or traditional religious values and morals are still widely diffused in Sweden. It is, indeed, striking how many of the leading critics and writers within the New Left have emerged from the milieu and homes where such beliefs have been strongly represented. Active moral engagement has also characterized earlier cultural transformations in Sweden. Liberal antitotalitarianism and relativism have already been mentioned as examples. One can also cite existentialism, which was a dominant force in the Swedish literary world of the 1940s. Thus, even though many adherents of the New Left wish to view their moral activity as a rebirth of social responsibility, just as many of their opponents seek to charge the Left with sectarian moralism and intolerant self-righteousness, the fact that the New Left is sustained by moral considerations is no departure from earlier traditions in Sweden.

THE ANARCHIST LEGACY

Until now I have considered the intellectual claim of the New Left to possess an objectively valid political "ideology" and its moral demand that others should likewise become politically conscious and active. Opposed to this aspect of the recent Swedish cultural debate is another movement whose relation to the New Left is not yet clearly defined. I am referring to the protest and anarchistic traditions which have recently emerged with new strength and apparently new ideas. These protest movements are Swedish versions of corresponding international phenomena and have assumed similar forms of expression. Within the artistic sphere such movements are related to dadaism and futurism, and can also be compared in Sweden with psychoanalytical and surrealist-influenced vitalism and primitivism which were important for Swedish literature and art during the 1920s and 1930s. The "new" movements in art during the 1960s, however, profess the same ahistorical and parvenulike desire as political radicalism to consider themselves something entirely new in relation to earlier Swedish traditions.

The relation between the current trends in art and the Socialist-inspired political movements is ambiguous. The artistic protest movement seeks to evade the form of political "consciousness" and participation demanded by the New Left, but it simultaneously criticizes the same "bourgeois" society against which the New Left directs its protests. Moreover, and equally important, its leaders are members of the same generation of young people seeking in common to define their own identity, role, and social tasks against a generation of predecessors whom they consider perfidious and spent.

The combination of artistic-literary protests and political anarchism is well known. The most recent preceding generation of writers in Sweden—those of the 1940s and to a certain extent of the 1950s—identified themselves to a considerable degree with what was then called anarcho-syndicalism. This was a combination of anarchistic individualism and syndicalistic utopian thought which envisioned the decentralization of society and the transfer of control over means of production to workers on the local level. Many of the leading theoreticians in the 1960s came initially from groups and journals espousing anarchistic programs. Contemporary theses concerning decentralized forms of direct (and industrial) democracy attest to continuity with these earlier forms of anarcho-syndicalism—even though the Socialist radicals refuse to concede the kinship. This refusal further reflects the lack of consciousness of tradition and appreciation for critical nuances in the contemporary Swedish cultural debate.

The anarchistic protest movement is also related to the Swedish New Marxism through its anti-intellectual and provolutional tendencies. The anti-intellectualism of modern anarchist leaders opposes the technology and bureaucracy of the present industrial state just as their predecessors had rejected earlier forms of analysis and critical knowledge. Many within the Swedish New Left movement have attacked the latter as well, depicting such thought processes as bourgeois formalism and Liberal irresponsibility.

Modern anarchism is related in yet another way to New Left Marxism. Both are opposed to what they consider social violence to man and seek in its place "authentic experience"—i.e., authenticity and development of the self—which they claim is denied them by contemporary society. In other words the modern antipolitical protest movement (anarchism) has joined the political protest movement (the New Marxism) in a common struggle against what the latter calls alienation. Neither these links nor the apparent similarities that such efforts against alienation and for authenticity share with existentialism have been clearly perceived and analyzed.

The struggle against alienation is thus a movement of many diverse strands in which dogmatic Marxists and antipolitical anarchists have converged. They are supported by a large number of other groups among today's youth who are inspired by the quest for equality and the renunciation of authoritarian and inhumane trends in the institutions of modern society. In connection with an historical formula, one could call this the third step in the revolutionary three-stage program of "freedom, equality, and fraternity." In this movement lies perhaps one of the most hopeful central points in the political engagement of the young generation—the vision of an "open society" or the utopia of humanitarian equality.

The Swedish New Left and the parallel anarchistic or antipolitical protest movements in the mid-1960s have thus been inspired by corresponding international phenomena. Although these protest movements seek to present themselves as entirely new phenomena, they nevertheless display a high degree of affinity with various older aspects of Swedish tradition. To a considerable extent, however, the leaders of the "new" movements are not conscious of these historical relations and have made little use of them in ways that might have accorded the Swedish variants of these international phenomena a greater independent individuality. Nor has the new radicalism attempted to draw on the unique features of the "Swedish experiment"—i.e., social-Liberal welfare reformism which was discussed above—to test the "new" thoughts and values in light of genuine Swedish conditions. Instead, leaders of the various radical protest movements have been content to find analogies with conditions in the Western and Communist industrial states where protest movements have had a more direct connection with the authoritarian, military, bureaucratic, or capitalist misuse of power on the part of the established regimes. They have underscored these analogies in a manner that has often been superficial, stereotyped, or abstractly speculative. Their actions reflect the lack of independence and uncertain cultural consciousness of a small country. This suggests, however, that moral indignation has probably been dominant in the protest movement. Moral engagement provides the most important source of strength of the new radicalism and has contributed to the enhanced political activity and sense of social responsibility among an elite of young Swedish intellectuals.

CONTRIBUTIONS OF THE CULTURAL DEBATE

Opponents have criticized the new radicalism for its lack of constructive determination. Although such criticism may be partially valid, it is hardly altogether justified. A lively and ambitious discussion has been conducted in a number of new journals and within groups and associations in which participants have attempted to formulate theories and programs for radical political activity. In their present form the "new" movements are only three to four years old, and they still exhibit elements of a generation gap and efforts to define their own identity in opposition to the established political and cultural circles. One hopes that the few years in which the new radicalism has existed have at least proved propitious for developments that can now lead to the advent of greater critical and constructive activity.

The major political parties in Sweden have confronted the new radicalism partially with criticism and partially with understanding. Leaders of the established parties have primarily reproached the New Left for its undeniable element of elitist thought and its antidemocratic inclination—based on the New Left's conviction that it possesses superior insights and knowledge—to dismiss its opponents without bothering to listen to them and to undertake instead direct democracy and anti-intellectual actions. The bourgeois or more Conservative parties have most often denounced the new radicalism, revealing a rigid lack of understanding of its motivation and aspirations, and have called for police action against its adherents. The Social Democrats have in general displayed greater sympathy with the demands of the new radicalism.

During the fall of 1968 a general election was held to the Swedish lower house of Parliament. Because the bourgeois opposition parties had gained strength in recent years and a change of government seemed possible, the election was a highly important one and the campaign proved livelier than usual. In this situation the political parties accorded particular attention to the opinion among members of the younger generation who were eligible to vote for the first time and could possibly constitute the crucial marginal voters. The youth associations of the political parties were elevated in importance and were supported in various ways by the parties. A certain rejuvenation was also discernible among the party candidates.

Divided in many factions, some members of the New Left aligned themselves with the Communist party while others leaned toward the Social Democrats. Although the New Left encompasses only a minority of younger voters, experience has shown that this minority—because it is intelligent and well informed—is more important than mere numbers might suggest. For this reason the New Left helped arouse Swedish interests—both before the election and after—in international questions such as the policies of the major powers and problems of the developing countries as well as in domestic issues such as questions of greater equality. Even though this heightened interest has only to a limited extent assumed the Marxist or Socialist forms advocated by the New Left, the diffusion of new levels of political consciousness is in itself a major accomplishment.

Notes

1. Recent Socialist criticism has been articulated in a number of journals (including *Zenit, Konkret, Clarté, Kommentar,* and *Komma*); newspapers (for example, *Tidsignal* and *Aftonbladet*); and books. Among the latter the most important include G. Therborn, *En ny vänster* (Stockholm, 1966), C. H. Hermansson, *Vänsterns väg* (Stockholm, 1965), and G. Palm, *En orättvis betrakelse* (Stockholm, 1966).

2. Herbert Tingsten, *Från idéer till idyll* (Stockholm, 1966).

3. A. Gramsci, *En kollektiv intellektuell* (Stockholm, 1967).

NILS ELVANDER

Democracy and Large Organizations

REPUTEDLY SWEDEN has the world's strongest and most highly developed system of interest associations. Every socio-economic group of importance has—or is in the process of forming—its own organization. These organizations have an extremely high percentage of members. Nearly 100 per cent of Sweden's industrial workers, over 90 per cent of state employees, and approximately 70 per cent of privately employed white-collar workers, for example, are organized in national unions.

As in other highly developed nations, innumerable so-called promotional organizations also exist in Sweden. Most of these are small and lack political significance. But some promotional organizations, e.g., those belonging to the temperance movement, are united in strong peak organizations and have exercised considerable influence in the political decision-making process.

The major interest organizations possess even greater capacity to influence political decisions. The most important of them comprise approximately twenty peak organizations which channel influence from various sectors of society to all parts of the political system. Since these large, politically influential organizations—along with the political parties—are the foundation on which Swedish political democracy rests, it is of primary importance to inquire how democracy functions *within* such organizations. The principal purpose of this essay is to undertake such an analysis in an attempt to formulate a theory of "broadened democracy" appropriate to advanced urban-industrial systems.

In the following discussion I shall use the term "large organization" to refer primarily to the large mass-interest associations within the labor, agricultural, and housing markets and to the consumer cooperatives. But in recent years problems of democracy have become more intensified even within other types of organizations such as private and public industrial corporations, local communes, and the political system itself. Hence I shall include these organizations in my analysis as well.

It should be noted that I define democracy as a form of government and that I place principal emphasis on two elements in democratic theory: (1) participation by the governed in the decision process and (2) a correspondence of views between the rulers and the governed. The social and psychological dimensions of democracy will not be discussed. Instead, I view them as necessary conditions for a well-functioning institutionalized democracy.

CENTRALIZATION AND CONSOLIDATION

A deeply rooted tendency exists among Swedish interest associations, as in other spheres of society, toward the centralization of power and the development of larger structures. In recent years this tendency has become even more accentuated. Especially within organizations on the labor market decision-making power has shifted from the lower units —e.g., the individual unions and business firms—to the peak organizations. On the latter level the center of power has moved in turn from the representative organs to the various executive councils and leading officials.

Simultaneously the consolidation of small local units into larger structures signifies another sort of concentration within the large mass organizations. Between the early 1950s and 1968, for example, the number of trade unions decreased from 9,000 to 3,300. Consumer cooperative associations, which numbered 600 at the beginning of the 1960s, are expected to diminish to approximately 20 by the middle of the 1970s. In many cases the new larger trade union and cooperative structures correspond to the boundaries of an entire province.

This process of structural consolidation is the explicit goal of conscious policy decisions. It is justified above all with arguments of greater efficiency. Since small organizations are considered incapable of providing their members with the kind of service they have a right to expect of their organization, larger structures must be created so that service functions can be delegated to full-time employees. Compensation for accompanying losses from a democratic perspective, e.g., reducing the number of elected group representatives and widening the gap between an individual member and his organization, is allegedly provided by the greater material advantages of membership. New methods of mobilizing members have also been employed (to which I shall return later).

A direct parallel to such developments exists on the communal level of government. Since World War II the Swedish Parliament has passed two major bills instituting a substantial decrease in the number of local communes through consolidation. The second of these measures, endorsed in 1962, calls for the merger of approximately 1,000 primary communes into 282 "communal blocs." Within these units cooperation will be successively intensified until the communes in each bloc voluntarily unite. The justification for this reform was largely the same as that underlying the consolidation of Sweden's interest associations. In refuting the charge of opponents that the merger of local government structures would weaken communal democracy, the proponents of reform maintain that the larger blocs actually represent a gain for democracy. They argue that through consolidation communal self-government obtained possibilities and resources to deal with important social questions that otherwise might have been relegated to the state bureaucracy.

The development toward larger units within interest associations and on the local government level is directly connected with the progressive implementation of representative democracy. Initially, collective wage decisions had been made within the trade-union movement on a decentralized basis of direct democracy. Individual trade unions had often decided the fate of contract proposals through a general referendum among their members. As early as the beginning of the twentieth century, however, union leaders had begun to reserve the right of decisions for themselves, and the vote of members became only advisory. After World War II referenda in contract decisions were virtually abandoned. In their place advisory conferences or representative assemblies were instituted which lack any power of decision. The driving force behind this development was the centralization of collective bargaining procedures, first to the level of national unions and from the middle of the 1950s onward to the peak Swedish Federation of Trade Unions.

A corresponding change has taken place within the local unions. Direct democracy in the small units has been replaced by indirect democracy in the larger structures. This transformation, which has its parallels in other organizations, means that Sweden's interest associations have adopted the same kind of decision processes that now prevail in the communal sphere of government. With the passage of the first consolidation bill of 1952, the last vestiges of popular participation in local decisions disappeared.

Even within the political system direct democracy in the form of referenda has declined in importance. Provisions for advisory referenda were provided by constitutional amendment after World War I, but the referendum procedure has been employed only three times since then. During the 1950s the bourgeois opposition strongly advocated strengthening the referendum institution. Non-Socialist leaders proposed, for example, that binding referenda should apply in questions of aprticular importance. The opposition viewed the referendum as an appropriate means to enhance Swedish democracy. Not without reason, however, the Social Democratic majority maintained that the real motive behind the non-Socialist demands was the opposition's desire to weaken the parliamentary position of the government. Political controversy over the referendum provisions and the way in which referenda were used during the 1950s—once concerning legislation to introduce right-hand traffic and later to implement a new supplementary pension reform—helped discredit the institution even in the eyes of the opposition. As a result interest in the referendum issue has declined appreciably in recent years.

No provisions exist in either law or practice for referenda on the communal level. The occasional local referenda that have been held—such as several involving the consolidation of communal units—were initiated solely on individual communal initiative. They have been accorded no political importance by the decision-making authorities.

IMPULSE FOR REFORM

Even a few years ago no one would have conceived of questioning the validity and effectiveness of representative democracy in Sweden. Its dominance in all areas of society appeared so self-evident that the debate on problems of democracy focused entirely on improvements within the framework of the representative system. But today the situation has changed significantly. In many ways the contemporary sociopolitical debate is tending toward a renaissance of direct democracy.

At a very minimum social critics have called for a thorough reconsideration of the existing forms in which the representative system functions. In a more radical fashion than earlier, the capacity of the individual to influence social development has occupied a central place in the Swedish debate. This has occurred because of greater awareness of the general tendency toward larger bureaucratic units and the increased centralization of power. In this sense Sweden appears to be on the threshold of a breakthrough to a new individualism.

In December 1969, for example, the sudden outbreak of a long wildcat strike of nearly 5,000 workers in the state-owned mining corporation LKAB called general attention to the problems of industrial and trade-union democracy. The strike was directed not only against intolerable working conditions but also against the lack of communication between the workers and management, as well as the trade-union leadership.

To a considerable degree the recent (and continuing) debate on problems of democracy in larger social structures has been inspired by the Swedish New Left. But the impulse for reform originating within the ranks of the New Left has almost exclusively concerned practical rather than theoretical issues. Preference for direct democracy, which is a common characteristic among the various leftist factions, has been expressed through concrete actions such as demonstrations and student revolts instead of attempts to formulate new theories of democracy as a form of government. Adherents of the New Left have not sought, in short, to clarify their definition of direct democracy.

In such manifestations of the New Left quest for direct democracy one is unable to discern answers to such questions as how far the demand for direct democracy can be carried or to what extent it is possible to vest decision functions in mass meetings and other forms of direct action. The strong reaction within the New Left movement against traditional representative democracy, the Marxist conception of a unity between "theory" and "practice," and the inspiration for New Left agitation provided by the Chinese cultural revolution are probably the most important reasons for the nearly total indifference displayed by members of the New Left toward the theoretical issues of democracy. But sooner or later every ideological movement that seeks to dismantle the power apparatus of society and replace it with purely voluntary institutions must confront such problematical questions.

Even the more moderate criticism of the representative system has revealed a strikingly untheoretical nature. The few constructive proposals for improvement that have been advanced to date have been motivated largely by practical considerations. Several examples will illustrate this.

In 1968 a leftist-led student revolt occurred in Sweden which was primarily directed against the university system but in broader perspective against capitalist society as well. Compared with other countries, where both the social system and university structures display considerably more authoritarian features than in Sweden, the Swedish revolt was modest. Nevertheless it had far-reaching effects. As a reaction to the activity of the New Left, the Conservative or moderate groups won a majority in subsequent elections to various student assemblies. On the initiative of the national government an attempt was made to broaden student influence within university institutions. Leaders of the Conservative and moderately radical students had no great difficulty in uniting with faculty members in arranging this reform. The problem of student influence will thus largely be solved within the context of representative democracy—e.g., through governing institutions that are composed of delegates from each of the major university sectors (administration, faculty, and student body).

Another significant victory for moderate student opinion—
represented by the principal student union organization and the Social
Democratic Student Association—was achieved when the government
abandoned an earlier commission proposal to create a new program of
studies that would have provided an established sequence of courses in
the philosophical faculties at the universities. Major features of the proposal, which had been drawn up within the central university administration on the basis of general guidelines established by an earlier parliamentary decision, were modified to accord with the wishes of the
more moderate students.

The course and outcome of the Swedish student revolt provide an
excellent example of the classical Swedish method of utilizing moderate
reforms and pragmatic adjustments to disarm critical attacks on the existing system. The extreme left, which had initiated the university reform process, has become increasingly isolated. Once its concrete demands were met, the broad mass of student opinion was satisfied. Some
of the leftist leaders have even helped implement the various reforms.
Herbert Marcuse would undoubtedly describe what has happened as a
typical manifestation of "repressive tolerance."

It should also be noted, as indicated above, that the process of revolution and reform was accompanied by a minimum of theoretical discussion. But the final result will probably be a discernible broadening of
democracy.

Within the university sphere the established authorities have thus
demonstrated a positive inclination to respond to criticism. The same
cannot be said, however, of the reaction of politicians and bureaucrats
to criticism of urban planning on the local level. Critics in both the leftist and non-Socialist parties have asserted that the technocratic power
structure constitutes the principal determining factor in urban planning
in the larger cities, with citizens exercising virtually no influence in decisions. To alleviate this imbalance they have demanded that experts
openly explain their values, politicians present alternative proposals to
the voters, and sufficient information and concrete possibilities be provided the citizens so that the latter can voice their opinion about the
value premises underlying the various alternatives. Such steps would
primarily serve to strengthen the representative system. But some social
dissidents have also raised the demand for direct democracy. For exam-

ple, critics have urged that inhabitants in a given urban district should be given the opportunity to influence detailed formulations of their environment through consultations with administrators and other forms of direct action. Alternatively, direct democracy could be achieved by making the politicians concerned directly accountable for their actions.

The politicians and experts who have been subject to such attacks have generally defended existing practices with two principal arguments. They have cited the need to maintain economic efficiency in urban planning and they have emphasized the formal democratic character of the decision process. With a few exceptions they have not sought a constructive discussion of the critics' proposals for broadening the democratic process. Even less have they actually sought to pursue concrete reforms.

In urban planning the Social Democrats, who for a number of years have had a majority or at least a dominant influence in the larger cities, have thus emerged as partial opponents of demands by critics for more intensified democracy. For reasons of partisan interest and ideology, however, they have not voiced similar opposition in the simultaneous debate on industrial and economic democracy. On the contrary, the Social Democrats have been the leading force in advocating reforms of the present economic system. In part the discussion has centered on means to increase employee influence within public and private corporations. Experimental forms of industrial democracy have recently been instituted within various state-owned enterprises. In addition agitation for economic democracy—involving in this case insight by the state and local communes into the decision processes of large private business firms—has been stimulated by a government commission report that documented the extent to which economic power is concentrated in the hands of a few large companies and banks. In all of these areas, however, reform proposals have been formulated solely within the framework of representative democracy. No proposals have been made to implement forms of direct economic democracy.

Finally it should be noted that political spokesmen have also formulated general programs to democratize virtually all social institutions: schools, hospitals, welfare services, prisons, the military, etc. Often such proposals call for democratizing social relations and eliminating authoritarian attitudes among responsible civil servants. Attempts such as these may prove significant for the future by creating better social and psychological requisites for broadened political democracy. But advocates of reform have generally failed to address themselves to the theoretical problems of democracy.

In summary, then, the intensive debate on means to broaden Swedish democracy has revealed a clear tendency toward direct democracy. Simultaneously the debate has been marked by a highly indeterminate and untheoretical character. The response of the established institutions to social criticism—to the extent that they have responded at all—has consistently been formulated in terms of representative democracy. Hence scant guidelines have been provided to formulate a "new" theory of democracy.

ORGANIZATION DEMOCRACY

What contributions have interest associations made to the contemporary debate on the democratization of society? Have they found cause to reappraise the forms of their own internal democracy? Can one discern within them any basis for a theory of broadened democracy? In attempting to answer these questions I shall restrict my discussion to the largest popular movements—the trade unions, cooperatives, and tenant associations—for which such problematical issues are most acute.

From the outset it should be noted that the larger interest associations have played only a minor role in the public debate on Swedish democracy. It has been above all adherents of the New Left (but also members of the Liberal and Conservative parties) who have raised charges of bureaucratization and democratic shortcomings within the major organizations. What the interest associations have done and what they intend to do in dealing with their internal problems, however, have not been accorded as widespread attention as the critical viewpoints in the mass media.

For some time it has been clearly perceived within the trade-union movement that individual members become more actively involved in union affairs in direct proportion to the organization's proximity to the concrete problems at their place of work. The more remote a union structure (such as the new larger regional units), the greater the disinterest among members. It is within the subunits of the national union organization that workers are most at home and feel that their interests can best be served. For these reasons the regional structures have been supplemented with a web of local units which have been established at all places of work where union members are employed.

This reform of the regional structures has also yielded increased resources for providing members with information, opportunities for specialized study, and other forms of union activity which were often nonexistent under the former system of small locals. Surveys within various trade unions indicate that aggregate activity among members is greater today than it was in previous decades when membership involvement was primarily limited to oftentimes sparsely attended annual meetings. Increased activity provides in turn enhanced possibilities for members to influence the policy of the regional and national union associations.

The question remains, however, whether such possibilities have been sufficiently utilized so that membership influence in larger questions of union policy—i.e., issues extending beyond specific places of work—can be articulated and communicated to regional and national leaders. Available studies suggest that much remains to be done to improve communications from members to union leadership. Information seems to flow effectively from the top of the union structure down to the local level, but leaders appear to be relatively poorly informed about opinions among the rank and file. The problem is difficult to solve, particularly since the distance between the individual member and the union leadership has increased with the introduction of the regional structures. Nevertheless present efforts within the trade-union movement to mobilize members through the subunits that are closest to them seem to be the only feasible means to resolve this issue.

COOPERATIVES

The Swedish cooperative movement confronts, with perhaps even greater magnitude, the same problems as the trade-union movement. The reason is that the process of concentration has gone even further among Swedish cooperatives than it has within the national trade-union association. Admittedly the responsible organs within the cooperative movement have for the time being rejected the extreme radical model of structural consolidation—which was strongly advocated by the leading figure in the Cooperative Association—that envisioned the creation of a single nation-wide organization. But even the alternative proposal to establish between fifteen and twenty-five associations by the mid-1970s will lead to considerable concentration.

The principal justification for this step is that consolidation of existing structures will result in greater economic efficiency. In this context one must recall that the cooperatives confront a special dilemma which other interest organizations are spared. They are a democratically based popular movement as well as a major business enterprise (Sweden's largest). In their latter capacity the cooperatives are highly competitive with private firms and chain stores. Since their competitors are not encumbered by considerations of democratic traditions and decision processes, they can concentrate on maximizing economic efficiency. If the cooperatives are to maintain and preferably increase their share of the market, they are forced to emulate the emphasis on efficiency among their private competitors. These factors create a persistent tension between economic considerations and internal democracy within the cooperative associations. As a result the danger arises that efficiency can become an end-in-itself and that the movement will submerge entirely in the bourgeois "hegemony" in society.

The continuing transfer of economic power to the central organization has made efforts to preserve and strengthen democracy within the cooperative movement extremely difficult. Recently it was decided that all industrial firms that are still owned by individual consumer organizations will be absorbed into the national structure. Various models for increased democratic control of the industries were discussed, but no realistic solution to the problem has yet been found. From a democratic perspective a considerable advantage could be gained, however, if effective channels of communication were established between the attitudes and wishes of members on the local level and leaders in the central representative organs who have the responsibility of determining the goals of the movement and providing directives to its professional employees.

In an attempt to promote such ends reforms have been initiated within the local structures in connection with the most recent decision on guidelines for consolidation. Conceived as a means to strengthen the democratic base organizations in the various cooperative associations, a network of local subunits or districts has been created that will serve as channels of information and contact among individual members. These district structures are conceived as natural meeting places which ideally should coincide with local community centers. Within the framework of such districts informal gatherings, study groups, and conferences dealing with consumer questions are designed to mobilize the individual members. Spontaneous initiatives of proposals and wishes among members will also be encouraged. In such ways cooperative leaders hope to complement and strengthen representative democracy in the large associations with a direct form of "grass roots democracy" which will emerge from the daily needs and interests of members.

If this experiment in grass roots democracy succeeds in widening the circle of active members and improving channels of communication to the more passive members (who always constitute the majority), the cooperatives will have provided a significant contribution in efforts to strengthen democracy and satisfy (at least to a degree) the demand for more direct democracy. Their example will inevitably be followed by other organizations. This has already occurred, for that matter, within the tenants' association, where small local study groups dealing with local living conditions have recently been established. Such groups can quite conceivably initiate steps to exert pressure on local urban authorities and infiltrate established institutions on behalf of tenant interests.

Thus it appears that the Swedish trade-union movement, cooperatives, and the tenants' association are well on their way toward creating new forms of membership activity which can strengthen internal democracy during their transition to larger organization structures. Moreover, various means have been discussed to improve the education level and salaries of appointed representatives within these associations so that they can devote themselves more fully to the demanding and time-consuming tasks of controlling group functionaries and serving as communication links between leaders and members. In this way it is hoped that the system of larger organization structures will not lead to bureaucratized authority.

A THEORY OF BROADENED DEMOCRACY

I am personally convinced that the larger popular organizations are moving in the right direction and that their practical measures have made a significant contribution—which has been accorded only marginal attention in the public debate—toward solving problems of democracy in contemporary Swedish society. I also believe that they have provided a valuable basis for a generally applicable theory of broadened democracy in advanced social systems. A basic thesis of such a theory could be formulated as follows:

Every attempt to strengthen democracy in a large organization— that is, mobilize as many passive members as possible and increase membership participation in the decision process—must begin with the daily needs and interests of members on the local level. If grass roots democracy in the small local units proves effective, it can be successively broadened to encompass more general questions and the transmission of an increased number of individual initiatives to higher levels. For this to be possible, however, certain social and psychological conditions must first be fulfilled. That a high degree of economic equality, universal education, and training to critical consciousness are necessary requisites for a well-functioning social democracy—as well as a political democracy—is generally recognized. Hence it will not be necessary to discuss these factors further. Instead, I shall limit myself to a few other important factors whose relation to democracy is often overlooked.

In the first place living conditions must be formulated in such a way that the citizens' sense of proximity to, and community with, each other and their social institutions is strengthened. This means that places of residence and work should be as close together as possible; the population in a given district should have a balanced age distribution and social composition; and sufficient access should exist to service and leisure facilities. A milieu of this sort can help overcome individual solitude and alienation and can facilitate more active participation in various organization activities as well as politics. It is necessary, in short, to regenerate important aspects of the former village community—to "recapture the old village within the confines of the city."

Another important condition for broadened democracy is that working conditions be humanized and that working hours be sharply reduced so that citizens will have more time and energy to engage in social issues extending beyond their day-to-day concerns. Within many areas of the Swedish economy the present pace of work is so fast and the production process is so demanding, both physically and psychologically, that it is wholly unrealistic to expect employees to devote their free time to participation in socio-political questions. Exacerbating this problem is the fact that reduced work hours have largely assumed the form of a five-day week. Moreover, an increasing number of people in the larger cities are forced to travel long distances to their place of work. The average employee thus has little available time for pursuits other than his necessary rest and recreation. I believe that this is a principal—but often overlooked—reason for the pervasive political apathy in modern industrial societies. For the present this factor imposes rigid limits on all attempts to vitalize democracy in such societies.

The second major thesis of a "new" theory of democracy is closely related to the first. It concerns how far the demand can be carried to achieve direct democracy. Historical experience demonstrates that all attempts in developed societies to base important decision functions on principles of direct democracy have led to confusion and anarchy which can be easily supplanted by the rule of an active minority. Since the time of Rousseau all dictatorial tendencies have arisen from the idea of the "general will." The theory and practice of the New Left only confirm this recurrent experience.

In light of the inherent dangers of direct democracy, one can only conclude that the representative system must be preserved. At the same time, however, representative democracy must be reformed in major aspects. This should occur primarily through the introduction of aspects of direct democracy which will strengthen the underlying structure of the representative system. Two kinds of methods for achieving this are conceivable. The first of these has already been discussed: The extension of grass roots democracy in large organizations can well be considered an infusion of direct democracy. Although principal decision functions should in general be reserved to the representative organs, small local groups can assume greater responsibility for making decisions in the future. The second method of reforming the existing system of representative democracy is to broaden the scope of referenda.

On the national political level binding referenda—and even a strengthened form of advisory referenda which could be initiated by a minority in Parliament—are incompatible with a parliamentary system of government and can weaken the power of the executive. But the situation is different on the communal level. There the characteristic Swedish pattern of coalition politics is entirely compatible with the advisory referendum procedure. In my opinion it should be possible for communal authorities to conduct advisory referenda on questions involving clearly defined alternatives that can be presented in easily comprehensible terms to the citizens. An example would be urban planning. This would be a better method to strengthen communal democracy than to replace the present practice of joint rule by the major parties with a parliamentary system. The latter proposal, which spokesmen for all the parties have intermittently advocated in recent years, could actually prove self-defeating in that control of the communal executive structures might be weakened—especially in communes with a strong, persistent Social Democratic or bourgeois majority.

Within the major interest associations it is, of course, unrealistic to propose a sweeping return to earlier referendum practices. Membership votes on contracts would in particular be incompatible with the present system of centralized wage negotiations. The existing system has immense importance for the peace and stability of the Swedish labor market, as well as for the prospects of promoting collective wage policies to benefit low income groups, and should not be subjected to the risk of any experiments with direct democracy. On the other hand it is wholly conceivable that the trade unions can make more extensive use of advisory referenda in more general policy questions. A practical and easily applicable alternative would be opinion surveys. (Such surveys have already been extensively utilized, for that matter, within the labor movement.)

It is tempting to consider how computer technology might accord direct democracy a more central role in the future. If every citizen had a small computer terminal in his own home—or at least had access to such facilities in a nearby community center—it would be possible to arrange frequent popular referenda on social questions. I would have no objection to such a practice provided that everyone could utilize the technique. But any such referenda would have to be solely advisory in nature, with decisions to schedule a referendum and formulate the questions remaining in the hands of the responsible political organs. Otherwise the process could degenerate into an anarchistic "Gallup democracy" controlled by powerful interest groups.

Here we touch on a central problem in democracy. Who shall determine which questions will be submitted to the people either in the form of a referendum or in context of an election? Who has the authority to formulate problems and determine what are socially relevant issues? Formally, the answer is self-evident; the politicians or the appointed representatives in the various social organizations have the right to decide such questions. But shouldn't the people have direct influence in the formulation of problems in a democracy? How can one prevent inaccessible experts and unaccountable economic interest groups from determining the conditions for, and the content of, politics over the heads of both politicians and the people?

To consider all aspects of these problematical issues would exceed the scope of this essay. Rather than attempt to answer such questions about actual freedom of opinion and power over the mass media, I shall concentrate instead on possible means to provide citizens with influence in formulating problems. One method is to combine advisory referenda with so-called popular initiatives. (The latter would encompass the right of a certain number of citizens to propose that a referendum be held on an issue formulated by a given group.) If this technique can be coupled with guarantees against its abuse by petty interests, it should, in my opinion, be tried. Another method, which can be viewed as a major alternative to the first one, would be to provide citizens, as well as organization members, greater opportunities to address initiatives to their elected representatives—and to political candidates during elections—and to insure that such initiatives are given serious consideration. This is related to what I have said above about the further development of grass roots democracy. But such provisions would also involve the election of delegates and the exercise of individual responsibility. And here I come to the third major thesis of a "new" theory of democracy, one which concerns the capacity of the governed to control their rulers.

PROPOSALS FOR POLITICAL ACCOUNTABILITY

If citizens and members of mass organizations are to achieve meaningful influence in the formulation of problems and hence actual power in their own right, they must have the possibility to elect candidates who are prepared to work for the realization of their desired goals. This does not imply the institution of a rigid mandate system. It is sufficient if the electoral system makes possible a personal choice among competing candidates. At present, however, Swedish voters are largely restricted to party lists of candidates. A stronger element of individual choice in elections would have the positive effect of improving contacts between voters and their representatives and thereby enhancing control by the former over the latter.

The capacity of voters to control the behavior of their representatives must be viewed as insufficient if deputies have virtually guaranteed mandates, that is, if they are reelected time after time without their position being seriously challenged either during nominations or at the polls. This is the case in Sweden—as in many other stable democracies —with respect to both political parties and interest organizations. The most suitable solution to this problem would seem to be for parties and organizations to formulate rules or to initiate practices that would limit mandates to a limited number of successive periods (possibly six to eight years in all).

Concomitant with the principal goal of strengthening control possibilities, restrictions on length in office would yield several important additional advantages. If representatives were granted full or part-time leave of absence during their elective tenure (during which time they would receive suitable remuneration), they could retain closer ties with their original profession. Later they might then seek reelection. Thus the estrangement of deputies from society and their jobs would be minimized. Such a system would also force representatives to maintain good contacts with voters if they are to be re-elected a second or third time, and would encourage the continual renewal and rejuvenation of elective assemblies.

In principle the same rules would conceivably apply to full-time appointed representatives, as well as members of the national government, communal officials, and leaders of interest organizations. For political and psychological reasons, however, a strict application of the principle of rotation in such positions is not possible.

Another, even more difficult question, is whether higher civil servants (with the exception of judges) and interest-group functionaries can be rotated in office. In Sweden such a practice would conflict with traditional policies, conceptions of the irremovability of public servants, and above all the notion of security in office. The national government has nevertheless proposed restrictions on the principle of irremovability; these, however, are stridently opposed by the white-collar unions.

Naturally it is possible to rotate public administrators from one office to another. This is already a common practice within the civil service. Unless one accepts a complete politicization of the administrative apparatus and the popular election of its incumbents, however, no rules restricting the period of administrative assignments or determining the placement of personnel can provide citizens with any influence or control possibilities vis-à-vis civil servants or public officials. What *can* be accomplished with such regulations are certain guarantees against the dictatorial exercise of power, lethargy in office, and commitments to vested interests—and that is quite enough. But the capacity of citizens to influence the behavior of experts must be achieved in other ways.

At stake is the necessity to ensure some kind of political accountability among leading experts in public administration, and to a certain degree within private bureaucracies as well, without subjecting such officials to the direct judgment of the people. This is the most central— and the most difficult—problem confronting democracy in contemporary societies characterized by large structures and advanced technology. If this problem is not solved, technical development threatens to transform democracy into an empty form.

There is no question that experts already exercise considerable (and rapidly increasing) influence within all areas of social life. Above all, in certain spheres of communal politics one can discern a clear tendency toward greater political dependence on the attitudes and advice of experts. The risks involved in such a development are considered less acute in private organizations where experts are recruited who share the ideology of the organization or at least can be trained to accept it. But the problem is much greater in the ostensibly apolitical national and communal administration structures. I do not wish to call into question the present system of a politically neutral public administration in which only the leading civil servants are—and should be—identified with the governing political party. But I do want to challenge the popular notion that a public servant can be apolitical in the sense that he is wholly detached from personal political values. I will assert outright that the myth of the apolitical expert is a deadly danger for democracy.

We must accept the indisputable fact that experts exercise major influence in policy formation in societies where questions have become increasingly more technically complicated. But we *can* demand that experts openly explain the values underlying their proposals to politicians as a basis for major decisions. This is the central and most crucial point in the recent criticism of urban planning in Sweden. Here can be found an indication of how the problem of holding experts accountable for their actions might be solved.

The solution lies in the necessity for experts to learn—through their professional training and the education they should receive from politicians—to articulate consciously their value premises and resist the temptation to "technocratize" questions of valuation. They should also be required to formulate solutions based on value premises other than their own. The question is not that experts should articulate their values in public. But they should be responsible for explaining them to the politicians; that should be an integral part of their job. The task of the politicians would then be to choose among the proposed alternatives and explain their decisions, and the value premises on which they rest, to the elected representatives—and in major questions even to the general public during elections and popular referenda. If the representatives or voters oppose major aspects of the decision, the political officials should resign. The experts, whose recommendations led to the decision, should also draw the necessary consequences. They should not be forced to resign, but they should modify their future actions to accord with the changed political situation. In this indirect manner, via politicans, public accountability of experts can become a reality.

I do not claim in this short sketch to have solved the most pressing problem of contemporary democracy. But I am convinced that this is the direction in which its solution must be sought. Better training of experts, aimed at increasing their awareness of their underlying values, and improved decision techniques can provide the basis for a more open political process in the future. Such a development would undoubtedly impose extensive demands on politicians with respect to both their ideological consciousness and their capacity to attain sufficient technical knowledge to evaluate independently the analysis of experts. In meeting such challenges of change, the political parties, above all, confront an educational task of considerable scope.

DEMOCRACY AND PRIVATE ENTERPRISE

I have attempted to provide some basic elements of a theory of democracy in societies characterized by large socio-economic organizations and advanced technical complexity. In my view heightened mass participation and public responsiveness can be attained in such societies through the successive expansion of grass roots democracy, a stronger infusion of direct democracy to complement the representative system, and greater accountability of representatives and experts. This theory can be applied to all the systems that have been discussed above: interest associations, local communes, the national political system, and political parties. But the question remains whether the theory is applicable to private enterprise. A closely related question involves an objection to the theory itself and the aspirations for which it is an expression: Is a broadened form of democracy compatible with the requirements of economic efficiency? Although limitations of space prohibit a thorough discussion of these important and difficult issues, I should like to indicate several future possibilities.

A good foundation for expanded grass roots democracy within private and public corporations already exists in the form of advisory councils—made up of representatives from both management and labor —which were instituted within all large enterprises in 1946. The status of these councils was strengthened in 1966 when the employer, employee, and white-collar associations agreed to grant them formal decision-making authority in various minor questions. In the future it should be possible to accord the advisory councils the right of codetermination in an increasing number of more important issues. It is also important that unions acquire representation in the planning organs of both private and public corporations where major questions are initially discussed and final decisions are often reached. On the other hand, it is not possible, as I have indicated above, to base to any considerable degree the influence of workers on forms of direct democracy such as the referendum. Instead, union organizations bear the major responsibility for maintaining close contacts with their members and communicating their desires to union representatives on the advisory councils and planning organs.

Another way in which employees could acquire greater influence has often been discussed in Sweden but has never been implemented in practice. This would be to allow the unions the right to appoint representatives directly to management councils. Until now union leaders have rejected such proposals on the grounds that if labor representatives sit on the opposite side of the bargaining table the capacity of the union movement to participate in wage negotiations would be weakened. But this situation could change if economic democracy were institutionalized through provisions for government and communal representation in the management boards of individual corporations. An effective form of economic democracy is, in any case, a necessary condition for the continued development of industrial democracy in the direction of actual rights of codetermination.

The most difficult question at present concerns possible means to ensure effective control by employee representatives and social structures over technical and economic experts within the large corporations. This problem is even more difficult within large corporations than it is within the political system because of the greater influence exercised by experts in the corporations. No realistic proposals have yet been made in the contemporary political debate to solve it.

Personally I can see no other recourse than to humanize the technological structure. This involves training technicians and economists to greater consciousness concerning both the role of values in technical-economic decision processes and the necessity of allowing social values to influence the goals and means of corporate activity. Innovation along such lines would impose demands on education and research at universities, technical colleges, and business schools, as well as on the formation of opinion through the mass media. The aim of humanizing technology should be to broaden the purpose of industry so that considerations of employment, employee satisfaction, social costs of investment in industrial expansion, and the effects of industry on environment can become increasingly important factors in economic planning. Maximizing profits should not be industry's exclusive goal.

This leads to a second question, namely, the relation between democracy and economic efficiency. As in other industrialized societies, Swedish industry has undergone successive concentration. Increased international competition has encouraged a broad wave of internal rationalization, fusions, and the abandonment of uneconomic enterprises throughout the country. This process is irreversible; even the government and the trade-union movement recognize its necessity. Nevertheless economic rationalization can be modified, and in certain cases slowed down, in response to social considerations. If one wishes to expand economic and industrial democracy, one must be prepared to pay a price. In the short run this would involve less efficiency in certain industries and perhaps even a less rapid expansion of the Gross National Product. Any major democratization of the economic system would presuppose that goals of industry be broadened and that efficiency criteria be modified in ways suggested above. But in the long run such changes are likely to prove advantageous even from the viewpoint of economic efficiency; industry can benefit significantly from increased employee enjoyment and motivation in work and rationalization problems can be solved through positive cooperation between industry and social organizations.

As long as the major industries, commercial enterprises, and banks are privately owned, democratization can hardly be carried as far within the Swedish economic system as within the political system, communes, and large organizations. Possibly the democratization process would be facilitated if industry were nationalized, but it is highly unlikely that political democracy—as it exists in Sweden today—could survive the violent political upheaval that such radical intervention in the social order would inevitably instigate. The dilemma might appear insoluble: The coexistence between an undemocratic economic system and an increasingly democratized socio-political system will continue. But the tension between the two worlds can be reduced. The economic system can be "socialized" in the sense that its functions are increasingly determined by the democratic values of society, indirect intervention by the state, and expanded government and cooperative industrial activity. More than any other country Sweden has moved furthest in such a direction. But much remains to be done.

Epilogue

Epilogue

WE ARE NOW in a position to consider some of the implications inherent in many of the essays in this volume. These essays
point to problems that deserve far greater attention than they have received up to now in the social-science literature. None of these is more
important for industrial-urban man than the possible transformation of
political structures within which he must seek to survive.

From a cross-national perspective the various countries reveal both
similar and contrasting patterns of post-industrial change. That the
United States, Great Britain, and Sweden share complex bureaucratic
organizations, an official commitment to welfare policies, and relative
affluence provides each of them with a common set of system capabilities for attaining potentially fundamental shifts in structured socio-economic and political relations. A growing critical awareness of the contradictions between such capabilities and the reality of persisting
poverty and social inequities led in both America and Western Europe
to the resurgence of ideological controversy during the 1960s. The efforts to adjust imbalances in the established industrial-welfare order
have lent added impetus to political change in all three countries.

At the same time differences in size, socio-political cohesion, legal
systems, class structures, ideological heritage, and government institutions have yielded significantly varied responses to the contemporary
crisis of modern society. Although the contributors to this volume are
not wholly representative of their respective intellectual communities,

the diversity of views among the American spokesmen and the general conformity of attitudes among the British and Swedish writers (with the principal exception of Lacey) reflect the disparate characteristics of their broader socio-political environments. In light of these profound national differences, the United States is likely to experience a more tension-laden transition to the post-welfare state than either Sweden or England.

To acquire a fuller understanding of the probable future of industrial-urban orders, it would be necessary to examine a still wider array of national patterns. It is particularly important to assess the emerging issue of the "new individualism," and the various forms the ideological and political struggles have assumed on its behalf, in Eastern Europe, the Soviet Union, and Japan.

THE LIMITATIONS OF PROJECTION

Addressing themselves to the prospects of change in advanced industrial-urban systems, the various essays raise important questions concerning the adequacy of the prevailing approaches among social scientists for the study of future political arrangements. Most of the contributors have tended, in one form or another, to base their analyses on present trends in each of the countries. Clearly, in studying the future one must begin with the present—and, as Anners has done, proceed to cast the problems of the future in terms of the past as well.

Yet one of the most critical problems facing scholars who are concerned with the study of futurology is the need to develop more fully and explicitly a wider range of theoretical and methodological tools than presently exist in the social sciences. While many of our contributors might not share our view, we believe that the problems of the post-welfare or post-industrial world cannot be adequately analyzed through reliance upon the dominant theoretical perspectives in contemporary sociology and political science.

For the past several decades the leading theoretical orientations in both fields have been structural functionalism and behavioralism. Although these perspectives differ markedly and the proponents of each school have carried on a running debate with each other, they nevertheless share a common characteristic: namely, a tendency to project the present into the future. Structural functionalists such as Talcott Parsons and system theorists such as David Easton have done so through their emphasis on "system maintenance." Assuming that systems (as well as their internal structures) seek to maintain themselves, structural functionalists have devoted much of their attention to such questions as boundary maintenance, adaptation, supports, demands, and policy outputs. In light of the criticism that such models of society and politics are too static, some writers, such as Gabriel Almond, have attempted to reinterpret structural-functional theory by incorporating certain developmental dimensions—e.g., in the form of "probabilistic functionalism." [1] Nevertheless they remain ensnared by many of their original premises about man and reality. Appraising, for example, the predictive utility of the system model for political development, Almond writes: "The classification of types of political systems constitutes in part a prediction that certain characteristics of capability, structure, and function will be associated with levels of development and autonomy." [2] His view of the future, in short, is based on an assessment of patterns of development in the past.

The behavioralists (or more narrowly the positivists), on the other hand, have concentrated on empirically describing or analyzing existing political patterns and then assuming that such empirical relations will persist in the future. A wide spectrum of sociologists and political scientists fall into this category. Many of those who study voting behavior, for instance, tend to project "what is" into "what will be." Also, some members of the social indicator school are working on a similar premise—that is, they believe that the existing indicators of political arrangements will provide social scientists and policy makers with meaningful guidelines to future political behavior.

The essays in this volume, however, underscore the fact that the future political system is open to a variety of possible patterns. That political analysts look upon the future in such diverse ways is, in our judgment, of considerable import—for it suggests that the future is by no means closed to man's control. From a theoretical point-of-view, therefore, extrapolations from the present provide no certain basis for predicting future socio-political structures or relations. Consequently, an understanding of the politics of the future requires greater attention to process analysis as a means to explore alternative models of post-welfare politics.

ALTERNATIVE PERSPECTIVES

A useful starting point in forming a more dynamic view of the possible range of future political arrangements is to adapt the modernization concept—which embraces the notion of increased control by man over his social, physical, and individual environments—to problems of advanced systems. Until now most scholars have tended to apply the modernization approach, or some kind of neo-evolutionary theory which it implies, largely to the less-developed nations of the third world. But we should recognize that industrial nations are also modernizing; they are also in a state of becoming. Implicit in this line of reasoning is a classification of systems into preindustrial, industrial, and post-industrial types (with a recognition that variations exist within each category).

As we noted in the Introduction, the post-industrial stage of modernization sets limits on industrial-urban systems, as well as opens up new options for man to restructure his socio-political and individual environments. In the first case, highly differentiated, technologically advanced societies must of necessity sustain certain kinds of structures—for instance, systems of education that perpetuate technical knowledge among at least part of the population. Moreover, increased international trade and communication—products of continuing industrialization and technological innovation—have established irrevocable trends toward greater interdependence among nations. Internal and international structural imperatives thus impose broadly similar constraints on the course of post-industrial change in all advanced nations.

Within these limits post-industrial modernization concomitantly makes possible alternative forms of socio-political organization in specific national systems and subsystems. The inherent tension between the claims of society for greater control over man's physical and social environments and the claims of the individual for control over his own environment (including life styles and the capacity to make meaningful political and economic choices) involves an ongoing struggle that may lead to various solutions. The future is not preordained.

In appraising the possible effects of alternative courses of post-industrial modernization, process analysis must incorporate new theoretical and methodological tools. A particularly promising basis for such a reorientation is the revival of dialectical reasoning—that is, the creation of utopian models as a means for attaining an alternative perspective on studies of the existing social and political order. Although dialectical analysis has appeared in a variety of forms throughout the evolution of Western political thought, one of the outstanding failures of dialectical theorists in the past—most notably many Marxists—was their reification of particular utopian models as projections of what *necessarily* must become the future. To avoid the danger of reifying utopian models of the post-welfare state, we have been especially interested in the use of countersystem analysis as a heuristic device for interpreting socio-political change. Briefly stated, countersystem analysis calls on the social scientist to construct logical counterparts to existing structures and value systems—but in the full realization that such countersystems will never become the social order of the future. The purpose of this procedure is to provide social scientists as well as political actors with a point of departure in evaluating the range of conceivable future politics and their consequences for group-individual relations.

The use of countersystem analysis raises several important issues for the study of incipient forms of post-industrial change. To be effective, countersystem analysis requires, first, that the scope and nature of empirical knowledge about present reality be broadened. New questions must be asked and new forms of data obtained—for example, concerning the role of the "living theater," music, and drugs as agents of resocialization. Only with this knowledge at hand is it possible to devise countersystems that can indicate which compromises between the ideal and the reality will work and which alternative arrangements seem bound to fail.

Second, it is imperative to recognize that efforts to operationalize particular countersystems may have unintended social consequences. Such has been the case with the communes and countercultures that have already emerged in some of the advanced Western nations. While the various countercultures are likely to exert at least indirect effects on the established industrial-urban order—as suggested by Alexander's

essay in this volume—it is equally plausible that the broader socio-political community may utilize such countercultures as a means of sustaining the system. That is, persons who live a counterculture existence
may fail to perceive that they, too, can be co-opted or isolated by the
very system they are seeking to challenge or remake.

THE CHANGING ROLE OF THE
SOCIAL SCIENTIST

If social scientists are to contribute to an understanding of post-industrial change, other modifications are in order. A process analysis
of politics suggests that the distinction behavioralists draw between
normative and empirical theory may not be a viable one. Such a position has been anticipated by Fred Riggs, who observes:

Perhaps most importantly, by raising some key theoretical issues [the study
of political development] may well bring normative political philosophy and
empirical political theory into closer relation to the central concerns of political science, for the study of political development raises again in urgent
form some of the perennial issues which have perplexed thinkers from Plato
and Aristotle to Bentley and Lasswell.[3]

The very notion that one must be highly cautious in extrapolating
from the present into the future, as so many structural functionalists
and behavioralists are prone to do, calls for some kind of normative
judgment concerning the kind of future that will best serve the needs
and expectations of post-industrial man. During the past several decades
social scientists have been able to avoid debating normative issues because most of them have generally accepted existing structural arrangements as the basis for both present and future policy decisions. But, as
the events of the 1960s dramatically demonstrated, the established industrial-welfare system has come under attack from a variety of fronts.
Under such circumstances concern with moral questions—ranging from
the status of minority groups to foreign policy issues—invariably comes
to the fore.

In light of the multiple possibilities for social reconstruction in the
post-industrial era, social scientists must reevaluate their role as analysts, critics, and policy advisers. We are of the persuasion that ideas do

have consequences and that social scientists are in a position to assist in determining the future through the intellectual skills at their disposal. As social scientists increasingly assume direct policy responsibilities in advanced industrial-urban nations, not only will their ideas acquire greater social impact but also the actions that flow from these ideas will more directly influence the course of political events than has heretofore been the case. With the increasing power of social scientists will come the need for even more meaningful criticism by scholars of both the actions of their colleagues as well as the ongoing social scene.

Greater awareness of the normative implications of social analysis for the future of politics requires a reformulation of the distinction between scholar and practitioner. Max Weber, perhaps more than any other writer in the twentieth century, established the tone for current political and social analysis by his insistence on a separation between the social scientist and the man of affairs. The most serious flaw in Weber's formulation—and it has led numerous social scientists astray—is his assumption that the social scientist's knowledge will inform his analysis of politics whereas his political involvement will not inform his social analysis. This position can be questioned on both theoretical and empirical grounds.

Such a dichotomy is refuted by Weber's own political and intellectual career, as well as those of other leading thinkers such as Marx and Durkheim. Some of Weber's political struggles in Germany seem to have had a major effect on his social scientific writings. Similarly Marx's personal, political, and intellectual battles are obviously intertwined. And Durkheim's concern with the Dreyfus affair indicates that politics may have informed his sociology more than some sociologists have been willing to recognize.

The fact that eminent social scientists in the past were forced through their personal political commitments to come to terms with significant intellectual issues is of considerable import for the changing role of social scientists today. Given their increased stature in the halls of political power, social scientists cannot escape the social consequences of their knowledge and theories. Nor can they avoid questions of responsibility. Within the decline of nationalism in advanced societies, one of the major problems facing social scientists will be defining their relations not only to the state they serve but also to mankind, which is, after all, their ultimate concern. Those social scientists in politically sensitive positions who attempt to resolve the inherent dilemmas of power and responsibility through creative intellectual ventures are thus likely to make some of the most innovative contributions to politics in the post-welfare state.

POST-WELFARE POLITICS IN
GLOBAL PERSPECTIVE

We conclude this volume on a note of caution. Although we are convinced that politics in the post-welfare state will increasingly become a major social issue, we must place it in global perspective. We cannot fault any of our contributors for having failed to do so; the original statement of the problem called on them to analyze only one particular society.

A much needed corrective to the present study—one that calls for another volume—is to assess the post-welfare state in relation to the international system, especially the preindustrial or industrializing nations. We would hypothesize that the constraints operative in modernizing states are quite different from those in the advanced industrial nations. Within developing societies the collectivity almost necessarily takes precedence over the role of the individual. For a system to industrialize rapidly, individuals must sacrifice many of their own interests; they must give up personal freedom of action so that scarce resources can be used to further the development of the industrial-urban order.

The radical protest movement in the Western industrial states poses a potential danger to international solidarity to the extent that some members of the New Left either turn inward and strive to resolve their own personal problems (or those of their own society) or romanticize links with the third world. Withdrawal into tribalism ignores such realities as world population problems and mass starvation, while the romantic idealization of the third world overlooks the fact that most of the nations therein seek the very way of life—i.e., affluence and material goods—that many of the radical youth in industrial societies are rejecting. Certainly the quest for a new individualism in the advanced nations has no real significance for most people in the third world.

Even though the crucial issues confronting the preindustrial and industrializing states are far removed from the existential concerns of many persons in the advanced nations, they will in the long run have grave consequences for the problems that have emerged in modern industrial-urban society. Unless the problems of the developing states can be satisfactorily solved, it is unlikely that the crisis of post-industrial modernization can be overcome. A viable post-industrial world will require a major restructuring of social and economic relations between the industrial and nonindustrial areas. Ultimately, no industrial nation can remove itself from the overriding concerns that beset most of humankind.

Notes

1. Gabriel A. Almond and G. Bingham Powell, Jr., *Comparative Politics. A Developmental Approach* (Boston, 1966), pp. 12–13.

2. *Ibid.*, pp. 322–23.

3. Fred W. Riggs, "The Theory of Political Development," in James C. Charlesworth, ed., *Contemporary Political Analysis* (New York, 1967), p. 327.

AFTER JESUS BEFORE CHRISTIANITY

AFTER JESUS

——BEFORE——

CHRISTIANITY

A HISTORICAL EXPLORATION OF THE
FIRST TWO CENTURIES OF JESUS MOVEMENTS

ERIN K. VEARNCOMBE, BERNARD BRANDON SCOTT,
HAL TAUSSIG, for the WESTAR CHRISTIANITY SEMINAR

HarperOne
An Imprint of HarperCollinsPublishers

HarperCollins books may be purchased for educational, business, or sales promotional use. For information, please email the Special Markets Department at SPsales@harpercollins.com.

FIRST EDITION

Designed by Bonni Leon-Berman

Library of Congress Cataloging-in-Publication Data is available upon request.

ISBN 978-0-06-306215-3

21 22 23 24 25   LSC   10 9 8 7 6 5 4 3 2 1

Many are the things that mortals,

seeing, can understand.

Without seeing, no one can tell

what the future is likely

to bring to pass.

SOPHOCLES, *AJAX*, LINES 1418–1420

This book is dedicated to the Jesus peoples and members of Anointed communities, wisdom schools, and Savior clubs in the first two centuries, whose voices we so long to hear and understand.

CONTENTS

FOREWORD
by Sue Monk Kidd

You are about to read a book that possesses the potential to re-write history, namely, the long-held "master narrative" of how Christianity came to be.

How do we perceive the founding story of Christianity? What really transpired during the first two hundred years after Jesus? Did early churches exist in the immediate aftermath of Jesus? Were there powerful, unseen dynamics behind the emergence of "Jesus groups"? Did these communities share a cohesive set of beliefs? What about women—were they "imperfect men" in need of fixing? Or boundary violators who sometimes led the way? Were "Jesus people" being martyred left and right by the Romans? Were there religious info-wars between the orthodox and the heretics? Did Christianity as we know it even exist in those pivotal two centuries?

The questions are formidable, tantalizing, disturbing, auda-cious, timely, and ultimately filled with hope. If I ask anything of you as you read the findings in these pages, it would be to not only allow the questions, but to love them.

...

On Easter Sunday, at the age of nine, I walked down the aisle of the First Baptist Church in my tiny hometown in Georgia and made what was known as a profession of faith.

It was 1957, a long while ago, but that experience, along with an event immediately preceding it, occupies a prime piece of real estate in my memory. I had dressed in a lavender dress, white gloves, Mary Jane shoes, and the pièce de la résistance, a matching lavender parasol. There was something about that last accoutrement that filled me with both joy and spunk. Earlier that morning, sitting in Sunday School class, seized by a combination of boldness, mutiny, and unfettered curiosity, I had opened the parasol, revealing its magnificent purple canopy. The act was met by a sharp reproach from the teacher and my beloved parasol's swift confiscation.

Shortly after this small kerfuffle, I strode down the aisle without my contraband where I was met by the minister, who asked a series of questions: Do you believe Jesus died for your sins? Do you believe God raised Jesus from the dead? Will you repent and accept Jesus as your Lord and Savior?

So began my religious life—in traditional, religious orthodoxy, in the beliefs and doctrines of the Baptist church of the 1950s in the American South. Yet hovering over it all was the lavender parasol, that small, prophetic moment of testing boundaries.

Throughout my adolescence and twenties, the orthodox master narrative that had been passed on to me that Easter Sunday became my lens for interpreting life. As a writer of stories, however, I'm aware that whether we're writing them, telling them, living them, or using them as a paradigmatic way to see and understand the world, a story always has a moment when the plot thickens. In other words, something happens. Otherwise, it's not much of a story. On the cusp of my thirtieth birthday, while reading a thin book titled *Letters to a Young Poet* by Rainer Maria Rilke, something happened. I came upon this profundity: "Try to love the questions."

The words initiated me into the freedom of unknowing. I began to probe the givens and fixed concepts that had shaped me. I began to love questions more than answers. I recovered the spirit of challenging sacrosanct boundaries. You could say, I got my parasol back.

...

Whether your relationship to the Christian religion is deep, shallow, past, present, or nil, the way you read this book matters. If you do so while loving the questions, the book will plunge you into the freedom of unknowing. This rare state of being is what allowed the Queen in *Alice's Adventures in Wonderland* to believe "six impossible things before breakfast." In our case, it will allow us to acknowledge a multitude of conclusions previously thought to be impossible because they've existed outside the traditional historical construct.

As our esteemed authors point out, the master narrative of the two hundred years after Jesus was conceptualized by looking back and molding events to fit the beliefs of an already established paradigm. In his book *Serendipities: Language and Lunacy*, Umberto Eco recounts how the thirteenth-century Italian explorer Marco Polo searched for unicorns and doggedly claimed to have found them. At the time, European culture accepted the existence of these mythical creatures. What he actually discovered were Asian rhinos, animals for which he had no image or language. Marco Polo fell victim to what Eco refers to as "background books." These invisible books, Eco writes, are our "preconceived notions of the world, derived from our cultural tradition. In a very curious sense we travel knowing in advance what we are on the verge of discovering, because past reading has told us what we are supposed to discover."

We see things not as they are, but as we are, the saying goes. It turns out, seeing is not believing so much as believing is seeing.

It's questions that will save us.

...

When I completed this book, I felt as if I'd uncovered an invaluable mosaic that had been lost in antiquity. Each chapter is a tile, a tessera dropped into place—one by one—until a new design of history comes into view. The picture reveals an era of immense social crisis transpiring across the Mediterranean world, giving rise to disparate "Jesus groups," an array of communities from wisdom schools to supper clubs. Displaced, oppressed, and terrorized, the people in these communities are in search of identity and belonging, of ways to resist violence, torture, and authoritarianism. They capsize the rules of gender. They create diverse documents—hidden transcripts, stories, poems, and songs that disguise their rebellion, offer them strategies and catharsis, inspire courage, and soothe their heartache. One such text, discovered in 1945 among the Nag Hammadi manuscripts, known as *The Thunder: Perfect Mind*, is an elegy I've read and reread for more than twenty years. Coming upon it within these pages was like seeing it in a thrilling new way. "I am she who exists in all fears and trembling boldness," the divine voice in the poem proclaims. I imagine "Jesus people" reading those words almost two millennia ago and finding bravery in them, just as I have.

The world today wrestles with its own social crises—terrorism; authoritarianism; displacement; racial, gender, and ethnic oppression; climate change; global pandemics; the breakdown of religious structures. I often feel that contemporary Christianity is at a turning point and a new Christian paradigm is struggling to be born. The reimagined history set forth here opens new possibilities. It makes room for spiritual flexibility.

Theoretical physicist Stephen Hawking defined genius as "radical humility." When you humble yourself to all that you don't know, he explained, you open yourself to what's possible. In that sense, and perhaps in other ways too, this book is a work of genius. I invite you into an experience of radical humility. Set aside your background books. Open your lavender umbrella. Feast on this stunning reconfiguration of history and dream with me what it means for the future.

Are you ready?

HOW THIS BOOK CAME INTO BEING

The time is right for this book.

Recent, surprising historical discoveries have opened up a wide, two-hundred-year-old gap between the historical Jesus and Christianity, and what is most surprising, this has gone almost unobserved. That is what this book seeks to remedy.

The Westar Institute is a research organization dedicated to cutting-edge scholarship on history and religion while also making that research accessible to readers outside the academy. Westar held the famous Jesus Seminar in the 1980s and 1990s that investigated which sayings and stories in the Gospels were most likely from the historical Jesus. In 2013, Westar decided to launch another seminar—the Christianity Seminar (hereinafter Seminar). The proposal, to put it simply, was to study *what came after Jesus.* Westar unfurled what could be at least ten years of work figuring out how Christianity came into being through a seminar of intergenerational and multidisciplinary scholars. In truth, we did not know what would happen. We even thought the name was problematic but did not know what else to call it.

What happened surprised us. Within our first several years, it became clear that the missing two hundred years between Jesus and Christianity was not just a holding pattern. Those two centuries after Jesus were not full of implicit Christianness, so to speak. That period had lots of new—not Christian—innovative peoples, groups, and movements inspired by Jesus but going in many different directions.

We did not rush to conclusions but began by examining twentieth-century scholarship about the first two centuries. Scholars had been drilling test wells in what they thought was the bedrock of Christianity and coming up dry or with something altogether different from the traditions, practices, and stories they expected to see. As we continued our investigations, we often found ourselves in disagreement, but we kept working together and listening to one another. Sometimes the arguments were fierce. We researched as thoroughly as possible. We tested new models for collaboration within the academic pursuit of knowledge, sometimes taking steps forward, though sometimes, it seemed, taking a step or two back. We sought to paint a nuanced yet straightforward picture of this time period through thoughtful, constructive scholarly conversation. We did not shy away from complicated and at times contradictory scenarios. We knew from the beginning we could not get it all right because too much was unknowable. Ours was an experiment in a conscientious rewriting of a history of these first two centuries of what might be called Jesus movements, although what to call "them" or "it" turned out to be one of our thorniest problems. Most of all, we wanted to write for you, the curious public, not just for scholars like ourselves. We believe this important research should be shared with the public and trust you will find it interesting, even if at times it is surprising or even shocking.

The method of all Westar Seminars is based on collegiality. We have long been an experiment in crowd-sourcing scholarship: we believe that knowledge is produced through discussion, through collaboration. The seven-plus years of meetings were based on about sixty-five scholarly papers that were shared, read, and discussed by seminar members in front of an average of 125 members of the public. After their discussions the Westar Institute provided ballots for the seminar members and the public in attendance on the main issues of each paper. In keeping with Westar principles, all ballots and results are available on the Westar website. These ballots and papers—and the hard work of seminar members—lie behind this book. In this way it is best to consider the Seminar and its members as the authors of this book.

We invite you on a journey into the unknown between Jesus and Christianity. We trust you will find it as exciting, disturbing, and at times thrilling as we have found it.

CONTRIBUTORS TO THIS BOOK AND SUPPORTING MEMBERS OF WESTAR'S CHRISTIANITY SEMINAR

For a more complete list of Westar fellows and seminar members, please visit www.westarinstitute.org. Every person that spoke up throughout the life of the seminar deserves acknowledgment and celebration. Westar thanks everyone at the seminar's table; in challenge and in affirmation, the voices present helped to newly hear voices past.

Al-Suadi Soham
Professor of New Testament
University of Rostock

Jason David BeDuhn
Professor, Comparative Study of Religions
Northern Arizona University

Arthur J. Dewey, ThD
Professor of Theology
Xavier University

Joanna Dewey, PhD
Harvey H. Guthrie Jr., Professor Emerita
Episcopal Divinity School

Susan M. (Elli) Elliott, PhD
Think Tank Analyst and Coordinator
Westar Institute

David Galston, PhD
Executive Director
Westar Institute

Glenna S. Jackson, PhD
Professor, Department of Religion and Philosophy
Otterbein University

Perry V. Kea, PhD
Associate Professor Emeritus
University of Indianapolis

Celene Lillie
Lecturer
University of Colorado, Boulder

Nina E. Livesey, PhD
Professor of Religious Studies
University of Oklahoma

Lane C. McGaughy, PhD
*George H. Atkinson Professor
of Religious and Ethical Studies
Emeritus*
Willamette University

Robert J. Miller, PhD
*Rosenberger Professor of Christian
Thought and Religious Studies*
Juniata College

Stephen J. Patterson
*George H. Atkinson Professor of
Religious Studies*
Willamette University

Shirley Paulson, PhD
Founder, Early Christian Texts
EarlyChristianTexts.com

Deborath Niederer Saxton, PhD
Affiliate Faculty
Christian Theological Seminary

Bernard Brandon Scott, PhD
*Darbeth Distinguished Professor
of New Testament Emeritus*
Phillips Theological Seminary

Christine Shea, PhD
Professor of Classics
Ball State University

Thandeka, PhD
President
Love Beyond Belief, Inc.

Hal Taussig, PhD
*Professor of New Testament,
Retired*
Union Theological Seminary

Erin K. Vearncombe, PhD
Assistant Professor
University of Toronto

Chad Venters, PhD
*Instructor of Humanities and
Philosophy*
Truckee Meadows Community
College

David Wheeler-Reed, PhD
Independent Scholar

AFTER JESUS BEFORE CHRISTIANITY

I

THE EXPERIMENT

The future is not inevitable; it is often random, a matter of accidents. Ours is an experiment in historical imagination into the possibilities of the past during the first two centuries of the Common Era (CE), as the time after the birth of Jesus is called. We begin in the years after the death of Jesus and move forward with an open mind. We begin before Christianity, not assuming anything about the phenomenon that emerged well after the death of Jesus. That sounds like common sense to most historians, but in this case it is unusual and not traditionally how Christian history has been done.

This experiment relies on reading history forward. Too often, we turn to look behind us. We fall victim to the fallacy of the inevitable. Because it happened, it had to happen; we use future events to understand the past. This fallacy is a constant temptation because it scares us back into what we already know, or into what we think we know. Questions like "How did we get to where we are now?" are interested more in the present than in the past.

Reading history backwards blinds us to the open character of the future. When we approach history backwards, we are always informed by the present. Here we are, in the twenty-first century, with our diverse forms, traditions, and structures of Christianity. The question up to this point has been "How did we wind up in this place?" We look to the past, seeking our links—here are the steps that got us here; here are the causes that led to these effects, with an emphasis much more on those effects (present) than causes (past). We have been trying to construct a building from the top.

A skyscraper, however, does not begin with its observation deck.

The "master narrative" of Christianity has been the traditional way in which history was read backwards. It refers to the conventional story of early Christianity, the notion that the origins of Christianity are settled, in need of no new data. This big story is stuck in our heads, not as fact, and despite our often knowing better. Here is the basic outline of the master narrative:

- Jesus came down from heaven to establish the Christian church. He was a fantastic person whose birth marks the very beginning of civilizations. He taught the truth and did god-sized things. He handed on his complete teachings to his most loyal followers, the apostles.
- These apostles then relayed correctly to the bishops of the early churches all of the great things Jesus said and did.
- These first bishops correctly passed down Jesus's teachings and magnificent deeds to the next two-plus centuries of bishops.
- The faithful line of bishops summarized perfectly Jesus's teachings and acts in the fourth-century Nicene Creed, which carried full truth and authority to the twenty-first century.

As the Christianity Seminar patiently examined the available evidence, the idea that the master narrative's assumption

that "Christianity" acted as a unified, continuous early tradition in unbroken line representing a single truth made little
sense. That is why members of the seminar questioned, and
ultimately rejected, the master narrative of Christianity's birth.

Much new research points to multiple and different stories of
Jesus peoples (not "Christians") in the first two centuries. The
seminar's work on these first two centuries resembles not a predestined master story but more a set of mosaic tiles in the process
of being pieced together. Many pieces are still missing, and at
times, some pieces pop into unexpected places. More accurately,
these vibrant, many-shaped tiles work to create not one story, but
many; the picture of the Jesus peoples of the first two centuries
ends up more like the view inside a kaleidoscope, the tiles shifting and the picture changing with each turn of the cylinder.

The master narrative did not happen because of any cache
of research. Instead, as later forms of Christianity began to
be viewed as more orthodox—advocating "proper" belief and
practice—this strand heavily influenced European and American societies, projecting their own power and belief systems
back onto the earliest centuries. Writers of the master narrative
reduced a wide variety of ideas, stories, and poetics to a simple
either/or of orthodoxy or heresy. This self-serving manipulation diminished the breadth of practice and experimentation
of the early Jesus peoples.

One of the core contributions of this book is its rejection
of the master narrative. We do not take this preexistent narrative for granted. This examination of previous assumptions
allows the reader to see clearly the many important experiments and diverse Jesus movements that have been lost in the
master narrative.

Reasonable, solid construction starts with foundations. Our
experiment is one of foundations, and only of foundations. So

if we do not assume we know the future, what can we reconstruct about the lived experiences of diverse peoples across the ancient Mediterranean? This question is in itself an exciting historical accomplishment.

This forward-looking approach to our evidence—evidence from new places, from new sources, in unexpected material forms—soon makes an essential circumstance clear. If we stand on the ground of Rome, of Athens, of urban and rural spaces across the Mediterranean in the first two centuries CE, we do not see anything resembling contemporary "Christianity," or, for that matter, "Christianity" as it was in the later ancient world, in the Middle Ages, or across human history. In the first two centuries, what we think of as "Christianity" did not exist.

WHAT WE DISCOVERED

What happens when we approach the first two centuries forward, rather than backwards? What happens if we start at the very beginning and see what happens from there, taking one careful step forward at a time, with minds open to an unknown, unassumed future? This groundbreaking, holistic approach yielded incredible and surprising results. The discoveries we encountered showed us, among other things, a world of Roman violence, the emergence of new genders and forms of family, and an Israel both creative and traumatized.

This framing for our experiment rests on new archaeological finds and possibilities for evidence that have dramatically opened up scholarship on the realities of the first two centuries. Ever since the discovery of the Nag Hammadi collection of ancient writings in 1945 in Egypt, which posited a much more diverse range of Jesus peoples in the early centuries after Jesus's death, researchers have advanced new perspectives and challenged conventional views of history. The substantial breadth and depth of this ongoing research helps us see very different realities occurring within the earliest Jesus peoples. Over the past eight years, the Westar Christianity Seminar that produced this book has reviewed the research from the past thirty to forty years and has consolidated and advanced the gains made.

In this chapter we introduce six surprising new discoveries of recent scholarship. The remaining chapters lay these insights out in greater detail. These six new perspectives are important because they transform how we think about the first two centuries CE and their relationship (or not) to the later phenomenon of Christianity. The first two centuries are not an interim or structured "origin" period that allowed Christianity to get its act together. No, with these new perspectives, the first two hundred years end up being an absorbing, unfinished story or, more accurately, a series of absorbing, unfinished stories.

A significant portion of the early, varied Jesus movements did not complete their journeys or continue their unfinished processes. Many of their stories have not yet been told. These six powerful and somewhat unfinished developments from the first two centuries allow for productive historical breakthroughs, though these breakthroughs are still incomplete. Our evidence is always in fragments, and we can work to make these fragments only meaningful, rather than whole. At the same time, these breakthroughs undo the necessity of fourth-, sixteenth-, or twenty-first-century Christianity as being perceived as perfect or complete. Their viability as loosely affiliated directions does not necessitate the inevitability of Christianity. Nor do these breakthroughs assume that there is, behind them, some essence of Christianity awaiting to emerge.

These discoveries undo much of the conventional picture of the first two centuries. They do not represent a uniform portrait, and indeed they often contradict one another. But they do open the door to possibilities for reimagining who these different groups were, enabling us to see these groups and peoples more clearly.

1. They Resisted the Roman Empire

A wide set of what we call Jesus clubs, movements for the Savior, communities of the Anointed, and schools of the Lord successfully resisted the Roman Empire. These peoples' resistance against Rome often kept violence at bay and gave their people courage and an experience of safety. A key dimension of their resistance to empire was invoking God's compassionate and strange empire, or kingdom, as later translators have it, in contrast to Rome's cruel and dominating one. These various groups made fun of Roman military power and mocked Rome's claim of divine power, even though they themselves had almost no power. The Empire of God challenged the Empire of Rome. Caesar Augustus as Lord conflicted with Jesus Anointed as Lord.

2. They Practiced Gender Bending

A wide range of Jesus peoples practiced gender bending—that is, gender roles were fluid and flexible. One of their primary identities was that they were neither male nor female, but all were "one" through different lived, experienced realities of gender pluralism. Women, and a significant number of men, rejected both male dominance and female passivity. A wide swath of Jesus groups rejected marriage and traditional families, with the envoy Paul often leading the way. Although some Anointed groups and individuals supported male dominance and demanded female obedience to men, many men shifted toward acting more vulnerable and less domineering. Women cut their hair and dressed like men. These gendered activities and actions brokered new possibilities for identity among various Jesus peoples, well beyond the regular masculine/feminine dichotomies of the first two centuries.

3. They Lived in Chosen Families

   With traditional families increasingly broken and dispersed, a variety of Jesus groups started living in experimental family groups. These new family groups were voluntary; that is, they lived together increasingly outside of blood or married relationships. Whereas previously the primary relations for living arrangements were extended families of multiple generations with cousins, aunts, and uncles in the mix, Jesus people associated daily with each other according to mutual support and affection. More and more "supper clubs" became crucial and core associations of daily life. Economic sharing provided ways that members of these groups bonded. In some cases, larger housing arrangements came into play for the groups through a donor exhibiting compassion. Although most of these new kinds of families were small, occasionally a wealthy person provided larger space for bigger groups.

4. They Claimed Belonging to Israel

   The largest and most common identity of Jesus groups was their allegiance to Israel, regardless of whether the groups or members came from Israel-based bloodlines. This bond applied whether they lived in geographical Israel or around the Mediterranean basin. Small and large groups understood themselves to be following the God of Israel, read Israel-based holy writings, prayed and meditated according to the various

Israel-based forms, bathed ritually according to Israel's traditions, and—perhaps most of all—gave allegiance to their Israel-born teacher and leader, Jesus. Since Jesus belonged to Israel by blood and practice, the larger Jesus movements assumed and explicitly practiced Israel's ways. But after the Bar Kokhba War (132–136 CE), the second major revolt against the Roman Empire of the people inhabiting the territory known as Roman Palestine, this allegiance was increasingly challenged.

5. They Had Diverse Organizational Structures

As was the case with larger Israel itself, the many different groups, schools, clubs, and Anointed communities had a variety of practices, beliefs, and organizational patterns. These peoples had no central leadership and so had neither interest in telling nor the ability to tell the myriad groups how to practice or what to believe. The models for such organization were local and occasionally regional, and so Jesus groups generally followed the diverse club organizational rules or the varieties of synagogue practices around the Mediterranean. The idea of Christian synods and ecumenical councils lay in the distant future. As occurred both in local clubs and in synagogue patterns, it was normal for different groups to dispute with one another about practices and beliefs.

6. They Had Persisting Oral Traditions

Writing did not dominate the life of the early communities of the Anointed to the same degree as surviving documents have dominated how we have imagined their life. There was nothing like the New Testament in the first two centuries CE. Throughout those centuries, Jesus peoples celebrating, arguing, and debating combined many forms of speaking and writing. Reading—as in all Mediterranean cultures—was done together publicly, especially when the few people who could read would read to a whole group. But often there was no reading. There was significant writing among the different groups, but this writing was part of a boisterous, complicated community dialogue, group reading, ritual practice, and—most of all—intense discussion. Much material overlapped Israel's developing readings of Torah, the Prophets, and Wisdom literature, the writings increasingly being set apart, designated as particularly meaningful for the life and identity of these peoples. Other writings were letters between communities, partially developed stories, and songs from within communities. Important writing was also done through a few words etched in stone and referenced as rules or statutes for Jesus clubs and associations.

These short descriptions of the Seminar's six major discoveries about the first two centuries of Jesus peoples show how dramatic the results of this experiment are. At the end of the second century, a wide range of possibilities and combinations of organization and meaning making were on the table. Our experiment is to explore the what, who, how, and why of those first two centuries, and to let these unique presences unfold in their astonishing variety. With this approach, we aim to deepen the understanding of the eclectic range of experiences, ideas, stories, and poetics that have been edited out of history, allowing ourselves to consider the breadth of practice and experimentation of the early Jesus movements. Walking forward in this way enables us to reconstruct the diverse experiments in identity, power, and belonging by those seeking to live in an Empire of God while negotiating the Empire of Rome. These major shifts in how to think about the first two centuries of the Common Era also suggest changes in how people see themselves and the world today. We welcome and encourage such reimaginations.

Papers Relevant to This Chapter by Seminar Participants

BeDuhn, Jason, Lillian Larsen, Nina Livesey, Brandon Scott, Hal
    Taussig, and Erin K. Vearncombe (the Christianity Seminar
    Steering Committee). "Summary, Westar 'Christianity Seminar'
    Trade Book on the Period 25–211 CE of 'Early Christ People';
    Content and Organization of Book: Product of Six Years
    of Seminar Research, Debate, Papers, Specific and Focused
    Seminar Session Spring 2018, and Three Years of Work by
    Seminar Steering Committee." Spring 2019.

Dewey, Arthur, Joanna Dewey, Lillian Larsen, Celene Lillie, and
    Jeffrey Robbins. "Individual Responses to 'Rewriting the First
    Two Centuries of Early Christ Movements: An Introduction.'"
    Spring 2018.

Taussig, Hal. "Rewriting the First Two Centuries of Early Christ
    Movements: An Introduction." Spring 2018.

2

IF NOT CHRISTIAN, WHAT?

When we survey the first two centuries of the Common Era, we find a great variety of people who are loyal to Jesus in different ways and to different degrees, addressing Jesus with a variety of titles. These peoples organized themselves into communities, clubs, groups of followers, and schools. Meals were their primary social engagement. They called themselves a variety of names: the Enslaved of God, the body of the Anointed, brothers and sisters, the Way—the list is extensive. They strongly identified with the traditions of Israel and often thought of themselves as part of Israel.

These peoples had no single name for themselves but a variety of names, and sometimes no name. The use of the term "Christian" was very rare, with no certain occurrence in the first century. Our first challenge, then, is figuring out what to call them, given that they did not call themselves "Christian" or "Christians." Previous scholarship has sometimes understood this problem but has never addressed it; the name "Christian" is still used to identify these diverse peoples, even with the acknowledgment that the word does not apply. We put a lot of importance in names, especially when we are trying to understand something. Naming something helps us to know it. If we try to name these peoples more accurately, our understanding of them may change dramatically.

Figuring out what to call these various groups and clubs requires us to answer three primary questions:

- What does the word "Christian" mean?
- What did it mean and how was it used in the first two centuries?
- What did these communities call themselves?

WHAT DOES THE WORD "CHRISTIAN" MEAN?

"Christian" in contemporary English refers to "one who believes or professes the religion of Christ; an adherent of Christianity," according to the *Oxford English Dictionary*, generally considered the authoritative historical dictionary of the English language. This definition, which is still current in the latest online version of the *OED*, was written by the dictionary's first editor, James Murray, in 1889 and has not changed since. The *OED* definition is nearly identical to the definitions of "Christian" in the current editions of the *Merriam-Webster Collegiate Dictionary* (2020) and the *American Heritage Dictionary* (2012). What is even more impressive is that Murray's *OED* definition is nearly identical to Samuel Johnson's definition of 1755 in his *A Dictionary of the English Language*, the first English dictionary: "professor of the religion of Christ." This consistency indicates a very stable definition from Johnson in 1755 to today. The definition represents a certain common sense; of course "Christian" has to do with "Christ" and the religion of Christ.

As obvious as this contemporary definition may seem, it

will not work for the first two centuries of the Common Era. This definition assumes an identifiable phenomenon called Christianity. But those who were loyal to Jesus had not yet definitely broken off from Israel to form separate associations or groups, much less a new religion. Also, the Greek word usually translated as "Christian"—*christianos*—has a very particular meaning in the first two centuries, a meaning that we lose when we transliterate, rather than translate.

The (now) English adjective "Christian" is not a translation of the Greek, but a transliteration. Transliteration means representing one language system in the terms and tools of another language system. "Christian" approximates the letters of the original language (Greek: Χριστιανός) in the letters of the Latin alphabet, that is, the Greek letter chi (Χ) is transliterated as "Ch"; the Greek letter rho (ρ), as "r"; and so on. This transliteration, rather than translation, of "Christian" does not tend to strike us as strange, but it should. The Greek word *christianos* is made up of two parts. *Christos* is a translation of the Hebrew word *messiah*, meaning "anointed with oil." In Israel, kings, prophets, and priests were anointed with oil. The Anointed One was the king; this term therefore had explicit, unavoidable political overtones. Proclaiming someone *messiah* or *christos*—an anointed one, a king of Israel—was bound to catch Rome's attention, and not in a good way.

The second part of "Christian" is the suffix -*ian*, which means "belongs to the party of." This suffix is used in both Greek and Latin with this meaning. The Gospel of Mark refers to the Herodians, or those who belong to the party of Herod, as among those who plot against Jesus: "And the Pharisees, having gone out, immediately held counsel with those who belonged to the party of Herod against him, concerning how to destroy him" (Mark 3:6).[1] Understood in these terms, the

translation of the Greek *christianos* into English is straightforward: "One who belongs to the party of the Anointed."

When the word began to be used in Latin, instead of translating the Greek word, it was transliterated; that is, Latin writers
simply used the Latin alphabet for the Greek letters. *Christianos*
in Greek became *christianus* in Latin. "Anointed" or "oiled" in
Latin is a very different word: *unctus*. The transliteration *christianos* to *christianus* looks simple, but it means that the new
Latin word is now a foreign word. *Christianus* has no meaning
in Latin, not a meaning like "anointed" or "oiled." It becomes
a loanword by transliteration, as *umbrella* (from Italian), *ballet*
(French), and *avatar* (Sanskrit) are loanwords, that is, words
integrated into one language from another, without translation
(Greek to Latin, or Italian to English).

The English word "Christian" meaning "one who believes or
professes the religion of Christ; an adherent of Christianity" is
far from the Greek meaning of "one who belongs to the party
of the Anointed." The process of transliteration from Greek
involved a loss of original meaning and the invention of new
meaning. Change in the meanings of words is a natural feature of languages, signed and spoken; languages are dynamic,
describing the realities they attempt to communicate; and, as
descriptive, languages are flexible and accommodating. Our
"new meaning" of "Christian" is not bad or wrong; it is just a
change. If we want to understand the many Jesus associations
and groups of the first two centuries, though, we need to use
and understand words in the ways that they were used and understood in those contexts during the first two centuries.

We will encounter and grapple with the significance of
transliteration in our interpretation of ancient phenomena in
different ways throughout this book. In this chapter, we are
wrestling with the word *christos* as naming an anointed king

of Israel. Other important transliterations we will encounter include "baptism" (a word that refers to "bathing" or "dipping" in Greek, see Chapter 12) and "heresy" (a word that simply means "choice," rather than some form of false belief or deviance, see Chapter 13).

WHAT DID IT MEAN AND HOW WAS IT USED IN THE FIRST TWO CENTURIES?

The New Testament's twenty-seven books contain approximately 138,015 words in Greek. "Approximately" may be surprising, but in fact ongoing work with ancient textual variation and with newly discovered fragments of canonical writings has shown that the collection called the New Testament is not as fixed as we might think. Among those approximately 138,015 words, *christianos* is found only three times. A comparison with other important words in the New Testament is revealing:

- "Jesus" is found 1,002 times
- "Mary" is found 54 times
- "Israel" is found 71 times
- "Judean/Jew" (the same word in Greek) is found 147 times
- "Disciples/students" (the same word in Greek) is found 241 times
- "Paul" is found 169 times
- "Believer(s)/those who trust" (the same word in Greek) is found 65 times

The word *christianos* never appears in the Gospels of Matthew, Mark, Luke, or John. Nor does it appear in the letters of Paul. Thus, apparently it is not a significant word in the vocabulary of the movement associated with those who belong to the party of the Anointed.

Three Uses in the New Testament

1. Acts of the Apostles 11:25–26

The first occurrence of the word *christianos* in the New Testament is often quoted in scholarship and popular discussion. It occurs in the Acts of the Apostles, the sequel to the Gospel of Luke that tells the story of the development of Jesus groups across the ancient Mediterranean. Following the ancient Greek meaning of the word, we translate *christianos* as "those who belong to the party of the Anointed."

> And going to Tarsus to look for Saul, Barnabas, when he had found him, brought him to Antioch. For an entire year they met with the assembly and taught a great many people, and it was in Antioch that the students were first called those who belong to the party of the Anointed. (Acts 11:25–26)

Christianos is not used in the surrounding story, and the sentence is an aside, almost a throwaway comment. The idea is not picked up again; the sentence seems to play no role in the narrative. The passive construction, "were called," suggests that the word is used by others. Translated in its first- and second-century context as "those who belong to the party of the Anointed," *Christianos* is not a term used by members of the groups, the insiders, but by those outside the group.

Notice the difference in meaning when "those who belong to the party of the Anointed" is used instead of the traditional transliteration "Christians." If we read this passage from Acts

and use "Christians" for the Greek word, the traditional transliteration makes it sound as though this event in Antioch marks
the coming out of the Christian religion. But our translation
has a different sense. In Antioch the students of the Anointed
were first called "those of the party of the Anointed." It notices
an important shift in perception from "students" to "party."
The passage sounds different and has a very different meaning,
read in translation.

2. Acts of the Apostles 26:27–29

In Paul's final trials before he is sent to Rome, he comes before
King Herod Agrippa II, the last Herodian king and a client ruler
of the Roman emperor. The king is also a follower of the traditions of Israel and parries a question from Paul about whether
he, the king, believes in the prophets of Israel. Paul is convinced
he does; Agrippa's belief is not called into question. Paul is really
asking a question about whether Agrippa believes Jesus fulfills
the prophecies of Israel's prophets:

> [Paul said,] "King Agrippa, do you trust the prophets? I
> know that you have trust." Agrippa said to Paul, "Are you
> so quickly persuading me to become one who belongs
> to the party of the Anointed?" Paul replied, "Whether
> quickly or not, I pray to God that not only you but also all
> who are listening to me today might belong such as I do—
> except for these chains." (Acts 26:27–29)

This second occurrence of the Greek word *christianos* provides more context for how the word functioned. In the standard
modern translations, Agrippa asks Paul, "Are you so quickly per-
suading me to become a Christian?" The modern reader understands this transliteration to mean, "Are you trying to persuade

me to convert to Christianity?" But our translation provides a different, more historically accurate meaning. Agrippa questions Paul, "Are you asking me, a client of the emperor Augustus, to join the party of the Anointed King of Israel?" That question is not only very different, but much more politically threatening and dangerous. The fact that Paul is in chains in this passage, on trial before Agrippa, highlights the political threat.

This translation also makes more sense in the context of the story. Paul does not claim that he is "Christian" in any part of his trial. Rather, he asserts his continuity with the people of Israel. He belongs to the party of the Anointed, commissioned to spread the word of the Anointed to Israel and the nations alike; he is not a "Christian." The transliteration makes no sense in Acts.

3. First Peter 4:14–16

The third occurrence of *christianos* in the New Testament comes in the First Letter of Peter. This letter was written in a context of persecution by the Roman state.

> If you are reviled for the name of the Anointed, you are
> blessed, because the spirit of glory, which is the Spirit of
> God, is resting on you. But let none of you suffer as a
> murderer, a thief, a criminal, or even as a mischief maker.
> Yet if any of you suffers as one who belongs to the party
> of the Anointed, do not consider it a disgrace, but glorify
> God because you bear this name. (1 Pet. 4:14–16)

While bearing the name of the Anointed, the letter writer asserts, members of this community will not be charged by the officials as murderers or thieves, that is, as common criminals, but as those who belong to the party of the Anointed. "Belonging to the party of the Anointed" is, from the magistrate's point of view, a criminal offense. Israel's kings were known as Anointed Ones; the word has clear political implications. Belonging to the party of the Anointed is therefore a threat to Rome's power.

Letters of Pliny and Trajan

Another early usage of *christianos*, at least as early as those in the New Testament, if not earlier, occurs in the early first century correspondence between Pliny (known historically as Pliny the Younger), a well-connected governor of a remote Roman province, and his superior, the emperor Trajan. They are writing about how to process those people Pliny calls *christiani*. This correspondence is in Latin, not Greek, so where the term appears, it is a transliteration from the Greek alphabet to the Latin.

Pliny writes describing his practice of dealing with *christiani* and asking for the emperor's guidance. When encountering the words "Christians" or "Christ" in the translation below, imagine the appropriate transliteration, *christiani* or *christus*, instead:

It is my custom to refer all my difficulties to you, Sir, for no one is better able to resolve my doubts and to inform my ignorance. I have never been present at an examination of Christians. Consequently, I do not know the nature or the extent of the punishments usually meted out to them . . . For the moment, this is the line I have taken with all persons brought before me on the charge of being Christians. I have asked them in person if they are Christians, and if they admit it, I repeat the question a second and third time, with a warning of the punishment awaiting them. If they persist, I order them to be led away for execution . . . There have been others similarly fanatical who are Roman citizens. I have entered them on the list of persons to be sent to Rome for trial.

. . . I considered that I should dismiss any who denied that they were or ever had been Christians when they had repeated after me a formula of invocation to the gods and had made offerings of wine and incense to your statue (which I had ordered to be brought into court for this purpose along with the images of the gods) and furthermore had reviled the name of Christ . . .

. . . They declared that the sum total of their guilt or error amounted to no more than this: they had met regularly before dawn on a fixed day to chant verses alternately among themselves in honor of Christ as if to a god, and also to bind themselves by oath . . . to abstain from theft, robbery and adultery, to commit no breach of trust and not to deny a deposit when called upon to restore it. After this ceremony it had been their custom to disperse and reassemble later to take food of an ordinary, harmless kind . . . This made me decide it was all the more necessary to extract the truth by torture from two slave-women . . . I found nothing but a degenerate sort of cult carried to extravagant length. (*Letters* 10.96)[2]

This translation from the Loeb Classical Library, considered in scholarship as the standard translation of ancient writings, employs the translation convention of "Christian," which we have seen is problematic. But this letter is in Latin, not Greek. The transition to Latin is where the transliteration problem originates. So, how did Pliny and Trajan understand this word? They clearly did not think it meant "Christian" in the sense of the *Oxford English Dictionary*.

Both Pliny and Trajan know this word; they do not have to explain it to each other. Belonging to this group is sufficient to be accused of breaking Roman law and being judged or punished by Rome, punished even by death. Pliny is enquiring of the emperor Trajan whether he is following correct procedure, like a good bureaucrat.

If the meaning of the Greek word *christianos*, "one who belongs to the party of the Anointed," is straightforward, the meaning of the Latin transliteration is less so. As we have seen, Greek *christos* is a translation of Hebrew *messiah*, both meaning "anointed." Neither Greeks nor Romans anoint their rulers, but whereas the Greeks *translated* the Hebrew, the Latins *transliterated* the Greek. Why?

Roman writers probably understood *christus* in Latin as the name or title of an individual. They recognized it as a foreign-sounding word, connected with strange superstitions from Israel, a place of continued rebellion. As the name originated in this place of rebellion, they probably recognized it as signaling rebellion or resistance, for which they were on the lookout with those connected to Israel's traditions.

There is one more possibility. *Christus* could be sounded as *chrestus* in Latin, which means "the good one." There is one important support for this possibility. The Roman historian and senator Tacitus, writing around 116 CE, shortly after Pliny's letter to Trajan, describes the great fire in Rome during the reign of Nero. Tacitus mentions *chrestiani* and *christus*. The confusion of *i* and *e* in Latin is common.

Tacitus also notes that this "degenerate cult"—the word "cult" here also potentially translated with an ancient meaning of "superstition"—had arisen first in Judea, a clear indication that it was Judean and then spread to Rome, "where all things horrible or shameful in the world collect and find a vogue," according to Tacitus (Tacitus was an upper-class snob).[3] As much as he hates Nero, he hates these foreign superstitions even more. Referring to the adherents of *christus* as degenerate and as superstitious are stereotypes that Pliny also uses. Furthermore, these stereotypes are often used by Roman writers in reference to Judeans. The orator Cicero, for example, refers to certain Judean practices as "outlandish superstition" and to Judeans as mass crowds, close-knit throngs prone to disruptive behaviors. Defying the will of the "crowd" of Judeans "that on occasion sets our public meetings ablaze" is "the height of responsibility" to Cicero, an act of public interest. Jerusalem, he states, is a city of "suspicion and slander" (*Pro Flacco* 67–68).[4]

Tacitus ties the term *christianus* to the traditions of Israel. He is making a distinction *within* various types of Judeans. *Christianus* is a type of Judean; any further meaning of "belonging to the party of the Anointed" or of "the good ones" is actually irrelevant to Tacitus. The association with Judea is enough. The transliteration of *christianos* (Greek) to *christianus* (Latin) is significant because it signals a Judean provenance, an association with a people of rebellion and resistance. "Christian," in Latin, refers to yet another troublesome group from the eastern Mediterranean. The meaning has nothing to do with who they are, but where they come from, and their resulting potential to cause trouble.

The Importance of Dating

In tracing this history of the term "Christian" and the political and cultural attitudes toward these people during the first two centuries, it's important to pinpoint when this shift began. To this point we have sidestepped the thorny and controversial issue of dating these early writings. But we can avoid it no more. The one date we know for sure is that Pliny was governor of the province of Bithynia between 111 and 113 CE. Pliny's governorship fixes the date of the Pliny-Trajan correspondence.

Traditionally, the Acts of the Apostles was understood as written by Luke, a follower of Paul. Since Acts does not record Paul's death, it was likely written before Paul's death (ca. 62–64 CE) and therefore in the late 50s CE. First Peter was taken as written by the Apostle Peter and so also had an early date. However, this dating scheme has been challenged and rejected by modern scholarship. The tendency in recent years has been to date both writings to the second century CE: according to the Westar Institute's Acts Seminar, a predecessor of the Christianity Seminar, the Acts of the Apostles should be dated after 125 CE.[5] First Peter is often dated after 150 CE.

Surprisingly, then, the likely earliest extant usage of "Christian" is in Latin, not Greek, and it is used by Pliny, an outsider, as an apparently bureaucratic term. Belonging to this party is clearly a chargeable offense. Since both the emperor Trajan and Pliny use the term and know its meaning, we obviously have here not the first usage. How much farther the word goes back is hard to know, but probably not much before 100 CE; otherwise, a usage would likely have turned up.

The statement "it was in Antioch that the disciples were first called *christianos*" (Acts 11:26) is often used to prove that "Christian" and "Christianity" were established usage before 70 CE. But what it really indicates is that Pliny, Tacitus, and the author of Acts shared a common early second-century Roman bureaucratic term.

The most prominent association of *christianos* in the second century is with people who are threatened, have been killed, or are willing to be killed by agents of the Roman Empire as a threat to empire. This association accords with the basic meaning of the word "one who belongs to the party of the Anointed." It is rarely, if ever, used to connote all those who belong to the Jesus movement.

The predominance of usage is in the late second century. Approximately 35 percent of all uses of *christianos* during the first two centuries were made by just two men, Tertullian and Clement of Alexandria, writers of the late second and early third centuries. In the extant literature, the word occurs about 215 times in the first two centuries, if one does not count Tertullian and Clement. The gospel that uses the word *christianos* the most, seven times, is the Gospel of Philip, also probably written in the late second century.

The lack of use of *christianos* in the first century and its infrequent use in the second century clearly indicates that it is not a significant word or identifier of the early Jesus movement. It most probably was an imperial Roman bureaucratic term used to identify a subgroup of the larger groups of Israel, specifically one that had the potential to cause trouble, like other groups from the region. This trouble-making affiliation made membership in this group a chargeable offense against the empire. Like many nicknames, the word was used against the group or party but then later was adopted as a badge of honor and symbol of resistance to dominant structures of power. That transition may well be evidenced in 1 Peter.

WHAT DID THESE COMMUNITIES CALL THEMSELVES?

If "Christian" has become the default term for the whole phenomenon and yet is inappropriate in the first two centuries, what words can we use to accurately represent the wide variety of those dedicated to Jesus or the Way or the Anointed during the first two centuries? These questions are particularly vexing because almost all current biblical scholars have overlooked them. Indeed, most of them simply use the word "Christian," often in quotation marks, when referring to the followers of Jesus in the first two centuries, noting that "Christian" may be inappropriate but not knowing what vocabulary might be more accurate. Even when the problem is acknowledged, a solution is never provided.

As this realization came clearly into focus, the Seminar refused to overlook this major problem. Our research, however, has not turned up a perfect answer. Our vocabulary is limited, and any word we choose seems to oversimplify or assumes too much. Even "Jesus peoples" assumes that Jesus was central to the lives and activities of these groups and movements, though that was not always the case, and there was no fixed idea of Jesus either, or why and how he was meaningful. We have two basic solutions: names these peoples themselves used and names we can use when they do not name themselves.

First- and second-century groups employed a range of names for themselves. Since these groups were very diverse, their names were also different. They did not all call themselves "those belonging to the party of the Anointed." It also is likely that many of these group names have been lost or never written down, so our policy has been that when a group uses a name for itself, we use that name as the group's descriptor.

At times we need a term for all the groups together. Even when we know the different groups had major and minor differences, sometimes we have to discuss what they hold in common. In these cases, we have employed several generalized phrases, like "Jesus peoples" or "followers of the Anointed." This solution is inadequate if for no other reason than these groups did not use these terms. Often, they were anonymous or their names were not recorded.

Many people identified with Jesus as a teacher while he was alive and after his death. With Jesus as their teacher, these people identified as "students." The primary word for "student" in Greek is translated traditionally as "disciple." In contemporary

English, however, "disciple" does not mean "student." "Disciple" is an ecclesiastical translation that sounds biblical and therefore out of the ordinary. The best translation is "student" as it's the most frequently used name for followers of Jesus Anointed in the first two centuries. When we read the Gospels in English substituting the more accurate "student" for the backwards-looking ecclesiastical translation of "disciple" ("backwards" as in interpreting history on the basis of what we know now, or contemporary categories), suddenly the writings feel different. New potential for meaning opens up.

Vocabulary drawn from the school environment is frequent. Jesus often is called a teacher, and drawing on this association, he is also called Wisdom, because he personified the wisdom characteristic of teachers. This identification is also more nuanced and more clever than being smart, but it also names a divine figure in Israel's holy writings. *Sophia* ("smart" or "wisdom") in Greek can mean a wise divine figure, as well as the quality of being wise. The Greek noun *sophia* is also feminine, opening up other ways of imagining Jesus. Calling Jesus *sophia*, a feminine divine term, is very different from the patriarchal vocabulary normally applied to Jesus. Likewise, the followers of Jesus, the wise teacher, are "the wise ones," or potentially "the wise women," given Wisdom's gendered identity.

In this same fashion other widely used names for Jesus have been overlooked. The Greek word *Christos* was one of the most significant names used to identify Jesus. As already noted, this Greek word translates the Hebrew *messiah*, and both words mean "someone anointed with oil" or "Anointed." In Hebrew culture, kings, prophets, and priests were anointed with oil, and Jesus was often identified with one or more of these roles. Eventually the root meaning of "anointed" slips away, and *Christos* more or less becomes Jesus's name, but it never completely loses the connotation of being anointed with oil as long as Greek was the dominant language of the movement. In English, Jesus Christ becomes his name, and "Christ" is free to take on a variety of meanings not found in Greek.

Seminar member Brandon Scott gave "Christian," a name applied to Jesus followers, a new twenty-first-century clarity. What emerges from his work is a wide set of evocative group names from Jesus's connections to kingship and prophet. "King" is especially resonant when one realizes that the Roman Empire destroyed the sovereignty of Jesus's homeland, while Jesus people sparked resistance to Rome. In other words, naming Jesus "King of Israel" is both silly, because Israel was ruled by Rome, and dangerous, because the title challenged that rule.

When groups proclaimed Jesus as Anointed One, that placed him in a role as a king or prophet of Israel over and against Rome's claims. Imagining Jesus as anointed king or prophet makes him a national figure of Israel, which then features Jesus groups as the followers of such a national anti-Roman leader. When they were called "adherents of the party of the Anointed One," "party" would be read as a party or group making claims of a political nature. As Part I of this book makes clear, under the leadership of Jesus as the Anointed King of conquered Israel, the Jesus people's resistance to Roman domination points to their national longing and identification with conquered Israel.

"The people of the Anointed" or "the people of the Anointed King" helps us see how the variety of Jesus people showed their political and social ambition, as well as hid such meanings. More variations of groups or Jesus movements came to expression in names like "Believers of the Anointed," "Confidants of the Anointed," "Friends of the Anointed," "Sisters and Brothers of the Anointed," and "Intimates of the Anointed."

Early on, people from other defeated peoples or nations also began thinking of themselves as Adherents, Confidants, and Faithful to the Anointed King or Prophet. While many of these followers were quite taken with imagining the crucified and risen Jesus as a political figure, it is also important to bear in mind that very few, if any, such groups were trying to defeat Rome militarily. On the other hand, it also is apparent that the groups that called themselves Adherents, People, Sisters and Brothers, or Intimates of the Anointed One had a significant political agenda of resistance that derived from following Jesus, both before and after his death. Just as our naming many different Jesus followers "students" or "wise ones" rather than the ecclesiastical "disciples" makes more sense, groups naming themselves Adherents, Confidants, and Faithful to the Anointed King or Prophet gives the groups political and social overtones.

The Seminar also found ten names of different groups in specific writings. These group names are especially fascinating in that none of them use the word "Jesus" but most of them seem to allude to activities or values of the various Jesus groups. Paul refers to a group that gathers under the leadership of a Corinthian woman called Chloe; the name of the group is Chloe's people (1 Cor. 1:11). In the Acts of the Apostles, a group or movement is called "the Way," with no other description (9:2). In the Acts of Paul and Thecla, apparently the young woman leader Thecla (and perhaps Paul) belong to a group that is called "the Enslaved of God" (37:3). From the somewhat extended description of Thecla's activities, these are a group of single women (and perhaps some men) who have left their families. Paul may have been the founder of this group of young women (and men) that Thecla leads. The composition called the *Shepherd of Hermas* (a second-century vision which identifies Jesus as an angel, sometimes included in manuscripts of the later New Testament) also uses the term "Enslaved of

God" (2:4). These groups are cited in multiple chapters of the work (1[38]10; 5[48]2). The Gospel of Truth describes a group and their duties to reach out to people in difficulty and trouble and says to them, "Say then from the heart that you are 'The Perfect Day'" (17:10, 11).

Colossians paints a picture of a group at the beginning and end of the letter that are faithful "brothers" of one another. This could be one of the chosen families that are not related by blood that are described in Chapter 10 of the present book or a larger movement across different geographical areas. There are many other writings in which groups call themselves "brothers," "sisters," "brothers and sisters," or "siblings," with Colossians being a kind of example of such group names or nicknames. Both James and 1 Peter address their letters to "the Migrants" (James 1:1; 1 Pet. 1:1). First Peter goes out of its way to underline this name by describing them also as "aliens." It seems most probable that this name in both writings is of a larger movement, not just of a small group.

The Gospel of Matthew, however, cites a particular group of celibate men that it names "the Children" (18:2–7; 19:10–15). When the Odes of Solomon addresses its group regularly as "Members," the meaning is a double one: it mostly uses the image of a group as parts of a body, but it also plays on the belonging character of people in close proximity to one another (3:2; 6:2; 8:14). The Letter to the Hebrews identifies two different groups, each with quite metaphorical names. "The Order of Melchizedek" is named after a king and priest from the ancient territory of Salem, and the writer of Hebrews clearly refers to Jesus Anointed as a priest in that order. In Hebrews, as well, there is another picture of a kind of Jesus group that the writer calls "the Altar" (13:9–16).

Although there must have been at least several hundred

different names for Jesus peoples during the first two hundred years of the Common Era, our research over the past two years of the Seminar has identified only twenty-four in actual documents. Nevertheless, the process of doing justice to the many different groups of those first two hundred years is now under way. The inaccuracy of thinking that these many Jesus peoples were all already Christians in the first and second centuries is behind us. Rethinking who they were and how they identified themselves is moving ahead. Naming is connected to identity. When we use an accurate name, we have a much better chance of understanding, or more respectfully, learning about identity.

The past forty years of research on the first two centuries of the Common Era has uncovered much viable connectivity among a great variety of clubs, families, movements, schools, communities, and groups associated with Jesus the teacher, the Anointed, Lord, and Savior. The remaining chapters of this book explore this fragile, multivalent vibrancy that occurred after Jesus and before Christianity.

Papers Relevant to This Chapter by Seminar Participants
Scott, Brandon. "If Not Christian, What?" Spring 2020.

PART I

LIVING
WITH THE
EMPIRE

3

ENGINE OF EMPIRE:
VIOLENCE

The crucifixion of Jesus is exhibit Number One for evidence of the violence at the heart of Roman rule. The basic facts about Roman crucifixion lay bare the charge: (1) crucifixion was the act of nailing a person to a makeshift tree until they slowly died; (2) Romans crucified hundreds of thousands of those they conquered; (3) such government crucifixions were intentionally undertaken as public torture and terrorism; and (4) many of the early communities of the Anointed emphasized the centrality of crucifixion for defining who they were. Early Anointed-association envoy Paul said, "I know nothing but Jesus Anointed and him crucified" (1 Cor. 2:2). The Gospel of Mark has Jesus saying, "Those who want to be a follower of mine . . . let them take up a cross" (8:34). Paul understands himself and his relationship to Jesus associations in terms of crucifixion: "I am crucified with the Anointed, and yet I am alive" (Gal. 2:20).

In this chapter's overview of this foundational dimension of the first two centuries, we first examine Rome's policy of violence and then the many rejoinders of the Jesus peoples living in and through this violence.

This statue shows the powerful Mesopotamian nation of Dakon under Roman rule. The exposed breast indicates military defeat as public spectacle.

Hal Taussig

ROME'S VIOLENT STRATEGY

An iron nail embedded in this right heel of a first-century person named Yehohanan, son of Hagkol, was found among a collection of bones north of Jerusalem. This is the only direct archaeological evidence of a crucifixion in the ancient Mediterranean.
Photo © The Israel Museum, Jerusalem / by Meidad Suchowolski

Although Roman violence was a primary concern for the early Jesus movements, Roman rulers did not focus on those movements. Violence was part of a larger Roman strategy that aimed to coerce conquered nations to think of themselves as half-human "barbarians." Jesus communities were seldom on Rome's radar during the first two hundred years CE; the empire thought of Jesus groups as a subset of conquered Israel.

Military Conquest and Torture

The city of Rome's domination began and ended with military conquest. Even in the centuries before the city grew into an empire, the city's armies secured most of what is now Italy. Its power then spread eastward through Greece and Asia Minor during the last two centuries before the Common Era. It was an empire before explicitly claiming the name. At this same time, Rome's leaders engaged in sporadic civil wars to claim authority over the city and its growing domain. All these real battles and wars—both around Rome and far away from it—damaged and finally destroyed the somewhat democratic Republic of Rome. The assassination of Julius Caesar in 44 Before the Common Era (BCE) was less what ended Rome's Republic and more a perfect picture of what Rome had become. Violence and combat became the trademark of Rome's rising power in the Mediterranean.

Although Roman generals nearly tore the empire apart as they competed for power and prestige, their armies nonetheless seized and held on to the whole of the Mediterranean basin and central Europe and then formed it into a permanent empire. With Rome as the capital, the empire was ruled by one dictator after another. Augustus Caesar ended Rome's disastrous civil wars by defeating Mark Anthony and Cleopatra at the sea battle of Actium (31 BCE). Rome named Augustus divine and bringer of "peace" whose military victories successfully eliminated any other competing nations for the next four hundred years. All over the empire, monuments celebrated the military victories of Augustus and the emperors who followed him.

Roman violence did not result in just dominion over a huge swath of territory. At least as important was the way violence became a signature for the Roman character itself. As Seminar member Celene Lillie's studies have demonstrated, the main stories of how Rome came into existence show rape as being an integral part of who the founders of Rome were.[1] Roman soldiers regularly raped enemy soldiers who survived their battles.

Although Rome had a relatively early code of written laws, lawyers, and judges, torture was a strong feature of its system—as was the case in most ancient governments. Roman citizens generally were not tortured, but no legal protections prevented conquered peoples from being tortured. Crucifixion was legal and designated as the punishment for noncitizens fomenting revolt against Rome. Roman officials were always on the lookout for potential rebellion in the empire. Both imperial officials and military members were known for practicing widespread torture and random crucifixions.

Vast Enslavement

A main prize of Rome's military conquests was an empirewide program of enslavement. After every major battle or war, Roman soldiers captured thousands of inhabitants of the subjugated territories and enslaved them to serve the empire's ever-expanding domination. Strategic to this larger program of enslavement was the transportation of many newly enslaved peoples to other parts of the empire. Following the Roman destruction of Jerusalem in 70 CE, almost one hundred thousand Judeans were sent to Rome to be enslaved.[2] Many of these enslaved people built the Colosseum, the amphitheater still central to tourism in central Rome today.

In addition to the huge number of enslaved people doing manual labor, many people of high social rank or status from the nations Rome seized were enslaved to help administer Roman affairs and imperial networks. They were displaced throughout the empire to staff remote villas and become the bureaucratic scribes who churned out the writing that managed the empire. The economy of the empire was built on, driven by, and grew by enslaving more and more people.

Besides being enslaved through warfare, people were enslaved for being in debt, committing or allegedly committing crimes, or being born of enslaved women. Slavery was everywhere throughout Roman society: both the government and private individuals engaged in the slave trade; most kinds of work received substantial support from the enslaved; the empire used the enslaved to construct huge monuments to Rome's glory. Silver mines in Spain were infamous for their harsh treatment of the enslaved. A tombstone of a four-year-old enslaved boy named Quintus Artulus (or Quartulus; the inscription is worn away in places), shown standing with his miner's hammer and basket, tells the tale of his early death in a mine.[3] Roman citizenship was tightly connected to ownership of the enslaved. Even relatively poor Roman citizens, by Roman standards, would have one or more enslaved people in their households.

Oppressive Taxation

The upper-crust members of the Roman Empire lived opulent lives and understood themselves as deserving of the wealth and resources of the nations Rome had conquered. Rome pillaged the art of Greece, the ancient treasures of Egypt, the silver mines in Spain, and the countryside from North Africa to Britain. But it was never enough.

Rome always asserted its right to take tribute from captured nations. As the empire grew, its administration became more elaborate. Provinces had different forms of taxation, some of which were under control of the Roman Senate and others under the control of the emperor. Often, provinces in the east of the empire remained under local control. Israel's Herod "the

Emperor Claudius triumphs in battle over the nation of Britain. A conquered nation was typically portrayed as a woman. This statue was publicly displayed in Asia Minor.

Hal Taussig

Great" is a good example of a client king who taxed his own country and gave much of it to Rome. He built not only a magnificent temple in Jerusalem, but other buildings throughout the empire. Governors were responsible for tax collection in their provinces and often viewed their appointment as a way to increase their personal fortune. The cruelty of this taxation was multiplied by the rights of the tax collectors to take additional sums for themselves.

Roman territories looked lavish in terms of the monuments and public works Rome built. But the result of taxation took a toll on both urban and rural areas. The notorious reputation of tax collectors among the population of Israel was typical of general resistance against Roman taxation. The gospel writings included in what is now the New Testament display much disdain for tax and tax collectors, and Jesus himself seems to have been in the middle of the fray, exhibiting sympathy for both impoverished populations and hated tax collectors.

Displacement of Peoples
Rome's policy was to displace the peoples it conquered—often, through enslavement. Rome's program of expanded road building and commerce pushed people into places other than where they had lived for centuries. The population of entire villages moved far away because work was available somewhere else. This lure of work in distant parts of the empire destroyed families, neighborhoods, and villages.

Rome also built many new cities and colonies either from scratch (the Decapolis region near Galilee) or from former cities destroyed by war (the rebuilding of Corinth). Many of these new cities were then populated by combinations of retired soldiers and conquered peoples who played major roles in the building of these cities.

Imperial Propaganda and Religious Dominion

Rome normally tolerated local religions while requiring participants to offer sacrifices to the honor of the emperor and to pray for him, so the many religions in the Roman Empire had roots in the conquered nations and tribes. Others, like Egypt's cults of Isis and Osiris, were ancient religions spread around the empire and were even welcomed in the city of Rome. Both the Babylonian and Egyptian versions of the religion of Israel derived from migrations from the homeland. Because of the breadth of the spread of the practice of Israel throughout the empire, Rome exempted Israelites from the requirement of sacrifice, but not from praying for the emperor.

Rome developed its own imperial religion in ways that supported its violence and power. Beginning with Augustus Caesar, most emperors were divinized to one degree or another, and votive offerings were made in temples and public venues, at meals, and in private villas. Most emperors were proclaimed gods after their death, and stars were named for them as the emperors were considered to be the stars, in and from which they continued to rule. At least as important were the monuments built around the empire that portrayed the emperor in the pose of one of the gods, often Zeus, or in warrior garb. The Sebasteion at Aphrodisias in Asia Minor, constructed by local officials, shows the emperor Claudius leaning over Britannia (the nation/woman) in a pose suggestive of rape.

The ancient Mediterranean of the first two centuries of the Common Era was a highly visual culture, and these images and stories of the divine emperor killing, raping, and ruling over the empire were perfect propaganda matches for the military and economic domination of the empire. Such demonstrative displays in public left no doubt that crucifixion, beatings, and theft of land were the divine privilege and role of Rome and its power.

CREATIVITY AND RESISTANCE

Early Jesus groups feared Rome's oppression and brutality. They responded to Roman violence with anger, but also through imagination, resistance, and humor. They did not follow a party line nor share common tactics against the empire. Despite how later Christianity and then scholarship ignored the challenge to Rome of early Jesus groups, scholarship in the past twenty-five years has begun recovering the creative resistance of these groups.

Jesus groups answered Roman violence with various strategies: some focused on resistance, others on creativity, and some employed both. In sly yet tangible ways, they worked to stop Rome from damaging their lives and to help people heal from torture and loss. At the same time, most Jesus peoples were even more drawn to joyful and imaginative ways of carving out their own spaces that left them freer to be lively and present. We suspect that these quite different groups, schools, and clubs leaned more toward aliveness, relationships, and community practices rather than what modern people might imagine as full-tilt battle against an evil empire. Chapter 4 takes a longer look at these community practices that carve out such spaces, but it is important first to see how these groups were both active and clandestine, sometimes in overlapping ways, in their opposition to Rome.

Resisting Empire

Telling the story of Jesus's crucifixion in an open way, and celebrating it, was an act of resistance to Rome. Jesus's crucifixion was not unique but was duplicated over and over throughout the empire, and the stories of Jesus being tortured to death allied his story with those of hundreds of thousands similarly executed.

Early Jesus groups dramatically described how their Anointed leader was crucified by Roman soldiers. They proclaimed openly that Jesus was an executed enemy of the state. Later Christians obscured Rome's violence by highlighting Jesus being crucified to save people from their sins. Without being sidetracked by that later Christian doctrine, most communities of the Anointed of the first and second century publicly acknowledged the paradox that Rome's defeat of Jesus the Anointed was actually Rome's defeat.

The stories of Jesus's death would have produced sympathy for other victims of Roman violence. This is clear in the stories of his death in the Gospels of Matthew and Mark, both of which describe Jesus being mocked as he was crucified and Jesus screaming out to God, "My God, my God, why have you abandoned me?" (Mark 15:34; Matt. 27:46). The empathy in these stories is anti-Roman.

Most of the stories of Jesus's crucifixion also proclaimed that Jesus was vindicated and raised up by God. This claim would have been understood as an anti-Roman claim of victory over Roman violence. Indeed, this was not just a claim of a victory over Rome, but a dramatic victory over one of Rome's most demonstrative methods of control and sovereignty. Like Jesus's successful resistance to crucifixion, the reports in the second century of Romans killing Jesus followers—who were later called "martyrs"—ended in those followers being raised up to their God's heavenly throne. These stories also exhibit resistance to Roman imperial claims.

There are many other expressions of resistance to Rome. The Gospel of Luke relates John the Baptist speaking about deep poverty and real hunger in the midst of Rome's ostentatious rule over Israel: "Anyone who has two tunics must share with the one who has none, and anyone who has something to eat must do the same" (Luke 3:11). To the Roman tax collectors he says, "Collect no more than what's appointed to you" (3:13). To the Roman soldiers known for their killing, beating, and stealing throughout the empire, he says: "No intimidation! No extortion! Be content with your pay!" (3:14).[4]

The Revelation to John angrily describes the death of many nations and Jesus peoples by a Rome "intoxicated with the blood of the holy ones and the blood of the witnesses of Jesus" (Rev. 17:6).[5] John demands protection for the Jesus people and vengeance against Rome: "Come out, my people, away from her [Rome], so that you do not share in her crimes . . . Her sins have reached up to the sky, and God has her crimes in mind. Treat her as she has treated others . . . Every one of her pomps and orgies is to be matched by a torture or an agony" (Rev. 18:4, 5, 7).[6]

Paul, a teacher, envoy, and letter writer, brags about having been beaten, thrown in prison, whipped, and stoned. He acknowledges similar violence against those who follow the Anointed, and he associates the Anointed's crucifixion with the cruelty most of them have experienced. Paul even cites a song about Jesus's death, praising him as an example when "he took the form of an enslaved person . . . even accepting death on a cross" (Phil. 2:7, 8).

Inventing a Life in the Face of Violence
The word translated as "gospel," meaning "good news" (derived from the Greek word *euangelion* and the Old English word *gōdspel*; see Chapter 4), occurs 101 times in the New Testament across eighteen books. Good news is not a religious expression but means what it says. It is an expression that celebrates a joyful event as a sort of public statement or proclamation. Often in imperial accounts, good news is the birthday of the emperor. Among the surprises in pursuing the writings created by the Anointed clubs, schools, and groups are the creative

and even comical ways they built their lives. This invention of different kinds of daily life looked with resistance into the face of Roman violence, creating unexpected, good news for these communities.

Two things help us understand good news in the ancient world. First, unlike so often in the contemporary United States, good news was not measured by the amount of money and property one had. Good news marked a significant event that changed the world, whether it was the birth of an emperor or the coming of the Anointed.

Second, most of the members of these groups—perhaps two thousand people twenty years after Jesus's death and maybe a total of twenty thousand fifty years later—were mostly peasants, day workers, the enslaved, and craftspeople. Although there were occasionally wealthy people in some groups, in many there were none. The communities called "the Migrants" and other gatherings were predominantly composed of people of meager means (a middle class in this era was nonexistent, the great majority of people being enslaved, laborers, and poor). Whatever good news meant for these various movements, it had more to do with the ways people lived together, the aliveness they experienced in community.

This good news was not about winning a great battle or gaining a material foothold. Nor was it about gaining assurance of life in the hereafter. What made a difference for these communities was caring for one another, bestowing forgiveness, being fed, finding a future, and being surrounded by companions. No wonder student sages mused, "You are the salt of the earth . . . the light for the world . . . Don't fret about your life—what you're going to eat or drink—or your body—what you're going to wear . . . Take a look at the birds of the sky: they don't . . . gather into barns . . . You are to seek God's domain, and . . . justice first, and all these things will come to you as a bonus" (Matt. 5:13, 14; 6:25, 26, 33).[7]

Stories of Jesus communities exhibit surprises in their daily lives: a worker makes serious mistakes in seeding his field, yet there is a harvest. A woman bakes a huge amount of bread as if she's expecting a party (Matt. 13:33). Small gatherings of people for supper don't have quite enough food or couches; other people crash the party, but everybody relaxes, reclines next to each other or on each other's lap, singing at the top of their voices with plenty to eat and drink (Luke 7:36–39; 12:17; 10:4–9). The country healer insists that it was the confidence of the sick person that made her better (Mark 5:34). Judeans and members of other nations figure out what and how they can eat together (Rom. 14:1–210). A large crowd listens to a teacher in the field, people get hungry, and somehow a small amount of shared food is more than enough (Matt. 14:13–21). A woman begs a healer to cure her daughter; the healer insults her; the woman persists; and when she returns home, her daughter is well (Mark 7:24–30). At a dinner party a young man falls asleep and then falls out of the window, but he is okay, and his companions carry him home (Acts 20:9–12).

Another hallmark of their lives was the "Empire of God"— traditionally translated as the kingdom of God. We lean toward the comic, ironic, and sociopolitical translation Empire of God because it captures the irony and opposition of this "God reality" to the violence of the Empire of Rome. It reminds us that when speaking of the Empire of God, the Empire of Rome is directly challenged. Moreover, the Greek word is the same in both cases. Stories and images about the Empire of God build upon small events in daily life, not long speeches about power and might, nor about the nature of God. Parables about the

realm or Empire of God were experiential snapshots, not theological dissertations or moral aphorisms. Empire of God—used
as often as "good news"—compared God's action to what happened in the ordinary field, market, and house.

Some groups used "good news" and "Empire of God," or
both, frequently in their daily conversations and weekly meals.
Others used them sometimes, and yet others rarely or never
used them. Some talked a lot about Jesus; others, somewhat;
and some, hardly ever. God was seldom the direct topic of exposition, except within the usage of Empire of God, in which
good news happened. Rather than a commonly shared vocabulary or set of beliefs, there was the experience of folks gathering
together for food, drink, and conversation.

This sharing of experience went on in the midst of the Roman
Empire's systemic violence and domination. So the clubs and
schools of the Anointed were an experience of good news and
God's empire in the face of Rome's violence. Their stories of Jesus's crucifixion and of others being tortured are featured in their
writings, as well as at their meal gatherings. As the wine flowed
and conversation unfolded, good news of God's empire emerged
in their everyday experience that challenged and mocked Rome's
empire.

This introduction to the gatherings of the Anointed points
toward a bondedness and a sense of belonging explored more
in Part II. In major and multitudinous ways, the early Jesus
movements resisted Roman domination and built alternative
lives related directly to the strength of their inventive and mul-
tiethnic communities.

Humor

Humor was a major part of these people's meals together. Although pietistic Christianity of our day has forgotten how

humorous the early Jesus people were, this wit and sparkle is
easily spotted in early writings. Jesus in the Gospel of Mark
critiques the idea that some food is unclean (that is, not appropriate) with potty humor: "It's not the things that come into
a person that are dirty, it's what comes out of a person that's
dirty" (Mark 7:15).

Perhaps the darkest joke in Mark's story makes fun of the
idea of happy or sad endings. Its madcap version of Jesus's resurrection (or mysterious lack thereof) doesn't let things get *too*
happy or *too* sad, but they are all confused. Mark's Gospel, a
writing of good news, was probably drafted in the aftermath
of Rome's grinding war against Israel in 68–70 CE and the
resulting Flavian propaganda. While Rome was arguing over
who was going to be the next emperor, Judea and the Galilee
had managed in 67 CE to free themselves from the empire. But
when Rome figured out who its next emperor was, it came back
and recaptured Israel in vicious fashion, ending with Jerusalem
in flames, the Temple destroyed, thousands of people crucified
by the Romans, and many more thousands carried off in enslavement (see Chapter 5).

In the wake of these events, Mark's good news—full of sad-
ness, healing, loss, and humor—was written. The truest vein of
humor aimed straight at the terror of such violence. In Mark,
Jesus heals many people; but strangely, when he does so, he commands them not to tell anyone about the healing. When no one
pays any attention to his directions, he becomes a famous healer.
Then Jesus is crucified and buried. None of Jesus's male followers come to his tomb, but several of his female followers do, to
anoint his dead body. When they approach the tomb, however,
they see only a young man, not Jesus. The young man tells the
women that Jesus has been raised to life and the women are to
tell his followers to meet him in Galilee where they used to be to-

gether with him. But the women are amazed and afraid, so they run off and never tell anyone about Jesus's resurrection. Now, for the first time, no one tells; no one ever knows that Jesus has been raised. And the reader is left to ask, "What happened?"

This is deadly serious comedy. It is about the horrible violence that happens to all the different kinds of people in Israel when the Romans retake Israel in 70 CE. This Gospel is written for the particular Jesus people(s) who have been damaged by Rome in the aftermath of the events of 70 CE. But the tragicomic and quizzical end to Mark's Jesus story has an incomplete resurrection and witnesses who crazily obey for the first time Jesus's instructions not to tell anyone. Significantly, it ends not with God wreaking apocalyptic vengeance on his Anointed's tormentors, but with women running away, afraid and saying nothing. It is incomplete good news in the middle of Rome's horrendous terror of 70 CE for those who have eyes to see and ears to hear.

The family movement called the Enslaved of God told stories about a first-century companion of Paul named Thecla with a similar mix of Roman violence and humor. In one of those stories, Thecla is sentenced to death in the arena for encouraging men and women not to get married but to join her and Paul in wandering around teaching and healing. The Roman soldiers strip Thecla naked and take her before the lions and bears. But hundreds of women in the arena throw perfume into the arena, and the animals lie down drowsily, leaving Thecla safe before them. She then escapes the wild beasts, which have suddenly lost their appetites.

In the Middle of Violence: Creativity and New Identities

Awareness of what Roman violence did to conquered peoples changes our thinking about how the Jesus communities came into being. The ruthlessness and oppression of Rome robbed millions of their identities. Rome successfully ravaged their bodies and psyches to the extent that they began to think of themselves as half-human barbarians, and others came to think of themselves as Roman. The central question was always how to respond to the violence of the Roman Empire.

But this is not the entire story. Adherents of the party of the Anointed developed various practices, communities, and ways of life that helped them to understand themselves in different and renewed ways. They resisted Roman violence, insults, and authoritarianism; and they built alternative identities for themselves that brought them vitality, a different sense of belonging, and internal resistance.

The standard way to describe how these peoples emerged has for centuries focused on the aspect of "believing in" Jesus. Curiously, this long-held model has had little to say about the Roman Empire or its violence. For the most part, it is ignored, except in the case of the deaths of community heroes later called martyrs. In the past twenty-five years, however, scholars have discovered the importance of the intensity of Roman violence and how much the writings and life of communities of Jesus Anointed were about resistance to Roman violence as well as aliveness and depth.[8] A more accurate picture would see the Jesus movements in the grips of Roman terror as a range of partially formed social identities that carry unresolved brokenness, authentic renewal, good news, and mixed messages. Rejecting a tendency to see Roman violence as simply devastating these groups or as these peoples always triumphing over Rome, we continue to take the effects of Roman violence seriously and explore the various dimensions of these emerging community identities. We do not see these peoples simply as the beginning of an otherworldly religion, but as complex, growing, and creative humans struggling toward the good news of the Empire of God.

Papers Relevant to This Chapter by Seminar Participants

Dewey, Arthur. "Switchback Codes: Paul, Apocalyptic and the Art of Resistance." Fall 2015.

Marshall, John. "Judean War and Judean Diaspora: Class and Networks." Fall 2015.

McGaughy, Lane. "God, Retaliation, and the Apocalyptic Scenario." Fall 2015.

Taussig, Hal. "What Do Fiction, Mass Crucifixions and Killer Seals Add Up To? Summarizing Break-Throughs in Martyrdom Scholarship Since 1990." Spring 2015.

Wendt, Heidi. "From the Herodians to Hadrian: The Shifting Status of Judean Religion in Post-Flavian Rome." Fall 2015.

4

GOSPEL OF EMPIRE, GOSPEL OF JESUS

GOSPEL AND GOOD NEWS

The first two centuries involved two "good news" parties: the Romans and the Jesus peoples. The meaning of "good news" presents us with a challenge of translation. In contemporary English there are two important translations of the Greek word *euangelion*. That word translates well in English as "good news," since its two Greek word stems are "good" and "news" or "announcement," and having a general expression of good news is useful for any language. But for this general meaning of "good news," there was another more specific meaning in the ancient world. *Euangelion* also referred to an official governmental announcement of some particular good news for the whole Roman Empire. So, for instance, the empire could wish an emperor an official and public "Happy Birthday" using the word "good news," in the sense of a proclamation.

For most English speakers in the twenty-first century, "gospel" is the most common translation of *euangelion*. Since there are writings called "gospels" and since those writings originate by and large in the first two centuries, those ancient writings probably were called gospels in the ancient world and even then were meant to be proclamations that brought good news about Jesus and the people who were around him and came after him. "Gospel" derives from an Old English word, however: *gōdspel*. This Old English word maintains the "good news" interpretation: *gōd* means "good"; and *spel*, "news."

These words in multiple languages may be somewhat confusing. This book mostly addresses the meaning of *euangelion* as the more ordinary meaning of "good news," news that simply designates something about life that is good. Some chapters occasionally use the word "gospel" for "good news" to refer to the ancient and modern writings called gospels. When readers and audiences encountered the word *euangelion* in the first two centuries, the meaning was "good news." "Gospel" as a technical term for early writings that told stories about Jesus came much later.

In the first two centuries, two distinct versions of "good news" go head to head. Rome announces a brash and powerful good news event about the beauty and might of the savior emperor, who destroys his enemies and makes everything right with the world, calling it peace. The budding Jesus schools, parties of the Anointed, and supper clubs, each with different names, announce good news that celebrates a crucified Anointed One and looks forward to a new creation, calling *it* peace.

During this time, tens of thousands of people recognize the "good news" that the Roman Empire announces. It is everywhere. It is the good news that the ruling government has saved all people in the Mediterranean. All these people are no longer in danger, for instance, from pirates on the open seas and thieves in their communities and homes. Civil war is at an end. The good news is that now people are safe. This good news spans thousands of miles. In addition, the government and its allies have built extensive and (mostly) safe roads to everywhere. There are magnificent cities with stunning buildings. Baths are built for all, and towering aqueducts carry water into the cities. Countless large and small boats carry goods all over the ocean. The golden age of *Pax Romana* was, indeed, peace for Romans. Empire certainly had its advantages.

The major caveat to this "peace," however, as described in Chapter 3, was that most people in the Roman Empire experienced it as oppression. For these people, the definition of "good news" came in smaller doses and was mostly experienced in communities. People in these small groups found good in relationships. They were thankful for the solidarity with others that provided them with help and support in daily life. These groups were known for their joy and compassion. They claimed a wisdom that pointed toward values of generosity, experiments in how to live, and bonding with one another. Their lives centered around regular meals together and public bathing in smaller groups. Most of them had an ongoing relationship with Jesus after his death, many of them focusing on Jesus as the Anointed King of Israel. Other groups formed local schools to explore their understanding of kindness, joy, Jesus's teachings, mutual support, and the reign of Israel's God in their world. Others became groups that lived together, often as ordinary families but many others as experimental families, living apart from bloodlines. These fresh practices, encounters, and developments were the other good news (explored more in the following chapters of this book).

The good news of Jesus and friends inspired people to resist Roman power and violence, creating new concepts of what should be considered "good news."

Good News Carved in Stone

"Good news" first appeared as a political term with Rome's first emperor, Gaius Octavian. The Senate gave him the title Augustus, "exalted one," for his defeat of Mark Anthony and Cleopatra, which ended a long-running civil war and brought peace to the empire. This was *Pax Romana*, the original good news of peace and salvation for all.

An inscription from the reign of Caesar Augustus from Asia Minor celebrates the birthday of the emperor as the good news:

> Since Providence, who has ordered all things and has great interest in our life, has perfectly ordered life by giving us Augustus, whom she filled with virtue that he might benefit humankind, sending him as savior for us and for those coming after us, that he might end war and arrange all things. Since he, Caesar, by his appearance, surpassed even our anticipations beyond all previous benefactors, he did not even leave to posterity any hope of exceeding what he has done. In this way the birthday of the god Augustus was the beginning of the good news for the world that existed because of him.[1]

The inscription, known as the Priene Calendar ("calendar" because Augustus ushers in a new age), piles on the accolades. Augustus is proclaimed as:

- The occasion of perfectly ordered life
- Savior of all
- Ender of war
- Greatest of all benefactors

- God Augustus
- The one whose birthday is the beginning of the good news for the world

If it's good, Augustus is the cause.

The Gemma Augustea

A small engraved onyx stone dating to the early first century CE encapsulates the Roman worldview of good news. It is commonly referred to as the Gemma Augustea. The delicacy

The Gemma Augustea (7.5 × 9 in.), attributed to the Roman workshop of the artist Dioskourides. Now part of the Kunsthistorisches Museum collection in Vienna.
Wikimedia Commons

and fineness of the engraving speaks for the prerogative and privilege of the people represented by, possessing, and viewing this gem. Its very richness speaks of empire. This beautiful household piece was probably commissioned by a member of the imperial family. Such portraits were widespread and a part of imperial propaganda.

The good news is framed in the tension between the upper panel, replete with success, leisure, and power, and the lower panel of struggle, pain, and implied death. On top is the world of power and peace; on the bottom is the world of imperial violence.[2]

The upper panel forms the focus of the composition. By design the eye is drawn to Augustus seated on a divan, dressed as the god Jupiter. To his left is the queenlike goddess Rome in battle garb, facing the emperor. They sit together on a divan like a married couple. Jupiter's eagle gazes up adoringly at the emperor. To the right of the emperor are three figures. The figure crowning Augustus with a wreath of oak leaves is the inhabited world (*oikoumene*), symbolizing the submission of the whole world to Augustus. The female figure seated next to the divan is Mother Earth, with a cornucopia and two children representing fertility. Increasing Roman fertility rates was a major part of Augustus's return to traditional Roman family values. The final figure on the right, between the inhabited world and Mother Earth, is the ocean (Neptune). Thus, all the creatures of the world, the earth, and the oceans support Augustus. The cosmos is his.

The upper and the lower panels appear separated as two different worlds. But there is a subtle and important connection between them: beneath the feet of Augustus and Rome are the shields of the defeated contestants, overlapping into the world of contest and turmoil below ever so slightly.

The lower panel pictures a military victory over the "barbarian" (non-Roman "other") nations. In contrast to the upper panel, there is no central organizing viewpoint; nothing detracts attention from Augustus above. The panel does divide into two sections, however. On the far right are two prisoners. Their nakedness and long hair symbolize that they are barbarians, probably Celts or Germans. Those barbarians who survive this battle will be enslaved for the greater glory of Rome. The woman is being pulled by her hair and the man is pleading for mercy.

The left side of the panel pictures a triumphant soldier raising the standard of victory. In the grouping of three men pulling on a rope, a central figure stands out and wears the helmet of Mars, the god of war. Below the standard are two more barbarians showing obvious signs of grief and despair. The unshown but implied scene is the binding of the barbarians to the victory standard.

The lower panel depicts a turbulent world of Roman victory and non-Roman defeat, despair, and desperation. The one figure with its back to the viewer is the goddess Diana with her hunting spears. She stretches out her hand to a fallen barbarian who kneels, pleading for mercy. Diana suggests the magnanimity of the Romans in victory, oddly paralleling the beauty of the carved stone itself and the serenity of the upper panel.

The suggested magnanimity of Diana is a ruse, however. The beauty of the carved gem should not cause us to miss the primary statement of Roman good news. Rome's good news is not just beautiful, muscular rule by the beautiful, muscular bodies of the emperor and supporting gods. The empire's good news is that the elite rule over the rest of the world with an iron fist by divine fiat. The Gemma Augustea pictures in miniature a world writ large. Roman peace and prosperity come through military might. The violence of military conquest is the engine that drives the empire. This gem, carved during the difficult and brutal Germanic wars led by Tiberius during the first century, reinforces the empire's right to carry on such brutal campaigns. Roman good news is for those in command, with misery for the rest. There is no doubt about the haunting message of this good news.

Good News in Speech

The promulgation of Caesar Augustus's good news prompted the various movements of the Anointed Jesus to claim their own good news. A version of their own celebratory inscription can be found in one of the letters of the teacher and envoy of the Anointed, Paul, to the holy ones in Corinth. This good news is not about the birthday of the savior of the world:

> I want you to understand better the meaning of the good
> news I preached to you, my friends, that you received
> and is the ground on which you stand and by which you
> are being saved . . . I passed on to you as of paramount
> importance what I also had received: that the Anointed
> died to free us from the seductive power of corruption
> according to the scriptures, and that he was buried, and
> that he was raised "on the third day" according to the
> scriptures. (1 Cor. 15:1–4)[3]

This good news also involves being saved, but its signs are very different. It is identified with the Anointed who was defeated and whom God vindicated. Even more, this God is aligned with the holy writings of a nation defeated and conquered by Rome. How is a defeated nation, a defeated Anointed King, a defeated God good news?

Practicing Good News

The new good news paved the way for an insistent and growing set of practices and lifestyles for surviving and being safer
during the first two centuries of the Common Era. This kind
of life had a great deal of integrity and was not delusional or
simply imagined. The good news of Chloe's people in 1 Corinthians, the gender creativity of groups of adult men called "the
Children" in the Gospel of Matthew, hundreds of groups called
"the Students of Jesus," and many different versions of the party
of the Anointed were joyful alternatives to the good news proclaimed by the Roman Empire. To discover these alternatives,
we follow their practices, what they did, and how they built
group cohesion.

Sharing Communal Meals

Communal meals are the practice that comes closest to being universally characteristic of the widest range of early Jesus
groups. These meals attracted people who had lost other connections through violence, poverty, or the disruption of family
connections. The exuberant moods of these meals, the chance
for people to have both light and heavy conversations, and
the humor characteristic of these meetings reframed what life
could be for the many people experiencing disruption. Eating
regularly in groups of six to fifteen developed intimacy, loyalty, community, shared values, and intelligence. Chapter 12
examines in detail communal meals and how they were both
a threat to the government and a way for people to build safe
connections.

Creating Wisdom Circles

Much of the Gospels of Matthew, Mark, Luke, and John in
the New Testament, as well as the Gospels of Mary and Thomas,

depict Jesus and his students teaching in marketplaces, at community meals, on roads, at seasides, and in fields. Their teaching was directed mostly to people at work, on the way someplace, or in their neighborhoods. The teaching and learning occurred in groups with lots of discussion. Our sources point strongly toward the teaching in the form of small sayings like parables, proverbs, questions and answers, and short stories, most not lasting more than two to three minutes. Topics of conversation were rarely formally philosophical and not explicitly about heaven or politics. Rather, the main topics were about work, nature, relationships, conflict, sickness, and possessions. The approach to all of these give-and-take discussions varied between debate, humor, and consensus.

It is hard to overestimate what these kinds of conversations can do for people who experience them day after day—as was the case in the first two centuries. Spending a great deal of time in dialogue leads to learning about life, people, and nature; building working relationships and friendships; learning skills in meaning making, strategic thinking, and community building. The ancients called this wisdom, so we might call these kinds of conversations "wisdom circles." Wisdom regularly explores long-term projects, God or some other kind of ultimate concept, and loss and pain. Such engagement with the everyday is good news.

Developing Identity by Belonging

As we saw in Chapter 3, living with and resisting violence—as well as the brokenness of families and nations and the difficulty of finding any sense of belonging—was a great challenge for people under the Roman Empire. By policy, Rome classified peoples it had conquered as barbarians, that is, not fully human.

Large portions of the population needed to rethink and reinvent themselves. Although many today see the development of identity as an individual task, that is not generally the case across humanity. Rather, growth and elaboration of identity are more often social and communal. Many of the Anointed groups created a sense of belonging by following Jesus as the Anointed King of subjugated Israel. This was an imaginative new identity or form of belonging. A fascinating aspect of this new identity/belonging was the announcement that people were no longer Judean or Greek, enslaved or free, woman or man, but they were all one in Jesus, the Anointed King of Israel (Gal. 3:28). The inventiveness of this new identity lay in its explicit invitation to all kinds of different ethnic, gendered, and enslaved people to think of themselves as a part of Israel, whose God was on their side.

On a less grand scheme, some women of Corinth had a new identity as "Chloe's people." They established new sexual and intellectual practices that changed their understanding of marriage. In following their teacher Paul away from marriage, the group identity of Chloe's people created a new space for them. Likewise, those who followed Thecla as the "Enslaved of God" eschewed marriage. When people in the letter *To the Ephesians* are called "the faithful brothers," this naming could very well refer to a specific kind of voluntary family group of only men who are claiming an identity of men who stand against traditional family. These men may be experimenting with a group identity different from the one they lost in either broken families or conquered nations.

Since there are so many groups, clubs, schools, and movements that did not have a particular name or whose name we do not know, how to characterize the new group identities or belongings of those people is difficult. Finding oneself in a group of compassion and new possibilities, though, is good news.

Building Confidence and Trust

Confidence and trust were two of the most important values in these early groups and movements. Roman propaganda worked tirelessly to persuade the conquered that they should fear the empire and that resistance put one in mortal danger. The Roman Empire could and did destroy those under its thumb. But the communities of the Anointed taught tirelessly that one should not be afraid, but confident. They contain many stories of women facing sickness, death, and danger who nevertheless stand firm with confidence. In these stories their confidence is rewarded, and they are seldom harmed. They trust in themselves or God, or both.

In the New Testament, the word "confidence" or "trust" occurs 252 times. A typical example is the story of the woman who has been bleeding for twelve years who touches Jesus and is healed. He tells her, "Daughter, your trust has cured you" (Mark 5:34). Pithy teachings of these groups constantly shout out encouragement of confidence and trust. Here are just a few:

Congratulations to those who grieve. They will be consoled.
  (Matt. 5:4)
Congratulations to those who hunger and thirst for justice. They
  will have a feast. (Matt. 5:6)
Don't fret about your life, what you're going to eat, or about your
  body, what you're going to wear. Remember, there is more to
  living than food and clothing . . . Think about how the lilies
  grow; they don't toil and they never spin. (Matt. 6:25, 28)[4]

Why is this ringing endorsement for confidence and trust so absent from most translations? The Greek word *pistis* is conventionally translated as "faith" or "belief." Recently, scholars agree that these conventional translations of *pistis* are misleading. The ancient meaning of *pistis* is properly translated in contemporary English as "confidence" or "trust," as in having trust in a particular person or people.

This kind of trust and confidence transforms community from being fearful to being loving. The practice of trust and confidence was the engine that put heart into these communities whose members found themselves belonging to one another. The wind goes out of the sails of life when *pistis* becomes "belief in" some truth instead of confidence or trust. In the first two centuries, even when groups believed different things, their practice of confidence was good news. And practice was what counted.

ASSESSING THE TWO KINDS OF GOOD NEWS

As the Gemma Augustea makes clear, Rome's definition of good news was more socially and politically powerful than that of the communities of Jesus Anointed. Rome's definition built more impressive cities and monuments, killed more people, and conquered far more nations. Rome saved more people from pirates on the open sea and kept more cities safe from invading armies. Roman infrastructure—water, roads, baths—improved many lives dramatically. But Rome also intentionally and accidentally broke apart millions of families, tribes, and nations.

We were tempted earlier in this chapter to write that the good news of Chloe's people, the Confident Party of the Anointed One, the Students, the Members from the Odes of Solomon, and other Jesus groups paled in comparison to Rome's good news. But when the practices of these plethora of communities is assessed, a lot more is revealed than just crazy clubs and exaggerated fantasies. When carefully examined, the practices of sharing communal meals, forming wisdom circles and schools, developing identities, and building confidence and trust can be seen as creating healthy communities with a wide range of examples of authentic good news. This kind of good news in many groups countered the violence and dominance of Rome. These practices taught groups and movements different values, communal skills, bright new ideas, and strategies of resistance that created new forms of safety. The strength and agility produced by these practices enabled these groups to survive and resist Roman damage. In the midst of social brokenness and state violence that was producing many difficulties and problems, real good news found a place. That is good news.

Papers Relevant to This Chapter by Seminar Participants

Dewey, Arthur. "Switchback Codes: Paul, Apocalyptic and the Art of Resistance." Fall 2015.

5

VIOLENCE IN STONE

MEMORIAL

The Arch of Titus, an honorific arch located at the head of the Roman Forum and built in 81 CE, is a vivid picture of the recapturing for Rome of the territory of Israel in the first century. The arch explains the real beginning of our larger rewriting: a context of massive crucifixion and of the wrecking of the central symbol of Israel's monotheism, the Temple in Jerusalem. These events were of crucial importance in the first two centuries for the many and varied followers of Abraham, Moses, and Jesus. The arch memorializes the emperor Titus's great accomplishment—the reduction of Israel, which had successfully broken away from Rome's control in 66 CE, to an enslaved state. The final act in this retaking of Judea was the siege and sacking of Jerusalem and then the destruction of the Temple of the Judeans. Since so little survives from the ancient world, that this arch of all arches should have endured into the twenty-first century is telling. This "accomplishment" of the emperor is carved into the surface of the arch, offering a concrete and complex depiction of Roman power and Israel's political disappearance for 1,950 years.

Monuments celebrating a conquering general's great victory always hide the pain of those who were defeated. The Arch of Titus is no different. It exults in the divinity of the conquering hero, while exhibiting the violence that lies at the heart of imperial Rome's *Pax Romana*, or Roman peace. It also foretells the violence the followers of Jesus Anointed are to face. But to ferret out this twisting and twisted story, we must coax the silent stones of the Arch of Titus to tell their story.

The arch was built shortly after the death of the emperor Titus in 81 CE by his brother, the new emperor Domitian. In the tradition of Roman emperors, Domitian declared his dead brother to be a god. There is a certain irony in this declaration, given the relationship between these brothers. Allegedly, Titus's last reported words were "I have made but one mistake."[1] Ancient Romans debated the meaning of these words and the circumstances of Titus's death—did Domitian poison his brother, or just abandon him when Titus fell ill? The Roman history writer Dio Cassius suggests that Titus's mistake was not killing his brother Domitian when he had the chance.[2] Violence lies at the very heart of the Roman Empire, within the imperial family itself—not the serene, beautiful portrait, certainly, that we viewed in the Gemma Augustea, in the previous chapter.

Before the Arch

What is knowable about the movements that traced back to Jesus before the building of the Arch of Titus is very limited and often buried in the obscurity of myth and legend. The first major effort to tell the story of the origins of Jesus and his legacy, a writing now known as Gospel of Mark, was most likely written about the time of the Arch's construction. The first story of the origins of the larger movement, the Acts of the Apostles, does not occur until the first quarter of the second century, well after the building of the arch.[3]

Paul, an envoy among the early Jesus followers, provides one of the few windows into how these groups viewed themselves before the Arch of Titus. Paul was neither founding nor joining a new religion. A Judean, he wanted to get the members of the nations into the covenant of Israel. He did not see this new covenant between the God of Israel and the nations as replacing the covenant between God and the people of Israel, but rather as the final fulfillment of God's promise to Abraham that he would be the father of many nations. Paul remained a part of the people of Israel, and according to his teaching, those members of the nations who trust in Jesus the Anointed became children of Abraham and a part of Israel, too.

During the period before the building of the Arch of Titus, various groups attached to Jesus are working out their identities within the people of Israel. There is no one set way of doing this. The debate over circumcision in Paul's letters, for instance, illustrates the different ways that followers of Jesus considered themselves as being part of Israel, as does the larger claim of the Gospel of Matthew that they, not the Pharisees, are the true Israelites. Group identity is not clear; that negotiation and experimentation will go on for a long time.

THE JUDEAN-ROMAN WAR

In 66 CE, a revolt broke out in Judea, the southern part of Israel. We are well informed about this revolt because a participant, Flavius Josephus, wrote a history of the events that has survived. His name "Flavius" indicates that his patrons, his essential social and financial supporters, were the Flavians, an important family in Rome. Indeed, the very general that the emperor Nero placed in charge of putting down the Judean revolt was Titus Flavius Vespasian, more commonly known simply as Vespasian. The emperor Titus was his son.

Josephus was born Yosef ben Matityahu (Joseph son of Matthias). He was a priest of Israel and reports that he was a Pharisee, a relatively new and innovative group within Israel in the first century. When captured by the Romans in 67 CE, however, he became an advisor to Vespasian and Titus, who in turn became his patrons. His allegiances, to say the least, are complicated. Josephus, as is clear from his name alone, was not a neutral observer. His history of the Judean War needs to be read with his specific allegiances in mind.

Josephus's patrons, the family named Flavian, was a plebeian family from Rome, that is, not part of Rome's aristocracy. They were actually the first plebeian family to rule the empire. The Flavians were the only dynasty in which succession was by natural birth alone without any adoption of extended family.

After several Roman disasters in putting down the revolt in Israel, the emperor Nero gave Vespasian four legions to command; he was a competent but not brilliant general. Most important, Nero thought Vespasian was no threat to his power so was not someone to be feared politically. Vespasian, however, was in no hurry to end the revolt because the Judeans needed to be punished; they needed to become an example of why revolt against Rome was unwise. Furthermore, Nero's grasp on power was tenuous, and Vespasian knew that interesting opportunities might present themselves to a Roman general with so many legions under his command.

Vespasian arrived on the scene in Judea to begin a slow,

gradual, and grinding reduction of the revolt. It was in the early stages of "pacification" (that is, the subjugation of Judean peoples through violence) that Josephus was captured.

Nero's suicide in 68 CE led to political chaos—a time known as the Year of Four Emperors, the last of whom was Vespasian. As things began to crumble, Vespasian saw his opportunity and seized it. In short order, his troops proclaimed him emperor, he turned against the third emperor Vitellius, made quick alliances with other generals in the eastern part of the empire, took Egypt, and defeated Vitellius. On December 21, 69 CE, the day following the defeat of Vitellius, the Roman Senate proclaimed Vespasian emperor.

With Vespasian in control of the empire and having the title of emperor, he needed a military victory to bolster and solidify his claims to authority. After all, what made an emperor an emperor was military might and victories. The Latin word *imperator*, which we translate "emperor" but might better be translated "conqueror," originated in a proclamation by the troops after a great military victory. With its basic meaning of commander or general, the title always retained a strong overtone of military victory.

To consolidate his rule, Vespasian dispatched his son Titus to bring the revolt in Judea to an end and plunder Jerusalem. Titus quickly brought the main elements of the revolt to a conclusion, but resistance had been long and fierce. Jerusalem had been in the hands of the Judean rebels for four years, since 66 CE. The city was strongly fortified by three walls.

At this point, Josephus's story of the war becomes important. After Josephus's capture, Vespasian gave him the high honor of Roman citizenship in 69 CE. Yosef ben Matityahu was now Flavius Josephus, a client of the emperor. Josephus was free to tell the story of this war and the history of the Judean peoples, but his audience was the emperor. Josephus becomes a historian, but his history is told for the empire, for the honor of Rome.

Josephus does offer a unique perspective as a historian: he was on the ground as a military commander and was familiar with both Judeans and Romans. He describes Titus's siege of Jerusalem under Vespasian in great detail: according to his history called *The Jewish War*, more than one million people were killed during the attack on and destruction of Jerusalem, and around one hundred thousand were enslaved. Numbers are very unreliable in ancient accounts, but it is clear that the number of people killed during this siege was extreme.

The Roman troops captured those fleeing from the city to gather food and began to crucify them before the city walls. According to Josephus, they crucified five hundred Judeans a day, so many that there was a shortage of wood in the area.[4] Josephus is at pains to indicate Titus's pity for those suffering, but nevertheless the slaughter continued. His story is an interesting mix of both honoring Rome and pitying the suffering Judeans. The sole purpose of these massive numbers of crucifixions, Josephus tells us, is to terrorize those remaining in the city:

> [Titus's] main reason for not stopping the crucifixions was the hope that the spectacle might perhaps induce the Jews to surrender, for fear that continued resistance would involve them in a similar fate. The soldiers out of rage and hatred amused themselves by nailing their prisoners in different postures; and so great was their number, that space could not be found for the crosses nor crosses for the bodies. (*The Jewish War* V.449–451)

When the Roman legions finally broke through the city walls, the rebels fortified the Temple, the heart of Judean ritual. According to Josephus, Titus's intention was to bring the revolt and the siege of Jerusalem to a quick end. A council of generals disagreed on the proper fate of the Temple, but Titus—at least according to Josephus—decided to keep the Temple intact:

> Titus, however, declared that, even were the Jews to mount it [the Temple] and fight therefrom, he would not wreak vengeance on inanimate objects instead of men, nor under any circumstances burn down so magnificent a work; for the loss would affect the Romans, inasmuch as it would be an ornament to the empire if it stood. (*The Jewish War* VI.241–242)

Titus implies that the Romans' war is with people, not with the house of a god. The beauty of that Temple, and the god it honored, could be incorporated into the empire, a visual celebration of Roman dominance over the known world.

But that is not what happened. Given Josephus's complicated and compromised relationship with the Flavians, especially Titus, some historians have doubted his view of Titus's motives. Did Titus really want to save the Temple? Given the way he so publicly acknowledged and celebrated its destruction, it is hard to imagine he did not intend it. On the other hand, Josephus was there and was close to Titus; what would he gain by undercutting Titus's propaganda victory? It is hard to decide. History is full of these unresolvable questions.

In Josephus's dramatic account of the destruction of the Temple, he writes: "At this moment, one of the soldiers, awaiting no orders and with no horror of so dread a deed, but moved by some supernatural impulse, snatched a brand from the burning timber and, hoisted up by one of his comrades, flung the fiery missile through a low golden door" (*The Jewish War* VI.252–253). Once the fire started, things merely got out of hand. According to Josephus, the Jerusalem Temple, the heart of Judean religious worship and tradition, was destroyed by accident.

THE ARCH OF TITUS

Accidental destruction: How does Josephus's history fit with the history depicted on the Arch of Titus? Are the stories of the arch and of Josephus the same? Is it odd that Titus's military campaign would be memorialized through an image of an accident? Or did Titus destroy the Temple on purpose, intentionally destabilizing the religious and social lives of the people of Israel?

The Arch of Titus was built to be seen. It dominates the highest point on the Via Sacra, marking a prominent entrance into the Roman Forum. It is 50 feet high, 13.5 feet wide, and 15.5 feet deep. On the attic of the arch, right at the top, is the original inscription:

THE SENATE

AND THE ROMAN PEOPLE

[DEDICATE THIS] TO THE DIVINE TITUS, SON OF VESPASIAN,

VESPASIAN AUGUSTUS

The interior of the arch consists of three panels, all in marble relief. The north panel pictures Titus as the successful general in his triumphal procession after the victory in Jerusalem. This triumphal march took place in 71 CE and was a joint victory for both Vespasian and Titus. Vespasian, however, is missing from this depiction.

Prominently on view, accompanying Titus in a chariot, is the goddess Winged Victory, who is crowning him with a laurel

A panel from the first century CE Roman monument the Arch of Titus. Riding in a chariot drawn by four horses, the goddess Victoria (Victory) crowns the emperor Titus. They ride the chariot into the conquered city of Jerusalem.

Daderot, Wikimedia Commons

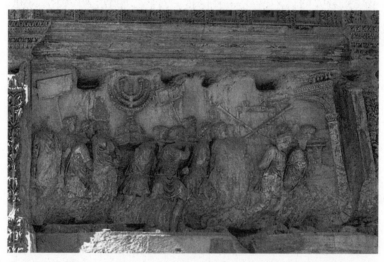

Known as the "Spoils of Jerusalem," this panel on the Arch of Titus depicts the sacred treasures of the Jerusalem Temple being carried into Rome as part of a triumphal procession. These treasures include a menorah, the Table of the Bread of the Presence, trumpets, and other sacred cups and vessels.

Jebulon, Wikimedia Commons

wreath, a sign of victory. The depiction of the victorious chariot
with its four horses and Winged Victory is a traditional cliché,
frequently found on coins and other items. But in the standard
mythology of the triumph, an enslaved person stands behind the
triumphing general, whispering to him, "Look behind you. Remember you are a man."[5] Significantly, in this visual version of
the mythology preserved on the arch, there is no enslaved person. This shifts the standard way of visualizing a triumph to emphasize Titus's divinity, as Winged Victory crowns him. Leading
the chariot is the goddess Rome in battle gear with bared breast,
symbolizing Rome's military might.

The south panel, immediately opposite the first one, depicts
the Roman legionnaires carrying in the triumphal procession
booty from the Temple in Jerusalem that will eventually be
placed in the newly built Temple of Peace in the Forum of Vespasian. The menorah stands out, along with golden trumpets
and the Bread of Presence table, so named for loaves of bread
that were always signaling the presence of God.

The panel in the vault depicts the raising into heaven
(*apotheōsis*) of Titus. Zeus in the form of an eagle bears him
aloft. This is the point of the arch and Domitian's point in its
construction—to announce the divinity of this brother, and by
association, his family and himself. While the divinity of the
triumphant general was temporary, the divinity proclaimed by
this arch was permanent. Titus was now one of the gods.

Logic of the Arch

The Arch of Titus tells the story of Titus's rising to the status of
a god, but it also lays out in stone the imperial logic of power and
divinity. Two panels depict Titus as a god: in the north panel,
where he is crowned by Winged Victory, and in the panel in the
vault, where he is shown ascending into heaven with Jupiter.

Titus is a god because he triumphed over the God of Israel. This triumph is evidenced in the south panel with its prominent display of the booty from the Judean Temple. This is the logic of Roman imperial might: we Romans must be in the gods' favor and Titus must be a god because we defeated your god. Without that triumph over the Temple, the earthly home of a god, Titus's claim to god-status is unconvincing.

The defeat of the Judeans featured prominently in the propaganda of the Flavians, further bolstering their claims to divinity. All three of the Flavians issued coins with the legend "Judea Captured."

One of the most famous edifices of the Roman world, the Colosseum, was intimately associated with the defeat of the Judean revolt and the destruction of Jerusalem's Temple. Origi-

From the inside of the arch, this relief shows the emperor Titus's *apotheōsis* or his being made into a god.
Martom Bax, Wikimedia Commons

nally known as the Flavian Amphitheater, the Colosseum stood near the Arch of Titus on the spot where the previous emperor Nero's enormous and notorious palace, the Golden House, had stood. The gigantic amphitheater supported the Flavian propaganda machine. According to a recent reconstruction of the original dedication, the cost of building the amphitheater came from Vespasian's share of the booty from the sack of Jerusalem.[6] The Roman Colosseum was built with stolen property. Furthermore, many of the twenty thousand enslaved Judeans Titus brought back to Rome were involved in the quarrying of the stone for the amphitheater and its construction.

ROME'S RESPONSE TO ITS OWN VIOLENCE

Roman elites were well aware of the empire's violence, but they had a solution. The emperors were very successful at co-opting others into the values of the empire. Along the Appian Way, one of the most important roads into Rome, stands a monument in memory of three men: Baricha, Zabda, and Achiba. These men, as argued by the classicist Mary Beard, were likely part of the Judean rebellion, brought to Rome in enslavement by Titus and sold to a Roman citizen by the name of Lucius Valerius.[7] Lucius Valerius eventually freed them and gave them Roman citizenship, shown on the monument in the attachment of Lucius Valerius to each man's name: the plain Judean name "Baricha" becomes "Baricha, freedman of Lucius Valerius." Judean and Roman identities become intertwined. By the mid-second century, half the population of the city of Rome were descendants of enslaved people. Some responded to Roman violence by eventually becoming citizens, while others joined communities of Jesus Anointed.

Flavian Propaganda

While Josephus may well be right about Titus's intention not to destroy the Temple, once it was destroyed, Titus doubled down. Its destruction had to be presented as a great Roman victory, hence Vespasian and Titus's triumph, the building of the Flavian Amphitheater, multiple coins celebrating *Judea Capta* (Judea's capture), and the Arch of Titus. The Flavian propaganda machine was on a roll.

Not rebuilding the Judean Temple was against long-standing Roman policy. Romans did not go to war against a nation's gods, but against its people. Destroyed temples were always rebuilt. Conquered people's gods were invited into the Roman pantheon. The emperor and the empire brought benefits.

In Josephus's extensive description of Titus's triumph, he enumerates the piles of booty from the conquering of Judea and the many golden vessels from the wasted Temple of Jerusalem, "and last of all the spoils, was carried the Law of the Judeans" (*The Jewish War* VII.150–151). This was war not only on the people of Israel but also on their God. Vespasian and Titus's triumph and not rebuilding the Jerusalem Temple set policy both for the Flavians and for the remainder of antiquity. All the subsequent emperors followed their lead. Upon the death of Domitian in 96 CE, the next emperor, Nerva, and the following Antoine dynasty of emperors continued the Flavian policy. After that, it became set in stone, almost literally.

AFTERMATH

Tensions remained strong in Judea, especially as Roman settlement increased, and the people of Israel were forced out of their homeland. The tensions reached a crisis when the emperor Hadrian (reign, 117–138 CE) built a new city named Aelia Capitolina at the site of the destroyed Jerusalem. This remained the official name for Jerusalem until the Arab conquest in 638 CE, when it was renamed Iliyā', the Arab name derived from the Roman name Aelia.

Hadrian escalated tensions yet again when he began the construction of a temple on the site of the old Judean Temple that he dedicated to Jupiter Capitolinus, named after the temple in Rome, which was the final destination of Vespasian and Titus's triumph and the principal temple of that city. The intended insult could not have been more direct. This was Roman erasure of Judean presence. This in turn provoked the Bar Kokhba War of Judean rebellion in 132–136 CE.

The political environment created by the Flavians and their successors is the context in which all the stories of good news, the gospels, were written and much of what later became the New Testament. The Roman Empire's stance toward the people of Israel also affected, shaped, and distorted the emerging Jesus peoples' movements as they interacted with their fellow inheritors of Israel's traditions and eventually grew into the Christian church.

All of this, as Josephus would have it, stemmed from a military accident—all from an unintended consequence: a fire accidentally started, a sacking of a city that got out of hand. History is not inevitable and historical events often are unintentional. Was the destruction of the Jerusalem Temple, like much of history, also unintentional? We cannot ever know for sure. The Arch of Titus, even with its mixed-up history, demonstrates how Rome's violent conquest of Israel provides a complicated, tangled frame for and a direction going forward for the Jesus peoples' agony and hope.

We don't have any images of crucifixions from the ancient

world, even though mass crucifixions are often described in literature. The Arch of Titus and the many other triumphal arches scattered around the Roman world are an effort to mask that horror in a fantasy of Roman glory. The massiveness and endurance of the arch demonstrates what those who chose to follow the Anointed King of Israel were up against. The arch announces how devastating is the power that will come down on those who resist. The Roman historian Tacitus quotes a British chieftain staring down ruin by Rome: "To plunder, butcher, steal, these things [Romans] misname empire: they make a desolation and they call it peace" (*Agricola* 30.5).[8]

Even though it falls outside of the first two centuries, one more issue remains that directly flows from the Arch of Titus. What had been the policy of the Flavians toward the Judeans became the policy of succeeding emperors throughout antiquity, and then of the Christian church afterward. The significance of this transfer of the anti-Jewish policy of the Flavians, first to the subsequent emperors and then to the Christian church, cannot be overestimated. This is the genesis of the twisted and tragic Christian church policy of anti-Judaism and anti-Semitism. The violence continues.

Papers Relevant to This Chapter by Seminar Participants

Scott, Brandon. "The Arch of Titus." Spring 2018.

———. "Review and Evaluation of Martin Goodman's *Rome and Jerusalem*: Impact on the Rise of Christianity." Fall 2015.

Wendt, Heidi. "From the Herodians to Hadrian: The Shifting Status of Judean Religion in Post-Flavian Rome." Fall 2015.

6

THE DEATHS OF HEROES

Living under *Pax Romana*, the Roman peace, could be dangerous. This peace brought many benefits, about which the emperors were always reminding their subjects, but was maintained by an overwhelming military force. Resistance could be lethal. The conquered nations all told stories of their heroes who died for the cause. Having heard of so much Roman cruelty in the previous three chapters, we turn now toward a major way conquered people, including Jesus peoples, coped.

THE NOBLE DEATH

Socrates
The most famous hero in the ancient world who died for a cause was not someone who died at the hands of an empire, but of a democratic government. The death of the Greek philosopher Socrates in 399 BCE became the archetype of all such "noble deaths." His death was much commented on in the ancient world and has continued to inspire thinkers and artists to this day. Socrates wrote nothing but was a frequent character in Plato's dialogues. Whether we are hearing Socrates's voice

or Plato's in these dialogues is highly debated, as in the various gospels concerning Jesus's voice.

Why did the ancients admire Socrates's death and think it so important? The primary reason was that he stood up to what he perceived to be the tyranny of the state. Socrates opposed democracy. He did not think that a vote of the majority was the correct way to determine the truth. That was available to only a few wise men after much hard work. The prosecutor brought two charges against Socrates: impiety against the pantheon of Athens' gods and corrupting the youth of the city. Socrates admitted that if he was let off with a lesser punishment than death, he would continue to teach the same things, as he said, to sting his fellow Athenians. He even described himself as the gods' greatest gift to Athens. A majority of the five hundred jurors voted for conviction.

In discussions with the prosecutor, Socrates joked that for his punishment he should get free meals from the city, an honor normally reserved for the city's benefactors and victorious athletes. He also offered to pay a fine, and his friends offered an even more substantial sum. The prosecutor remained firm, insisting on the death penalty. Ironically, more jurors voted to sentence Socrates to death than voted for conviction.

His friends pleaded with him to flee the city into exile, which was expected by all and was a well-established tradition. But Socrates had taught that it was the duty of all citizens to follow the laws of the city, so he refused to go into exile. Instead, he drank the poison hemlock, bringing about his death. Taking the hemlock was his individual decision as to what was just and good. By this act, standing up to tyranny became the fundamental aspect of the noble death.

A second aspect of the noble death is that it demonstrates self-mastery, a primary value in both Greek and Roman education. Self-mastery included control of the self and control of the passions. The emphasis was not on abstract knowledge, but on self-control that ensured integrity and overall character. Death, of course, was the last challenge to self-control. To take control of one's own death would be the ultimate sign of controlling the passions, of self-mastery.

This self-mastery is clearly evident in the account of Socrates's last hours in Plato's writing *Phaedo*. After Socrates took his bath, his gathered friends began to cry. Socrates said: "Really, my friends, what a way to behave! Why, that was my main reason for sending away the women, to prevent this sort of disturbance; because I am told that one should make one's end in a tranquil frame of mind. Calm yourselves and try to be brave!" (*Phaedo* 117d–e).[1]

Self-control and mastery of the passions are male virtues, and so Socrates not only excludes the females so that a quiet, controlled atmosphere will prevail, but he accuses the men of behaving like women. Plato remarks, "We controlled our tears": self-mastery prevails.

Plato remarks that Socrates "quite calmly and with no sign of distaste . . . drained the cup in one breath" (*Phaedo* 117c). As Socrates dies, he remains calm the entire time. His last words are to his student Crito, "We ought to offer a cock to Asclepius," the god of healing (*Phaedo* 118a). He dies remaining faithful to his civic duties.

Taking control of one's death in the face of tyranny also demonstrates one's good name. Even the jailer testifies to Socrates's good name: "I have come to know during this time that you are the noblest and the gentlest and the bravest of all the men that have ever come here" (*Phaedo* 116c). At the very conclusion of *Phaedo*, the writing's last words echo the jailer's testimony: "Such . . . was the end of our comrade, who was, we may fairly say, of all those whom we know in our time, the bravest and also the wisest and most upright man" (*Phaedo* 118).

Other Noble Deaths

The philosopher Zeno (ca. 430 BCE), who lived before Socrates, was involved in a conspiracy to overthrow the tyrant Nearchus. When tortured to reveal the names of his fellow conspirators, he refused. But he told the tyrant he did have another secret to reveal. When the tyrant leaned in to hear, Zeno bit his ear and did not release his bite until he died and the tyrant had lost his ear.

Rome also had its famous examples of noble deaths— including one from the legendary beginnings of Rome that exhibits the noble death of a woman. The noblewoman Lucretia (died 510 BCE) was beautiful and described as a good, faithful wife. Late one night, Sextus Tarquinius, son of the king, at sword point threatened to frame her for adultery if she did not submit to him. Tarquinius raped Lucretia and left, "exulting in his conquest of a woman's honour."[2] She summoned her father and husband and confessed what had happened, asking, "What can be well with a woman when she has lost her honour"?

Lucretia threatened to take her life as her father and husband pleaded with her that the rape was not her fault, but to no avail. "Though I acquit myself of the sin," she said, "I do not absolve myself from punishment." She then plunged a dagger into her chest to demonstrate her virtue. Her kinsmen took revenge, and this led to an outrage on the part of the general populace, which revolted and overthrew the monarchy. Thus began the Roman Republic. A deeply troubling story of sexual assault became a pivotal part of the founding myth of the Roman Republic.

Lucretia's death at her own hand demonstrates the perfidy

and corruption of the Roman kings and leads to their over-throw. It also shows, in this ancient context, her control of her own destiny, even though she is a woman—again, this story must be read in its ancient context—and it preserves and rein-forces her good name and honor, which the rape by Tarquinius had challenged.

The telling of these stories of noble deaths reinforces the cause against tyranny, and the memory of them creates a way for others to envision how to resist tyranny. Lucretia's story is disturbing on many levels, but as an ancient "noble death," we read it in this important context of resistance.

DYING FOR TORAH AND ISRAEL

The people of Israel had their own stories of noble deaths as they struggled against tyranny. The galvanizing moment was the at-tack of Antiochus IV Epiphanes on the very life of the nation of Israel. While exactly what happened has never been success-fully reconstructed, the stories that were told became critically important. The way it was remembered and retold fashioned a new way of viewing Israel's relation to suffering at the hands of tyrants.

Following what he thought was a revolt, Antiochus Epiph-anes ("God Manifest") attacked Jerusalem in 168 BCE and desecrated the Temple. He followed this up with an effort to suppress and abolish the religious life and practice of Israel. He forbade worship in the Temple, as well as circumcision. This was unprecedented in the ancient world and goes against the usual policy at the time, which was to respect the religious prac-tices of conquered populations. The extreme character of An-tiochus's prohibitions led to the Maccabean revolt (beginning in 167 BCE), a brief respite of independence, and then Roman intervention (63 BCE).

These memories provoked a series of stories about those who suffered death during all this mayhem because they refused to cooperate with the decrees of Antiochus. In 2 Maccabees, written sometime in the first century BCE, there appears the story of a mother and her seven sons whom the king tortures to death. He forces them to eat pork to violate Torah. They all refuse, are tortured, and die.

As the second son dies, he calls out to the king, "You accursed wretch, you dismiss us from this present life, but the King of the universe will raise us up to an everlasting renewal of life, because we have died for his laws" (2 Macc. 7:9).[3] This story sees the issue as a direct contest between two kings: King Antiochus IV Epiphanes and the King of the universe. This poses the problem of theodicy, that is, the existence of a good and compassionate God despite the existence of evil. To die as Socrates did for the truth is one thing, but to die for God's law, to die because one is righteous, calls into question the character and very existence of the God of the universe. Being raised up to eternal life is the solution to this problem and argues that Antiochus's offense will not hold.

The youngest son in his speech notes how the death of his brothers is redemptive for the nation of Israel:

> I, like my brothers, give up body and life for the laws of
> our ancestors, appealing to God to show mercy soon to
> our nation and by trials and plagues to make you confess
> that he alone is God, and through me and my brothers to
> bring to an end the wrath of the Almighty that has justly
> fallen on our whole nation. (2 Macc. 7:37–38)

Their noble deaths are not in vain but will benefit the people. The nation deserves to suffer, but the sons' deaths will relieve that need.

The cycle of stories of a mother and her seven sons is retold in 4 Maccabees, written probably in the first century CE. The mother's speech to her sons directly picks up the themes of a noble death:

> My children, noble is the struggle, and since you have
> been summoned to it to bear witness for our nation,
> fight zealously for our ancestral Law. Shameful were
> it indeed that [an] old man should endure agonies for
> piety's sake, while you young men were terrified of
> torments. (4 Macc. 16:16–17)[4]

The cause for which they are dying is directly stated, the ancestral law, and thus their cause is just. They must be noble and not be frightened by torture. To encourage them, the mother rehearses the sacrifices made by their ancestors. The sons stand in a noble tradition, and their deaths will ensure that tradition has a future:

> Remember that it is for God's sake you were given a share
> in the world and the benefit of life . . . for whom our
> father Abraham ventured boldly to sacrifice his son Isaac,
> the father of our nation; and Isaac, seeing his father's
> hand, with knife in it, fall down against him, did not
> flinch. Daniel also, the righteous one, was thrown to the
> lions, and Hananiah and Azariah and Mishael were cast
> into the fiery furnace, and all endured for the sake of
> God. (4 Macc. 16:18–22)

She then applies this same lesson to her sons, saying:

> "Therefore, you who have the same faith in God must
> not be dismayed. For it would be unreasonable for you
> who know true religion not to withstand hardships."
> With these words the mother of the seven exhorted each
> one and persuaded them to die rather than transgress the
> commandment of God. (4 Macc. 16:22–25)

The multiple tellings of this cycle of stories over several centuries points to their continued importance and applicability as a vehicle for understanding the nation of Israel's dealing with a succession of empires, culminating in Rome. The influence of these stories would be considerable going forward in the early Jesus movement as a way of understanding Jesus's crucifixion and then later the deaths of his followers at the hands of Roman authorities for their allegiance to the Anointed of Israel. The noble death model was probably the earliest way by which followers of Jesus began to come to terms with his crucifixion. They drew on a general cultural model and directly from the Maccabean tradition. The tradition of Israel had already thought through this issue.

DYING FOR A FUTURE

In Paul's Letter to the Romans is a fragment of what might be an early "hymn." Since the language is distinctly not Paul's, he appears to be quoting something else: "through the deliverance which is in the Anointed Jesus whom God has put forward as a means of propitiation" (Rom. 3:24).

This passage has often been the go-to text for the idea of sac-
rificial atonement that eventually developed in the Christian
church, but that is not its correct context. Instead, it belongs
to the noble death model. "Propitiation" refers to an act that
gains the favor of the gods. In this case, the execution of Jesus is
described as God putting him forward. The propitiation is not
offered *to* God but *by* God. Why is God putting Jesus forward?
To ensure the future of the people. The closest parallel to the
language of Romans is in 4 Maccabees 17:20–22, where the
narrator is describing the effects of the death of the seven sons
who died for Israel (emphasis added):

> These then, having consecrated themselves for the sake of
> God, are now honored not only with this distinction but also
> by the fact that through them our enemies did not prevail
> against our nation, and the tyrant was punished and our land
> purified, since they became, as it were, a ransom for the sin
> of our nation. *Through the blood* of these righteous ones and
> through the *propitiation* of their death the divine providence
> recused Israel, which had been shamefully treated.

The noble death tradition with a strong presence in the
larger Mediterranean world, as well as an important place in
Israel's understanding of its dealing with the oppression of various empires, naturally aligns with Jesus's crucifixion and provides a way of understanding this tragedy.

Communal Meals and the Noble Death Tradition
As we have seen, communal meals were an important element
in the social formation of the communities of Jesus Anointed
(see more in Chapter 12). These meals also drew upon the noble

death tradition and were often an important aspect of it. The retelling of stories of a person's life and death served to keep the memory and the good name of that person alive after that person's death. These tellings happened most often at meals.

Meals are an important aspect of the commemoration of a hero's noble death because they remind the participants that the hero died resisting the tyrant for the future possibility of the community, whether that community be the community of Socrates or the community of Israel or the community of the Anointed.

Paul introduces his comments about the communal meal in 1 Corinthians 11:23–26 with a stereotyped sentence for the passing on of tradition: "I received from the Lord the same thing I passed on to you" (v. 23).[5] The bread symbolizes the Lord Jesus's body: "This means my body broken for you" (v. 24). "Broken for you" indicates the bloody character of Jesus's death, as well as drawing from the noble death tradition of dying "for" the community, language in line with that we saw in 2 and 4 Maccabees.

The wine coming after the meal indicates that it is a libation; the pouring of the wine is a standard part of the memorial meal. The "new covenant" referenced in 1 Corinthians 11:25 is effected by Jesus's bloody death by crucifixion: "This cup means the new covenant ratified by my blood." In both the bread and wine, heroic language is evoked; there is the explicit call to remember. The hero's noble death of resistance to the tyrant must be remembered to have its effect.

The language in this meal is memorial and mythic, not factual. The memory keeps alive the resistance of original noble death and points to its founding function for the new Anointed peoples and communities: "Do it to remember me" (1 Cor. 11:24, 25).

Paul adds a final comment: "So every time you eat this bread and drink this cup you are proclaiming the death of the Lord until the day when he returns" (1 Cor. 11:26). Apart from the heroic tradition, Jesus's "death" can be understood in a bland sense. Jesus did not simply die; he was crucified, executed by the empire. So, death has a more fulsome and terrifying sense here. His body was broken, his blood was shed. Furthermore, it was the "Lord" who was crucified. "Lord" is one of the titles of the emperor. Lords are not crucified; they do the crucifying. The phrase, "the death of the Lord" in the context of what this meal is remembering is highly provocative, almost oxymoronic. The hero's death points to a future people who will be joining Jesus's meal tradition.

A standard part of Roman banquets was a libation for the emperor, which was almost like our playing of the national anthem before sporting events. To not offer the libation to the emperor was close to treason. But this libation is offered in memory of a Lord, an Anointed king, who was put to death by the emperor of Rome. The meal memorializes a conflict between empires. The provocative, dangerous, and even seditious nature of these meals in memory of an executed criminal is often overlooked.

Passion Accounts

How the passion accounts of Jesus's suffering and death came to be is a controversial and debated topic, with no agreed way forward. The controversy testifies to the multilayered aspect of the growth of the accounts. They also apparently developed after the destruction of the Jerusalem Temple in 70 CE, with the Gospel of Mark being the earliest one (that we know of today). As such, this is the telling we will follow. The elements of the noble death tradition are clearly evident: the hero has a final meal with his followers, the trial points to the innocence of the hero, and the death is depicted in heroic terms. We briefly examine each of these.

The Last Supper

The meal scene in Mark is elaborated from the memorial meal of the dying hero we examined above. The move is from mythic language to actual narrative account. In the process there are several significant changes. "On the night he was betrayed" or "handed over," which opens Paul's account of the memorial meal (1 Cor. 11:23), indicates that God handed the hero over; but now a person is named as the betrayer, Judas. In Mark's story, Judas makes a deal with the Jerusalem priests, and in the garden of Gethsemane he hands Jesus over with the sign of a kiss. Jesus says at the meal's end: "The Human One departs just as the scriptures predict, but damn the one responsible for turning the Human One in! That man would be better off if he'd never been born!" (Mark 14:21).[6] This saying implies that Jesus's fate is divinely willed.

In the transformation of the memorial meal into a narrative of the Last Supper, the libation of wine after the meal disappears. In the Gospel of John the meal is even more radically transformed, almost along the lines of one of Plato's dialogues. Jesus carries on an elaborate series of speeches that take up nearly a quarter of the gospel (John 13–16). What is missing is the memorial meal itself.

The Innocence of the Hero: The Importance of Self-Mastery in Trial

The purpose of a trial in the noble death tradition is to demonstrate the innocence, nobility, and goodness of the victim. Often in the trial the offender makes his (or her) case.

In the Gospel of Mark, Jesus remains strangely silent but his silence demonstrates his self-mastery and elegantly speaks against his chief accusers, the Jerusalem priests. The Roman official in charge, Pilate, is the character who actually is tested in the narrative, and his failure to render justice implies Jesus's innocence. The charge is presented at the very beginning of the trial:

> And Pilate questioned him: "*You* are 'the King of the Judeans'?"
>
> And in response he says to him, "If you say so."
>
> And the chief priests started a long list of accusations against him. Again Pilate tried questioning him:
>
> "Don't you have some answer to give? Look at the long list of charges they bring against you!" But Jesus still did not respond, so Pilate was astonished. (Mark 15:2–5)

Pilate's astonishment or wonder marks him as a neutral judge or observer in this telling. Pilate proposes a strange substitution. He will release Jesus instead of a dangerous prisoner:

> "Do you want me to set 'the King of the Judeans' free for you?" (You see, he realized that the chief priests had turned him over out of envy.) But the chief priests incited the crowd to get Barabbas set free for them instead. (Mark 15:9–11)

In the context of the noble death tradition, the Barabbas story is very intriguing. He had committed murder during an insurrection; that is, he really was guilty of sedition, the charge against Jesus. This becomes an exchange of the truly guilty for the truly innocent. His name is the giveaway. *Barabbas* in Aramaic means "son of the father."

Pilate now knows the true intention of the priests and knows that Jesus is innocent. He challenges the stirred-up crowd:

> "What do you want me to do with the man you call 'the King of the Judeans'?" And they in turn shouted, "Crucify him!"
>
> Pilate kept saying to them, "Why? What has he done wrong?" But they shouted all the louder, "Crucify him!"
>
> And because Pilate was always looking to satisfy the crowd, he set Barabbas free for them, had Jesus flogged, and then turned him over to be crucified. (Mark 15:12–15)

Pilate fails the test; he demonstrates lack of self-mastery by giving in to the priests and the crowd. His failure vindicates Jesus.

The Heroic Death: Jesus's Execution

During the execution, the condemned is to show courage, not to break under duress. The priests and those crucified with Jesus taunt him, but Jesus does not respond.

The Gospel of Mark's account of Jesus's execution plays against the noble death tradition. Jesus does not die calm and reassured, in charge of his dying. Instead, "Jesus shouted at the top of his voice, 'Eloi, Eloi, lema sabachthani' (which means 'My God, my God, why have you abandoned me?')" (Mark 15:34).

These final words of Jesus run counter to the expectations of a noble death and have long bothered readers, including those ancient writers who used Mark's story. The Gospel of Luke and the Gospel of John both replace the problematic saying with one that is more in line with the expectations of a noble death.

Then Jesus shouted at the top of his voice, "Father, into your hands I entrust my spirit!" Having said this, he breathed his last. (Luke 23:46)

When Jesus had taken some wine, he said, "Now it's complete." Lowering his head, he handed over the spirit. (John 19:30)

In the Gospel of Mark, the Roman official who was in charge of Jesus's execution, upon seeing Jesus die this way, responds, "This man really was God's son!" (Mark 15:39). The exclamation mark in this translation is an interpretation that makes this statement a confession and so brings our reading in line with a noble death narrative (if only Greek had punctuation!). But it stands in the Gospel without interpretation. It could just as easily be read as sarcasm, which would be the more likely interpretation. What about this scene would persuade a hardened Roman trooper that a man dying in despair is a son of god? The author of Mark provides no way out of the interpretive conundrum.

The author of Matthew's Gospel does interpret the centurion's saying as a confession, actually a group confession, noting that the centurion and those with him were filled with awe. In the Gospel of Luke's account, the official proclaims that Jesus was innocent, remaining true to the expectations of a noble death. In the Gospel of John, Jesus's mother, other women, and his favorite disciple gather around the cross, like the way Plato's friends gather around him in his prison cell.

Why would the author of Mark's Gospel alone diverge from the expectations of Jesus dying a noble death? For the same reason that this Gospel ends with women finding the tomb empty and going away telling no one. The readers of this Gospel must make their own decision as to what happened and why.

This survey of the different stories of Jesus's death shows how the stories of heroic noble deaths in the ancient Mediterranean are present in each Gospel. This signals how a larger pattern of noble heroes dying for resisting tyranny and ensuring the integrity of those who came after is a basic part of all the versions of Jesus's death.

DYING FOR TRUTH

The tradition of a noble death in defiance of tyranny has a long and deep tradition within the various cultures of the Mediterranean world. Dying for truth was a noble idea. The people of Israel adapted this tradition to their experience when Antiochus IV Epiphanes tried to destroy their religious practice and life, and that became a model for later generations dealing with other forms of tyranny. The early followers of Jesus employed the noble death tradition, particularly as expressed in the Maccabean tradition, to turn the catastrophe of Jesus's execution into the death of a hero that marks the beginning of communities of the Anointed.

This same tradition will be employed by later followers of Jesus in the second century as they confront yet more Roman imperial tyranny. They will call it martyrdom. We follow that second-century development in Chapter 18.

PART II

BELONGING
AND
COMMUNITY

TESTING GENDER, TESTING BOUNDARIES

In Chapter 2 we considered Pliny the Younger's correspondence with the emperor Trajan early in the second century CE. Recall that Pliny is concerned about how to deal with the people he calls *christiani*:

> It is my custom to refer all my difficulties to you, Sir, for no one is better able to resolve my doubts and to inform my ignorance. I have never been present at an examination of *christiani*. Consequently, I do not know the nature or the extent of the punishments usually meted out to them, nor the grounds for starting an investigation and how far it should be pressed. (*Letters* 10.96)

In the course of this letter, Pliny mentions that to get information about these people, he has tortured two enslaved women, named as officials (or perhaps, according to the original Latin, promoters) of this group. Although historians have paid attention to Pliny's casual note about torture, the fact that these officials were two enslaved women has been overlooked.

Leaders who happened to be women, and to be enslaved women specifically, deserve special attention. Women's leadership in religious groups was not uncommon in the ancient

Mediterranean, so perhaps Pliny and Trajan would not have blinked at the existence of two female officials, or two prominent female promoters, among these *christiani*. The enslaved status of the two leaders is more surprising. In the ancient world, the enslaved were not granted full human status and were more often called "bodies" than humans. How, then, should we interpret the roles and situations of these anonymous women, enslaved people and promoters of a Jesus group? Pliny drags them out into the most public of spaces, into the very gaze of the emperor himself. Surely, then, they are more than worth our gaze.

This letter begs a consideration of the importance of gender in early Jesus groups. Contemporary understandings of gender are not the same as those of the ancient Mediterranean world, and we should not read the ancient world in modern terms. Gender is a social concept, not a physical, biological, or anatomical one.

Because gender is a social concept, embedded in specific social contexts, it has not had a stable meaning over human history. What gender "is"—how we make and shape it, how we use and act upon it in our daily lives—has changed dramatically over time. As an everyday social reality, gender, though unstable, is still a very important category to consider. Keeping ancient understandings of gender firmly in mind will allow us to see meanings and possibilities within early Jesus groups and schools of the Way that we could not otherwise see. Above all, viewing the various ways they constructed gender will highlight just how diverse these movements really were.

GENDER AND LEADERSHIP: A CASE STUDY

How gender was viewed in early communities of the Anointed opens up real, lived possibilities for visibility, agency, and leadership, new spaces to imagine and exert power and authority. Women's leadership in early Jesus associations was and still is a hotly contested topic, and existing ancient writings do not paint a cohesive or coherent picture of what gendered activities looked like within these groups. Two writings, however, can help us start to define and explore this topic: Gospel of Mary and 1 Timothy. First Timothy, included in what would become the New Testament, has been a major influence on historical constructions of Christian gender relations. Gospel of Mary, a fragmentary text dating to the late first or early second century, has not had the same voice throughout history; lost for centuries and then found at the end of the nineteenth century, it became a focus of scholarly discussion only in the late 1990s. These two texts present very different, and equally important, depictions of women's leadership in the early movements of the Anointed and the roles and possibilities defined in, through, by, or in spite of gender.

Equality in Gospel of Mary

A brief overview of Gospel of Mary will make its importance in conversations about gender clear. The beginning of this gospel is lost; as it now exists, it starts in the middle of a teaching about the nature of sin. The Savior, as the Anointed One is called in this gospel, concludes his teaching and then departs, leaving his followers pained and weeping, despairing of their next move. "How shall we go to the nations and proclaim the good news of the Child of Humanity? If they did not spare him, how will they spare us?" the Savior's followers worry (Gos. Mary 5:1–3).[1]

As followers weep, Mary stands in the midst of this group of the Savior. She comforts and encourages them, exhorting them not to doubt, for the Savior's "grace will be with you and shelter you." She then "turned their heart to the Good," and calming down, they begin to discuss the Savior's teachings (5:4–10).

Peter asks Mary to teach them, saying, "Sister, we know that the Savior loved you more than the rest of the women. Tell us the words of the Savior which you remember, which you know and we do not, nor have we heard them" (6:1–2). Mary obliges and begins to tell the followers about a vision she had of the Savior, and the Savior's response to that vision.

Mary concludes her instruction. Andrew responds with disbelief: "Certainly these teachings are strange ideas," he states (10:2). Peter, though he had asked Mary to teach them, then turns on her, sneering, "Did the Savior really speak with a woman without our knowing about it? Are we to turn around and all listen to her? Did he choose her over us?" (10:3–4). Mary weeps. "My brother, Peter, what are you thinking?" she cries. "Do you think that I have thought this up myself in my heart, or that I am telling lies about the Savior?" (10:5–6). Levi stands to support Mary, arguing:

> Peter, you have always been an angry person. Now I see you
> contending against the woman like the adversaries. But if
> the Savior made her worthy, who are you, then, to reject her?
> Surely the Savior's knowledge of her is trustworthy. That is
> why he loved her more than us. Rather, let us be ashamed.
> We should clothe ourselves with the perfect Human, acquire
> it for ourselves as he commanded us, and proclaim the good
> news, not laying down any other rule or other law beyond
> what the Savior said. (10:7–13)

Levi has the last word; after he speaks, the members of this group of the Savior go out to teach, and the gospel ends.

Mary is presented very simply in this gospel: she is Mary, a woman. There are no other descriptors. No mention is made

A strong nation, represented as a woman, thrives even when other nations were defeated by the empire.

Hal Taussig

of which Mary she is; no mention of whether she is a virgin, a mother, a sex worker, a wife—nothing. Mary is known by her activities: she is obviously a leader. She is a teacher, revealing and relaying words of the Savior unheard by the other followers. She is a seer, describing a vision of the Lord. She is an authority, exhorting the followers of the Savior to action when they would fear and despair, giving focus and stability to the group.

Mary is also granted special, superior authority in this writing. Peter states that the Savior loved Mary more than "the rest of the women," implying, significantly, that other women were part of the Savior's core group of followers. Levi then offers an important corrective to Peter's statement. He affirms that the Savior loved Mary "more than us"—more than any of his followers, female or male.

Gospel of Mary ends with Levi putting Andrew and Peter in their places; Levi defends Mary, dressing down the male followers, offering a new gendered possibility for men. As Seminar member Celene Lillie argues, Levi "provides an alternative position and attitude for men. While Andrew and Peter are defended, particularly at the end of the text when they attempt to police Mary and strip her of her authority, Levi holds that it is legitimate to believe a woman."[2] Mary is a legitimate leader, both on her own terms, given her activities among the followers, but also on the basis of the fundamental teachings of the Savior. Levi's statement demands that all accept Mary as such. Mary is to be believed and respected.

According to Gospel of Mary, women were held up as authorities in groups of the Savior; in the words of the Savior, they were teachers and leaders. Prohibiting women's leadership was actually a characteristic of "the adversaries": "Now I see you contending against the woman like the adversaries," Levi

responds to Peter. While Peter might try to distinguish between men and women and between male and female activities
or roles, those distinctions do not, and must not, hold. Levi reminds the group of the Savior that their primary concern is to
"clothe ourselves with the perfect Human," to acquire true humanity—a status without gendered parameters. Followers are
not to "lay down any other rule or other law beyond what the
Savior said." Women and men have equal right to teach and to
lead. This equal right derives from a shared focus beyond gender: a focus on the attainment of true, perfect human status.

The Prohibitive 1 Timothy
First Timothy, a letter attributed to Paul but written by a later
writer, offers an entirely different position regarding women's
leadership. This mid-second-century letter is best known for
its verses that place limits on women's activities in a Jesus
community, prohibiting their very right to speech, not once,
but twice:

> I desire, then, that in every place the men should pray,
> lifting up holy hands without anger or argument; also that
> the women should dress themselves modestly and decently
> in suitable clothing, not with their hair braided, or with
> gold, pearls, or expensive clothes, but with good works, as
> is proper for women who profess reverence for God. Let
> a woman learn in silence with full submission. I permit
> no woman to teach or to have authority over a man; she
> is to keep silent. For Adam was formed first, then Eve;
> and Adam was not deceived, but the woman was deceived
> and became a transgressor. Yet she will be saved through
> childbearing, provided they continue in faith and love and
> holiness, with modesty. (1 Tim. 2:8–15)[3]

The letter writer prescribes and prohibits; he tells women what to wear and what not to wear, what to do and what not to do. Above all, he tells women to be silent.

First Timothy sounds very different from Gospel of Mary, to be sure, but also very different from the Paul of other letters. First Corinthians assumes that women are visible and active within Chloe's people in Corinth, leading prayers and prophecy. Chapter 16 of Paul's Letter to the Romans lists a significant number of female leaders and officials of Jesus associations there, eight by name. In Philippians Paul speaks to Euodia and Syntyche, two women who "worked with me in the good news," "co-workers," he calls them (Phil. 4:2–3). Galatians 3:28, one of Paul's most famous sayings, speaks directly to the significance—or rather, the insignificance—of gender in his Jesus communities in the context of belonging: "You are no longer Judean or Greek, no longer enslaved or freeborn, no longer 'male and female.' Instead, you all have the same status in the service of God's Anointed, Jesus." Paul is reimagining creation here, playing with the wording of Genesis 1:27: "So God created humanity in his image, in the image of God he created them; male and female he created them." A new creation, with a new view of gender: Paul's position in Galatians is radical.

Where Galatians reimagines creative boundaries, 1 Timothy rigidly proscribes them. This letter seems to have more in common with the biblical letters Colossians and Ephesians, letters also attributed to Paul but authored by others, in the judgment of most scholars. Colossians and Ephesians include a household code—a list of ideal relationships within the main family unit, the household. Colossians 3:18–4:1 and Ephesians 5:22–6:9 both begin with a command for wives to be subordinate to their husbands, while husbands are to love their wives. "For the husband is the head of the wife as also the Anointed is the head of the assembly, the Savior of the body," declares the writer of Ephesians, continuing, "Just as the assembly is made subject to the Anointed, so also are wives, in everything, to their husbands" (Eph. 5:22–24). Children are to obey their parents, and fathers should not treat children too harshly. The enslaved are to obey their masters, the male heads of the household, and the heads of household should treat the enslaved fairly.

First Timothy, like a household code, does place some limits on men. The letter focuses on group leadership, not household leadership, so the emphasis is on authority figures in the Jesus community: bishops and deacons, both male leadership categories in 1 Timothy. Men are given prescriptions and prohibitions in 1 Timothy; as the approved authorities of the Jesus group, their behaviors and inclinations also require policing. This policing is directed inward, toward group-specific ideals: deacons are told to hold "to the mystery of trust with a clear consciousness" (1 Tim. 3:9). This policing is also directed outward, toward larger social norms: bishops and deacons are to maintain standard households, the foundational units of Greek and Roman social life. Bishops must also be "well thought of by outsiders" (3:7), so that they, and presumably their communities, are not shamed, not disgraced. The letter writer is very concerned about how others see the community.

Men are policed in 1 Timothy as the only ones authorized for leadership within Jesus groups. Women in 1 Timothy are not authorized for anything except childbirth. Women are to be invisible in public and in the activities of the community. They are commanded to be silent.

As case studies on gendered possibilities for authority and leadership in the early Jesus groups, Gospel of Mary and 1 Timothy appear to be complete opposites. On the one hand, Gospel of Mary affirms that Jesus upheld women as equal, even superior, leaders. The goal of this group of the Savior was the attainment of true humanity, outside of or aside from a male-female binary. On the other hand, 1 Timothy appeals to Genesis 2–3 to deny women any right to activity within the community: women are to be seen but not heard, and preferably not seen, either. Surely 1 Timothy would fall into the category of "adversary" mentioned in Gospel of Mary!

What are we to do with these opposing writings when attempting to understand the groups of the Savior and Jesus clubs of the first two centuries?

TENSION, AMBIGUITY, PARADOX

The Question

These two writings and, by extension, the Jesus movements that produced them, seem to have nothing in common. Can the figure of Mary, and the list of women teachers and leaders in the Letter to the Romans, possibly connect to the proscriptive, prohibitive 1 Timothy, a letter that explicitly states that women are not to teach, nor even speak? Can we usefully compare the boundary challenge of Galatians 3:28, Paul's statement about all belonging in and through the Anointed, to the rigidity of the household codes of Colossians and Ephesians? No, Gospel of Mary and 1 Timothy imagine entirely different gendered possibilities. No, the form of belonging proposed in Galatians does not compare to the division that Colossians and Ephesians prescribe. These writings cannot be held in common. They speak of and to deep differences in the understanding of gender, and the possibilities gendering does or does not allow, in very different ways.

Most discussions of the writings of the early Jesus movements have not accounted for this difference. Conversation about these writings has centered on unanswerable questions when it comes to gender. "Is the New Testament (the New Testament being seen as one coherent volume, here) negative toward women?" is one such question that is often asked and one about which everyone has strong feelings, on one side or the other. Yes, the New Testament is negative toward women. No, while the New Testament contains some problematic passages, it can and should still be interpreted as positive toward women. The New Testament is both. Should we ask this question at all?

We like asking questions that have yes or no, good or bad, right or wrong answers because they seem simpler. We want to find a clear answer, on one side or the other. This good/bad positioning is a fine place to start an argument; it is always important to notice a surprise or discrepancy within a given source. Such positioning is not a place where we can end, however. The basic question remains: So what? What kind of meaning can be generated when the presentation of those stereotypes is examined more closely?

Nothing particularly new will be learned when binary questions are asked about gender in the diverse writings of the early Jesus movements. Are these writings negative toward women? Absolutely, and absolutely not. Ask the opposite question: Are these writings positive toward women and women's roles? Again, absolutely, and absolutely not. Where, then, can binary questions and answers lead? How can we engage these writings more deeply?

The Loss of Visibility and Agency of Women in 1 Corinthians

Understanding the "yes and no," the binary, is step one. The writings of the early people of the Way, some of which were later included in the New Testament, contain contradictory depictions of women and of gender, not just between biblical writings, but within them, individually. Paul's first letter to Chloe's people in Corinth presents readers with such tension, a tension both intriguing and challenging. In chapter 7 of 1 Corinthians, Paul offers Chloe's people some advice about marrying or remaining

This small detail from a once large Roman fresco from the turn of the first century CE depicts an unidentified woman sipping from a cup and looking out from a balcony.

Woman on a Balcony, courtesy The J. Paul Getty Museum (Gift of Barbara and Lawrence Fleischman)

single: he would prefer it if everyone in the community could remain single, but if singleness is not possible, it is reasonable for community members to marry. When married, husbands and wives should grant one another their "conjugal rights." Paul then states, "the wife does not have authority over her own body, but the husband does" (v. 4). That representation of authority, husband over wife, is not surprising for ancient Greece and Rome. Next, however, Paul affirms, "likewise, the husband does not have authority over his own body, but the wife does." The statement that a woman has authority over the body of the husband, the head of the household, is not only much more surprising, but really radical. The male head of the household was the primary authority figure in ancient Rome, wielding power over the other men, women, children, and the enslaved in his house.

Paul then moves to a discussion of situations in which a man or woman marries someone who does not follow the Anointed. Paul declares, "the husband who is not a member is consecrated through his wife and the wife who is not a member is consecrated through her husband . . . After all, wife, what do you really know about whether you will save your husband; or what do you really know, husband, about whether you will save your wife?" (1 Cor. 7:14, 16). The reciprocity expressed here, the rights for both wives and husbands, is remarkable.

Later in this same letter, the situation shifts. First Corinthians 11:2–11 offers some confusing instructions concerning women's head coverings in public gatherings. A man should not veil his head, Paul writes, "since he is the 'image and reflection' of God"; but, he continues, "woman is the reflection of man, because man did not come into being from woman, but woman from man. And man was not created for woman, but woman for man" (vv. 7–8). This declaration does not sound much like 1 Corinthians 7, where husbands and wives were created for the sake of each other with a carefully balanced mutuality. This difference is so great and the ideas seem to disrupt the overall argument of the letter to such an extent that many biblical scholars therefore consider this section to be an addition by a later author.

Paul continues his case for the veiling of women in the activities of Chloe's people with an argument about what he calls "nature": "You be the judge: is it proper for a woman to pray to God with her head unveiled? Does not nature itself teach you that if a man wears long hair, it is degrading to him, but if a woman has long hair, it is her glory? For her hair is given to her for a covering" (1 Cor. 11:13–15). There is nothing natural about hair length; Paul's argument rests on a social convention of gender. It was socially acceptable for men to have short hair and women to have long hair.

Where Paul previously upsets social convention in 1 Corinthians 7, here in chapter 11 he, or perhaps a later editor of Paul's letter, reinforces it. In ancient Greece and Rome, socially "decent" adult women covered their heads in public. A covering indicated a woman's social status as true "woman": a Greek woman was not actually called such until she had given birth to her first child within the bonds of marriage. "Woman" was a status a person became. The proper sexual status or sexuality of the Greek woman, as a woman, was made visible by her covered head.

In Paul's context, adult women active in public with uncovered heads were sexually and socially transgressive—they violated expected norms. New groups like Chloe's people were always viewed with suspicion in ancient Greece and Rome, and this suspicion often included charges of sexual immorality. In 1 Corinthians 11, Paul, or a later author, tries to reign in the free activities of Chloe's people, activities that would be labeled as sexually, and therefore socially, deviant. Mutuality in marriage is one thing; implications of transgressive sexuality due to uncovered heads is quite another.

Women in this letter, and in this particular chapter of the letter, are envisioned as present and visible in the community. They are active during communal gatherings, participating in prayer and prophecy. But how do we resolve the gendered ambiguity in the letter? Is Paul stating, "Yes, women, you are free to participate, but could you maybe tone it down a little bit? Could you observe a bit of normal social protocol?" Or, is this passage even from Paul? Is it perhaps an addition by a later editor of Paul adjusting Paul's letter to a new situation? These two solutions are, of course, not the only options; 1 Corinthians 11 can easily lead us down a rabbit hole of interpretation. We cannot satisfy all our curiosity.

First Corinthians 14 is less ambiguous. "Women should be silent during the meetings," the writer asserts. "They are not allowed to speak, but must be subordinate, just as the Law says. If there is something they want to know, they should ask their husbands at home" (vv. 34–35). These statements leave no room for interpretation. Women are not to be heard. They are not to be active participants in the community's ritual life. They do not even have the right to ask questions.

First Corinthians 11:2–11 and 1 Corinthians 14:33–36 both seem out of place in the argument of the letter and therefore are likely additions to the letter made after Paul's time. Several translations, such as the New Revised Standard Version, place 1 Corinthians 14:33–36 in parentheses to highlight the dubious or perhaps later (post–second century) authorship of those verses. Some interpreters go further and think that these verses should be removed from the letter entirely, since they only harm readers. But does removing the offending verses solve the issue, even if Paul did not write them? How can or should chapters 7, 11, and 14 of 1 Corinthians make sense together? An early editor of the letter thought that these passages all made sense together, from Paul.

RECONCILING THE CONTRADICTIONS

First Corinthians is just one example of contradiction at most, ambiguity at best, within a single writing. Such ambiguity is often found in studying and interpreting ancient writings, which have an internal history and social situation that are not always apparent to later readers. The ambiguity of 1 Corinthians and the ambiguities about gender within other early Jesus associations force a move away from yes/no, good/bad, right/wrong questions and answers. Simple questions like, "Did the early Jesus movement value women? Did the movement prioritize women's roles? Did Paul like women?" can be answered only, "Yes, no, and both."

More than anything, "yes and no" tell us that the early groups of the Savior were incredibly diverse. The imagined community that found 1 Timothy meaningful was likely not the same group of the Savior that found Gospel of Mary meaningful. This conclusion is important in and of itself, for it argues against the popular notion that "Christianity" was some kind of unified "whole" from the start and that fragmentation or disunity—diversity—came later. There was no such thing as "Christianity" in the first centuries of the Common Era.

Papers Relevant to This Chapter by Seminar Participants

Dewey, Joanna. "Women: Their Visibility and Agency and Loss of Agency in Early Christian Texts." Fall 2018.

Lillie, Celene. "Thinking Through Gender in the Second Century Jesus Movements." Fall 2018.

Wheeler-Reed, David. "Re-Reading *Regulating Sex* One Year Later." Fall 2018.

8

FORMING NEW IDENTITIES
THROUGH GENDER

Seeing gender in the groups of the Savior enables us to see the testing of boundaries. The lack of clear boundaries for identity, group belonging, and cohesion prompts gender-boundary violation. This disruption demonstrates, in a way nothing else can, the multiplicity of the early Jesus movements. Boundary maintenance or protection was not something that many Jesus peoples were particularly interested in. Yet gender was and is all about boundaries: their definition, maintenance, and defense. The use of gender by these groups became the ultimate tool for testing boundaries, for slipping a toe across a line, for withdrawing and creating new boundaries, for disordering the social world around them.

This disordering of the social world is made possible through the manipulation of gender by and through women. Women of the early communities of the Anointed test the social fabric, probe its weak spots, and thereby imagine alternative warps and wefts. Gospel of Mary, 1 Timothy, Galatians, Colossians, Ephesians, and even Pliny's letter to Trajan all share in common a socially male interest in fixed, stable boundaries. They

Thecla, a teacher and healer, was thrown into a pool in a Roman arena as a means of execution. But she survived with the help of many women cheering for her, and, so her story goes, the beasts of the arena were killed by lightning. She stayed in the water with the animals and baptized herself (see Chapter 13).
Sarah Sexton Crossan

also share in common a socially female interest in instability, in challenging boundaries. The author of 1 Timothy, co-opting the voice of Paul, commands, "Let a woman learn in silence with all subordination" (1 Tim. 2:11). The need for this prohibition, of course, suggests that women were not "learning in silence" at all. "Let us teach!" or "We are teaching!" are the imagined other sides of this silenced story.

This boundary challenge is present in an Anointed community writing from the first two centuries called Acts of Paul and Thecla. Paul's main goal in this story concerns marriage: he aims to free young people from the violence and patriarchy of the married state. Thecla is the one who takes this teaching to heart and suffers the brutal consequences. She abandons the path set out for her by society and violates boundaries. She is then abandoned by her family, tortured by political authorities, and even abandoned by Paul himself. She exemplifies the price paid by those who violate the fixed male boundary.

GENDER IN GREECE AND ROME

The male focus on fixity and female interest in instability makes sense when considered in the context of Greek and Roman ideas about gender. The ancient Mediterranean was a "one-sex" world in which men were the "reality," fully formed physically and socially. Women were imperfect men, unfinished, their genitals inappropriately inverted: "the female is as it were a deformed male," Aristotle affirmed in *Generation of Animals*.[1] According to the physician Galen, born in Pergamon in the second century CE, women and men did not have different organs or body parts; men's organs were properly external and public, while a woman's were turned inside. He writes:

> All the parts, then, that men have, women have too, the difference between them lying in only one thing, namely, that in women the parts are within [the body] whereas in men they are outside, in the region called the perineum. Consider first

whichever ones you please, turn outward the woman's, turn inward, so to speak, and fold double the man's, and you will find them the same in both in every respect.[2]

Galen goes on to compare a woman's inward-facing parts to the eyes of a mole: while moles cannot use their eyes to see, the eyes still exist, unopened, "left there imperfect."

Similarly, the second-century CE physician Soranus builds upon the work of an earlier physician named Herophilus, whose late fourth-/early third-century BCE work, though surviving only in quoted fragments, showed a particular focus on gynecology. Soranus quotes:

And in his *Midwifery* Herophilus says that the uterus is woven from the same thing as the other parts, is regulated by the same faculties, has the same material substances at hand, and is caused to be diseased by the same things . . . Accordingly, says Herophilus, there is no affection peculiar to women, except conceiving, nourishing what has been conceived, giving birth, "ripening" the milk, and the opposites of these. (*Gynecology* 3.3)[3]

Medical works from the first two centuries suggest that men and women were not understood as different kinds of bodies. The difference between men and women was of degree, a vertical axis with "man" at the top and "woman" as a progressive movement downward or away.

This one-sex perception of human bodies played out socially in significant ways. Men, genitals-turned-out, belonged to the public sphere, while women, genitals-turned-in, belonged to the private sphere. The ancient understanding of the body was profoundly social rather than physical or biological. Our use of the words "male" and "female," "man" and "woman" in this book attempts to align with these social categories as understood and used in the first two centuries.

The male body was the "normal" body, the exemplar of the complete or perfect body, but it was not a "natural" body, as we would understand that term. "Natural" here really means socially natural, or socially appropriate and acceptable. Acquiring this natural or socially acceptable body required constant work. Infants were bathed, massaged, and swaddled so that their bodies literally could become molded, shaped into acceptable male and female characteristics. The reference to Mary's swaddling of Jesus, her wrapping of Jesus in bands of cloth (Luke 2:7), takes on a different meaning when viewed from this perspective: Mary is forming his body so that Jesus can eventually take the shape of a man. Jesus's swaddling is an act of masculinization.

Nobody—no *body*—could ever achieve masculinity in its fullness, could ever actually become or be male. Like the body of an elite athlete, the ancient body required constant, strategic work. Care of the body focused on the appropriate expression of social norms. The Latin word *vir* means "man" but specifically refers to an adult male, over twenty years old, married to a woman, freeborn, not enslaved, a Roman citizen, engaged in military activity, and expressing virtues such as courage and honor. The word constructs not simply "male" but a web of social relationships. The word is not about biological sex, but social status.

Ancient men were also defenders of boundaries. Male bodies were associated with qualities like hardness, hotness, solidity, and definition. The male body should protect itself, its household, and its empire from external threat. Male bodies perceived to be without such qualities and therefore potentially violable were subject to ridicule. One of the worst insults in antiquity was the charge of effeminacy, the labeling of a man as being feminine or womanly.

By contrast, the female body, as an imperfect male body, was a violation and violator of boundaries. The female body was constantly penetrated by social and physical forces; it was leaky, porous, cold, soft, wet, moving across and between spaces. The female body was dangerous, therefore, in its potential to transgress, to go beyond or violate boundaries. All kinds of leaky female bodies appear in the writings of Jesus groups. Mark's Gospel relates the story of the woman "suffering from hemorrhages"; no matter what treatments physicians offer, her leakiness becomes worse and worse. She approaches Jesus knowing that he can stop her leakiness and restore her boundaries. "If I could just touch his clothes," she avows, "I'll be cured!" (Mark 5:28). The miracle of Jesus in this context is the restoration of boundaries to this particularly porous woman. In giving the woman's body some clearer boundaries, Jesus also restores her to social acceptability. Healing her body is a social healing.

Men's bodies were firmly bounded; women's bodies were transgressive and thus required bounding or "fixing." The Greek word for a woman's head covering or veil, *krēdemnon*, makes this point quite clearly. While used most often to refer to a veil, the same word also refers to a city's fortifications or battlements, and to the lid or stopper of a wine jar. Could the implications of the different uses of this term—a defense, a wall, a stopper, a lid, a woman's head covering—be any clearer?

The construct of gender enabled the embodiment of social realities. Men (again, understanding this word as a specific social construct from a specific time and place) were active, public, authoritative, and bounded. Women were passive, private, submissive, and in need of bounding. Gender was completely bound up with social position and power. Gender is obviously, then, a hugely important tool, perhaps the most important tool, as a person or group explores and defines identity.

TESTING AND QUEERING BOUNDARIES

Given the default understanding of gender in the ancient world, the interest of the early Jesus movements in boundary testing and violation allows us to see something not apparent without the lens of gender. Writings that appear to have nothing in common, on one level, all point to the use of gender as a means of testing boundaries. Specifically, *women* test boundaries.

Female boundary testing, such a prominent feature of this diverse collection of writings, really makes good sense. Women were boundary violators, characterized negatively by instability. These early Jesus schools and associations employ an ancient social construction of gender in a very positive way. Of course, women are testers of boundaries—that's who women *are*. In the early groups of the Savior, this boundary testing is used to achieve constructive or affirming ends. It is central to the experience of these groups, for both women and men.

Much of this boundary-testing activity is best understood as a queering of ancient structures of gender. The word "queer" has different modern meanings, but for the purposes of this chapter, queering refers to a disruption of conventional, normative ideas about gender, sex, and sexuality, especially ideas that make heterosexuality the norm from which all other forms of sexuality deviate. Queering opens possibilities for new modes of identity and belonging. Queering questions, challenges, resists, deconstructs, and disassembles categories we think we know—man, woman, male, female—and renders them "other." This strangeness is what opens new social spaces in which to experiment. There is nothing natural about gender. While contemporary contexts operate as though the male/female binary still directs social life, these categories are not the only possibilities for social existence and never have been. Just because we *say* that something is male or female does not mean that that thing actually *is* male or female.

By exploring how gender functions among the early peoples of the Way, it becomes apparent that they queered gender and, as a result, imagined new space for social existence and identity. Scholar Virginia Burrus makes this landmark argument in an examination of narratives about martyrs.[4] Previous scholars who considered gender and sexuality in the martyrdom stories insisted that these stories actually reproduce and therefore affirm conventional ideas of gender. The goal of martyrdom, according to the competing arguments, was the final achievement of the status of "man." The martyrs are shown to be active, courageous, strong, in control, and dominant—all qualities of the ideal Greek or Roman male. The martyrs are like gladiators, athletes, or soldiers; again, all roles open exclusively to men.

Burrus, however, takes a closer look at just who these supposed "men" were in the martyrdom accounts. Who are these bodies that are associated so strongly with conventional symbols of masculinity? Burrus notices that these bodies are entirely unconventional for their social context: the bodies of the martyrs are old, disabled, enslaved, female, maternal, children. The bodies are non-men, according to Greek and Roman social norms. What could such a privileging of non-male and non-masculine bodies mean?

The most prized male virtue in the ancient Mediterranean world was courage. Courage is actually synonymous with manliness in this context; the Greek word for courage, *andreia*, is formed from a root meaning "man" (*andr-*). Courage, therefore, is equivalent to "being a man," a skill that takes practice and discipline and is never fully mastered. Burrus examines the concept of courage/manliness in a story about nine Judean martyrs that appears in 4 Maccabees, a text likely written in the first century CE (see Chapter 6). This narrative is the origin story of all martyrdom stories that are to come. It presents itself as a philosophical treatise about the relationship between reason and emotion, highlighting rational judgment as the pinnacle of virtue. The author demonstrates the sovereignty of rational judgment through descriptions of the violent deaths at the hands of imperial authorities of Eleazar, seven unnamed brothers, and finally, the young men's mother, also never named.

The story in 4 Maccabees is set in Judea during a period when it was under the control of the Seleucid Empire. The ruler, Antiochus IV Epiphanes, is remembered for his cruelty. In 4 Maccabees, Antiochus is introduced as "an arrogant and terrible man" who banned religious observance. When his decrees were ignored, "he himself, through torture, tried to compel everyone in the nation to eat defiling foods and to re-nounce Judaism [ancestral practice]" (4 Macc. 4:26).[5] Eleazar is brought before the king. He is "a man of priestly family, learned in the law, advanced in age, and known to many in the tyrant's [Antiochus's] court because of his philosophy" (5:4). Antiochus repeatedly draws attention to Eleazar's age, calling him an "old man," noting his gray hairs, urging him to consider his "years" and "old age" to compel Eleazar to eat pork and meat sacrificed to idols. Eleazar turns Antiochus's ridicule around: "You, O king, shall not defile the honorable mouth of my old age, nor my long life lived lawfully. My ancestors will receive me as pure, as one who does not fear your violence even to death. You may tyrannize the ungodly, but you shall not dominate my religious principles, either by words or through deeds" (5:36–38).

Antiochus does not respond well to Eleazar's refusal to eat his unclean meat. Eleazar is stripped, tortured, beaten, and burned. Despite his agony, Eleazar is "courageous and noble." He is "unmoved"; "he kept his reason upright and unswerving." The narrator repeatedly references both Eleazar's courage and old age at once: "Like a noble athlete the old man, while being beaten, was victorious over his torturers; in fact, with his face bathed in sweat, and gasping heavily for breath, he amazed even his torturers by his courageous spirit" (6:10–11). Eleazar is remembered as a glorious war general: "No city besieged with many ingenious war machines has ever held out as did that most holy [old] man . . . he conquered the besiegers with the shield of his devout reason" (7:4–5).

The mother in the narrative receives the highest praise. She not only watches her seven children die before Antiochus, but she persuades them to die rather than give in to the empire's demands. She then casts herself into flames so that no one can touch her body, completely and fully in control of herself. She is "of the same mind as Abraham" (14:20), "mother of the nation, vindicator of the law and champion of religion" (15:29), the ultimate athlete "who carried away the prize of the contest in [her] heart" (15:29). She is "more noble than males in steadfastness, and more courageous [manlier] than men in endurance" (15:30).

Manliness and courage are synonyms. What is courage, in this context? What is true manliness? Eleazar, the seven brothers, their mother: they are not powerful individuals in their social worlds. They are not kings, like Antiochus. Since courage equals manliness in the ancient world, we would expect this manliness to manifest itself as active, dominating, aggressive, and penetrating. Masculinity is about domination. Antiochus, then, should be the ultimate man in this story. Instead, the aged Eleazar and the mother emerge as the true men. The virtue of *andreia* is wholly redefined. Eleazar, the brothers, and the mother do not become "men" in any conventional kind of way; they do not become penetrators, and they do not dominate. Manliness actually becomes completely disconnected from domination. Fourth Maccabees presents a total reversal of the gendered ideal.

Burrus argues that this redefinition of a gender category, the redefinition of "man," must be seen in light of the politics of 4 Maccabees, which presents a vivid depiction of violence under imperial rule. The challenging and threatening life of Judeans under the Roman Empire demands a reimagining of social possibility. For Burrus, 4 Maccabees exposes a time when "the excesses of imperial rule have rendered masculinity *qua* domination deeply problematic, posing the challenge of imagining masculine virtue otherwise."[6] The pervasive conventions of male and female can no longer stand, given the brutality of life under those conventions. No one should be a man if the ideal man is a vicious tyrant like Antiochus. In queering gender, the story gives readers a way to imagine what life could look like apart from imperial rule, what life *should* look like. The reimagination of gender is also a reimagination of social possibility, of a way to resist, to keep living in a world of crushing oppression.

QUEERNESS AND STORIES OF MARTYRDOM

Fourth Maccabees is just one example of a martyrdom story that queers gender. Martyrdom stories told by the Jesus schools and associations follow in the tradition of 4 Maccabees. Queering disrupts the principles and realities of the worlds behind these narratives. As a tool for disruption, gender becomes an essential opportunity to envision alternatives. In the story of the Letter of the Churches of Vienne and Lyons, preserved in the writings of fourth-century historian and bishop Eusebius, the unexpected body of a chronically ill enslaved woman, Blandina, is at the center. Blandina is "filled with such power that those taking turns to inflict every form of torture on her from dawn to dusk failed and gave up, confessing that they were defeated and had nothing left to do to her . . . her entire body was torn and laid open."[7] Blandina, "like a noble athlete," gained new strength, we are told, in her declaration of her group identity: "I am of the party of Christus; we do nothing to be ashamed of" (5.1.17–19).[8] We see a different facet of martyrdom in the second-century story of the *Martyrdom of Polycarp*, in which the elderly bishop Polycarp, entering the arena to be burned alive, is told by a "voice from the sky" to "make yourself manly!" (9.1). Being a man here seems synonymous with being a follower of the Anointed: being a man is about patience, endurance through suffering, quiet calm, and confidence.

We see these traits exemplified by a woman in *Acts of Perpetua and Felicitas*, when Perpetua has a vision in which she takes on an Egyptian gladiator; as she is stripped in preparation to fight, she becomes male: "I became a man" (10.7). The Latin reads *facta sum masculus*, "I become male" or "I am made male." *Facta* is a feminine word form indicating a feminine identity for the speaker, Perpetua. *Masculus* means "male" or "masculine" and identifies the speaker as masculine. Perpetua, in three words, *facta sum masculus*, is both female and male. This story is full of gender fluidity and ambiguity.

TRANSFORMING BOUNDARIES AND IMAGINING NEW ALTERNATIVES

Gender in the writings of the early Jesus movement is blurred and tested. This queering at its core is a disruption. Gender is something always under construction, and therefore always under threat in the social worlds of the groups of the Savior. That threat, that constant risk, is in these narratives an *opportunity*. They use, even exploit, that risk in order to test new, unconventional modes of existence. For people without social power, without any other means of changing their circumstances or shaping their identities, gender was a tool at everyone's disposal. For people living under empire, under oppression and violence, the boundary-testing potential inherent in the construction of gender became a powerful tool for imagining something other, for representing one's self, one's identity, through newly imaginative means.

"Queering" was not a term that these movements would have used of themselves. The application of this modern analytical category of queer to the narratives discussed in this chapter builds on contemporary queer theory. Gender was a foundational part of ancient Mediterranean social life in very specific ways. When that context is carefully and thoughtfully considered, the use of queering as a lens to examine these narratives and understand these peoples becomes dynamic and constructive. When the context is clarified, a context so different from our own contemporary constructions of gender, the queer lens can accurately apply. We can see through the glass clearly. And what we see is transformative.

Stories help us to understand our social worlds differently and to make arguments about these worlds. Narratives represent their social worlds, not completely, but significantly. They offer arguments about those social worlds. Through their representation and argument, they give readers new opportunities to offer their own representations and arguments. The entanglement of narrative and social world is appropriate across very different cultural worlds. The use of the modern category of queer helps us to understand these worlds. When we read the

writings of the early Jesus people, we can know them better—
again, not completely, but significantly.

Specifically, knowledge of these early peoples of Wisdom
comes through in their use of gender in their writings. The
different kinds of gendered possibilities in this literature, possibilities as wide-ranging as those from 1 Timothy to Gospel of
Mary, all explore boundaries, testing and fortifying, construct-
ing and deconstructing, re-creating and reconfiguring. Women
in particular, as porous, leaky bodies, have the potential to disrupt these lines and offer social alternatives. Gender in these
writings stimulates imagination.

Gender was not significant among early Jesus clubs only in
writing, however, but also as a lived reality in their actual experience of diversity and fluidity in social roles. Women are
named often in Paul's letters as leaders and are named in the
same way as male contemporaries; Paul applies the same terms
to men as to women. The visibility of women in many schools
of the Savior associated with Paul was a taken-for-granted reality. Indeed, women in Paul's time were relatively common
religious leaders, but later their roles were minimized or erased.
Junia is named as an apostle in Romans 16:7. Junia, a female
name, was turned into Junias, a male name, in later biblical
manuscripts and translations, and Paul's fellow female apostle
disappeared. Paul took women's leadership in his Jesus groups
for granted. Beyond the New Testament writings, clearly
women were more prominent in these early associations than
has traditionally been recognized.

There is no straightforward answer to binary questions
about whether the early movements of the Way were positive
or negative about and toward women. We have seen that the
evidence makes that either/or way of asking the question problematic, or even the wrong question to ask. We cannot survey

all of the writings of early Jesus groups that use gender, but the writings surveyed here tell us the following:

- The early Jesus groups, schools, and clubs were diverse and multiple.
- Gender demonstrates, as no other category or mode of questioning can, the interest among these communities in testing boundaries and imagining alternative life possibilities.
- This boundary testing was a "queering" of identity among these peoples, groups, and movements, a disruption of their status quo. There is no question that people of diverse gender identities were active and visible within the earliest groups of the Savior.

These writings are complex and challenging. But the more we question, the more we begin to see, the more possibility we see in the bodies of, for example, those two enslaved women mentioned in Pliny's letter to the emperor. Gender had the capacity to dismantle forms of social domination, and thereby allow people to reimagine life apart from the empire.

Papers Relevant to This Chapter by Seminar Participants

Burrus, Virginia. "The Gender of Martyrdom." Fall 2018.

Dewey, Joanna. "Women: Their Visibility and Agency and Loss of Agency in Early Christian Texts." Fall 2018.

Lillie, Celene. "Thinking Through Gender in the Second Century Jesus Movements." Fall 2018.

9

BELONGING TO ISRAEL

In the late second or early third century CE, a man named Publius Aelius Glykon built a limestone coffin for himself and his family on a hill outside Hierapolis, an ancient city located in what is now western Turkey. Glykon's sarcophagus is part of an impressive necropolis system, an ancient cemetery, on the outskirts of the city. While made for the dead, Glykon's sarcophagus tells an interesting story about the dynamics of belonging for the living. The inscription on his family tomb reads:

> This grave and the burial-ground beneath it along with the base and the burial-place which is round about it belongs to Publius Aelius Glykon (son of) Zeuxianos Aelianus and to Aurelia Amia, daughter of Amianos the son of Seleukos. In it he will bury himself and his wife and his children, but no one else is allowed to be buried here. He bequeathed to the solemn leadership of the purple-dyers 200 denarii for grave-crowning, in order that it would give from the interest a portion for each to gain in the seventh month during the festival of Unleavened Bread. And likewise he bequeathed to the association of carpet-weavers one hundred and fifty denarii for grave-crowning, so that the proceeds from the interest should be divided, half

during the festival of Kalends, in the fourth month, on the eighth day, and half during the festival of Pentecost.[1]

Glykon leaves money to the local association of purple-dyers, people who dyed cloth with expensive purple for a living, for taking care of his tomb. This money should accrue interest and through the interest, enable the association to contribute to the festival of Unleavened Bread, a Judean religious festival. To the association of carpet-weavers, he leaves money for a grave ceremony marking the festival of Pentecost, another Judean festival, as well as Kalends, a Roman festival for the new year.

While Glykon does not explicitly name himself as Judean, the request for grave ceremonies on two Judean holy days certainly aligns his family with Israel in a way that will hold this bond of belonging into Glykon's indefinite future. This bond with Israel is cemented outside of the land of Israel; Glykon lives in Hierapolis, in Asia Minor, not in Roman Palestine. He is a Judean in diaspora.

Glykon also declares his Romanness, by his status as a Roman citizen with his three names, Publius Aelius Glykon—a definitive marker of his citizenship—and by leaving money to recognize Kalends. Glykon's identity is also local. He is part of the Greek urban context of Hierapolis, given his interaction with the local associations of purple-dyers and carpet-weavers. Here, then, we see a significant level of interaction and integration: Judean, Greek, and Roman all intertwine as important terms of identity. Glykon located himself and his family within Judean, Greek, and Roman modes of belonging.

Glykon's inscription on his tomb points to the complicated, variable, and even seemingly contradictory ways in which people found belonging in the first two centuries. Prior to the Roman Empire, the essential mode of belonging in the ancient

Mediterranean was nation, one's "people." The contemporary word "ethnic" derives from the ancient Greek word for nation/people, *ethnos*. Belonging to a people meant also belonging to a particular place, a geographical space. It likewise meant honoring the gods of that place, even outside the boundaries of geography.

The Roman Empire, however, compelled a reimagining of these ties to nation and people, requiring honors to the new god, the emperor. Belonging to the Roman Empire meant weakening local ties and affiliations over time as nations were brought into the cosmopolis of Rome. The fundamental belonging to people, however, did not just disappear. Glykon's presentation of his social and spatial identities testifies to the importance of people, of physical or local space, and of empire. All kinds of new definitions of belonging were under way during the first two centuries of the Common Era in order for people to learn to live with Rome's effort to amalgamate all nations, all peoples.

Like Glykon, the multiple Jesus peoples and associations identified with the people of Israel. These identifications were expressed in different ways, but there was no clearer agreement among the followers of the Anointed in the first two centuries than this: "We belong to Israel, even if we weren't born into Israel. We are people of Israel." Even as the conquered people of a former nation in Asia Minor or North Africa, and despite Rome's claim that all were barbarians compared with Rome, the adherents of the Anointed belonged to the small, defeated nation of Israel, as did the Anointed, the Savior, Jesus.

ISRAEL AND "JEWS" IN THE FIRST TWO CENTURIES

Who was who in Israel during the first two centuries was decisively different from the way it is in the twenty-first century.

Coin issued by Emperor Vespasian celebrating the defeat of the Judeans.
Classical Numismatic Group, Wikimedia Commons

Today, being a "Jew" or "Jewish" can mean being a member of the Jewish religion, the Jewish state, or both. But in the first century both those words were rarely used for referring to national or religious identities.

In the first two centuries, saying that you belonged to Israel or identifying as Judean were the clearest ways to say who you were. These statements of belonging were also the main ways one identified oneself even when one did not live in geographical Israel, as was the case for the majority of Judeans. At that time "Israel" was more "all the people of Israel," no matter where they lived.

The word for "Judean," typically translated in our twenty-first-century language as "Jewish," was the first-century way many people in southern Israel identified and also the way for some people who identified religiously or politically with southern Israel. The identification is primarily of people, rather than geography. Since this is a very particular title for people of southern Israel in the first century, scholars now use the word "Judean" (rather than "Jewish") for this group. In the mid-to-late second century, more people of Israel were switching to calling themselves "Jews" or "Jewish," as the reality of a nation of Israel faded because of Rome defeating it twice. This was the same word as "Judean" but by the end of the second century it had a broader meaning than referring to someone from southern Israel.

In ancient Greek, the language that all these people spoke, the term *Ioudaios* was the most common word used to reference a person who belonged to Israel, or a Judean. In this book, we have translated *Ioudaios* as Judean. *Ioudaios* includes the overlapping meanings explained above.

Six primary groups of people or individuals identified themselves in three major ways at various times and places:

- The non-Greek people who lived in geographical Israel: "people of Israel"
- The people who worshipped Israel's God but did not live in Israel: "people of Israel"
- The historical Jesus: "people of Israel"
- Most non-Greek people who lived in southern Israel during the first century: "Judeans"
- More and more people in the second century who worshipped Israel's God: "Jews"
- Paul, who lived in Asia Minor during the first century: "people of Israel"

PAUL AND BELONGING TO ISRAEL

Paul is the earliest writer interested in finding a place for his clubs of Jesus followers in the early Roman Empire. Paul consistently gives the Jesus followers a new, stronger sense of identity through modeling his sense of ethnicity, of peoplehood, of ties to land, tradition, and practice. In many of his letters, Paul identifies himself using ethnic/geographic descriptors for Judea: Judean, Israelite, Israel, and Hebrew. "Are they Hebrews? So am I!" Paul asserts in 2 Corinthians 11:22, in the face of competition from other envoys of good news. "Are they Israelites? So am I! Are they descendants of Abraham? So am I!" Similarly, in Philippians 3:4–6, Paul declares:

> . . . though I, too, have confidence in [my] body. If anyone else seems to have confidence in their body, I have more: circumcision on the eighth day; of the people of Israel, the tribe of Benjamin; a Hebrew (born) of Hebrews; according to the Law, a Pharisee; according to zeal [or "honor," potentially, or "rivalry"], one persecuting the assembly [of Jesus followers]; according to righteousness under the Law, one becomes faultless.

Throughout the letters Paul writes to different clubs in Asia Minor and Rome, whose identities have been shattered by Roman violence, he invites these people to follow Jesus and become a part of the people of Israel now scattered all over the world. Many take him up on this invitation. Like Paul, they listen to the stories of Israel in its holy writings and claim the lineage of Abraham and hold on to the writings of Isaiah, Genesis, and Exodus. They take seriously the invitation in Isaiah that all the people of the world are welcomed to be a part of that nation of Israel.

In our contemporary contexts we no longer understand the ancient world as the collection of nations/peoples to which Paul refers forty-five times in his letters. We have lost this sense of people or nation in our reading of Paul, and in our reading of how people figured out their identities under empire more broadly. This situation is most unfortunate, given Paul's frequent reference to the idea. The word "nation," *ethnos*, in the first two centuries, when those nations had been subsumed by the Roman Empire, still means "nation." But Paul knows that it also means the sense of ethnicity, of peoplehood, of ties to land, tradition, and practice. We should not lose sight of these dynamics of belonging in Paul's letters.

The Greek word *ethnos* in New Testament translations is often rendered "gentile," often capitalized ("Gentile"). In this sense it refers to a person of non-Jewish faith. In later interpretations of writings of early Jesus peoples, it took on the sense of being a Christian, that is, not a Jew. This sense is wholly missing from the first two centuries. Normally in Greek the word refers to a nation or people, and this is its usage in the Greek writings of the first two centuries. It carries no sense of distinguishing those who follow Jesus from those who do not, and much less any such anachronistic understanding of "Christian" versus "Jew."

Paul works to identify himself and others using ethnic descriptors, specifically, the Judean national identity. When we encounter these identifications in Paul, our aim as readers is to consider what is behind them. When Paul identifies himself or others as belonging to peoples, ethnic groups, or devastated nations, how does he position these peoples, in relation to one another, and what might this positioning tell us about belonging? For those who lost their nation to Rome, the word now also has the meanings of adherence to Paul's Anointed groups and to other clubs on the ground in the first-century Mediterranean basin.

Paul's implications when he asserts his Hebrew or Israelite identities are clear: he is not to be considered as inferior to his competitors, belonging to some lesser national heritage than Greece or Rome—no indeed! He is of the nation of Israel, of the people of Judea. Look again at his words from Philippians quoted above: "If anyone else seems to have confidence in their body, I have more: circumcision on the eighth day; of the people of Israel, the tribe of Benjamin." But his next move in this letter places this primary identification in a new context: "But whatever gains these were to me, because of the Anointed, I now consider loss" (Phil. 3:7). The social advantage Paul claims because of his national identity becomes intertwined with what he calls "the knowing of the Anointed Jesus" in Philippians 3:8. This "knowing" also appears to take precedence over the honor brought through national identity. Philippians presents us with an interesting dynamic of group identity. How should we understand Paul's model of belonging? What is the relationship between belonging to a nation and belonging to an association of the Anointed?

These verses from Philippians voice a certain tension in what belonging means under the power of the Roman Empire. In the first-century Mediterranean, tensions developed between the loss of nationhood for many people and the new reality of a universal power everywhere one looked. Empire produced a sense of both location and dislocation. The continued pull toward national affiliation struggled with the push toward primary affiliation with Rome. Philippians makes clear that nation still exerted a significant amount of pull. National belonging was a central experience of ancient social life. Members of associations of the Anointed found this belonging in Israel. More or less, all first- and second-century writings related to Jesus or the Anointed honored various traditions of Israel. As people began to identify with Jesus and/or the Anointed, including many people not related by blood with Israel, they also began to understand that they belonged to greater Israel.

Usually, Paul emphasizes that participation in associations of the Anointed involves adoption of the God of Israel, an ethnic or national God, and the rejection of other ethnic forms of worship or cultural practices. Belonging to Paul's groups involves "turning to God from idols, to serve the living and true God" (1 Thess. 1:9). In Paul's view, before membership in Paul's groups, people served the wrong gods, or honored gods in incorrect ways: "You know that when you were among the nations," Paul reminds his addressees in 1 Corinthians 12:2, "being diverted, you were led to idols without speech." Learning to be a part of the greater Israel that had spread around the Mediterranean basin involved proper connection to the God of Israel.

In Paul's writings, consistently, the Judean "nation" also appears at the top of an ethnic ladder of peoples.[2] The ladder is relatively short: Israel, Israelites, or Judea at the top, and all others together at the bottom. Paul offers a simple Judeans-and-others dichotomy. He adopts the perspective of the superior ethnic group, the top of the ladder: belonging to Israel is best, followed by Greek identity, perhaps, but basically by everyone else. Rome is definitely not at the top of this ladder. These ethnic identifications imply the superiority of the people of Israel over inferior "peoples" or "nations"; out of these inferior nations, though, some have turned to this superior God, and the superior national belonging, of Israel.

Belonging to Israel is at the top of Paul's world.[3] Those peoples who turned to the God of Israel became associated with Israel through shared cultural practice, despite their origins among other peoples. Paul indicates that belonging to Israel is something groups can do, through the proper honor of the

God of Israel, regardless of origin. Paul has this capacity for belonging in mind in his famous statement in Galatians 3:28: "There is neither Judean nor Greek, there is neither enslaved nor free, there is neither 'male and female,' for all of you are one in the Anointed Jesus." This is not a statement about belief, about what it means to believe in the Anointed Jesus. Neither is this a statement about a fundamental equality, an erasure of human difference or some kind of reformation of contemporary "Judaism," such that everyone, Jew and non-Jew alike, might adhere to the God of Israel through faith.

In its specific context, this statement follows from Paul's strategic attempt to persuade his audience from the nations that they do not need to adopt Torah regulations concerning practice, especially the practice of circumcision. Since everyone can belong to the God of Israel, the claim to belong to different nations no longer holds. There is no difference between Judean and Greek in that both can be equally saved or condemned. Participation in the national identity of Israel on the basis of honoring God: this form of belonging is open to all.

Affiliation with Paul's group is about connection, about belonging, but about belonging in the midst of difference. Identification with the Anointed involves belonging to Israel, being in relationship to Israel. This vocabulary is not about religious beliefs, but about the making and remaking of group identities through practice. This is a vocabulary for figuring out and defining group belonging.

What kind of belonging is Paul working toward here? Again, most first- and second-century literature about Jesus or the Anointed honored the traditions of Israel. Identification with the nation of Judea, with the people of Israel, was key to Anointed-belonging. This more national mode of belonging, though, existed in a context of the loss and erasure of national belonging under empire. The issue here is not about belief, about dogmatic concerns, but rather about redefining group belonging amidst the destruction of conventional ways of thinking about one's identity.

On the one hand, for Paul, belonging to larger Israel identifies and defines who the members of his Jesus associations are. Members of Paul's clubs are not necessarily ethnically or nationally Judean, but they are children of Israel. In Paul's context, we are dealing with two primary dynamics of human geography: First, there are many birthright people of Israel who have been displaced from the territory of Israel. Many thousands of people from Israel now live in Egypt, Syria, Greece, and Asia Minor. There is already a new model for who can belong to Israel: an Israel in diaspora.[4] Second, Rome has intentionally displaced many of the nations it conquered. The many nations who used to exist now are scattered around a Mediterranean ruled by the empire. Because this displacement often happened violently, these displaced peoples do not accept the possibilities of becoming Roman or living under Roman governance. Many people in the first two centuries are looking for a new kind of national belonging.

In his Letter to the Romans, Paul claims a space for his gospel that closely resembles the Roman "inhabited world," or *oikoumene*, the space of empire (see Chapter 4): "For I will not venture to speak of anything except what the Anointed has accomplished through me to win obedience from the nations, by word and deed, by the power of signs and wonders, by the power of the Spirit of God, so that from Jerusalem and as far around as Illyricum I have fully proclaimed the good news of the Anointed" (Rom. 15:18–19). This statement has a clear imperial context and consequence. As the Roman emperors triumphed over the inhabited world with the permission and support of the gods, so Paul's gospel, his good news of the Anointed, triumphed over this same space, with the permission of the God of Israel.

Consideration of nation in Paul's writings enables us to understand that his use of words like "Israel" did not mean he was participating in an ideological disagreement about abstract entities but was trying to help associations of the Anointed feel like they were in shared or adopted national/ethnic space.[5] Paul uses both the idea of "nation" and that of "empire"—the two main group affiliations of the time. These affiliations existed in tension. Paul's intention is not opposition to the larger people of Israel, nor is it the creation of a universal religion. Neither is it an eradication of difference. At issue in Paul's writings is the matter of identification, the matter of struggle, clash, and claim at issue in belonging.

Israel was not the only place where those who had lost their nation could find a new sense of belonging. In the first two centuries members of other former nations also found belonging in new ways. Some groups claimed community in stories and rituals of the ancient Egyptian goddess Isis and her brother Osiris. Not unlike the fascination with Israel, in Isis and Osiris there were also stories of remaking oneself that found resonance across Asia Minor, Greece, and Syria. In one primary ancient story Isis found the dismembered body of her brother Osiris and put it back together into a living whole. No wonder defeated nations joined clubs honoring the Egyptian glory of Isis and Osiris. Likewise, in North Africa, Macedonia, and Greece, the loss of so many different national practices sparked all kinds of clubs that rebirthed older stories and retooled practices of Eleusis and Dionysos to claim new ways of belonging.

It makes sense that new clubs with practices originating

in Greece and Egypt provided a new kind of reassurance for the national identities that Rome assaulted. Greece and Egypt were historic and legendary powerhouses in the ancient world. Even though in the first two centuries Rome controlled both nations, everyone in the Mediterranean knew how famous, honored, and ancient the Egyptians and Greeks were. Their civilizations had been known for their architecture, literature, religion, and politics for many centuries, or—in the case of Egypt—for millennia. For nationalities crushed by Rome to associate their new identities with reimagined parts of Egypt or Greece was far more attractive than remaking one's self as part of Israel. Israel was a small nation that hardly ever conquered anything and instead was often conquered. Why then did so many groups turn to belonging to Israel in the first two centuries?

MODELING ONE'S SELF AFTER ISRAEL

Bringing nation or people (*ethnos*) into our Jesus-group vocabulary helps us to see important dynamics of belonging in and to the Roman Empire. Being part of the empire means finding ways to deal with the disruption and rethinking previously meaningful ethnic ties and national affiliations. The mechanism some used to deal with this disruption across diverse communities of the Anointed was to identify as children of Israel.

There are three main attributes these peoples find in Israel. First, Israel has only one God, and it is a God that claims to rule the world with goodness. This first honor does not come without some argument and second thoughts. What proof does one have that Israel's God rules the earth? After all, the Roman emperors look more powerful than Israel's God. But honoring one God began to make more sense to those who lived in the Mediterranean basin in the first two centuries. Before the Roman Empire, the world seemed smaller. Most nations had relatively small gods that moved in smaller circles. When the people of Israel praised the One God and everything that God had made, first- and second-century philosophers paid some attention. It seemed to make more sense that the bigger world, which one had come to know in the large empire, would have one divine ruler. The philosophers of this enlarging world noticed that the Roman emperor was sometimes too stupid, often too cruel, and occasionally too inattentive to effectively rule an increasingly large world. When the Greek and Roman philosophers heard about one God that created all things and demanded goodness and justice from all people, they saw something in Israel that they admired, even if Israel did not win many battles.

Second, as the Roman Empire grew and the people of Israel spread to almost all parts of the Mediterranean, people talked more about the curious long list of commandments to do good that the people of Israel tried to follow. Both ordinary people and philosophers noticed that Israel's law of five books, the Torah, had quite high standards for ethics and behavior. Indeed, people of non-Israel ethnicity around the empire started going to synagogues to learn more about these commandments. They were surprised that the Israel people in the synagogues did not require non-Israel people to follow all their rules. As non-Israel people also learned of the teachings of Jesus and Jesus movements, they assumed that this also belonged to Israel's God and Israel's high ethical standards.

Third, Israel's holy writings—those stories about the creation of the world, the ways the national God saved and punished the people of Israel, and the long list of commandments—became more familiar to different groups in the Roman Empire. Israel's writings repeatedly commanded Israel to honor other peoples and to feed them when they were hungry. Teachers of groups of the Anointed that included mostly non-Israel people joining Israel engaged in discussions about God's goodness and the behavior Israel's God required. Other peoples considered Israel's writings as important gifts to the larger world, and the wisdom literature of Israel celebrated broad swaths of other peoples' wisdom writings.

Although Rome had humiliated Israel as a people in ways similar to the other nations, its long history and engagement in the world resulted in some part from the larger Mediterranean world acknowledging Israel's gifts, strengths, and wisdom. Biblical scholar and author Burton Mack has pointed to the deep connections between Israel and the other Mediterranean peoples:

> The Jews thought in terms of creation . . . How to find the key that would make it possible to see the world as a whole again, account for the human diversity and cosmic expanse that had come into view and understand all the powers that had been unleashed as capable of working together for human well-being? . . . The story of Noah, also, was a good place to reflect on the standing of the nations in the eyes of the God of Israel. The rainbow's promise was not the private property of the Jews . . . What about the way God treated Abraham as a sign that the gentiles must be welcomed into the family of God?[6]

It was this dynamic in the larger Roman world that found those overwhelmed nations and ethnicities discovering new possibilities in belonging to or being connected to Israel.

A MESSY BLEND

A sense of the first two centuries as producing a joining of the broken nations following their Jesus-related companions into a larger Israel is emerging in historical research among both Jewish and Christian scholars. Jewish scholar Daniel Boyarin played a key role in the Seminar's study of these two hundred years of blended Israel, fractured nations, and Jesus movements.[7] Boyarin has argued that for at least the first four centuries, there was no "parting of the ways" between what has been mistakenly understood as two different religions— Judaism and Christianity. The first two centuries were mostly an intermingling and cohabitation of Jesus peoples and Israel.

Boyarin encourages us to discard a "parting of the ways" model in favor of an understanding of nation, people of the Anointed, and people of Israel, in their own diverse forms and varied collectives, as participating in a series of complex encounters with empire—specifically with the imperial reality of triumph over nation and people. When we recover the sense of nation in the writings of the Jesus movements in the first and second centuries of the Common Era, we get a much stronger picture of the situation on the ground, a picture of the significance of belonging to Israel. Being an adherent of the Anointed, following Jesus, meant identification with larger Israel—part of a complex dance of national and imperial belonging.

Papers Relevant to This Chapter by Seminar Participants

Boyarin, Daniel. "The Christian Invention of 'Judaism.'" Fall 2016.

Harland, Philip A. "Climbing the Ethnic Ladder: A Portrait of Interactions Between Judeans and Other Peoples." Fall 2016.

Kotrosits, Maia. "Devising Collectives: Losing the Nation in the Story of Judaism and Christianity: A Response to Daniel Boyarin's *Dying for God: Martyrdom and the Making of Christianity and Judaism* and *A Traveling Homeland: The Babylonia Talmud as Diaspora*." Fall 2016.

Livesey, Nina. "Difference and Similarity: A Review of Daniel Boyarin's *A Radical Jew: Paul and the Politics of Identity* and *Border Lines: The Partition of Judaeo-Christianity*." Fall 2016.

———. "Does Paul Speak from the Heart?" Spring 2018.

Marshall, John. "Judean War and Judean Diaspora: Class and Networks." Fall 2015.

IO

EXPERIMENTAL FAMILIES

Fairly early on in the writing we now know as Gospel of Matthew, Jesus stands outside, teaching a mixed crowd. As he teaches, his mother and brothers arrive on the scene and ask to speak to him. Told of their arrival, Jesus rejects them, asking, "Who is my mother, and who are my brothers?" Gesturing to his students, he states that his true family members, his chosen kin, are those who "do the will of God," named as Jesus's "father in the sky," his celestial or divine father (Matt. 12:48–50).

Jesus's apparent rejection of his mother, brothers, and sisters in Matthew is a radical move. The family was the heart of social, economic, religious, and political life in the first two centuries, and rejecting this heart would have put Jesus at enormous social risk. Jesus appears to alleviate this particular social risk, however, in choosing his family members for himself: his students are his true, chosen family.

Jesus's rejection of his kin is even more dramatic, and surprising, given that the entire Gospel is presented as the story of Jesus's family. The opening line of Matthew reads, "An account of the family of Jesus the Anointed son of David son of Abraham" (1:1). After this opening comes a long list of fathers and sons—forty-two generations in all. The final generation offers a puzzle: "And Jacob the father of Joseph the husband of Mary, of whom Jesus was born, who is called Anointed" (1:16). Is Jesus related to Joseph? No other birth announcement is presented this way. This final puzzle aside (for now), the Gospel writer makes it clear that Jesus's family, his long line of ancestors, is the ultimate point of this story. This is a story about family. Yet later in the story, he rejects his closest family.

The complicated family story that is the Gospel of Matthew is just one of many complicated family stories we find in the writings of the early communities of the Anointed. When these writings are approached with ancient families in mind, family dynamics pop into view just about everywhere. Family was central to the founding and shaping of Jesus groups and schools in the first two centuries. Paul often refers to an assembly or association formed around a household: Aquila and Prisca, "together with the assembly at their house," send greetings to Chloe's people in Corinth (1 Cor. 16:19); Paul asks those belonging to the Anointed in Rome to send greetings to this same assembly at Prisca and Aquila's house as well (Rom. 16:5). Paul's Letter to Philemon, as it is typically titled, is not just written to Philemon, but also to Apphia, whom Paul names as his sister; to a man named Archippus; and to the whole assembly in Philemon's house (Philem. 2). Colossians, a letter attributed to Paul, mentions the assembly in the house of a woman named Nympha (Col. 4:15).

Acts of the Apostles highlights the centrality of the household to the growth of early Jesus groups. When a prominent local figure belongs to the Anointed, that person's whole household tends to belong along with them. Successful local businesswoman Lydia is initiated into an association of the

Anointed, and her whole household is then initiated as well (Acts 16:15). Paul and Silas tell a prison guard that if he trusts Jesus, "you will be kept safe, you and your household." The guard takes them to his house, cleans the wounds they sustained in prison, "and he was initiated at once, with all those belonging to him, and he brought them up into his house, and set food before them, and he rejoiced, with all his household, that he had trusted God" (Acts 16:31–34). In Acts 18:8, Crispus, a local leader of a synagogue, trusts the Anointed, "together with all his household." The affiliation of a head of a household with an association of the Anointed often, though not always, implies the affiliation of everyone in that household with that same association.

The language of family is used in many different writings of the first two centuries to identify group members, though these group members are not factual kin. Paul often refers to God as the father of a Jesus club and to the members of that club as siblings (for example, in 1 Thess. 1:3–4). Similarly, in Gospel of Thomas, Jesus teaches his students, "When you come to know yourselves, then you will become known, and you will realize that it is you who are the sons of the living father" (3), and later, "The one who knows the father and the mother will be called the child of a whore" (105). Although the members of these communities are not formally related by blood, the language of family indicates a status as chosen family.

The language of family is also used to break or to challenge factual and conventional bonds. Jesus's challenge in Matthew was reproduced from the earlier Gospel of Mark. Though Mark's account is not as specific as Matthew's, Jesus's claim envelops the crowd as a whole in Mark, rather than the students alone (Mark 3:31–34). In Acts of Paul and Thecla, the heroine, Thecla, is first introduced by listing her family connections: she is a virgin, the daughter of Theocleia, and engaged to Thamyris. She gives up all family and household connections to follow Paul. The reader hears that upon her disconnection, "those who were in the house wept bitterly, Thamyris for the loss of a wife, Theocleia for that of a child, and the maidservants for that of a mistress. And there was a great outpouring of lamentation in the house" (ch. 10).[1] In order to follow Paul, Thecla breaks all the social bonds that characterized life in the ancient world: her roles as daughter, future wife, and slave owner are denied. Throughout her story, Thecla takes on new, independent social roles: she becomes a teacher, leader, and healer.

Households are joined and abandoned; familial bonds are created and destroyed. Clearly, family structures were extremely important to group being and belonging. Less clear, however, are how and why family structures were so important. Family is the central point of intersection of a complex network of social experiments. What made the family, specifically the ancient Roman concept of the household, such an important tool for belonging in the first two centuries?

THE ANCIENT HOUSEHOLD

This chapter uses the word "family" to refer to the social arrangement that lay at the center of ancient Mediterranean life, but family had a very different set of meanings in the ancient world than now. The fourth-century BCE Greek philosopher Aristotle's description of family summarizes the ideal model for that world. He discusses the family, more accurately called the

FVRIA·ƆL·P·FVRIVSPL·FVRIAƆL·FVRIAƆE·C·SVLPICIVSCI

Archaeological evidence speaks of the importance of groups that pushed the boundaries of the conventional Roman household. This funeral monument from the first century depicts a chosen household of freed people: three women and two men, freed from the household of the Furii. The man on the right is a freedperson from the household of the Sulpicii. The personal names of these individuals are not given—only their identifications with the households in which they were formerly enslaved. While their relationships to one another are unclear, their representation together on this monument shows that they belonged with and to one another.

household, in his work *Politics*; even before reading further, the context suggests that family is connected to politics:

> And now that it is clear what are the component parts of the state, we have first of all to discuss household management; for every state is composed of households . . . the household in its perfect form consists of enslaved and freemen. The investigation of everything should begin with its smallest parts, and the primary and smallest parts of the household are master and enslaved, husband and wife, father and children. (I.ii.1253b)[2]

Aristotle states that the structure and running of a household is a microcosm for the effective running of the state. The philosopher then names enslaved and freed people as central to the household before naming any other role or figure. A family, then, is not made up simply, or even primarily, of kin or blood relations. Aristotle breaks the household down into three sets of relationships: master and enslaved, husband and wife, father and children. Each of these three relationships revolve around one central figure: the male head of the household, who is a slave owner, a husband, and a father.

Though from an earlier time, Aristotle's depiction of the family, the household, is representative of the elite male ideal of family that heavily influenced cultural thought and practice under the Roman Empire. The household was a network of people and property in relation to one another, of both membership and ownership. Mark 10:29–30 offers a succinct portrait of this network: "Jesus said, 'Truly I say to you, there is no one who, having left house or brothers or sisters or mother or father or children or lands because of me and because of the proclamation, who will not receive a hundredfold now in this time, houses and brothers and sisters and mothers and children and lands.'" House and land are an integral part of this view of family and, in this case, connect to an image of subsistence living that characterized life for the vast majority of people in rural areas of the empire.

House, land, wife, and children, as well as enslaved and freed people, dependent workers, clients and even members of the same trade or local occupation in attached shops and work-rooms, property, enslaved and free laborers, kin—all existed in hierarchical relationship to one person: the male head of the household, or in Latin, the *paterfamilias*. The *paterfamilias*, dominating social space and social activity, subjected all to his power. Westar Institute scholar Susan M. (Elli) Elliott describes how the Roman household was an enactment of the honor and virtue of the *paterfamilias* in her book *Family Empires, Roman and Christian*. Walking past the front entrance of a wealthy household, a passerby would see the *paterfamilias* in a central officelike space, granting or prohibiting access to himself. Clients, including formerly enslaved people who, though legally free, still existed in subordination to the *paterfamilias*, mingled in a wide-open space in front of the him, waiting to pay him honor. The enslaved bustled about this space working, looking for a corner in which to rest, trying to carry on their own relationships when these relationships received no recognition under the law. Children, enslaved and free, played together on the floor. The household's deities held a prominent place in a shrine where they received adornments of flowers and food offerings as devotions from household members. The funeral masks of ancestors peered down from the walls, still present and observant.[3]

The *paterfamilias* was his own kind of household god, and gods filled the Roman household, overseeing every act and aspect. The *paterfamilias*, taking the role of household priest, led the household in performing devotion to the various gods of the family and ensuring prosperity, household honor, and the continuation of the family line.

The *paterfamilias* was in charge of the maintenance of the moral order of the household. Each member of the household was required to perform specific virtues, virtues we find reflected in writings of some communities of the Anointed. Colossians, Ephesians, 1 Timothy, and 1 Peter contain "household codes," definitions of proper virtue through relationship. The household codes still follow the threefold pattern of Aristotle: master and enslaved, husband and wife, and father and child: "Wives, belong to your husbands as to the lord, for the husband is the head of the wife just as the Anointed is the head of the assembly" (Eph. 5:22–23). "Children, obey your parents, for this is right. 'Honor your father and your mother,' this is the first command with a promise, 'that it may be well with you and that you may live long on the earth'" (Eph. 6:1–3). The *paterfamilias* is to rule the social hub of the household with honor, duty, justice, and mercy. Wives should perform virtues of modesty, proper shame, and obedience; children should be dutiful; and the enslaved are to be obedient. These virtues were all directed toward the maintenance of proper, stable social relations.

The primary importance of the household was as social model, as Elliott points out. It gave the ancient world a particular shape, describing an ordered social world. This shape was used to justify larger social institutions, including the empire itself.

If the household was the microcosm of larger political structures, the empire was the household played out in its largest, most dramatic form. When Nero became emperor in 54 CE, he sent out a proclamation, the good news of his accession, still preserved on a papyrus text found in ancient Egypt:

> Owed to the forefathers, the revealed god Caesar has gone to them. And the one for whom the entire inhabited world looked and hoped, the Emperor, has been proclaimed; the good divine power of the inhabited world and the source of all things good, Nero Caesar, has been proclaimed. Wherefore we should all give thanks to all the gods, wearing wreaths and sacrificing oxen. Year one of Nero Claudius Caesar Augusts Germanicus, the 21st of the month of Neus Sebastus.[4]

Dynamics of family shape this proclamation. Nero first honors the former Emperor Claudius, "the revealed god Caesar," in the context of his ancestors. Most interestingly, Nero presents himself as "the good divine power of the inhabited world." He names himself the guardian and guiding god of the empire.

Nero is the ultimate *paterfamilias*: the head of the household of empire.

HOUSEHOLD OF THE ANOINTED

Those belonging to the Anointed used the primary building block of social life, the household, to define what this belonging essentially meant. Almost every writing we have from these diverse communities presents family in some way and thus necessitates a reading through a household lens.[5] For example, Elliott's careful reading of Paul's letter to the Jesus association at Philemon's house helps us to see the complex ways in which even a single association both relied on and pushed back against the norms of family.[6] The letter is short and can be summarized succinctly: while in prison, Paul wrote to an association of the Anointed Jesus in the household of Philemon, a *paterfamilias*. Paul has met Onesimus, an enslaved person in Philemon's household. The circumstances of the meeting are ambiguous: how they met, why they met—we have none of those details. Paul is sending Onesimus back to the household in the hope that Philemon will change his behavior toward Onesimus, or perhaps his fundamental relationship with Onesimus. Again, what this change involves is not specified.

From the very beginning the audience of this letter is drawn into a complex network of relationships. Although this writing is typically called the Letter of Paul to Philemon, from the perspective of the ancient household, this title is misleading. First, Paul is a co-sender of this letter; Timothy is also named in the letter's opening and is named as Paul's chosen brother: "Paul, a prisoner because I serve the Anointed Jesus, and Timothy our brother" (Philem. 1). Paul could be making a claim as a *paterfamilias* here himself; as Elliott suggests, "Paul uses his imprisonment for the cause of the Anointed/Christ as a credential in a way that appeals to basic Roman values, displaying the *virtus* (manliness, courage, self-sacrifice) that was an essential part of Roman identity and a virtue expected of a *paterfamilias*."[7] Even though he is not the head of the household, Paul seems to be asserting himself through his command of virtues that should be more readily attributed to Philemon.

Philemon is also not the sole addressee. The letter is written "to our beloved coworker Philemon and sister Apphia and our co-soldier Archippus and to the assembly in your house" (Philem. 2). Already, our household lens reveals more complexity than we might otherwise be able to see. Philemon is named as a *paterfamilias*, certainly. He is the head of the household where the Jesus association meets. The "your house" here is singular, referring to the household of not several, but one: the house is Philemon's. The relationship of Apphia and Archippus to this house, however, is unclear. Apphia is not addressed as Philemon's wife. Their address on equal terms with Philemon suggests that they are also leaders of this group for the Anointed Jesus. Philemon could be the patron of this association, allowing members to meet within his house but not exercising sole authority over them. All of these members were meant to receive and hear this letter.

Philemon may be a *paterfamilias*, patron and co-leader with Apphia and Archippus, but he is not the ultimate authority; he is not the master of this assembly. He is subject to a household himself. In verse 3 of the letter, Paul names God as the father of the association: "Grace to you and peace from God our father and the lord, Anointed Jesus." The reference to God as father is a not-so-subtle challenge to Philemon's concept of his own social power, and also a challenge to the emperor as father. God is the ultimate *paterfamilias*. Paul reminds Philemon that they are of shared association and purpose, members of the same intentional community. They are chosen family.

The focus of the letter is Onesimus, enslaved in Philemon's household. We never hear Onesimus himself. The voices of the enslaved are hidden in these ancient writings. We never hear how or why Onesimus leaves Philemon's household to find Paul in prison, and we need to be careful to avoid the trend in the history of interpretation that reads Onesimus as a "runaway slave"—this reading privileges the voices of slaveholders.[8] Paul refers to Onesimus as his child in the letter, and to himself as Onesimus's father: "I appeal to you for my child, Onesimus, the one whose father I became in prison" (Philem. 10). Paul actually says that he "begot" Onesimus. If Onesimus is Paul's son, his relationship to Philemon's household is contested.

The Letter to Philemon, though only twenty-five verses long, is full of plays with, against, through, and toward power. Paul frames these power plays in the language of family: Who is the *paterfamilias*? Where does authority really lie? Ultimately, for Paul and for many of the schools of the Savior in the first two centuries, the true *paterfamilias* is God. Even the household codes of Colossians and Ephesians—two writings later attributed to Paul, but of unknown authorship, after Paul's time—while upholding the dominant social values of slaveholding, marriage, and fatherhood, subordinate existing social relationships to God as *paterfamilias*: "So then you are no longer refugees and migrants, but you are citizens with the holy ones and members of the household of God, built upon the foundation of the messengers and prophets, the Anointed Jesus being the cornerstone" (Eph. 2:19–20). People and property, a house and its members.

Household is subordinate to counterhousehold. Here, that counterhousehold refers to the household of a different deity. The model is not new: the Roman household was a hierarchy under the gods. The emperor, as god, was the ultimate head of household and of empire-as-household during these first two centuries. In these associations of the Anointed, a god is still the *paterfamilias*. But this god is no longer the Roman emperor. Ephesians in particular describes an alternative household empire structured very much like the Roman household empire, under a different god.

The experiment with family expressed in Philemon is subtler than others we find among the schools, associations, and parties of the Savior. We need to remember that there were many non-father-based groups in the greater set of groups and families. The teacher Paul also was known as an opponent of some versions of the *paterfamilias* model. Women like Chloe and Thecla led family groups and (in the case of Thecla) family movements without a *paterfamilias* playing a role at all. As is laid out in a number of chapters in the present book, a major contribution of the many early Jesus movements was their rejection of father-led families.

CHOSEN FAMILY

The writings of the Jesus peoples in the first two centuries tell stories of family. These stories describe factual and chosen households, holding cultural and countercultural modes of belonging in tension. The language of family declares both social legitimacy and social nonconformity.

This language of family was so important to the ways in which early communities of the Anointed experimented with their relationships to one another because it was the same language people used to think about and experience social life under empire as a whole. Calling the leader of a Jesus association "father," as many associations did, had specific social consequences: Was that father a *paterfamilias*, a head of a household, or was this new chosen father standing in tension with the standard understanding of a *paterfamilias*? Paul's greetings to various Jesus associations at the conclusion of his Letter to the Romans suggests that some associations met in households in which the *paterfamilias* was not a member of the group. How did that situation work itself out? In the midst of their earthly push-and-pull, these associations consistently displaced the ultimate patriarch, the Emperor-God, with the God of the Judeans. The writer of Ephesians calls God "the father from whom every fatherhood of the sky and on earth is named" (3:14–15). The displacement of emperor also would not have gone without social consequence.

The Tenuous Role of Women in the Family Unit

Family is a thorny, ever-changing concept. It is everywhere, though, in the writings of the communities of the Anointed, and we cannot understand the experiments in group belonging these communities undertook without it. The Gospel of Matthew, again, offers an insightful example. As we have seen, Matthew is a story about family—Jesus's family. The audience is given this context in the very first line: "An account of the family of Jesus the Anointed" (1:1). What follows is a list of forty-two generations from Abraham, the "father of many nations," through David, ancient Israel's definitive king, to Jesus. It is easy for the eye to skip through these generations—the long list of "so-and-so was the father of so-and-so," et cetera. If we read each name one by one, however, we find five unusual,

unexpected ancestors in Jesus's epic history—five women:
Tamar, Rahab, Ruth, Bathsheba (the wife of Uriah), and Mary:

... and Judah the father of Perez and Zerah by Tamar (v. 3)

... and Salmon the father of Boaz by Rahab (v. 5)

... and Boaz the father of Obed by Ruth (v. 5)

... and David the father of Solomon by the wife of Uriah (v. 6)

... and Jacob the father of Joseph the husband of Mary, of whom
Jesus was born, who is called Anointed One (v. 16)

These five women are named as being pivotal to Jesus's an-
cestry, as foundational to the story of Jesus's family. According
to the conventions of genealogies, their names were not necessary; the father-son line was the important one to preserve.
Most of the generations listed in Matthew follow the simple
father-son paradigm, "and so-and-so the father of so-and-so."
Who were these women? What makes them of central importance to this account of the family of Jesus?

These mothers and grandmothers of Jesus share one thing
in common: Tamar, Rahab, Ruth, Bathsheba, and Mary were
all forced to engage in very risky sexual activity in order to
ensure their survival. These risks were conditioned by their
patriarchal surroundings: survival under the systemic violence
of patriarchy meant that they had to behave in ways that their
societies defined as being indecent, immoral, disreputable,
impure, and unholy. Tamar dresses herself as a sex worker
and sleeps with her father-in-law, Judah, in order to find safety
and security for herself in a world that had made these promises and taken them away from her (Gen. 38). In Joshua, sex
worker and property owner Rahab, both because of and in
spite of her marginal status as sex worker and foreigner, aligns
herself with the God of Israel, ensuring her family's future by

saving Israelite spies (Josh. 2:1–24; 6:15–25). Ruth, an immigrant and a widow, chooses to live with and provide for her mother-in-law, Naomi, in Israel. She has two ways of living available to her: agriculture or marriage. She risks everything by sleeping with Boaz, who has the freedom and independence to decide to marry her (Ruth 1–4). Bathsheba is identified in Matthew's genealogy not by name, but as the property of her husband, Uriah. Bathsheba seems to be at the mercy of powerful men around her: David saw her bathing and "sent messengers to get her" (2 Sam. 11:4). David ensures her husband's death, and then takes Bathsheba for himself. Bathsheba is portrayed only in her vulnerability to male power.

Mary has no voice in Matthew, though as scholar Marika Rose argues, her presence in Jesus's genealogy is "most disruptive . . . Mary's role is to ensure that the one who (for Matthew) fulfills that line belongs there only by adoption."[9] Mary is pregnant with a child outside of her engagement to Joseph. Joseph marries her and so ensures her (highly) relative safety—a social status of respectability—within patriarchy. Mary's child is Joseph's by adoption (it should be noted that most of the Roman emperors were adopted into the line of succession!) and thus is part of the ancestral line of Israel by adoption. Jesus, according to Rose, "is more truly the child of these scandalous women than he is of the respectable patriarchs." Rose continues, "Like so many of these holy mothers, [Jesus] has no property but his own body, which he puts at risk in order to secure the future of those he loves; and the fatal violation of his body on the cross is the realization of the threat of death which lurks more or less explicitly in the background of each woman's story."[10]

While Mary is only spoken to in Matthew, her endurance of risk, her fundamental insecurity, forms the basis for the entire story of this early Gospel.

CONCLUSION

Under a household lens, Gospel of Matthew can and must be read as an ultimate experiment with family, an experiment that in many ways challenges the prevailing social model of the *paterfamilias* and of patriarchal descent. Jesus is an adopted son. His mother and his adoptive grandmothers were women who had to endure social violence, take risks, and express vulnerability to survive, and only four of these women are named, five recognized. This writing, itself adopted by different Jesus groups, would have had a profound impact on group belonging and organization. It is just one example of many forms of experimental family we find across the diverse communities of the Anointed and related groups in the first two centuries.

Chapter consultant:

Susan M. (Elli) Elliott

Papers Relevant to This Chapter by Seminar Participants

Elliott, Susan M. (Elli). "Introduction: Family, Religion, and Politics—Then and Now." Spring 2016.

———. "Transforming Family Relationships—Paul's Letters." Spring 2016.

Larsen, Lillian. "Re-defining Monastic 'Solitude': Fictive (and/or Factual) Family." Spring 2016.

JOIN THE CLUB

Chosen family was one way in which Jesus groups organized themselves. Another prominent organizational form was the association or club. Belonging to an association was a crucial way for people to find security, safety, and social place, especially for members of the under-heard: the enslaved, day laborers, and migrants from across the empire, among others. Exploring what these clubs were, how they were created, and how they functioned in the first and second centuries of the Common Era will help us to understand how Paul established his Anointed associations in particular.

THE SITUATION AT CORINTH

The ancient city of Corinth was located at the entrance of the Greek Peloponnesus, a peninsula extending from the mainland like an immense four-toed foot. About forty-five miles due west of Athens, Corinth was set astride two major ports, one on either side of a narrow geographical filament holding this foot to mainland Greece. An important commercial city, Corinth during the first and second centuries was a dynamic mix of people and practices—Greek, Roman, and otherwise—and home to impressive temples, baths, marketplaces, and theaters.

As we have seen, this vibrant city was also home to an equally alive Anointed association: Chloe's people. In a letter to this association, Paul remarks that news of the group's activities has been passed along to him by "Chloe's people," naming Chloe as a group leader or patron. "It has been reported to me by Chloe's people," writes Paul, "that there are divisions among you, my brothers and sisters" (1 Cor. 1:11). Paul wrote to this association at least four times, each letter addressed to a different situation within the community. On this occasion, Chloe's people report that members of the association are claiming allegiance to competing group leaders and teachers: "I belong to Paul!" some are shouting, and "I belong to Apollo!" or "I belong to Cephas!" Still others cry, "I belong to the Anointed!" (1 Cor. 1:12).

After much discussion of the challenges in this community, many caused by these disorderly factions, Paul counsels what he calls the superior or perfect way forward: love. "If I speak in the tongues of men and of angels, but have not love," Paul declares, "I am a noisy gong or a clanging cymbal . . . If I give away all I have, and if I deliver my body to be burned, but have not love, I gain nothing. Love is patient and kind; love is not jealous or boastful; it is not arrogant or rude . . . So trust, hope, love, these three, stand fast; but the greatest of these is love," Paul concludes (1 Cor. 13:1, 3–5, 13).

These verses from Paul's letter to Chloe's people, some of Paul's most famous verses, are best known from readings at contemporary wedding ceremonies. "Love is patient, love is kind," reads a sweaty second cousin to a fidgeting congregation, everyone eager for cocktail hour and the reception. Taken out of their context, apart from the rest of the letter, they do sound like a nice summary of the strength and singular importance of love. Paul's statements are made in a very specific context, however; earlier in his letter, Paul states that he wishes association members would remain unmarried, as Paul himself has.

Paul's statements about love are directed toward the activities of the Anointed association as a whole, toward group practice and the ways in which group members are to belong to and with one another. The Greek word Paul uses for love— *agape*—is associated most commonly, especially in the writings of early Anointed communities, with the love of humans for God. If association members approach group activities from the perspective of love for God, if they start with proper honor being paid to God, then their group practice will cohere. The group will come and stick together.

The verses that lead in to this description of love, while left out of readings at weddings, make Paul's point about love as group belonging clear. Paul states that all group members "are the body of the Anointed and individually members of it" (1 Cor. 12:27); this statement forms the heart of Paul's argument. He then lists various positions within the assembly/association: envoys, prophets, teachers, miracle workers, healers, helpers, administrators, and speakers of tongues. Everyone has their proper role to play within the Anointed community; no one can take on all roles. Group survival depends on respect for and observance of proper roles, the desire to play these roles properly.

When Paul talks about membership in the body of the Anointed, he is referring to an association. Many people across the Roman Empire in the first two centuries belonged to an association: a private, unofficial club, guild, or society whose members were organized around a particular neighborhood, a specific trade or occupation, worship of a particular god, a national identity, a household, or a combination of these forms of belonging. Chloe's people, for example, could have been an association structured in and around Chloe's extended household.

FINDING BELONGING IN AN ASSOCIATION

Associations were an essential mode of social belonging in the ancient world. The ancient words for "association" demonstrate the centrality of group belonging and activity: *collegium* is the standard Latin term, with the sense of colleague, collegiality, or fellowship. *Koinonia*, one of the most common Greek words for an association, means fellowship, partnership, or communion. Other words used to identify associations include "assembly," "meeting" or "company" (*synodos*), "fellow workers" (*synergasia*), and "a bringing together" or "assembling" (*synagoge*). These latter three club designations start with *syn*, Greek for "with," signaling the essential "with-ness" at the heart of these groups. This "with-ness" or bringing together usually involved eating together: club members met regularly for banquets, to celebrate festivals and observances for their club god or gods, to host burials for deceased members, to honor group officials and patrons, and to simply meet and network together. Meals were so important to these clubs that often they were named dining, banquet, or supper clubs, or the club itself was referred to with the Greek word for meal. Members were often required to pay club dues in support of these varied activities and were expected to follow certain rules of behavior.

The rules for membership in these clubs were varied. Some groups were exclusive to men; others were exclusive to women. A club record from Lanuvium in Italy recognizes the patronage of a man, Gaius Sulpicius Victor, toward a "women's assembly."[1]

A man named Thallos dedicated this monument to the god Zeus the
Highest, and to his association. This marble monument, dating from
between 150–30 BCE and found in modern-day Turkey, offers a vivid
portrait of club religious and social life.
British Museum

Women also served as benefactors of male and mixed associations; a marble slab from second-century Histria, a Greek colony on the Danube, records that a woman named Aba paid for feasts, prayers, and processions and gave members from a number of male associations—a club of local craftsmen, a neighborhood club, a club of doctors, and a club devoted to the hero-god Herakles—wine and money, "something which had never been done by anyone else before."[2]

Women were also leaders of various associations. A second- or third-century CE grave inscription from Smyrna, a city on the coast of modern Turkey, highlights the association leadership of a woman named Rufina:

> Rufina, Judean head of the synagogue, prepared the burial niche for her freedmen and the enslaved in her house. No one else has the authority to bury anyone else here. Now if anyone dares to do so, he will pay fifteen hundred denarii to the most holy treasury and one thousand denarii to the people (ethne) of the Judeans. A copy of this inscription was stored in the archives.[3]

Many Judean associations in the first two centuries were called synagogē: clubs organized around the honor of the Judean God and the particular Judean national/ethnic identity. The term was not exclusive to Judean clubs, however; records of synagogues of barbers, small-wares dealers, and shippers honoring the sea god Poseidon show that the term in the early centuries simply meant "a bringing together."

Clubs sometimes included the enslaved among their membership; enslaved members could belong to a club's household, if the association was formed out of someone's house, but household affiliation was not always relevant. Another record from a Lanuvium club, inscribed on a marble plaque in the second century CE, states:

> It was voted further that if an enslaved member of this association dies and his master or mistress unreasonably refuses to relinquish the body for burial, and he has not left written instruction, a funeral with an image of him will be held . . . It was voted further that if any enslaved member becomes free, he must give an amphora of good wine.[4]

These club votes suggest that enslaved people, apart from the households in which they were considered property, were full club members, honored equally.

As these examples suggest, our knowledge of these clubs comes largely from epigraphic evidence, that is, inscriptions on stone. These inscriptions often record the rules for club activities, procedures for meals or festivals, or recognition for honors given to specific members, among other subjects. They were displayed in club meeting spaces as a reminder of the rules; members were sometimes required to touch the stones before participating in group activities, ensuring that members kept the rules in mind while also displaying their proper conduct to other members. "During the monthly and annual sacrifices," reads the rules of an association based in the household of a man named Dionysios in the second or early first century BCE, "may those men and women who trust themselves touch this stone on which the instructions of the god [Zeus] have been written, so that those who obey these instructions, and those who do not obey these instructions, may become evident."[5]

PAUL AND THE *IOBACCHOI*

We get a sense of association life through an impressive stone inscription from Athens that records a list of club activities. Dating to 164/165 CE, this large, inscribed column would have been placed prominently in the club meeting space. The inscription on the column states that an assembly centered on the worship of the god Bacchus, an assembly calling themselves the *Iobacchoi*, "followers of Bacchus," met under the leadership of a new vice priest, Claudius Herodes. Herodes read the group statutes for approval by the group priest and the group president. The president announced: "To whomever it seems good that the statutes that have been read out should be ratified and inscribed on a monument, raise your hand!"[6] All group members raised their hands. This process, itself inscribed on the monument, makes it clear that all group members were responsible for knowing the club statutes.

The inscription goes on to state that all new members must register with the group priest and then be approved by a vote of the *Iobacchoi*, "if he appears to be worthy and suitable for the meeting place of Bacchus." If voted in, the new member pays an entrance fee, including an extra drink offering if the new member's father was not part of the group. Household ties play a role in this assembly but are not necessary for membership.

Members meet together, the inscription reads, on the ninth day of every month and for special festivals and feasts for the god Bacchus. Every member must contribute a certain amount of wine each month and "shall speak and act and be zealous for the association." The next section of the inscription offers a particularly vivid picture of association life:

In the gathering no one is allowed to sing, cause a disturbance, or applaud. Rather, with all order and decorum members shall speak and do their parts, as the priest or the head of the bacchic devotees directs. None of the *Iobacchoi* who has not paid the contributions for either the meetings on the ninth of the month or the annual festival is permitted to enter into the gathering, until it has been decided by the priests whether he should pay the fee or be allowed to enter anyway. Now if anyone begins a fight or is disorderly or sits in someone else's couch or insults or abuses someone else, the person abused or insulted shall produce two of the *Iobacchoi* as sworn witnesses, testifying that they heard the insult or abuse. The one who committed the insult or the abuse shall pay to the common treasury twenty-five light drachmas, or the one who was the cause of the fight shall either pay the same twenty-five drachmas or not come to any more meetings of the *Iobacchoi* until he pays. If someone comes to blows, the one who was struck shall file a report with the priest or the vice priest, who shall without fail convene a meeting and the *Iobacchoi* shall judge by a vote with the priest presiding.

Bacchus was the god of wine, fertility, and partying. Clubs dedicated to Bacchus likely had some very good times. These good and drunken times could surely lead to altercations, and the *Iobacchoi* are clear that disorderly behavior will not be tolerated. The extensive discussion of disorderly conduct indicates that it probably happened a lot. This club performed a reenactment of stories about Bacchus as its central practice: the priest told the story of Bacchus, and club members gave a dramatic performance of the story, rotating between roles such as the goddess Aphrodite or Palaimon, a child god of the sea who liked to ride upon a dolphin. Food, specifically the meat from sacrifices, was distributed to group members according to a prescribed protocol.

Paul's instructions to Chloe's people, along with his command that the letter be read out loud, should be understood as performing the same function as the statutes approved by the *Iobacchoi* and set up within their clubhouse. Like the statues, Paul directs that club activities should follow a certain order:

> When you come together, each one has a hymn, a lesson,
> a revelation, a tongue, or an interpretation. Let all things
> be done for edification. If any speak in a tongue, let there
> be only two or at most three, and each in turn, and let
> one interpret . . . If any one thinks that he is a prophet, or
> spiritual, he should acknowledge that what I am writing to
> you is a command of the Lord. If any one does not recog-
> nize this, he is not recognized." (1 Cor. 14:26–27; 37–38)

Paul lists disorder, fighting, unequal distribution of food at meals, drunkenness, arrogant talk, jealousy, and rivalry among the problems of this club, all stemming from the poor leadership of club officials.

THE ANOINTED'S SUPPER CLUB

Meals are a particularly important facet of establishing who has real or ultimate leadership over club practice. Paul admonishes, "in eating, each goes ahead with his own meal, and one is hungry and another is drunk. What! Do you not have houses to eat and drink in? Or do you despise the assembly of God and humiliate those who have nothing?" (1 Cor. 11:21–22). Paul reminds the association of their proper practice:

I received from the lord the same thing I passed on to
you, that on the night when he was handed over, the lord
Jesus took bread and after he gave thanks he broke it and
said, "This means my body broken for you. Do this to
remember me." And in the same way he took the wine
cup after the meal and said, "This cup means the new
covenant ratified by my blood. Whenever you drink this,
do it to remember me." So every time you eat this bread
and drink this cup you are proclaiming the death of the
lord until the day when he returns.

It follows that anyone who eats the bread or drinks the
cup without considering its meaning will be guilty of
demeaning the body and the blood of the lord. A person
should think about what he is doing before he eats the
bread and drinks from the cup . . . So then, my friends,
when you gather to eat, wait on one another. Any of
you who thinks only about his own hunger should eat
at home, so that your gathering together does not bring
condemnation upon you! (1 Cor. 11:23–28, 33–34)[7]

Jesus Anointed is presented in these verses as the initiator
and ongoing host of the club banquet, meaning Jesus Anointed
is the real leader of this group. Dishonor or insult to a club
member is an insult to the club's divine host.

Paul's presentation of this divinely hosted banquet runs
parallel to association practice more widely. Many clubs celebrated their meals in honor of their club gods and in the
assumed presence of their club gods. Club participation,
therefore, could put members directly in the presence of, and
in relationship to, honored divine beings. Aelius Aristides, a
well-known public speaker in the second century, wrote about

the Egyptian god Sarapis in terms similar to Paul, emphasizing partnership with the host deity:

> People make this god [Sarapis] alone a full partner in sacrifices, inviting him to the meal and making him both chief guest and host. So while different gods contribute to different club feasts, he is the one who completes all feasts and has the rank of leader of the banquet for those who assemble at times . . . He is a participant in the libations and the one who receives the libations. He comes to the celebration and invites those celebrating, who perform a dance under his direction. (*Orations* 45.27–28)[8]

Sarapis plays a very similar role, in club suppers, as the Anointed plays at the feast of Chloe's people. The Anointed invites those celebrating and leads the supper and the association, both participating in the supper and being the one honored at the supper. Celebration with gods and heroes was certainly an important strategy in encouraging group belonging.

The participation of gods in association meals is represented on a monument from sometime in the first century BCE to the second century CE, now in the British Museum and depicted earlier in this chapter. At the top of the monument, an inscription reads that a man named Thallos, a club official, dedicated the monument to Zeus the Highest and to his club. Below the inscription stand three large gods: Zeus, Artemis, and Apollo. Each of the gods holds out a bowl in which they are to receive offerings of wine. Beneath the gods a row of club members recline on couches to eat a meal, as was customary. The bottom row of the monument depicts the meal's entertainment: two musicians, a dancer, and a man mixing the wine. Again, the meal both honors these gods and depicts them as participants, reaching out to drink the wine alongside the reclining banqueters.

SAFETY IN NUMBERS

The *Iobacchoi* inscription goes on to state that anyone causing a disturbance during a meal, if they refuse to leave on their own accord, will be thrown out by "horses," a euphemism for bouncers:

> The officer in charge of order shall be chosen by lot or be appointed by the priest, bearing the wand of the god for anyone who is disorderly or creates a disturbance. Now if the wand is laid on anyone . . . the one who made the disturbance shall leave the banquet hall. If he refuses, those who have been appointed by the priests as "horses" shall take him outside of the door.

These details, read alongside the rules for group membership and for required and prohibited behaviors, speak to an essential benefit of belonging to a club: safety. Club officials carefully vetted new members, who were often approved by a club vote. Club practice demanded that members uphold standards of behavior, such as not causing fights or disturbances, not sleeping with other people's spouses, not wishing one another harm, or not participating in club activities knowing of any deceit or ill will toward any group member. Those causing disturbances will be thrown out of meals; those knowing of or guilty of any deceit will be thrown out of the association. Official bouncers and watchmen guard club space.

Among the benefits of club membership—lively meals, networking, the honor of acting as a priest or official—safety, group trust, was of top rank. Scholar Andrew Monson calls associations "trust networks," groups bonded by norms of safety and shared expectation: "By joining an association," Monson writes, "members signal to others that they are trustworthy and share the values of their peers. The rules of associations represent agreed norms of ethical behavior and embody shared values."[9] Members could trust one another to behave properly, but more than that, to provide one another with tangible forms of support: an equal share at meals, protection from cruel heads of household, assurance that their bodies would be properly honored after death, and protection from the gods. This form of trust, of support, was no small thing, given the precarious character of life during the first two centuries. Safety through group belonging made life less threatening and more livable.

Understood as a trust network, Paul's charge that Chloe's people love one another makes perfect sense. "If I speak in the tongues of men and of angels, but have not love," he writes, "I am a noisy gong or a clanging cymbal . . . Make love your aim, and earnestly desire the spiritual gifts, especially that you may prophesy" (1 Cor. 13:1; 14:1). Paul speaks of love in the context of the important group practices of prophecy and speaking in tongues. Love is about the unity of the body of the Anointed. If club members try to perform these activities but their underlying trust network is broken, none of the practices will work properly. Paul's lines about love speak to the issues fracturing club life: jealousy, arrogance, disrespect. As a trust network, the association will dissolve if these issues are not checked. This letter to Chloe's people speaks to the kind of trust, of mutual belonging, required for association life. Clubs were meant to be a refuge, a safe haven in precarious circumstance. Clubs were meant to be unified, not fractured, bodies.

The importance of trust to these groups found expression

in the language they often used for one another. Many associations were structured as chosen families, calling themselves "brotherhoods" and referring to members as siblings and adopted siblings. Association leaders could also be called mothers or fathers. While clubs were often formed out of particular households, the use of the language of family often did not relate to actual family members. An association of immigrants in what is now southern Turkey called one another brothers; a club devoted to "the Highest God" named each other adopted brothers; a man who donated several rooms, including a dining room, to a Judean bringing-together was called the father of the synagogue.

Other clubs used the language of friendship, calling one another friends or companions. In the same way, Paul uses the language of chosen family—members are called brothers and siblings, God is named as father—throughout this letter to Chloe's people, and in his letters to other Anointed associations as well. This language reflects the strength of this form of belonging, the social surety that association membership could provide.

CONCLUSION

Club members understood their voices to be temporary, heard only by their friends. While clubs might receive an occasional letter from an emperor recognizing impressive club honors paid to him or his imperial cult, clubs operated unofficially and mostly locally. Clubs gave voice to women, to the enslaved, to rag dealers, clothing cleaners, basket weavers, and grave diggers. Their statutes were often inscribed on stone, but they were for use by club members only, set up inside their meeting places or memorialized on a tomb, papyrus copies filed and lost in local archives. They were not meant for a master narrative. Outside of their clubs, the voices of rag dealers were not expected to be heard.

When we explore the evidence from clubs in our reading of first- and second-century Anointed associations, we keep our experiment on track. History tends to preserve only the voices it wants to hear. The voices that remain are intentional, almost always those of the powerful, those with access to resources, the elites. These winning voices also look backward, validating events and their interpretations, speaking to a constructed historical master narrative. That they should win was inevitable.

As records of the voices of the under-heard, such a wide, diverse cross section of ancient society, association rules, and registers provides us with a more reliable picture of first- and second-century Mediterranean life than what we find in the writings or histories of the social elite—writings from a narrow minority, free, fully resourced, and from an almost entirely male perspective. Reading Paul alongside association records gives us a much clearer understanding of what was happening in the associations of the Lord Jesus Anointed and why. Not every Anointed community was an association, to be sure. But undoubtedly, many Anointed communities structured themselves on this form of belonging, a belonging prioritizing group trust and social safety. Evidence from Paul's letters to the community at Thessalonica suggests that this group was also structured as an Anointed association. Such associations and early Judean synagogues also find their place among the varied, vibrant lives of ancient supper clubs, fellowships, and bringings-together.

12

FEASTING AND BATHING

THE SPIRIT AND PRACTICE OF COMMUNAL FEASTING

In the Gospel of Thomas, Salome says to Jesus, "Who are you mister? You have climbed onto my couch and eaten from my table" (61:2).[1] For modern readers, these words of Salome, one of Jesus's woman companions, may say more about the first two centuries of Jesus peoples than almost any other writing.

Her words present a graphic picture of the long and boisterous meals these people shared together. And, shocking for most of us, they lay down together as they ate, drank, talked, and feasted. The Gospel of John's description of this Mediterranean practice is vivid: "While at dinner, the student Jesus loved leaned back on Jesus's breast" (John 21:20).

These meals were the heart of all the gatherings of groups associated with Jesus Anointed. They were lush, entertaining, full of conversation, expressive, long, and embodied. Recognizing that members of these groups spent most of their time together at meal gatherings helps us understand what they stood for, how they thought of themselves, and what their core values were. The one thing that unified all the groups of this movement was that they regularly dined with each other.

Reclining: Meals on the Couch

This story from Gospel of Thomas can tell us even more. Both men and women attended these meals. While some groups insisted that women sit rather than recline, it was most common for women to recline, as in the Gospel of Thomas story of Salome. Salome is surprised that Jesus reclines at dinner with her, and challenges him: "Who are you mister?" This challenge is telling, since most reclining groups separated women and men on different couches and encouraged women to recline with women and men with men, as Jesus did with his favorite student in the Gospel of John.

Salome's attitude of challenging a man, especially in a semi-public situation, is less normal for that time, yet the way their conversation unfolds indicates that both are comfortable with conflict and real exchange. This story signals that the larger situation of these meals may have included regular substantive conflict and lively conversation among the meal community and between men and women.

The exchange between Salome and Jesus in Gospel of Thomas can tell us even more about how these meals provided the context for exploring the possibilities of stronger communication, community building, and complex gender relationships. What follows Salome's initial challenge to Jesus about his eating her food and lying on her dining couch illuminates new possibilities:

A typical Mediterranean meal of the first and second centuries.
Romney Oualline Nesbitt, copyright © 2002 Romney Oualline Nesbitt and Dennis E. Smith

Jesus said to her: I derive from the One who is connected
to all. I was given some of the things of my Father.

(Salome:) I am your follower.

(Jesus:) Because of this, I say: When one becomes whole,
one will be full of light. When one is in parts, one will be
full of darkness. (61:2, 3)

This exchange deepens the tension of living in community,
of connecting to one's meal group, of experiencing oneself as
both women and men together, of joining oneself to the One
who is connected to everything.

The tension between Salome's challenge to Jesus as he climbs
upon her couch and Salome's status as one of Jesus's followers remains. Jesus's connection to the One who is connected to the All

underscores the development of community at meals. And Jesus being given "some" (not all) of the things of the Father makes the relationship between Salome and Jesus more human. In this scene and this gospel writing, Jesus does share divinity with God, but not nearly as much as in the writings of the Gospel of John or the Gospel of Truth. This relationship to divinity opens up between Salome and Jesus a space shared by both humans and God. In all this connectivity, tension remains concerning whether the individuals and the meal community itself are "in parts" or "becoming whole." In this example of meal community in Gospel of Thomas, the connectivity is understood as practice. Everyone reclining together—and in this case, Jesus climbing up on Salome's couch—is a normal part of the practice of being in community. This practice is an analogue to a deeper experience of being one with "the One who is connected to all."

The exchange between Jesus and Salome demonstrates several kinds of practice. The back-and-forth about who can do what as Salome and Jesus challenge each other within the meal group expands traditional sexual and teacher-student roles. The meal also gives them real practice with new models for how women and men relate. Eating together invites practice in learning what it means to come from a larger oneness. As the back-and-forth makes a whole out of Jesus and Salome, Jesus says the result is reclining fully "in light" together.

This story from Gospel of Thomas enables modern readers to view practices of these Jesus clubs, schools, and communities from the early centuries that are very different from those of today.

Feasting in the Mediterranean

Mediterranean people in general intentionally exaggerated the importance of relaxation and ease when they ate together. They took their time to enjoy their food and wine. Joyful celebration was foundational, even in the midst of the tension of life under empire. Although research indicates these early groups of Jesus peoples had exuberant and jubilant meals, as the conversation between Salome and Jesus shows, it was not always sweetness and light. Fierce arguments, as well as shortages of food, were well known.

Other groups besides Jesus peoples gathered and acted in a similar way: reclining, drinking, singing, discussing, and arguing. Members of extended families and neighborhood groups; workers such as carpenters, shipbuilders, and bricklayers; and members of various religious groups shared meals as a regular practice. Associations and clubs of various types hosted such meals.

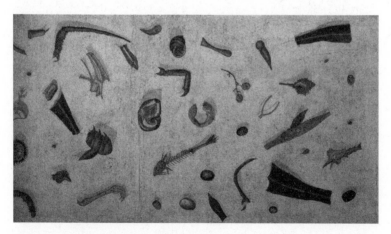

The diners belonging to Chloe's people, parties of the Anointed, and the Order of Melchizedek reclined around the room, and as they ate they threw their food remains on the ground in the center of the room. Mostly at mid-course, volunteer servers let dogs into the room to eat the scraps. This mosaic (a Roman copy of a Greek original) depicts the leavings from such a meal.
Alf van Beem

So important was dining in the first and second centuries that it was defining for most people. Reclining while eating expressed the significance of leisure and ease. The Greeks, who began this style of feasting centuries before, insisted that the meal expressed equality. Initially, equality found expression only among wealthy, free Greek males. By the first century, however, the enslaved, women, and other ethnicities also could be full participants, although full participation was often a matter of principle rather than of practice. This participation became an inherent principle of the communities of the Anointed.

Many Jesus movements expanded what it meant to recline together and share food equally. While these meals did have a set of general rules, many gatherings elaborated what they did, how they did it, and what it meant. In this way, their identities emerged through participating in their festive meals.

More Kinds of Meals

The picture in Gospel of Thomas of such meals illustrates the broad pattern of Mediterranean meals in general and among Jesus communities. Two other kinds of meals among Jesus peoples show how different the basic reclining communities could be, and how different the various Jesus-related communities' ideas and constituents were.

Levi's Feast for Jesus

Different communal emphases emerge in different writings. Although the basic framework for these meals is the same, the focus shifts. Gospel of Thomas focuses on spiritual oneness, learning from gender tensions, and what Jesus and his followers have in common.

A story in the Gospel of Luke has a different tenor. This story should not be understood simply as being about the historical

Jesus, but about how this particular community emerged in the second century.

> And Levi gave Jesus a great banquet in Levi's house, and a large group of toll collectors and others were dining with them.
>
> The Pharisees and their scholars would complain to his followers: "Why do you people eat and drink with tax collectors and sinners?"
>
> In response Jesus said to them, "Since when do the healthy need a doctor? It's the sick who do. I have not come to enlist religious folks to change their hearts, but sinners." (5:29–32)[2]

The drama in this story revolves around what happens at meals when a group experiences being shunned or mocked. Many other writings make this same point: good things happen when people alienated from one another eat together. Meaning and benefit emerge in meals when those of different classes, ethnicities, and social standing eat together.

However, this attractive and compelling practice of diversity by groups of the Anointed had some problematic examples as well: women were sometimes silenced or not allowed to recline; enslaved peoples might be denied complete equal status; festive meals sometimes provoked clashes between ethnicities. This meal story in Gospel of Luke holds up an interaction with despised people, while the meal story in Gospel of Thomas deals with a oneness of spirit and a focus on getting to know one another across gender.

Synagogue of the Womb of All That Grows

In the Nag Hammadi manuscripts, a small document called *Prayer of Thanksgiving* illustrates an even wider range of what people can learn from meals during this period. It is highly likely that the group who used this prayer had a significant relationship to Jesus peoples, because this document was found in a collection of writings that belonged to Jesus groups. This document presents a prayer that might be said at a meal much like the meals in Thomas and in Luke. How many groups, or what size communities, prayed this meal prayer is unknown, but the fact that the fifty-two documents found along with this prayer were probably stored in a later Christian desert monastery suggests that many groups did so.

Prayers such as *Prayer of Thanksgiving* are best described as "prayers of larger Israel." More or less all Jesus peoples of the first and second centuries thought of themselves as belonging to greater Israel, even when they did not have parents of descent from Israel (see Chapter 9).

As we have seen elsewhere in this book, during this time conquered nations experienced difficulty and sorrow around who they were. *Prayer of Thanksgiving* is a prayer of defeated Israel, regardless of the group's composition. Celene Lillie translates the prayer as follows:

We give thanks to you, every life and heart stretches toward you,

O name untroubled, honored with the name of God, praised with the name of Father.

To everyone and everything, comes the kindness of the Father, and love and desire.

And if there is sweet and simple teaching, it gives us mind, word, and knowledge; mind that we may understand you; word that we may interpret you; knowledge that we may know you.

We rejoice and are enlightened by your knowledge.

We rejoice that you have taught us about yourself.

We rejoice that in the body you have made us divine through your knowledge.

The thanksgiving of the human who reaches you is this alone: that we know you.

We have known you, O light of mind.

O light of life, we have known you.

O womb of all that grows, we have known you.

O womb pregnant with the nature of the Father, we have known you.

O never-ending endurance of the Father who gives birth, so we worship your goodness.

One wish we ask: we wish to be protected in knowledge.

One protection we desire: that we not stumble in this life.[3]

Following the prayer is this line: "When they said these things in prayer, they welcomed one another, and they went to eat their holy food, which had no blood in it." The reference to "no blood" in the holy food suggests that this group followed procedures held by early Judean synagogues. Many synagogues in the first two centuries were not buildings, but groups, since the word "synagogue" is a transliteration of the Greek word that means "meeting." As in Thomas and in Luke, going to a synagogue and belonging to Israel can be applied to most of the groups we have encountered in this book. Understanding this group as belonging to the people of Israel is standard for the Jesus peoples of the first two centuries.

This prayer exhibits a range of social inventiveness, visionary spirituality, and theology. Its openness and imagination are part of a signature innovation of broader Israel and the energy of the larger meal movements in the first and second centuries.

Its energy of receiving the "kindness," "love," and "desire" of

God in "everyone and everything" fits well with the concerns of Israel, as represented by Jesus or Philo, a first-century Judean philosopher from Alexandria. The prayer's praise for the "light of life" and the "womb of all that grows" overflows with vitality and fertility. That this document proclaims "every life and heart stretches toward you, / O name untroubled" indicates deep receptivity to a large world and a generous and open-ended divinity. Its courageous resistance to violence and its joyfulness are at home within the encouragement of leisure, social openness, debate, and embrace of diverse peoples that meals of the Anointed expressed.

Feasting with God

Even though these examples of meals have a similar shape and interest in Jesus, they exhibit very different causes and values and produced different kinds of communities and movements. Even more variety of festive meals existed among other Jesus peoples, synagogues, clubs, and schools of the Anointed than we can explore. These widely different meals created an extraordinarily creative set of cultures in the first two centuries—ones that were resistant, lively, and innovative.

Key to the present book's larger understanding is that groups gathered regularly for communal meals. The first two hundred years after Jesus are unintelligible without these vigorous and intense gatherings at meals. The broad differences between the meal portraits we have explored also begin to show that such meals both held these many differences together and also encouraged a great variety of ideas and expressions.

The Decline of Vibrant Meals

For most of the first two centuries of the Common Era, the many different types of groups associated with the Anointed had meals as their primary gathering. So when did the shift in practice move to other forms of communal eating?

This work has unfolded relatively slowly but since about 2015 has resulted in a series of key conclusions. Andrew McGowan sketches out a clear portrait of the first four hundred years of the Common Era in his paper "Changing Courses: Eucharistic Origins":

1. The only known practice of Jesus communities for the first ninety years was the festive meal. It was perhaps one of the most profound dimensions of those early movements.

2. All of those groups continued to meet around meals for something like the first 235 years of the Common Era. Everyone participated in these meals. But in some places, probably beginning in the early second century, a minority of groups and clubs had occasional larger early morning gatherings in town halls. These morning meetings were too large to achieve the intimacy of the communal meals, but there was often a mini-meal at those morning meetings. The mini-meals were understood to be subsidiary to the regular and ongoing evening meals. Regular reclining meals remained the primary practice of these groups.

3. McGowan tends to think that many meals groups continued through the 200s and into the 300s, but sometime in the third century some groups discontinued the evening meals because their groups were too large for them.

4. Probably by the mid-fourth century only a minority of these groups shared meals anymore; by this time, most of them thought of themselves as "Christian."

5. By the sixth century the vast majority of Christians worshipped in churches without anything but a token piece of bread and a cup of wine to eat and drink.[4]

So ended the central dynamic—the festive communal meal—of the communities of Jesus Anointed in the first two centuries.

THE SPIRIT AND PRACTICE OF BATHING

Not nearly as regularly but just as expressively as the meals, most Jesus-related groups practiced bathing as a part of their life together. The joy of bathing ran deep alongside the joy of feasting.

We know most about bathing practices connected to the people of Israel who lived all around the Mediterranean. Stories about Jesus bathing with others are found throughout the diverse writings of these clubs and groups. Acts of the Apostles has ten different stories that make direct reference to Judean-like bathing outside of geographical Israel. However, especially in Acts, these bathings are mistakenly translated "baptism" and take on the meaning of being a Christian ritual associated with becoming a Christian. This imposes a later Christian meaning on the practice of bathing by the communities of Jesus Anointed.

Roman emperors always listed baths as one of their great gifts to the people of the empire. By the end of the second century, the city of Rome had more that three hundred baths. Imperial baths were large complexes with three main rooms: a central atrium, a hot bathing room, and a cold one. These were places not only for bathing but also for socializing.

Since baths needed lots of water, the emperors built large aqueducts to supply cities with water. The ruins of some of these enormous stone engineering projects dominate landscapes to this date. There was no real practical need for all the stonework; it was part of Roman propaganda. The baths and aqueducts demonstrated concretely Roman ownership, power, and stability. The empire was here to stay.

The common meaning of the Greek word *baptizo* (baptism) is "bathing," "washing," "immersing," or "thoroughly dipping." It is an ordinary word, used to describe ordinary washing and bathing of both objects and people. Ordinary usage of the words *baptizo* and *baptisma* do not refer to ritual.

To make basic sense of the references to "*baptizo*-ing" in the writings of the groups of the Anointed of the first and second centuries, it is best to use the basic meaning of washing and bathing. To call these events "baptisms" is inappropriate for two reasons. First, it is not a translation but a transliteration. Like the word "Christian," the English word "baptism" imposes a later Christian meaning on the practice of bathing by the communities of Jesus Anointed. The proper translation for the word in all writings of the Jesus communities of the first two centuries is "bathing" or "washing."

Not unlike the communal meals we have just examined, these bathings were often social and relaxed. The late second-century Jesus movement writer Tertullian listed the places such bathing could happen as "in a sea or a pool, a stream or a fount, a lake or a trough" (*On Baptism* 4).[5] Archaeological digs have revealed that many neighborhoods in Israel had small baths next to, and often almost as large as, houses. Pools were often found between houses in neighborhoods. People from various households bathed together (the men and the women at separate times). Besides these Judean baths, many other groups in the empire engaged in this practice: Isis cults and Mithraic, Bacchic, and Eleusian groups also held regular or occasional washings as a part of their group life.

Ritual was a major aspect of ordinary, daily life. Social bathing took on a variety of meanings, rooted in the importance of cleaning oneself. Metaphorically, bathing became a sign of moral cleanness and purity of heart and mind, differentiating the bathers from corruption in its many forms. People washed themselves regularly of such physical, moral, attitudinal, and social "dirtiness."

Since most bathing was social, a variety of different types of uncleanliness would be present. Some bathers had minor regrets and worries; others needed to recuperate from dirty or humiliating work; still others were experiencing significant pain or only needed to wash their bodies. Bathing events involved group reflection, small talk, silence, joy, ponderings, prayers, and storytelling. They mixed losses and wounds with relaxation, comfort, social give-and-take, and the sensuousness of water. There was also a sense of release, lamentation, and long-term resolve. The first-century historian Josephus wrote of washings by "John the Bather," whom we more traditionally know as John the Baptist, that were "a consecration of the body implying that the soul was already thoroughly cleansed by right behaviour," meaning that those who bathed were committed to "lead righteous lives, to practice justice towards their fellows and piety towards God, and so doing to join in baptism" (*Antiquities* 18.117).[6]

One special occasion was when a washing of one's past life as a person became intentionally part of a new way of life. Both non-Israel women and men bathed upon the occasion of joining the community of Israel, with its new demands and reliefs. Although men also were circumcised as a part of joining the community of Israel, the washing—again, always with a group—was the pivotal moment for women becoming a part of the people of Israel. This washing away of losses, uncleanness, and indignity formed the basis for membership in greater Israel.

This snapshot of ancient Mediterranean bathing offers a chance to rethink the logic of so-called baptism during the first two centuries. While this practice resembles many similar bathings of Mediterranean peoples, its more immediate antecedent was the washing practices in Israel and more specifically in Galilee where Jesus movements first existed.

John the Bather aka John the Baptist

The stories associated with the first-century Israel leader called John the Bather show us how bathing in different Jesus groups became a crucial practice. The context for John's practice was that the people of Israel needed to be cleansed from the humiliation, anger, and pain resulting from Rome's violent conquest and occupation of Israel; they also needed to be bathed clean of their collaboration with their Roman occupiers.

Rome's client king of Israel built Roman baths during the early occupation of Jerusalem. The building of these baths around the Jerusalem Temple as a part of a Roman renovation of the Temple met with protests by devotees of the Temple. The Roman bathing pools around the Temple were deemed especially offensive, because many experienced Roman rule as sullying Israel's sense of purity before God. The stories about John the Bather indicate or imply his joining the protests and setting up a competing bathing away from the corrupt Roman baths around the Temple.

Setting up these alternate bathings was a brilliant spiritual and political move on the part of John the Bather. Gospel stories tell of John leading hundreds of people from Jerusalem to the fabled Jordan River at the edge of the desert, a several days' walk from the city. There they bathed in the fresh running water to cleanse themselves of the dirty military occupation of their land, and to avoid the sullied bathing pools around Jerusalem's Temple. Not unlike Israel's march to the Jordan twelve hundred years before to claim the land as its home, these stories portray the people walking to wash themselves clean of ordinary uncleanliness, the dirty business of Roman rule, and the brokenness of Israel's identity. John's teaching and washing enabled them to make deep changes in their actions and thinking.

The drama of this bathing carried with it emotional and spiritual comfort, release, and community. Tens or maybe hundreds of people bathing together in the mother river of the land of Israel brought a sense of safety, belonging, and renewal to the traumatized people in Jerusalem and surrounding areas. Perhaps most of all, this bathing washed away at least some of the humiliation, pain, and loss of people living under a relentlessly cruel and arrogant tyrant. On all these levels, the bathing poured over the pilgrims the salve of healing in free-flowing water.

Sorting out the details of John the Bather's story is difficult. Maybe only seventy-five people or maybe more than a thousand went to the Jordan River. Maybe it's just a story. In any case, he became so beloved by the people of Israel that Gospel of Matthew has Jesus saying, "Among those born of women no one greater than John the Bather has appeared" (11:11). The Romans, however, hated him, and inevitably ordered his death.

Downstream in the Second Century

More than half of all the accounts of bathings in the New Testament appear in the Acts of the Apostles. In Acts, most likely a second-century document, bathing was done as a part of people being washed clean of their faults and failures and celebrating this major change in their lives. In at least twelve different stories in Acts, after someone changes their way of life and resolves to lead a better one, bathing marks, as Josephus wrote, "a consecration of the body implying that the soul was already thoroughly cleansed by right behaviour." Both Israel's practice of ordinary washings and the dramatic elaborations of such washings by John the Bather shaped the bathings narrated in Acts. The pictures and stories of washing in Acts are stories of people who change their way of life by practicing an Israel-based and John-the-Bather–based innovation in the name of Jesus Anointed.

Bathing Practices in the Second Century

Thus we can understand, in its proper context, the courageous, renewing, and imaginative practice of a besieged people through a retooling of a routine practice. What, then, about later Christian baptisms and how Israel's bathings relate to them? A number of questions remain open and unsolved.

It is now clear that ordinary ritual bathing practices and John the Bather's experimental practices were practices of occupied Israel. In the second century, however, these bathing practices of Jesus groups moved beyond celebrations of people's resistance to Roman violence. The mid-second century, after the Bar Kokhba War of 132–136 CE, was marked by people's gradual increasing loyalty to various schools, clubs, and movements associated with Jesus, and the bathings increasingly express intentional membership in specific groups or movements. The bathing celebration focused more on membership and loyalty. Of course, there was very little or no talk of "Christian" or "Christianity"; but there was an increasing attention to declaring one's loyalty to Jesus, the God of Israel, and particular communities during the bathings. What remains to be sorted out is exactly how and when the shift from bathings to Christian baptism occurred.

CONCLUSION

Both bathing and communal eating practices of Jesus groups during the first two centuries of the Common Era were important community activities. The bathing practices in particular had a strong effect across broad swaths of these communities as people strove against imperial pressure. Both of these practices healed and energized otherwise broken people and relationships, providing them with a sense of belonging to a safe community.

Papers Relevant to This Chapter by Seminar Participants

Al-Suadi, Soham. "The Ritual of the Hellenistic Meal: Early Christian Everyday Practice as an Exegetical Challenge." Fall 2017.

Larsen, Lillian. "Monastic Meal Rituals." Fall 2017.

McGowan, Andrew. "Changing Courses: Eucharistic Origins." Fall 2017.

Patterson, Stephen J. "Baptism: A Pre-History." Fall 2017.

Smith, Dennis. "In the Beginning Was the House: How Social and Identity Formation of Early Christ Groups Took Place." Spring 2016.

Taussig, Hal. "Washing Dogma Off Baptismal Practices of the First Two Centuries." Fall 2017.

PART III
_____

REAL VARIETY, FICTIONAL UNITY

INVENTING ORTHODOXY
THROUGH HERESY

To call someone a heretic is a very grave insult and accusation. Why? Simply put, because it puts that person outside of the bounds of the group, indicating that he or she has deviated from the group's true beliefs. Originally a religious term, and today even a Christian term, it has spread its tentacles from the religious sphere into a variety of other aspects of modern life. Politics is a great example. Republicans whom other Republicans deem insufficiently "Republican" are called "RINOs," or Republican in Name Only—a contemporary kind of heretic.

There is an irony here. How did the Jesus movement, which was open to the varied elements of the Roman world and all different peoples, move to exclude that diversity in favor of orthodoxy—that is, so-called proper belief that excluded many? Orthodoxy told this story as the exclusion of heresy that corrupted the purity of original teachings. The fourth-century church historian Eusebius used this as his main narrative line.

The teacher Thecla of the group the Enslaved of God was continually arrested for being a single public woman teacher who refused to be married. Her teaching was never stopped, and she died of old age. Here she prays among the beasts in the arena.

Sarah Sexton Crossan

THE ORIGINS OF HERESY

The English word "heresy" is a transliteration of the Greek *hairesis*, whose basic meaning is "choice," particularly intellectual choice. Often it refers to teachings of the Greek philosophical schools or to those who follow a particular school or system of thought, with the common translation of "party" or, more negatively, "faction." The Acts of the Apostles uses this term in precisely this way: "But the high priest rose up and all who were with him, that is the party [*hairesis*] of the Sadducees" (5:17). This could just as easily be translated as "school" or "philosophy." This is precisely the way the first-century Judean historian Josephus uses this word in describing the four schools or philosophies of first-century Israel.[1]

Paul, the envoy of the Anointed, uses *hairesis* in a slightly different fashion, although well within standard usage. "First of all, I hear that when you meet as a community there are divisions [*hairesis*] among you and to some extent I believe it" (1 Cor. 11:18). The context indicates that Paul views this as negative, so "divisions" is an acceptable translation. The sense is that Paul fears the Corinthian community is dividing into schools. There is no indication, however, that he thinks one of the schools or divisions should be excluded from the community.

The sense of *hairesis* as intellectual choice or school remained dominant through most of the second century. The strong negative sense of "heresy" becomes evident only in the late second century in the writing of the north African teacher Tertullian called *Concerning the Prescription of Heretics*: "The heretic is no longer considered a member of the party of *Christus*" (16.2). Now the heretic is excluded from the community and identified with those who follow false gods and Judeans.

When writers in later centuries, including even modern scholars until recently, looked back on those writers before Tertullian, they anachronistically read earlier usage as identical with Tertullian's. Translations also reflect this anachronistic reading of the second-century writers. This is very clear in the writings of the Greek bishop Irenaeus. Markus Vinzent in his paper for the Christianity Seminar pointed out how translation can change the meaning of a writing. If one translates *hairesis* as "heresy," as has been traditionally done, the sense is very different from the sense one gets if one uses "school" instead. This makes a big difference in our understanding of Irenaeus, an important teacher in the mid-second century, in his writing:

> Many offshoots of numerous schools (heresies) have already been formed from those schoolmasters (heretics) we have described. This arises from the fact that numbers of them— indeed, we may say all—desire themselves to be teachers, and to break off from the particular school (heresy) in which they have been involved. Forming another teaching out of another opinion, and then another from another, they insist upon teaching something new, declaring themselves the inventors of an opinion which they may have been able to call into existence. (*Against Heresies* 1.28.1)[2]

The context clearly indicates that Irenaeus is dealing with schools of thought and the dynamic of how schools and teachers operate. They inherently create competition for new teachings. Like Paul, Irenaeus finds these schools and teachings problematic, but he does not appear to view them as outside the group, as Tertullian does at a later period. Their error needs to be exposed and corrected. This is indicated in the complete title of Irenaeus's book: *On the Detection and Overthrow of the So-Called Knowledge.* The traditional English title, *Against Heresies* (from the Latin title *Adversus Haereses*), was formulated several centuries after the work's composition after the debate between teachers and schools at the time of Irenaeus had escalated into expulsion from the church of those who disagreed with the developing orthodoxy. In this much later period, the Greek *hairesis* was transliterated into Latin as *haereses* and subsequently into English as "heresy." This transliteration process almost guarantees an anachronistic reading of earlier authors. (See Chapter 2 for how this plays out with the word "Christian.")

RIVALRY IN PHILOSOPHICAL SCHOOLS

The way forward is to reject the either/or of heresy versus orthodoxy, the creation of later centuries, and look at the evidence from the first two centuries without prejudice as to a predetermined outcome. Where did these different teachings come from?

The significance of philosophical schools as the primary social environment for the development of teachings in the early Jesus movements is often overlooked.[3] Such schools had a long tradition in Greek and Roman culture. Plato's academy existed well into the first century BCE. Schools in this context did not have formal curricula but were an informal grouping of teachers and students who shared a common interest.

Israel also had well-established schools. The Judaean historian Josephus refers to the four schools of Israel. The Pharisees were one of those schools, and the later rabbis, especially after the Bar Kokhba War (132–136 CE), reorganized the life of

204 AFTER JESUS BEFORE CHRISTIANITY

Israel around Torah and its study. Jesus in the gospels is often called a teacher, and his followers are referred to as students, or in church-speak as "disciples." The Gospel of Matthew ends with the resurrected Jesus telling his students, "You shall go and make students of the nations . . . Teach them to observe everything I have commanded you" (28:19, 20). This Gospel understands the task of Jesus's followers to be a school task. The various writings associated with John would also appear to be the product of a school. Thus, the school model goes back to the very beginning of the Jesus movements.

Following the Bar Kokhba War, the rise of schools within the movement became much more evident. The continuous interaction and debate between rival schools highlighted the difference in teachings between schools and teachers. This, of course, was normal school practice. These differences in teachings would in time escalate to differences in doctrine, an ecclesiastical word for "teachings." In the mid-second century, Justin Martyr addresses Marcion in a now lost work titled *To Marcion*, indicating that it is a conversation between two teachers, a conversation in which according to the rules of rhetoric, Justin will try to persuade Marcion. Tellingly, the fourth-century church historian Eusebius knows this is the title of Justin's work, but oftentimes when not quoting from it, he refers to it as *Against Marcion*, reflecting the heresy-orthodoxy divide of his time. In Justin's later *First Apology* and *Second Apology* he turned more decisively against Marcion, but it still remained a serious and critical debate among teachers.

Even later in the second century, Irenaeus writes of the many different and lively schools within the Jesus movement. He argues that schools break up and divide out of the desire of students to become teachers themselves. This desire led to the rise of new teachings. Thus, the internal dynamics of the schools, the competition between different teachers, and the desire of students to become teachers gave rise to new teachings and new schools supporting those teachings. The schools and their teachers were a driving force in a dynamic movement creating difference within the movement, according to Irenaeus.

Significantly, the interschool debates about teachings arose not from theological issues, like the oneness of God, but from the actual practices of the communities of the Anointed. This should not be surprising, as the Jesus movement, just like the Judean movement, was more about correct practice (ortho-praxis) than correct belief (orthodoxy). What unified both movements was practice. On the road to Christianity in the third and fourth centuries, that relationship would reverse. As illustrations of this dynamic, we look at two issues: death at the hands of the Roman officials and gender.

Self-Mastery and Noble Death
To understand the "noble death" (see Chapter 6), it's impor-tant to understand that a major goal of Greek and Roman ed-ucation was training in self-control or self-mastery—control of the passions. The emphasis was not on abstract knowledge, but control of the self that ensured integrity and overall char-acter. This goal was held in common by many followers of the Anointed who adapted it to their own needs. Paul in Ga-latians 3:24 refers to the law as a teacher for the nations. The purpose of the law was to teach the nations mastery of their passions. His whole understanding of the purpose of the law for the nations in his Letter to the Romans is undergirded by the notions of self-mastery. For Paul, the efforts of the nations to employ the law as a method of self-mastery of the passions

led to a misuse of the law. They became invested in doing the law, what Paul calls "works of the law." For Paul, self-mastery is achieved by emulating the assurance of Jesus.

In Favor of Seeking a Noble Death

In the second century, the notion arose that a noble death at the hands of Roman officials ensured eternal health and salvation for the soul and body's fleshly resurrection (see Chapter 18). The value of suffering was in its ability to control the passions. Deborah Saxon traces this process in her paper for the Seminar "What's at Stake When 'Heresy' Sells?"

According to Saxon, *1 Clement*, written in the second century, holds up the deaths of the envoys Peter and Paul as examples for the Corinthian community:

> We should set before our eyes the good apostles. There is Peter, who because of unjust jealousy bore up under hardships not just once or twice, but many times; and having thus borne his witness he went to the place of glory that he deserved. Because of jealousy and strife Paul pointed the way to the prize for endurance. (*1 Clem.* 5:3–5)[4]

Just as jealousy led to the execution of the envoys, so will it undermine the Corinthian community. But the envoys' patient endurance demonstrated in their deaths their self-control, which will win out with eternal reward, as stated of Paul further along in *1 Clement*: "He taught righteousness to the whole world, and came to the limits of the West, bearing his witness before the rulers. And so he was set free from this world and transported up to the holy place, having become the greatest example of endurance" (5:7).

Ignatius, writing about the same time as Clement, plays with the same themes. He sees his upcoming execution as a training in self-control:

> For even though I have been bound in the Name, I have not yet been perfected in Jesus Anointed. For now I have merely begun to be a student, and I speak to you as my fellow learners. For I need to be trained by you in faith, instruction, endurance, and patience. (*To the Ephesians* 3.1)[5]

He uses the school language of a student in training. All this suffering is so that he can be perfected in the virtues of self-mastery.

In this model, execution and those who followed the executed attained all virtues. Execution by Rome validated the truth of their position. Their opponents were accused of disloyalty and lack of courage for avoiding execution. Irenaeus clearly makes this argument:

> Some of these men have proceeded to such a degree of temerity, that they even pour contempt upon the witnesses, and vituperate those who are slain on account of the confession of the Lord, and who suffer all things predicted by the Lord, and who in this respect strive to follow the footsteps of the Lord's passion, having become martyrs of the suffering One. (*Against Heresies* 3.18.5)[6]

This becomes the standard argument, repeated over and over, from the second century until, well, almost forever. The position of this "pro-execution" group is that suffering teaches patience, which controls desire, thereby producing self-mastery.

Suspicious of Seeking Execution

This attack on those suspicious of dying in the arena is, of course, from the point of view of their opponents. What, then, is the contrary argument?

A second- or early third-century CE writing known now as *Testimony of Truth* helps us to understand this alternative position. *Testimony of Truth* came to light among the Nag Hammadi manuscript discoveries of 1945. Although this manuscript was seriously damaged, what remains is very interesting, including its retelling of the Garden of Eden story from the perspective of Eden's snake. The modern editors assigned the present title on the basis of its contents, which emphasizes truth and truth-telling: "This therefore is the true testimony. When man knows himself and God who is over the truth, he will be saved and he will be crowned with the crown unfading."[7]

This statement can serve as a summary of the author of the *Testimony*'s position. Saxon's work is key in identifying how this writing crafts a self-mastery counterargument to those favoring dying as a witness. Salvation is knowledge, not theoretical knowledge, but knowledge as experience that engages with self-control. That will win the athlete's crown, the same crown associated with the witness. All those involved in this debate agree that self-mastery is the goal, and they basically agree on what constitutes self-control: the traditional stoic control of the passions. The debate in the *Testimony* is over how that is achieved:

> And this is what the Son of Man reveals to us: It is fitting for you (pl.) to receive the word of truth. If one will receive it perfectly—. But as for one who is [in] ignorance, it is difficult for him to diminish his works of [darkness] which he has done. Those who have [known] Imperishability, [however,] have been able to struggle against [passions].

Just as the witness is perfected by suffering, the knower is perfected by the word of truth, knowing "Imperishability" (God). The knower will win the struggle with the passions. In the hand of the opponents, the knower becomes a gnostic and identified with the modern invention of Gnosticism (see Chapter 14). The author of *Testimony of Truth* attacks those who seek execution by quoting the martyr's confession:

> The foolish, thinking [in] their heart [that] if they confess, "We are Christians," in word only (but) not with power, while giving themselves over to ignorance, to a human death, not knowing where they are going nor who the Anointed is, thinking that they will live, when they are (really) in error, hasten towards the principalities and the authorities. They fall into their clutches because of the ignorance that is in them.

This is a remarkable passage. The witnesses are foolish and have completely misunderstood how salvation is achieved. They are ignorant and the victims of ignorance. This in turn leads to a denial of the resurrection of flesh: "[Do not] expect, therefore, [the] carnal resurrection, which [is] destruction."

Both sides in this argument agree on the goal—salvation as defined by self-control—but they disagree on how this is achieved. For one group it is through suffering, which builds endurance and patience and controls desire. The witness is the archetype. On the other side, the knower achieves these same goals reached by knowledge though the revelation of the Word, experiencing God. That knowledge brings control of the passions. By the end of the second century this divide became explicit, whereas it had been more fluid through the mid-second century.

Gender in Acts of Paul and Thecla

The title Acts of Paul and Thecla tells so much. Although Paul's name in first place indicates his priority as a male over a female, Thecla actually dominates the story. She is its true hero. As so often, things are not as they appear. A recently discovered fresco in Ephesus epitomizes the problem. It pictures Thecla's mother and Paul making the sign of preaching to Thecla in a burning house. But some later vandal, thinking that this indicates that Paul and a female are equal, has scratched out the eyes of the female character, attempting to disappear her, just as orthodoxy has attempted to scratch out heresy along with her. But the real story is more complex. Tertullian is the first author to remark on Thecla's story only to attack it, while Gregory of Nazianzus in the fourth century withdrew to her tomb for three years of prayer. (Thecla remained a popular saint whose tomb in Seleucia was venerated until well into the sixth century.)

The dating of Acts of Paul and Thecla is difficult to ferret out, but the text surely was in widespread circulation in Asia Minor by the mid-second century. In form it is a romance tale with high interest in legendary and miraculous details. Men are always falling in love with the beautiful virgin Thecla. It contains the first existing description of Paul: "a man small in size, bald-headed, bandy-legged, of noble mien, with eyebrows meeting, rather hood-nosed, full of grace" (Thecla 3).[8]

Bearing witness before the Roman officials is neither praised nor criticized in the narrative, but it is part of the story's subtext. Very early in the story Paul's message is summarized as "the word of God about abstinence and resurrection" (Thecla 5). One has to wonder whether the author of these Acts had actually read or even knew Paul's letters (see Chapter 15). Both abstinence and resurrection are strongly connected to a noble death. Abstinence is an example of self-mastery, overcoming the passions and desire, while resurrection is the reward for dying as a witness.

When Thamyris, who is engaged to Thecla, denounces Paul before the proconsul, he accuses Paul of making "virgins averse to marriage." When the proconsul questions Paul, he responds, "The living God . . . has sent me that I may rescue them from corruption and uncleanness and all pleasure, and from death, that they may sin no more" (Thecla 17)—all of which call for self-control. But when Thecla, remaining faithful to Paul's teaching about virginity, refuses to marry Thamyris, the proconsul condemns her to die by fire. Thecla maintains her self-mastery despite her sentence, not requiring the vision sent to her of the Lord as Paul to shore up her resolve: "As if I were unable to endure, Paul has come to look after me" (Thecla 21). When Thecla is brought naked before the proconsul to be burned, the procounsel "wept and admired the power that was in her" (Thecla 22). She is not defeated; she is not a victim. When the fire threatens to consume her, God causes a great thunderstorm to swamp the theater, so that Thecla is saved, and the spectators are threatened with drowning.

After her miraculous deliverance, Paul continues to worry about her purity: "Times are evil and you are beautiful. I am afraid lest another temptation come upon you worse than the first and that you do not withstand it but become mad after men" (Thecla 25). Right on cue, Alexander, one of the chief men of Antioch, sees Thecla and falls madly in love with her. He forces himself on her, but she strongly resists and makes a laughingstock of him in public. He brings her before yet another Roman official who condemns her to die with the beasts:

> Thecla . . . was stripped . . . and was thrown into the
> arena. And lions and bears were let loose upon her. And

a fierce lioness ran up and lay down at her feet . . . And a
bear ran upon her, but the lioness went to meet it and tore
the bear to pieces. (Thecla 33)

As the beasts keep coming, Thecla sees a pit of water and
says, "Now it is time to wash myself." So she throws herself in
the water, saying, "In the name of Jesus Christ I baptize myself
on my last day" (Thecla 34).

This remarkable self-baptism demonstrates how totally in
control Thecla is. Paul should have had no need to worry about
her purity. Her self-control over her passions and desires is complete. The purpose of dying in the arena was to purify the soul
for immortal life. In Thecla's case this is modified because she is
not executed. But her miraculously prevented death testifies to
her purity, and she acknowledges that this is her last day. So, this
formula combines both the position of those who see suffering as
the way of purification and the knowers who see revelation and
wisdom as the way. She both suffers and sees a vision. She does
not have to die but will go on to preach the word of God.

The women in the crowd, seeing Thecla enter the pit of
water, worry that she is going to drown herself.

She then threw herself into the water in the name of Jesus
Christ, but the seals, having seen a flash of lightning,
floated dead on the surface. And there was round her a
cloud of fire so that neither could the beasts touch her nor
could she be seen naked. (Thecla 34)

Like a true knower, only Thecla can see what is really happening. Everyone else sees dead seals and her nakedness obscured.
Her purity remains protected.

The tale of Thecla is a marvelous antidote to the debates raging in the schools of the Anointed and wisdom circles in the second century. Both sides can find something of worth in her story, which probably accounts for its popularity and longevity. Her self-mastery is complete. She is not afraid and speaks boldly. She never appears as a passive victim. She even at one point dresses as a man (Thecla 40). She resists the power of the empire, both in the presence of its officials and in its effort to destroy her in public spectacles of violence. The emphasis on her virginity and refusal to marry wellborn men rejects the empire's "family values," in which marriage and bearing children was a requirement of wellborn women. Yet she becomes a substitute daughter to her wellborn matron Tryphaena. She does not desire execution nor resist it. Her deliverance twice from death is interpreted as proof of her purity and her resurrection even before her baptism. Baptism and resurrection (the last day) are elided in this tale. The tale has all the earmarks of a witness story but without the execution. At story's end she converts her mother and "enlightened many by the word of God; then she rested in a glorious sleep" (Thecla 43).

Yet even though Paul plays a minor role in her story, seemingly lurking in the background to pop out at the appropriate moment, he is the one at the end who commissions her: "Go and teach the word of God" (Thecla 41). Just as the author of Acts subordinated its hero Paul to the twelve in Jerusalem, so this tale puts Thecla in that same apostolic line through a commission from Paul. But that self-baptism or washing continues to unsettle the story, pointing to the fluidity and experimentation so characteristic of the early stages of the Jesus movement.

CONCLUSION

Throughout the first and second centuries, we see not only a great deal of diversity, but also fluidity and experimentation in all aspects of the life of the communities of the Jesus movements.

Members of early Jesus communities grew up within greater Israel and identified with Israel's tradition. Israel had long dealt with its diversity by orthopraxy, not orthodoxy, that is, by correct practice and not correct teaching. The Jesus groups initially followed in this tradition. But competition between teachers for new teachings created new schools and began to shift the balance more toward teachings than practice. Irenaeus is a good example of the shift as he begins to sift through various teachers and schools. By the time of Tertullian at the end of the second century, the teachers he does not agree with are being excluded. Now we are on the way to the anathemas of the creeds. Heresy is a Christian invention. Significantly, Judaism and the rabbis, faced with the same conditions, did not take the same route.

We have seen how *hairesis*, which means choice, and by extension school, shifts from a neutral term to an indication of division to finally a negative term that excludes the other. But as categories, heresy and orthodoxy, false teaching versus true teaching, obscure our understanding of the first two centuries. In this period, the two categories are anachronistic and read the future into the past. The real situation is more complex and calls for a more radical solution. The categories themselves need to disappear. The real situation is fluid, exhibiting a great deal of experimentation. We do not have heresy and orthodoxy in competition but a whole series of schools and teachers engaged and interacting in conversation, debate, and experimentation. Only toward the end of the second century did things begin to settle out, and then only tentatively.

Papers Relevant to This Chapter by Seminar Participants

Iricinschi, Eduard. "How Gullible Were the Women of Late-Antique Rhone and Asia Minor? Redescribing the Valentinian Marcosians in Irenaeus of Lyon's *Against the Heresies*." Fall 2019.

Miller, Robert J. "Prophecy, Christology, and Anti-Judaism in Justin Martyr." Spring 2017.

Niederer Saxon, Deborah. "What's at Stake When 'Heresy' Sells?" Fall 2019.

Toft Rosland, Kristine. "A New Beginning: Reading the *Apocryphon of John* as *Genesis* Fanfiction." Fall 2019.

Vinzent, Markus. "Orthodoxy and Heresy: Misnomers and Misnamers." Fall 2019.

Wilhite, David E. Is Jesus YHWH? Two De-Judaizing Trajectories of Marcion and Justin." Spring 2019.

DEMOLISHING GNOSTICISM

On November 16, 1953, the preservation of an ancient collection of documents related to early Jesus peoples made the front page of the *New York Times*. "Gnostic Gospels of 150 A.D. Found," read the title of journalist Michael L. Hoffman's article, with the sub-headline, "Throw Light on Early Christianity." Hoffman's article discussed a "book" of writings found in the Nag Hammadi collection of manuscripts in the Egyptian desert. This collection was a library, of sorts, preserved for almost two thousand years and found accidentally when a man went digging for fertilizer. Instead, he turned up a red clay jar full of papyri: fifty-two texts, collected inside thirteen leather-bound volumes. The tale of discovery is thrilling: it involves four-thousand-year-old gravesites, illegal smuggling, fire, suppression, revenge, and even murder.

Hoffman's *New York Times* article is particularly interesting because of how it frames this collection. Hoffman starts his report with two very basic categories, categories that seem to be decidedly distinguished from one another: Gnosticism and Christianity. On first read, the article seems clear that Gnosticism and Christianity were separate phenomena, though they existed in the same space and time. Hoffman describes Gnos-

ticism in a short paragraph in brackets as a kind of explana-
tory aside: "Gnosticism was a mystic religious movement that
existed side by side with early Christianity and was influenced
by it. It reached its height in the second century." This "mystic
religious movement" was not Christian, though Christianity
affected this movement. The statement implies that Christianity was not likewise influenced by Gnosticism; the influence
was one way.

A reread of Hoffman's article is confusing, however. The article starts by saying that "a book of early Christian writings,
some of which date from about 150 A.D.," was found. So, a
Christian collection. The next sentence, though, states that the
book "is one of thirteen volumes of Gnostic manuscripts containing forty-eight texts or Gospels." This statement expresses
some judgment about these texts as not being Christian, given
the hesitancy here to call them "Gospels," and the title of
"Gnostic." So, *not* a Christian collection.

Next, readers find that definition of Gnosticism in brackets,
one that clearly separates Gnosticism from Christianity. Later,
though, Hoffman references early Christians "who followed
this line of spiritual development"—that is, Christians who
located themselves within a "Gnostic experience." We're left
asking whether these newly discovered texts are Christian or
(g)not? What, exactly, is the relationship of these so-called
Gnostic writings to Christian gospels? Of Gnosticism to Christianity? Can one be Christian and Gnostic, or are they separate? If separate, did one influence the other, or is evidence of
mutual influence to be found?

The Gnosticism-Christianity questions raised by Hoffman's front-page *New York Times* article are the questions
that have preoccupied scholarship on early Christianity for
the past two centuries. It isn't surprising, then, to find these

questions between the lines of this news article. While these categories sometimes blur together, it is apparent that Gnosticism is *bad*, signaled in the article by the word "unorthodox," and contrasts with Christianity, *good* and, of course, "orthodox." He points out first that scholars know little about the manuscripts found at Nag Hammadi, though scholars immediately labeled these writings as Gnostic. Second, to quote Hoffman, scholars know little about ancient Gnosticism itself in any kind of "original and pure form." Why was the Nag Hammadi collection called Gnostic, when scholars knew so little either about the writings or about Gnosticism? What made, and continues to make, Gnosticism an important category of scholarship on the first two centuries of the Jesus movements? Finally, and most important, *if we don't know what Gnosticism is, why are we so sure that it was important?*

THE MYTH OF GNOSTICISM

A lot has changed since 1953, of course. Many of the writings from the Nag Hammadi find are now available not just to scholars, but also to the public, in a variety of online forms and forums. A lot has *not* changed, however. It seems like, at this point, we should at least know what Gnosticism is. Strangely, even since the publication of the manuscripts discovered at Nag Hammadi in 1945, our understanding of Gnosticism has not substantially advanced.

We continue to rely on some basic stereotypes about Gnosticism, stereotypes that have not changed or been proved. These stereotypes include claims that Gnosticism is a religion of body-haters, people who believe that material existence is evil, and that God cannot be known through the body. It is a religion of social deviance born of cosmic duality: this visible world, created by a lower god, is bad, devoid of beauty, order, true ethics, anything that reveals true divinity. Our human task is to escape this world through the acquisition of knowledge. Specifically, we must know our true divine essence; this knowledge of our true selves will free us from our gross natural flesh. These stereotypes of Gnosticism form an intact myth. Discussion of Gnosticism in both scholarly and popular contexts has combined these stereotypes into a seemingly coherent narrative—the myth of Gnosticism.

Here we encounter a major problem: while different scholars, writing some sixteen to nineteen centuries after the Gnostic phenomenon, have discussed this narrative of Gnosticism as if it existed for some people in the first centuries of the Common Era, there are no documents that verify the story. This myth of Gnosticism does not actually exist. It's like a myth of a myth. On a theoretical level, the myth exists. We can look up "Gnosticism" in the *Oxford English Dictionary* and find our Gnostic stereotypes, neatly packaged. Gnosticism has been made to exist, has been made a *thing*, a category. It exists, and has existed, as a tool with which to think.

Gnosticism is impossible to find in any practical way, however. The writings we have called Gnostic might contain some of the elements of the myth, to some degree, but never all of them, and never in the same way. You can't find this myth in any given so-called Gnostic writing. For example, a commonly cited element in the Gnostic myth is world hating: the world in which we live was created by a lower, generally mean divinity, and because of that bad start, the world is a fundamentally bad place. The powers of this world are unequivocally evil; our own material bodies are evil. The world is a dark prison from which we need to escape.

When we start to look at actual Gnostic writings, however, this fundamental pessimism is not there. The writings really do not seem to be all that different from other writings of the time period that were also interested in the workings of power in the world: the evils of power, the negotiation of power, possibilities of power as and for good. The more individual writings called Gnostic are examined, the more they seem to reflect commonly shared values and concerns, questions and desires, reflection on and struggle with human morality. Even the word itself, Gnosticism, does not seem to have been used until the time of theologian Henry More, in the seventeenth century—more than a millennium after the apparent existence of the phenomenon.

The nonexistence of the Gnostic myth in the ancient world should be deeply disturbing. Why have we insisted on the existence of this monster, if this monster has never, not once, fully crawled out of the water, never heaved its ancient body onto the reedy banks to stretch out its head in the heat of a summer sun? None of our evidence suggests that there was an actual, historical phenomenon any time in the first through the third centuries of the Common Era called Gnosticism. Let's explore why it has been used as a scholarly category and why we invented Gnosticism.

THE LIMITS OF CATEGORIES

We invented Gnosticism not because it was a "thing" that we observed, but rather because it was a word that we used to think with. Specifically, it helped us make distinctions. Gnosticism became important as a powerful word to help us create categories and boundaries, not to describe an objective reality.

At its core, it was a word used, in the eighteenth through the twenty-first centuries, to create an "other" over against the self of Christianity.

Biblical scholarship is just beginning to see this significance of Gnosticism, not as an objective, historical phenomenon but as a category of language used to think with. Karen L. King in her book *What Is Gnosticism?* challenges the category of Gnosticism and traces the history of the use of the word "gnostic" from its first use by Irenaeus, the second-century bishop of Lyons, to modern times.[1] Irenaeus was interested in promoting the unity of a "church" over against the divisiveness of "others," of schools or what are later called "heretics" (see Chapter 13). He calls people "Gnostics," but we do not find people calling themselves "Gnostics," in the same way that we do not find people calling themselves "Christian." Irenaeus never used the word "Gnosticism." The term becomes significant in biblical scholarship from the nineteenth century onward, when Gnosticism is used as a substitute term, in scholarly discourse, for heresy.

Scholars examining the histories of religions became interested in the idea of Gnosticism, looking to trace its origins—the origins of a "thing" that scholars identified as an "it," and therefore an "it" with a beginning—against the more perfect Christianity. King is clear about the impact of this work when she states, "The fixation on origins has tended to distort the actual social and historical processes of literary productions because the purpose of determining the origin of Gnosticism is less historical than rhetorical . . . it is aimed at delimiting the normative boundaries and definition of Christianity."[2]

King's revelation in *What Is Gnosticism?* is this acknowledgment of Gnosticism as a kind of Shakespearean tragedy—a King Lear, an idea lurching wildly, not without discipline or insight so much as tortured by fatally flawed assumptions. Scholars have made a thing where no such thing existed, building off later categories of orthodoxy and heresy, in order to continue to produce a narrative of "Christianity." These later categories—categories created by the historical "winners," those who got to define "right" and "wrong" belief, and "Christianity" itself, in future historical periods—miss the messiness of the first two centuries. The term, and the category, no longer works; it obscures much more than it clarifies and presumes agreement, a sameness, where no such sameness existed. There was a great deal more dynamism, a great deal more variability and diversity in the first two centuries, than the category allows. What do we call "it," if not Gnosticism, then?

A NEW APPROACH

Help with this question of categories comes from an unexpected source: fantasy writer Ursula K. Le Guin. Included in her 2012 compilation of short stories *The Unreal and the Real* is an imitation of scholarly research and writing, a parody of academic work Le Guin titled "The Author of the Acacia Seeds, and Other Extracts from the *Journal of the Association of Therolinguistics*."[3] This fictitious journal is situated in a (sadly) fictitious academic discipline; "therolinguistics" refers to the study of animal languages.

Le Guin first walks us through a research project on Ant, a language more written than spoken, and mainly written on seeds. Then a fictitious scholar announces an expedition to Cape Crozier in the Antarctic, inviting colleagues interested in the study of penguin languages to join. Penguin, it seems, has a great deal of potential as a field of study. This potential opened up when scholars shifted away from comparing Penguin to Dolphin languages, toward a comparison between Penguin and the script of a goose, the Low Greylag. Penguin seemed to resemble Dolphin in form; both languages were written in water, through the movement of groups of flipper-based writers. Both "scripts" are movement-based and collective. The long-standing parallel to Dolphin never made much sense of the content of Penguin "sea writings," however, and scholars had all but abandoned study of Penguin script.

The fictitious Professor Duby then shakes up the study of Penguin entirely, asking what would happen if Penguin were studied not from the perspective of Dolphin, or other mammals of similar habitats, like seals, but from the perspective of Bird? A shift in category, from sea mammal, to bird, changes the type and quality of evidence available about the object of study (the penguin) dramatically.

Le Guin's story poses a wonderful "what if" question: What if we think about Penguin from a new perspective, in the context of a totally different—but not at all shocking—category? Le Guin's imaginary history of scholarship, though, never thought about Penguin as Bird. The comparison to Dolphin seemed to work, as the *form* of the "script" was similar (water writing, through the movements of a group), but we never learned much about *content*.

The story offers a helpful corrective for our approach to so-called Gnostic writings, inviting us to ask our own "what if?" From the moment of their discovery in 1945, the Nag Hammadi collection was called Gnostic, but what if they are not Gnostic at all, but simply part of the diverse literature of the early Jesus movement in the second and third centuries? What if we released them from their Gnostic category and thought of them from an entirely new category?

The imposition of the label or category of Gnostic on the Nag Hammadi writings and other previously discovered writings has impeded, blocked, and caricatured our attempts to make these writings meaningful. These documents offer important information about the many different Jesus movements, Wisdom schools, and adherents of the Anointed in the second century. The writings are much more complex, much more diverse, than that category allows. We need to allow ourselves a big "what if?" with these texts. What if they are not, have never been, could not be, Gnostic? How would we read them then? What would we learn, what would we see? What knowledge could we produce, as a result?

IF NOT GNOSTIC, WHAT?

What if these texts are not Gnostic, but . . . what, exactly? Le Guin's story offered a corrective category for Dolphin: Bird. Penguins are birds, after all. It is not clear, though, if we have such a corrective category in our case. If the category Gnostic has impeded our study of these various first- and second-century texts, it is not obvious that "Jesus peoples" should be the corrective. It is difficult to frame a comparative statement, "Bird is to Dolphin as ___ is to Gnostic." How to fill in the blank?

Perhaps we do not need to fill in the blank at all. Perhaps we can retrain ourselves to think without categories, without the almost knee-jerk reaction of placing things within boxes so that we might therefore come to know them. We will have to come to know things differently. That new way of knowing will be a huge challenge, given our current intellectual habits.

When we reject, or at least test, our boundary-based ways of thinking, so much potential for meaning opens up—we can come to know differently, to see and know a totally new range of possibilities. If there are no constants, no essences, no unchanging forms, we can appreciate variability. We might consider Charles Darwin here, the "father" of evolutionary biology: Darwin rejected constants and unchanging forms, seeing, instead, variability within populations. He didn't assume he knew what a finch was, in some unchanging form, as a species, an essence; he saw populations full of diversity, variability. No two finches are exactly the same.

King is proposing a model for approaching these writings-previously-known-as-Gnostic on the basis of population thinking, specifically as a population of writings. This population displays a great deal of similarity, but seldom, if ever, sameness. At its edges, we find a great deal of difference. We need to approach these members of the population one by one, study them on their own terms. As King contends in the introduction to her book *The Secret Revelation of John*:

> I think initially we need to refer to individual texts. That is, rather than generalize about what Gnostics believe . . . —especially as opposed to what Christians believe—I think it best to talk about particular texts. The goal is not to create the perfect category (an impossibility in any case), but to make these texts available for critical and constructive work, whether in historical reconstruction or theology.[4]

In setting aside categories like Gnostic and Christian, these first- and second-century shadows without forms, the writings will be allowed to speak for themselves, without preconception. It is challenging work, this un-learning. But given the dangers of maintaining our categories, our task is clear: we need to start, restart, by *not knowing* these writings at all.

The primary means of not knowing this diverse group of Jesus- or Anointed-referencing writings from the first and second centuries is to set aside the name of Gnostic, this category that has given scholarship on the writings its fundamental shape. In this chapter, then, we have done to Gnosticism in the first and second centuries what our first two chapters did to Christianity in these same two centuries. In both cases we have decided to learn about these two centuries without the made-up twinned words "Christianity" and "Gnosticism."

By designating the writings found at Nag Hammadi as Gnostic, these writings were also considered to be "bad," erroneous, because Gnostic was oppositional to Christian. The writings would just be examples of error, of heresy, of false forms of Christianity. We know, though, that Gnosticism is not an adequate category for the analysis of early Anointed movements. Setting aside the Gnostic name allows us to see that these writings really resist any easy categorization, easy naming or definition. All the Nag Hammadi writings have in common, at their core, is that they were found in the same jar in the Egyptian desert.

GNOSTIC VERSUS WHAT?

King's work on the Nag Hammadi text called The Secret Revelation of John has allowed us to see how important it is to get rid of the term Gnostic. This writing was popular in the ancient world, as it has survived in multiple copies; the Nag Hammadi collection itself included three. It is often discussed as a primary example of Gnosticism. How do we know The Secret Revelation of John is really Gnostic if we have never had the opportunity to see it as anything else?

King's work offers the first comprehensive study of a supposed Gnostic writing that does not make Gnosticizing assumptions. The [Gnostic] Secret Revelation of John is very different from The Secret Revelation of John. Not surprisingly, when our approach to the writing is left blank, unconditioned, we can know this writing in entirely new ways and understand much more of the writing itself.

Reading afresh, The Secret Revelation might strike us as familiar or resonate with us in a particular way. King translates the first lines of this writing as follows:

> Now it happened one day when John the brother of James, the sons of Zebedee, was going up to the temple, a Pharisee named Arimanios approached him. And he said to him, "Where is your teacher, the one whom you used to follow?" He said to him, "He returned to the place from which he came." The Pharisee said to me, "This Nazorene deceived you with error. He filled your ears with lies, and he shut your hearts. He turned you from the traditions of your fathers." When I heard these things, I turned from the temple to the mountain which was a place of desert. And I grieved greatly in my heart, saying, "How was the Savior appointed? Why was he sent into the world by his father who sent him? Who is his father? And of what sort is that aeon to which we will go? He told us that the aeon is modeled on that indestructible aeon, but he did not teach us about what sort the latter is."[5]

This scene seems reasonably conventional: we have a conversation between a Pharisee (Arimanios) and a follower of the Savior (John). We find a lot of debates with Pharisees in the canonical Gospels, so nothing about that context seems unusual.

We also have a lot of references to people and nation in this passage: Nazareth, the Jerusalem Temple, "traditions of your fathers." Nazareth was not considered an honorable place, so Arimanios is starting with a strong put-down here in calling Jesus, here identified as "the Savior," "this Nazorene." Arimanios is really challenging John's sense of belonging, his sense of place within the collectivity of Israel. It starts, geographically, at the Temple in Jerusalem, which did not exist after its destruction in 70 CE. We don't know why John is going up to the Temple, but Arimanios stops him in his tracks, and his accusations cause John to lose his certainty, to turn from the Temple and retreat to the desert. John then asks questions about origins and belonging: "How was the Savior appointed? Why was he sent into the world by his father who sent him? Who is his father?" The crisis of Jesus's death, followed by Arimanios's attack, destroys John's confidence.

The writing is framed as working through the uncertainty of belonging to the people of Israel. After the Judean-Roman War and the destruction of the Jerusalem Temple, the meaning of belonging to Israel was in a state of crisis. The Secret Revelation of John could be read as a response to this crisis, a way to work through the question of belonging to Israel when Israel, as a geographic or physical place, a homeland, was devastated. A reading of these opening lines without any decided category, without any prereading, as it were, offers rich meaning relating to social belonging. How do I belong, John asks, when my conventional ways of belonging have been shaken up, destroyed?

In response to his anxiety about belonging, John receives a vision in which he is offered a mode of counterbelonging, a location of community in a "world above." An interesting Father-Mother-Son trinity tells John:

"[The Unity] is a monarchy with nothing ruling over it. It is the God and Father of the All, the holy, the invisible, who exists over the All, the one who [. . . there is a gap in the text here] in corruption, existing as pure light, into which it is not possible for any light of the eye to gaze. It is the Spirit. It is not appropriate to think about It as God or that It is something similar. For It surpasses divinity. It is a dominion having nothing to rule over it. (Secret Revelation 4:2–5)[6]

A monarchy, a dominion, *with nothing ruling over it.* In the context of the Roman Empire, that mode of belonging, that kind of belonging "upward" or location of sovereignty in a world above, would definitely have sounded appealing.

This vision of a monarchy with nothing ruling over it in the Secret Revelation belongs to a literature of belonging, writings that work through what it means to identify with a particular group once old or familiar boundaries have been erased—writings like the book of Revelation, for example, and the Letter to the Hebrews in the Bible. King's reading of the Secret Revelation refuses conventional classifications. It does not present us with some kind of mystical, inaccessible sort of treatise, but with a relatable consideration of how to understand our social lives and location in the face of a violent, imperfect, sometimes dark world.

This meaning is not apparent if we hold on to our Gnostic category. King's work enables us to understand The Secret Revelation of John in its own world, a world of lived experience. Instead of Gnosticism, we see these poignant expressions of power negotiation in the face of dominance and crises of belonging, the working out of what belonging means, specifically belonging to Israel, in a situation where it might have felt like God had abandoned the people. We see this vital, urgent, complex wrestling with human experience, experience of power, history, commitment. Reading without the categories—it is a totally new, exciting way of knowing this text.

CONCLUSION

The movement of Gnosticism to the scholarly sidelines removes a confusing category from our ongoing work of rethinking the history of early Jesus schools and associations. We are moving from an idea that Gnosticism was a real force, the primary "heresy" that threatened the "pure" trajectory of Christianity, to the actuality, on the basis of evidence for the absence, the nonexistence, of Gnosticism. We must rethink the entire assumption that a unified heretical Gnosticism played a primary role in how the first two centuries unfolded. Using Gnosticism as an analytical category seems to hide more than it reveals, and if we really want to understand the writing called Gnostic, we need to set aside that designation.

A lot changes when we do this. For one thing, without this falsely constructed version of a crucial battle in the second and third centuries between early orthodox Christians and fiercely competitive and heretical Gnostic Christians, the picture of orthodoxy versus heresy becomes a much shakier enterprise. The Anointed groups of the first two centuries are no longer about a pure church based on a preordained belief system, over and against sneaky, corrupting Gnosticism.

Second, the wealth of Nag Hammadi documents and other writings previously labeled as Gnostic provides a wealth of new stories to both the public and scholarship. These writings offer important information on the second century to a broad reach of readers from very different perspectives. King's reading of

The Secret Revelation of John begins to show us what might happen when we integrate these documents into a more diverse and complex description of emerging phenomena. It is essential that we not impose categories on these writings, so that they can start to speak for themselves.

Papers Relevant to This Chapter by Seminar Participants

Brakke, David. The *Gospel of Judas*, 'Gnostics,' and 'Sethians': An Emendation to My Argument in *The Gnostics*. Fall 2014.

Kotrosits, Maia. "But What Do We Call It?: 'The Secret Revelation of John and Crises of Categories.'" Fall 2014.

Scott, Brandon. "What Categories Are Left?" Fall 2014.

Taussig, Hal. "Questioning the Category of Gnosticism." Fall 2014.

Williams, Michael. "Are You, or Have You Ever Been, a Gnostic?" Fall 2014.

15

PAUL OBSCURED

Paul dominates the New Testament. He is credited as the author of as many as fourteen letters and is the hero of the second half of the book of Acts. Many of the core debates over Christian doctrine revolve around interpreting Paul: faith versus works, free will versus grace, letter versus spirit. So, if one thinks of the New Testament as a record of the beginnings of Christianity, one naturally assumes that Paul's voice and authority held center stage right from the start.

But that assumption is wrong. Paul's own letters show that he struggled to find an audience and had trouble holding on to supporters. A former persecutor of Anointed followers, he proved to be a quarrelsome thorn in their side when he joined their ranks. Although he had never known Jesus "in the flesh," he claimed a superior intimacy with the Anointed through his personal call. At the time of his death, Paul might have had good reason to feel alone and abandoned, with many Jesus followers having turned their backs on him. What is more, a long silence follows his life when Paul was all but forgotten, except in a handful of communities that remembered him as their founder. Nearly a hundred years after his death, in the mid-second century, he began to be name-checked by an aggressive group of partisans who had rediscovered his legacy. But others reacted either with hostility or with relative indifference to this obscure character from the past.

Paul's place in the New Testament has led the public, theologians, and biblical scholars in the past to imagine his influence everywhere in the period between his life and the later formation of the New Testament. Pick up popular or scholarly books on the Apostolic Fathers or other second-century authors from the nineteenth century forward, and you will see scores of references to Paul. But once we realize that the New Testament did not yet exist in the second century, we can begin to see that the words attributed to Paul's influence usually are nothing more than short turns of phrase, stock metaphors, or popular images both Paul and the other authors draw from the culture around them. When we search these other second-century writings for Paul's substantive or distinctive ideas, we typically do not find them.

Even those who knew of Paul and mentioned him may not have known his writings. Acts purports to tell Paul's story but, notoriously, never once mentions him writing letters. Our tendency is to think that everyone in these religious circles read Paul, especially those who, like the author of Acts, thought highly of him. But the absence of engagement with Paul's big ideas in many of the writers suggests either that they did not know his letters or, even more intriguingly, did not think his letters mattered much to communities other than the ones to which they were addressed.

Writings in the ancient world did not have the wide distribution and circulation that they have today, and this was especially true of letters that were not composed with a larger audience in mind. Paul's reputation as a heroic envoy and community founder had wider circulation than his writings, which after all were directed to the occasional affairs of individual

communities. Special circumstances and motives had to intervene to collect and "publish" those letters as something worth
the attention of a wider audience.

COMMUNITY FOUNDER

Most second-century writings by those belonging to communities of the Anointed do not mention Paul. It may be that
such silence is not particularly significant in compositions such
as the *Teachings of the Twelve Apostles*, *Barnabas*, the *Shepherd
of Hermas*, a good number of the apologists, and the letters of
John, 1 Peter, or Hebrews.

Three writers dated to the mid-second century do mention
Paul explicitly: Clement of Rome, Ignatius of Antioch, and
Polycarp of Smyrna. Since so many second-century writings
make no reference to Paul, it is important to take a closer look
at what these writers do say about him. And perhaps more to
the point, what they do not say about him.

The trio of teachers Thecla, Paul, and Theocleia, Thecla's mother.
Sarah Sexton Crossan

Clement of Rome

Clement, an early leader in the Roman community, sees Peter and Paul together as famous martyrs in the memory of his own Roman community. But Paul alone gives him a connection to his Corinthian compatriots, since Paul founded their community and therefore had authority for them. Since Clement seeks leverage with the Corinthians, he explicitly cites and endorses statements of Paul that serve this purpose. He has a copy of 1 Corinthians, probably not because Paul's letters were in wide circulation as a collection, but because, as Clement tells us, he has been approached by a group of Corinthian leaders seeking his intervention. Apparently, they gave Clement a copy of Paul's letter to their community as a useful reference point for him to use in his own correspondence. Clement alludes to no other letter of Paul's besides the one to Clement's own Roman community, and his presentation of ideas and ideals of that Roman community shows little influence from Paul. Clement refers to Paul, but only to confirm the relationship between the Corinthians and himself.

Ignatius of Antioch

Although scholars recently have doubted the integrity or even authenticity of Ignatius's letters, they do provide some useful evidence of Paul. As with Clement, Ignatius acknowledges Paul without making substantial use of him. He refers to Paul explicitly only twice. Like Clement, he knows of Paul in tandem with Peter, as a pair of martyrs associated with the community at Rome (*To the Romans* 4.3). He refers to Paul alone when writing to the community of followers at Ephesus, which he thinks was founded by Paul. He calls them "fellow initiates of Paul, (a man) sanctified, approved, worthy of blessing, in whose steps may it be mine to be found when I reach God, who in every letter remembers you in the Anointed Jesus" (*To the Ephesians* 12.2).[1] On the basis of the last remark, Ignatius seems to know that Paul wrote letters to the communities he founded, which he may have learned of as he was passing through territory where many of these communities resided. Yet it is unlikely that Ignatius had read Paul's letters, since he mistakenly says that Paul mentioned Ephesus "in every letter." For Ignatius, therefore, Paul, known as a community founder of the revered past, appears to be primarily a famous name to drop.

Further supposed influence of Paul on Ignatius's thought takes the form merely of a common stock of phrases that we have every reason to think were not unique to Paul ("inherit the kingdom of God," "not to please men, but to please God," "not through human beings, but through God"). Phrases like "fighting wild beasts," "things visible and invisible," "every tongue testify" are found even as part of the discourse of other groups besides the followers of Jesus. Paul-like phrasing turns up also in other authors who never mention Paul by name (the cross as a "scandal," becoming a "new human being," or "Jews and Gentiles in one body"). Paul does not represent a significant influence on Ignatius, or a special authority for him. Consistently with what we observed in the case of Clement, Ignatius brings Paul up when writing to the one community, of the six he addresses, that Paul himself founded.

Polycarp of Smyrna

When writing to the community of Jesus Anointed in the city of Philippi founded by Paul, Polycarp, like Ignatius and Clement, has good reason to cite the authority of Paul. He is "their" envoy of the Anointed, and his letter to them is the one that provides some of Polycarp's ideas and phrasing, even though he appears to know that Paul wrote other letters, too (*To the Philippians* 3.1–2).

A Pattern

A clear pattern therefore emerges among the three principal identifiable authors who recognize Paul as an authority before 180 CE. These authors cite Paul when writing to communities he founded. This citation honors the founding figure of the local association. But how do we know that Paul was an authority for Clement or Ignatius or Polycarp in other circumstances? Did Polycarp, for example, refer to Paul or use his ideas in letters that he wrote to communities that did not have Paul as their founder?

Writing a generation later, Irenaeus mentions in his letter to Florinus that Polycarp wrote multiple letters. The fact that only this one letter was preserved draws our attention to how later church leaders chose what to preserve. This one letter of Polycarp, widely regarded as a not particularly scintillating piece of writing, may have been preserved and valued precisely because it happened to refer to Paul. Polycarp's other letters possibly contained no further reference to him. Perhaps they even contained elements that did not align with later orthodoxy and could serve no useful purpose for those who were choosing what to copy from earlier literature.

By looking only at what later orthodox collectors allow to slip past, we are misled in our reconstructions of the period. In that way we may have been overgeneralizing from a few isolated scraps that later church leaders found to be useful. When we consider how much of early writings are lost, we must recognize how skewed our picture is by preservation that might have been inclined to save anything with positive reference to Paul. They are far from Paul in their thinking, and they treat him primarily as a founding figure, not as a theologian. They handle his letters as charter documents for specific communities, mined mostly for encouraging words, not for core doctrines, and certainly they do not treat them as "scripture."

PAUL AS A PROBLEM

Other second-century writings grapple in varying degrees with Paul. Several of these writings were later included in the New Testament.

The author of 2 Peter famously grabs the bull by the horns and refers to the difficulty of understanding Paul. This is a polite way of saying that one should not try too hard to do so and should focus instead on his more banal, edifying remarks. Although Paul is not mentioned by name, a convincing case can be made that this author levels subtle criticism at Paul for some of his more radical statements, by alluding to and refuting specific passages in Paul's letters. James takes a broader swipe at faith/belief as a sufficient basis for righteousness; and James 2:20–23 plays a different Abraham story off against the one Paul uses in Galatians and Romans. Both of these writers know Paul as a writer of letters but find the content of his letters problematic.

Writing in the name of Paul, the writers of 1 and 2 Timothy and Titus clearly promote Paul, but only by tampering with his image in a way that makes him more palatable. Third Corinthians, the Acts of the Apostles, and the Epistle of the Apostles follow the same path. Those writers all make Paul stand out from the disciples of Jesus as a special case and the ultimate hero toward which the trajectory of the early tradition heads. Yet at the same time, they strip Paul of his major distinctive ideas and conform him to the image of a generic moralizing preacher. In fact, they go out of their way to emphasize that he is neither original nor independent from the twelve disciples. His dependence on them is particularly stressed in 3 Corinthians, the Acts of the Apostles, and the Epistle of the Apostles. These works, like Clement, Ignatius, and Polycarp, celebrate Paul primarily as the founder of communities and as a martyr.

The Epistle of the Apostles follows this strategy with a heavier hand than the other writings. Paul's origins as an enemy of Jesus's followers are discussed at much greater length than in Acts, and his dependence on the instruction of the disciples is emphasized much more. His independent inspiration by Jesus, which was of paramount importance to Paul, is all but erased. The Acts of the Apostles handles this issue more subtly but yields the same result. Paul's visionary relationship with Jesus is effectively reduced to a single call and, in direct contradiction to Paul's own testimony in Galatians, is followed by instruction at the feet of the Jerusalem disciples.

The question is, why would these second-century promoters of Paul feel they had to redeem him from himself? What was offensive in Paul as he presented himself in his own letters? And who was the audience for whom they needed to make Paul more palatable by reducing him to a figurehead who mouths words that have nothing to do with the historical Paul? The answers must be sought in the traces that have survived of two other views of Paul: the zealously anti-Paul groups on one side and the zealously pro-Paul followers of Marcion on the other.

Anti-Paul Voices
Many writings attack Paul, both in fiction and in direct debate. One author who perhaps slipped through later censorship of overtly anti-Pauline writings was Hegessippus, who journeyed to Israel to collect traditions of Judean followers of Jesus. Their communities had been decimated by the Romans during the Bar Kokhba War (in the 130s CE). While not mentioning Paul by name, Hegessippus appears to directly reject a statement matching Paul's words in 1 Corinthians 2:9 as "twisted" and contrary to a saying of Jesus.

Other voices of this anti-Paulinism slipped past later Christian censorship by being incorporated into a popular spiritual novel, surviving in two alternative fourth-century editions. In this fictionalized story of the adventurous missionary work of early followers of Jesus, the hero Peter joins repeated verbal battle with an opponent named Simon Magus, the arch-heretic, whom the reader easily recognizes to be a thinly disguised Paul. In the end, Peter emerges triumphant, with the Paul-like opponent defeated and discredited.

For those represented in the novel by Peter, Paul represents a dangerous corruptor trying to lead the faithful astray. The image of Paul offered in several of the second-century compositions discussed before are tailor-made to win such an audience over to a more favorable opinion of him. Rather than the Paul in Galatians, who openly brags about telling Peter off to his face, the authors of the Acts of the Apostles and the Epistle of the Apostles offer a Paul who follows Peter's lead at every step. Rather than the Paul of 2 Corinthians who boasts of his independent authority through visions, they offer a Paul who receives authorization from Jesus's disciples. Rather than the Paul who has unique things to say, they depict a Paul whose words are indistinguishable from any of the disciples of Jesus. By this dramatic makeover, they salvage the figure of Paul at the cost of anything recognizable of the man who wrote the authentic letters of Paul.

Pro-Paul Voices

Marcion (about 90–160 CE) is the earliest figure to have treated Paul's Epistles as authoritative (see also Chapter 16). Marcion places Paul's letters in a definitive collection, with a specific order, and uses them as "scripture." He is the earliest witness to the existence of 2 Corinthians, 1 and 2 Thessalonians, Colossians, Philippians, and Philemon, as well as their Pauline authorship. Finally, he is the only writer before Irenaeus and Tertullian to make extensive, rather than superficial, use of Paul's own words and ideas.

The network of Marcion's Jesus clubs that stretched across the Roman Empire testify to his success as a community organizer. But he also provoked controversy. Many communities resisted his attempts to unify the movement under a consistent set of beliefs and practices. Paul's letters had an integral role in those attempts, as an important set of documents from the previous century. Marcion used Paul to establish the rules for gaining and maintaining membership, conducting club ritual and social activities, and knowing what to expect in this life and the next.

For some, rejecting Marcion's version of what it meant to follow Jesus also meant rejecting Paul. That would include others who might not have had such strong objections to Paul himself, if he were not so closely associated with Marcion. Unfortunately, and suspiciously, what individuals of the latter type had to say has not survived.

Since Justin Martyr, a major writer among mid-second-century communities of the Anointed, explicitly mentions his opposition to Marcion multiple times, what should we make of Justin's complete silence on Paul in his surviving work? In some of that work, for example his *Dialogue with Trypho*, Paul would have served as a useful ally, since Paul interprets Israel's scriptures concerning the Messiah in a similar way.

Remarkably, many anti-Marcionite tracts no longer exist, and one must wonder why. Did they perhaps go too far in some of their remarks, and attack not only Marcion but his chief authority figure Paul? If that were the case, that would explain why tracts against Marcion may have been considered largely worthless to later generations, and why those generations stopped copying and circulating them.

REHABILITATING PAUL'S LEGACY

A century after his death Paul held an ambiguous or even ambivalent status. The impression is not of an ancient and well-established authority stretching back to his own time, but rather of a recent introduction that various leaders feel compelled to stage-manage and resolve. The flurry of literary activity, all dated approximately to the mid-second century, bears witness to a significant adjustment of traditions to make room for Paul.

Outside of Marcion's circles, those who want to make room for Paul value him as a legendary founder of non-Judean communities a century earlier, not as a theologian. His Epistles are understood as a chronicle of his work of founding communities; only Marcion shows much interest in Paul as a theological witness. This legendary Paul is featured in the Acts of Paul and a few other apocryphal acts. But even this figure of Paul is debated. The Acts of Paul pictures him as socially radical, rejecting family and marriage and traditional gender roles, while the Pastoral Epistles support social conservatism.

This abstracted memory of Paul of the mid-second century almost certainly results from the aftermath of Rome's Bar Kokhba War against Israel. This war marked a devastating setback for Israel and heightened prejudice and persecution beyond the homeland. In these circumstances, non-Judean followers of Jesus found themselves separated and often alienated from their Judean associates by various forces.

Two paths of adaptation emerged in the mid-second century. Marcion took up the cause of Paul, the envoy of the Anointed to the nations, and projected the separation from Israel back to the very beginnings of the Jesus movement, as something intended from the start. The message of Jesus, Marcion argued, had always been outside of Israel's religion.

Other Jesus groups, however, including the dominant group in Rome, chose a different path. They appropriated Israel's tradition and arrogated it to themselves as True Israel, spiritual Israelites replacing ethnic Israelites. Leaders such as Justin Martyr developed the argument that the Judeans were not entitled to their own tradition, as it was predestined for the nations. This theme of God's rejection of Israel, of course, would be utterly abhorrent to Paul (Rom. 11:26). Yet it becomes the plot of Acts (see especially Acts 13:46–47, as it recounts, in the person of Paul no less, the transfer of the message of Jesus from Israel to the nations).

In this new synthesis, Paul retains his status as the founding "Envoy of the Anointed to the Nations," reflecting Paul's missionary work and the communities that traced their origins back to him. These non-Judean communities, probably a minority among Jesus followers before the Bar Kokhba War, in its aftermath looked more and more to be its future. Paul now took on greater importance, as hindsight made him the advance scout for a way that only now took center stage. The Epistle of the Apostles seems to encapsulate this transition. The twelve disciples become the revered spiritual ancestors from an exotic Judean culture who sanction in advance its appropriation by the nations. Paul is not allowed to be original even in the mission to non-Judeans, as he is anointed for the task by Peter himself. This new synthesis of traditions found fixed expression in the dual stories of the deaths of Peter and Paul. Their joint portrait was copied almost as an emblem of the new Roman orthodoxy, and their connected mention in

Clement, Ignatius, and Polycarp belongs to this same promotional project.

Why did these domesticators of Paul retain his Epistles? What the two sides had in common was the status of the Epistles as foundational charter documents of a non-Israel religion of Jesus among the nations. Since there were no other documents from the first generations of the movement that proposed such a shift from Israel to the nations, Paul's writings must suffice. Whether it was specifically Marcion's activity that demanded a response or the historical circumstances that these writers shared with Marcion, the result was a flurry of activity in the mid-second century to address, champion, domesticate, or reject Paul.

The result of these shifts can be seen in the first two authors who treat Paul's letters as something approximating "scripture"—Irenaeus and Tertullian, writing two and three generations later than Marcion, respectively. They accept Paul as an important authority when they can quote him in support of their views. But neither of them works with a set and sequence of the Epistles. Irenaeus undertakes no analysis of Paul's letters, which remain an amorphous, undefined set of resources for his theology. Tertullian brings to its culmination the domestication of Paul, by reading the figure from Acts and other mid-second-century rehabilitative efforts into selected passages from the Epistles.

We probably owe to Marcion, therefore, the prominence of Paul in the later Christian tradition. Marcion's opponents had incorporated Paul within the broader group of apostles, remembering him as an early community founder and martyr. His letters were treated as edifying correspondence documenting his organizational work and relations with his communities. In those communities, no doubt the Epistles were treasured as charter documents, kept in the community bookchest and taken out for consultation to settle issues of community governance and practice. That is where "letters of a just man named Paul" were kept by the community at Scillium in North Africa in 180 CE.

To make use of Paul and reclaim him from the Marcionites, other communities could not simply dismiss his Epistles, once they became aware of them and confirmed that other communities revered them as their charters. But they made Paul more palatable and usable by adding previously unknown "private" letters to Paul's communities. The Pastoral Epistles (I Timothy, II Timothy, and Titus) conveniently aligned Paul more closely with their own brand of the Jesus movement. The Pastorals, unknown to Marcion, are first clearly referenced by Irenaeus, two generations after Marcion. They were either composed or added to the corpus of Paul's letters for the express purpose of countering Marcion and domesticating Paul from radical interpretation. The emerging authority of Paul led, therefore, to the creation of different collections of his Epistles, varying in content and adapted to the needs of different concerns within the Jesus movements.

Paul's association with the controversial Marcion did not drive others away from Paul, for the simple reason that those others needed him as the "envoy of the Anointed to the nations," who had created a distinctive form of following Jesus that grew in significance after Israel and those associated with Israel suffered violent setback after setback. He was the founder of key communities with which they wished to be in communion and also an "ancient" authority dating back to the first generation of the movement, few of whose participants put quill to papyrus. Finally, his heroic reputation as a martyr already had a life of its own, separate from a reputation as a writer and theologian. Paul was destined to become "all things to all people," used in various ways as needed, read in light of other ways of following Jesus than his own.

In the end we are confronted with a variety of Pauls. The Paul who emerges from a reading of his own letters, and the one taken by scholars and theologians alike to be the "real" Paul, was an accidental Paul—a Paul of specific circumstances and moments in a career that certainly had much more to it. Despite many of the second century either not knowing Paul or viewing him as a problem associated with problematic ideas and practices, some reinvested his letters with authority and reinterpreted those letters. Paul was controversial in his own day and remained so. Opinions varied about Paul in his own day, in the second century, and would continue to vary in the future.

Chapter contributor:
Jason BeDuhn

Papers Relevant to This Chapter by Seminar Participants
BeDuhn, Jason. "The Contested Authority of Paul in the Second Century." Fall 2017.

16

JESUS BY MANY OTHER NAMES

The second century represents a wide and at times wild variety and diversity of angles on the figure of Jesus, some that clearly extend images originating in the first century and others that create entirely new views. What it lacks is a unified image. The organization of this chapter reflects that very diversity. To present an overly organized, unified picture would betray the multiplicity of the second century.

FIRST-CENTURY PORTRAITS OF JESUS: GENDER-BENDER

Among the most interesting portraits of Jesus and Jesus's teachings are those focused on gender. The parables of Jesus, as characteristic of Jesus's style of teaching, especially in the gospel writings of Matthew, Mark, Luke, and Thomas, come as close to Jesus's perspective of himself as we can reasonably get. Although the parables are not generally read in terms of gender, several of these stories raise provocative questions about male and female roles. In the Parable of the Lost Coin, a woman loses one of ten silver coins and searches her house to find it. Recovering the coin, she throws a neighborhood party. In this story, a woman's role conforms to female expectations. What is unusual here is the casting of a woman in a lead role, especially a woman doing an ordinary thing. The lead role in stories of the time should really be played by a king, as indicated in many rabbinic parables. In that time period, a woman was an inappropriate image for the Empire of God, or any empire for that matter.

Parables may appear simple, but many explore gender in a provocative fashion. The Parable of the Leaven, a story told in a single line—"The empire of heaven is like leaven that a woman took and mixed in with three measures of flour, until all of it was leavened" (Matt. 13:33; Luke 13:21)—ups the ante. It compares the empire of heaven to a woman and leaven, a symbol of moral corruption. In the Parable of the Prodigal Son (Luke 15:11–32), the father, who is the real star of the show, runs to greet his lost son, a betrayal of his male dignity. In the confrontation with his elder son, the father refuses to stand up to the elder's broadside attack. Instead, he refers to his oldest son as "child," a word usually associated with the infant of a nursing mother. His male-father dignity is so undercut that he "becomes" a mother. Real gender-bending is going on here.

The Q Gospel, a group of sayings that provided source material for Luke and Matthew, combines the Parable of the Lost Coin with the Parable of the Lost Sheep, a story in which a man leaves ninety-nine sheep behind to find one that is lost. Like the woman upon finding her coin, when he returns home he celebrates the finding of the sheep with friends. Gender pairing in parables like this appear in several first- and second-century writings. While both figures play typically gendered social roles in the parables—a woman at home, a shepherd in a field—their juxtaposition implies their equality. If we can see Jesus in these stories, this Jesus is one who challenged gender roles.

Gender pairing also appears in the writings of Paul and later in the Gospel of John. In 1 Corinthians 7, Paul makes a series of radical pairings that have gone almost unremarked upon. "But because of cases of sexual immorality, each man should have his own wife and each woman her own husband," Paul declares (1 Cor. 7:2).[1] In the ancient world, a husband owns his wife; she is his property. That relationship is clearly reflected in the first part of this pairing. The second part, however, challenges male ownership of the female in saying that the wife also owns her husband. No other writer in the ancient world says anything that radical about marriage. That this is Paul's intention is made clear in verse 4: "For the wife does not have authority over her own body, but the husband does; likewise the husband does not have authority over his own body, but the wife does." Again, male claims to exclusive authority are undone.

Paul's declarations about gender roles in 1 Corinthians find reflection in the body of Jesus as presented in Paul's Letter to the Galatians. In this letter, Paul famously states, "There is no longer Jew or Greek, there is no longer slave or free, there is no longer male and female; for all of you are one [in the Anointed Jesus]" (Gal. 3:28).[2] Judean, Greek, enslaved, free, male, and female are all integrated in the body of the Anointed Jesus. Jesus's body merges with and becomes these things, according to Galatians. Jesus's body, in this writing, is both male and female. Paul plays off of Genesis 1:27 in this letter, reversing the creation of "male and female" by incorporating them into one body. Galatians undoes the binary gender pairing and presents Jesus as this undoing.

Another overlooked gender pairing occurs in John 20. After the student whom Jesus loved and Peter go to the tomb and find it empty, Jesus appears to Mary Magdalene in the garden. She thinks he is the gardener, but when he speaks, she recognizes him. The risen Jesus then commissions her to announce his resurrection to "my brothers." She tells the good news to them with a phrase associated with resurrection appearances, "I have seen the Lord" (v. 18). This puts her on the same level as all the other students, giving her an apostolic claim. She proclaims the resurrection to the students, upending the male hierarchical order.

The late second-century writing *2 Clement* cites "the Lord himself" making a bi-gendered connection explicit:

> When "the two are one," we are speaking truth among ourselves. The "outside of ourselves" is the body, whereas the inside is the soul. The body is therefore no longer the basic factor establishing one's identity. Rather our soul, then, should be made manifest by our good works. In that way, it makes sense that when a brother sees a sister, he doesn't think of her as a female, and that a sister seeing a brother wouldn't think of him as a male. This is what ushers in the Father's realm. (*2 Clem.* 12:3, 5, 6)[3]

Paul also had a very similar saying. In his Letter to the Galatians he connected the idea of gender blending to the ancient Hebrew scripture Genesis 1:27: "So God created humankind in his image, . . . male and female he created them." Paul affirmed for the Galatians that indeed, there was no longer a division between male and female. The body of the Anointed, so prominent in 1 Corinthians, is viewed by Paul as both male and female.

The Gospel of Thomas, written in the late first or early second century, follows along this same female-male pattern with a saying (no. 22) nearly identical to that of *2 Clement*. Jesus, seeing some nursing infants, tells his students that the nursing infants are like those who gain entrance to the empire of heaven. Jesus lists a series of inversions: two becoming one, upper becoming lower, the inside as the outside, and male and female being a single one. This inverted and collapsing view of male and female is well established from Paul into the late second century.

Contradictory influences also developed, even while other gender-bending depictions persisted. When Paul's followers conceived Jesus's body as "male and female," they saw it as a reflection of ideas from Genesis. This ideal was understood, after all, to be a divine image in Hebrew scriptures. However, Rome's patriarchal domination, operating at all levels of society, seeped gradually into the images of Jesus. The gender bending in the parables went unseen, and the author of Ephesians wrote "Wives, be subject to your husbands" (5:22), reinstituting the patriarchal order. Mary Magdalene disappeared as the one who proclaimed the resurrection to the students. Her presence was there to be seen, but it gradually disappeared.

SECOND-CENTURY PORTRAITS OF JESUS

Savior as True Human

The second century accommodated many and contradictory ideas, sometimes in direct conflict, sometimes in coexistence, some creatively new, and some from the earliest followers of Jesus. The Gospel of Mary, written in the first half of the second century, was discovered at the end of the nineteenth century. It combines the first-century tradition of Jesus as a teacher of wisdom with a strong dose of popular Greek philosophy. The focus of that mixture turns on the Savior's teachings about life beyond the body and the soul that moves beyond the body. The Greek philosopher Plato had made a clear distinction between the eternal and immutable and the finite, mutable world, and the Savior in this gospel appears mostly to agree. Although the first several pages are missing in the surviving Coptic text, the gospel picks up with Jesus teaching that the material sense of things would dissolve back into its own proper root, and that the soul and the mind would be found as the entities with ultimate spiritual value. Significantly, the Gospel of Mary does not use the name "Jesus" at all, but only "Savior."

Ancient pages from The Secret Revelation of John describing Jesus: "And behold a child appeared to me. Then he . . . changed into the form of an old man . . . I did not understand this wonder, whether it was a woman having many forms (who) said to me I am the Father, the Mother, and the Son." (3:4–8, 12)

Wikimedia Commons

The meaning of gender is woven neatly into the fabric of this story also with the absence of the male patriarchal model. First, God is not identified by a male name such as Father but is recognized more distinctly as the Good. Second, the maleness of the Savior's body becomes either irrelevant or disappears, even though his authority predominates.

In the Gospel of Mary—which is presented as a postdeath story—the Savior turns the attention of the students from the nature of his resurrected body to the care of the soul and mind, either of men or of women. The nongendered soul, while it moves toward its complete freedom, explains to the people that "you (those who are learning) mistook the garment I wore for my true self" (Gos. Mary 9:2).[4] This garment that is shed while the soul is progressing upward appears to present only an outward image of gender and identity. It is the outer garment that distorts the true image of the soul. When the Savior finishes teaching his students and leaves them, the students "were distressed and wept greatly. 'How are we going to go out to the rest of the world to announce the good news about the Realm of the child of true Humanity? . . . 'If they did not spare him, how will they spare us?'" (Gos. Mary 5:1, 2).

Then a woman steps forward to comfort and take a leadership role. Mary (representing one of the first-century Marys—most likely Mary Magdalene) speaks with the authority of a second-century man, addressing the students' fear of Roman violence: "Do not weep and be pained, nor doubt . . . But rather let us praise his greatness for he has prepared us and made us Humans" (Gos. Mary 5:6, 7). In the face of her confidence, some of the men are offended (see Chapter 7).

Two of the male students represent two conflicting reactions to the idea of female leadership. Peter, representing the patriarchal norm, is annoyed that Jesus would have trusted his greatest spiritual teachings to a woman. But Levi recognizes the obstruction that the gender role has caused in the mission entrusted to them through the Savior. "Rather," he exclaims, "we should be ashamed and, once we have clothed ourselves with the perfect Human, we should do what we were commanded" (Gos. Mary 10:11, 12). That perfect human seems more similar to the "neither male nor female, but also male *and* female" ideal than the socially constructed gender Peter was reacting to.

The Rescuer

The Letter of Peter to Philip, a document written by an anonymous second-century writer, envisions the crucifixion of Jesus as a way of helping those who feared their own crucifixions. To gain legitimacy and authority, the author used two highly respected envoys to present a new image of Jesus. The goal was to make sense of the ongoing violence of the Roman Empire in the face of no realistic hope. Peter writes a letter to Philip, who had become estranged from the envoys after the Savior's death. Peter begs Philip to return to fellowship, because they urgently need each other. Keenly aware of Roman rulers' willingness to kill them, just as they had killed Jesus, this group of envoys turns to the Lord in prayer for answers.

This pointed story of the envoys for Jesus being fearful of being killed can be understood clearly only in the Roman context. As we explored in Part I of this book, violence was an everyday occurrence in the Roman Empire. The cruelty and aftermath of atrocities formed the backdrop for everyday life. Stories of a good and faithful teacher of Israel who had been brutally and unjustly crucified resonated in many corners of the Mediterranean world. The senseless world of torture, humiliation, enslavement, and random crucifixions continued to stoke the Roman power engine several generations after Jesus's death.

The shame and humiliation of crucifixion were as intentional and intense as its cruel physical torture. But Jesus's crucifixion ironically triggered the opposite of Roman intentions. The Romans' anticipated destruction of both the body and memory of Jesus failed. Instead of silencing him, his death resulted in stories and songs of hope, inspiration, and a commitment to remembering him throughout the Mediterranean area. People who needed an expression of their own devastation found stories of Jesus filling those needs. These stories of Jesus—crucified and resurrected in body and spirit—opened up the possibilities of his divine, saving, guiding, healing, encouraging presence existing and comforting people more than a century after his death.

Others who took hope from Jesus's story created very different images. Here was a hero who came to terms with death but *without* total victory. These were people who continued to experience injustice and violence but whose reshaping of Jesus's story gave them hope when no end to the suffering was in sight. Some conceived this crucified and resurrected Jesus as the one divinity to be revered. Others respected him as a teacher and healer. Not everybody thought he was the most important character of the time, because his death by crucifixion was one of thousands during the period. But the images of his memory grew to fit the needs of the time.

The Letter of Peter to Philip aimed to propose a new social cohesion among these key envoys of Jesus the Anointed, who could unite in their response to the violence they faced. The contents of the letter soon shift from a message to Peter to a narrative that reveals new images of the Master. After Philip receives the letter, he departs quickly and joins Peter and his fellow envoys. And as soon as they gather on the Mount of Olives, they pray: "Child of life, Child of immortality, who dwells in the light; the

Child, Anointed of immortality, our rescuer, give us your power for they seek to kill us" (134:2–9).

In response to their prayer, Jesus Anointed appears to them as "a great light," and his voice, emanating from the light, explains that they also will suffer. But he instructs them to participate in the Savior's mission for the whole world. New images of Jesus emerge from this letter: Jesus appears as a great light, with a distinctive voice. He is now "the Savior of the whole world," not just for his people. His counsel to his followers, despite the likelihood that they will suffer just as he did, is to preach and heal, also just as he did.

This portrait draws no particular attention to the Hebrew scriptures, but it is an image of a Savior—"Child of life, Child of immortality, who dwells in the light; Child, Anointed of immortality, our rescuer"—attentive to the dire needs of the day. The writer of the letter imagines Jesus's suggestion that his own suffering and that of these second-century followers were part of the strategy that countered the violence of the Roman rulers, but it was not a mandate to die. The Letter of Peter to Philip ends with Jesus's envoys following Jesus's light-filled instructions to go out into the streets and to the Temple to teach and heal the ordinary people (132:18, 19).

Jesus as Parent

The Gospel of Truth, which like most gospels makes no explicit claim for authorship, provides a frame for yet another kind of image of Jesus from the second century. Although Jesus is present in almost every one of the twenty-six chapters of this gospel, he is called "Jesus" only once, "Jesus Anointed" only once, and "Savior" once. Two extensive chapters lay out the case that "the name of the Father is the Child" (Gos. Truth 23, 24).

From the tone of the Gospel of Truth, we can surmise that the group for whom this "sermon" was written had experienced physical torture and injustice, but Jesus's role as teacher and "Mother" carries special meaning. As a teacher of parables, Jesus is a guide; in a cosmic role, he teaches the correction of the "transgression" that made humanity ignorant. As "the Mother," he fulfills the role of the Word. His death became a means for processing and strategizing about the terrible losses in the lives of the people who knew this gospel:

> They nailed him (Jesus) to a tree, and he became the fruit of
> the Father's knowledge. However, it (the fruit) didn't cause
> destruction when it was eaten, but those who ate it were
> given joy in the discovery. He discovered them in himself
> and they discovered him in themselves. (Gos. Truth 3:5–7)[5]

This figure whose death on a tree makes him into the fruit of the Father is one of the most imaginative second-century portraits. As the "Word," "Mother," and "Father, "His love made a body for the Word . . . and walks in creation as the fruit of (God's) heart and the face of his love" (Gos. Truth 10:1–5).

Here, the figure suffered an unjust death and overcame the shame and threat to his mission by becoming the fruit of knowledge. Engaging in that fruit brings joy, not death, while sharing in his persecution brings about the discovery of unity with him. In a major difference with the Letter of Peter to Philip, there is hardly any mention of threat or pain in death.

Noble Death

Other second-century writers conceived contrasting and even conflicting images of Jesus that pertained more to Jesus's unique relationship to God, while still based on the idea of the "noble death" of Jesus (see Chapter 6).

Ignatius, the bishop of Antioch, executed in the early second century, left reflections on the subject of his death. Ignatius's letters, probably written in the mid-second century, use the simple name of "Jesus" very rarely and the simple name of "the Anointed" hardly at all. His preferred names are the combined "Lord Jesus Anointed" and "Jesus Anointed." His image of Jesus was personal but fit with the shifting sands of cultural meaning. Jesus's crucifixion shaped Ignatius's attitude toward his own impending death and inspired his life purpose to become a "true student of Jesus Anointed." In his letter *To the Ephesians* he wrote that his "hoped-for success as a witness" would allow him to become a student—and to know his identity as a "self" totally committed to the Anointed (21:2). In his imitation of the Anointed, Ignatius conceived suffering as an opportunity to present his image of the Savior as one who exercised proper self-control under persecution.

Ignatius's embrace of his own death at the hands of Roman officials represents a major cultural shift of the second century. Not only adherents of the Anointed, but society in general had begun drifting toward the idea of suffering as an identity marker (see Chapter 19). It is difficult to know when Ignatius's writings became widely known. But eventually, at least by the beginning of the third century, they formed part of a basis for shifts in the political, social, and religious realms, and the noble death of the witness became a focus of identity as one who suffers.

Ignatius's Lord Jesus Anointed is very different from the Savior of the Gospel of Mary, the Mother and Father of the Gospel of Truth, and the shining light of the Letter of Peter to Philip. Jesus is present in these texts in many different ways.

Enslaved Savior

Another shift in the second-century kaleidoscope produced markedly different images of Jesus. The widely circulated Secret Revelation of John was, as far as we know now, the first writing of the followers of the Savior to incorporate into a single document the nature of God and evil; the origin of the world; and salvation from human sin, suffering, and death. The narrative framework sets out the Savior as the teacher and expounder of wisdom. However, it makes no mention of the Savior's death or any encouragement for martyrdom.

Instead, the Savior is represented as a teacher in a postdeath scene, explaining why a proper understanding of the goodness of God and the fraudulence of evil was necessary for salvation. The bodily image of the Master is somewhat blurry to the second-century author, because in the opening scene, when John (the student of the Savior) is found grieving over Jesus's death, the Savior appears to him in a vision. First, a child appears as the heavens open and the earth quakes. Then the messenger becomes like an old person, and then he appears as enslaved. Nonetheless, John recognizes him as his master, the Savior, and the rest of the book comprises his revealed teaching.

After his lessons on the origin of the world and the distinction between the all-harmonious realm governed by infinite Spirit and the deceiving nature of the counterfeit spirit, John presses the Master to explain how humans can be saved. Salvation in the second century did not deal with God's judgment but was more readily conceived as an escape from fear, disease, chaos, emotional torment, physical danger, and death. The Roman emperor himself was often addressed as "Savior" as he saved the empire from these dangers.

In The Secret Revelation of John, the Master demonstrates the saving power that extends directly from the Mother-Father-God through various representations of a Savior. At times "the Savior" takes on the role of Epinoia, the light who enlightens the deceived sufferer. Sometimes Sophia (Wisdom) and sometimes Pronoia (Foreknowledge) provide what is most needed. While the name Jesus occurs only in the closing of the document, he is variously called "Nazarene," "Savior," "Lord," "Anointed," and "Master."

Spiritual Body

Marcion of Sinope (90–160 CE), one of the most important second-century writers, is known now only through the voice of his opponents. He was a teacher and an excellent organizational leader with a large following. His ideas represent a unique overlap between such writers as Ignatius and the author of The Secret Revelation of John.

Marcion came from Pontus on the Black Sea, a backwater in the Roman Empire, far from the main religious scene. Relatively few Judeans lived in Pontus, so he had little access to Judaism or Israel's scriptures. But Jesus's crucifixion left a deep impression on him—as it had for Ignatius. However, for Marcion it marked a clean break from the Hebrew world of Jesus's contemporaries and ushered in a new era.

When Marcion went to Rome, he may have gained greater access to wider views of Jesus. What is more certain, though, is that he derived his image of Jesus from parts of a version of what was later recognized as the Gospel of Luke and Paul's letters, which writings he considered to be the only legitimate voices of authority. These few resources became the basis of Marcion's highly ordered teaching system (see Chapter 15).

According to Marcion, Jesus was the God who descended into the world and was a stranger sent to save those trapped in this imperfect world, similarly as he appeared in The Secret Revelation of John. Jesus was crucified and arose from the dead, and in his new spiritual body, he exercised the power to save all who believed in him.

Even more important for Marcion, Jesus was *not* the same as the God of the Hebrew prophets. That "God" had nothing to do with Jesus's new gospel of God as Love. The prophet Isaiah had proclaimed that God said he created "darkness" and "woe" (Isa. 45:7). Jesus may have belonged to Israel, but Marcion emphasized some differences between Jesus and scriptural understandings of Judeans. Jesus, as Marcion saw him, was breaking with some Judean interpretations of holy writings.

Anointed Lord

A decade or so after Marcion had been in Rome, Justin Martyr (100–165 CE) rose to prominence with yet another, radically different image of Jesus. His picture builds upon the opening of the Gospel of John, announcing that the "Word [Logos] was with God, and the Word [Logos] was God" (John 1:1). For Justin, Jesus was the embodiment of this Word. Since Jesus "was in the beginning with God," and "All things came into being through him" (John 1:2, 3), for Justin, logically, Jesus would be this God, or "the Lord."

The Greek word *kyrios* (Lord) was what the Greek translators of Hebrew holy writings used for the Hebrew name of God, represented by the four Hebrew letters *Y, H, W,* and *H*. From the Greek translation, Justin reasoned that Jesus, the "Lord," would actually be that Word that *was* God and *with* God, and therefore he was the preexistent God.

Contrary to Marcion, who thought the new idea of God was not at all like the God of the Hebrew writings, Justin thought the Hebrew scriptures made perfect sense. But Judean interpretation had made a major mistake in failing to recognize the presence of God in Jesus Anointed as proclaimed in their own scriptures. In fact, Justin argued, "Anointed" has the same meaning as "Lord" (*kyrios*) as evidenced *throughout* the Hebrew scriptures. Judeans, according to Justin, were missing this key teaching in their own writings.

He turned to one of the Psalms to offer an example. In his book *Dialogue with Trypho*, Justin converses with an imagined character named Trypho, a Judean, and explains how the Anointed was the very Lord prophesied throughout the ancient scriptures. He reminds Trypho of Psalm 24:3: "Who shall ascend the hill of the Lord? / And who shall stand in his holy place?"

The Hebrew YHWH is translated into Greek *Kyrios*, Lord. Trypho and his Judean colleagues thought that "Lord" in this case referred to the Hebrew king Solomon, but Justin saw it as clear evidence of prophecy for the coming of the Anointed. The same reasoning works for the last verse: "Who is this King of glory? / The Lord of hosts, / He is the King of glory" (Ps. 24:10).

Again, in Hebrew, the "Lord of hosts" is YHWH, and the Greek translation is *Kyrios t n dyname n* (Lord of hosts). From this, Justin concludes that "Lord" refers to Jesus the Anointed. David E. Wilhite, in his paper for the Seminar, concludes that for Justin, the primary person encountered in the Hebrew holy writings named God is Jesus Anointed. He does not assume that God the Father and God the Son are distinct. In fact, those distinctions, based on the father/son metaphor, were introduced later on the way to a Trinitarian theology to solve the problem created by Justin's *Kyrios* understanding of Jesus Anointed as being identical with God.

People from different cultures and communities within the Roman Empire picked up on different and at times conflicting parts of the story. While Justin differed with Marcion over the "right" way to understand Jesus in light of the Hebrew scriptures, others turned their attention to the meaning of Jesus's teachings and/or death to find meaning in their own lives. And for different reasons, both Justin and Marcion encouraged the separation between people of Israel who were followers of Jesus the Anointed and those who were not followers of Jesus the Anointed.

CONCLUSION

A variety of portraits of Jesus arose during the first and second centuries. Evidence of first-century acknowledgment of the prominence and value of women and the meaning around Jesus's crucifixion engendered novel interpretations and new sources of authority. The image of the second-century Jesus, however, particularly moved in many directions. Unlike historical assumptions of forty years ago, it no longer makes sense to think of the second century as a time in which orthodoxy was establishing itself and what was later thought of as heresy was being dismantled. Nor can the second century's many different ideas about and practices of gender be characterized as headed definitively toward male dominance or gender equality. As Chapters 7 and 8 explored, it is best to see second-century Jesus movements, clubs, schools, and groups as offering a full range of gender experiments.

Ignatius and Justin, who in later centuries were identified as the "winners" of various philosophical debates and as two of the "church fathers," did not represent a majority of second-century opinion, but they embodied some of the innovations of the period. Ignatius's promotion of the noble death idea encouraged self-identification with suffering, in contrast to The Secret Revelation of John's awakening to false powers that cause suffering and resistance to them. Justin's conflating the "Lord" of the Hebrew holy writings with the coming of the Anointed highlighted a dominant male figure who made no room for the worth of women.

The implications from the variety of images of Jesus from the second century surprise us. First, Jesus often was not the dominant figure in the writings and narratives produced by these second-century movements. Second, Jesus's death and its aftermath stirred the imagination more in the second century than his life and ministry. Third, the kaleidoscopic images cannot be confined to a polarity between old and new, right and wrong, orthodox and heresy. The second century was rich with multiple images of Jesus.

Chapter contributor:

Shirley Paulson

Papers Relevant to This Chapter by Seminar Participants

Miller, Robert J. "Prophecy, Christology, and Anti-Judaism in Justin Martyr." Spring 2017.

Smith Wilson, Justine. "Gospel of Judas and the Ravenmocker." Spring 2019.

Wilhite, David E. "Is Jesus YHWH? Two De-Judaizing Trajectories of Marcion and Justin." Spring 2019.

PART IV

FALLING INTO WRITING

HIDING IN PLAIN SIGHT

In Part I we pointed to how Rome's violence was a crucial factor in how so many different Jesus peoples, clubs, groups, schools, and movements emerged. How does that key theme and reality of Roman violence on the Jesus peoples fit with everything else we have learned?

The answer in this chapter brings new aspects of the impact of imperial violence forward, beyond what we saw in Part I. First, the clash between Rome's violence and the clubs, movements, and followers associated with Jesus still defines who these various groups were. Second, there is still no "party line" about Rome among the many communities of the Savior. Certainly, more overt voices become insistent about the damage Rome continues to do. At the same time, complicated ongoing relationships between Roman virtue and violence are emerging.

Third, and most important, during the first two hundred years of the Common Era, one major tactic of resistance to Roman aggression emerged: the hidden transcript—that is, alternative stories that are "hidden" behind a more obvious one.

WHAT ARE HIDDEN TRANSCRIPTS?

The way that Jesus groups in the first and second century resisted violence resembles a worldwide pattern of how subjugated populations resist domination. More than a decade's worth of research shows how many oppressed peoples and groups around the world create "a secret" language that makes fun of those dominating them and helps them process some of their loss and trauma.

Credit for uncovering these behaviors belongs to political scientist and cultural anthropologist James C. Scott. Scott, the author of *Domination and the Arts of Resistance: Hidden Transcripts*, has marshaled a wide range of examples of the mockery of oppressive rulers. For instance, the intense interest in spirit possession in many cultures points directly to a hidden transcript occurring as a woman's "spirit talk" in public, and protects her from spousal abuse:

> In the case of spirit possession, a woman seized by a spirit can openly make known her grievances against her husband and male relatives, curse them, make demands, and, in general, violate the powerful norms of male dominance. She may, while possessed, cease work, be given gifts, and generally be treated indulgently. Because it is not she who is acting, but rather the spirit that has seized her, she cannot be held responsible for her own words. The result is a kind of oblique protest that dares not speak its own name but that is often acceded to if only because its claims are seen to emanate from a powerful spirit and not from the woman herself.[1]

Scott and those who have elaborated on his proposals have found many such examples in carnivals of Europe and Latin

America. The festive spirit of the carnival and the chance to wear costumes and masks give oppressed groups an opportunity to express their discontent with and critique of their political reality. Under the cover of masks, costumes, and festivities, they can speak "normally suppressed speech and aggression," as Scott puts it. In a carnival atmosphere, such criticism on one level appears to be just fun and festivity, even while speaking truth to power.

Although many of the early stories and writings about the many Jesus clubs, groups, schools, and movements of the first two centuries portrayed in the previous chapters are read today as "holy" and "solemn" literature, it seems likely that ancient readers saw some of them as comical, irreverent, and resistant hidden transcripts—potentially carnival-like in their disdain for authority.

The differences in many Jesus groups of the first two centuries paint a vibrant kaleidoscope in their approaches to responding to and surviving violence. This multicolored collage does not demonstrate common creeds or ideologies as much as a wide range of hidden transcripts. As a first example, we turn to a hidden transcript (this one twisted and darkly humorous, as hidden transcripts often are) found in the Gospels of Mark, Matthew, and Luke.

A MAN GOES CRAZY: *EXORCISM OF THE "DEMONIAC"*

The story begins with a man who is sick and appears to be possessed, so much so that his misery is beyond bearing and he retreats to live among the tombs. His agony is so intense that he is often found smashing himself with rocks, perhaps to distract himself from the terrible pain. The story is set in northern

Israel, not far from where a Roman military unit called a legion is stationed. As we will discover, it looks like this man's pain has to do with the thousands of soldiers in his neighborhood and their violent behavior. Perhaps they had they beaten him or had killed or maimed his family members, friends, and/or neighbors.

The hidden transcript within this story proposes, subtly, that this man's possession comes mostly from the presence of the occupying Roman army around the Sea of Galilee, where the man lived. Literally, the man says what has driven him crazy is "legion," the normal word for a large Roman military unit. And indeed—according to the symbolic, fanciful, and analytic way the story unfolds—the man is relieved of his pain when the "spirits" of the occupying army are transferred by a healer from the man to pigs in fields nearby. When those spirits of the occupying army are transferred to the pigs, the man's possession is gone, and the pigs run down a steep bank and drown in a lake.

In this story, the man is, in a way, saved from the violence the army subjected him to when the pigs/soldiers drown in the lake, although the occupying army remains. The man returns to his right mind, although the people of the area are not pleased and fearful. Are they worried that the healer will make trouble for them? Is the formerly possessed man himself a sign of such trouble-making? Somewhat puzzled, but certainly relieved, the receivers of this story wonder about the dead pigs and the real, occupying army that could still make other people crazy and hurt themselves.

The story accurately addresses the profound damage an occupying army can do to the population it controls. It gives such a population a way to think about how to cope, escape some of the pain, express anger, and even laugh a bit when it portrays the similarities between that occupying army and a group of pigs—animals considered unclean in Hebrew writings. Any suspicions Roman authorities might have about the story's strange mix-up of pigs and armies would be hard to prove. The people listening to the story are not really worried about whether the story is encouraging a calamity in which Roman soldiers run into a lake and drown. Rather, the people under the thumb of the Roman army can tell the story of the pigs drowning and laugh at the way it links pigs and soldiers. The nagging questions about the fact that the army is still ruling the countryside in the middle of the satisfaction of the giggles about pigs/soldiers drowning remind the story's audience that all still is not right. The man is "healed" of this possession, but the real soldiers still occupy the land.

The artful hiddenness of these powerful portraits of loss, trauma, and violence allowed the residents of the Roman Empire to think and feel deeply about their circumstances without getting themselves into trouble, through their stories, with their Roman rulers. The cleverness of these ancient stories was by and large so successful that their subtle meanings and hidden messages about violence are easily lost to the modern reader. In large part, the ingenuity of these ancient experiences and expression has made it difficult for moderns to see the violence at all. Instead, contemporary eyes often see in these ancient writings only modern Sunday school lessons for children, theological treatises, or quaint tales of Roman customs.

The ways modernity has looked past and covered over the deep social and interior ancient work on how to live with heartache and torture is strong enough that we take up here a kaleidoscope of examples in the writings of the first two centuries. The stories may seem unfocused, yet persistent images, stories, worries, and fantasies about violence show up in them. Many do seem to focus on, if only involuntarily, Roman violence, damage, and power. As it turns out, these stories show surprising twists, humor, and melancholy, alongside anger and rawness. They offer practices and participatory theatrics for the many different Jesus groups. Rather than mounting the barricades for social change or erecting buildings for formal ritual, these hidden transcripts are more like songs to sing, stories to tell, and namings of children after their uncle or cousin killed by marauding soldiers.

SWEET FRAGRANCE AND NIGHTMARES: THE GOSPEL OF TRUTH

The first sentence of the mid-second-century Gospel of Truth is "The good news of truth is joy" (1:1).[2] Discovered in the Egyptian desert, but written with full consciousness of Roman violence, this text surprises in how it lives with pain and loss. At the same time, it fills its readers with joy and beauty. It overflows with a sense of fulfillment and sensuousness, sounding alternately like a poem, a letter, or an ecstatic sermon.

Although the Gospel of Truth reads like a mix of poetry and ecstasy, just under the surface of its lush language are signs of trauma and violence. In the middle of images of beauty, praise of kindness, joy, and leisurely relief, one finds less present but sure signals of nightmares and torture:

> . . . as if they were sleeping and found themselves in
> disturbing dreams—running someplace or powerless while
> pursued, coming to blows or themselves beaten, falling from
> heights or flying through air without wings. Or sometimes
> as if people are trying to kill them or killing their neighbors,
> smeared with their blood. Those in the midst of all this
> confusion see nothing for these things are nothing.

. . . the beloved Child . . . spoke new things . . . He did
away with torture and torment for they caused those
needing compassion, those in transgression and bonds,
to stray from his face. He dissolved them with power and
reproached them with knowledge. He became a way for
those who were ignorant, discovery for those searching and
strength for those who were shaken, purity for those who
were defiled. (14:12–15; 16:2, 6, 8–10)

On one level, everything in the Gospel of Truth is sweetness and light, but nightmares and torture are not far away.
Here the hidden transcript is the imperial violence, silently
breathing its threat, through the fragrance of all people and
the strength of the beloved Child. "The Father's children are
his fragrance, for they are from the beauty of his face. Because
of this, the Father loves his fragrance and discloses it everywhere" (19:4, 5). God's children are everywhere, and they are
the actual fragrance of God and light.

This same combination of over-the-top sensuous goodness
with an undertow of haunted violence occurs in what has become the most modernly heralded part of the Gospel of Truth:

Say then from the heart that you are the perfect day and
within you dwells the light that never ends. Speak of the
truth with those who seek it and of knowledge of those
who have sinned through their transgressions. Strengthen
the feet of those who stumble and stretch your hands
to those who are weak. Feed those who are hungry and
give rest to the weary. Raise those who wish to arise and
awaken those who sleep—for you all are understanding
drawn forth. If strength does these things, strength
becomes stronger. (17:10–16)

This passage exhibits one of the most explicit pictures of people reaching out to others in need and working together. The vibrant confidence of this document translates overtly on a communal level and perhaps a societal one. That multiple and different early manuscripts of the Gospel of Truth exist could suggest that this may be one of the most unambiguous statements of social action for goodness. Even in this assertion, this Jesus-related movement is not far from having strong subliminal awareness of social transgression, weakness, and hunger. It gives attention to these broken parts of life, but only in terms of the communities' need to address them.

This gospel blends poetry, sermonizing, songs, and parables and gives voice to a strong social range. Within and across these poems and songs is also a storyline, an implicit narrative. The through-line of this story runs as follows:

> He was nailed to a tree and became the fruit of the Father's knowledge.
>
> It did not cause destruction when it was eaten,
>
> But it caused those who ate it to come into being
>
> And find contentment in its discovery.
>
> And he discovered them in himself,
>
> And they discovered him in themselves
>
> —the uncontainable, the unknowable . . . one who is full and made all things.
>
> All things are in that one and all things have need of him.
>
> He came into their midst and spoke a teacher's words . . .
>
> After all these, the little children came . . .

ɩWhen they had been strengthened . . .

They knew and they were known . . .

The sound walks through creation as the fruit of creation's heart and the face of its love.

This active word bears all things, choosing and receiving all things,

Bringing them back to the Father, the Mother, Jesus of boundless sweetness.

God opens his bosom . . . and reveals a hidden self.

This hidden self is the Child of God,

So that through God's compassion,

The generations learn about God. (4:5–8; 5:8, 10, 11, 12; 10:5, 7, 8)

The Gospel of Truth is one big hidden transcript, reflecting both a larger story and a social vision, but focusing only implicitly on the Roman violence described systematically in the first two chapters of the book. This is almost, but not quite, the same art of resistance to Roman violence as seen in Luke's "The Man Goes Crazy." The hidden transcript of the Gospel of Truth, however, differs from Luke's story in that the transcript is almost doubly hidden: the Gospel of Truth has power and beauty around every corner, and violence is hidden in the past or in dreams. So, as we proceed through four other hidden transcripts of resistance and resourcefulness, we do so suspecting that each social hidden strategy is different. There is no single guiding story against violence. We find instead creative commitments to difference and to communal strength through challenging times.

A SINGER IMAGINES THE
DESTRUCTION OF ROME: REVELATION OF JOHN

A song that imagines that Rome is on fire and all its power has been destroyed offers another, very different hidden, though much less hidden, transcript. The song, from the Revelation to John, was probably written several decades after Rome was damaged by a fire set perhaps by those against Roman rule and centuries before Rome was destroyed. Our shortened telling is from chapters 17 and 18 of this late first-century vision. Although written near the height of Roman domination, the story is told in far-off Babylon, destroyed and rebuilt repeatedly during the centuries before the Common Era. The composer of this song imagines that Babylon stood on seven hills, just like ancient Rome.

The song can be summarized as follows: one of seven angels takes a dreamer to a lonely place and points out a giant sex worker riding on a monster. The angel says to the dreamer that the giant woman is Babylon the Great and that the seven heads of the monster on which she rides are seven hills. The angel identifies the giant woman as the great city that holds sway over all the rulers of the earth. Then another angel descends from the sky and sings of how Babylon the Great has fallen. All the wealth that she had now is now destroyed. In a single hour all the ships carrying great commerce have been destroyed. Another voice from the sky announces that God has remembered the cruelty of Babylon in order to destroy it and will reward the dreamer and his people to make up for all the torture and misery they have experienced.

The song rages against the violence of this great city that rules over all the earth. It promises revenge and reward for those who have been tortured and are in misery. The song continues: "She has fallen. She has fallen . . . Alas! Alas! Great city! City clothed in fine linen, and purple and scarlet cloth! City adorned with gold ornaments, and precious stones, and pearls! In a single hour your vast wealth has vanished!" (Rev. 18:2, 16–17). There is little, if any, sign in the late first century that Rome can be destroyed or punished. Only in the eye of this dreamer can the people Rome pillaged be restored. Nevertheless, the song paints a massive tableau in which the reigning city is annihilated and the dreamer's people are saved.

Indeed, nothing like what the song described happened. How, then, should we interpret this song of the Great City's destruction and those who heard it? Did anyone sing along? Did the raging song provide catharsis to those who had suffered so much at the hands of Roman imperial power or other violence, as New Testament scholar Adela Yarbro Collins has suggested?[3] Was this song a way of escaping the violence—if only in reading, singing, or performing it? In many situations of violence, the anger and fantasy in hidden transcripts help people survive unthinkable damage and loss.

These two chapters in Revelation may be the closest that any writings of the first two centuries come to calling for an attack against Rome. The voice of the dreamer claims that he has been punished for his teachings. On the other hand, the song does not present an explicit attack on Rome but focuses instead on the much more ancient city of Babylon in a faraway time and place. Rather than humor and healing, the response to violence in this writing is anger, fantasy, and outrageous hope. It is a hidden transcript because it calls this imagined destroyed city "Babylon," but its location on seven hills clearly marks its setting as Rome.

DIVINITY HIDDEN IN RUBBLE—
THE THUNDER: PERFECT MIND

Our final example of responding to violence with hidden transcripts is a long poem presented in the voice of a divine figure. Not unlike many ancient Mediterranean divine voices from literature of the first and second centuries, this divine figure announces itself in long stanzas full of self-praise. Although only one ancient manuscript exists of this poem called *The Thunder: Perfect Mind*, there are many similar long poems in Egyptian literature and the Hebrew scriptures, as well as the somewhat shorter yet clearly similar Gospel of John. The first verses of *The Thunder* are especially similar to these other collections of that time:

> I was sent out from power
>
> I came to those pondering me . . .
>
> Look at me . . .
>
> Audience, hear me.
>
> Don't chase me from your sight . . .
>
> I am the first and the last. (1:1–3, 5)[4]

Although found among the Nag Hammadi manuscripts, *The Thunder*'s date of composition could be anywhere from the first century BCE to the fourth century CE. Even with this lack of clarity concerning its time of composition, it still falls within the time of the Roman Empire, and its discovery along with many other Jesus-related writings near a fourth-century Christian monastery points in that direction.

The figure introduced in *The Thunder: Perfect Mind* has many divine relatives. One specific family tree of the Mediterranean divine family helps make sense of this poem. That tree consists mostly of divine females who give long speeches about how powerful, beautiful, and wise they are. Two examples from that family tree are Isis and Wisdom/Sophia.

The ancient Egyptian goddess Isis also became very popular during the first two centuries in Greece, North Africa, and Rome. The North African second-century writer Lucius Apuleius hears her in this voice:

> I am she that is the natural mother of all things, mistress and governess of all the elements, the initial progeny of the worlds, Queen of heaven . . . At my will the planets of the air, the wholesome winds of the seas, and the silence of the underworld be disposed . . . my divinity is adored throughout the world . . . the Athenians call me Cecropian Artemis . . . they call me Queen Isis. (*Metamorphoses* 11.47)[5]

Wisdom/Sophia is a similar figure who appears in the Hebrew Bible and some Christian Bibles. She speaks poetically in *Sirach*:

> "Over the waves of the sea, over all the earth,
>   and over every people and nation I have held sway.
> Among all these I sought a resting place . . . ;
> Come to me, you who desire me,
>   and eat your fill of my fruits.
>
> Those who eat of me will hunger for more,
> and those who drink of me will thirst for more."
>   (*Sir.* 24:6–7, 19, 21)[6]

Although the divinity at the beginning of *The Thunder: Perfect Mind* sounds powerful and dominating—"I am the first and the last"—the writing quickly moves to images that are much closer to the pain and vulnerability of the Gospel of Luke and the Revelation to John. The divine voice of *The Thunder* proclaims:

I am she who is honored and she who is mocked . . .

I am a sterile woman and she who has many children . . .

I am the enslaved woman of him who served me . . .

I am she who is disgraced and she who is important . . .

Do not be arrogant to me when I am thrown to the ground . . .

Do not stare at me in the shit pile, leaving me discarded . . .

Do not stare at me when I am thrown out among the condemned

Do not laugh at me in the lowest places

Do not throw me down among those slaughtered viciously . . .

In my weakness do not strip me bare

Do not be afraid of my power . . .

I am she who exists in all fears and in trembling boldness . . .

I shall shut my mouth among those whose mouths are shut

and then I will show up and speak

Why then did you hate me, you Greeks?

Because I am a barbarian among barbarians?

. . . Hear me in tenderness, learn from me in roughness

I am she who shouts out and I am thrown down on the ground

I am the one who prepares the bread and my mind within.

(1:5, 7, 10; 2:10, 12–15, 17, 18; 3:2–3; 4:24–25)

This voice is never safe from danger of all kinds: chase, enslavement, beating, slaughter, hatred, weakness, and stripping bare. On the other hand, "trembling boldness" is all around. Even when in danger or disgrace, she is not to be pitied. She has substantial power.

The voice of *The Thunder: Perfect Mind* seems to live in the mire of humiliation and violence. This voice—usually female—cries out in pain, fears being overwhelmed, and experiences loss and loneliness. At the same time, she sounds like a goddess and almost certainly is modeled in part on Isis. But Isis never lost a battle and was always in control, while the voice of *The Thunder* is both divine and human. She is honored and mocked, disgraced and authoritative, exalted and thrown to the ground. Although she is at the same time divine and violently humiliated, these conditions are not treated as opposites. The tension between being divine and being beaten happens often. The experience of violence, slaughter, and disgrace is mentioned somewhat more than being powerfully divine. When she is divinely strong, she has the character of "the one who prepares the bread and the mind within," of one who has many experiences, like the crazy man and the people in the Gospel of Truth who have nightmares and are fragrant, just like God. When the people of the Anointed and the Enslaved of God faced Roman violence, their sense of their own power resembled Jesus and the voice of *The Thunder*.

Although *The Thunder: Perfect Mind* does not mention Jesus at all, the voice in the writing resembles the way Jesus is portrayed in the Gospel of John. There, Jesus regularly proclaims in a divine voice "I am." Yet even with his divine authority, Jesus cries when his best friend dies and he is finally tortured to death on the cross. These two figures are more or less alone in the ancient world as being both divine and overwhelmed by violence.

Like the Gospel of Luke, the Gospel of Truth, and the Revelation to John, *The Thunder* takes the notion of hidden transcripts against Roman violence and develops it extensively. None of these documents simply expresses fright, and all of them hide the way they manifest their resistance to Rome. The character of each of these expressions has both courage and fear.

MAKING SENSE OF AND RESISTING VIOLENCE

The artful hiddenness of these portraits of loss, trauma, and violence allowed their readers to think about and explore deep emotions about their own circumstances without putting those readers, and the writers, at increased risk with their Roman rulers. For us the cleverness of these ancient stories is so successful that their hidden meanings and messages about violence are almost completely lost. As James C. Scott points out, hidden transcripts are subtle, subliminal strategies for living with and resisting violence.

The examples we have examined show that making sense of violence was very important to ancient writers and readers alike. These people needed to come to grips with seeing neighbors, strangers, or members of their own families humiliated, tortured, enslaved, and killed. But at the same time, as some of these various groups grew larger, they also had to create ways to deflect some of the public awareness of what was often resistance to Rome. The clever, if indirect, ways that the groups addressed a wide variety of violence testifies to how much resistance mattered to them. The hidden transcripts of these stories, their tricky language, indicate these people's commitment to speaking about violence as a way to cope with it.

Instead of reducing the meaning of Jesus's experiences of violence and death to a sacrifice for sins, a wide range of writings see his death as an effort to make sense of people's pain and loss, sometimes through such hidden transcripts. These hidden transcripts about violence become a cipher for understanding the trauma in people's lives and their attempt to find a voice in a landscape of violence.

Such hidden transcripts, however, do not provide a standard or single correct interpretation of what to do with violence. In the story of the crazy man, the "demoniac" in the tombs, the way to face violence is by cleverly associating the villainous, violent soldiers with pigs, laughing darkly about the story and celebrating a recovery (at least a temporary one) from the violence. The subtle merging of sweet fragrance and horrible nightmares in the Gospel of Truth holds in tension the ingenuity of the Anointed movements and the violence of Rome. In the case of the dreamer in the Revelation to John, the strategy of facing violence has to do with being angry at Rome and having confidence in God's revenge. In *The Thunder: Perfect Mind*, the approach to humiliation and violence is to merge "all fears and trembling boldness" in a (nameless) divine figure.

In no case does one find a tragic approach to violence among the various Jesus peoples. And in no case is violence completely and successfully solved. What this group of movements, schools, and clubs shares is a courageous and clever response to and plan for experiencing almost inevitable violence. All of these expressions about the experience of violence make some kind of provisional advance in the ongoing struggle. There is no reason to apply this almost accidental bundle of writings and communities to all of the Anointed-related writings of the first two centuries. On the other hand, neither is there reason to ignore their temporary ways of dealing with the violence in the lives of the people of the time, of which hidden transcripts are one.

Papers Relevant to This Chapter by Seminar Participants

Taussig, Hal. "Hidden Transcripts of Violence and Partial Recovery." Spring 2017.

18

ROMANCING THE MARTYR

DYING HAPPILY EVER AFTER

According to the *Acts of Perpetua and Felicitas*, a story set right at the turn of the third century, a mass execution of women and men who asserted their belonging to the party of Christus took place in the Roman city of Carthage, on the northern coast of Africa. Roman officials killed Perpetua and Felicitas alongside a group of other heroes from their community. The story asserts that these heroes sought their own deaths and had a great desire to die for their cause.

The story ends in intense violence. Within the arena, a man named Saturus is bitten by a leopard and then thrown, unconscious, onto a pile of bleeding bodies, awaiting a final cut of his throat. The frenzied crowd demands to watch the executioner's sword finish off those bodies, so the martyrs regain consciousness, stand and move into the open, and kiss each other goodbye. Without movement or speech, the necks of many of these heroes are slit, but Perpetua "had yet to taste more pain," the audience is told with relish. Perpetua "screamed as she was struck on the bone; then she took the trembling hand of the young gladiator and guided it to her throat. It was as though so great a woman . . . could not be dispatched unless she herself were willing" (*Perpetua* 21).[1] Perpetua, both seeking and in control of her own death, is the actual victor of the contest.[2]

So ends the Acts of Perpetua and Felicitas: in violent, spectacular, intentional death. The audience is clearly meant to interpret this finale as happy. "Ah, most valiant and blessed martyrs!" the story concludes. "Truly are you called and chosen for the glory of Christ Jesus our Lord! And anyone who exalts, honors, and worships his glory should read . . . these new deeds of heroism!" (*Perpetua* 21). Everything ends as it should. The heroes are in their proper place, having died noble deaths and achieved their goal. The audience is left with role models for future life, and for future death. Everyone lives and dies happily ever after.

Death, however, even noble death, is not an obvious goal for the living. The *Acts of Perpetua and Felicitas* is part of a later compilation of writings now known as the *Acts of the Christian Martyrs*, though these writings initially circulated independently. "Martyr" is a Greek word with a long history of meaning "witness." These "witness stories," as we might more appropriately call them, or perhaps simply "acts," began to circulate mainly in the second century of the Common Era as letters. Eventually, over a long period of time, these letters came to define later understandings of the perpetually thorny word "Christian": a sufferer, one who endures pain and dies willingly, holding Jesus as both model for imitation and ultimate goal. Entire communities grew up around witness stories; the Acts of Paul and Thecla was a particularly popular narrative, though relatively few are familiar with it now. Acts became hugely important to the growth and institutionalization of the later phenomenon of Christianity, and suffering, broken bodies became central to the development and understanding of group commitment, identity, and belief.

THE DISINTEREST OF EMPIRE

Although each of these witness stories concludes with this not-happy happy ending, heroic death seeking was not a lived reality for the large majority of Jesus groups. We do not know whether Perpetua and Felicitas were historical people. Where and when persecution did occur, it was local, not imperial or systemic; it was unorganized and random. Roman officials did execute people who asserted their membership in communities of the Anointed, but execution was not generally sought. Pliny, the Roman governor of Bithynia and Pontus in the early second century, writes to Emperor Trajan because he does not know what to do with the people he calls, in Latin, *christiani* (see Chapter 2). Though a Roman governor, the main administrative power for an important imperial place, Pliny had never been to a trial of one of these people, suggesting that such trials cannot have been that widespread or significant, from an imperial perspective. Because he has never seen such a trial, Pliny does not know how to punish *christiani*, how to investigate them, or even whether investigation needs to be pressed to any great length.

As we have seen, Pliny uses the word *christianus* in Latin with reference to a person who is part of a rebellious, resistant group from Judea. He has executed people who maintain an identity as part of this potentially trouble-making group: "with all persons brought before me on the charge of being Christians [read, here, 'members of a rebellious Judean group' or 'members of the party of Christus']," Pliny recounts, "I have asked them in person if they are Christians [i.e., members of this party], and if they admit it, I repeat the question a second and third time, with a warning of the punishment awaiting them. If they persist, I order them to be led away for execution" (*Letters* 10.96).[3] Pliny has a handle on those who persist in their identification with this group, but he does not know what to do with new, less clear-cut situations. A pamphlet circulating through his province lists names of accused Christus-party members. Informers whisper in his ear. Men, women, young, old, rich, poor, urban, rural: too many people are implicated. The accused who deny that they are members of this party and honor the emperor are released; those who say that they used to be members but are no longer, Pliny also dismisses. What to do with the others? "The question seems to me to be worthy of your consideration," Pliny writes to Trajan, "especially in view of the number of persons endangered."

Trajan's response validates Pliny's actions. "It is impossible to lay down a general rule to a fixed formula," he replies:

> These people must not be hunted out; if they are brought before you and the charge against them is proved, they must be punished, but in the case of anyone who denies that he is a *christianus*, and makes it clear that he is not by offering prayers to our gods, he is to be pardoned as a result of his repentance however suspect his past conduct may be. But pamphlets circulated anonymously must play no part in any accusation. They create the worst sort of precedent.

The emperor is clear: while asserting an identity as a member of this disruptive people is a crime, and a crime punishable by death, it is not a crime the empire has an interest in actively seeking out. Imperial authorities are not "Christian" seekers. Membership in an Anointed group or school is not a death sentence.

The large disinterest of the empire in those who identified as *christianus* is reflected in a variety of writings from the early centuries. The story of Perpetua's noble death is dated to 202–203 CE, though we can't verify the dates, the person, or the time when the story began to circulate. Though this story is right on the edge of our two-century time frame, it is representative of other acts circulating during the second half of the second century, witness stories such as the *Letter of the Churches of Vienne and Lyon* and the *Acts of Polycarp*.

The regular visits to heroes in prison in these witness stories indicate that imperial officials were not that interested in pursuing communities of the Anointed. Perpetua, in the *Acts of Perpetua and Felicitas*, persuades a prison official to allow her brothers and other people to visit, and they enjoy a meal together; her visitors then freely depart. A second-century writer named Lucian relates the story of Peregrinus Proteus, a man who, for a time, identified as a so-called Christian and was imprisoned. Prison was not a solitary experience for Proteus: "from the very break of day aged widows and orphan children could be seen waiting near the prison, while officials [of the Anointed group] even slept inside with him after bribing the guards. Then elaborate meals were brought in, and sacred books of theirs were read aloud" (Peregrinus 12).[4] Lucian was a satirist, and he did not have a high opinion of Peregrinus Proteus nor of Jesus peoples. Lucian's description of Proteus's visitors while in prison, though, and the casual interactions depicted between those visitors and prison officials is indicative, as in Perpetua's case, of a general apathy toward Jesus-followers.

"Christian" seeking (using, again, Pliny and Trajan's bureaucratic construct of that word) was not the norm of the empire. Perpetua's and Lucian's stories also suggest that unlike the storied heroes, death seeking was not the norm for the majority of Jesus groups, even Jesus groups affiliated with a heroic witness. Perpetua's brothers and friends do not throw themselves into the prison cell with her; they eat together, and then they leave. Lucian's visitors to Peregrinus Proteus are incredibly numerous. Members of Anointed communities travel from across the empire to support Proteus in prison, donating large amounts of money to his cause. Again, they do not lock themselves in with Proteus; they come and go as they please. They are able to belong to Anointed communities in public, without fear.

SUFFERING DEATH DESPISERS

Lucian offers an important description of these people who visit Proteus: "the poor wretches have convinced themselves, first and foremost, that they are going to be immortal and live for all time, in consequence of which they despise death and even willingly give themselves into custody, most of them" (Peregrinus 13). If arrested—if accused specifically of identifying themselves as a member of an Anointed group—they give themselves up to imprisonment. They do not flock to prisons. More interesting, though, in this description is Lucian's comment that these people "despise death." They are not death seekers, perhaps, but they are death despisers.

This preoccupation with suffering and death is not about martyrdom, as that word came to be understood in the third and fourth centuries. This preoccupation connects Jesus groups to the earlier hero and noble death stories (see Chapter 6), but not as heroes themselves. People naming themselves as belonging to the party of Christus were not systemically persecuted in the first two centuries. The preoccupation with death is *voiced* through these hero stories, but not *lived* through them.

Lucian is not the only writer from the first two centuries to comment that members of Jesus associations "despised death." Second- and early third-century Latin writer Tertullian, a so-called Christian himself (his use of this term is ambiguous and sometimes inconsistent), calls association members "sworn to one purpose, so ready for death itself" (*Apology* 37.3).[5] Another second-century writer, Justin Martyr, a philosopher and member of a school of the Anointed, invents a debate between himself and a fictitious challenger. His challenger remarks that those belonging to the Anointed have "invented an Anointed One, for whom you give up your lives" (*Dialogue with Trypho* 8). Suffering and death seem central to party-member representation, to understandings of who Jesus groups, those belonging to the Anointed, and followers of the Savior were during these first two centuries. While these followers were not dying in large numbers or dying by spectacular or official means, suffering and death were still central to their understanding of who they were and what made their association with Jesus meaningful. The development of elaborate stories of Christus followers seeking death and dying through these violent means builds belonging in group clubs and schools around meaningful experiences of suffering.

This centrality of pain and death to Anointed-group identity during the first two centuries helps us to understand the widespread popularity of the witness stories as stories, rather than as lived experiences. The stories that Wisdom schools told about themselves were stories of suffering with happy endings in death. As Westar scholar Judith Perkins argues, "suffering was the message encoded in nearly all of the Christian representation of the period."[6] The "suffering self," to use Perkins's term, was not a required self. There were many different options for thinking about who these diverse Jesus peoples were and how they might understand themselves. It was the choice, Perkins argues, that many of these groups made. The suffering self was not, though, an obvious choice.

Under the early Roman Empire, stories of pain and suffering grew in importance. More and more people and groups began presenting themselves, through their writings, as sufferers. Paul, envoy to Jesus associations across the ancient Mediterranean, was the consummate sufferer: in his second letter to Chloe's people in Corinth he presents himself as having three times been beaten with rods, once stoned, and three times shipwrecked and adrift at sea; in constant danger from rivers, bandits, and Jesus association members, non-members, and false members; and sleepless, cold, naked, hungry, thirsty, and broken (2 Cor. 11:23–27). Perkins points to an emerging consciousness of pain and suffering across the empire during the first two centuries. Broken bodies, bodies in pain, were becoming visible in new ways and in new places, among all kinds of groups and peoples.

These stories of pain, suffering, and death later collected in the *Acts of the Christian Martyrs* were not isolated in the empire; they were not unique. The violence represented within them was also not new. Noble death, this form of witness, had a history in Judea. The kind of violence detailed in witness stories was not exceptional. A witness story is a redirected story of empire. It is a story of violence and death and of honor and glory, told over and over across the ancient Mediterranean, in different forms, through different kinds of media (see Chapter 6).

Perpetua's guiding of the executioner's hand to her throat would have been a familiar image in the early empire. The Sebasteion at Aphrodisias, a monument to the emperor—a visual representation of empire—depicted Emperor Claudius raising his arm above a woman representing conquered Britannia (see Chapter 3). Though his hand has been lost to time, he appears ready to bring down a sword and slice open her throat. Coins circulated across the empire showing a female Judea seated and bound, captive to Roman victory, sometimes with a Roman soldier standing behind her, ready to subdue. A defeated gladiator

A Roman gladiator. There are many stories of people who volunteered to enter the arena to be killed rather than deny Jesus Anointed.
Jona Lendering

in the arena, if not killed in battle, waited for the sponsor of the games—in Rome, most often the emperor—to decide whether or not his life should be spared; if the sponsor gave a thumbs-down, the victorious gladiator would then slit the loser's throat. If we read Perpetua's guiding of the executioner's hand to her throat in this context of the propaganda of conquered nation and people, her death as a member of a disruptive Judean group makes perfect sense.

"I AM . . ."

Many of these stories of heroes, later called martyr stories, turn around a bold statement of group affiliation, most commonly translated as "I am Christian." Voiced in Greek or Latin, this late second-century statement should be treated with care. While normally translated as "I am Christian," the declaration does not include the constellation of meaning associated with the word "Christian" in the present. Still, members of Jesus clubs and schools, parties of the Anointed, and other forms of Jesus families were asserting themselves in this way at this time. How exactly we should treat this declaration during this period remains an open question within scholarship, and the people who made it certainly meant different things. There is no one meaning to ascribe to it. "I am Christian" is certainly, though, more a statement about membership in a particular group or chosen family than about belief, practice, or personality. The "I am" statement is equivalent to "I belong to."

In Perpetua's case, for example, the Roman official, a governor named Hilarinus, demands that Perpetua offer proper honor to the emperor in the form of a sacrifice. When she refuses, Hilarinus asks, "Are you a Christian?" Perpetua replies,

"I am Christian" (*christiana sum*, in Latin; *Perpetua* 6). This statement is enough for Hilarinus to pass sentence not only on Perpetua, but on the other members of her community: "we were condemned to the beasts." Why? What is the nature of the accusation, exactly? What does Perpetua mean in her statement of belonging, her impenetrable "I am Christian" declaration?

This claim, "I am Christian," is not without imperial precedent, though the "Christian" is, rather, "Roman." The historian Livy, writing in the late first century BCE into the early first century CE, tells the story of one Gaius Mucius, later known as Mucius Scaevola, in his epic *History of Rome*. In 508 BCE, Rome, besieged by Etruscans, is slowly starving to death. Mucius, frustrated and eager to prove himself, sets out to kill the Etruscan king by himself. He kills the king's secretary by accident and is caught as he tries to flee the chaotic scene. Brought before the king, he cries, "I am Roman! A citizen; men call me Gaius Mucius." He continues, "I can die as resolutely as I could kill: both to do and to endure valiantly is the Roman way" (*History* 2.12).[7]

Both Mucius's declaration of his membership to/in Rome and of his willingness to suffer and die bear striking parallels to the witness stories popular among Jesus associations. The primary importance of group affiliation, "I am Roman!," is repeated in these stories with the same grammatical structure as "I am Christian!" Mucius desires to suffer in order to show his allegiance to Rome and, through this allegiance, to Roman virtue. When the king orders Mucius to be thrown into the fire, Mucius decides to burn himself voluntarily: "Mucius, exclaiming, 'Look, that you may see how cheap they hold their bodies whose eyes are fixed upon renown!' thrust his hand into the fire that was kindled for the sacrifice. When he allowed his hand to burn as if his spirit were unconscious of the sensation, the king was almost beside himself with wonder" (*History* 2.12). The "they" to whom Mucius refers here are Romans; this renown is glory, honor. Mucius suffers for the purpose of honor; he seeks to embody what he calls "the Roman Way."

Read alongside Mucius's declaration, Perpetua's statement becomes clearer. Perpetua's "I am Christian" is a form of opposition to "I am Roman." If we hear her voice in Latin, using *Christiana* in its bureaucratic sense, like Pliny, Perpetua is stating, "I am of the party of Christus." This statement throws the term back in Hilarinus's face, like a rebuke. It is a statement of both belonging (I am of the party of Christus) and antibelonging, or intentional estrangement (I am not Roman).

THE PERFORMANCE OF BELONGING

Mucius's suffering for honor, virtue, or the Roman Way resonates with what we know about gladiators and gladiatorial combat in the first two centuries. Earlier gladiators had predominantly been enslaved, participating in spectacular combat involuntarily. When Rome moved from republic to empire, men started to volunteer for the role. As Westar scholar Elli Elliott has convincingly argued, the role of gladiator gave men (specifically; gladiatorial combat was a highly gendered activity) an opportunity to demonstrate key Roman virtues of courage and strength and, through the performance of virtue, to acquire honor to which they would otherwise not have access.[8] Public honor was highly prized in ancient Rome and was available in limited supply; your honor-gain meant someone else's honor-loss. The voluntary gladiator chose to fight, and potentially die;

death becomes intentional. A defeat, rather than a humiliation, became an opportunity to demonstrate virtue: the gladiator could play to the crowd, offering his neck willingly, demonstrating a courage audience members longed to possess themselves. The gladiator was both ultimate subject to empire, especially to the violent humiliation of empire, and, equally, ultimate subject of and in empire. The gladiator performed empire; the gladiator performed belonging to Rome.

Like Mucius and the gladiator, those local heroes later known as martyrs were also suffering and dying bodies. This suffering and dying became its own performance of group belonging. Although members of Jesus schools were not being rounded up and executed in significant numbers during the first two centuries, they were experiencing pain and suffering under the violent conditions of the growing empire. As Perkins states, "the centrality of pain, suffering and death in early Christian representation suggests that Christian 'reality' was unrelentingly filled with risk, pain and death."[9] The importance of suffering and death in the stories the Anointed told about themselves—stories that were not necessarily historically true but represented truths about group understanding and attachment—points to a reimagination of honor, a reimagination of power, and ultimately, a reimagination of possibility.

If the honorable body in the Roman Empire was that of the freeborn male citizen, the bodies that are central to the witness stories, and the behaviors of these bodies, certainly cannot be associated with conventional forms of honor. The *Acts of Perpetua and Felicitas* centers on Perpetua, a woman in her early twenties breast-feeding an infant son. Perpetua rejects her father, the male head of her household and, as male head of a household, an institution: the *paterfamilias* was the foundation of the entire Roman system of power (see Chapter 10).

Perpetua gives thanks for her separation from this convention-ally powerful institution, her father. Her father makes a second visit to the prison, warning Perpetua that she "will destroy all of us!" if she insists upon dying (*Perpetua* 5). Perpetua con-tinues to deny her father throughout the story, even as he is eventually beaten in front of her. Throughout the narrative, she upsets the household, the basic structure of Roman social and imperial life.

Perpetua is a powerful figure, and she becomes increasingly powerful as her story develops. Later in the story, she has a dream in which she becomes a gladiator. In her vision, she is taken to the arena to fight an Egyptian man "of vicious ap-pearance." When her clothes are stripped off in preparation for combat, "suddenly," Perpetua states, "I was a man." They begin to fight. Perpetua narrates:

> We drew close to one another and let our fists fly. My oppo-nent tried to get hold of my feet, but I kept striking him in the face with the heels of my feet. Then I was raised up into the air and I began to pummel him without as it were touching the ground. Then when I noticed there was a lull, I put my two hands together linking the fingers of one hand with those of the other and thus I got hold of his head. He fell flat on his face and I stepped on his head. (*Perpetua* 10)

Victorious, Perpetua receives her award, a branch with golden apples, and wakes up. She realizes that her true victory will be not over beasts—or over Rome, for that matter—but over "the slanderer," the unclean spirit or devil, himself.

Felicitas is an enslaved woman and is pregnant when ar-rested. She gives birth in prison, and a prison official snidely remarks that she will suffer much more in the arena than in childbirth. "What I am suffering now," she responds, "I suffer by myself. But then another will be inside me who will suffer for me, just as I shall be suffering for him" (*Perpetua* 15). When she is thrown into the arena naked, the crowd is horrified: Felicitas is portrayed as "a woman fresh from childbirth with the milk still dripping from her breasts." That spectacle was too much. Perpetua and Felicitas are dressed, returned to the arena, and tossed to a wild cow. Perpetua, seeing that her tunic is torn, tries to cover her exposed thighs. She then asks for a pin to fix her hair, "for it was not right that a martyr [read "witness"] should die with her hair in disorder, lest she might seem to be mourning in her hour of triumph" (*Perpetua* 20).

Both Perpetua and Felicitas find social power through the course of their suffering. Perpetua in particular is a broken body that, through its brokenness, itself works to break dominant hierarchies and conventional social structures. As she rejects social norms, she increases in power; each time she rejects her father, he becomes smaller, weaker, less effectual. They both give up her basic identity as his daughter. The deaths of Perpetua and Felicitas in the arena at the conclusion of the story are portrayed as victories, not defeats. They are not victims of empire. They are its new conquerors. Their ending could not be more noble; it could not be happier.

THE ROMANCE OF DEATH

Perkins compares these "happy endings" of the *Acts of the Christian Martyrs* to those of the Greek romances that were popular at the same time. The typical romantic finale is summarized characteristically at the conclusion of romance writer Chariton's writing *Callirhoe*: "I think that this last book will prove the most enjoyable for my readers, as an antidote to the grim events in the preceding ones. No more piracy or slavery or trials or fighting or suicide or war or captivity in this one, but honest love and faithful marriage" (8.1).[10] Perkins's translation of this happy ending reads "*lawful* love and *sanctioned* marriage," a translation that points more directly to the social norms the typical romantic ending is meant to uphold.[11] At the conclusion of a romance, everything and everyone are in their proper place. The social world is ordered. All is as it has been, and as it should be.

From the perspective of the Greek romance, the ending of the martyr story could not seem less happy. Nothing is in its proper place. The social world is completely disordered. Nothing is as it has been. But . . . it is as it should be.

The endings of these stories make sense in their depictions of gruesome yet intentional and triumphant death, in that death in this literature is representative of social bodies, not physical ones. Early Jesus schools, groups of the Savior, and chosen families were not death seekers—at least, not in a literal sense. The spectacular death seeking of these stories represented a kind of social death seeking. The pain and suffering in the stories granted a worth to the experienced pain and suffering in and among the Jesus peoples. These stories, part of the tradition later called martyrdom, were primarily representational, a means to understand culture and context and the place of Jesus peoples within them rather than a reality of that culture and context. Pain and suffering in empire, though, was real. Everyday suffering, through the spectacular suffering of local heroes, was given new worth, a new meaning. It need not be viewed as humiliation, but as endurance, a forward-looking endurance with an honorable end.

This death seeking was also focused on the death, or denial, of certain social norms. Perpetua is fundamentally antisocial, as are most of the early Anointed heroes; she rejects forms of family, of gender, of all kinds of dominant structures of power. This rejection is the "happy ending" of the hero. Perkins argues that this ending, "just as it was in the Greek romances, was a social judgement. It disclosed an audience approving their hero's dissociation from human society, his rejection of its immanent worth."[12] The deaths of the heroes both recognized lived experience under empire and rejected this experience.

These stories offered a reimagination of power. The representation of violence and the purpose of violence in the *Acts of the Christian Martyrs* would have been familiar to readers in the ancient Mediterranean of the first two centuries. These readers experienced empire and the propaganda of empire through many different types of media: monuments to imperial violence, coins, gladiatorial combat. Representations of violence, as well as forms of experienced violence, pervaded ancient Mediterranean life. The *Acts*, however, repurpose these stories so that dominant forms of social power might be disrupted and potentially displaced.

The second-century stories of the noble deaths of heroes were so popular and so important for the emerging group identities of Jesus schools because they use familiar tools to redirect a familiar story. As violent representations of empire expressed and depicted a certain power relation, the relation of emperor and empire to the known, and conquered, world, so the stories express and depict a parallel power relation. The emperor is no longer the one honored, however. The glory is not for Rome. "Oh, most honorable and fortunate witnesses!" concludes the account of Perpetua. "Truly are you called and chosen for the glory of Christ Jesus our Lord!" (*Perpetua* 21).[13]

These stories are told to honor a different ultimate ruler: a different God.

During the first two centuries of the Common Era, diverse peoples began to make pain and suffering visible in new ways. Schools of Wisdom were particularly drawn to this visibility, representing suffering bodies as significant tools for thinking about and for imaginatively reordering their social worlds. Stories about suffering and noble death, particularly the dramatic, vivid stories of those later known as martyrs, helped to give worth to everyday suffering, and to shape many Jesus followers as certain kinds of people, interested in certain kinds of things: interested in brokenness, interested in power, interested in the intersection between the two. As inhabitants of empire, those belonging to the Anointed redirected familiar stories and media forms as one strategy, among others, of making sense of lived experience in new ways.[14] The stories became, with their re-purposing of the ancient happy ending, the new romance: the romance of the martyr.

Papers Relevant to This Chapter by Seminar Participants

Daniel-Hughes, Carly. "Producing and Contesting Martyrdom in Pre-Decian Roman North Africa." Spring 2015.

Elliott, Susan M. (Elli). "Gladiators and Martyrs: Icons in the Arena." Spring 2015.

Taussig, Hal. "What Do Fiction, Mass Crucifixions and Killer Seals Add Up To?: Summarizing Break-Throughs in Martyrdom Scholarship Since 1990." Spring 2015.

BETTER THAN A NEW TESTAMENT?

The birth name of "The Artist Formerly Known as Prince" was Prince Rogers Nelson. As he and his music rose to prominence in the 1980s, he became known as just "Prince"—playing coolly with the fact that hardly anyone knew that that was in fact his first name. Even now, posthumously, he is mostly known as "Prince." By the 1990s, for various reasons, he became uneasy with "Prince," claiming instead a symbol as his preferred name. This symbol—a stylized combination of the conventional icons for female and male gender—had no sound or pronunciation associated with it and was impossible to reproduce in any print typeface. So media adopted the clumsy "The Artist Formerly Known as Prince" for the rest of the decade, until the artist reclaimed "Prince" in the 2000s. Continuing his play with language and social boundaries, the artist wrote about his unpronounceable symbol, "It's all about thinking in new ways, tuning in 2 a new free-quency."[1]

This chapter demands a similar experiment with language, names, and boundaries. Given all the surprises in this book, here in the final chapter, the history of the New Testament turns out to have two of the biggest surprises of this whole volume.

The first surprise is this: There was nothing like a New Testament in these first two hundred years. This must be told. Quickly.

The second shocker: The writings of these first two centuries (very much like Prince's music and the "unpronounceable symbol" that followed it) were so dynamic and flexible that they could hardly be called "books." In contrast to how Bibles are understood to bring every important thought together, these first two centuries of writings kept spinning out into a wide variety of new forms of awareness. This chapter explores the imaginative and quirky way these writings unfolded. We imagine and reimagine what "writing" actually is and what writing means. As Prince stated, we will be "tuning in 2 a new free-quency."

BUT FIRST, NO NEW TESTAMENT

The first sign that no New Testament existed in the first two centuries is that few people in these movements could read or write; literacy was minimal. Most people of the time were subsistence farmers, weavers and other artisans, day laborers, and merchants. They were known for their ingenuity and aliveness, but few were wealthy and even fewer were authors. In the first and second century one might be able to do the minimal necessary reading for marketplace transactions without ever going to school. People who did not write much, or at all, still were highly skilled at communication in daily life.

Probably neither Jesus nor the great majority of his followers knew how to read or write. In the first hundred years of the Common Era there is only one story in which Jesus reads, and one in which he writes, bending to draw with his finger on the ground. More to the point, neither Jesus nor most who came after him in the first two centuries focused on writing or reading. They were busy with pithy parables, pointed assertions, clever blessings, and miniature pictures—expression and thought that happens outside the boundaries of writing. The only writer we know about during the first sixty years after the death of Jesus is Paul, who writes letters to specific groups, most of whose members cannot read. Instead, the letters are read to them when they gather to eat and drink, enjoy one another's company, sing songs, and listen to a story or a letter. Paul writes about their daily lives together—the writing is about practice and not philosophy or theology.

These groups and makeshift schools were awash in new ideas and practices. But writing, especially writing in the way we tend to think about it in our contemporary world, was rarely the way these thoughts and actions came to the fore. Instead, these people rushed into expressive conversations and attended weekly gatherings where they could speak and listen. Of course, some of these good ideas and beautiful odes would eventually get written down in letters, short stories, and musings, but they were sidebars compared to the riptide of conversations at group meals, in workshops, and in the middle of the marketplace.

With the growth of Jesus movements by the end of the first century, some writings, and even some with longer stories, were read aloud to others. Many of these writings were probably sets of rules and codes of conduct for Jesus clubs and associations, rather than stories about the Anointed. We do not possess anything from these groups that was actually written during the first century. We are not sure how many writings were produced by the end of that century. The earliest manuscripts of first-century writings are second-hand, third-hand, fourth-hand, or fifth-hand copies from the mid- to late second century. Most of the actual "early" manuscripts of first-century writings were copied during the fourth through sixth centuries. The earliest partial copies from first-century writings are a few tiny papyrus scraps of several sentences only, dated to the second century and later.

That the members of the many different groups associated with Jesus in these first two hundred years did not read and write strikes twenty-first-century readers as bizarre or perhaps impossible. Since the writings of the first twenty generations of the movement are the main way we know anything about and understand these Jesus groups, it is difficult today to think that the real people of that time sang, worked, and hung out together but rarely read or wrote. The rare person who had learned to read knew it was a civic duty to read aloud so that others could hear stories, club rules, thoughts of someone else, tombstone epitaphs, and expressions of protest. If we moderns think that reading and writing were important to those early clubs, groups, and schools, we miss most of who they were and how they became excited about Jesus, new kinds of family, or God.

That such groups wanted to be guided primarily by a list of readings they themselves had written during these first two hundred years seems highly unlikely to participants of the Seminar. The New Testament came into being sometime between the mid-fourth and the seventh century, depending on what exactly one means by "New Testament." Even though much evidence supports this position, it surprises most people.

IF NOT EARLY, WHEN?

New scholarship by the Seminar in 2020 has underlined that even though there were more writings associated with Jesus groups and schools in the second century than in the first, the larger Jesus-related movements continued to be primarily oral and community-based. Inasmuch as they sometimes had "holy writings" in the first two centuries, these were mostly spoken from memory, or one person read aloud to a larger group. The Seminar approved new scholarship by Jason BeDuhn that clearly showed that most second-century writings were not read by communities at large, and some should be considered to be something like mere notes. In his recommendations to the Seminar, BeDuhn says clearly, "(I)t is inappropriate to speak of Christian 'scriptures' in the second century."[2] No one in the second century would have proposed a collection of writings of twenty or thirty documents to act like a "New Testament"; there was little interest in a written religious authority in the second century; no one proposed it and no one assembled something like a New Testament.

By the end of the second century, Irenaeus, the leader of a Jesus assembly in Lyon (now in southern France), mentions the four Gospels that are now considered part of the canon: Matthew, Mark, Luke, and John, in that order. Irenaeus's mention of these writings has generally been understood as proof that four "canonical" gospels existed by that time. Close attention to Irenaeus's words, however, suggests a very different situation:

Matthew published a written gospel among the Hebrews in their own dialect, while Peter and Paul were proclaiming the gospel in Rome and founding the assembly. After their deaths, Mark, the student and interpreter of Peter, also handed down Peter's proclamation to us in written form. Luke, the follower of Paul, put the gospel proclaimed by Paul down in a book. Then John, the student of the Lord, the one who reclined on the Lord's breast, he also published the gospel, while living in Ephesus of Asia. (*Against Heresies* 3.1.1)[3]

Irenaeus, a tenacious promoter of a certain kind of Jesus people, mentions four "authors"—Matthew, Mark, Luke, and John—and he grants these writers times and places. However, his language concerning what these writings were varies widely and certainly is not suggestive of the stability of the Gospels now associated with the New Testament canon. As scholar Matthew D. C. Larsen has pointed out, only Luke is called a "book" by Irenaeus. Matthew and John are "published," or in the public domain; Mark is something "handed down" in some sort of written form, though the Greek word here translates best to "writtenly."[4] Far from offering a picture of a stable four-book set of Gospels, Irenaeus's statement actually indicates that these writings existed in a variety of forms, as different kinds of written objects that represented different kinds of writers, stories, traditions, and situations.

Yes, here we have a real surprise. The first two centuries did not come close to producing any kind of New Testament.

NOT-BOOKS

It turns out that what happened with first- and second-century writings may be more remarkable, meaningful, and moving than we have previously imagined. Endlessly searching for a "New Testament" has limited our ability to see and appreciate the diverse forms and functions of early writings in their full creative capacities.

Irenaeus's naming of three gospels and one object handed down "writtenly" has long been taken as confirmation of what we yearned for: a bounded collection of four stable Gospels. Reading Irenaeus, scholars proclaim, "The Gospels are finally named!" as if we had been waiting for this moment all along.[5]

This interpretation of Irenaeus reads history backwards, starting with much later understandings of the words "author," "book," and "publication" as well as the biblical canon. Irenaeus's statement has echoed loudly throughout history probably because it seems to approve our own way of knowing these writings. We know these four Gospels, and it's nice that Irenaeus knew them, too. Our knowledge is validated.

Most second-century writers refer to a range of written traditions, called gospels, "the gospel," memoirs, memorials, words, and voices. Irenaeus has been allowed to speak loudest because he tells us what we like to think we know. When other, equally important voices have the chance to speak, what we hear is much different. After taking seriously the lack of "New Testament" in the first two centuries, we now turn to view that many of these early writings were not writing down the answer but opening up new possibilities and experiences.

One of the authors of the present book, Erin K. Vearncombe, proposed that many "writings" of the first two centuries are a thorough mix of conversation, physical objects, community, and writing, in which the writing was not the deciding factor in terms of meaning.[6] In cultures where the great majority of people do not read or write, life becomes meaningful in ways that involve writing alongside all kinds of other ways of expressing learning and belonging. Books or scrolls are important not just because of what is written in them, but as objects. These objects in and of themselves create meaning, possibility, and community. Meaningful and productive parts of living combine reading and writing with many other actions and conversations. That kind of meaning making makes these writing-objects, Vearncombe maintains, texts with which "one expects to cooperate in the production of meaning." Once one understands that many of the writings of these peoples were less books or essays and more events, ongoing conversations, songs, theatrics, or unfinished letters, then one can approach what the "writings" of these early centuries were like.

The current breakthrough into these eventful "writings" is happening mostly because scholars are paying very close attention to the exact words about this early partly written material. As we have seen, Irenaeus uses a wide variety of words, including "gospel," "proclamation," "book" (and only in the case of Luke), and "publication" to refer to "things" that were written, handed down, given up, or, in the case of Mark, ambiguously "writtenly," which could be interpreted as "sort of written" or "in the form of notes." An opponent of the Jesus movement, Celsus, criticized what they wrote, claiming that these peoples "as if in a drunken brawl with one another, alter and remodel the gospel from its original written form— three times, four times, many times—so that they might be able to give a rebuttal in the face of critical accusations" (Origen, *Against Celsus* 2.27).[7] Writing, in form and function, was much more fluid during the first two centuries than we have previously understood.

Focusing on Mark, Vearncombe states, "The writing we now call 'the gospel according to Mark' did not exist as such in the first two centuries." This nonexistence of Mark does not mean that the writing-now-called-Mark was somehow missing in action during the first two centuries; instead, it was important as a non-book or not-book, as an "object, writtenly." What do we call Mark, if not a writing? Vearncombe writes, "'The-textual-object-we-now-call-Mark' sounds a bit too much like 'the-artist-formerly-known-as Prince.'" The problem of what to call the diverse writings of the first two centuries recalls the related problem of what to call the Jesus peoples, groups, and schools of this same period. Without an appropriate symbol at our disposal, we struggle with language, not wanting to fall into the traps of "book," "text," or modern concepts of authorship.

As we undo the modern perception that people during the first two centuries wrote lots of books, essays, creeds, and reports, it is helpful to recall the present book's earlier chapters about meals and supper clubs (see Chapters 11 and 12). In those chapters it is clear that members of the many different Jesus movements gathered almost exclusively at festive meals. Discovering now that their "writings" were not books for intellectuals matches well with the activities of their boisterous banquets.

COMMUNAL "WRITINGS" IN THE FACE OF TRAUMA

Vearncombe's research focuses on how these writings were less books and more physical *things*. In her studies of Mark, she notices how often the writing sounds like a memorial for people who had died—how often bodies are broken, Jesus warns of death, and he predicts his own crucifixion in this gospel. In her inspection of first- and second-century memorials of stone and statuary and the role writing plays in those memorials, she notes, "the epitaph does not exist apart from its material context, the tomb itself." Many small and large "graves" are no more than a written epitaph. These "graves" allowed and encouraged people to visit the cemeteries often and participate in the drama of the deceased person's life, offering food and wine and remembering a life as part of a community. Writing and sculpture on a grave together tell stories and recall group belonging. This function of writing as memorial points to parallels between written portraits of people's lives in Mark, especially Jesus's life, and stone and statuary memorials.

The word usually translated as "tomb" in Greek means, more accurately, "memorial" or "memory marker." Many inscriptions on grave monuments from the ancient Mediterranean basin begin with the words "memorial of" followed by a person's name. One such memorial inscription from the second century BCE remembers the priestess Stratonike and her involvement in the ritual activities of a local association. The inscription on the monument is worth reproducing in full:

> It was resolved by the association of hero-devotees who gather together for Harpalos (senior), Athenodoros (senior), Meno-dote and Zostas: Since it was announced that the priestess Stratonike—daughter of Athenodoros and mother of both Harpalos (junior) and Athenodoros (junior)—has left us, who was beautiful and good and behaved in an honor-loving manner towards both the association and each member individually during the gathering of the association. She conducted her entire life in an honorable manner, always seeking to maintain her propriety and love of humanity in a manner worthy of her ancestors and she was god-fearing.
>
> Then it is just and appropriate, since she is irreproachable, for her to be honored by the associates in the following manner: that a day may be observed for her whenever the rest of the sacrifices are performed, just as is also done for her ancestors (i.e., those heroes listed at the opening); that she also be crowned with a gold crown worth ten gold coins; that a painted portrait be set up in the heroes' shrine; and, that a slab of white stone be set up with the decree inscribed on it, in order that she herself might possess an eternal memorial of

her benevolence toward everyone. Furthermore, men are to be sent who, meeting with Harpalos and Athenodoros (i.e., her sons), will explain the honors which have been decreed and will comfort her sons appropriately to endure her deification (*apotheōsis*) which has taken place, of one who was affectionate towards her children and was blameless by all people during her life-time.[8]

This monument was close to another naming additional members of Stratonike's family, as well as sixty-five other active members of this association. When family and club members visited Stratonike's monument, according to Vearncombe, both the monument and writings "were culturally accepted and expected means for interaction with the dead. Memorialization in a material, visual format was essential to both the dead and the living, as . . . actively celebrated by the living, after one's death." This material memorialization expands the many combinations of writings and sculptures from being a story about the deceased to being an interaction and conversation with the deceased.

The connection between the Gospel of Mark and these physical, visual monuments and memorials is made clear when Vearncombe asks about what happens to group remembering when the usual means for remembering are not available:

What happens if there is no body for a tomb—only empty space? The textual tradition we now call Mark highlights this absence: at the (non-)end of the text, the body of Jesus is gone, and Mary Magdalene, Mary the mother of James, and Salome run from the empty tomb in terror, saying nothing to anyone. Absent body, absent followers, absent speech.

Words have meanings like the rungs of a descending ladder.[9] The top rung, the first step, is the meaning most commonly associated with a word. The word usually translated as "tomb" means, on its top rung, "memorial" or "means of remembrance"—words that have the physical connotation of tomb or monument. Farther down the ladder, this word can also mean "written reminder" and even "notes." Staying on the top rung, we can interpret Mark as a memorial: a material memorial to a missing Messiah.

Perhaps over generations of storytelling about Jesus and visiting the memory of him through other people addressing his questions or groups singing, the presence of Jesus lives on. "Extended epitaph," Vearncombe suggests, is a much more appropriate name for the Gospel of Mark, or simply, "memorial." Making Jesus stories into writing created a way for members of Jesus associations to remember him and respond to a situation of absence. Stories about Jesus handed down "writtenly" were meaningful because they created a real, lived opportunity to remember, or for memorialization, in the way in which remembrance was meant to be carried out in the first two centuries. For Vearncombe, Mark is a memorial: a tomb created "writtenly."

Approached as memorial, Mark suddenly bears a striking resemblance to the monument for the priestess Stratonike. Her family, including the chosen family of her association, needed a way to remember her. She has died, but she is also absent— her body has been "taken up," according to the inscription on her monument. The monument, Vearncombe argues, "is established in order to ensure that members of the association will have and adhere to particular guidelines for Stratonike's memorialization, or for remembering her appropriately." People will explain the honors that are to be maintained for Stratonike and to comfort her family in the reality of her missing body.

The parallels to Mark's story of Jesus are strong. As a memorial for a missing body, this written "thing," the Gospel of Mark, allows Jesus associations, like the association of Stratonike, to continue in community, to continue their group activities in a structured way. The "thing" that is the Gospel of Mark is the thing that happens when the actual community's time together adds to and redoes the stories.

As Vearncombe's understanding becomes clear, it is probably less proper to call this early form of Mark's Gospel "less than final" and more correct to call it "more alive." We are now close to something alive for the experiences of a variety of first- and second-century Jesus peoples. Not a book, for sure, and just barely "writing," as it hangs brightly in the rawness of real people. These early "less than writings" are not a hefty, if meandering, New Testament. Rather, they seem sometimes more vibrant in the space between life and death in the early centuries.

Vearncombe points toward another way that the tenuous status of the "writing" of Mark positively affects the people of the first two centuries. A number of studies of Mark underline that it is responding to situations of disaster, at least implicitly related to the two unsuccessful wars of Israel against Rome, the countless acts of tortures by the empire, and the destruction of the Jerusalem Temple. Vearncombe finds "disaster response" in the frayed texts of early Mark.

Clearly in the versions of Mark that we now read, the absence of Jesus after his death has the potential to be a disaster. This disaster is evident not only in Mark's open ending ("he is not here," Mark 16:6), but across the story. In present story time the "bridegroom" has been taken away (2:20), followers in Judea are fleeing without even grabbing their clothes (13:14–16), the shepherd is struck and the sheep are scattered (14:27), and the disciples, confronted with a missing body, feel abject terror (16:8). There is no validating presence of the risen Jesus in this textual object. Both content and composition in this story make Jesus's absence palpable.

The reading of Mark at these early stages of writing, then, serves as an extended epitaph for a larger disaster happening to many people. The absence of Jesus and the disasters of both Jesus movements and other larger disasters are processed in provisional, yet dramatic, memorial writing.

CONCLUSION

These first two hundred years of the Common Era are not the territory of something (to be) called the "New Testament." There is little organization or dogma, as people and groups work on defining their identities in unsteady but creative times. The writings, the people, and the identities are fresh, free, and incomplete. Some of us will wish for a more quickly formed finality of the New Testament, and perhaps read backwards into statements like that of Irenaeus on Matthew, Mark, Luke, and John. Others of us will be happy to discover this resourceful open-ended space of sort-of-writing, continuing our experiment of reading forward and taking history one step at a time. "Tuning in 2 a new frequency," as The Artist Formerly Known as Prince put it, thinking not about "texts" but about dynamic "objects, writtenly," we find exciting and diverse possibilities for meaning making in the first two centuries.

Papers Relevant to This Chapter by Seminar Participants

BeDuhn, Jason. "Becoming a People of the Book: Texts, 'Scripture,' and 'Canon' Among Christ Groups in the Second Century CE." Spring 2020.

Shea, Chris. "Some Observations on the Evolution and Politics of Roman Imperial Canons." Spring 2020.

Taussig, Hal. "Scripture and Resistance Hybridity: Without Canon." Spring 2020.

Vearncombe, Erin K. "Gathered Around Absence: A First-Century Approach to the Text Known as 'Mark.'" Spring 2020.

20

CONCLUSION

Assumptions are dangerous things to make, and like all dangerous things to make—bombs, for instance, or strawberry shortcake—if you make even the tiniest mistake you can find yourself in terrible trouble. Making assumptions simply means believing things are a certain way with little or no evidence that shows you are correct, and you can see at once how this can lead to terrible trouble. For instance, one morning you might wake up and make the assumption that your bed was in the same place that it always was, even though you would have no real evidence that this was so. But when you got out of your bed, you might discover that it had floated out to sea, and now you would be in terrible trouble all because of the incorrect assumption that you'd made. You can see that it is better not to make too many assumptions, particularly in the morning.

LEMONY SNICKET, *THE AUSTERE ACADEMY*[1]

It is time to consider our results. We began with our hypothesis: Christianity was not the inevitable future. An examination of available evidence from the first two centuries suggests that the futures of the diverse Jesus groups and Anointed communities across the Mediterranean basin were open and full of possibility and difference. Some of these possibilities may have overlapped in different ways, but these possibilities make it clear that there was no organized or cohesive phenomenon called Christianity in the two centuries after Jesus.

We tested our hypothesis with evidence. The evidence, fragmentary as it may be, is startling. However we might think of the various peoples of these two hundred years, they were neither a religion nor preludes to a religion. Yes, there were jumbles of peoples with various interests in Jesus stuff and Anointed activities. Evidence makes it clear, though, that these various groups, schools, clubs, and movements cannot be summarized together as something like "Jesus peoples," much less as Christian. They were too diverse and had too many other dimensions to their lives.

These jumbles of peoples accomplished a great deal in the midst of dramatic, unsettled times. Their collective experiences and accomplishments between Jesus's death and the beginning of the third century are told in moving and creative ways, some through story, others through what we have called "objects, writtenly." Central to this experiment was the assessment of these experiences on their own terms, rather than on the terms of a Christianity still unborn. Our experiment looked forward, not back.

Our looking forward required a deep questioning of long-held assumptions, an active process of unknowing. It required a willingness not just to look past ourselves, but to un-see ourselves in a history many of us might claim as our own. The goal was to see not the familiar, not the practices, structures, or stories that might remind us of what we know now, the things we are comfortable knowing, the things we understand. We did not set out looking for practices and offices that are now established; we did not set out even to look for their origins, hints of institutions yet to come. We did not set out to find priests and bishops, sacraments, or churches. We did not set out to find these things, and we did not find them.

Rather, the goal was the nourishment of an ongoing willingness to see and respectfully attempt to understand the "other"—many others. To not believe that things are or have to be a certain way. To hear voices completely different from our own, and completely different from those of our present moments. The goal was to hear voices that have gone unheard: the voice of a rag dealer who joined an Anointed supper club. The voice of a female head of household, supporting a Jesus group in her home, despite and against the norm of the Roman father-centered family.

Our unknowing, however, is not an act of deconstruction. It is a radical act of imaginative construction. The construction of new, authentic, exciting possibilities for meaning is enabled when we ask, "What can we understand about the lived experiences of the diverse peoples who associated, in different ways, with Jesus across the ancient Mediterranean, when we start assuming nothing?" We have, essentially, discovered that the bed has indeed floated out to sea. What's more, it is not just a bed anymore. It is also a boat. A raft. The immense hump of a whale. A small island refuge. The haunt of a wandering albatross.

CONNECTING THREADS

In any self-respecting experimental report, results are followed by discussion. After the findings are reported, those findings need to be interpreted. Connections need to be made. Experimental limitations and future possibilities for study need to be acknowledged.

Certainly, our hypothesis—that Christianity was not the inevitable future—has been proved. The Anointed communities of the first two centuries, in their many structures of and for group belonging, do not suggest a nascent singularity called Christianity. The results of our experiment are indeed so diverse that making any single overarching claim to meaning is challenging and risks the integrity of those results. These groups were loosely or occasionally interconnected; gathered around similar, but not identical, practices such as meals; and focused on Jesus Anointed in sometimes very different ways. No single name or form of these groupings gained considerable traction in the first two centuries.

The elements that stand out from our study of those committed to the heritage of Jesus in the first two centuries will likely be different for each reader, and that possibility is exciting. There are so many new stories to tell. Among these new stories, though, are several important connecting threads, threads that are themselves closely woven together into a tight, if motley, fabric. Integral to the fabric is empire.

Responding to Empire
In the first century CE, Rome had conquered all the nations around the Mediterranean and consolidated them into an empire. From the Romans' point of view they were masters of the

whole world—in the words of Virgil, empire without limit. While empire brought some benefits to citizens, the overarching violence of empire led many nations, institutions, communities, and families to experience great loss and trauma.

Underlying everything we have found is the Roman Empire. The influence of empire is everywhere in early Jesus-group representations of life and practice. Empire actually initiates what one might call the Jesus-group process through the crucifixion of Jesus. The empire's ongoing violence toward parties of the Anointed became a primary factor in the self-understanding of these communities: they were ones who suffered.

Responses to empire were varied. While some parties of the Anointed actively worked to resist empire, other communities sought simply to survive within it, or to use the tools of the empire for redefined ends. The Revelation to John offers a vision of Rome's fleets burning up, an explicit image of a desired destruction of empire. The Gospel of Mary offers comfort and encouragement in the face of violence: Mary provides strength to those students of the Savior who cry out in fear at his death. The envoy Paul's identification with Jesus's crucifixion—"I am crucified with the Anointed One, nevertheless I live" (Gal. 2:19)—leads association members to a consciousness of the interdependence of being hurt and being alive. The many ways in which Jesus groups deal directly or indirectly with Jesus's execution create a wide social consciousness of oppression.

Seeking Refuge

The life of these groups came out of surviving in the context of the Roman Empire. Their concern was about what to do, how to care for one another. Compared with what they practiced, what they believed was of relatively little concern.

These communities experimented in many different ways.

They organized themselves into and around families. They looked at times like clubs and associations, formed schools out of which came new wisdom. They played with gender and sexual boundaries, with some forsaking marriage. They did not seem to be looking for *the* way, but for a whole variety of ways. Women were prominent leaders, patrons, and participants. Belonging to Israel was strongly felt.

These experiments in community life functioned as refuges, as safe places amidst imperial violence. These communities did not espouse one single, systematic approach to dealing with violence; they did not have enough social power to do so. Likewise, the emergence of refuge was not the direct result of ethics or religion. Different groups employed different strategies to create safe places. Varieties of social cohesion were at the heart of group practice.

The creation of refuge played with and built upon existing, everyday social realities. Associations provided ready models of social safety. Households were repurposed and reimagined. Nations in diaspora, especially Judea, pulled toward group belonging. Gender was bent to allow for alternative possibilities for living. A recognition of experienced pain, suffering, and fear allowed for new forms of social cohesion.

The biggest experiment concerned the representation of safety itself. Generals, kings, and emperors had long been heralded as saviors, fathers of nations, deliverers from evils. Emperors were the divine good powers of the entire inhabited earth. Zeus, the *paterfamilias* of the Greek pantheon, ruler of the gods, was a savior. The emperor, *paterfamilias* of Rome, ruler of defeated nations, was a savior.

Jesus groups in the first two centuries radically changed this image of a savior. The savior of these communities was a crucified man: a man tortured and executed through means the empire deemed ultimately humiliating. This crucified man was a source of refuge and bringer of safety. This man's god, the God of the Judeans—the God of a defeated, humiliated nation—was honored as parent of the known world.

While the meaning of the word "salvation" now lies blanketed in belief, its ancient heart meant keeping safe, a means or way of safety. Understood this way, the Anointed communities of the first two centuries certainly were interested in salvation. They were deeply invested in the communal work of keeping safe.

Families That Eat Together . . .

The extent to which communal meals provided the social context for the development of Anointed communities cannot be overestimated. Sharing a meal was the practice that really made these groups happen. The Anointed-group practice of community meals popped up around the empire, forming a diverse set of social organizations in villages, towns, and cities. While many different clubs celebrated meals that connected people, Jesus communities were especially attracted to this practice, and it was their most characteristic trait. Writings from these communities present Jesus as host, guest, and chief honoree of the meal, building off the meal practices of neighboring groups.

The life that grew up in the practice of these meals provided a safely ordered space in a precarious and dangerous world. The requirement of a certain set of participant behaviors, both moral and practical, ensured that guests at the meal would receive a certain level of respect, honor, and reciprocity from other group members. Adhering to group standards led to the cultivation of specific dispositions focused on caring for others and honoring God.

Although communal meals strongly contributed to who these diverse groups were, the practice did not last. This primary way of belonging fell out of practice during the third century. Initially, these chosen families that ate together, stayed together. If there is an essence of this movement in the first two centuries, it is their common meal practice, and it disappeared in the third century. Why this essential practice disappeared from group life at that time is a question for our next experiment.

Haunt of the Albatross

Study of the ancient world involves us in a strange paradox: the more we learn, the more we realize we do not know. Our experiment's conclusion is one of humility at what we cannot know, while realizing that this humility, this recognition of our ignorance and limitations, is also often the long and winding, sometimes torturous, path to knowledge. Most of our evidence is fragmentary or missing from the historical record. Much of the evidence we do have may be misleading, promoting only the voices of history's most powerful, those in a position to say whose voices are heard and whose should be silenced.

We can, however, and should find power in our vulnerability to the unknown past. In considering new forms of evidence and reconsidering evidence we thought we knew, in considering evidence on its own terms, and on equal terms, so many new and vital voices throng to our attention. These Anointed communities in the first two centuries of the Common Era told many more stories than just the ones now collected in the New Testament, so privileging only those writings later deemed canonical drastically skews the evidence, misreading the evidence of the communities it claims to represent.

Opening our ears to these voices requires a great intellectual shift. If we are to really think about what happened between two imperial moments—when the Roman Empire crucified an insignificant Galilean peasant and when the emperor Constantine favored emergent Christian practice about three hundred years later—we can no longer look for essences. We cannot take for granted that the bed remains in the corner, no matter how long we have believed it to be there. We need to wake up to find ourselves at sea, the albatross slowly drifting overhead.

Any experiment worth its salt should be reproducible. A strong hypothesis is one subject to testing; a strong hypothesis needs to be ready to be proved wrong. Our evidence is out there. It has not received sufficient attention in the past, but we invite you to consider it now. We must continue to listen for these buzzing, urgent voices. These voices can and need to reshape our understanding of group experience and belonging in the two vibrant centuries after Jesus, before Christianity.

NOTES

Chapter 2: If Not Christian, What?

1. Unless otherwise indicated, translations of ancient texts are those of: Erin K. Vearncombe, Hal Taussig, and Bernard Brandon Scott. Because there is no canon of the New Testament in the first two centuries of the Common Era, we have treated canonical and noncanonical books the same typographically, meaning that none of these books are italicized. They should be treated the same, so they should look the same in our text.
2. Pliny the Younger, *Letters, Volume II: Books 8–10. Panegyricus*, trans. Betty Radice, Loeb Classical Library 59 (Cambridge, MA: Harvard Univ. Press, 1969).
3. Tacitus, *Annals: Books 13–16*, trans. John Jackson, Loeb Classical Library 322 (Cambridge, MA: Harvard Univ. Press, 1937), XV.44.
4. Cicero, *In Catilinam 1–4. Pro Murena. Pro Sulla. Pro Flacco*, trans. C. MacDonald, Loeb Classical Library 324 (Cambridge, MA: Harvard Univ. Press, 1976).
5. See Dennis E. Smith and Joseph B. Tyson, eds., *Acts and Christian Beginnings: The Acts Seminar Report* (Salem, OR: Polebridge, 2013).

Chapter 3: Engine of Empire: Violence

1. Celene Lillie, *The Rape of Eve: The Transformation of Roman Ideology in Three Early Christian Retellings of Genesis* (Minneapolis: Fortress, 2017).
2. The historian Josephus recounts that ninety-seven thousand people were taken prisoner—read, enslaved—at the conclusion of the siege of Jerusalem in 70 CE (*The Jewish War* 6.9.3). For more on enslavement in the Roman world and in early Christian contexts, see Jennifer A. Glancy, *Slavery in Early Christianity* (Oxford: Oxford Univ. Press, 2002).
3. Inscription is published as CIL II 3258. The tombstone dates to the second century. Currently the stone is part of Madrid's National Archaeological Museum collection.
4. Translation from the New Jerusalem Bible.
5. Translation from *A New New Testament*.
6. Translation from the New Jerusalem Bible.
7. Translations from Robert J. Miller, ed., *The Complete Gospels: The Scholars Version*, 4th ed. (Salem, OR: Polebridge, 2010).

8. See, for example, Maia Kotrosits and Hal Taussig, *Re-reading the Gospel of Mark Amidst Loss and Trauma* (New York: Palgrave Macmillan, 2013).

Chapter 4: Gospel of Empire, Gospel of Jesus

1. Translation from Frederick W. Danker, *Benefactor: Epigraphic Study of a Graeco-Roman and New Testament Semantic Field* (St. Louis: Clayton Publishing House, 1982), 216–217.
2. For a thorough examination of the Gemma Augustea, see Susan M. (Elli) Elliott, *Family Empires, Roman and Christian. Vol. I: Roman Family Empires: Household, Empire, Resistance* (Salem, OR: Polebridge, 2018), preface.
3. Translation lightly adapted from Arthur J. Dewey, Roy W. Hoover, Lane C. McGaughy, and Daryl D. Schmidt, trans., *The Authentic Letters of Paul: A New Reading of Paul's Rhetoric and Meaning, the Scholars Version* (Salem, OR: Polebridge, 2010).
4. Translations from Robert J. Miller, ed., *The Complete Gospels: The Scholars Version*, 4th ed. (Salem, OR: Polebridge, 2010).

Chapter 5: Violence in Stone

1. Dio Cassius, *Roman History, Vol. VIII: Books 61–70,* trans. Earnest Cary and Herbert B. Foster, Loeb Classical Library 176 (Cambridge, MA: Harvard Univ. Press, 1925), LXVI.26. On Titus's death, see also Suetonius, *Lives of the Caesars, Volume II,* trans. J. C. Rolfe, Loeb Classical Library 38 (Cambridge, MA: Harvard Univ. Press, 1914), *Deified Titus* 10.
2. Dio Cassius, *Roman History* LXVI.26.
3. This is according to the Westar Institute's Acts Seminar: Dennis E. Smith and Joseph B. Tyson, eds., *Acts and Christian Beginnings: The Acts Seminar Report* (Salem, OR: Polebridge, 2013).
4. Josephus, *Jewish War, Vol. III: Books 5–7,* trans. H. St. J. Thackeray, Loeb Classical Library 201 (Cambridge, MA: Harvard Univ. Press, 1928), V.449–451. Further quotations from Jewish War are from this edition.
5. This tradition is preserved in the writing of the second-century Carthaginian Tertullian, *Apology* 33.
6. Amanda Claridge, *Rome: An Oxford Archaeological Guide* (Oxford: Oxford Univ. Press, 1998), 278.
7. See Meet the Romans with Mary Beard, "All Roads Lead to Rome" (episode 1), BBC Two, https://www.bbc.co.uk/programmes/b01ghsjx.
8. Tacitus, *Agricola. Germania. Dialogue on Oratory,* trans. M. Hutton and W. Peterson, Loeb Classical Library 35 (Cambridge, MA: Harvard Univ. Press, 1914).

Chapter 6: The Deaths of Heroes

1. Plato, *Phaedo,* in *The Last Days of Socrates: Euthyphro, the Apology, Crito, Phaedo,* trans. Hugh Tredennick (Harmondsworth: Penguin, 1969). Further quotations from *Phaedo* are from this edition.
2. Quotations from Lucretia's story are from Livy, *History of Rome, Vol. I: Books 1–2,* trans. B. O. Foster, Loeb Classical Library 114 (Cambridge, MA: Harvard Univ. Press, 1919), I.i.57–58.
3. Translations of 2 Maccabees are from the New Revised Standard Version.
4. Translations of 4 Maccabees are from H. Anderson, "4 Maccabees: A New Translation and Introduction," in James H. Charlesworth, ed., *The Old Testament Pseudepigrapha. Vol. 2: Expansions of the "Old Testament" and Legends, Wisdom and Philosophical Literature, Prayers, Psalms, and Odes, Fragments for Lost Judeo-Hellenistic Works,* Anchor Bible Reference Library (New York: Doubleday, 1985).
5. Translations of 1 Corinthians are from, or lightly adapted from, Arthur J. Dewey, Roy W. Hoover, Lane C. McGaughy, and Daryl D. Schmidt, trans., *The Authentic Letters of Paul: A New Reading of Paul's Rhetoric and Meaning, the Scholars Version* (Salem, OR: Polebridge, 2010).
6. Gospel translations in Chapter 6 are from Robert J. Miller, ed., *The Complete Gospels: The Scholars Version,* 4th ed. (Salem, OR: Polebridge, 2010).

Chapter 7: Testing Gender, Testing Boundaries

1. Translations of Gospel of Mary are from Celene Lillie, "The Gospel of Mary," in *A New New Testament: A Bible for the Twenty-First Century Combining Traditional and Newly Discovered Texts,* ed. Hal Taussig, 224–226 (Boston: Houghton Mifflin Harcourt, 2013), with some emendations. Lillie's 2018 paper for the Seminar, "Thinking Through Gender in the Second Century Jesus Movements," was essential to the writing of this chapter.
2. Celene Lillie, "Thinking Through Gender."
3. This translation of 1 Timothy is from the New Revised Standard Version.

Chapter 8: Forming New Identities Through Gender

1. Aristotle, *Generation of Animals,* trans. A. L. Peck, Loeb Classical Library 366 (Cambridge, MA: Harvard Univ. Press, 1042), II 737a.
2. Galen, *On the Usefulness of the Parts of the Body* 14.6, trans. Margaret Tallmadge May, referenced in Elaine Fantham, Helene Peet Foley, Natalie Boymel Kampen, Sarah B. Pomeroy, and H. A. Shapiro,

Women in the Classical World: Image and Text (New York: Oxford Univ. Press, 1994), 201.

3. Trans. Heinrich von Staden, referenced in Fantham et al., *Women in the Classical World*, 194.

4. Virginia Burrus, "The Gender of Martyrdom," paper presented at the Westar Institute Annual Meeting, Christianity Seminar, Denver, November 2018.

5. Translations of 4 Maccabees in this chapter are from the New Revised Standard Version, with adaptations by the authors shown in square brackets. The NRSV sometimes uses terms we find inappropriate for ancient contexts, such as the word "Judaism" in this particular quotation. "Judaism" as such was not a fixed "entity" or institution in this time period. While the NRSV reads "Judaism," we believe "ancestral practice" would be a more appropriate translation for the context.

6. Burrus, "Gender of Martyrdom."

7. Translation from Burrus, "Gender of Martyrdom."

8. This line is adapted from Herbert Musurillo, *The Acts of the Christian Martyrs* (Oxford: Clarendon, 1972). Musurillo's text presents Blandina as saying "I am a Christian," but we know from our work in Chapter 2 that this translation is not accurate.

Chapter 9: Belonging to Israel

1. Translation is that of the authors. Another (though similar) translation by Philip A. Harland and the original Greek text, as well as images of the tomb, are available at Associations in the Greco-Roman World, "[152] Grave of Glykon with Bequest to Purple-Dyers and Carpet-Weavers (161–250 CE); Hierapolis–Phrygia," http://philipharland.com/greco-roman-associations/152-grave-of-glykon-involving-purple-dyers-and-carpet-weavers/. Highly recommended reading is Philip A. Harland, *Dynamics of Identity in the World of the Early Christians: Associations, Judeans, and Cultural Minorities* (New York: T&T Clark International/Continuum Press, 2009). See also Philip Harland, "Acculturation and Identity in the Diaspora: A Jewish Family and 'Pagan' Guilds at Hierapolis," *Journal of Jewish Studies* 57, no. 2 (2006): 222–244, https://doi.org/10.18647/2670/JJS-2006.

2. This idea of an "ethnic ladder" comes from Philip A. Harland, "Climbing the Ethnic Ladder: A Portrait of Interactions Between Judeans and Other Peoples," paper presented at the Westar Institute Annual Meeting, Christianity Seminar, San Antonio, November 2016.

3. Again, for more on this idea of ethnic hierarchy, see Harland, "Climbing the Ethnic Ladder."

4. In her book *Rethinking Early Christian Identity: Affect, Violence, and Belonging* (Minneapolis: Fortress, 2015), Maia Kotrosits considers the language of diaspora, specifically Israelite diaspora and experiences of trauma in and through diaspora, to help us to work through these questions about belonging. The Seminar takes a different direction on those questions in this book.

5. See Caroline Johnson Hodge, *If Sons, Then Heirs: A Study of Kinship and Ethnicity in the Letters of Paul* (Oxford: Oxford Univ. Press, 2007).

6. Burton L. Mack, *Who Wrote the New Testament? The Making of the Christian Myth* (San Francisco: HarperOne, 1996), 30–31.

7. Daniel Boyarin, "The Christian Invention of 'Judaism,'" paper presented at the Westar Institute Annual Meeting, Christianity Seminar, San Antonio, November 2016. See also these responses to Boyarin's work: Maia Kotrosits, "Devising Collectives: Losing the Nation in the Story of Judaism and Christianity: A Response to Daniel Boyarin's *Dying for God: Martyrdom and the Making of Christianity and Judaism* and *A Traveling Homeland: The Babylonia Talmud as Diaspora*," paper presented at the Westar Institute Annual Meeting, Christianity Seminar, San Antonio, November 2016; and Nina Livesey, "Difference and Similarity: A Review of Daniel Boyarin's *A Radical Jew: Paul and the Politics of Identity and Border Lines: The Partition of Judaeo-Christianity*," paper presented at the Westar Institute Annual Meeting, Christianity Seminar, San Antonio, November 2016.

Chapter 10: Experimental Families

1. Translation of Acts of Paul and Thecla from J. K. Elliott, "The Acts of Paul and Thecla," in *The Apocryphal New Testament*, ed. J. K. Elliott (Oxford: Clarendon, 1993), 366.

2. Translation lightly adapted from Aristotle, *Politics*, trans. H. Rackham, Loeb Classical Library 264 (Cambridge, MA: Harvard Univ. Press, 1932).

3. Susan M. (Elli) Elliott, *Family Empires, Roman and Christian. Vol. I: Roman Family Empires: Household, Empire, Resistance* (Salem, OR: Polebridge, 2018), ch. 3 (n.p.).

4. P.Oxy. 7 1021, from Oxyrhynchus, Egypt, dated November 17, 54 CE. Notification of accession of Nero. Greek text available at Papyri.info, http://papyri.info/ddbdp/p.oxy;7;1021.

5. The term "household lens" comes from Lillian I. Larsen, "Re-defining 'Solitude': Monastic Registers of Fictive (and Factual) Family," *Forum* 9, no. 1 (2020): 77–102, here 90.

6. See Elliott, *Family Empires*, chs. 14 and 15.

7. Elliott, *Family Empires*, ch. 15.

8. Elliott, *Family Empires*, ch. 14.

9. Marika Rose, "Holy Mothers of God: Sex Work, Inheritance, and the Women of Jesus' Genealogy," *Theology & Sexuality* 25, nos. 1–2 (2019): 1–20, here 7, doi: 10.1080/13558358.2019.1652031.

10. Rose, "Holy Mothers," 11–12.

Chapter 11: Join the Club

1. *Corpus inscriptionum latinarum* (CIL) XIV 2120. Consilio et Auctoritate Academiae Litterarum Regiae Borussicae Editum. Berlin: Georg Reimer, 1863–1974. Available from Last, Richard, trans., "Honors for C. Sulpicius Victor with Reference to a Women's Assembly (curia) (ca. 200 CE), Lanuvium - Campania," Associations in the Greco-Roman World, Accessed July 23, 2021, HYPERLINK "https://urldefense .com/v3/__http://philipharland.com/greco-roman-associations/a -womens-assembly-curia-ca-200-ce/__;!!PH0vZokp8wwQNw!ijDv nYWS5iITU8KAw0Z0Y21gDN1GuJ9nGlSeqmo2L9svOj8l4-nme FKz6RzfGstUgafqUA$" http://philipharland.com/greco-roman-asso ciations/a-womens-assembly-curia-ca-200-ce/.

2. IHistria 57, Associations in the Greco-Roman World, "Honorary Decree for Aba with Mention of Associations (150–200 CE); Histria–Scythia and Moesia," trans. Philip A. Harland, http://phili pharland.com/greco-roman-associations/honorary-decree-for-aba -150-200-ce/.

3. ISmyrna 295 = IJO II 43, second–third century CE. From Richard S. Ascough, Philip A. Harland, and John S. Kloppenborg, "Family Grave of Rufina the Head of the Synagogue," in *Associations in the Greco-Roman World: A Sourcebook* (Waco, TX: Baylor Univ. Press, 2012), 120.

4. CIL XIV 2112. Translation from Associations in the Greco-Roman World, "Regulations of the Worshippers of Diana and Antinoüs (136 CE), Lanuvium–Campania," trans. John S. Kloppenborg, http:// philipharland.com/greco-roman-associations/310-regulations-of- the-worshippers-of-diana-and-antinous/.

5. TAM V 1539. Translation from Associations in the Greco-Roman World, "Divine Instructions for the Household Association of Dionysios (late II–early I BCE), Philadelphia–Lydia," trans. Philip A. Harland, http://philipharland.com/greco-roman-associations /divine-instructions-for-the-household-association-of-dionysios/.

6. Kirchner, Johannes, ed. *Inscriptiones Atticae Euclidis anno anteriores* (*IG* II²). 4 vols. Berlin: Walter de Gruyter, 1913–1940. 1368.

7. All references to this inscription are from the translation of Richard S. Ascough, Philip A. Harland, and John S. Kloppenborg, "Regulations

of a Bacchic Association–The Iobacchoi," in *Associations in the Greco-Roman World*, 13–16.

8. Translation from Robert J. Miller, ed., *The Complete Gospels: The Scholars Version*, 4th ed. (Salem, OR: Polebridge, 2010).

9. Translated in Richard S. Ascough, Philip A. Harland, and John S. Kloppenborg, "Aelius Aristides of Smyrna (Ionia), Orations 45.27–28," in *Associations in the Greco-Roman World*, 246.

10. Andrew Monson, "The Ethics and Economics of Ptolemaic Religious Associations," *Ancient Society* 36 (2006): 221–238, here 233–234, doi: 10.2143/AS.36.0.2017836.

Chapter 12: Feasting and Bathing

1. Translations of Gospel of Thomas are by Justin Lasser, "Gospel of Thomas," in *A New New Testament: A Bible for the Twenty-First Century Combining Traditional and Newly Discovered Texts*, ed. Hal Taussig, 15–26 (Boston: Houghton Mifflin Harcourt, 2013).

2. Translation from Robert J. Miller, ed., *The Complete Gospels: The Scholars Version,* 4th ed. (Salem, OR: Polebridge, 2010).

3. Translation of Prayer of Thanksgiving by Celene Lillie, "The Prayer of Thanksgiving," in *A New New Testament: A Bible for the Twenty-First Century combining Traditional and Newly Discovered Texts*, ed. Hal Taussig, 7 (Boston: Houghton Mifflin Harcourt, 2013).

4. See also Andrew Brian McGowan, *Ancient Christian Worship: Early Church Practices in Social, Historical, and Theological Perspective* (Grand Rapids, MI: Baker, 2014).

5. Translation of Tertullian, *On Baptism,* by S. Thelwall, in *Ante-Nicene Fathers*, Vol. 3, ed. Alexander Roberts, James Donaldson, and A. Cleveland Coxe (Buffalo, NY: Christian Literature Publishing, 1885); revised and edited for New Advent by Kevin Knight, http://www.newadvent.org/fathers/0321.htm.

6. Josephus, *Jewish Antiquities, Vol. VIII: Books 18–19,* trans. Louis H. Feldman, Loeb Classical Library 433 (Cambridge, MA: Harvard Univ. Press, 1965).

Chapter 13: Inventing Orthodoxy Through Heresy

1. See Josephus, *Jewish War* 2.119–166; *Jewish Antiquities* 13.171–173; 18.11–22.

2. Translation from Markus Vinzent, "Orthodoxy and Heresy: Misnomers and Misnamers," paper presented at the Westar Institute Annual Meeting, Christianity Seminar, San Diego, November 2019.

3. For a treatment of the importance of schools and school models in later antiquity, see Lillian I. Larsen and Samuel Rubenson, eds., *Monastic Education in Late Antiquity: The Transformation of Classical Paideia* (Cambridge: Cambridge Univ. Press, 2018).
4. *First Letter of Clement*, in The Apostolic Fathers, Vol. 1, ed. and trans. Bart D. Ehrman, Loeb Classical Library 24 (Cambridge, MA: Harvard Univ. Press, 2003).
5. Ignatius, *To the Ephesians*, in Apostolic Fathers.
6. Irenaeus, *Against Heresies*, trans. Philip Schaff, "ANF01. The Apostolic Fathers with Justin Martyr and Irenaeus," Christian Classics Ethereal Library, https://ccel.org/ccel/irenaeus/against_heresies_iii/anf01.ix.iv.xix.html.
7. Translations of *Testimony of Truth* by Søren Giversen and Birger A. Pearson, "The Testimony of Truth," Gnostic Society Library: The Nag Hammadi Library, http://gnosis.org/naghamm/testruth.html.
8. Translations of Acts of Paul and Thecla from J. K. Elliott, "The Acts of Paul and Thecla," in *The Apocryphal New Testament*, ed. J. K. Elliott, 364 (Oxford: Oxford Univ. Press, 1993).

Chapter 14: Demolishing Gnosticism

1. Karen L. King, *What Is Gnosticism?* (Cambridge, MA: Belknap, 2003).
2. King, *What Is Gnosticism?*, 189.
3. Ursula K. Le Guin, "The Author of the Acacia Seeds," in *The Unreal and the Real: The Selected Short Stories of Ursula K. Le Guin* (New York: Saga, 2012), 617–625.
4. Karen L. King, *The Secret Revelation of John* (Cambridge, MA: Harvard Univ. Press, 2009), ix.
5. King, *Secret Revelation*, 26.
6. King, *Secret Revelation*, 28.

Chapter 15: Paul Obscured

1. Translation of Ignatius, *To the Ephesians*, from Paul Trebilco, *The Early Christians in Ephesus from Paul to Ignatius* (Grand Rapids, MI: Eerdmans, 2007), 686.

Chapter 16: Jesus by Many Other Names

1. Except where otherwise noted, translations in this chapter of canonical writings—writings now found in the Hebrew Bible and the "New Testament"—are from the New Revised Standard Version, with adaptations by the authors shown in brackets.

2. This translation is by the book editors, and is therefore not from the NRSV, as has been otherwise noted for other translations in this chapter.
3. Translation from Michael W. Holmes, *The Apostolic Fathers: Greek Texts and English Translations,* 3rd ed. (Ada, MI: Baker Academic, 2009).
4. Translations of the Gospel of Mary are from Karen L. King, *The Gospel of Mary of Magdala: Jesus and the First Woman Apostle* (Santa Rosa, CA: Polebridge, 2003).
5. Translations of the Gospel of Truth, with some adaptations, by Celene Lillie, "The Gospel of Truth," in *A New New Testament: A Bible for the Twenty-First Century Combining Traditional and Newly Discovered Texts*, ed. Hal Taussig, 230–241 (Boston: Houghton Mifflin Harcourt, 2013).

Chapter 17: Hiding in Plain Sight

1. James C. Scott, *Domination and the Arts of Resistance: Hidden Transcripts* (New Haven: Yale Univ. Press, 2008), 141, 143.
2. Translations of the Gospel of Truth by Celene Lillie, "The Gospel of Truth," in *A New New Testament: A Bible for the Twenty-First Century Combining Traditional and Newly Discovered Texts*, ed. Hal Taussig, 230–241 (Boston: Houghton Mifflin Harcourt, 2013).
3. This is cleverly developed by Adela Yarbro Collins in *Crisis and Catharsis: The Power of the Apocalypse*, 152–154, 161, 166 (Philadelphia: The Westminster Press, 1984).
4. Translations of *The Thunder: Perfect Mind* by Hal Taussig, Jared Calaway, Maia Kotrosits, Celene Lillie, and Justin Lasser, "The Thunder: Perfect Mind," in *The Thunder: Perfect Mind: A New Translation and Introduction.* Hal Taussig et al. (New York: Palgrave MacMillan, a division of St. Martin's Press. 183–188).
5. Lucius Apuleius, *Metamorphoses or the Golden Ass*, translation adapted by Paul Halsall from the translation of Adlington (1566) in comparison with that of Robert Graves (1951). Paul Halsall, "Lucius Apuleius (c. 155 CE): Isis, Queen of Heaven," Fordham University, Ancient History Sourcebook, https://sourcebooks.fordham.edu/ancient/lucius-assa.asp.
6. New Revised Standard Version translation.

Chapter 18: Romancing the Martyr

1. Translations of the *Acts of Perpetua and Felicitas* are from Herbert Musurillo, trans., *Acts of the Christian Martyrs* (Oxford: Oxford Univ. Press, 1972).

2. Building on Judith Perkins, Carly Daniel-Hughes supports this reading in her paper for the Seminar, "Producing and Contesting Martyrdom in Pre-Decian Roman North Africa," presented at the Westar Institute Spring Meeting, Christianity Seminar, Santa Rosa, CA, March 2015.
3. Translation of Pliny, *Letters,* LCL 59.
4. Lucian, The Passing of Peregrinus. Translations here and following from *Lucian, Vol. V,* trans. A. M. Harmon, Loeb Classical Library 302 (Cambridge, MA: Harvard Univ. Press, 1936).
5. From Minucius Felix Tertullian, *Apology. De Spectaculis. Minucius Felix: Octavius,* trans. T. R. Glover and Gerald H. Rendall, Loeb Classical Library 250 (Cambridge, MA: Harvard Univ. Press, 1931).
6. Judith Perkins, *The Suffering Self: Pain and Narrative Representation in Early Christianity* (London: Routledge, 1995), 23.
7. Translation adapted from Livy, *History of Rome*, LCL 114.
8. See Susan M. (Elli) Elliot, "Gladiators and Martyrs: Icons in the Arena," *Forum* 3, no. 6 (2017): 29–59.
9. Perkins, *Suffering Self,* 15.
10. Chariton, *Callirhoe*, ed. and trans. G. P. Goold, Loeb Classical Library 481 (Cambridge, MA: Harvard Univ. Press, 1995).
11. Perkins, *Suffering Self,* 26, uses Reardon's translation in B. P. Reardon, ed., *Collected Ancient Greek Novels* (Berkeley: Univ. of California Press, 1989).
12. Perkins, *Suffering Self,* 27.
13. As adapted from Musurillo: "The Martyrdom of Perpetua and Felicitas," from *The Acts of the Christian Martyrs,* trans. Herbert Musurillo (Oxford: Oxford Univ. Press, 1972).
14. Daniel-Hughes, "Producing and Contesting Martyrdom," offers a helpful overview of responses that contested or countered so-called martyrdom.

Chapter 19: Better than a New Testament?

1. Quoted in Jessica Lussenhop, "Why Did Prince Change His Name to a Symbol?" BBC News Magazine, April 22, 2016, https://www.bbc.com/news/magazine-36107590.
2. Jason BeDuhn, "Becoming a People of the Book," paper presented at the Westar Institute Spring Meeting, Christianity Seminar, online, May 2020.
3. Translation adapted from Matthew D. C. Larsen, *Gospels Before the Book* (Oxford: Oxford Univ. Press, 2018), 93.
4. Larsen, *Gospels Before the Book*, 95–96.

5. "The Gospels Are Finally Named! Irenaeus of Lyons," is actually the title of a blog post by Bart D. Ehrman on his eponymous blog The Bart Erhman Blog: The History & Literature of Early Christianity, November 18, 2014, https://ehrmanblog.org/the-gospels-are-finally-named-irenaeus-of-lyons/.
6. Erin K. Vearncombe, "Gathered Around Absence: A First-Century Approach to the Text Known as 'Mark,'" paper presented at the Westar Institute Spring Meeting, Christianity Seminar, online, May 2020. All citations of Vearncombe in this chapter refer to this paper.
7. Translation from Larsen, *Gospels Before the Book*, 150.
8. This translation of ILydiaHM 96 is from Associations in the Greco-Roman World, "Posthumous Honors by Heroists for Stratonike the Priestess (II BCE); Koloe area–Lydia," trans. Philip A. Harland, http://philipharland.com/greco-roman-associations/posthumous-honors-by-heroists-for-stratonike-ii-bce/.
9. This image comes from Philip Pullman's novel *The Golden Compass* (New York: Alfred A. Knopf, 1995), ch. 9, "The Spies." Lyra, the main character, describes how she interprets the symbols on a special piece of equipment in her possession called an "alethiometer": "I kind of see 'em. Or feel 'em rather, like climbing down a ladder at night, you put your foot down and there's another rung. Well, I put my mind down and there's another meaning, and I kind of sense what it is. Then I put 'em all together. There's a trick in it like focusing your eyes."

Chapter 20: Conclusion

1. Snicket, Lemony. *The Austere Academy: Book the Fifth* (New York: HarperCollins, 2000), 187.

ANCIENT WRITINGS IN TRANSLATION: A GUIDE

This bibliography will enable readers to follow up on the discussions in this book by reading the primary sources, in translation, from or associated with the early groups of Jesus Anointed followers: gospels, acts accounts, histories, and letters by leaders of these groups, and the like. Individual writings (for example, the Gospel of Mary or the Acts of Perpetua and Felicitas) are noted in chapter endnotes. This guide is to collections of various ancient writings associated with or important for the study of the groups of Jesus Anointed.

A NOTE ON TRANSLATIONS

The Italian proverb *"Traduttore, traditore"* (to translate is to betray) sums up the problem with translations. All translations are mistranslations. Readers need to keep this in mind. Mistranslation is not deliberate but results from the inevitable fact that words and grammar do not have an exact correspondence between languages. So-called word-for-word or literal translations are actually impossible. Translation is always interpretation, whether or not it is admitted to be such. Also, a language over time shifts and changes, which is why we always need new translations.

Biblical translations have a way of taking on a "sacred" character, but they are still just translations. Reading multiple translations is always a good strategy.

COLLECTIONS OF ANCIENT WRITINGS

Perseus Digital Library, http://www.perseus.tufts.edu/hopper. This
website covers the history, literature, and culture of the Greco-Roman
world. It is an important resource when dealing with the ancient world.

A New English Translation of the Septuagint. Edited by Albert Pietersma
and Benjamin G. Wright. New York: Oxford Univ. Press, 2007. The
Septuagint is a Greek translation of the Hebrew Bible. It is the sacred
writings of ancient Israelite and Judean communities, as well as those
of Jesus Anointed. The Hebrew text on which it is based, as well as the
books included, differs from the Masoretic Hebrew tradition that has led
to much conflict between Catholic and Protestant editions of the Bible.

Early Jewish Writings, http://www.earlyjewishwritings.com. This
website provides digital access to many early Jewish writings. Currently
missing are the Dead Sea Scrolls (claimed to be forthcoming).

BibleGateway, https://www.biblegateway.com. This website provides easy
access to multiple versions of the Bible in English, as well as several
foreign languages. It allows users to read multiple versions of a given
biblical passage side by side so that users can compare translations.

Bible, King James Version (1611). Authorized by King James VI, the
translators of the New Testament were excellent Greek scholars
who were still part of the living tradition of ancient rhetoric. While
antiquated in many ways, this translation is often worth looking
at because of the translators' understanding of rhetoric and as an
important point in the history of translation into English. Many
English versions of the Bible are revisions of the King James Version.
Available on many internet sites.

The HarperCollins Study Bible: Fully Revised & Updated. Edited by
Harold W. Attridge and Wayne A. Meeks. San Francisco: HarperOne,
2006. General reference Bible using the New Revised Standard
Version. Includes articles, introductions, and notes by scholars for the
Society of Biblical Literature.

*The Old Testament Pseudepigrapha. Vol. 1: Apocalyptic Literature and
Testaments. Vol. 2: Expansions of the "Old Testament" and Legends,
Wisdom and Philosophical Literature, Prayers, Psalms, and Odes,
Fragments of Lost Judeo-Hellenistic Works.* Edited by James H.
Charlesworth. Garden City, NY: Doubleday, 1983 and 1985. Although
not produced by groups of Jesus Anointed followers, these writings
often influenced them. The translations are excellent, with strong
introductions and notes.

Early Christian Writings, http://www.earlychristianwritings.com/intro
.html. This website collects in digital format all known so-called

Christian writings from the first two centuries, as well as a selection
from the third century. An Index (http://www.earlychristianwritings
.com/index.html) lists all these writings in chronological order.
Provides easy digital access to a great many writings.

Ante-Nicene Fathers. Edited by Alexander Roberts and James Donaldson.
10 vols. Edinburg: T&T Clark, 1867 and 1873. US edition, 1885,
edited by Cleveland Coxe. As its subtitle of the 1885 edition indicates,
this contains "The Writings of the Fathers Down to A.D. 325." The
translation is antiquated but more important is missing all the
writings that have been discovered since the late nineteenth century. It
is still available in reprint editions, free on Kindle, and on the internet
(https://en.wikisource.org/wiki/Ante-Nicene_Fathers). Even given its
limitations, it is still worth consulting.

*New Testament Apocrypha. Vol. 1: Gospels and Related Writings. Vol.
2: Writings Relating to the Apostles; Apocalypses and Related Subjects.*
Edited by Edgar Hennecke and Wilhelm Schneemelcher. Philadelphia:
Westminster, 1963 and 1965. A translation of the standard German
collection of New Testament apocrypha. Good introductions.

The Apocryphal New Testament. Edited by J. K. Elliott. Oxford:
Clarendon, 2005. A translation similar to that of Edgar Hennecke
and Wilhelm Schneemelcher and based on the earlier work of M. R.
(Montague Rhodes) James (1924).

*The Authentic Letters of Paul: A New Reading of Paul's Rhetoric and
Meaning*. Edited by Arthur J. Dewey, Roy W. Hoover, Lane C.
McGaughy, and Daryl D. Schmidt. Salem, OR: Polebridge, 2010.
A completely new translation of Paul's letters that pays attention to
their rhetoric. It breaks away from the King James tradition. With
introductions and notes.

The Gnostic Society Library, http://gnosis.org/library.html. A major
digital archive of all Nag Hammadi documents discovered in the
past century. Although committed to a twenty-first-century "gnostic"
interpretation, this website provides good scholarship and translations.

The Nag Hammadi Library in English. Edited by Marvin Meyer and
James M. Robinson. San Francisco: HarperCollins, 2009. New
translations and introductions to all the writings discovered in 1945 at
Nag Hammadi, Egypt, a major find.

*A New New Testament: A Bible for the 21st Century Combining Traditional
and Newly Discovered Texts*. Edited by Hal Taussig. Boston: Houghton
Mifflin Harcourt, 2013. New translations of ten new writings
alongside traditional New Testament writings.

The Complete Gospels. Edited by Robert J. Miller. Salem, OR: Polebridge,
2010. A translation with introductions and notes to all the early extant
gospels. The translation breaks with the King James Version tradition.

The Apostolic Fathers. Vol. 1: I Clement, II Clement, Ignatius, Polycarp, Didache; Volume II. Epistle of Barnabas. Papias and Quadratus. Epistle to Diognetus. The Shepherd of Hermas. Translated Bart D. Ehrman. Cambridge, MA: Harvard Univ. Press, 2003. Part of the Loeb Classical Library, a standard collection of Greek and Latin writings with English translations on facing pages. This collection of early Christian writings dates from the seventeenth century.

The Acts of the Christian Martyrs. Herbert Musurillo. Oxford: Clarendon, 1972. Greek and Latin texts with translations and short commentaries. The standard for dealing with these writings.